BRITISH COLUMBIA
Pages 242–275

WASHINGTON
Pages 170–193

BRITISH
COLUMBIA

Vancouver

Seattle
WASHINGTON

Portland

OREGON

OREGON
Pages 86–115

EYEWITNESS TRAVEL GUIDES

PACIFIC
NORTHWEST

EYEWITNESS TRAVEL GUIDES

PACIFIC
NORTHWEST

Main contributors:
STEPHEN BREWER,
CONSTANCE BRISSENDEN,
ANITA CARMIN

DK

LONDON, NEW YORK,
MELBOURNE, MUNICH AND DELHI
www.dk.com

Produced by International Book Productions Inc.,
Toronto, Ontario, Canada

Project Editor Barbara Hopkinson
Art Editors James David Ellis, Barbara Hopkinson
Editors Judy Phillips, Sheila Hall, Debbie Koenig, Tara Tovell
DTP Designers Dietmar Kokemohr, Nicola Lyon
Picture Research and Permissions Diana Bahr

Main Contributors
Stephen Brewer, Constance Brissenden, Anita Carmin

Photographers
Bruce Forster, Gunter Marx, Scott Pitts

Illustrator
William Band

Production Controller
Shane Higgins

Reproduced by Colourscan, Singapore
Printed and bound by Graphicom, Verona, Italy

First American Edition, 2003
03 04 05 06 07 10 9 8 7 6 5 4 3 2 1

Published in the United States by DK Publishing, Inc.,
375 Hudson Street, New York, New York 10014

Published in Great Britain by Dorling Kindersley Limited.

ISSN 1542-1554

ISBN 0-7894-9680-1

**The information in every
DK Eyewitness Travel Guide is checked regularly.**
Every effort has been made to ensure that this book is as up-to-date
as possible at the time of going to press. Some details, however,
such as telephone numbers, opening hours, prices, gallery hanging
arrangements and travel information are liable to change. The
publishers cannot accept responsibility for any consequences arising
from the use of this book, nor for any material on third party
websites, and cannot guarantee that any website address in this
book will be a suitable source of travel information. We value the
views and suggestions of our readers very highly. Please write to:
Publisher, DK Eyewitness Travel Guides,
Dorling Kindersley, 80 Strand, London WC2R 0RL, Great Britain.

◁ **Beautiful vineyards in the Okanagan Valley, British Columbia**

Windsurfers and kayaks, Vancouver

Contents

Introducing the Pacific Northwest

Emmons Glacier, Mount Rainier National Park, Washington

Guitar from the collection at the Experience Music Project, Seattle

Chinese Buddhist Temple, Richmond, British Columbia

TRAVELERS' NEEDS

Victorian home in the Nob Hill neighborhood of Portland

Freshly caught crab

View of the Seattle Center

Sea kayaks at Snug Harbor, San Juan Island, Washington

HOW TO USE THIS GUIDE

THIS GUIDE HELPS YOU to get the most from your visit to the Pacific Northwest. It provides detailed information and expert recommendations. *Introducing the Pacific Northwest* maps the region and sets it in its historical and cultural context. Features cover topics from wildlife to geology. The three area sections, as well as the three city sections, describe important sights, using maps, photographs, and illustrations. Restaurant and hotel listings can be found in *Travelers' Needs*. The *Survival Guide* offers tips on everything from public transport to using the telephone system.

PORTLAND, SEATTLE, AND VANCOUVER

The center of each of these cities is divided into several sightseeing areas, each with its own chapter. A last chapter, *Farther Afield*, describes sights beyond the central areas. All sights are numbered and plotted on the chapter's area map. Information on each sight is presented in numerical order, making it easy to locate within the chapter.

Sights at a Glance lists the chapter's sights by category, such as Museums and Galleries; Historic Buildings and Churches; Parks and Squares; Gardens and Viewpoints; and Shops.

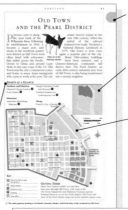

All pages about Portland have orange thumb tabs. Seattle's are purple, and Vancouver's are green.

A locator map shows where you are in relation to other areas of the city center.

1 Area map
For easy reference, sights are numbered and located on a map. City center sights are also marked on Street Finders: Portland (pp80–85); Seattle (pp164–9); Vancouver (pp236–41).

2 Street-by-Street map
This gives a bird's-eye view of the heart of each sightseeing area.

A star indicates a sight that no visitor should miss.

A suggested route for a walk is shown in red.

3 Detailed information
The sights in the three main cities are described individually. The address, telephone number, opening hours, and information on admission charge, tours, wheelchair access, and public transport are provided. The key to the symbols is on the back flap.

1 Introduction
The landscape, history, and character of each state or province is outlined here, showing how the area has developed over the centuries and what it has to offer to the visitor today.

PACIFIC NORTHWEST AREA BY AREA
In this book, the Pacific Northwest has been divided into the two states and one province, each of which has its own chapter. Portland, Seattle, and Vancouver are dealt with in separate chapters. Interesting sights to visit are numbered on a pictorial map.

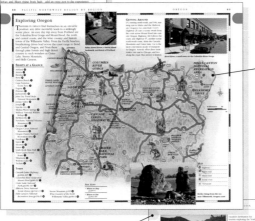

2 Pictorial map
This shows the road network and gives an illustrated overview of the region. Interesting places to visit are numbered, and there are also useful tips on getting to, and around, the region by car and public transport.

Each area of the Pacific Northwest can be quickly identified by its color coding, shown on the inside front flap.

3 Detailed information
Noteworthy towns, cities, and other places to visit are described individually. They are listed in order, following the numbering on the pictorial map. Within each sight there is detailed information on interesting buildings and other attractions.

A visitors' checklist provides all the practical information needed to plan your visit.

4 Top sights
These are given two or more pages. The most interesting town or city centers are shown with sights picked out and described; parks have maps showing facilities, major exhibits, and the main roads and trails.

INTRODUCING THE PACIFIC NORTHWEST

Putting Oregon and Washington on the Map

Nestling in the northwest corner of the United States and containing pristine expanses of forest, mountains, and desert, Oregon and Washington are two of the country's most beautiful states. Oregon's population of some 3 million, and Washington's, of just over 6 million, are concentrated in and around the major cities. The region's economic base is as diverse as its landscape, with manufacturing, retail and services, tourism, agriculture, and forestry particularly strong industries.

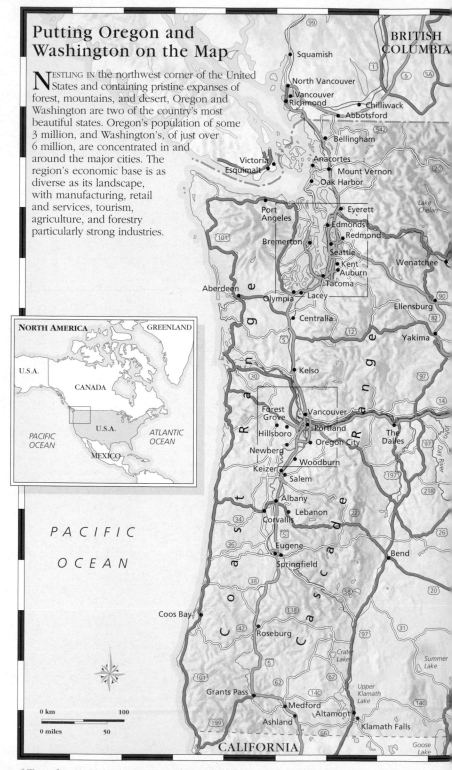

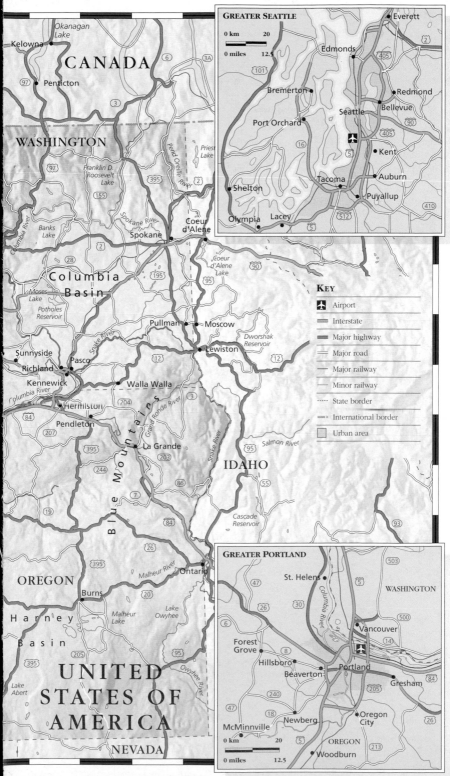

GREATER SEATTLE

0 km   20

0 miles   12.5

Everett
Edmonds
405
2
Bremerton
Redmond
Seattle
Bellevue
Port Orchard
90
405
16
Kent
Tacoma
Auburn
Shelton
Puyallup
410
Olympia   Lacey
512
5

KEY

✈ Airport
— Interstate
— Major highway
— Major road
— Major railway
— Minor railway
---- State border
--- International border
☐ Urban area

CANADA

Okanagan
Lake
Kelowna
6
3A
97   Penticton
3
WASHINGTON
Priest
Lake
97   Franklin D.
Roosevelt
Lake
395   2
155
Banks
Lake
Spokane River
28   Coeur
d'Alene
Spokane
C o l u m b i a   Coeur
B a s i n   d'Alene
Lake   90
Moses   195
Lake   95
Potholes
Reservoir   Pullman   Moscow
Dworshak
Reservoir
Sunnyside   12
Snake River   Lewiston   12
Richland   Pasco
Kennewick
Columbia River   Walla Walla
Hermiston   204   Grand Ronde River   3
84   B   Salmon River
Pendleton   l   95
207   u
395   e   La Grande   **IDAHO**
203
244   M   86   55
o
7   u
19   n
t   84
a
i   26   Cascade
n   Reservoir
395   s   93

OREGON

Malheur River   Ontario
Burns   20
H a r n e y   Malheur   Lake
Lake   Owyhee
B a s i n   205   95
UNITED
395
Lake
Abert   **STATES OF**
Owyhee River
AMERICA
NEVADA

GREATER PORTLAND

503
St. Helens   5
47   **WASHINGTON**
26   30
Columbia River
6   500
Vancouver
Forest   14
Grove   8   ✈   Portland   205
Hillsboro   84
Beaverton   Gresham
240
47
18   Newberg   Oregon
McMinnville   City   26
5   **OREGON**   213
0 km   20   Woodburn

0 miles   12.5

Putting British Columbia on the Map

BRITISH COLUMBIA, Canada's westernmost province and the country's gateway to the Asia-Pacific region, is home to over 4 million people. Traditionally strong industries such as forestry, mining, and fishing remain vital to the province's economy, though recent years have seen a boom in the high-tech, film, and eco-tourism areas. Hydroelectricity and natural gas are other important resources. The beauty of the British Columbian wilderness – from the rugged coastline to the commanding mountain ranges – is preserved in the province's 675 parks and protected areas.

Pelly Mountains

Tungsten

YUKON

Teslin

Liard

Kechika

Atlin Lake

Juneau

Cassiar

Stikine

BRITISH COLUMBIA

37

ALASKA (U.S.A.)

Coast

PACIFIC OCEAN

Terrace

Prince Rupert

Skeena

Kitimat

Haida Gwaii (Queen Charlotte Islands)

0 km   150
0 miles   100

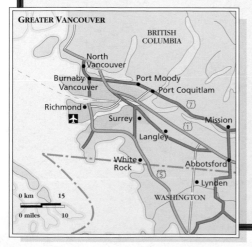

GREATER VANCOUVER

BRITISH COLUMBIA

North Vancouver

Burnaby
Vancouver

Port Moody

Port Coquitlam

Richmond

7

Surrey

Mission

1

Langley

White Rock

Abbotsford

5

Lynden

WASHINGTON

0 km   15
0 miles   10

Vancouver Island

KEY

✈ Airport

▬ Major highway

▬ Highway

═ Major road

— Major railway

— Minor railway

----- Provincial border

–•–• International border

▢ Urban area

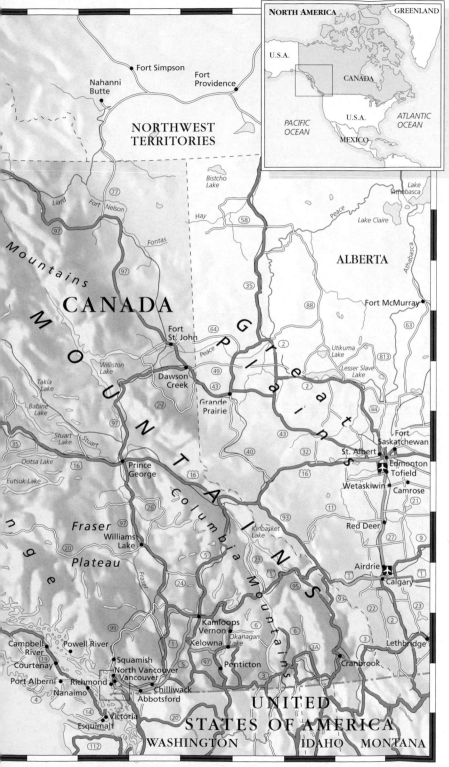

NORTH AMERICA

GREENLAND

U.S.A.

CANADA

PACIFIC
OCEAN

U.S.A.

ATLANTIC
OCEAN

MEXICO

Fort Simpson

Nahanni
Butte

Fort
Providence

NORTHWEST
TERRITORIES

Bistcho
Lake

Lake
Athabasca

Liard

Fort Nelson

Hay

Peace

Lake Claire

ALBERTA

Mountains

Fontas

Fort McMurray

CANADA

M
O
U
N
T
A
I
N
S

Williston
Lake

Fort
St. John

Peace

Grande
Prairie

Utikuma
Lake

Lesser Slave
Lake

Athabasca

Takla
Lake

Dawson
Creek

G
r
e
a
t

Babine
Lake

Stuart
Lake

Stuart

Fort
Saskatchewan

St. Albert

Edmonton
Tofield

Ootsa Lake

Prince
George

Columbia Mountains

Wetaskiwin

Camrose

Eutsuk Lake

P
l
a
i
n
s

Fraser

Kinbasket
Lake

Red Deer

R
a
n
g
e

Williams
Lake

Plateau

Fraser

Airdrie

Campbell
River

Powell River

Kamloops
Vernon

Kelowna

Okanagan
Lake

Calgary

Lethbridge

Courtenay

Port Alberni

Nanaimo

Squamish

North Vancouver
Vancouver

Richmond

Chilliwack
Abbotsford

Penticton

Cranbrook

Esquimalt

Victoria

UNITED
STATES OF AMERICA

WASHINGTON

IDAHO

MONTANA

A PORTRAIT OF
THE PACIFIC NORTHWEST

SOME OF NORTH AMERICA'S MOST RUGGED *and spectacular terrain unfolds across the Pacific Northwest. Settled by Europeans barely 150 years ago, the region has cradled Native cultures for thousands. The region is now also home to three of the continent's most sophisticated cities – Portland, Seattle, and Vancouver – surrounded by soaring mountains, dense forests, and sparkling water.*

The Pacific Northwest, comprising Oregon, Washington, and British Columbia, is richly varied – with its desert, mountain, and seashore landscapes, its mild and extreme climates, and a cosmopolitan mix of cultures and ethnicities. The region straddles two nations – the US and Canada – and comprises 526,000 sq miles (1,362,240 sq km), making it larger than France, Germany, and Italy combined. The one quality that characterizes all of the Pacific Northwest is its natural beauty, the result of eons of geological rumblings that have imprinted the region with lofty mountains, deep gorges, rocky shorelines, and mighty rivers.

One of Washington's prized apples

NATURAL WONDERS
The call of the wild is the draw for many travelers to the Pacific Northwest. Although highways, suburban sprawl, large-scale ranching, logging, dams, and other encroachments have all had a negative impact on this great wilderness, enough of its many natural wonders – such as 800-year-old Sitka spruce in the coastal rainforests – remains intact to offer a welcome escape from the stresses of the 21st century.

Another characteristic of the Pacific Northwest is its infamous weather. It can indeed rain for days on end here, but the weather varies as much as the topography docs. Whereas west of the mountains the north Pacific Ocean currents ensure wet and mild winters and pleasant summers, an entirely different climate is revealed east of the mountains. On the eastern plateaus and steppes, temperatures dip to well below freezing in the winter, often accompanied by heavy snow, and soar in the summer. In the central mountain region, inland deserts experience harsh winters – resulting in frequent road closures – and dry hot summers.

Sailboats in a regatta held on the waters of Burrard Inlet, British Columbia

◁ The striking landscape of the John Day fossil beds in central Oregon

Local hikers on a trail near Bellingham, Washington

OUTDOOR ACTIVITIES

Pacific Northwesterners claim to enjoy their cloudy skies and drizzly days. In defiance of the elements, many residents adopt the "grunge" look (hiking boots and heavy socks, khaki shorts, and flannel shirt) year-round and enthusiastically embrace the outdoors. The region offers some of the world's best white-water rafting, kayaking, hiking, skiing, fishing, scuba diving, windsurfing, and rockclimbing. For those who prefer more placid pursuits, such as sitting beside a still mountain lake or a rushing stream, or strolling along a remote surf-pounded beach, the opportunities here are seemingly endless.

CITY LIFE

All this natural beauty provides a backdrop for the urban sophistication of the Pacific Northwest's three major cities, Portland, Seattle, and Vancouver. Here residents have worked together to preserve the scenic virtues and old quarters of their cities while accommodating new growth. Portland has

Portlanders relaxing at a local café and wine bar

converted much of its downtown riverfront into parkland and laid the tracks of an efficient rapid transit system. Due to the efforts of residents, Seattle has restored its historic Pike Place Market, the colorful and quirky heart of the city, and Vancouver has incorporated striking new architecture into a landscape dominated by mountains and inlets.

Of course, the residents of each city tend to claim that theirs is the most beautiful and livable in the Pacific Northwest, if not in all of North America. Each has its own unique virtues. Portland takes first place for careful urban planning, for containing urban sprawl, and for preserving a charming small-town atmosphere. Seattle, with its imposing skyline, is the largest of the three cities. Well known for its high-tech industries, it also offers a vibrant music and theater scene. Cosmopolitan Vancouver, nestled between the Strait of Georgia and the Coast Mountains, arguably enjoys the best setting.

ART AND CULTURE

Long gone are the days when the Pacific Northwest was considered a poor country cousin in terms of the arts. Highly regarded and wide-ranging collections of art now hang in many museums throughout the region, and excellent concert halls and other venues play host to world-renowned orchestras and performing artists, and to stellar home-grown talent. Unforgettable experiences such as a classical concert beneath a canopy of ponderosa pines at the annual Britt Festivals in Jacksonville, Oregon; an evening of jazz with a sunset backdrop of Seattle's Elliott Bay; or a Shakespeare play at a waterfront park in Vancouver, bring artistic flair to some of the most spectacular settings in the world.

Tourists at the top of Seattle's Space Needle

ECONOMY AND INDUSTRY
While the economies of the major coastal cities are healthy, the interior regions are suffering from high unemployment as traditional industries such as mining and logging decline and the economy shifts to one based largely on services and technology. In coastal areas, the fishing industry too has seen increasingly hard times. Fruit cultivation remains a major Pacific Northwest industry, its orchards yielding some of the most prized fruit in the world.

The emergence of high-tech companies in the region (some 3,000 software and e-commerce businesses are in the Seattle area alone) began with the rise in the 1980s of Microsoft, now employing 25,000 Washingtonians. In 1995, entrepreneur Jeff Bezos opened the doors to the online shopping business, founding Amazon.com in his Seattle home. Aerospace giant Boeing operates several plants in western Washington. Manufacturing facilities for computer industry giants Intel, Epson, and Hewlett-Packard are located in Oregon's Willamette Valley; sportswear chain Nike is also based in Oregon.

Vancouver has benefited from its recent incarnation as Hollywood North: movie companies inject $3 billion annually into the local economy.

The increase in white-collar jobs has led to an influx of professionals into the three cities, not only expanding the urban areas but also raising the standard (and the cost) of living within them.

Amid this economic transformation, the tourist industry has consistently thrived. Increasing numbers of tourists come to enjoy what locals have long considered their greatest resource: the Pacific Northwest's natural beauty.

PEOPLE AND POLITICS
Some 13 million people call the Pacific Northwest home. Portland, Seattle, and Vancouver are among the fastest-growing cities in North America. After a US-wide spike in growth in the 1990s, the Hispanic population is today Oregon's largest ethnic group, having increased by 144 percent to represent 8 percent of that state's population. And Hispanics now represent 7.5 percent of Washington's population. Vancouver has swelled in size and prosperity in recent years with the arrival of Asian immigrants, particularly from mainland China, Hong Kong, India, Philippines, and South Korea. The First Nations and bands of the Pacific Northwest, many continuing to live in traditional communities, are recovering from a decline in population that occurred after European settlement.

Portland, Seattle, and Vancouver tend to be liberal in their politics, other areas of the region, conservative. Even so, a unique political climate emerges in the Pacific Northwest. Oregonians are the first in the US to have approved assisted suicide for the terminally ill; Washingtonians have elected the US's first Asian-American governor; and British Columbians have bounced between right- and left-leaning parties, often bucking the national trend.

A lunchtime concert at Pioneer Courthouse Square, Portland

Geology of the Pacific Northwest

No SMALL AMOUNT of geological activity has shaped the present-day Pacific Northwest. One hundred and fifty million years ago, much of the western part of the region was at the bottom of the sea. Over the eons, the North American continental landmass crept westward and collided with the landmass moving eastward across the Pacific Ocean, forcing the Earth's crust upward and creating the coastline of the Pacific Northwest as we know it today. Meanwhile, the eruption of volcanoes thrusted up mountain peaks, and glaciers and ice sheets advanced and retreated, carving out deep gorges and canyons. As recent volcanic eruptions and earthquakes in the area attest, the Pacific Northwest is still a geologically active region, and its topography will no doubt continue to change as a result.

Washington's Mount Rainier – the most active volcano of the Cascades

Fossil records are found throughout the Pacific Northwest, with its sedimentary rock bearing traces of plant, marine, and animal life from as long ago as 136 million years. The world-renowned John Day Fossil Beds National Monument in Kimberly, Oregon, and the fossil beds at Burgess Shale near Field, British Columbia, are both extensive repositories of this ancient past.

SEDIMENTARY ROCK

As the Pacific plate periodically lurched eastward, sedimentary rock from older coastal mountains was uplifted to form the peaks of the Rocky and Cascade mountain ranges. Layers of the sedimentary rock, such as sandstone and shale, that were formed about 15 to 20 million years ago can be seen when visiting the ranges.

Volcanoes such as Mount St. Helens are formed when a plate descends (subducts) beneath another plate and it begins to melt, The molten rock rises to the surface to form a volcano. In the Pacific Northwest, volcanoes began erupting about 55 million years ago. The Cascade Mountains in Oregon and Washington, the Blue Mountains in Oregon, and the Olympic Mountains in Washington are in the Ring of Fire, a zone of volcanic activity that partially encircles the Pacific Ocean.

Glaciers *are masses of ice that advance and retreat, scooping out deep gorges and sculpting jagged mountain peaks. Continent-sized glaciers are known as ice sheets. About 15,000 years ago, the Cordilleran ice sheet covered much of Washington and British Columbia; it was 4,000 ft (1,219 m) thick in places. When it melted, the raised water levels of the Pacific Ocean filled two of the deepest gouges, creating Puget Sound and the Strait of Juan de Fuca.*

Gorges were formed *at the end of the last ice age, when massive floods were triggered periodically by melting glaciers. These floods etched out deep narrow chasms such as the one shown here, or much wider ones such as the Columbia River Gorge, which forms the boundary between Washington and Oregon.*

PLATE TECTONICS

Three main forces are responsible for the formation of mountain ranges such as the Rockies or the Cascades. First, large areas of the Earth's crust (known as tectonic plates), constantly moving together and apart, created uplift. Second, the North American plate, subducted by the Pacific plate, caused a chain of volcanoes to form from the molten rock of the oceanic crust. Third, erosion caused by ice ages deposited sedimentary rocks on the North American plate, which was then folded by more plate movement between 50 and 25 million years ago.

Volcanoes   **North America plate**
Pacific plate

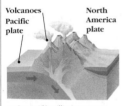

1 Some 150 million years ago, the Pacific plate moved east, adding to the molten rock from great depths of the North American plate. This then rose up to form the Western Cordillera Mountains.

Pacific plate   **Sediments**

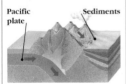

2 The Cordilleras were eroded over millions of years and during various ice ages. This led to sediments being deposited in the sagging, wedge-shaped crust east of the mountain range.

Cordillera Mountains   **Rockies**

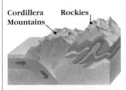

3 Around 50 million years ago, the Pacific plate continued to push east, forcing the Cordillera range eastward, compressing sedimentary rocks, folding and uplifting them to form the Rockies.

Wildlife of the Pacific Northwest

THE LANDSCAPES OF the Pacific Northwest are the most varied in North America. The cold waters of the Pacific Ocean fill sheltered bays and wash onto great lengths of sandy beach, dense old-growth forests carpet the Coast and Cascade Mountains, and arid plateaus and high deserts spread across the eastern parts of the region. Over the past 150 years, settlers have created new landscapes, including the fertile farmland of Oregon's Willamette Valley and the expanses of orchards and wheatfields in eastern Washington and British Columbia. These landscapes – lush river valleys and harsh deserts alike – provide rich habitats for a great diversity of wildlife, and viewing these animals is a rewarding part of a visit to the Pacific Northwest.

Sea lions make their homes on rocky outcroppings along the Pacific shore.

Pacific salmon migrate from cold ocean waters, where they feed until maturity, into the inland streams, rivers, and lakes of their birth where they spawn, then die. Once they have reached fresh water, they stop feeding and live on their stored body fats. The fish often make journeys of more than 1,000 miles (1,600 km), swimming up rapids and bypassing dams. Each of the five species of Pacific salmon – sockeye, pink, chum, coho, and chinook – has a distinct appearance and life cycle. The pinks, for example, live up to two years and weigh little more than 5 lbs (2.3 kg), while the chinook can reach 120 lbs (54 kg) in weight and live up to seven years.

ELK

Elk reside in the subalpine forests of the Rockies and eastern Oregon mountains. During the mating season in the fall, males become aggressive and fight for herd domination. The nasal, whining sound they emit, known as "bugling," should be taken by humans as a warning.

Sea otters were rendered almost extinct in the 19th century by trappers who obtained enormous prices for their pelts but are now making a comeback along the Pacific Northwest coast. These creatures eat the equivalent of a third of their weight a day, providing quite a show as they feed. A sea otter lies on its back and, using its paws, smashes crabs, mussels, and other shellfish against a rock it has placed on its chest. Otters are easily spotted, lolling on rocks or floating asleep on the water, their bodies entwined in kelp to keep them from drifting.

Whales *belonging to over 20 species pass Vancouver Island, the Olympic Peninsula, and the Oregon coast as they travel between the Arctic and their breeding grounds off southern California and Mexico. It is estimated that 20,000 gray whales and 2,000 orcas make the 5,500-mile (8,850-km) trip each year. The whales migrate south from December to early February and return north from March through May.*

Bald eagles, *once common thoughout North America, are now mainly found in the Pacific Northwest, in coastal areas or near large inland lakes. The bald eagle is regarded as a symbol of strength and independence, and was designated as the national bird of the US in 1782. Contrary to what its name implies, this eagle is not actually bald; the term comes from the Old English word "balde," meaning white.*

Beavers *are very industrious, using their sharp upper teeth to fell small trees, which they then float to a chosen dam site. The lodges they build within the dam can be as wide as 16 ft (5 m).*

Moose, *distinguishable by their magnificient spreading antlers, are often spotted grazing by streams, ponds, and other marshy areas.*

Grizzly bears, *weighing up to 800 lbs (350 kg) and standing as tall as 8.8 ft (2.68 m), roam remote parts of the northern Cascades and the Rockies. Far more common is the black bear, smaller than the grizzly but imposing nonetheless.*

Flora of the Pacific Northwest

D EEP FORESTS, wildflower-filled alpine meadows, and grass-covered steppes are all typical of the Pacific Northwest. Although vastly different, these landscapes are often found in close proximity to one another. The moist, temperate climate of the region's coastal areas fosters an abundance of plant life, including the towering trees, mosses, and shrubs that thrive in centuries-old forests, such as the rainforest in British Columbia's Pacific Rim National Park Reserve. In Washington's Skagit Valley, tulips covering thousands of acres bloom each spring. In the Cascade and Rocky Mountains, and in the deserts and steppes east of the mountains, the terrain is less hospitable and only the hardiest plants survive. But even here, alpine meadows and stands of juniper that scent the high desert attest to the rich diversity of the region's flora.

Wildflowers
The moist climate of the coastal forests and high-country meadows provide perfect growing conditions for colorful wildflowers, such as wood lilies, asters, Jacob's ladder, and purple mountain saxifrage.

Lichens
Hardy lichens – along with mosses, liverworts, ferns, skunk cabbage, and orchids – flourish in the dampness of rainforests that grow along the coast of the Pacific Ocean.

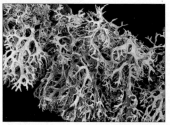

Sagebrush
The arid environment of the Columbia River basin and the high plateaus of Oregon and Washington support only vegetation that can survive with little moisture, such as sagebrush.

MOUNTAIN FORESTS
Many of the trees in the rugged mountain forests are several centuries old. Douglas firs can live as long as 1,200 years and grow to be 260 ft (79 m) tall. Fallen logs foster young trees which, if they survive 200 years, will earn "old-growth" status.

Deciduous Forests
*Deciduous trees grow
in river valleys in the
Pacific Northwest.
In the fall, these trees
provide a brilliant show
of color, all the more
dramatic because the
multihued leaves are
usually set against
a backdrop
of evergreen trees.*

Ferns
*Lady's fern and
deer fern are
among the many
species that grow in
the region. In the
Hoh Rainforest,
ferns grow taller
than the hikers.*

Pines and Junipers
*Ponderosa pines, lodge-
pole pines, and junipers
have long roots that tap
subterranean water
tables. With flat needles
that retain moisture,
junipers can survive on
just 8 inches (20.5 cm)
of precipitation a year.*

Rainforests
*Rainforests carpet much of the Pacific
Northwest, on British Columbia's
Vancouver Island and Queen
Charlotte Islands, and along the
Pacific coast. These lush green forests
of Sitka spruce, Douglas fir, red cedar,
Pacific silver fir, western hemlock
and yew can receive more than
150 inches (381 cm) of rain per year.*

Native Peoples of the Pacific Northwest

FOR THE NATIVE PEOPLES of the Pacific Northwest, 15,000 years of a bountiful life and rich cultural tradition were abruptly upset when European traders and settlers began arriving in the late 18th century. Diseases introduced by these newcomers all but obliterated many First Nations. Those who survived were forced to surrender their lands and ways of life, and move to government-designated reservations. Today, although indigenous people continue to fight against racism and for their self-determination, Native traditions are increasingly recognized as a vital part of the region's rich heritage. Native cultures and history can be explored in such places as the Royal British Columbia Museum, in Victoria *(see pp252–3)*, Whatcom Museum of History and Art, in Bellingham, Washington *(see p180)*, and Oregon's Museum at Warm Springs *(see p102)*.

A stone inukshuk, sign of friendship

Totem poles *are among the best-known artifacts created by the Native peoples of the Pacific Northwest. Each pole depicts a legend; magical birds and beasts mix with semi-human figures to tell a story in carved panels arranged in sequence up the pole. Other elaborate carvings, such as those on masks, ornaments, and utensils, often also represent real and supernatural beings.*

ARTISANS AND BUILDERS

The trunks of cedar trees were used by Pacific Northwest Natives to carve masks, cooking utensils, wooden chests, elaborate dwellings up to 500 ft (150 m) long and aptly called longhouses, and magnificent dugout canoes, used for transportation, hunting, and fishing.

Respect for the land *underpins the spirituality and way of life of Native peoples of the Pacific Northwest. Nature provides all, so long as nature's balance is not disturbed. Chief Seattle once said: "We are part of the Earth and it is part of us. The perfumed flowers are our sisters; the deer, the horse, the great eagle, these are our brothers. The rocky crests, the juices in the meadows, the body heat of the pony, and man – all belong to the same family."*

Canoes made of birch bark or dug out of massive cedar logs provided an essential mode of transportation on the many rivers which formed a network of trade routes throughout the Pacific Northwest. Canoes ranged in size from small vessels for personal use to large and elaborately decorated ceremonial canoes.

Wigwams were built as dwellings by tribes living in the interior, such as the Nez Percé, Yakama, Cayuse, Shoshone, and Modoc. More permanent longhouses were preferred by many of the tribes that settled along the Pacific Northwest coast from southern Alaska down to Oregon. They include the Tlingit, the Tsimshian, the Haida, the Kwagiutl, the West Coast, and the Coast Salish.

NOTEWORTHY CHIEFS

Chief Seattle (1786–1866), leader of the Duwamish and Suquamish tribes, was just six years old when he witnessed the arrival of Captain Vancouver in Puget Sound. He frequently petitioned American and British authorities for Indian rights and urged peaceful coexistence with settlers.

Chief Joseph (1840–1904) was the renowned leader of the Nez Percé tribe. In 1877, his tribe was forced out of its beloved Wallowa Valley in Oregon. The tribe fled, fighting, and Chief Joseph showed great skill leading his warriors in battle against the American troops until his defeat the same year.

Chief Joe Capilano (1840–1910) was born on what is now Vancouver's North Shore. An esteemed Suquamish chief, he and his wife Mary, known as the "Indian Princess of Peace," visited King Edward VII in Great Britain in 1906 to present a petition for Indian rights.

Landscapes of the Pacific Northwest

THE PACIFIC NORTHWEST is blessed with an abundance of dramatically different landscapes. Seashores give way to coastal mountains, which drop into the Fraser Plateau in British Columbia, into Puget Sound in Washington, and into the Willamette Valley in Oregon. The peaks of the Cascade Mountains bisect both Oregon and Washington, and the majestic Rockies rise in eastern British Columbia. Other distinct landscapes are the Columbia Plateau's layers of ancient lava that spread across eastern Oregon and Washington, and the high, arid deserts of central and southern Oregon.

Sea Stacks
Portions of wave-eroded headlands that remain as offshore mounds rise majestically from the surf of the Pacific Ocean. The stacks are most numerous along the southern Oregon coast near Cape Blanco and off Washington's Olympic Peninsula.

Coasts
In Oregon and southern Washington, sandy beaches and rocky headlands extend for more than 450 miles (725 km) along the coast. The Strait of Juan de Fuca etches Washington's northern coastline with a succession of bays and inlets, while in British Columbia, 10,340 miles (16,640 km) of shoreline wrap around inlets, fjords, and islands.

MOUNTAIN RANGES
The Coast and Cascade ranges form a spine of mountains that rises almost continuously from southern Oregon to northern British Columbia. Much of the lower slopes of the mountains is carpeted with forests that give way to alpine meadows, then to glaciers.

The Canadian Rockies
With their dominating peaks and vast ice fields, the Rocky Mountains cover a large part of British Columbia. Thirty mountains of this immense range are more than 10,000 ft (3,048 m) high.

Mountain Areas
The mountains in the Pacific Northwest form a barrier that traps great amounts of moisture, which in winter can cause heavy snowfall on peaks such as Oregon's Diamond Peak.

Gorges
Gorges reveal the dramatic geological history of the region. Over the course of thousands of years, rushing rivers have carved away rock and earth, leaving behind huge gorges as well as long and narrow chasms, such as Oregon's Oneonta Gorge in the Columbia River Gorge National Scenic Area.

Waterfalls
The spectacular Lower Kentucky Falls in Oregon's Siuslaw National Forest is one of thousands of waterfalls in the Pacific Northwest. The Kentucky Creek runs through old-growth forest before spilling over a cliff, plummeting 75 ft (23 m), then an additional 25 ft (8 m), to the rocky slopes below.

Dry Lands and Desert Country
East of the mountains, the terrain tends to be flat, and precipitation can average as little as 12 inches (30.5 cm) a year. As a result, the landscape here is vastly different from that found in the mountain and coastal regions. In eastern Oregon, steppes and deserts are covered with juniper and sagebrush. Rocky outcroppings, usually composed of volcanic basalt, are also common here, and vegetation is often sparse.

Famous People

THE RESIDENTS OF THE PACIFIC NORTHWEST have cultivated a rich tradition of excellence in the arts,
sciences, public service, and creative entrepreneurship.
Some Pacific Northwesterners were drawn to the region
from other parts of the US and Canada; others were
born and bred in the Pacific Northwest and continue
to call it home. Whichever the case may be, all have
left their mark on the region, and indeed, the world.
Long at the forefront of environmentalism and entrepreneurship, the Pacific Northwest continues to nourish
some of the best creative talents of this century.

**Emily Carr, portrayer of remote
Pacific Northwest Native villages**

AUTHORS AND ARTISTS

THE VILLAGES and totems of
the Pacific Northwest's
Native peoples were por-
trayed in fluid brush strokes
by painter and writer Emily
Carr (1871–1945) *(see p250).*
However, she was 57 years
old before her striking can-
vases garnered critical acclaim.
Carr's 1941 short story collection *Klee Wyck* is considered
a Canadian classic.

Modernist architect
Pietro Belluschi
(1899–1994) came
to Portland from
his native Italy in
the 1920s and was
soon designing the
elegant, spare build-
ings – including the
Portland Art Museum
– for which he earned
world approval.

The "Father of
American Gastron-
omy," Portland chef and cook-
book author James Beard
(1903–85) reminded his fellow
Americans of their culinary
heritage with his focus on
fresh local ingredients.

Raymond Carver (1938–88)
often set his rich short stories

and poems in his
native Oregon and
other Pacific North-
west locales.

Heat, gravity, and
centrifugal force
are the hallmarks
of Dale Chihuly's
art. Born in
Tacoma in 1941, he is
one of the world's lead-
ing glass sculpturists.

Also hailing from
Tacoma, Gary Larson
(b.1950) delighted read-
ers for 14 years with his
zany portrayals of
animals with human
quirks in *The Far Side*
cartoon strip,
launched in 1980.

**Master guitarist
Jimmy Hendrix**

ENTERTAINERS

RAISED IN TACOMA, singer
and actor Bing Crosby
(1903–77) embodied the image
of the happy-go-lucky
guy, notably as jaunty
Father O'Malley in
the acclaimed 1944
film *Going My Way.*
His recording of
"White Christmas"
remains the most
popular song ever,
the only single to
make American pop
charts 20 times.

Hollywood also
claimed Seattle-
born cult figure
Frances Farmer (1913–70) as
one of its most promising
actresses in the 1930s and
1940s, though she is perhaps
better known for her battle
with mental illness and the
brutal treatment she received
in state institutions. Farmer's

**Dale Chihuly,
leading glass artist**

life was detailed in her auto-
biography *Will There Be a
Morning?* and in the movie
Frances, starring Jessica Lange.

Crime-fighting superhero
Batman of the 1966–8 TV
series was in real life Walla
Walla native Adam West
(b.1928). His debonair looks
and flair for tongue-in-cheek
comedy made him perfect for
the role, though being type-
cast as the Caped Crusader
eventually brought his
career to a grinding halt.

James Marshall Hendrix
(1942–70), better known
as Jimi Hendrix, was born
in Seattle. After releasing
chart-topping singles,
breaking concert
attendance records,
and selling millions of
albums, Hendrix became a
rock legend and one of the
most influential guitarists
of all time. Seattle's Experience Music Project *(see
pp146–7)* holds the world's
largest collection of Hendrix memorabilia.

The creator of the
wildly popular TV
show *The Simpsons*
was born and raised
in Portland. Matt Groening
(b.1954) is behind the antics
of Homer, Marge, Lisa, and
Maggie (named after Groening's own family members),
and, of course, Bart (loosely
based on himself), enjoyed
weekly by 60 million viewers.

At the age of 16, rock star
Bryan Adams (b.1959) made

**British Columbia's world-class
jazz vocalist Diana Krall**

Terry Fox, running across Canada to raise money for cancer research

his singing debut with Vancouver band Sweeney Todd, going solo a year later. In 1990, Adams was awarded the Order of Canada, and in 1991 received a Grammy Award for "(Everything I Do) I Do It for You."

Actor Michael J. Fox (b.1961) left Vancouver for Hollywood in 1979 to star in popular TV shows *Family Ties* and *Spin City,* as well as in several films. In 1998, he announced that he was afflicted by Parkinson's disease, and cut back on his acting career.

Jazz vocalist Diana Krall (b.1964) began studying classical piano at the age of 4, and landed her first piano gig when she was 15, in a restaurant in her hometown of Nanaimo, British Columbia. Her breakthrough album *All for You* was released in 1996; *When I Look in Your Eyes* won Krall the 2000 Grammy Award for Album of the Year.

Popular music was redefined in the 1990s when limelight-shy singer Kurt Cobain (1967–94) cofounded the Seattle-based grunge band Nirvana, which went on to release the multiplatinum-selling album *Nevermind.*

HUMANITARIANS

ABIGAIL SCOTT Duniway (1834–1915) published the Portland weekly *New Northwest,* which promoted equal rights for women. As a suffrage leader, she played an important role in gaining women the right to vote in Idaho (1896), Washington (1910), and Oregon (1912).

A resident of Port Coquitlam, BC, Terry Fox (1958–81) lost his right leg to cancer at age 18. He became a national hero when, in 1980, he pledged to run across Canada to raise money for cancer research. He was forced to quit his Marathon of Hope after 143 days and 3,339 miles (5,373 km) when cancer appeared in his lung. Annual Terry Fox Runs continue to this day around the world, and have raised more than $300 million for cancer research.

SCIENTISTS AND ENVIRONMENTALISTS

PORTLANDER LINUS Pauling (1901–1994) is the only person to win two unshared Nobel prizes – for chemistry in 1954 and for peace in 1962. An outspoken pacifist, Pauling and his wife, Ava Helen, presented to the United Nations in 1958 a petition signed by thousands of scientists calling for an end to the testing of nuclear weapons, thereby raising awareness of their dangers. The Pacific Northwest is known for its passionate environmentalism; one of the movement's most respected spokespersons is David Suzuki (b.1936). A Vancouverite who was interned with his family during World War II, Suzuki is an internationally recognized geneticist and host of the award-winning TV series *The Nature of Things.* In 1990, in response to thousands of letters, he and his wife Tara Cullis set up the David Suzuki Foundation to help find solutions to the environment crisis.

David Suzuki, respected enviromentalist

POLITICIANS

Amor de Cosmos, BC premier, 1872–4

AMOR DE COSMOS (1825–97), British Columbia's second premier, was born William Smith but changed his name to reflect his love of "order, beauty, the world, the universe." Although a founding member of the Confederation League, an organization created to campaign for BC's union with Canada, de Cosmos's increasingly erratic behavior led to his removal from public life in 1882.

In 1926, Seattleites elected Bertha Landes (1868–1943) mayor. The first female executive of a major US city, Landes and her corruption-free administration served as encouragement for other women to enter politics.

Tom McCall (1913–83), Oregon's governor from 1967 to 1975, was a staunch supporter of measures to regulate land use and protect the environment. In 1971 he enacted the US's first mandatory bottle-deposit law in a fight against his state's growing litter problem.

ENTREPRENEURS

MICROSOFT, THE world's foremost computer software company, was founded by Bill Gates (b.1955) and Paul Allen (b.1953) *(see p159).* Gates and his wife also established the Bill and Melinda Gates Foundation, which contributes millions of dollars to charities. Allen, owner of the Seattle Seahawks football team, is a philanthropist and founder of the Experience Music Project *(see pp146–7).*

Jeff Bezos (b.1964) is the founder and chief executive officer of Amazon.com, the world's largest online retailer, headquartered in Seattle. The multibillionaire has been called the king of cybercommerce; *Time* magazine named him Person of the Year in 1999.

THE PACIFIC NORTHWEST THROUGH THE YEAR

Hot air balloon, Oregon

THE IMAGE of the Pacific Northwest's weather as consistently wet is rooted as much in myth as in fact. Rain is a distinctive presence in only half of the Pacific Northwest – the part west of the mountains that divide the region. The weather in this western, coastal section remains mild throughout the year, and snow is rare in all but the higher elevations. In the mountains, winter snowfall is heavy, much to the delight of skiers. East of the mountains, where cold and heat reach extreme levels, winter snowfall can be heavy but summers can be bone dry. In spite of the variable weather throughout the Pacific Northwest, the unique rewards of living and traveling in the region are many. Even in the damp and most heavily populated western sections, rain doesn't prevent residents and visitors alike from heading outdoors to enjoy a large variety of entertaining festivals and events.

SPRING

MARCH AND APRIL bring the signs of spring to the lower elevations of the Pacific Northwest. A number of festivities celebrate the region's lush gardens as they come into bloom in an array of magnificent colors.

MARCH

Playhouse International Wine Festival *(Mar or Apr)*, Vancouver, BC. A week of wine tastings at Canada Place *(p202)* and other locales.
Great Gorge Grape and Gouda Gala *(mid-Mar)*, The Dalles, OR. Local vintners and cheesemakers offer tastings.
Sandhill Crane Festival *(late Mar)*, Othello, WA. Witness the sounds and rituals of 25,000 migrating cranes.

Blossoming fruit trees in April, the Hood River Valley, Oregon

Victorian Festival *(late Mar)*, Port Townsend, WA *(pp176–7)*. All things Victorian are celebrated in this historic seaport.

APRIL

Skagit Valley Tulip Festival *(Apr)*, Skagit Valley, WA. A month-long festival of arts and crafts fairs, barbecues, and walking tours amid 1,000 acres (405 ha) of tulips.
Victoria International Blossom Walks *(mid-Apr)*, Victoria, BC. Fitness and flowers for walkers.
Hood River Valley Blossom Festival *(third weekend)*, Hood River Valley, OR. Arts and crafts fairs and tours of orchards and wineries in towns along the Hood River.
Washington State Apple Blossom Festival *(late Apr–early May)*, Wenatchee, WA. Parades, a carnival, and concerts to usher in spring.

MAY

Seagull Calling Festival *(first Sat)*, Port Orchard, WA. A waterfront festival centered on a seagull-calling contest.
Bloomsday Run *(first Sun)*, Spokane, WA. A 7.5-mile (12-km) race through downtown, with more than 50,000 runners.
Cinco de Mayo Festival *(early May)*, Portland, OR. Four days of Mexican food,

A perfect rose, the International Rose Test Garden, Portland

art, music, and dance on the Portland waterfront.
Annual Rhododendron Festival *(third weekend)*, Florence, OR. A parade and carnival to celebrate the rhododendron blossoms.
Northwest Folklife Festival *(Memorial Day weekend)*, Seattle, WA. Dance, exhibits, and workshops at one of the largest free events in the US.
Brookings Azalea Festival *(Memorial Day weekend)*, Brookings, OR. Blossoms and food in a coastal town famous for its azaleas.
Blessing of the Fleet *(late May)*, Westport, WA. A parade and a blessing of the town's famous fishing fleet.
Vancouver International Children's Festival *(late May)*, Vancouver, BC. Local, national, and international performing artists present theater and music for children.
Portland Rose Festival *(late May–mid-Jun)*, Portland, OR. Parades, concerts, races, and a carnival in honor of the rose.

SUMMER

SUMMER IN MUCH of the Pacific Northwest is not assuredly sunny. But locals don't hesitate to venture outdoors for a variety of activities and events, including wine festivals, rodeos, plays, and concerts under the stars.

JUNE

Bard on the Beach Shakespeare Festival *(Jun–Sep)*, Vancouver, BC. Lively plays at Vanier Park *(pp220–21)*.
Sisters Rodeo *(mid-Jun)*, Sisters, OR *(p102)*. Rodeo held every year since 1940.
Britt Festivals *(mid-Jun–early Sep)*, Jacksonville, OR *(p108)*. Music concerts from classical to pop under the ponderosa pines and stars.
JazzFest International *(late Jun)* Victoria, BC. Jazz and blues concerts at venues all over town.
Pi-Ume-Sha Treaty Days *(late Jun)*, Warm Springs, OR *(p102)*. A powwow, parade, and rodeo mark the treaty that formed the Confederated Tribes of Warm Springs.
Oregon Bach Festival *(late Jun–mid-Jul)*, Eugene, OR *(p101)*. A series of concerts honoring J.S. Bach.
Summer Nights at the Pier *(late Jun–Aug)*, Seattle, WA. Waterfront concert series, with lovely sunset views over the Olympic Mountains.
Hoopfest *(last weekend)*, Spokane, WA. The US's largest three-on-three basketball tournament.

Costumed dancer, Caribbean Days Festival, North Vancouver

JULY

Seafair *(Jul)*, Seattle, WA. Waterfront festival including a torchlight parade, hydroplane races, and an air show.
International Folk Music Festival *(Jul)*, Vancouver, BC. An annual folk festival, in Jericho Beach Park.
Canada Day *(Jul 1)*, across British Columbia. Parades, live music, and evening fireworks.
Williams Lake Stampede *(Jul 1 weekend)*, Williams Lake, BC. Rodeo fun at one of North America's largest stampedes.
Waterfront Blues Festival *(early Jul)*, Portland, OR. Five days of blues from local and nationally acclaimed artists.
Washington Mutual Family Fourth *(Jul 4)*, Seattle, WA. Over 5,000 fireworks over Gas Works Park *(p155)*.

Ripe peaches in the Okanagan Valley, BC

Bite of Seattle *(mid-Jul)*, Seattle, WA. A popular two-day event with food from more than 60 restaurants.
Oregon Coast Music Festival *(mid–late Jul)*, Charleston, Coos Bay, and North Bend, OR. Classical music and jazz performed next to the Pacific Ocean.
Caribbean Days Festival *(late Jul)*, North Vancouver, BC. Celebration of all things Caribbean, with colorful costumes and great music.
International Pinot Noir Celebration *(late Jul)*, McMinnville, OR *(p100)*. Pinot noirs coupled with food from noted local chefs.
Molson Indy Vancouver *(late Jul)*, Vancouver, BC. High-speed car races through the city's downtown streets.
Celebration of Lights *(late Jul–early Aug)*, Vancouver, BC. Spectacular fireworks competition at English Bay.

AUGUST

Penticton Peach Festival *(early Aug)*, Penticton, BC. A charming festival celebrating the local peach harvest.
Mount Hood Jazz Festival *(early Aug)*, Gresham, OR. Two days of mellow jazz and local wines.
ExtravaGAYza! Parade and Festival *(early Aug)*, Vancouver, BC. Fun and fanciful events for Gay Pride Week.
First Peoples Festival *(early Aug)*, Victoria, BC. Three days of art, food, and performances by First Nations peoples.
Omak Stampede and World Famous Suicide Race *(mid-Aug)*, Omak, WA. A rodeo, stampede, and daredevil horse race.
Oregon State Fair *(late Aug–early Sep)*, Salem, OR *(p100)*. Twelve days of Oregon produce and livestock, rides, concerts, and food.
Evergreen State Fair *(late Aug–early Sep)*, Monroe, WA. Arts and crafts, rides, races, and rodeo events.

Steer roping at the Sisters Rodeo, held mid-June in Sisters, Oregon

Ride at the September Pacific National Exhibition, Vancouver, BC

FALL

Fall foliage can be quite spectacular in the Pacific Northwest, as brilliant reds and yellows stand out against evergreens. Colorful landscapes are the backdrop for events celebrating the harvest of cranberries, oysters, and other regional specialties.

SEPTEMBER

Pacific National Exhibition *(late Aug–early Sep)*, Vancouver, BC. One of Canada's largest fairs, with big-ticket entertainment, rides, pavilions, and agricultural exhibits.

Bumbershoot *(Labor Day weekend)*, Seattle, WA. A mix of music and film at the Seattle Center *(pp142–3)*.

Classic Boat Festival *(early Sep)*, Victoria, BC. Racing of classic sailboats and power-boats in the Inner Harbour.

Puyallup Fair *(early Sep)*, Puyallup, WA. An important state fair with rides, exhibits, a rodeo, and live music offered over 17 days.

Oktoberfest *(mid-Sep)*, Mount Angel, OR. Bavarian food and plenty of beer.

Pendleton Round-Up *(mid-Sep)*, Pendleton, OR *(p111)*. A rodeo featuring calf-roping, bull-riding, and a town full of real cowboys.

Indian-style Salmon Bake *(third Sat in Sep)*, Depoe Bay, OR. Fresh salmon cooked over an open fire beside the town's tiny harbor.

OCTOBER

Okanagan Wine Festival *(early Oct)*, Okanagan Valley, BC. Vineyard tours and wine tastings at harvest time.

OysterFest *(early Oct)*, Shelton, WA. A weekend of oyster shucking, wine tastings, and cooking contests.

Annual Cranberrian Fair *(mid-Oct)*, Ilwaco, WA. Music, dancing, craft displays, and cranberry tastings to celebrate the local harvest.

Vancouver International Writers Festival *(third week)*, Vancouver, BC. Readings by Canadian and international writers.

Northwest Bookfest *(late Oct)*, Seattle, WA. An indoor street fair for book-lovers, featuring many author readings.

NOVEMBER

Cornucopia *(mid-Nov)*, Whistler, BC *(pp256–7)*. A festival featuring fine dining, wine tastings, and seminars.

Christkindlmarkt *(weekend after Thanksgiving)*, Leavenworth, WA *(p186)*. An open-air market with decorated booths selling German treats, such as bratwurst

Seattle Marathon *(Sun after Thanksgiving)*, Seattle, WA. A chance for more than 10,000 participants to run off Thanksgiving excesses.

Climate

Climate varies widely across the Pacific Northwest. Coastal areas, such as Portland, Seattle, and Vancouver, are mild and wet, while inland deserts, such as the areas around Spokane and Kamloops, have seasonal extremes. Climates of mountain ranges in the Pacific Northwest, represented here by the Cascade Mountains, have divergent microclimates.

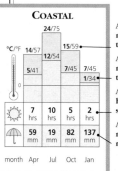

COASTAL

°C/°F	Apr	Jul	Oct	Jan
Average daily maximum temperature	14/57	24/75	15/59	7/45
Average daily minimum temperature	5/41	12/54	7/45	1/34
Average daily hours of sunshine	7 hrs	10 hrs	5 hrs	2 hrs
Average monthly rainfall	59 mm	19 mm	82 mm	137 mm

Average daily maximum temperature
Average daily minimum temperature
Average daily hours of sunshine
Average monthly rainfall

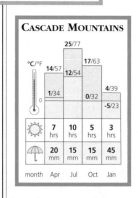

CASCADE MOUNTAINS

°C/°F	Apr	Jul	Oct	Jan
	14/57	25/77	17/63	4/39
	1/34	12/54	0/32	-5/23
	7 hrs	10 hrs	5 hrs	3 hrs
	20 mm	15 mm	15 mm	45 mm

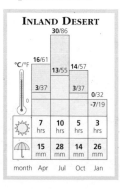

INLAND DESERT

°C/°F	Apr	Jul	Oct	Jan
	16/61	30/86	14/57	0/32
	3/37	13/55	3/37	-7/19
	7 hrs	10 hrs	5 hrs	3 hrs
	15 mm	28 mm	14 mm	26 mm

In December, a cheering Christmas Lighting Festival in Bavarian-themed Leavenworth

WINTER

WHEN SNOW covers the region's mountains, many Pacific Northwesterners take to downhill ski slopes or cross-country trails. In mild coastal areas, where winter days are short and rainy, unique Christmas celebrations provide a cheerful glow.

DECEMBER

Portland Parade of Christmas Ships *(Dec)*, Portland, OR. Gaily decorated boats sail down the Willamette River.
Van Dusen Botanical Gardens' Festival of Lights *(Dec)*, Vancouver, BC. Thousands of lights glitter throughout 55 acres (22 ha) of lush plantings in this botanical garden during the month before Christmas.

One of many ski competitions held in the region during winter

Christmas Lighting Festival *(first three weekends in Dec)*, Leavenworth, WA. Visitors enjoy roasted chestnuts, bratwurst, strolling carolers, and twinkling lights against the snow-capped Cascade Mountains in a Bavarian-style town.
Christmas Carol Ship Parade of Lights *(three weeks before Christmas)*, Vancouver, BC. Beautifully decorated vessels light up local waters.

JANUARY

Eagle Festival and Count *(early Jan)*, Brackendale, BC. Festival centered on a competition to count the number of bald eagles settling for the winter on the Squamish River.
Chinese New Year *(late Jan or early Feb)*, Vancouver, BC. Almost two weeks of colorful festivities, including dance, music, and a parade celebrate the new lunar year.

FEBRUARY

Northwest Flower and Garden Show *(third week of Feb)*, Seattle, WA. Full-scale landscaped garden displays and a flower show featuring creative designs attract flower-lovers to this event.
Oregon Shakespeare Festival *(mid-Feb–early Nov)* Ashland, OR *(p108)*. Classic and contemporary plays draw actors and spectators from around the world to this highly acclaimed drama festival.

PUBLIC HOLIDAYS

UNITED STATES

New Year's Day
(Jan 1)
Martin Luther King Day
(3rd Mon in Jan)
Presidents' Day
(mid-Feb)
Easter Monday
(variable)
Memorial Day
(last Mon in May)
Independence Day
(Jul 4)
Labor Day
(1st Mon in Sep)
Columbus Day
(2nd Mon in Oct)
Election Day
(1st Tue in Nov)
Veterans' Day
(Nov 11)
Thanksgiving Day
(4th Thu in Nov)
Christmas Day
(Dec 25)

CANADA

New Year's Day
(Jan 1)
Good Friday
(late Mar or mid-Apr)
Victoria Day
(Mon before May 25)
Canada Day
(Jul 1)
Civic holiday
(1st Mon in Aug)
Labor Day
(1st Mon in Sep)
Thanksgiving Day
(2nd Mon in Oct)
Remembrance Day
(Nov 11)
Christmas Day
(Dec 25)
Boxing Day
(Dec 26)

THE HISTORY OF
THE PACIFIC NORTHWEST

THE VAST LANDSCAPES *of the Pacific Northwest bear the imprint of the geological forces that carved deep gorges and thrust up soaring mountain peaks. The imprint left by Native peoples who lived in harmony with the land for thousands of years is less visible. In the early 19th century, after explorers had opened up the territory, settlers began to arrive and the modern Pacific Northwest was born.*

Enough is known about the early inhabitants of the region to suggest that many enjoyed a good life among the natural riches. The earliest inhabitants were likely nomadic hunters who, 15,000 to 25,000 years ago, crossed a land bridge across the then-dry Bering Strait from Russia to North America.

British explorer Captain James Cook

These early societies left various traces of their presence. Among intriguing finds is a 14,000-year-old spear point left embedded in fossilized mastodon bones. Sagebrush sandals, on display at the University of Oregon Museum of Natural History, are possibly the world's oldest, revealing that 9,000 years ago the art of shoemaking was practiced. Other signs that the region was long settled can be found in oral traditions, rife with tales of the eruption of Mount Mazama, which occurred 8,000 years ago. Rock carvings and paintings in Petroglyph Provincial Park, near Nanaimo, BC, are thought to be at least 3,000 years old.

EARLY LIFE

Food and other resources were abundant for tribes living in the forests west of the Cascade Mountains. Many tribes lived in well-established settlements, fished the rivers for salmon, and, in long dugouts, set out to sea in search of whales. They also cut timber for longhouses – massive dwellings that could house as many as 50 to 60 people. Tribes living in the harsher landscapes east of the mountains had fewer resources at hand and migrated across high-desert hunting grounds in search of bison, deer, and other game. In spring and summer, they moved up mountain slopes to pick berries and dig roots. By the 19th century, tribes

◁ **A contemporary illustration of Captain George Vancouver's ship, HMS *Discovery***

A Shoshone hunting elk with bow and arrow

World, the British, too, wanted a share of the riches. The mission of Sir Francis Drake (1540–96), financed by Queen Elizabeth I, was to sail up the west coast of North America, plundering gold from Spanish galleons. After claiming the land around San Francisco Bay for Britain, Drake sailed up the Oregon coast, as far north as the Strait of Juan de Fuca, first navigated by Juan de Fuca in 1592. Drake then traveled across the Pacific Ocean back to England.

In the 1770s, Captains George Vancouver (1758–98) and Peter Puget (1765–1822) accompanied Captain James Cook (1728–79) on a voyage along the Pacific Northwest coast in search of the fabled Northwest Passage. The explorers sailed up the coasts of Oregon, Washington, and British Columbia. In 1791, Vancouver and Puget also charted what are now Puget Sound (Washington) and Vancouver (British Columbia).

Captain George Vancouver

living in the high deserts had acquired horses and rode them east to the Great Plains to hunt bison, which had become extinct farther west.

For many tribes, life was so bountiful that a tradition of potlatch evolved. At these elaborate ceremonies, which marked important occasions and which were centered around a feast, the host chief would offer gifts with the expectation that the recipients would eventually repay the gesture with loyalty and gifts at a subsequent potlatch.

ARRIVAL OF EXPLORERS

Native peoples thrived in the Pacific Northwest until the 18th century, disturbed only by occasional incursions by explorers and traders. In the 16th century, the first Europeans began exploring the coastline in search of the Northwest Passage, a sea route that would provide a passage between Europe and the Far East.

The first European to sight the Pacific Northwest was Spanish explorer Juan Rodriguez Cabrillo, who sailed with his crew from Mexico to southern Oregon in 1543. Once the Spanish had gained a stronghold in the New

Ship caught in the ice along the northern Pacific coast

TIMELINE

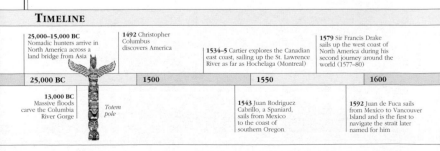

25,000–15,000 BC
Nomadic hunters arrive in North America across a land bridge from Asia

1492 Christopher Columbus discovers America

1534–5 Cartier explores the Canadian east coast, sailing up the St. Lawrence River as far as Hochelaga (Montreal)

1579 Sir Francis Drake sails up the west coast of North America during his second journey around the world (1577–80)

| 25,000 BC | 1500 | 1550 | 1600 |

13,000 BC
Massive floods carve the Columbia River Gorge

Totem pole

1543 Juan Rodriguez Cabrillo, a Spaniard, sails from Mexico to the coast of southern Oregon

1592 Juan de Fuca sails from Mexico to Vancouver Island and is the first to navigate the strait later named for him

Simon Fraser and companions on the Fraser River

However, they did not notice the Columbia River, discovered the following year by Captain Robert Gray, an American fur trader from the East Coast, who named the river after his ship, *The Columbia Rediviva.*
Other American vessels soon arrived in search of animal pelts and other bounty. The Spanish, who had been attempting to establish strongholds along the Pacific coast for centuries, retreated to their claims in California.

In 1793, Scotsman and Montreal fur trader Alexander Mackenzie crossed Canada to British Columbia, proving that an overland trade route was feasible. Mackenzie was also the first European to navigate the Peace River, the only river in British Columbia that drains into the Arctic Ocean.

From 1805 to 1808, Simon Fraser (1776–1862), a partner in the fur-trading North West Company, was charged with extending the company's trading activities west of the Rocky Mountains to the Pacific Ocean, and exploring a river thought to be the Columbia. In this capacity, Fraser established Fort McCleod, Fort St. James, Fort Fraser, and Fort George, all in British Columbia.

Fraser's major accomplishment though, was to be the first to navigate the longest river in British Columbia, now known as the Fraser River, which courses through the rugged BC interior to the Pacific Ocean.

LEWIS AND CLARK

US President Thomas Jefferson called on his former secretary, Meriwether Lewis, and Lewis's friend, William Clark, to find an overland route to the Pacific Ocean. The pair and an entourage of 33 set out from St. Louis, Missouri, in May 1804 and walked, rode horseback, and canoed to the Oregon coast, which they reached a year and a half later, in November 1805. The only female member of the expedition was Sacagawea, a young Shoshone woman who proved to be an invaluable guide and translator. The famed expedition set the stage for the rapid settlement of the Pacific Northwest. The expedition members not only plotted the first overland route across the US, mapping unexplored territory and collecting data on Native peoples and wildlife, but they also published journals that sparked a wave of migration from the east.

William Clark, explorer

Pioneer log cabin, Champoeg State Park, Oregon

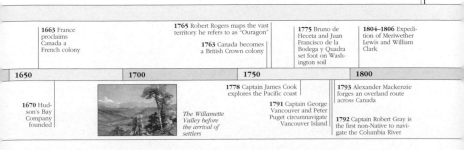

1663 France proclaims Canada a French colony

1670 Hudson's Bay Company founded

1765 Robert Rogers maps the vast territory he refers to as "Ouragon"

1763 Canada becomes a British Crown colony

The Willamette Valley before the arrival of settlers

1778 Captain James Cook explores the Pacific coast

1791 Captain George Vancouver and Peter Puget circumnavigate Vancouver Island

1775 Bruno de Heceta and Juan Francisco de la Bodega y Quadra set foot on Washington soil

1804–1806 Expedition of Meriwether Lewis and William Clark

1793 Alexander Mackenzie forges an overland route across Canada

1792 Captain Robert Gray is the first non-Native to navigate the Columbia River

1650	1700	1750	1800

A BATTLE FOR THE SPOILS

The battle to control the Pacific Northwest was waged by the British and the Americans not with gunfire but through trade. The expedition of Lewis and Clark opened up the region to US fur traders. They could now compete with the British, who dominated the lucrative pelt trade. In 1811, the American John Jacob Astor established a fur-trading post, Astoria, at the mouth of the Columbia River. Although US President Jefferson had hoped that Lewis and Clark's expedition would displace the British, the British-owned Hudson's Bay Company effectively continued to rule the Pacific Northwest until the middle of the 19th century. The company controlled both the growing population of settlers and much of the trade activity. Company headquarters at Fort Vancouver, overlooking the confluence of the Columbia and Willamette Rivers, and at Fort Victoria, on Vancouver Island in British Columbia, were the region's major settlements. Hudson's Bay Company trading posts became such common sights in the wilderness that it was quipped that the initials "HBC" stood for "Here Before Christ."

Territorial tensions between Britain and the US erupted in the War of 1812. Although neither side "won" this war, the dominance of the British was later undermined when thousands of American farmers migrated westward along the Oregon Trail. Britain and America divided the spoils of the Pacific Northwest in 1846, using the 49th parallel as the

Sir James Douglas of the Hudson's Bay

new boundary, with the land to the north (British Columbia) being claimed by Britain, and that to the south (Oregon) by the US. Oregon, which included the present-day states of Oregon, Washington, and Idaho, became a US territory in 1848. The Oregon Territory was itself divided in 1852, with lands north of the Columbia River forming the new Washington Territory. Oregon gained statehood in 1859, Washington in 1889. British Columbia and Vancouver Island joined to become one colony in 1866, and joined the Dominion of Canada in 1871.

Those who profited least from the division of spoils were the Native peoples. Already decimated by diseases introduced by settlers, such as smallpox, measles, and influenza, they were forcibly removed from the lands they had inhabited for millennia and resettled on reservations.

THE GREAT MIGRATIONS

Between 1843 and 1860, more than 60,000 settlers embarked on a six-month, 2,000-mile (3,218-km) trek from Independence, Missouri, across the US along the Oregon Trail mapped by Lewis and Clark in 1804–1805. Many settlers left the trail

Astoria, founded by John Jacob Astor in 1811

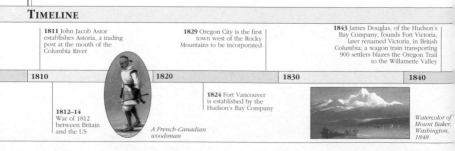

TIMELINE

1811 John Jacob Astor establishes Astoria, a trading post at the mouth of the Columbia River

1829 Oregon City is the first town west of the Rocky Mountains to be incorporated

1843 James Douglas, of the Hudson's Bay Company, founds Fort Victoria, later renamed Victoria, in British Columbia; a wagon train transporting 900 settlers blazes the Oregon Trail to the Willamette Valley

1810   **1820**   **1830**   **1840**

1812–14 War of 1812 between Britain and the US

A French-Canadian woodsman

1824 Fort Vancouver is established by the Hudson's Bay Company

Watercolor of Mount Baker, Washington, 1848

Fort Vancouver, a strategically located trading post, in 1848

in Idaho and headed south to California. Most of those who continued west to Oregon followed the Snake River to the Columbia River, where they put their wagons on rafts. The downstream trip across dangerous rapids led to the mouth of the Willamette River and, just upstream, the trail's end at Oregon City. Rather than pay the exorbitant fee of $50 to float a wagon down the river, some settlers opted for the treacherous climb across Barlow Pass on the flanks of Mount Hood, one of the peaks of the Cascade Mountains.

The reward for those who made the arduous trek to Oregon's fertile Willamette Valley was a land grant of 350 acres (140 ha). Many settlers staked their claims in Oregon, while others made their way farther north and settled in Washington. With its strategic location at the confluence of the Columbia and Willamette Rivers, Portland became the region's major port and most important city.

By the 1870s, transcontinental railroads were steaming across the US and Canada, making the Pacific Northwest accessible to hundreds of thousands more settlers. Trains began crossing Canada between Montreal and Vancouver in 1886, opening up British Columbia to mass settlement.

In the US the arrival of the railroad was especially beneficial to the tiny settlement of Alki-New York in Washington, which soon burgeoned into Seattle, and eventually outstripped Portland as the Pacific Northwest's major port and center of trade.

GOLD RUSHES

Gold fever gripped the Pacific Northwest in 1848, when gold was discovered in California's Sierra Nevada mountains. Many of the new settlers who had staked land claims in Oregon headed south, lured by the hope of making their fortune.

Romantic vision of the westward trek, painted c.1904

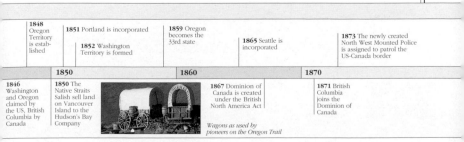

| 1848 Oregon Territory is established | 1851 Portland is incorporated | 1859 Oregon becomes the 33rd state | 1865 Seattle is incorporated | 1873 The newly created North West Mounted Police is assigned to patrol the US-Canada border |
| | 1852 Washington Territory is formed | | | |

| **1850** | | **1860** | | **1870** |

| 1846 Washington and Oregon claimed by the US, British Columbia by Canada | 1850 The Native Straits Salish sell land on Vancouver Island to the Hudson's Bay Company | | 1867 Dominion of Canada is created under the British North America Act | 1871 British Columbia joins the Dominion of Canada |

Wagons as used by pioneers on the Oregon Trail

Government House, New Westminster, BC, in 1870

In fact, two-thirds of the male population of Oregon followed the lure of gold. Many returned soon afterward with gold nuggets in their pockets. The Gold Rush moved north in 1851, when prospectors found gold in southern Oregon, and farther north again, to British Columbia's Fraser River, in 1858. Canadian prospectors also struck it big in 1860 in the Cariboo Mountains, in the BC Interior.

The Klondike, in Canada's Yukon Territory, was the stage for the next frenzy of gold fever. Once prospectors stepped off ships in Seattle and San Francisco, in 1896, with gold they had found along Bonanza Creek, the word was out. More than 100,000 prospectors flooded into the Klondike gold fields, and Vancouver and Seattle prospered by supplying and housing the miners and banking their finds.

Portland, City of Roses

MODERN TIMES

By the early 20th century, the Pacific Northwest was celebrating its prosperity. Portland hosted the Lewis and Clark Exposition in 1905, honoring the pair's voyage 100 years earlier. The city put up new buildings downtown, planted thousands of roses, and laid out new parks for the event. Many of the thousands of exposition visitors stayed in the newly dubbed "City of Roses," and the population doubled to more than 250,000 by 1910. Seattle, having quickly rebounded from an 1889 fire that leveled all of downtown, followed suit in 1909 with the Alaska-Yukon-Pacific Exposition.

These expositions set the stage for the region's growth throughout the 20th century. The Boeing Airplane Company, founded in Seattle in 1916 and rivaling the state's timber industry in economic importance, created tens of thousands of jobs through its military and commercial aircraft contracts. During World War II (1939–45), factories in the Pacific Northwest produced aircraft, weapons, and warships for the Allies' war effort. When Seattle-based Microsoft took off in the 1980s, this ushered in a wave of high-tech business. Vancouver became the focus of world attention when 21 million visitors attended festivities at Expo '86 to celebrate Canada's 100th anniversary. In the years immediately following, there was a huge surge in population growth, business development, and cultural diversification.

Historic cannery along the British Columbia coast

TIMELINE

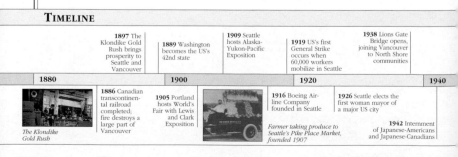

1897 The Klondike Gold Rush brings prosperity to Seattle and Vancouver

1889 Washington becomes the US's 42nd state

1909 Seattle hosts Alaska-Yukon-Pacific Exposition

1919 US's first General Strike occurs when 60,000 workers mobilize in Seattle

1938 Lions Gate Bridge opens, joining Vancouver to North Shore communities

1880   **1900**   **1920**   **1940**

The Klondike Gold Rush

1886 Canadian transcontinental railroad completed; fire destroys a large part of Vancouver

1905 Portland hosts World's Fair with Lewis and Clark Exposition

1916 Boeing Airline Company founded in Seattle

1926 Seattle elects the first woman mayor of a major US city

Farmer taking produce to Seattle's Pike Place Market, founded 1907

1942 Internment of Japanese-Americans and Japanese-Canadians

Mount St. Helens before its cataclysmic explosion

In the late 1990s, trade liberalization and the globalization of goods manufacturing increasingly became topics for public debate. On the streets of Seattle, in December 1999, more than 30,000 protested against the World Trade Organization and its policies on multinational corporations, environmental and labor laws, and subsidies for developing countries.

The Pacific Northwest has also had its share of natural disasters in recent years. Washington's Mount St. Helens *(see pp192–3)* erupted violently in 1980; an earthquake triggered the largest avalanche in recorded history, killing 57 people as well as millions of birds, deer, elk, and fish. Floods and avalanches devastated parts of Oregon and Washington in February 1996, as a result of heavy rains and melting snow caused by unusually mild temperatures; the swelling of the Willamette River and its tributaries forced the evacuation of residents in low-lying areas, stranded hundreds of drivers, and resulted in at least one fatality. On the evening of February 28, 2001, Seattle was rocked by a Mardi Gras riot and then a 6.8-magnitude earthquake. The façades of many of the

historic red-brick buildings in Pioneer Square were destroyed by a combination of the rioters' violence and the effects of the quake.

For the Native peoples of the Pacific Northwest, the 20th century brought gains as well as losses. Fishing rights were restored, but the construction of dams along many rivers destroyed some traditional fishing grounds and greatly diminished salmon runs. The casinos on Native lands brought economic benefits to some tribes but not to others. With the Nisga'a Treaty, drawn up in 2000, the Canadian and BC governments acknowledged that 744 sq miles (1,927 sq km) of crown land in northern British Columbia belongs to the Nisga'a Nation.

Snowy owl, endangered species

Keeping the landscape pristine in the Pacific Northwest continues to be both a source of pride and an ongoing bone of contention. Conservationists fight to curtail lumbering operations and limit growth, while loggers and ranchers often resist government intervention in their affairs. This conflict between the need to protect the environment and interests in capitalizing on the region's natural resources is likely to continue well into the 21st century.

Airplanes on the Boeing assembly line, Seattle

1962 Seattle's Century 21 Fair and opening of Space Needle	*Mount St. Helens after the eruption*	**1980** Mount St. Helens erupts in Washington	**1999** Protesters shut down World Trade Organization talks in Battle of Seattle	**2000** The Nisga'a Treaty awards land in northern BC to the Nisga'a Nation

1960   **1980**   **2000**

1949 Seattle earthquake ruins many historic buildings in Pioneer Square

1971 Environmental group Greenpeace founded in Vancouver

1986 Vancouver hosts Expo '86; Microsoft world headquarters established in Redmond, Washington

1995 Amazon.com launched from Seattle

2002 Seattle football and soccer fans celebrate opening of Seahawks Stadium

Jeff Bezos, founder of Amazon.com

THE PACIFIC
NORTHWEST
REGION BY REGION

The Pacific Northwest at a Glance

A N AREA OF many contrasts, the Pacific Northwest has much to offer visitors. From Portland, Seattle, and Vancouver, its vibrant and attractive cities, many of the region's impressive natural wonders are only a short excursion away. Imposing mountain ranges, vast stretches of deserts, deep, wild canyons, crystal-clear lakes, and a magnificent coastline ensure that there is a sight or activity to suit every taste. While in summer wildflowers carpet alpine meadows, in winter, visitors and locals take advantage of the snow-covered slopes to enjoy winter sports. On the West Coast, whale-watching enchants visitors year-round.

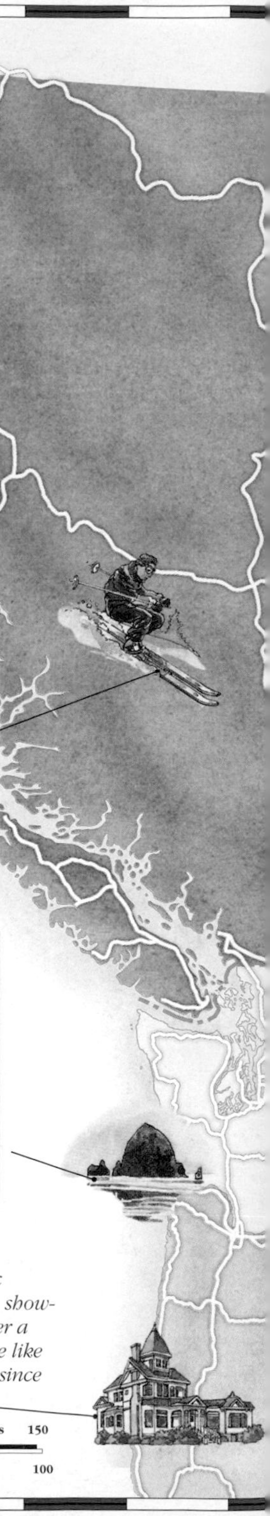

Alta Lake, *in Whistler, British Columbia, offers many summer activities in a town which, in winter, is one of the world's most popular ski destinations (see pp256–7).*

Cannon Beach *is just one of the many beautiful stops along the Oregon coast offering breathtaking vistas of sand, sky, and sea-stacks that rise out of the ocean (see p92).*

Deepwood Estate *(1894), one of Salem's many historic buildings, is now a museum showcasing period pieces that offer a glimpse of what life was once like in this city, Oregon's capital since 1851 (see pp100–101).*

0 kilometers   150

0 miles   100

◁ Coaling station in Nanaimo, Vancouver Island, British Columbia (1859)

Sinclair Pass, *located on the parkway that cuts through British Columbia's Kootenay National Park, is surrounded by the high walls of Sinclair Canyon, a red limestone gorge. It is just one of many natural wonders that attracts visitors to this national park, which covers 543 sq miles (1,406 sq km) of diverse terrain (see p265).*

Fort Steele Heritage Town *is a re-created BC mining town. The original town of Fort Steele was established in 1864 after gold was discovered nearby. When its fortunes faded, it became a ghost town – until reconstruction began in 1961 (see p264).*

Whatcom Museum of History and Art, *in Bellingham, Washington, houses many excellent exhibits on the Native peoples of the Pacific Northwest coast (see p180).*

Canoe Ridge Vineyard *is owned by the well-known Washington winery Chateau Ste. Michelle, the oldest winery in the state (see p181).*

Granite, *in Oregon, once a thriving gold rush town, is now a ghost town (see p112).*

PORTLAND

Portland's Best

ORTLAND ENHANCES its beautiful natural surroundings with a healthy dose of urban vitality and a relaxed yet sophisticated lifestyle. Spectacular parks and gardens flourish throughout the City of Roses. Historic landmarks and neighborhoods show off the city's commitment to preserving its rich past, while Pioneer Courthouse Square, a bustling pedestrian-only space in the heart of what is now the city center, reflects the effective urban planning that makes Portland so pleasant. Meanwhile, the city continues to enhance its many charms with locales such as the Pearl District, a neighborhood currently being fashioned out of an old industrial area.

One of Portland's many roses

Pearl District
Portland is reclaiming this former industrial district as its new neighborhood for art galleries, boutiques, restaurants, and sophisticated urban living (see pp54–5).

Portland Streetcar
Modern, low-slung trams link Nob Hill, the Pearl District, and downtown Portland. Not only is a ride a handy way to get around town, but it's free within the city center (see p63).

Governor Hotel
Early-20th-century grandeur prevails at the Governor Hotel. Murals in the lobby honor an earlier chapter of local history – the Lewis and Clark Expedition (see p60).

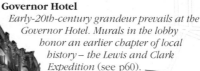

Portland Art Museum
The holdings of the oldest art museum in the Pacific Northwest include European paintings, Asian ceramics, and Native American basketry (see p62).

South Park Blocks
A farmers' market is held here every Saturday in this green ribbon of elm-shaded lawns laid out in 1852 (see p62).

| 0 meters | 200 |
| 0 yards | 200 |

◁ **Downtown Portland's skyline at twilight**

Powell's City of Books
The largest bookstore in the US houses more than a million volumes (maps of the store are provided at the front door) and is one of Portland's most popular spots (see p55).

Classical Chinese Garden
This 15th-century Ming-style walled garden, with its tile-roofed pavilions, embodies traditional Chinese concepts of harmony and tranquility (see p54).

Pioneer Court-house Square
At the city center is a welcoming expanse of brick paving where Portlanders gather, come rain or shine (see p60).

Governor Tom McCall Waterfront Park
Portland has reclaimed this 1.5-mile- (2.5-km-) long stretch of Willamette River waterfront as a park, waterside promenade, and locale for the Rose Festival and other public celebrations (see pp64–5).

Keller Auditorium
Keller Auditorium hosts Broadway shows and other big productions; the adjacent Ira Keller Memorial Fountain suggests the waterfalls of the Cascade Mountains (see p65).

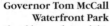

OLD TOWN
AND THE PEARL DISTRICT

PORTLAND GREW UP along the west bank of the Willamette River. Following its establishment in 1843, it became a major port, and docks in the riverfront quarter now known as Old Town were often lined with schooners that sailed across the Pacific Ocean to China and around Cape Horn to the east coast of the US. Old Town was the city's commercial center and home to many Asian immigrants who came to work at the port. The city

Glass art at the Saturday Market

center moved inland in the late 19th century, when the arrival of the railroad reduced river trade. Declared a National Historic Landmark in 1975, Old Town is now once again a popular part of the city. Many 19th-century buildings have been restored, and a Chinese-American community still thrives here. The Pearl District, an early-20th-century industrial area west of Old Town, is also being transformed into a trendy neighborhood.

SIGHTS AT A GLANCE

Gardens and Districts
Classical Chinese Garden ❷
Pearl District ❹

Museums
American Advertising Museum ❸

Oregon Maritime Center and Museum ❶
Portland Institute for Contemporary Art ❺

Shops
Powell's City of Books ❻

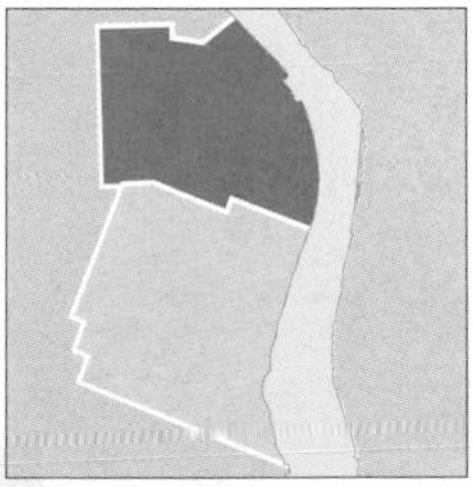

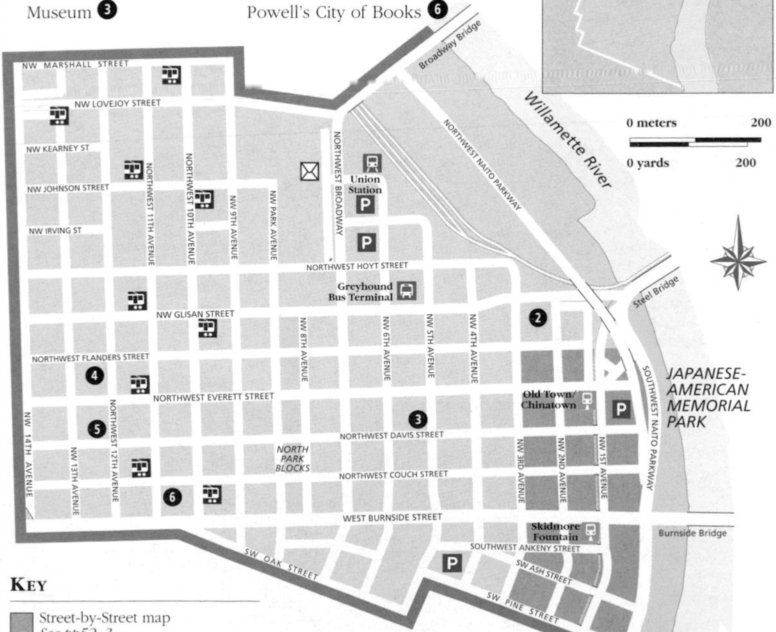

KEY

▢	Street-by-Street map *See pp52–3*
🚊	MAX station
🚏	Streetcar stop
🅿	Parking
⊠	Post office

GETTING THERE
Metro Area Express (MAX) red and blue lines pass through Old Town, with stops at the Old Town/Chinatown and Skidmore Fountain stations. Portland Streetcar serves the Pearl District; Old Town and most of the Pearl District stops are in the Fareless Square zone.

◁ **The main gateway leading to Portland's Saturday Market, held both days of the weekend in Old Town**

Street-by-Street: Old Town

Metal pennant at Portland's Saturday Market

Elegant brick façades and quiet, narrow streets belie Old Town's raucous, 19th-century frontier-town past, when the district hummed with traders, dockworkers, shipbuilders, and sailors from around the world. While the saloons and bordellos that once did a brisk business are long gone, Old Town is still known for harboring some of the city's wilder night life. The street life here can be colorful, too, especially on weekends, when the Saturday Market takes over several blocks, as well as during the many festivals held year-round on the nearby waterfront.

Chinatown Gate
This multicolored, five-tiered, dragon-festooned gate is the official entryway to Chinatown, home to many immigrants from Asia for more than 135 years.

NORTHWEST 4TH AVENUE

NORTHWEST 3R

SOUTHWEST ANKENY STREE

SOUTHWEST ASH STREET

SOUTHWEST PINE STREET

SOUTHWEST OAK STREET

The New Market Block
This group of Italianate buildings is typical of the cast-iron and brick structures built after fire destroyed much of Portland in the 1870s.

Star Sights

★ **Classical Chinese Garden**

★ **Oregon Maritime Center and Museum**

★ **Portland Saturday Market**

Skidmore Fountain
Built in 1888 as a place for citizens and horses to quench their thirst, this elegant fountain and the adjacent plaza are at the center of Old Town.

0 meters		100
0 yards		100

KEY

- - - Suggested route

LOCATOR MAP
See Street Finder map 2

★ **Classical Chinese Garden**
*In this one-block-square walled
enclave, stone paths wind through a
beautiful landscape of water, stone,
plantings, and Chinese pavilions* ❷

★ **Portland
Saturday Market**
*On Saturdays and
Sundays, over 300
vendors gather here
for America's largest
handicrafts market.*

**Governor Tom McCall
Waterfront Park Walkway**
*This path extends along the east side
of the river from Burnside Bridge to
RiverPlace Marina (see p65).*

★ **Oregon Maritime Center
and Museum**
*One of the best things about this infor-
mative little maritime museum is where
it's housed – aboard the tugboat* Portland, *which is docked in the Willamette
River alongside the waterfront* ❶

Oregon Maritime Center and Museum **❶**

113 SW Naito Pkwy. **Map** 2 E4.
❪ (503) 224-7724. **❑** Skidmore
Fountain (red, blue lines). **◯** 11am–
4pm Fri–Sun. **●** major hols. **▨**
w oregonmaritimemuseum.org

THIS SMALL but colorful
museum is housed aboard
the *Portland*, a stern-wheel,
steam-powered tugboat – the
last to be in operation in the
US when it was decommis-
sioned in 1982. The ship is
now permanently moored
alongside Governor Tom
McCall Waterfront Park *(see
pp64–5)* where docks once
bustled with seafaring trade.

Visits include a climb up to
the captain's quarters and the
wheelhouse, which provides
a captivating view of the river,
the downtown waterfront,
and the bridges that span the
Willamette River. Visitors can
also descend into the huge
below-decks engine room.

In the main cabin, historic
photographs, paintings,
models of ships, navigation
instruments, and other marine
memorabilia record the pre-
railroad days when Portland,
with its key position at the
confluence of the Willamette
and Columbia Rivers, flourished as a major West Coast
seaport. Visitors also get a
glimpse of maritime life in
Portland throughout the 20th
century, during which the city
was an important shipping
center and its shipyards were
some of the largest in the
world. Portland continues to
be a major port today.

**Ship's wheel on board the Oregon
Maritime Center and Museum**

**An intricately carved pavilion at
the Classical Chinese Garden**

Classical Chinese Garden **❷**

NW 3rd Ave & NW Everett St.
Map 2 D3. **❪** (503) 228-8131.
❑ Old Town/Chinatown (red, blue
lines). **◯** Apr–Oct: 9am–6pm daily;
Nov–Mar: 10am–5pm daily.
● Jan 1, Thanksgiving, Dec 25.
▨ **❧** partial. **▨ ❑ ❑**
w www.portlandchinesegarden.org

ARTISANS AND ARCHITECTS from
Suzhou, Portland's sister
city in China, built this walled
garden in the late 1990s. The
gardens, which cover one
entire city block, or 40,000
sq ft (4,000 sq m), are located
in Portland's Chinatown.

The landscape of stone
paths, waterfalls, lily pads,
bamboo, a bridged lake, and
tile-roofed pavilions is classic
15th-century Ming Dynasty
style and provides a tranquil
glimpse of nature amid urban
surroundings. Hundreds of
plants grow in the garden,
many of which are indige-
nous to Southeast China.
Towering, artfully placed
rocks mimic mountain peaks,
below which water flows
through lily ponds and
gurgles across rock gardens.
Mosaic-patterned footpaths
winding through stands of
bamboo and across wood and
stone bridges lead to nine pavilions, intended to be places
for rest and contemplation.
One of the ornate pavilions
contains a teahouse that serves
tea and *dim sum*.

Throughout the garden,
poems and literary allusions
are inscribed on rocks, entry-
ways, plaques, and above
doors and windows.

American Advertising Museum **❸**

211 NW 5th Ave. **Map** 2 D3.
❪ (503) 226-0000. **❑** Old Town/
Chinatown (red, blue lines). **◯** 11am–
5pm Thu–Sat. **●** major hols. **❧ ❑**
w www.admuseum.org

PORTLAND MAY BE across the
country from New York
City, where the nation's
major advertising firms line
Madison Avenue, but it is
home to the only museum in
the US devoted entirely to
advertising. Displays in the
bright, ground-floor space
trace the subtleties and
excesses of the art of persua-
sion from 1700 to the present
– from quaint broadsides to
Burma Shave roadside signs
to MTV-inspired video clips.
Visitors will encounter the
fast-talking Starkist tuna, the
well-remembered Alka-Seltzer
indigestion sufferer who
groans, "I can't believe I ate
the whole thing!" and many
other notable characters
from the annals of American
advertising.

**Burma Shave signs in sequence at
the American Advertising Museum**

Pearl District **❹**

W Burnside to NW Lovejoy Sts, from
NW 8th to NW 15th Aves. **Map** 1 B3.
▣ to NW Glisan St.

PORTLAND'S "NEWEST" neighborhood occupies an old
industrial district on the north
side of Burnside Street, between Chinatown to the east
and Nob Hill *(see p68)* to the
west. Galleries, shops, design
studios, breweries, cafés,

The Pearl District's First Thursday, showcasing the work of local artists

restaurants, and clubs – especially hip and trendy ones – occupy former warehouses, factories, and garages. Meanwhile, buildings are being renovated as apartments, and new residential blocks are going up all the time. Visitors may notice many similarities to urban renewal projects in other cities such as Boston, New York, and London, but the Pearl District is still relatively free of large-scale commercialism.

One of the most enjoyable times to visit the neighborhood is during a First Thursday event (the first Thursday of every month), when the many art galleries remain open late to show the latest pieces. Art galleries have played such an important role in the development of the Pearl District that Jameson Park is named after William Jameson, the first art dealer to set up shop in the area.

One of the many specialty shops in the Pearl District

Portland Institute for Contemporary Art ❺

219 NW 12th Ave. **Map** 1 B3.
📞 (503) 242-1419. 🚈 to NW Everett St. ⏱ noon–6pm Wed–Sat. 🔴 major hols. ♿ Ⓦ www.pica.org

PORTLAND'S VENUE for the latest trends in art does not have a permanent collection but hosts six exhibitions a year, on themes such as contemporary artists from the Pacific Northwest and the connection between art and the human body in motion. The institute also provides a stage for performing artists from around the world, and has sponsored appearances of new-music composer Philip Glass and the experimental performance-art troupe, Dumb Type.

Powell's City of Books ❻

1005 W Burnside St. **Map** 1 B4.
📞 (503) 228-4651. 🚌 20. ⏱ 9am–11pm daily. ♿ Ⓦ www.powells.com
See **Shopping in Portland** p76.

THE LARGEST BOOKSTORE in the US houses more than one million volumes on a wealth of subjects. The store welcomes 6,000 shoppers each day, and has become one of Portland's most beloved cultural institutions.

Despite its size, Powell's is easy to browse in: the 3,500 sections are divided into nine color-coded and well-marked rooms, and knowledgeable staff at the information desks possess the remarkable ability to lay their hands on any book in the store. The in-store coffee shop allows browsers to linger for hours, making Powell's a popular hangout any day of the year. Indeed, it's open all 365 of them.

Entrance to Powell's City of Books, the largest bookstore in the US

CITY OF BRIDGES

Portland, the City of Roses, is also called the City of Bridges because the east and west banks of the Willamette River are linked by eight bridges. The first to be built was the Morrison, in 1887, though the original wooden crossing has long since been replaced. Pedestrian walkways on many of the bridges connect the Eastbank Esplanade on the east side of the river with Governor Tom McCall Waterfront Park on the west side. The Steel Bridge affords the most dramatic crossing: a pedestrian path on the lower railroad deck seems to be almost at water level; when a ship needs to pass, the entire deck is lifted into the bottom of the roadway above.

St. Johns Bridge, built in 1931

DOWNTOWN

WITH THE DECLINE of river traffic in the late 19th century, Portland's center moved inland to the blocks around the intersection of Morrison Street and Broadway. The 1905 Lewis and Clark Exposition brought new prosperity and new residents to the city: downtown became a boomtown. Steel-frame buildings with façades of glazed, white terra-cotta tiles (Meier and Frank department store is a fine example) began to

Allow Me **sculpture by Seward Johnson**

rise; they continue to give the downtown a bright, distinctive look. In recent years, urban planning efforts have earned Portland's downtown a reputation as one of the most successful city centers in the US. The area around Pioneer Courthouse Square is the city's commercial and cultural hub, while many government offices are housed in innovative new buildings to the east, near historic Chapman and Lonsdale Squares.

SIGHTS AT A GLANCE

Buildings, Churches, and Museums

Governor Hotel ❸
Keller Auditorium ⓰
KOIN Center ⓯
Mark O. Hatfield
 US Courthouse ⓭
Multnomah County
 Library ❹
Old Church ❽
Oregon Historical Society ❻
Pioneer Courthouse ❷
Portland Art Museum ❼
Portland Building ⓫
Portland Center for the
 Performing Arts ❺

Parks and Squares

Chapman and
 Lonsdale Squares ⓬
Governor Tom
 McCall Water-
 front Park ⓮
Pioneer
 Courthouse
 Square ❶
RiverPlace
 Marina ⓱
South Park
 Blocks ❾

Other Attractions

Portland
 Streetcar ❿

KEY

▨	Street-by-Street map See pp58–9
▣	MAX station
▣	Streetcar stop
ℹ	Information
P	Parking
🚓	Police station

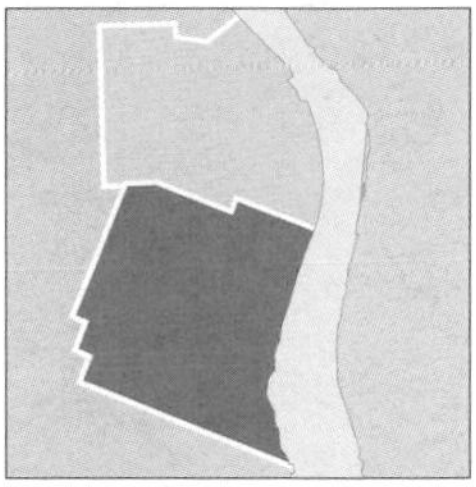

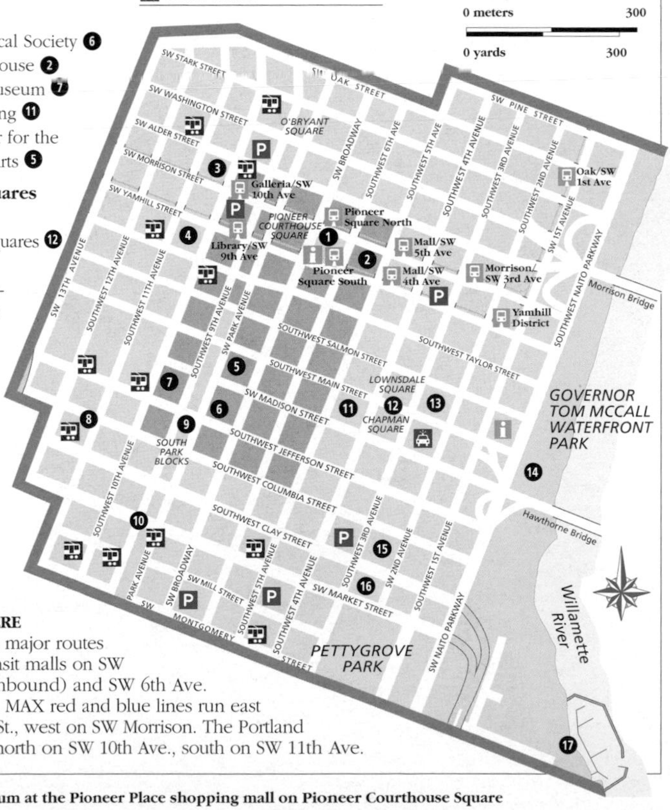

0 meters 300
0 yards 300

GETTING THERE

Buses on most major routes stop at the transit malls on SW 5th Ave. (northbound) and SW 6th Ave. (southbound). MAX red and blue lines run east on SW Taylor St., west on SW Morrison. The Portland Streetcar runs north on SW 10th Ave., south on SW 11th Ave.

◁ **Light-filled atrium at the Pioneer Place shopping mall on Pioneer Courthouse Square**

Street-by-Street: Downtown

The top of the Weather Machine

ONE OF THE MOST APPEALING characteristics of Portland is the way the city combines cosmopolitan sophistication with a relaxed, low-key ambience. Nowhere is this more in evidence than on the attractive downtown blocks that surround Pioneer Courthouse Square. Broadway and the streets that cross it here are lined with department stores and boutiques, office complexes, hotels, restaurants, theaters, and museums, many occupying well-restored century-old buildings. Busy and vital as these downtown blocks are, sidewalks are shaded, parks are plentiful, and glimpses of the hills and mountains that encircle the city are easy to come by.

★ Portland Art Museum
The holdings of the oldest art museum in the Pacific Northwest range from Monet paintings to Native American crafts ❼

Oregon Historical Society
Huge murals on the façades of this complex depict scenes from the Lewis and Clark expedition and other great moments in Oregon history. Inside is a wealth of memorabilia from the early days of the state ❻

★ South Park Blocks
Daniel Lownsdale laid out these city blocks as parkland in 1848. A local farmer's market is held here Saturdays ❾

KEY

- - - Suggested route

| 0 meters | 80 |
| 0 yards | 80 |

STAR SIGHTS

★ Pioneer Courthouse Square

★ Portland Art Museum

★ South Park Blocks

Portland Center for the Performing Arts
Portland's main venue for theater, music, and dance lights up a stretch of Broadway. The marquee of its Arlene Schnitzer Concert Hall has been shining brightly since 1927, when the theater opened as the city's foremost movie palace and vaudeville house ❺

Weather Machine

A whimsical, 25-ft- (8-m-) tall sculpture comes to life every day at noon, when figures emerge from its top to announce the weather for the next 24 hours.

Jackson Tower, built by the Reid brothers in 1912 for a newspaper magnate, features glazed terra cotta as a decorative element for its steel frame.

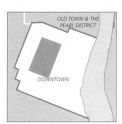

LOCATOR MAP
See Street Finder map 1

American Bank Building

This classical building, finished in 1914, features Corinthian columns at its base and is decorated with terra-cotta eagles and griffins.

★ Pioneer Courthouse Square

This one-block-square open space is the heart of Portland, where fountains splash and Portlanders gather for free lunchtime concerts, flower shows, and other events, or simply for a chance to sit and enjoy their city ❶

Pioneer Courthouse
The octagonal tower of the first federal building in the Pacific Northwest has been a fixture of the Portland skyline since 1873 ❷

Pioneer Courthouse Square, a popular public gathering place

Pioneer Courthouse Square ❶

SW Broadway & Yamhill St. **Map** 1 C5.
📞 (503) 223-1613. 🚊 Pioneer
Square (red, blue lines). ♿

Pioneer courthouse Square resembles the large central plazas of many European cities, which was the intent of the city planners who designed this brick-paved pedestrian-only square in the mid-1980s. Despite its recent vintage, the square stands on hallowed Portland ground: the city's first schoolhouse was erected on this site in 1858, and the much-admired Portland Hotel stood here from 1890 to 1951, when it was demolished to make way for a parking lot.

According to plan, Pioneer Courthouse Square has become the center of the city, a friendly space where Portlanders gather to enjoy a brown-bag lunch or free outdoor concert. Architectural flourishes include a graceful, amphitheater-like bank of seats, a fountain that resembles a waterfall, and a row of 12 columns crowned with gilt roses.

Underground spaces adjoining the square accommodate offices and businesses, including the Portland Visitors Association Information Center, a coffee shop, and a branch of Powell's bookstore (see p55) that specializes in travel books. The most compelling aspect of the square, though, is the lively presence of the many residents who use the space.

Pioneer Courthouse ❷

520 SW Morrison St. **Map** 1 C5.
📞 (503) 326-5830. 🚊 Pioneer
Square (red, blue lines). ◑ 9am–5pm
Mon–Fri. ● Sat–Sun & major hols. ♿

Completed in 1873, Pioneer Courthouse was the first federal building to be constructed in the Pacific Northwest and is the second oldest federal building west of the Mississippi River. The trees planted here at that time are still standing. The Italianate structure, faced with freestone and topped by a domed cupola, houses the US Court of Appeals and a branch of the US Post Office. A climb to the cupola rewards visitors with a panoramic view of Portland. Historic photographs next to each window show how the same view looked in the city's early years.

Governor Hotel ❸

611 SW 10th Ave. **Map** 1 B5.
📞 (503) 224-3400. 🚊 Galleria/SW
10th Ave (red, blue lines). 🚏 to SW
Alder St. ♿ See **Where to Stay**
p282. 🌐 www.govhotel.com

The hotel opened as the Seward Hotel in 1909 and, after sitting empty in disrepair for years, as the Governor Hotel in 1991. The expedition of Meriwether Lewis and William Clark (see p37), whose 1804–1806 journey across the US and down the Columbia River put Oregon on the map, figures prominently in the Governor Hotel.

A sepia-colored, four-section mural in the newly renovated lobby shows a map of the Lewis and Clark expedition and depicts scenes from the explorers' journey: Native Americans fishing at Celilo Falls on the Columbia River, Meriwether Lewis trading with members of the Nez Percé tribe in present-day Idaho, and the guide Sacagawea (see p37) surveying the Pacific Ocean. Even the lampshades pay tribute to the pair – they are decorated with excerpts from the explorers' journals.

The hotel incorporates the ornate former headquarters of the Elks Lodge as its west wing, built in the luxuriant style of the pre-Depression early 1920s to resemble the Palazzo Farnese, in Rome. Mahogany detailing, leather chairs, fireplaces, and warm tones create an atmosphere of old-fashioned opulence.

The luxurious lobby of the Governor Hotel, evoking an earlier age

The light-filled stairwell of the Multnomah County Library

Multnomah County Library ❹

801 SW 10th Ave. **Map** 1 B5. 🔵 (503) 988-5123. 🚊 Library/SW 9th Ave (red, blue lines). 🚋 to SW Taylor St. 🕐 9am–9pm Tue–Thu, 9am–6pm Fri–Sat, 1–5pm Sun. ⬤ major hols. ♿ 🏢 ⓦ www.multcolib.org

ALFRED E. DOYLE, the architect whose work in Portland includes such landmarks as the Meier and Frank department store and the drinking fountains that grace downtown streets, chose limestone and brick for this distinctive Georgian structure. The building, completed in 1913, is the headquarters of the 17-branch county library system, established in 1864 and the oldest library system west of the Mississippi.

Construction cost $475,000 and was marred by accusations that materials were being diverted to private hands. Renovations, completed in 1997, amounted to $25 million. Notable holdings

The New Theatre in the Portland Center for the Performing Arts

of the collection, which is valued at $1.9 million, include one of the two known copies of the original Portland charter, housed in the John Wilson Rare Book Room.

Portland Center for the Performing Arts ❺

1111 SW Broadway. **Map** 3 B1. 🔵 (503) 248-4335. 🚋 to SW Main St. ♿ 📷 ⓦ www.pcpa.com

SINCE THE MID-1980s, the Portland Center for the Performing Arts has been the city's major venue for theater, music, and dance. The complex consists of the Arlene Schnitzer Concert Hall and the New Theatre Building, on Broadway, and the Keller Auditorium, a few blocks east at Southwest 3rd Avenue and Clay Street (see p65). In the New Theatre Building, the 916-seat Newmark Theatre and the 292-seat Dolores Winningstad Theatre open off a dramatic, five-story, cherry-paneled rotunda capped by a dome designed by glass-artist James Carpenter.

The Arlene Schnitzer Concert Hall occupies a former vaudeville house and movie palace built in 1927. Its ornate, Italian Rococo Revival interior has been restored, and it is now the home of the Oregon Symphony. The marquee continues to illuminate Broadway with 6,000 lights, and it now props up a 65-ft- (20-m-) high sign that screams "Portland" in blue neon.

Oregon Historical Society ❻

1200 SW Park Ave. **Map** 3 B1. 🔵 (503) 222-1741. 🚊 Library/SW 9th Ave (red, blue lines). 🚋 to Jefferson St. 🕐 call for hrs. ⬤ major hols. 📷 ♿ 🏢 ⓦ www.ohs.org

EIGHT-STORY murals by Richard Haas on the west and south façades of the Oregon Historical Society depict the Lewis and Clark expedition (see p37), fur trading, and other important events that have shaped the history of Oregon. On display in the galleries, which extend through three buildings, are some of the 85,000 objects that make this museum the largest repository of Oregon historical artifacts. The exhibits, which include maps, paintings, photographs, and historical documents, change frequently since space does not allow for the display of the entire collection at once.

On permanent display is the penny that the founders of Portland, Asa Lovejoy and Francis Pettigrove, tossed to decide on the city's name (the other contender was "Boston"). Other exhibits here include Native American crafts, models of ships, memorabilia tracing the state's rich maritime history, and the multimedia exhibit Portland!, devoted to the history of the city. The journals of pioneers can also be viewed in the society's research library.

Decorative murals on the façade of the Oregon Historical Society

The Portland Art Museum's gallery of late-19th-century European art

Portland Art Museum ❼

1219 SW Park Ave. **Map** 3 B1.
[(503) 226-2811. **▣** Library/SW 9th Ave (red, blue lines). **▥** to Jefferson St. **◯** 10am–5pm Tue–Wed & Sat, 10am–8pm Thu–Fri, noon–5pm Sun.
◑ Dec 25. **▨ ▤ ▣ ▯**
Ⓦ www.pam.org

T HE OLDEST art museum in the Pacific Northwest opened in 1892, introducing the citizenry to classical art with a collection of plaster casts of Greek and Roman sculpture. Today, the 32,000-piece-strong collection, which places the museum among the 25 largest in the country, is housed in a building designed by modernist architect Pietro Belluschi.

A sizable collection of European paintings, including works by Van Gogh, Picasso, masters of the Italian Renaissance, and French Impressionists, hang in the second-floor galleries. Works by Rodin and Brancusi fill the sculpture court; modern and contemporary galleries house works by Frank Stella and Willem de Kooning; and a new wing is devoted to historical and contemporary photographs, prints, sculptures, and drawings by artists from the Pacific Northwest. The Grand Ronde Center for Native American Art displays masks, jewelry, totem poles, and other works by artists from more than 200 indigenous groups throughout all of North America.

The museum is an important stop for traveling exhibitions.

Old Church ❽

1422 SW 11th Ave. **Map** 3 A1.
[(503) 222-2031. **▥** to SW Clay St.

T HE ROUGH-HEWN wood exterior lends this church a distinctly Pacific Northwestern appearance. Completed in 1883, the Old Church reflects a Victorian Gothic Revival style, also known as Stick or Carpenter Gothic style, with exaggerated arches, a tall steeple, and sleek, elegant windows. On Wednesdays at noon, the historic Hook and Hastings Tracker organ is put into service for free concerts.

The Gothic Revival–style Old Church with its decorative arches

South Park Blocks ❾

Bounded by SW Salmon St & I-405, SW Park & SW 9th Aves. **Map** 3 B1.
▥ to stops between SW Salmon & SW Mill Sts.

I N 1852, frontier businessman and legislator Daniel Lownsdale set aside the blocks between Park and 9th Avenues as parkland. After the city council authorized the landscaping of these blocks, landscape designer Louis G. Pfunder planted 104 Lombardy poplars and elms between Salmon and Hall. The so-called South Park Blocks continue to form a 12-block ribbon of tree-shaded lawns through the central city, running past the Portland Art Museum and the Portland Center for the Performing Arts *(see p61)* and into the campus of Portland State University. In this city forested by so many evergreens, the blocks of deciduous trees are refreshingly pleasant in the fall, when the foliage turns vibrant colors. Particularly vivid is the area around Madison Street, where the First Congregational Church rises above the trees.

Notable statuary along the blocks includes, between Madison and Main Streets, a dour-looking US president Abraham Lincoln (1861–5) by George Fite Waters, who was a student of Rodin. One block south is the 18-ft- (5.5-m-) tall bronze equestrian *Rough Rider*, a statue of President Theodore Roosevelt (1901–1909), by his friend and hunting partner Phimister Procter.

Among the most distinctive ornaments are the Benson drinking fountains. In 1917, lumber baron Samuel Benson commissioned prominent architect A.E. Doyle to design these graceful, four-bowled fountains. He placed 20 of them throughout the South Park Blocks and the rest of downtown to quench the thirst of Portland residents who might otherwise be tempted to frequent saloons. Since then, 20 more fountains have been added.

Offerings at the Saturday farmers' market, South Park Blocks

Portland Streetcar ⓾

East- & southbound on NW Lovejoy St & 11th Ave, north- & westbound on 10th Ave & NW Northrup St. **Map** 1 A2–3 B2. ⭘ 5:30am–11:30pm Mon–Thu, 5:30am–1am Fri, 7:30am–1am Sat, 7:30am–10:30pm Sun.

HORSE-DRAWN streetcars began running along Front Street in the 1870s. By the early 20th century, electric streetcars were rumbling all across Portland, bringing downtown within easy reach of newly established residential neighborhoods. Automobiles had put the streetcars out of service by the 1950s, but in the late 1990s, city planners turned to streetcars again as part of a public transport scheme intended to reduce traffic congestion and ensure the vitality of the central business district.

Portlandia watching from the Portland Building

The Czech-built streetcars travel a route that links the Nob Hill shopping and residential neighborhood, the Pearl District, the western edge of downtown, and the campus of Portland State University. A ride on the streetcar and transfer to buses and MAX lines *(see Getting Around Portland, p78)* are free within the city's Fareless Square zone.

Czech-built Portland streetcars, environmentally sound transit

Portland Building ⓫

1120 SW 5th Ave. **Map** 3 C1.
☎ (503) 823-5111. ▦ Transit Mall.
⭘ 9am–5pm Mon–Fri. ⬤ major hols.

THE PORTLAND Building, designed by New Jersey architect Michael Graves, has been featured on the covers of both *Time* and *Newsweek* and was called Portland's "Eiffel Tower" by the city's former mayor Frank Ivancie. The building has been controversial ever since it was completed in 1982. Displaying an experimental combination of architectural styles, this first large-scale postmodern office building in the US has been hailed as a major innovation in contemporary urban design and a credit to forward-thinking Portland. It has also been denounced as just plain ugly. The use of muted colors and ornamental swags and pilasters lends a certain playfulness to the exterior, while the 15-story building's relatively modest height and multiple rows of small square windows suggest practicality and a lack

The landmark Portland Building, home to City of Portland offices

of pretension, as befits the home of government offices.

More ostentatious is *Portlandia*, a 36-ft- (11-m-) tall statue fashioned from 6.5 tons of copper that emerges from a second-floor balcony above the main doors. The figure crouches, with one hand extended and the other brandishing a giant trident. Completed by sculptor Raymond Kaskey in 1985, *Portlandia* is modeled on Lady Commerce, the symbolic figure that appears on the city seal and that supposedly welcomed traders into the city's port. After New York City's Statue of Liberty, *Portlandia* is the largest copper statue in the US.

A small gallery on the second floor of the Portland Building displays plans, models, and other material related to the design and construction of the building and the *Portlandia* statue.

PORTLAND THE GREEN

Justifiably, Portland's abundant parks and gardens are often described in superlatives. The city can make claim to both the largest forested city park in the US, 5,000-acre (2,025-ha) Forest Park, and the smallest park in the world, 452-sq-inch (0.3-sq-m) Mills End Park *(see p65)*. The city boasts some of the nation's largest and most extensive rose test gardens *(see p72)*, one of the world's most renowned rhododendron gardens *(see p74)*, one of the finest Japanese gardens outside Japan *(see p72)*, and the largest classical Chinese garden outside China *(see p54)*. Many of the other parks and gardens included in the city's 36,000 acres (14,600 ha) of greenspace have no such claims attached, but they are nonetheless pleasant places in which to enjoy the great outdoors.

Mill Ends Park, the world's tiniest park

Chapman and Lownsdale Squares ⑫

Bounded by SW Salmon & SW Madison Sts, SW 3rd & SW 4th Aves. **Map** 3 C1. 🚇 *Mall/SW 4th Ave (red, blue lines).*

IT IS ONLY FITTING that Daniel Lownsdale should have a one-block-square park named for him. The tanner who became one of Oregon's early legislators had the foresight to set aside a parcel of downtown for the South Park Blocks *(see p62),* and he did much to encourage trade on the nearby waterfront by building a wood-plank road into the countryside so that lumber and other goods could be transported to the Portland docks.

Judge William Chapman, for whom the adjoining square is named, was one of the founders of the *Oregonian* newspaper. Along with Terry Schrunk Plaza – a third, adjacent parklike block – the squares provide a soothing stretch of greenery in Portland's quiet courthouse and government-building district. The neighborhood was not always so sedate though: anti-Chinese riots broke out here in the 1880s, and the area was raucous enough in the 1920s that Chapman Square was declared off-limits to men so that women could enjoy the space in safety.

Portland's popular Elk Fountain, built in 1852, near the courthouse

The limestone, aluminum, and glass Mark O. Hatfield US Courthouse

Mark O. Hatfield US Courthouse ⑬

1000 SW 3rd Ave. **Map** 3 C1.
📞 *(503) 326-8000* 🚇 *Transit Mall.*
🕐 *7:30am–4:30pm Mon–Fri.*
⬤ *major hols.* ♿

NAMED FOR a popular Oregon governor and senator, the Mark O. Hatfield US Courthouse defies any preconceived notion that a government building is by definition unimaginative. Designed by the New York firm of Kohn Pedersen Fox and completed in 1997, the courthouse presents a bold and handsome façade of glass, aluminum, and limestone. A ninth-floor sculpture garden provides excellent views of both the river and one of Portland's most beloved pieces of statuary, the **Elk Fountain**, which stands across the street.

Erected in 1852 on land where elk once roamed freely, for many years the Elk Fountain provided citizens' horses with a place to drink. When automobile traffic began to increase in the early 20th century, the fountain stood in the path of a proposed extension of Main Street. Angry citizens protested plans to move the fountain; it now stands in the middle of the street.

Governor Tom McCall Waterfront Park ⑭

Bounded by SW Clay & NW Glisan Sts, SW Naito Pkwy & Willamette River. **Map** 4 D1. 🚇 *Skidmore Fountain, Morrison/SW 3rd Ave, Yamhill District (red, blue lines).*

THIS 1.5-MILE- (2.5-km-) long park on the west bank of the Willamette River covers 23 acres (9 ha) of land that once bustled with activity on the Portland docks and which, from the 1940s to the 1970s, was buried beneath an expressway. The city converted the land to a park as part of an urban renewal scheme and named it for the environmentally minded Tom McCall, Oregon's governor, 1967–75.

The park is a much-used riverside promenade and the locale for many festivals. One of its most popular attractions is **Salmon Street Springs**, a fountain whose 100 jets splash water directly onto the pavement, providing easily accessible relief on a hot day. The foot of nearby Southwest Salmon Street was once the roughest part of town. Here, drunken revelers were routinely knocked unconscious and then taken aboard ships as involuntary crew members.

The Battleship Oregon Memorial, Gov. Tom McCall Waterfront Park

A block away, at the foot of Southwest Taylor Street, is **Mills End Park**, measuring only 452 sq inches (0.3 sq m). The park is the former site of a telephone pole, removed in the late 1940s. Local journalist Dick Fagan began planting flowers on the patch of earth and writing articles about what he dubbed the "World's Smallest Park," which it officially became when the City of Portland adopted it as part of the park system in 1976.

The **Battleship Oregon Memorial**, built in 1956, honors an 1893 US Navy ship. A time capsule sealed in its base in 1976 will be opened in 2076.

Keller Auditorium, part of the Portland Center for the Performing Arts

Keller Auditorium ⑯

222 SW Clay St. **Map** 3 C2. ☎ *(503) 248-4335.* 🚌 *Transit Mall.* ♿

WHEN A BROADWAY road-show or other big production comes to Portland, the 3,000-seat Keller Auditorium often plays host. Built in 1917 on the former site of an exhibition hall and sports arena known as the Mechanics' Pavilion, the auditorium was completely remodeled in the late 1960s, gaining clean sightlines as well as excellent acoustics. The auditorium is part of the Portland Center for the Performing Arts *(see p61)* and is home to the Portland Opera, the Oregon Ballet, and the Oregon Children's Theatre.

Across the street is the **Ira Keller Memorial Fountain**, a waterfall cascading over 18-ft (5.5-m) concrete cliffs into a pool crisscrossed with platforms laid out like stepping stones. The fountain, enclosed by a delightful garden, successfully presents a typical Pacific Northwest experience – that of emerging from the shade of trees to the sight, sound, and spray of a plunging torrent. Completed in 1970, the fountain was designed by Angela Danadijieva. Originally called the Forecourt Fountain, it was renamed in 1978 to honor civic leader Ira C. Keller.

RiverPlace Marina ⑰

SW Clay St & Willamette River. **Map** 4 D3. 🚌 *95X, 96.* 🍴 🚹

RIVERPLACE MARINA is a commercial and residential complex on the west bank of the Willamette River, situated at the southwest end of Governor Tom McCall Waterfront Park.

Among the amenities here are upscale shops, several restaurants, including Portland's only floating restaurant, and one of the city's higher-end hotels, RiverPlace Hotel *(see p283)*. The complex also has sloping lawns, riverside walks, and a large marina. Sea kayaks are available for rental, providing an alternative way to view the river and city.

The multifunctional KOIN Center, rising 29 stories above Portland

KOIN Center ⑮

222 SW Columbia St. **Map** 3 C2. 🚌 *Transit Mall.*

LIKE THE Portland Building *(see p63)*, the KOIN Center is designed in the postmodern style, which incorporates a plurality of architectural styles in one structure. However, this 29-story blond-brick tower capped by a pyramidal blue steel roof has elicited none of the controversy that the Portland Building has. Instead, the KOIN Center, designed by the Portland firm of Zimmer Gunsul Frasca and completed in 1984, is considered a model urban complex. The building houses residences, offices – including those of the television station for which it is named – and shops, as well as a popular movie theater.

Ira Keller Memorial Fountain, across from Keller Auditorium

Farther Afield

By the late 19th century, Portland was fast growing from a small riverfront settlement surrounded by forests into an important port city. It expanded westward into Nob Hill, where wealthy merchants settled, and eastward across the Willamette River. In 1871, the City created Washington Park, now Portland's favorite green retreat. Crystal Spring Rhododendron Garden, to the south, is another tranquil spot. Numerous important events in Oregon's history transpired just south of Portland. Oregon City, at the end of the Oregon Trail, was the site of the first meeting of the territory's provisional legislature, in 1843. At Aurora, a Utopian society once thrived, and at nearby Champoeg State Heritage Area, pioneers voted to break from Britain.

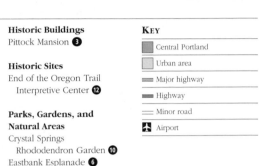

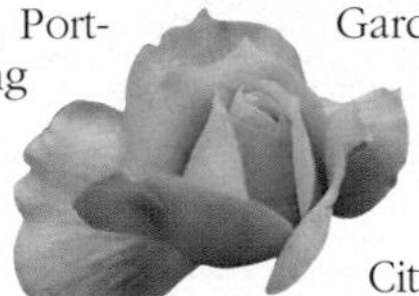
A rose in Washington Park

Sights at a Glance

Towns and Neighborhoods
Aurora 14
Hawthorne District 8
Nob Hill 4
Oregon City 13
Rose Quarter 5
Sellwood District 9

Institutions
Reed College 11

Museums
Oregon Museum of Science and Industry 7

Historic Buildings
Pittock Mansion 3

Historic Sites
End of the Oregon Trail Interpretive Center 12

Parks, Gardens, and Natural Areas
Crystal Springs Rhododendron Garden 10
Eastbank Esplanade 6
Sauvie Island 1
Washington Park pp70–73 2

Key
Central Portland
Urban area
Major highway
Highway
Minor road
✈ Airport

5 miles = 8 km

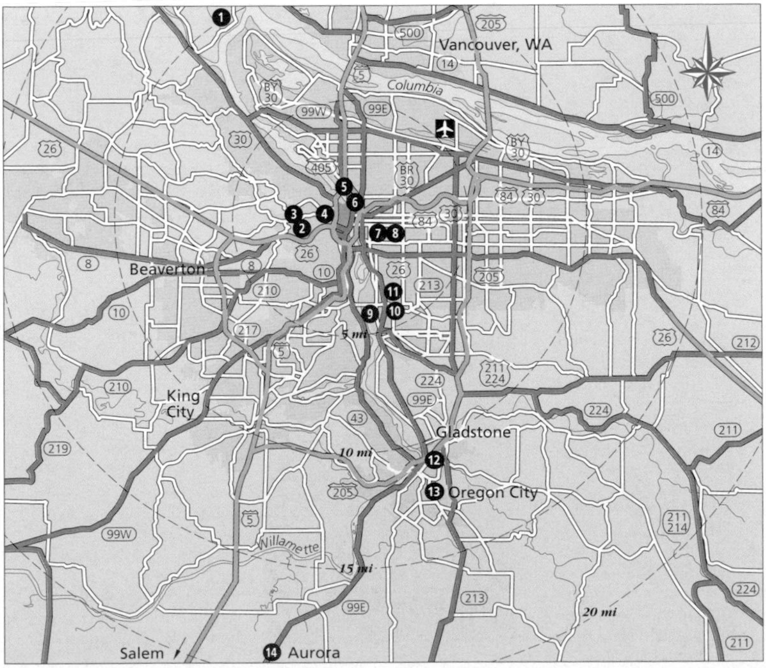

◁ **View of downtown Portland as seen from the International Rose Test Garden in Washington Park**

**One of several beaches along
Sauvie Island's Columbia River side**

Sauvie Island ❶

🛈 *18330 NW Sauvie Island Rd,
(503) 621-3488.* 🚌 *17 NW 21st Ave/
St Helens Rd.* ⭘ *4am–10pm daily.*

SAUVIE ISLAND comprises
24,000 acres (9,700 ha)
of low-lying land at the confluence of the Willamette and
Columbia Rivers, just 10 miles
(16 km) from downtown Portland. With rich soil that supports many berry farms and
orchards, the southern half of
the island is primarily agricultural. The northern half is set
aside as the **Sauvie Island
Wildlife Area**, managed by
the Oregon Department of
Fish and Wildlife. Birdwatch-
ers come to see some of the
estimated three million birds –
including swans, ducks, and
cranes – that stop here on
their spring and fall migrations.

During the summer, swim-
mers and sunbathers enjoy
beaches on the island's
Columbia River side, and
anglers fish for sturgeon and
salmon from the shores and
from boats in nearby channels.
The island's **Bybee House
Museum**, a Greek Revival–
style house built in 1858 by
James Y. Bybee, is surrounded
by orchards with flourishing
fruit trees, brought by pioneers on the Oregon Trail.
An adjoining barn built in 1960
houses antique farm equipment, including a chuckwagon.

🏛 **Bybee House Museum**
Howell Territorial Park. 📞 *(503) 222-
1741.* ⭘ *Jun–Labor Day: noon–5pm
Sat–Sun.* 🎟 *(by donation).*

Washington Park ❷

See pp70–73.

Pittock Mansion ❸

3229 NW Pittock Dr. 📞 *(503) 823-
3624.* 🚌 *77.* ⭘ *Jun–Aug: 11am–
4pm daily; Sep–Dec & Feb–May: noon–
4pm daily.* ⬤ *Jan, Thanksgiving
weekend, late Nov & major hols.* 🎟
♿ *(partial; call 48 hrs ahead).* 🅿 📷
🆆 *www.pittockmansion.com*

HENRY PITTOCK, who came
west on the Oregon Trail
as a young man and founded
the *Oregonian* newspaper,
commissioned this mansion in
1914 for his wife Georgiana
and himself. Designed by San
Francisco architect Edward
T. Foulkes, the house is
still the grandest resi-
dence in Portland.
Perched on a 1,000-ft
(305-m) summit in the
West Hills, it commands
superb views of
the city and snow-
capped mountain
peaks. The man-
sion's gardens are
a good picnic
spot.

Guided
tours show off
the mansion's
remarkable embellishments.
Among them are a marble staircase, elliptical drawing room,
and circular Turkish-style
smoking room. Family artifacts
decorate the home. The furnishings, though not original
to the house, reflect the finest
tastes of the Pittocks' time.

**The sweeping entrance of the
imposing Pittock Mansion**

**A turn-of-the-19th-century
house in Nob Hill**

**A Nob Hill mansion, typical of
those in the fashionable district**

Nob Hill ❹

*W Burnside to NW Pettigrove Sts,
from NW 17th to NW 24th Sts.*
🚊 *to NW 23rd St.*

ALSO KNOWN AS Northwest
23rd in reference to its
main business street, Nob
Hill is a gracious, late-
19th-century
neighborhood
of shady streets,
large wooden
houses, and
apartment
buildings. With
its proximity to
downtown and
its inherent
charms, Nob
Hill has become
one of the city's
most popular
commercial and
residential neighborhoods
over the past two decades. A
slightly bohemian atmosphere,
together with upscale shops
and restaurants, make Nob Hill
a pleasant place to stroll.

Northwest 23rd Street from
West Burnside to Northwest
Lovejoy Streets is the neighborhood's commercial core. The
side streets are lined with
lovely old houses. The 1892
Victorian gingerbread **Pettigrove House** (2287 Northwest
Pettigrove Street) was the
home of Francis Pettigrove,
the city founder who flipped
a coin with fellow founder Asa
Lovejoy to determine the city's
name. Pettigrove won and
choose the name of a city in
his native Maine (Lovejoy preferred "Boston"). Northwest
Johnson Street between Northwest 22nd and 23rd Streets is
lined with many fine houses
from the 1880s, when Nob Hill
first became fashionable.

Rose Quarter ❺

1 Center Ct. 🚇 *Rose Quarter (red, blue lines). See Entertainment in Portland p77.*
🌐 www.rosequarter.com

Portland's major venues for sports, big-ticket entertainment events, and conventions are clustered in the Rose Quarter, a commercial riverside area on the east bank of the Willamette River. Portlanders come in droves to the otherwise quiet neighborhood to attend Portland Trail Blazer basketball games, Portland Winter Hawks ice hockey games, and major pop and rock concerts by the likes of Paul McCartney and Bruce Springsteen at the **Rose Garden Arena**. Designed by the Kansas City firm of Ellerbe Becket, the arena was completed in 1996. It features a unique "acoustical cloud" made up of 160 rotating acoustic panels which can be tailored to the needs of the specific event.

The smaller, nearby **Memorial Coliseum** (300 Winning Way) once hosted these events. Its glass-fronted hall, designed by New York firm Skidmore, Owens and Merrill and completed in 1960, is now used for conventions and trade shows.

The **Lloyd Center**, just east of the Rose Quarter, is recognized as the US's first covered shopping center. Although such malls are now ubiquitous, the Lloyd Center retains an old-fashioned charm, with more than 200 shops and restaurants lining handsome, well-planted walkways that radiate from a skating rink.

Portland's cityscape, the Eastbank Esplanade in the foreground

Eastbank Esplanade ❻

Bounded by Willamette River & I-5, Steel & Hawthorne Bridges. 🚇 *Rose Quarter (red, blue lines).* 🚌 *14.*

This pedestrian and bicycle path following the east bank of the Willamette River between the Steel and Hawthorne Bridges was part of a massive riverfront redevelopment. While the esplanade's unobstructed views of downtown Portland and the opportunity it provides to enjoy the river are compelling reasons to visit, the walkway is an attraction in its own right. A 1,200-ft (365-m) section floats on the water, and another cantilevered portion is suspended above one of the city's original commercial piers.

The esplanade provides access to four of the city's major downtown bridges, linking the walkway to Governor Tom McCall Waterfront Park *(see pp64–5)* on the west bank of the river. The most dramatic crossing is via the Steel Bridge Riverwalk, perched just 30 ft (9 m) above the water.

Oregon Museum of Science and Industry ❼

1945 SE Water Ave. 📞 *(503) 797-4000.* 🚌 *83, 14.* 🕐 *Sep 3–Jun 14: 9:30am–5:30pm Tue–Sun; Jun 15–Labor Day: 9:30am–7pm daily.* ● *major hols.* 🎟 ♿ *(partial).* 🎫 *of submarine.* 🖥 📷 🌐 www.omsi.edu

Commonly referred to as OMSI, the Oregon Museum of Science and Industry is one of the top science museums in the US. The multiple exhibition halls and science labs of this world-class tourist attraction house hundreds of interactive exhibits. Visitors may enjoy hands-on experiences in subjects such as physics, chemistry, space exploration, computers, and mathematics. A favorite is the earthquake simulator, in which visitors are shaken and rattled while learning about the tectonic plates that continue to shift beneath Portland.

The Murdock Planetarium, a state-of-the-art facility, places OMSI at the forefront of astronomical education, and an Omnimax theater with a five-story screen takes audiences on exciting adventures in locales ranging from the ocean floor to a mountain summit.

Moored alongside the museum is the USS *Blueback*, first launched in 1959 and the last diesel submarine to be used by the US Navy. Guided tours provide a chance to look at downtown through a periscope and to experience the claustrophobic conditions in which 85 submariners once lived for months at a time.

An interactive exhibit at the Oregon Museum of Science and Industry

Washington Park ❷

T HOUGH A PARK FIRST TOOK SHAPE in the western hills of
downtown Portland in 1871, it was not until 1903 that
Washington Park acquired much of its present appearance.
This was the year Boston landscape architect John Olmsted
came to Portland to help plan the Lewis and Clark Exposition
and lay out a parks plan for the young city. Reflecting Olmsted's suggestions, Washington Park has developed, over
the years, to encompass gardens, open spaces, great groves
of evergreens, a zoo, and recreational facilities. Today, the
park is one of Portland's most popular outdoor playgrounds.

**Sign at Washington
Park's Oregon Zoo**

★ Hoyt Arboretum
*More than 8,000 trees and
shrubs from around the
world grow in this arboretum; they can be appreciated
along the 10 miles (16 km)
of well-marked hiking trails.*

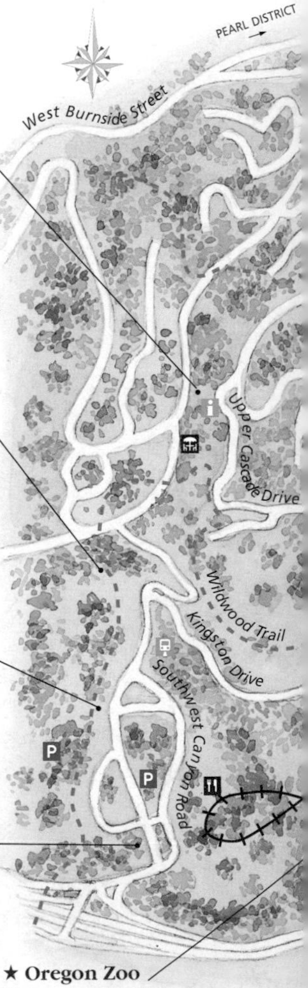

**Vietnam Veterans
Living Memorial**, a ring of
dramatic black granite blocks,
honors Oregonians who served
in the Vietnam War.

World Forestry Center
*This renowned center includes a discovery lab and
a museum, with its "talking" 70-ft (21-m) Douglas fir
that explains how trees grow and excellent exhibits on
rain- and old-growth forests.*

**CM2 – Children's Museum 2nd
Generation** is an exciting interactive
museum designed for children from
ages six months to ten years.

STAR SIGHTS

★ **Hoyt Arboretum**

★ **International
Rose Test Garden**

★ **Japanese Garden**

★ **Oregon Zoo**

★ **Oregon Zoo**
*Oregon's most-visited
attraction, famous for its elephants, is a noted research
institute, harboring over 50
threatened and endangered
species on 64 acres (25.5 ha)
of forested hillside.*

★ **Japanese Garden**
Plants, stones, and water are arranged to reflect the essence of nature in five distinct traditional Japanese gardens.

0 meters 400
0 yards 500

★ **International Rose Test Garden**
Award-winning roses from around the world, a grass amphitheater, and a walkway honoring every queen of the city's annual Rose Festival since 1907, are among the treasures of this 4-acre (1.5-ha) garden, the oldest public garden of its kind in the US.

Wildwood Trail, a 23-mile (37-km) portion of the 40-Mile Loop, runs the length of Washington Park and into Forest Park to the north, winding past Douglas firs and wildflowers.

Washington Park and Zoo Railway
Three trains – the old-style Steamer, the sleek 1958 Zooliner, and a circus train known as the Oregon Express – meander through the park's lush landscape, offering great views of downtown Portland, Mounts Hood and St. Helens, and the zoo.

Exploring Washington Park

Hiking on a forest trail beneath a canopy of old-growth pine trees or coming upon a meadow filled with wildflowers, visitors may find it hard to believe that 320-acre (130-ha) Washington Park is surrounded by the city. Wild as the hilly terrain is in places, however, the park also contains some of the city's best-tended gardens and the always busy zoo, as well as large expanses of manicured lawn. Scenic roadways, an extensive trail system, and even a miniature railway make it easy to explore the park and enjoy its diverse experiences.

Elephant in the Oregon Zoo

Roses in full bloom in the International Rose Test Garden

International Rose Test Garden

400 SW Kingston Dr. **C** (503) 823-3636. ◯ dawn–dusk daily. & ◻

A magnificent treat for all those who love flowers, this garden is the oldest continuously operated rose test garden in the US. It can trace its beginnings to a summer day in 1888, when Georgianna Pittock, wife of pioneer publisher Henry Pittock (see p68), invited her friends to display their prize roses in a tent on the lawn of her mansion. The enthusiasts formed the Portland Rose Society in 1888, planted roses along city streets, and dubbed Portland the "City of Roses." In 1917, the society established the rose garden in Washington Park, on a terraced hillside commanding memorable views of the city and Mount Hood. Today, the garden's 8,000 bushes and 525 species come into bloom in a spectacle of color every June, in

time for the city's annual Rose Festival pageant (see p30).

In the All-American Rose Test Garden, new varieties of roses are carefully observed for two years, as a panel of judges evaluates them for color, form, fragrance, and other criteria. The evaluations are then combined with those of judges at 23 other test gardens around the country to determine the best roses. The City of Portland also chooses its own favorites; these annual winners are on display in the Gold Medal Garden.

Only at the Shakespeare Garden do roses not take center stage – this pleasant bower is planted with flowers mentioned in the bard's plays.

The Rose Society also maintains gardens in Peninsula Park, in north Portland, and in the neighborhood of Ladd's Addition (see p74), in southeast Portland.

Japanese Garden

611 SW Kingston Dr. **C** (503) 223-1321. ◯ Apr–Sep: noon–7pm Mon, 10am–7pm Tue–Sun; Oct–Mar: noon–4pm Mon, 10am–4pm Tue–Sun. ● Jan 1, Thanksgiving, Dec 25. ◧ mid-Apr–Oct: 10:45am & 2:30pm daily. ◻ ⓦ www.japanesegarden.com

This lovely, manicured landscape, spread across hilly terrain adjacent to the International Rose Test Garden, is said to be one of the most authentic Japanese gardens outside of Japan and is certainly one of the most tranquil spots in Portland. Within the garden, designed by noted Japanese landscape architect Takuma Tono, meticulously tended plantings surround ponds, streams, rock formations, and pavilions.

Paths wind through four distinct landscapes: the Tea Garden, built around a ceremonial tea house; the Strolling Pond Garden, where zigzagging bridges cross carp-filled pools and iris beds; the Natural Garden, where trees, shrubs, ferns, and mosses grow in their natural state alongside ponds, streams, and waterfalls; and the Dry Landscape Gardens, in which raked gravel simulates the sea and plantings depict a sake cup and gourd to wish the visitor happiness. The wood, tile-roofed entrance gate can be reached by a short uphill climb on a woodland path or via a shuttle bus that departs every ten minutes from the parking lot below.

Stone pagoda in the Japanese Garden

The authentic and tranquil Japanese Garden, designed by Takuma Tono

Stately conifers in the plantings of the Hoyt Arboretum

Hoyt Arboretum

4000 SW Fairview Blvd. *(503) 228-8733.* ⏰ *dawn–dusk daily.* 🏛 *Apr–Oct: 2pm Sat–Sun.* w *www.hoytarboretum.org*

In the groves and meadows of this 175-acre (70-ha) arboretum grow 218 species of conifers (which is the world's largest such collection), dozens of species of wildflowers indigenous to the Pacific Northwest, and other trees and plants gathered from around the world.

The visitors' center – the departure point for tours – also provides maps of the many trails that crisscross the arboretum and detailed lists of the trees and plants to be found along the way.

At the south end of the Hoyt Arboretum, the **Vietnam Veterans Living Memorial** – a subdued assemblage of lawns, gardens, and six granite slabs inscribed with the names of veterans – commemorates those Oregonians who were killed or reported missing during the Vietnam War.

Oregon Zoo

4001 SW Canyon Rd. *(503) 226-1561.* ⏰ *Apr–Sep: 9am–6pm daily; Oct–Mar: 9am–4pm daily.* ⚫ *Dec 25.* 🏛 ♿ ▯ ▮ w *www.oregonzoo.org*

In 1887, pharmacist Richard B. Knight donated a grizzly bear and a brown bear to the city. A zoo has been located in Washington Park ever since, moving to its present location on the hillsides and ravines of the south side of the park in 1959. More than 1,000 birds, mammals, reptiles, and invertebrates – representing 200 species – live in the zoo, many in spacious, naturalistic habitats. The Oregon Zoo, home to the largest breeding herd of elephants in captivity, is noted for its efforts to perpetuate some 21 endangered and 33 threatened species.

Among the zoo's most popular denizens are the Humboldt penguins from Peru that live in the Penguinarium; the sea lions and sea otters in Steller Cove; the impalas and giraffes that graze in the zoo's African Savanna exhibit; and the wolves and grizzly bears of the Alaskan Tundra exhibit. The Cascade exhibit provides a look at the goats, otters, elk, and other animals that roam the Pacific Northwest wilds.

World Forestry Center Museum

4033 SW Canyon Rd. *(503) 228-1367.* ⏰ *Memorial Day–Labor Day: 9am–5pm daily; Labor Day–Memorial Day: 10am–5pm daily.* ⚫ *Thanksgiving, Dec 25.* 🏛 ♿ ▯ Trees steal the show at this museum devoted to the world's forest resources. At the center of the main floor of the stylishly designed timber building is the 70-ft (21-m) "talking tree," which, at the push of a button, explains how a tree grows and lives. On display around the tree is an outstanding collection of petrified wood – wood that has been buried for thousands of years and transformed into mineral deposits.

Upstairs, photographs, slide shows, and text panels explore the importance of old-growth forests and tropical rainforests. The Forest Discovery Lab provides hands-on exhibits to help youngsters appreciate the forests around them. The museum also hosts many special exhibits.

The timbered exterior of the World Forestry Center Museum

Children's Museum 2nd Generation

4015 SW Canyon Rd. *(503) 223-6500.* ⏰ *9am–5pm Mon–Thu & Sat, 9am–8pm Fri, 11am–5pm Sun.* ⚫ *some school hols.* 🏛 ▯ ▮ w *www.portlandcm2.org*

When it was established in 1949, the Portland Children's Museum was one of the first of its kind in the US. In 2001, the museum moved to its current location and was renamed the Children's Museum 2nd Generation.

"Play" is the operative word at the museum, as youngsters turn cranks and operate valves to send water cascading through Water Works, use giant rain sticks to make music in the Zounds! exhibit, perform medical operations in the Kids' Clinic, and in other creative ways explore the world around them.

One sea lion draped over another in Stellar Cove at the Oregon Zoo

Street shopping in Portland's funky Hawthorne District

Hawthorne District ⑧

NE Hawthorne Blvd, from SE 17th to SE 39th Sts.

A N EAST-SIDE RESIDENTIAL and business area somewhat reminiscent of parts of Berkeley, California, the Hawthorne District is hip, funky, and bustling with young people, many of whom attend nearby Reed College. Hawthorne Boulevard is lined with coffee-houses, clothing boutiques, bookstores, bakeries, delis, and restaurants, several serving ethnic foods, including Vietnamese, Indian, Lebanese, and Ethiopian. Buskers add their sounds to the area's vibrant street scene.

The district's surrounding residential neighborhoods date from the early 20th century and were among Portland's first so-called "streetcar suburbs." Of these, Ladd's Addition is one of the oldest planned communities in the western US. Built in a circular grid of streets that surround five rose gardens, the plan was considered radical when it was laid out in 1939. Today, the area boasts many styles of 20th-century architecture: bungalow, craftsman, mission, colonial revival, and Tudor.

To the east, Hawthorne Boulevard ascends the slopes of Mount Tabor, an extinct volcano whose crater is now surrounded by a lovely forested park, popular with picnickers. Walking trails are to be found throughout the park.

Sellwood District ⑨

SE 13th to SE 17th Aves, from SE Tacoma St to SE Bybee Blvd.

S ELLWOOD, A QUIET residential neighborhood on a bluff above the Willamette River in the southeast corner of the city, has become the antiques center of Portland. Long gone are the days when Sellwood was a bargain-hunter's paradise, but shoppers continue to descend upon Sellwood's 30 or so antique shops – many of which occupy old Victorian houses along Southeast 13th Avenue, known as **Antique Row**. They may then enjoy a meal in one of the area's many restaurants or in the adjoining Westmoreland neighborhood.

The riverbank just below the Sellwood bluff is made festive by the presence of the Ferris wheel, roller coaster, roller-skating rink, and other attractions of **Oaks Park**, a shady amusement park that opened during the 1905 Lewis and Clark Exposition (see p40).

Chairs for sale in front of shops in Sellwood's Antique Row

Crystal Springs Rhododendron Garden ⑩

SE 28th Ave, near SE Woodstock Blvd. ☎ (503) 771-8386. 🚌 19. ◯ dawn–dusk daily. 🎫

T HIS 7-ACRE (2.8-ha) garden is laced with trails that cross streams, pass beneath misty cascades, and circle a spring-fed lake that attracts ducks, geese, herons, and many other kinds of birds and

waterfowl. The garden erupts into a breathtaking blaze of color from March through June, when hundreds of species of rare rhododendrons and azaleas – one of the world's leading collections of these woodland plants – are in bloom.

The serene lake at Crystal Springs Rhododendron Garden

Reed College ⑪

3203 SE Woodstock Blvd. ☎ (503) 771-1112. 🚌 19. ◯ dawn–dusk daily. 🌐 www.reed.edu

E STABLISHED IN 1908 with a bequest from Oregon pioneers Simeon and Amanda Reed, Reed College occupies a wooded, 100-acre (40-ha) campus at the edge of Eastmoreland, one of Portland's most beautiful residential neighborhoods. Brick Tudor Gothic buildings, along with others designed in traditional Northwest timber style, are set amid rolling lawns surrounding the "canyon," a wooded wetland; shade is provided by 125 species of maples, cedars, and other trees. This setting seems to have a beneficial effect on the college's 1,400 students – Reed has produced the second highest number of Rhodes scholars of all US liberal arts colleges.

One of the several brick Tudor buildings on Reed College campus

Artifacts of early pioneers, End of the Oregon Trail Interpretive Center

End of the Oregon Trail Interpretive Center ⑫

1726 Washington St, Oregon City.
☎ (503) 657-9336. ◯ Mar–Oct: call for hrs. ● Nov–Feb: Mon–Tue; Jan 1, Thanksgiving, Dec 25. 🎫 ♿ 🏠
🄦 www.endoftheoregontrail.org

ALTHOUGH MANY of the pioneers who crossed the country on the Oregon Trail went their separate ways once they passed into eastern Oregon, for those who continued westward across the Cascade Mountains, Abernethy Green near Oregon City was the end of the trail. Here they stocked up on seeds and provisions and set up farmsteads in the fertile Willamette Valley.

The End of the Oregon Trail Interpretive Center tells the story of life on the trail in three oversized, 50-ft- (15-m-) high covered wagons that encircle Abernethy Green. Exhibits of artifacts and heirlooms, hands-on experiences in which visitors choose supplies and pack a wagon, and mixed-media shows bring the hardships of the trek to life.

Oregon City ⑬

Road map 1 A3. 🏠 26,000. 🚹 1810 Washington St, (503) 656-1619.

TERMINUS OF the Oregon Trail and capital of the Oregon territory from 1849 to 1852, Oregon City's past prominence is largely due to its location beside the 40-ft (12-m) Willamette Falls, which powered flour and paper mills. The mills brought prosperity to the city, which was the site of the first meeting of the territory's provisional legislature, in 1843.

Clackamas County Historical Society Museum traces this history from the days when John McLoughlin, an Englishman sympathetic to the cause of bringing Oregon into the US, settled the town in 1829. In 1846, the "Father of Oregon" built the then grandest home in Oregon, now the **McLoughlin House National Historic Site**. Stairs and an elevator connect this historic area, located on a bluff, to the commercial area by the river below.

🏛 **Clackamas County Historical Society Museum**
211 Tumwater Dr. ☎ (503) 655-5574.
◯ 10am–4pm Mon–Fri, noon–4pm Sat–Sun. ● major hols. 🎫
🏯 **McLoughlin House National Historic Site**
713 Center St. ☎ (503) 656-5146.
◯ call for hrs. ● major hols. 🎫

The stately McLoughlin House (1846) in Oregon City

Aurora ⑭

Road map 1 A3. 🏠 630. 🚹 21558 Hwy 99 E, (503) 678-2288.

THE TOWN of Aurora traces its roots to the Aurora Colony, a Utopian community founded by Prussian immigrant William Keil in 1852. Similar to Shaker communities in the east, it was a collective society based on the principles of Christian fundamentalism and shared property. The colony thrived for more than a decade, until it was decimated by a smallpox

epidemic. Exhibits tracing the colony's history fill the **Old Aurora Colony Museum**'s handsome white-frame buildings. Many of Aurora's other historic buildings now house antique shops.

Nearby **Champoeg State Heritage Area** is the site of an 1843 convention at which settlers voted to break from Britain and establish a provisional American government in Oregon. By that time, Champoeg was a thriving trading post on the banks of the Willamette River, having been established by the Hudson's Bay Company in 1813. The town that grew up around the trading post was abandoned as a result of devastating floods in 1861 and 1890; the park now comprises 650 acres (265 ha) of meadows and stately stands of oaks and evergreens.

Displays in the visitors' center pay tribute to the Calapooya Indians, who once lived here on the banks of the river, and to the traders and pioneers who came in the wake of the Hudson's Bay settlement. Its historic buildings include a jail, a schoolhouse, a barn, and several early dwellings.

🏛 **Old Aurora Colony Museum**
212 2nd St. ☎ (503) 678-5754.
◯ 10am–4pm Tue–Sat, noon–4pm Sun. ● major hols. 🎫
🌿 **Champoeg State Heritage Area**
Rte 99 W, 12 miles (7.5 km) west of Aurora. ☎ (503) 678-1251.
◯ dawn–dusk daily. 🎫 🏠

Picturesque cottages in Aurora's National Historic District

Shopping in Portland

O NE OF THE MANY PLEASURES of shopping in Portland is the fact that no state sales tax is levied. Another is the convenient location of the city's commercial areas in or near downtown. Portland has its share of nationally known department stores and chains, but it also has many specialty shops, often selling locally manufactured goods.

SHOPPING DISTRICTS

D OWNTOWN, NEAR Pioneer Courthouse Square, is the city's main shopping district. Major department stores are here, as are jewelry and clothing stores, and other specialty shops. In Nob Hill, Northwest 23rd Avenue west of Burnside is lined with an eclectic mix of chic and trendy shops specializing in home furnishings, clothing, gifts, and gourmet foods. The Pearl District *(see pp54–5)* has a concentration of commercial galleries, along with shops offering designer furniture and wares.

In Sellwood *(see p74)*, antique stores line Southeast 13th Avenue. A funky counterculture holds sway on nearby Southeast Hawthorne Boulevard *(see p74)*, with book, music, and vintage clothing shops. At Portland Saturday Market *(see p53)*, over 300 artisans gather on weekends to sell their work.

Gallery art on a First Thursday

DEPARTMENT STORES AND SHOPPING CENTERS

F OUNDED IN PORTLAND over 100 years ago, **Meier and Frank** is famous for its constant sales on everything from socks to refrigerators. **Nordstrom**, a Pacific Northwest chain based in Seattle, is well

Wares of all kinds on display at the popular Saturday Market

Sign atop one of the unique Made in Oregon stores

known for its quality clothing for men, women, and children, and superb service, while **Saks Fifth Avenue** offers designer labels and fine accessories. More than 70 upscale retailers are housed in the three-level **Pioneer Place**. The 170 stores in **Lloyd Center** encircle an ice-skating rink.

SPECIALTY SHOPS

S PECIALIZING IN items "made, caught, or grown" in the state, such as local jams and preserves, and smoked salmon, **Made in Oregon** also stocks a selection of products from the Pendleton Woolen Mills *(see p111)*, as does the **Portland Pendleton Shop**.

An excellent selection of wines produced from the bounty of the state's many acclaimed vineyards is to be found at **Oregon Wines on Broadway**. There is a wine bar adjacent to the shop. **Columbia Sportswear** specializes in athletic wear made in the Pacific Northwest. Portland's very own **Norm Thompson** carries classic casual and outdoor clothing with a Pacific Northwest look. It also has a highly successful worldwide mail order business.

Powell's City of Books, with its inventory of over one million new and used books, is said to be the world's largest bookstore.

DIRECTORY

DEPARTMENT STORES AND SHOPPING CENTERS

Lloyd Center
NE Multnomah St & NE 9th Ave.
📞 *(503) 282-2511.*

Meier and Frank
621 SW 5th Ave. **Map** 1 C5.
📞 *(503) 223-0512.*

Nordstrom
701 SW Broadway. **Map** 1 C5.
📞 *(503) 287-2444.*

Pioneer Place
700 SW 5th Ave. **Map** 1 C5.
📞 *(503) 228-5800.*

Saks Fifth Avenue
850 SW 5th Ave. **Map** 1 C5.
📞 *(503) 226-3200.*

SPECIALTY SHOPS

Columbia Sportswear
911 SW Broadway. **Map** 1 C5.
📞 *(503) 226-6800.*

Made in Oregon
921 SW Morrison St. **Map** 1 B5.
📞 *(503) 241-3630.*
(One of several locations)

Norm Thompson
1805 NW Thurman St.
📞 *(503) 221-0764.*

Oregon Wines on Broadway
515 SW Broadway. **Map** 1 C5.
📞 *(503) 228-4655.*

Portland Pendleton Shop
900 SW 5th Ave. **Map** 3 C1
📞 *(503) 242-0037.*

Powell's City of Books
1005 W Burnside St. **Map** 1 B4.
📞 *(503) 228-4651.*

WHAT TO BUY

W INE CONNOISSEURS will not want to miss the offerings of Oregon's vineyards, especially the pinot noirs. Smoked salmon and oysters from Oregon waters also rank high among local delicacies. A wool blanket or plaid shirt or scarf from Oregon's famed Pendleton Woolen Mills *(see p111)* is high on the list of popular gifts, as is the art – including masks, carvings, and jewelry – of Native Americans of the Pacific Northwest.

Entertainment in Portland

P ORTLAND HAS A VIBRANT and growing cultural scene. The performing arts thrive in the many venues located throughout the city, with theater and music offerings being especially plentiful. And, of course, Portland has its fair share of big-ticket rock concerts and professional sports matches.

INFORMATION

T HE FREE WEEKLY *Willamette Week* newspaper runs comprehensive entertainment listings. The *Oregonian*, the city's major daily, prints listings in its Friday edition. The **Portland Oregon Visitors Association** also provides information on events around town.

BUYING TICKETS

T ICKETS FOR MANY EVENTS can be purchased by phone or in person from **Ticketmaster** and **Fastixx**. **Ticket Central**, a service of the Portland Oregon Visitors Association located at Pioneer Courthouse Square *(see p60)*, sells tickets to a variety of performances. Same-day half-price tickets are often also available. It is closed on Sundays, so buy tickets for Sunday on Saturday.

FREE EVENTS

E VERY WEDNESDAY at noon, **The Old Church** (tel. 503/ 222-2031) hosts a free organ concert. Free noontime concerts are also held at **Pioneer Courthouse Square** *(see p60)*.

During summer, the **Oregon Zoo Amphitheater** (tel. 503/ 226-1561) is the setting for free concerts several nights a week.

THEATER

T OPPING THE LIST of Portland's theater troupes are the **Artists Repertory Theatre,** the oldest theater group in the city; **Portland Center**

The modern Rose Garden Arena, in the Rose Quarter complex

The façade of the Portland Center for the Performing Arts

Stage, with a repertoire of classic and contemporary plays; and **Tygres Heart Shakespeare Company**, presenting acclaimed interpretations of the bard's works.

DANCE

B ASED AT the **Portland Center for Performing Arts**, the **Oregon Ballet Theatre** performs classical and contemporary pieces, including the *Nutcracker* during the holiday season and new works showcased in late spring.

MUSIC

T HE OLDEST SYMPHONY orchestra on the West Coast, the **Oregon Symphony** has garnered considerable praise over the past two decades under conductor and music director James DePreist. The **Portland Baroque Orchestra** presents a program of early music, fall through spring, while the **Portland Opera** stages five works a year.

The **Crystal Ballroom**, opened in 1920, hosts popular musical acts; it is famous for its "floating" dance floor, which rests on ball bearings.

A favored jazz haunt of locals is **Jazz De Opus**, in Old Town, where music can

DIRECTORY

TICKET OUTLETS

Fastixx
(*(800) 922-8499.*

Ticket Central
(*(503) 275-8355.*

Ticketmaster
(*(503) 224-4400.*

THEATER

Artists Repertory Theatre
(*(503) 241-1278.*

Portland Center Stage
(*(503) 274-6588.*

Tygres Heart Shakespeare Company
(*(503) 222-9220.*

DANCE

Oregon Ballet Theatre
(*(503) 222-5538.*

Portland Center for the Performing Arts
(*(503) 796-9293.*

MUSIC

Crystal Ballroom
(*(503) 225-5555.*

Jazz De Opus
(*(503) 222-6077.*

Oregon Symphony
(*(503) 228-1353.*

Portland Baroque Orchestra
(*(503) 226-6635.*

Portland Opera
(*(503) 241-1802.*

SPORTS VENUES

PGE Park
(*(503) 553-5510.*

Rose Garden Arena
(*(503) 321-3211.*

be enjoyed seven nights a week, accompanied by a selection of seafood and steak specialties.

SPECTATOR SPORTS

T HE ROSE GARDEN Arena, part of the Rose Garden complex *(see p69)*, is home to the Portland Trailblazers basketball team and Portland Winter Hawks hockey team.

Fans can watch the Portland Beavers play baseball at **PGE Park**, its recent $38.5 million renovation now complete.

Getting Around Portland

Old-fashioned streetcar near Jameson Square

THE RESULTS OF PORTLAND'S EFFORTS to prevent urban sprawl and congestion are noticeable in the compact metropolis. Central Portland is easy to navigate. One can walk just about anywhere, and extensive bus, light rail, and streetcar systems put most places within easy reach. Not only is public transportation readily available, in much of the city center it is also free.

Bicycle parked on a Portland downtown street, a common sight

STREET LAYOUT

THE WILLAMETTE RIVER, which is spanned by eight downtown bridges, divides Portland into east and west. Burnside Street bisects the city into north and south. As a result, Portland is divided into quadrants, reflected in street addresses, most of which begin with a "Northwest," "Northeast," "Southwest," or "Southeast."

Avenues in Portland are numbered and run north–south; streets are named and run east–west. The streets north of Burnside run alphabetically, making them easy to find – for example, Couch is next to Burnside and Davis is next to Couch. South of Burnside, however, street names run in a random order. Street numbers that are odd are usually on the west and north sides, even numbers usually on the east and south.

Several highways crisscross Portland. The I-5, the main West Coast north–south route, runs through the city, while the I-84 runs from the east bank of the Willamette River east toward Idaho and beyond. The I-205 forms a perimeter around the city's outskirts and runs by the airport; the I-405 loops around the southern and western edges of downtown.

WALKING

PORTLAND'S DOWNTOWN is so compact that it is easy to get almost anywhere on foot, and walkways on the bridges make most eastside neighborhoods accessible to pedestrians. Powell's City of Books (*see p55*) offers a free walking map. Maps are also available at the **Portland Oregon Visitors Association**, at Pioneer Courthouse Square (*see p60*).

BICYCLING

PORTLAND IS a bicycle-friendly city. Bikes are permitted on public transit, most public buses are equipped with bike racks, and many streets have designated bicycle lanes.

Helmets are mandatory for cyclists under 16 years of age, and all cyclists who ride after dark must equip their bicycles with a red reflector that can be seen from the rear and a flashing white light that is visible from ahead. The **Bicycle Transportation Alliance**, a cycling advocacy group, provides route maps and other useful cycling information.

TAXIS

TAXIS DON'T CRUISE the streets in Portland looking for fares as they do in many other cities. You can find a cab outside major downtown hotels or call one of the city's taxi companies. Fares can be paid with major credit cards.

PUBLIC TRANSIT

PORTLAND'S PUBLIC TRANSIT is free within the 300 blocks of the Fareless Square, in the city center. The Fareless Square is bordered by the I-405 to the south and west; Northwest Irving Street to the north; and the Willamette River to the east, with the exception of the Rose Quarter and Lloyd Center, which also fall within the zone.

The Portland transportation authority, **Tri-Met**, provides three types of public transit: light rail, buses, and streetcars.

The Metro Area Express (MAX) light rail system serves the Portland metropolitan area. Its blue-line trains run through downtown between Hillsboro in the west and Gresham in the east, while the red line connects downtown with the airport. The yellow line, opening in late 2004, runs across north Portland, from the Rose Quarter to the Expo Center.

Trains run roughly every 10 to 15 minutes, with a reduced late-night schedule.

Most **Tri-Met** bus routes include stops along the downtown transit malls on

A MAX train servicing Portland's historic Old Town

5th and 6th Avenues, from which many downtown attractions are an easy walk.

The Portland Streetcar travels through central Portland and makes many stops along 10th and 11th Avenues.

Outside the Fareless Square, the fare on MAX trains, buses, and streetcars varies depending on the distance traveled. There are three zones; the adult fare for one zone is $1.25, increasing to $1.55 for three zones. The fare is reduced for seniors and for children between the ages of 7 and 18. As many as three children under age 7 can ride for free when accompanied by an adult. Transfers are free and allow for interchangeable travel on the three forms of transit. Books of ten tickets are available at a discount. All-day tickets offering unlimited rides anywhere in the system and three-day Adventure Passes are also available. MAX tickets must be validated at one of the machines located throughout the trains.

Tri-Met buses, MAX trains, and Portland Streetcars accommodate passengers with disabilities: buses are equipped with lifts, and trains and streetcars have ground-level entrances that allow passengers in wheelchairs to wheel onto the cars.

DRIVING

COMPARED WITH many other cities, Portland is relatively easy to drive in. Some of the major arteries out of downtown – such as US 26 West, I-84, I-85, and Macadan Boulevard – can become congested between 5 and 6pm, but at most other times, barring accidents and road work, traffic flows easily.

The many one-way streets downtown ease traffic congestion. Cars are prohibited on parts of 5th and 6th Avenues designated as transit malls, which accommodate public trains and buses. It is legal to make a right turn on a red light, but only after coming to a full stop.

Speed limits are generally 25 mph (40 km/h) in residential areas, and 20 mph

Portland Streetcar at the Portland State University Station

(32 km/h) in business and school districts. Drivers and passengers are required to wear seatbelts and motorcyclists must wear helmets.

If you need assistance, maps, or guidebooks, contact the local office of the **American Automobile Association**.

PARKING

METERED STREET parking is available downtown, but the ease of finding a space greatly depends on the time of day. The parking time permitted varies from 15 minutes to three hours, one hour being the norm. An economical alternative is one of the city's many Smart Park garages.

On a few streets, the city is introducing a park-and-display system. Machines accept payment in cash or by credit card and issue a ticket – valid for up to three hours, depending on the amount paid – to be displayed on the inside of the windshield. Metered parking

Union Station, with its prominent tower, welcoming train passengers

is generally in effect Monday through Sunday, from 8am to 6pm, excluding state holidays.

TOWING

PARKING WARDENS are a vigilant presence on downtown streets. Check posted street parking regulations, as they may limit parking during rush hours or specify other regulations, such as stopping being permitted only to load or unload. If your car has been towed, call the **Portland Police Auto Records**. A processing fee and towing charge, payable by cash or money order, will be levied.

<table>
<tr><td colspan="1">

DIRECTORY

USEFUL NUMBERS

American Automobile Association
📞 *(503) 111-6734* or *(800) 452-1643.*

Bicycle Transportation Alliance
📞 *(503) 226-0676.*

Portland Oregon Visitors Association
📞 *(503) 275-8355* or *(877) 678-5263.*

Portland Police, Auto Records Department
📞 *(503) 823-0044.*

Tri-Met Customer Service
📞 *(503) 238-7433.*

TAXIS

Broadway Cab
📞 *(503) 227-1234.*

Radio Cab
📞 *(503) 227-1212.*

</td></tr>
</table>

PORTLAND STREET FINDER

THE KEY MAP BELOW shows the area of Portland covered by the *Street Finder* maps, which can be found on the following pages. Map references for sights, hotels, restaurants, shops, and entertainment venues given throughout the Portland chapter of this guide refer to the grid on the maps. The first figure in the reference indicates which map to turn to (1 to 4), and the letter and number that follow refer to the grid reference on that map.

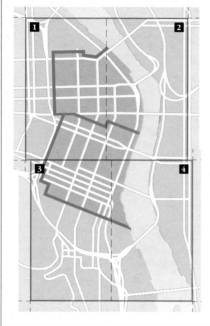

KEY TO STREET FINDER

▪	Major sight
▪	Minor sight
▪	Station building
🚆	Train station
🚌	Bus station – long distance
🚋	Streetcar
Ⓜ	MAX
🅿	Parking
ℹ	Information
✚	Hospital
🚔	Police station
✝	Church
⊠	Post office
═	Railroad line
→	One-way street

SCALE OF MAPS 1–4

0 meters   150
0 yards   150

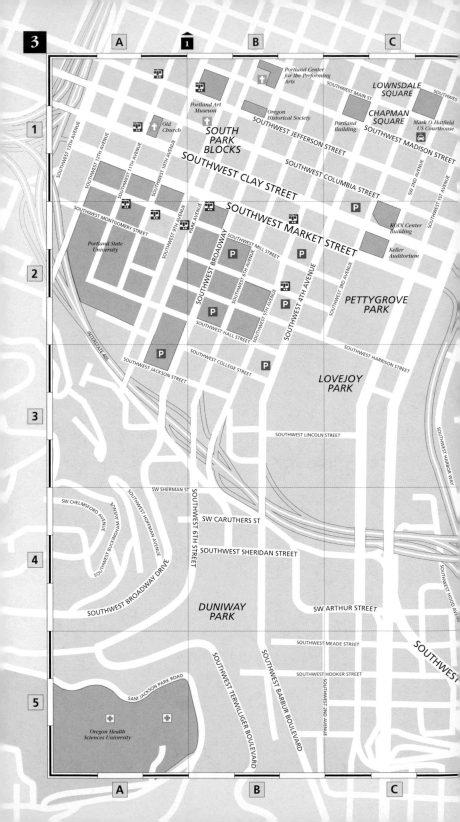

D   E   2   F   4

SW TAYLOR ST

SOUTHWEST NAITO PARKWAY

ION STREET

i

GOVERNOR
TOM McCALL
WATERFRONT PARK

SOUTHEAST BELMONT STREET

SOUTHEAST WATER STREET

SOUTHEAST 1ST AVENUE

SOUTHEAST YAMHILL STREET

SOUTHEAST TAYLOR STREET

SOUTHEAST 3RD AVENUE

MARTIN LUTHER KING JR BOULEVARD

1

SOUTHEAST SALMON STREET

SOUTHEAST MAIN STREET

SOUTHEAST MADISON STREET

Hawthorne Bridge

P

SOUTHEAST HAWTHORNE BOULEVARD

SOUTHEAST 2ND AVENUE

SOUTHEAST CLAY STREET

2

Willamette River

EASTBANK
ESPLANADE

SOUTHEAST MARKET STREET

SE MILL STREET

SOUTHWEST
MONTGOMERY
STREET

RiverPlace
Marina

SOUTHEAST STEPHENS STREET

SE HARRISON ST

SOUTH WEST RIVER DRIVE

3

INTERSTATE 5

Marquam Bridge

Oregon Museum
of Science
and Industry (OMSI)

SW MOODY STREET

Willamette River

4

SOUTHWEST MOODY AVENUE

EWAY

LLY AVENUE

Ross Island Bridge

5

OREGON

OREGONIANS AND THEIR VISITORS *alike run out of adjectives to describe the scenic wonders contained within the 97,000 sq miles (251,200 sq km) of the tenth largest US state. Here, snow-capped mountains pierce the clouds, waves break on rocky shores, rivers sprint through gorges, dense forests cling to ravines, and desert vistas stretch beneath skies that, indeed, are not cloudy all day.*

A forest-cloaked headland, tidal estuary, or stretch of isolated beach appears around every bend of the 350-mile (560-km) Oregon coastline. In the north, the mighty Columbia River flows through a magnificent gorge where waterfalls plummet from cliffs. Those traveling alongside the river follow in the footsteps of explorers Lewis and Clark, who canoed the rushing waters in 1805. The Snake River, a tributary of the Columbia River, tumbles through inhospitable desert at the bottom of 8,000-ft (2,440-m) Hells Canyon, the deepest gorge in North America.

Looking at such rugged landscapes, it is easy to imagine the hardships hundreds of thousands of pioneers encountered as they migrated west along the Oregon Trail. Then, of course, there are the mountains – the Coast range taking shape above coastal headlands, the Cascades peaks soaring above the central valleys, the Wallowas and Blues rising from high desert country in the east. These landscapes provide more than memorable views. Hiking trails lace the forests, and rushing white-water rivers, such as the Rogue and Deschutes, brim with trout, salmon, and sturgeon, attracting white-water rafters and anglers. Lakes sparkle with crystal-clear water; the most awesome of them, Crater Lake, is the deepest in North America. And the slopes of Mount Hood are covered with snow – and skiers – all year.

Oregon serves up cosmopolitan pleasures, too. Portlanders are quick to claim their city as one of the most sophisticated and cultured anywhere. But even out-of-the-way places, such as Ashland, of Shakespeare Festival fame, stage notable events.

Wherever a traveler goes or whatever a traveler does in Oregon, the glimmer of a distant mountain peak and the scent of pine in the air will add an extra zest to the experience.

Cowboys in the sagebrush-dotted ranching settlement of Jordan Valley

◁ The Heceta Head Lighthouse (c.1894), Florence, casting the strongest light on the Oregon coast

Exploring Oregon

Travelers in Oregon will find that almost any drive
inevitably takes them through beautiful landscapes.
From Portland, day trips can easily be made to the
Columbia River Gorge and Mount Hood, to the north and
central coasts, and to the wine country and historic towns
of the Willamette Valley. From the Pacific beaches, breathtakingly scenic drives lead across the Coast Range to Bend
and Central Oregon, and from there
through pine forests and high desert
country to such natural wonders as
Crater Lake, Steens Moun-
tain, and Hells Canyon.

Bybee Howel House, a Sauvie Island
landmark, northwest of Portland

SIGHTS AT A GLANCE

Tours

ASTORIA **❷**

Columbia River

COLUMBIA
RIVER
GORGE

CANNON BEACH **❸**

101

30

TILLAMOOK **❹**

McMINNVILLE **⑭**   PORTLAND

THREE CAPES
SCENIC ROUTE **❺**

18

205

216

LINCOLN CITY **❻**

SALEM **⑯** **⑮**

SILVERTON

101

22

26

NEWPORT **❼**

34

NORTH
WILLAMETTE
VALLEY

20

YACHATS **❽**
CAPE
PERPETUA **❾**

36

13

5

SISTERS **⑲**

19

FLORENCE **⑩**

EUGENE **⑰**

126

CASCADE
LAKES
HIGHWAY **㉓**

BEND **㉑**
㉒

NEWBER
NATION.
VOLCAN
MONUM

⑪

OREGON DUNES
NATIONAL
RECREATION AREA

58

38

138

⑫
BANDON

42

230

97

5

62

CRATER
LAKE
NATIONAL
PARK

㉔

101

62

Upper
Klamath
Lake

140

199

46

㉖ JACKSONVILLE
ASHLAND

66

㉕

㉗

OREGON CAVES
NATIONAL MONUMENT

GETTING AROUND

I-5, running north–south, and I-84, running east to Idaho and the Midwest, are Oregon's two major routes. Hwy 26 runs through lovely landscape from the coast across Mount Hood into eastern Oregon. Hwy 101 follows the coast; Hwy 97, another scenic north–south route, skirts the Cascade Mountains and Crater Lake. Car is the most convenient way to travel in Oregon. Amtrak offers three train routes: one east to Chicago, two along the coast. Bus service is limited.

Hood River, a small town on the Columbia River Gorge

HELLS CANYON NATIONAL RECREATION AREA

PENDLETON
32

JOSEPH 34
35 WALLOWA LAKE

JOHN DAY FOSSIL BEDS NATIONAL MONUMENT
31

33 ELKHORN DRIVE

John Day River

RAS WARM NGS

H ROCK E PARK

0 kilometers   50

0 miles   40

MALHEUR NATIONAL WILDLIFE REFUGE
30

Malheur Lake

Lake Owyhee

Owyhee River

STEENS MOUNTAIN
28

JORDAN VALLEY
29

KEY

	Highway
	Major road
	Minor road
	Scenic route
☀	Viewpoint

Rocks rising from the sea near Tillamook, Oregon coast

Columbia River Gorge and Mount Hood Driving Tour ❶

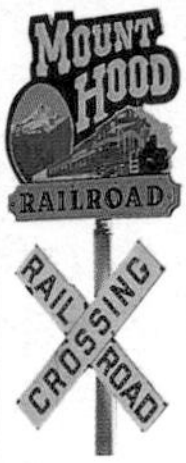
MOUNT HOOD
RAILROAD
RAIL ROAD
CROSSING

Mount Hood Railroad sign

THIS EASY OUTING from Portland encompasses a diverse sampling of Oregon scenery, including the banks of the Columbia River as it flows through a magnificent gorge and the spectacular summit of Mount Hood. Along the way, the route takes in five waterfalls, the bountiful orchards that surround the Hood River, and picturesque Timberline Lodge. Other features of this tour include scenic overlooks, rushing streams, mountain lakes, enormous glaciers, and dense forests.

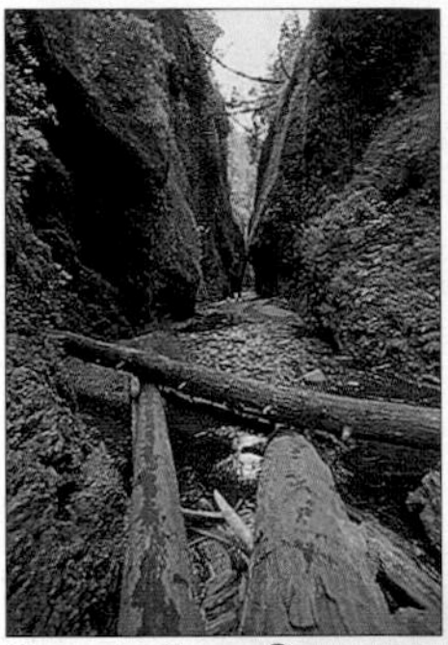

Oneonta Gorge ③
Hardier hikers will enjoy walking through this dramatic gorge. It can also be viewed at the south end of a trail starting in Horsetail Falls.

Bonneville Dam ④
A tour of this 1930s dam reveals massive hydroelectric powerhouses, as well as underwater views of migrating salmon, and a fish hatchery.

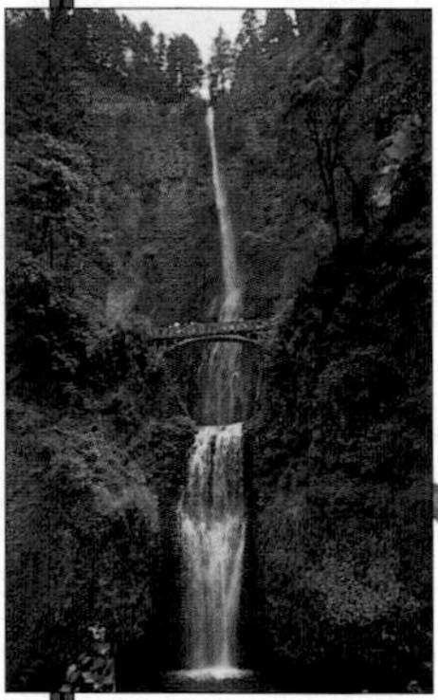

Multnomah Falls ②
The fourth highest waterfall in the US tumbles 620 ft (186 m) in two picturesque cascades.

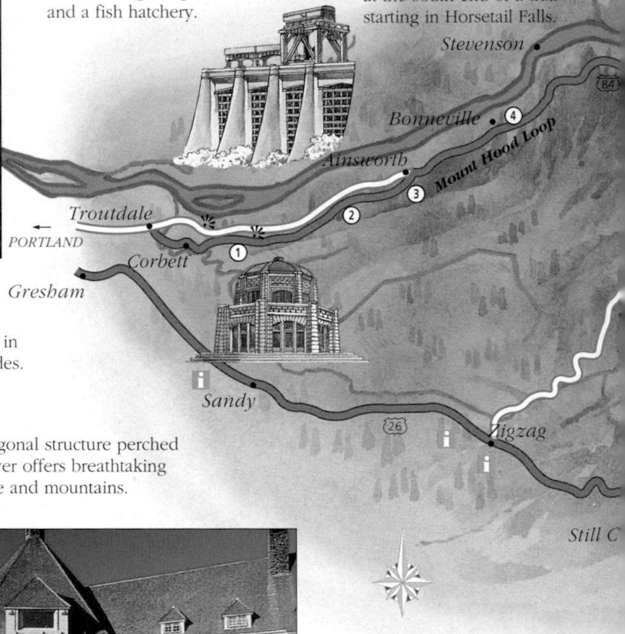
Stevenson
84
Bonneville
4
Mount Hood Loop
Ainsworth
3
2
Troutdale
PORTLAND
1
Corbett
Gresham
Sandy
26
Zigzag
Still C

Vista House ①
This historic, octagonal structure perched high above the river offers breathtaking views of the gorge and mountains.

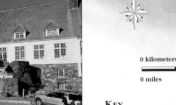

0 kilometers 15

0 miles 10

KEY

- Tour route
- Other road
- Viewpoint
- Information

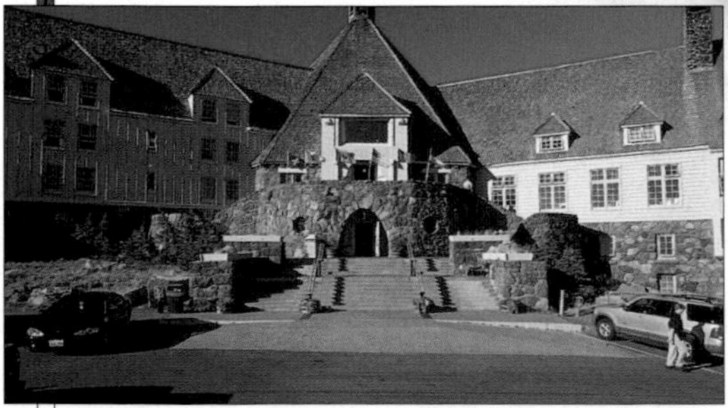

Timberline Lodge ⑪
Artisans hired by the federal Works Project Administration crafted every detail of this beautiful 1930s ski lodge, from the wrought-iron door handles to its massive wood beams.

Ruthton Point [5]
This cape situated in a small state park makes a perfect stopping-off point from which to view the mighty Columbia River Gorge and surrounding Cascade mountain range.

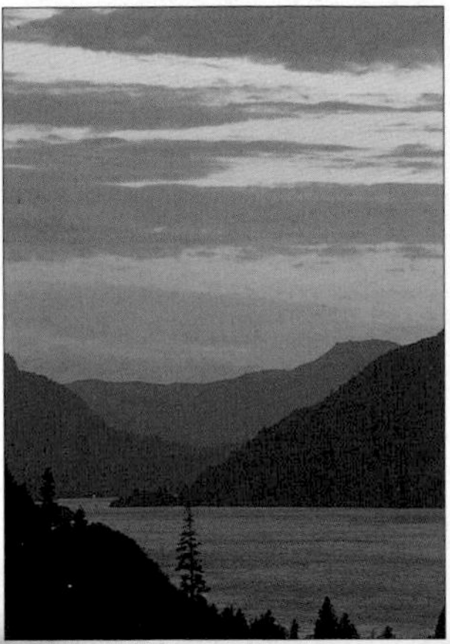

Tips for Drivers

Tour length: *146 miles (235 km).*
Starting point: *I-84 in Portland.*
Stopping-off points: *The most scenic places to enjoy a meal are the two historic lodges on the loop, one at Multnomah Falls in the gorge and the other at Timberline atop Mount Hood. At both, salmon, trout, and other fresh Pacific Northwest cuisine can be enjoyed in front of a blazing hearth.*

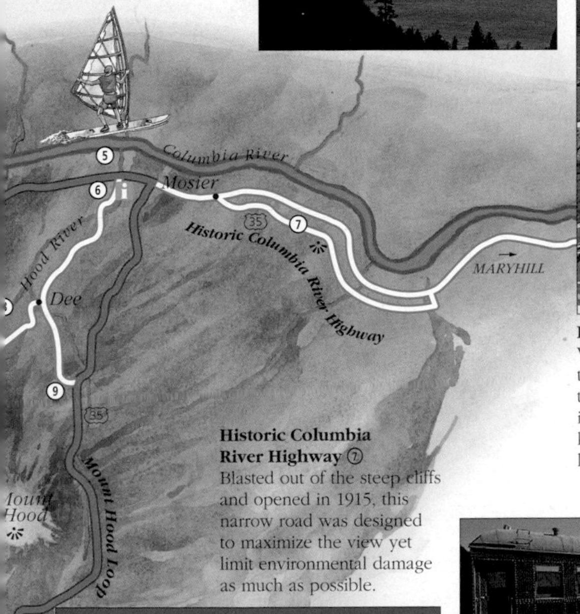

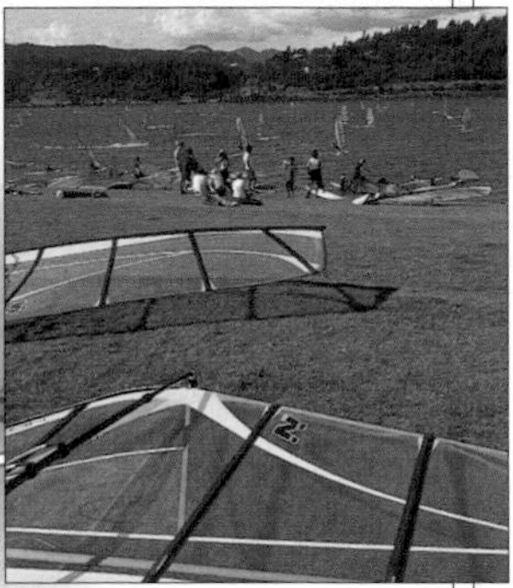

Hood River [6]
Winds and river currents create the ideal conditions that render this riverside town the windsurfing capital of the world. Landlubbers enjoy the bounty of local fruit orchards.

Historic Columbia River Highway [7]
Blasted out of the steep cliffs and opened in 1915, this narrow road was designed to maximize the view yet limit environmental damage as much as possible.

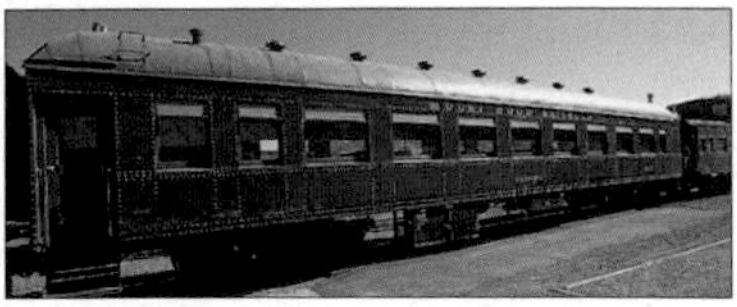

Parkdale [9]
This pretty little town on the eastern slopes of Mount Hood is the terminus of the Mount Hood Scenic Railway, which passes through apple and pear orchards to the Hood River.

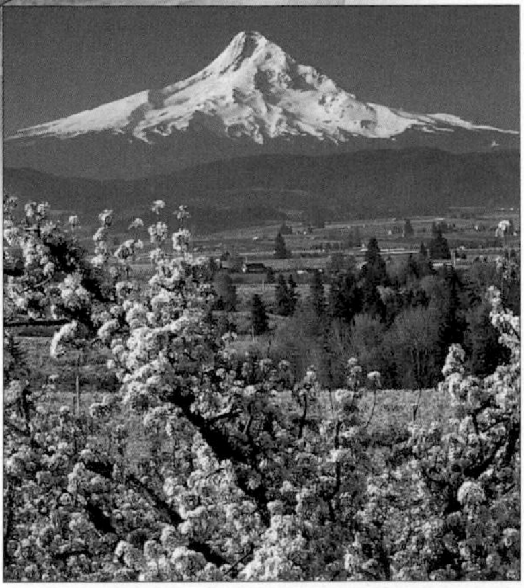

Hood River Valley [8]
This beautiful and fertile valley offers blossoming fruit trees in season and magnificent views of majestic Mount Hood throughout the year.

Barlow Pass [10]
Wheel tracks still rut this section of the Oregon Trail, which is so steep that wagons were often lowered down the hills with ropes.

Astoria ❷

Road map 1 A3. 🏠 10,000. 🏢 111
W Marine Dr, (800) 875-6807.
Ⓦ www.oldoregon.com

Throughout the damp winter of 1805–1806, explorers Lewis and Clark *(see p37)* passed the time making moccasins, preserving fish, and recording in their journals accounts of bear attacks and the almost continual rain at a crude stockade near Astoria. This stockade has been authentically rebuilt at **Fort Clatsop National Memorial**.

In 1811, John Jacob Astor sent fur traders around Cape Horn to establish a trading post in this location at the mouth of the Columbia River, making Astoria the oldest American settlement west of the Rocky Mountains.

These days, the town is a major port for fishing fleets and commercial vessels; its Victorian homes climb a hillside above the river. One such home, the stately **Captain George Flavel House Museum**, retains the cupola from which the captain and his wife once observed river traffic. An even better view can be enjoyed from atop the 164-step spiral staircase of the **Astoria Column**, encircled with bas-relief friezes paying homage to the Pacific Northwest's history – from habitation by early Native Americans to the arrival of the Great Northern Railway in 1892.

The town honors its seagoing past at the **Columbia**

The Astoria Column, with a scenic lookout of the port at its top

Cannon Beach's famous Haystack Rock at sunset

River Maritime Museum, where riverside galleries house fishing dories and Native American dugout canoes. The lightship *Columbia*, berthed in front, once guided ships across the treacherous area at the mouth of the river – a worthy undertaking since the more than 200 shipwrecks in the past century have earned for local waters the moniker "graveyard of the Pacific."

🚩 Fort Clatsop National Memorial
3 miles (5 km) southwest of Astoria, off Hwy 101. 🎫 *(503) 861-2471.*
⬜ *mid-Jun–Labor Day: 8am–6pm daily; Labor Day–mid-Jun: 8am–5pm daily.* ● *Dec 25.* 🏷 🔲 🚹

🚩 Captain George Flavel House Museum
441 8th St. 🎫 *(503) 325-2203.*
⬜ *10am–5pm daily.* ● *Jan 1, Thanksgiving, Dec 24 & 25.* 🏷

🏛 Astoria Column
Atop Coxcomb Hill, off 16th St. 🎫 *(503) 325-2963.* ⬜ *7am–dusk daily.*

🏛 Columbia River Maritime Museum
1792 Marine Dr. 🎫 *(503) 325-2323.*
⬜ *9:30am–5pm daily.* ● *Thanksgiving, Dec 25.* 🏷 🔲 Ⓦ www.crmm.org

ENVIRONS: Fort Stevens State Park, 10 miles (16 km) west of Astoria, dates back to the Civil War, when it guarded the Columbia River from Confederate incursions. The only time the fort actually saw action, though, was on June 21, 1942, when a Japanese submarine fired 17 rounds toward the concrete bunkers that were still buried in the dunes.

🍂 Fort Stevens State Park
Off Hwy 101. 🎫 *(503) 861-1470.*
⬜ *dawn–dusk daily.* ● *Dec 25.* 🏷
🚹 Ⓦ www.visitftstevens.com

Cannon Beach ❸

Road map 1 A3. 🏠 1,200. 🏢 2nd
& Spruce Sts, (503) 436-2623.
Ⓦ www.cannonbeach.org

Despite its status as Oregon's favorite beach town, Cannon Beach retains a great deal of quiet charm. The surrounding forests grow almost up to Hemlock Street, where buildings clad with weathered cedar shingles house art galleries.

Haystack Rock, one of the tallest coastal monoliths in the world, towers 235 ft (72 m) above a long beach and tidal pools teeming with life.

Ecola State Park, at the beach's north end, carpets Tillamook Head, an 1,100-ft (335-m) basalt headland, with verdant forests accessible via Tillamook Head Trail. Viewpoints look across raging surf to **Tillamook Rock Lighthouse**, built in 1880 and soon known as "Terrible Tillie," as waves, logs, and rocks continually washed through the structure. Decommissioned in 1957, the lighthouse is now a private mortuary. Tillamook Rock, a wildlife refuge closed to the public, is home to nesting murres and cormorants.

🍂 Ecola State Park
2 miles (3 km) north of Cannon Beach, off Hwy 101. 🎫 *(503) 436-2844.*
⬜ *dawn–dusk daily.* 🏷

Picturesque house on Cannon Beach's Hemlock Street

Packaging cheese at the Tillamook County Creamery Association

Tillamook ❹

Road map 1 A3. 🏠 6,000. ✈ 3705 Hwy 101 N, (503) 842-7525. ⓦ www.tillamookchamber.org

TILLAMOOK SITS ABOUT 10 miles (16 km) inland from the sea in rich bottomland fed by five rivers that empty into Tillamook Bay. Green pastures, nurtured by more than 70 inches (178 cm) of rain a year, sustain 40,000 cows that supply milk for the historic **Tillamook County Creamery Association**. Here, visitors can view the facilities and sample its output of 78 million lb (35 million kg) of cheese per year, including smoked cheddar and pepper jack.

During World War II, Tillamook was the base for giant blimps that patrolled the coast for Japanese submarines. One

of the hangars – at 1,100 ft (335 m) long and 15 stories tall, the largest wood structure in the world – houses the **Tillamook Air Museum**, which boasts a fine collection of flying boats, early helicopters, and some 30 other restored vintage aircraft.

🏛 **Tillamook County Creamery Association**
4175 Hwy 101 N. ☎ (503) 815-1300. ◷ mid-Jun–Labor Day: 8am–8pm daily; Labor Day–mid-Jun: 8am–6pm daily. ● Thanksgiving, Dec 25. ⓦ www.tillamookcheese.com

🏛 **Tillamook Air Museum**
6030 Hangar Rd. ☎ (503) 842-1130. ◷ 10am–5pm daily. ● Thanksgiving, Dec 25. 🎦 ⓦ www.tillamookair.com

Three Capes Scenic Route ❺

Road map 1 A3. *Oregon State Parks Association* ☎ (800) 551-6949. ⓦ www.oregonstateparks.org

ALONG THIS 35-mile (56-km) loop that follows the marshy shores of Tillamook Bay, roadside markers recount the fate of Bayocean, a resort that thrived in the early 20th century but was washed away in winter storms. For most of the drive, though, nature is the main attraction.

One of the several beaches on the Pacific coast, north of Tillamook

The rocks below **Cape Meares State Scenic Viewpoint** and Cape Meares Lighthouse are home to one of the largest colonies of nesting seabirds in North America. In **Cape Lookout State Park**, trails pass through old-growth forests to clifftop viewpoints – good places to spot migrating gray whales – and to a sand spit between the ocean and Netarts Bay. In the **Cape Kiwanda Natural Area**, waves – turbulent at times – crash into massive sandstone cliffs and offshore rock formations. Pacific City, at the route's south end, is home to a fleet of fishing dories that daringly ply the surf on their way out to sea.

The **Oregon State Parks Association** provides detailed information about the sights along this stunning route.

Massive sandstone cliffs at Cape Kiwanda, along the Three Capes Scenic Route

Colorful kites at one of Lincoln City's many kite shops

Lincoln City **6**

Road map 1 A3. ⚑ 7,000. ℹ️ 801 SW Hwy 101, (541) 994-3070. ⓦ www.lcchamber.com

LINCOLN CITY is a long stretch of clutter and congestion along Highway 101. The town does, however, boast several natural attractions. Formerly called Devil's River and abbreviated by Christians who disliked the name, the D River flows only 120 ft (36 m) – from Devil's Lake to the Pacific Ocean – making it the world's shortest river. The 7.5-mile- (12-km-) long beach, littered with driftwood and agates, is popular with kite enthusiasts who enjoy the strong winds off the sea.

To the north, the steep cliffs of **Cascade Head Preserve** rise out of the surf, then give way to mossy rainforests of Sitka spruce and hemlock and a maritime grassland prairie. Many rare plants and animals, including the Oregon silverspot butterfly, thrive in the preserve, which can be explored on steep but wellmaintained trails.

🐾 Cascade Head Preserve
2 miles (3 km) north of Lincoln City, off Hwy 101. 📞 (503) 230-1221. ⓞ dawn–dusk daily. **Upper trail** ⓞ Jan–mid-Jul.

ENVIRONS: At Depoe Bay, a little fishing port 12 miles (19 km) south of Lincoln City, rough seas blast through narrow channels in the basalt rock, creating geyser-like plumes that shoot as high as 60 ft (18 m). A local amusement is watching the fishing fleet "shoot the hole," or navigate the narrow channel that cuts through sheer rock walls between the sea and the tiny inland harbor, which lays claim to being the smallest navigable harbor in the world.

More excitement may be in store at the Otter Crest State Scenic Viewpoint atop Cape Foulweather, so named by Captain James Cook in 1778 because of the 100-mph (160-km/h) winds that regularly buffet it. This promontory provides an excellent view of the adjacent **Devil's Punchbowl State Natural Area**, where the foaming sea thunders into rocky hollows formed by the collapse of sea caves. Tidal pools on the rocky shore below are known as marine gardens because of the colorful sea urchins and starfish that inhabit them.

🌿 Devil's Punchbowl State Natural Area
15 miles (24 km) south of Lincoln City, off Hwy 101. 📞 (800) 551-6949. ⓞ dawn–dusk daily.

Newport **7**

Road map 1 A3. ⚑ 10,500. ℹ️ 555 SW Coast Hwy, (541) 265-8801. ⓦ www.newportnet.com

THIS SALTY OLD port on Yaquina Bay is home to the largest commercial fishing fleet on the Oregon coast and supports many oystering operations. The town is well accustomed to tourists, too. Shingled resort cottages in the Nye Beach neighborhood date from the 1880s, and in the late 1990s travelers came from around the world to visit Keiko, an orca whale that resided in the internationally renowned **Oregon Coast Aquarium** and gained stardom in the *Free Willie* films. Keiko has since been returned to his native Iceland, but the aquarium still teems with visitors and sealife. Rockfish and anchovies swim around pier pilings in the Sandy Shores exhibit, jellyfish float through the Coastal Waters exhibit, and sea horses and sea dragons cling to sea grass in Enchanted Seas. In Passages of the Deep, sharks

Fish market sign in Newport

Picturesque fishing boats moored in Newport's harbor

swim alongside glass viewing tunnels that are suspended in a 1.32-million-gallon (5-million-liter) tank. Outdoors, tufted puffins and murres fly through North America's largest seabird aviary, and sea otters, sea lions, and seals frolic in saltwater pools.

At the **Hatfield Marine Science Center**, headquarters of the University of Oregon's marine research programs, thoughtful exhibits encourage visitors to explore oceanic science in many fascinating ways, from viewing plankton through a microscope to spotting patterns of sand build-up in time-lapse photography. An octopus that occupies a tank near the entrance is referred to as the "tenacled receptionist."

Yaquina Head Outstanding Natural Area, a narrow finger of lava that juts into the Pacific Ocean on the north end of town, makes it easy to watch marine animals in their natural habitats. Platforms at the base of Yaquina Head Lighthouse are within close sight of rocks where seabirds nest and sea otters sprawl in the sea spray. Wheelchair-accessible paths lead to the edge of tidal pools occupied by kelp crabs, sea urchins, sea anemones, sea stars, and octopi. The interpretive center looks at human and nonhuman inhabitants of the headland; shell debris attests to the presence of the former more than 4,000 years ago.

Newport's working waterfront stretches along the north

The quiet and unspoiled shoreline near Yachats

side of Yaquina Bay. Here, the masts of the fishing schooners tower over shops and restaurants, and crab pots and pesky sea lions trying to steal bait are as much of an attraction as underwater shows and waxwork replicas of sea animals.

Oregon Coast Aquarium
2820 SE Ferry Slip Rd.
(541) 867-3474. Memorial Day–Labor Day: 9am–6pm daily; Labor Day–Memorial Day: 10am–5pm daily. Dec 25. www.aquarium.org

Hatfield Marine Science Center
2030 SE Marine Science Dr.
(541) 867-0100. Memorial Day–Sep: 10am–5pm daily; Oct–Memorial Day: 10am–4pm Thu–Mon. Thanksgiving, Dec 25. www.hmsc.orst.edu

Yaquina Head Outstanding Natural Area
3 miles (5 km) north of Newport, off Hwy 101. (541) 574-3100. dawn–dusk daily. **Interpretive center:** 10am–4pm daily. **Lighthouse:** noon–4pm daily (weather permitting).

Yachats **8**

Road map 1 A3. 635. 241
Hwy 101, (541) 547-3530.
www.yachats.org

THE TOWN OF Yachats (pronounced "ya-hots"), once home to the Alsea people who gave Yachats its name, is the sort of place a shore-lover dreams about: small, unspoiled, and surrounded by forested mountainsides and surf-pounded, rocky headlands. In the center of town, the Yachats River meets the sea in a little estuary shadowed by fir trees and laced with tidal pools. The rocky shoreline and a stunning sunset can be admired from the **Yachats Ocean Road State Natural Site**, a seaside loop on the south side of town.

Yachats Ocean Road State Natural Site
South of Yachats River, west of Hwy 100. (541) 997-3641. dawn–dusk daily.

ORCAS

The largest members of the dolphin family, orcas are found throughout the world's oceans, especially in cold waters. They are also known as killer whales. Along the coast of

Orcas swimming in the cold waters off the coast of Oregon

the Pacific Northwest, transient orcas roam the ocean from California to Alaska in groups of up to 60 whales. Resident orcas, on the other hand, remain faithful to a given location; up to 300, organized into matrilinear pods, live off Vancouver Island (see pp254–5) in summer.

Shark-watching from the Oregon Coast Aquarium's suspended tunnel

Heceta Head Lighthouse, near Cape Perpetua, in operation since 1894

Cape Perpetua Scenic Area ⑨

Road map 1 A4. *Interpretive center*
(541) 547-3289. ◯ *Memorial Day–Labor Day: 9am–5pm daily; Labor Day–Memorial Day: 9am–4pm Sat–Sun.* ⬤ *major hols.* 🎫 🎥

Cape Perpetua is the highest – albeit often cloud-shrouded – viewpoint on the coast. A road ascends to the top at 800 ft (245 m), but those with time and stamina may prefer to make the climb on trails that wind through the old-growth rainforests from the interpretive center. An easy hike of about a mile (1.5 km) along the Giant Spruce Trail leads to a majestic, 500-year-old Sitka spruce.

From Cape Perpetua, Hwy 101 descends into **Heceta Head State Park**, where trails offer spectacular ocean views. Birds nest on the rocks and sea lions and gray whales swim just offshore. High above the surf rises Heceta Head Lighthouse, first lit in 1894 with a beacon that can be seen 21 miles (34 km) out to sea. Guided tours are likely to include imaginative accounts of hauntings by the wife of a lightkeeper; despite this ghostly presence, the lightkeeper's house is a popular bed-and-breakfast.

A herd of Steller sea lions inhabits the **Sea Lion Caves**, the only rookery for wild sea lions found on the North American mainland. An elevator descends 208 ft (63.5 m) from the clifftop to platforms near the floor of the 12-story cavern. Some 200 animals live in the cave during fall and winter; in spring and summer they breed on rock ledges just outside the entrance, where they also bear and nurse their young. Burly bulls weighing up to 2,000 lb (900 kg) boisterously guard groups of 15 to 30 cows and the newborn pups.

🌿 **Heceta Head State Park**
Hwy 101, 19 miles (30.5 km) south of Yachats. *(541) 547-3696.*
◯ *dawn–dusk daily.* **Lighthouse**
🎫 🎥 *Memorial Day–Labor Day: 11am–5pm daily; Labor Day–Memorial Day: call for times.*
🦭 **Sea Lion Caves**
91560 Hwy 101 N, 11 miles (17.5 km) north of Florence.
(541) 547-3111. ◯ *Jul–Aug: 8am–dusk daily; Sep–Jun: 9am–dusk daily.* ⬤ *Dec 25.* 🎫 🚻

Florence ⑩

Road map 1 A4. 🏘 7,000. 🚌 270 Hwy 101, *(541) 997-3128.*
🌐 www.florencechamber.com

It is easy to speed through Florence en route to the nearby sand dunes. The old town, though, tucked away along the banks of the Siuslaw River, warrants a stop. Many of its early 20th-century brick and wood buildings now house art galleries, and a sizeable commercial fishing fleet docks alongside them. The fishing boats not only add a great deal of color to the surroundings but also provide the bounty that appears in the riverside fish markets and restaurants.

Fishing boats in the harbor at Florence, on the Siuslaw River

Environs: At nearby **Darlingtonia State Natural Site**, a short trail loops through a bog where Darlingtonia, also known as cobra lily, thrive. These rare, tall, carnivorous plants are reminiscent of the human-eaters of horror films. Their sweet smell traps insects, which fall to the bottom of the plant stem where they are slowly digested.

🌿 **Darlingtonia State Natural Site**
5 miles (8 km) north of Florence, off Hwy 101. *(800) 551-6949.*
◯ *dawn–dusk daily.* ♿

Dune buggy, Oregon Dunes National Recreation Area

Oregon Dunes National Recreation Area ⑪

Road map 1 A4. 🚌 855 Highway Ave, Reedsport, *(541) 271-3611.*
◯ *dawn–dusk daily.* 🎫
🌐 www.fs.fed.us/r6/siuslaw/oregondunes

Massive sand dunes stretch south from Florence for 40 miles (64 km). The desert-like landscape has been created over thousands of years, as winds, tides, and ocean currents force sand as far as 2.5 miles (4 km) inland and sculpt it into towering formations that reach heights of as much as 300 ft (90 m). Not just sand but streams, lakes, shore pine forests, grasslands, and isolated beaches attract a wide variety of recreation enthusiasts to this area.

Boardwalks make it easy to enjoy stunning vistas from Oregon Dunes Overlook, about 20 miles (32 km) south of Florence, whereas the mile-long Umpqua Scenic Dunes Trail, 30 miles (48 km) south of Florence, skirts the tallest dunes in the area.

Sea stacks rising majestically from the ocean off Bandon, the lights of houses seen in the background

Bandon ⑫

Road map 1 A4. 👥 *2,600*. ℹ️ *300 2nd St, (541) 347-9616.* Ⓦ *www.bandon.com*

THE SMALL TOWN of Bandon, near the mouth of the Coquille River, is so weather-beaten, it is difficult to imagine that 100 years ago it was a major port of call for cargo ships and passenger liners plying the route between Seattle and Los Angeles. These days, Bandon is famous for its cranberries, which are harvested in bogs north of the town.

Craggy rock formations rise from the sea just off Bandon's beach. These wind-sculpted shapes include Face Rock, allegedly an Indian maiden frozen into stone by an evil spirit. A wilder landscape of dunes and sea grass prevails at **Bullards Beach State Park**, which lies across the marshy, bird-filled Coquille Estuary from Bandon.

🌿 Bullards Beach State Park
2 miles (3 km) north of Bandon, off Hwy 101. Ⓒ *(541) 347-2209.* ⭕ *dawn–dusk daily.*

ENVIRONS: In the early 1900s, lumber baron Louis J. Simpson built Shore Acres, an estate atop oceanside bluffs outside the town of Coos Bay, 25 miles (40 km) north of Bandon. It is now the site of **Shore Acres State Park**. Simpson enhanced this magnificent spot with formal gardens of azaleas, rhododendrons, and roses. An enclosed observatory offers visitors a stunning view of the ocean, while interpretive panels educate them about the history of the site. Although the mansion is long gone, the gardens continue to thrive next to **Cape Arago State Park**, where seals and sea lions bask in the sun on offshore rocks.

Cape Blanco State Park, 27 miles (43 km) south of Bandon, is the westernmost point in the 48 contiguous states and one of the windiest spots on earth, with winter gusts exceeding 180 mph (290 km/h). The park's lighthouse is the oldest on the Oregon coast, having been first lit in 1870.

Hwy 101 nears the California border in a stretch of dense forests, towering cliffs, and offshore rock formations. Some of the most spectacular scenery is within the boundaries of the **Boardman State Scenic Corridor**, 4 miles (6.5 km) north of Brookings – a little town where warm winter temperatures contribute to the town's fame as supplier of 90 percent of the Easter lilies grown in the US.

🌿 Shore Acres State Park
Cape Arago Hwy, 13 miles (21 km) southwest of Coos Bay. Ⓒ *(541) 888-3732.* ⭕ *8am–dusk daily.* ♿

🌿 Cape Arago State Park
End of Cape Arago Hwy, 15 miles (24 km) southwest of Coos Bay. Ⓒ *(800) 551-6949.* ⭕ *dawn–dusk daily.*

🌿 Cape Blanco State Park
9 miles (14.5 km) north of Port Orford, off Hwy 101. Ⓒ *(800) 551-6949.* ⭕ *dawn–dusk daily.* **Lighthouse** ⭕ *Apr–Oct: dawn–dusk Thu–Mon.*

🌿 Boardman State Scenic Corridor
Hwy 101, 4 miles (6.5 km) north of Brookings. Ⓒ *(800) 551-6949.* ⭕ *dawn–dusk daily.*

Driftwood on the beach near Bandon, looking toward the town

Wine Country of the North Willamette Valley ⑬

Wine grapes on the vine

THE RICH, WET, TEMPERATE VALLEY that surrounds the Willamette River as it flows north from Eugene to join the Columbia River has yielded a bounty of fruits and vegetables for 150 years, ever since Oregon Trail pioneers began farming the land. Two decades ago, the valley's soil was also found to be ideal for growing grapes, especially the pinot noir, pinot gris, riesling, and chardonnay varietals.

Now, vineyards carpet the rolling hillsides, especially in Yamhill County. Though the wine country of North Willamette Valley is not as developed as that of Napa Valley, its output is arguably just as good. It is easy to conduct a taste test since dozens of wineries are conveniently located just off Hwy 99W between McMinnville and Newberg.

Farms dotting the valley slopes of Yamhill County

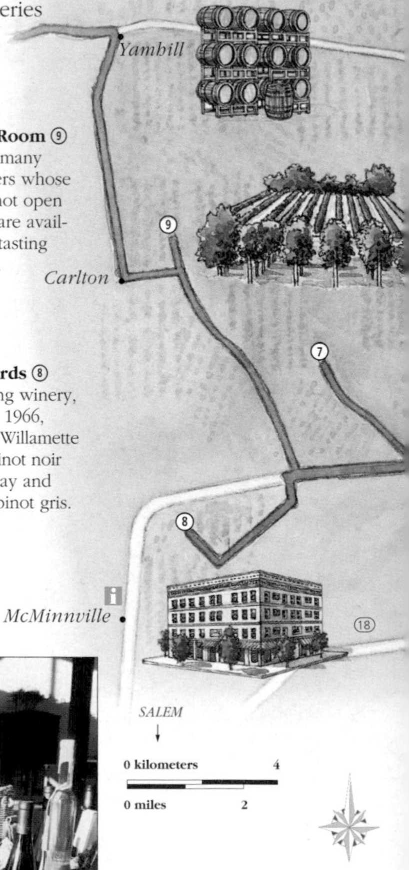

The Tasting Room ⑨
The wines of many small producers whose wineries are not open to the public are available here for tasting and purchase.

Eyrie Vineyards ⑧
This pioneering winery, established in 1966, produced the Willamette Valley's first pinot noir and chardonnay and the US's first pinot gris.

Typical of the valley, the lush vineyards at Domaine Serene

Yamhill

Carlton

McMinnville

SALEM

0 kilometers 4

0 miles 2

Chateau Benoit ⑦
The views of the Willamette Valley are one attraction of this hilltop winery; several fine white wines are another.

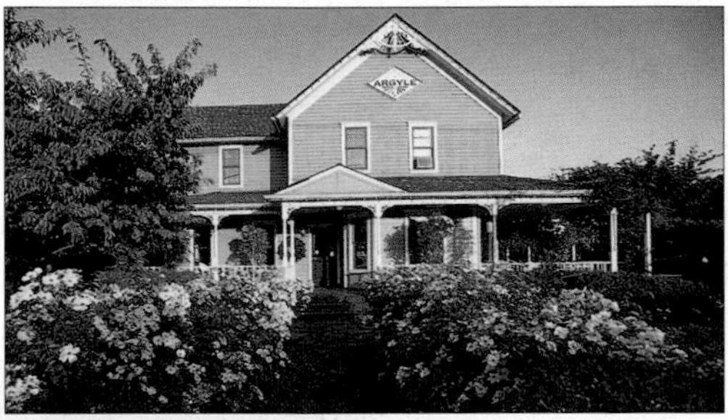

Tips for Drivers

Tour length: *About 35 miles (56 km).*

Starting point: *On 99W a few miles east of Newberg, which is 38 miles (58 km) west of Portland.*

Stopping-off points: *Dundee boasts many well-known restaurants, of which Tina's is arguably the star. Newberg, McMinnville, and Yamhill also have good places to eat.*

Argyle Winery ③

With 235 acres (95 ha) of vineyards, this winery specializes in sparkling wines. The tasting room is in a picturesque Victorian farmhouse.

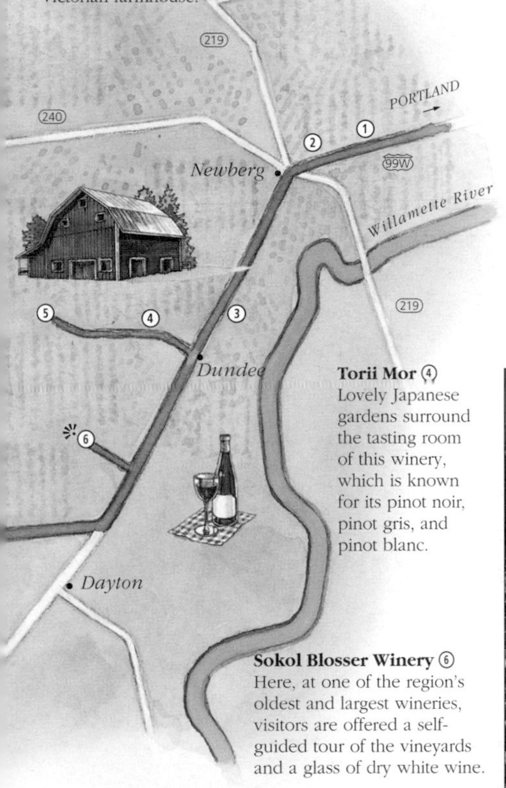

Hoover-Minthorn House ①

An orphaned Herbert Hoover, who would become the 31st US president, came west from Iowa to live with his aunt and uncle in this handsome house in 1885, at the age of 11.

Rex Hill Vineyards ②

Shady hillside gardens and an antiques-filled tasting room warmed by a fire are lovely spots to taste this winery's award-winning pinot noirs.

Torii Mor ④

Lovely Japanese gardens surround the tasting room of this winery, which is known for its pinot noir, pinot gris, and pinot blanc.

Sokol Blosser Winery ⑥

Here, at one of the region's oldest and largest wineries, visitors are offered a self-guided tour of the vineyards and a glass of dry white wine.

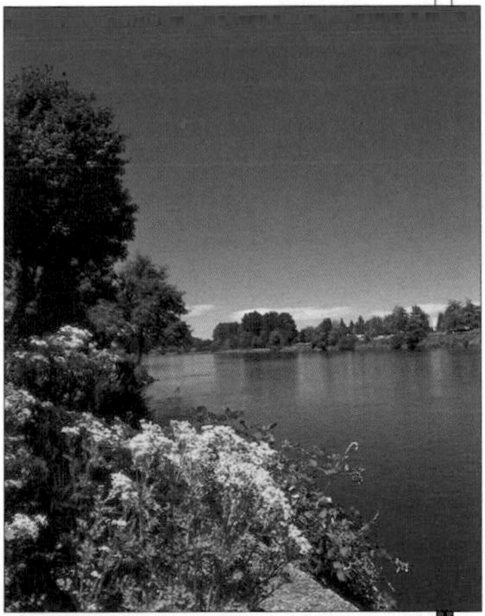

The Willamette River, meandering through the fertile North Willamette Valley

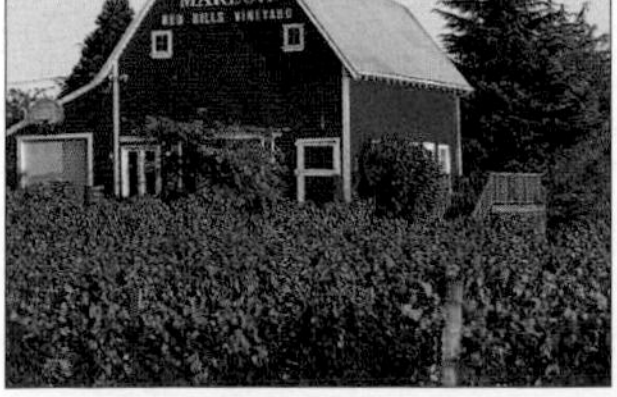

Maresh Red Barn ⑤

Wines from Maresh vineyard grapes, custom-made by three Oregon wineries, are on offer here. The vineyard, Oregon's fifth, grows pinot noir and pinot gris, among other varietals.

Key

- Tour route
- Other road
- Viewpoint
- Information

Howard Hughes' "Spruce Goose" at the Evergreen Aviation Museum

McMinnville ⑭

Road map 1 A3. 7,500. 417 NW Adams St, (503) 472-6196. www.mcminnville.org

IN THIS PROSPEROUS town surrounded by the Willamette Valley vineyards, the Downtown Historic District is graced by the old Oregon Hotel, McMinnville Bank, and many other late 19th- and early 20th-century buildings. The excellent reputation of ivyclad Linfield College, chartered in 1858, has long put McMinnville on the map, but these days the university shares the honor with the "Spruce Goose." This wooden flying boat, built in the 1940s, is housed in the **Evergreen Aviation Museum**, where its 320-ft (97.5-m) wingspan spreads above early passenger planes, World War II fighters, and other vintage aircraft.

🏛 **Evergreen Aviation Museum**
500 NE Cat. Michael King Smith Way. (503) 434-4180. 9am–5pm daily. major hols. www.sprucegoose.org

Silverton ⑮

Road map 1 A3. 7,500. 426 S Water St, (503) 873-5615. www.silvertonor.com

THIS PLEASANT OLD farming town in the foothills of the Cascade Mountains is the entryway to 8,700-acre (3,520-ha) **Silver Falls State Park**, the largest state park in Oregon. The Trail of Ten Falls follows Silver Creek through a temperate rainforest of Douglas firs, hemlocks, and cedars to the trail's cataracts; the largest of them, South Falls, plunges 177 ft (54 m) down a mossy cliff into a deep pool.

At the southern edge of Silverton is the **Oregon Garden**. Rising high above the groomed landscape is a magnificent stand of 100-year-old oaks. The **Gordon House**, set in a shady grove near the garden's entrance, is the only structure in Oregon designed by renowned architect Frank Lloyd Wright.

The 1894 Deepwood Estate in Salem

🌳 **Silver Falls State Park**
Hwy 214, 10 miles (16 km) east of Salem. (800) 551-6949. dawn–dusk daily.
🌳 **Oregon Garden**
879 W Main St. (503) 874-8100. Mar–Oct: 9am–6pm daily; Nov–Feb: 9am–3pm daily. **Gordon House**: Mar–Oct: 10am–5pm daily; Nov–Feb: 10am–3pm daily. Jan 1, Thanksgiving, Dec 25. www.oregongarden.org

Salem ⑯

Road map 1 A3. 121,000. 1313 Mill St SE, (503) 581-4325. www.scva.org

SALEM WAS a thriving trading post and lumber port on the Willamette River when it became the capital of the Oregon Territory in 1851.

At the edge of Bush's Pasture Park stands **Asahel Bush House**, an 1878 home with ten marble fireplaces and a conservatory said to be the first greenhouse west of the Mississippi River, and the historic **Deepwood Estate**. The **Mission Mill Museum** preserves some of the state's earliest structures: the 1841 home of Jason Lee, who helped found Salem; the 1847 home of state treasurer John Boon; and the Kay Woolen Mill, where waterwheels from the 1890s remain intact. The state's early history is also in evidence around the **Oregon State Capitol**.

A gilded pioneer stands atop the rotunda of the building. Marble sculptures of a covered wagon and of Lewis and Clark (see p37) flank the entrance, and the murals inside depict Captain Robert Gray's discovery of the Columbia River in 1792.

On the Willamette University campus is **Waller Hall**, the oldest college building in Oregon, constructed in 1867; and the striking **Hallie Ford Museum of Art**, which houses an outstanding collection of 20th-century Native American basketry and paintings.

The Oregon State Capitol Building in Salem

🏛 Asahel Bush House

600 Mission Street SE. ☎ *(503) 363-4714.* 🕐 *May–Sep: noon–5pm Tue–Sun; Oct–Apr: 2–5pm Tue–Sun.* ● *major hols.* 🚫📷 ☞

🏛 Deepwood Estate

1116 Mission St SE. ☎ *(503) 363-1825.* 🕐 ***Grounds**: dawn–dusk daily. **House**: May–Sep: noon–5pm Sun–Fri; Oct–Apr: noon–5pm Tue–Sat.* ● *major hols.* 🚫📷 ☞

🏛 Mission Mill Museum

1314 Mill St SE. ☎ *(503) 585-7012.* 🕐 *10am–5pm Mon–Sat.* ● *major hols.* 🚫📷 ☞

🏛 Oregon State Capitol

900 Court St NE. ☎ *(503) 986-1388.* 🕐 *7:30am–5:30pm Mon–Fri, 9am–4pm Sat, noon–4pm Sun.* ● *major hols.*

🏛 Waller Hall

900 State St. 🕐 *8am–5pm Mon–Fri.*

🏛 Hallie Ford Museum of Art

700 State St. ☎ *(503) 370-6855.* 🕐 *10am–5pm Tue–Sat.* ● *major hols.* 🚫📷 ♿ 🛍

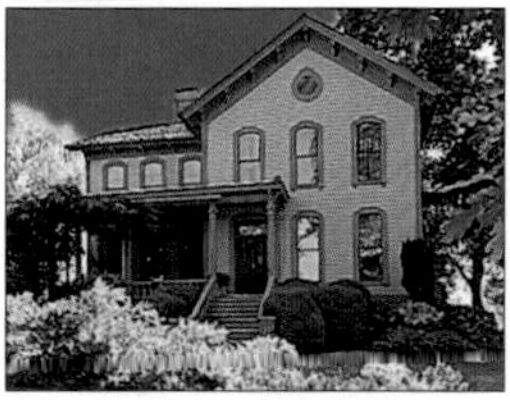

Asahel Bush House, built in 1878, a historic landmark in Salem

Eugene ⑰

Road map 1 A4. 👥 *130,000.* [i] *190-115 W 8th Ave, (541) 484-5307.* [W] www.eugene.com

The University of Oregon brings no small amount of culture and animation to the second largest city in Oregon, which straddles the banks of the Willamette River at the south end of the river valley. The peak-roofed, glass-and-timber **Hult Center for the Performing Arts**, designed by the New York firm Hardy Holzman Pfeiffer Associates and completed in 1982, is considered to be one of the best-designed performing arts complexes in the world. The **University of Oregon Museum of Natural History** counts among its holdings the world's oldest shoes – a pair of sandals dating from 9500 BC.

Local artisans sell their wares weekly at the **Saturday Market**, a large collection of stalls on the downtown Park Blocks; and the **5th Street Public Market**, a collection of shops and restaurants in a converted feed mill, bustles with locals and the more than 17,000 university students who make good use of the city's many bicycle and rollerblading paths, pedestrian malls, and parks.

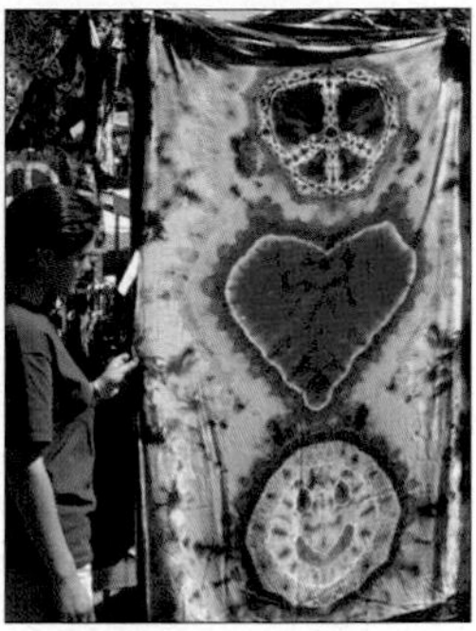

Local arts and crafts at the Saturday Market in Eugene

🏛 Hult Center for the Performing Arts

1 Eugene Center. ☎ *(541) 682-5087.* [W] www.hultcenter.org

🏛 University of Oregon Museum of Natural History

1680 E 15th Ave. ☎ *(541) 346-3024.* 🕐 *noon–5pm Tue–Sun.* ● *major hols.* 🛍 [W] http://natural-history.uoregon.edu

🛒 Saturday Market

8th Ave & Oak St. ☎ *(541) 686-8885.* 🕐 *Apr–Nov: 10am–5pm Sat.* [W] www.eugenesaturdaymarket.com

🛒 5th Street Public Market

High & 5th Sts. 🕐 *10am–9pm daily.* [W] www.5thstreetmarket.com

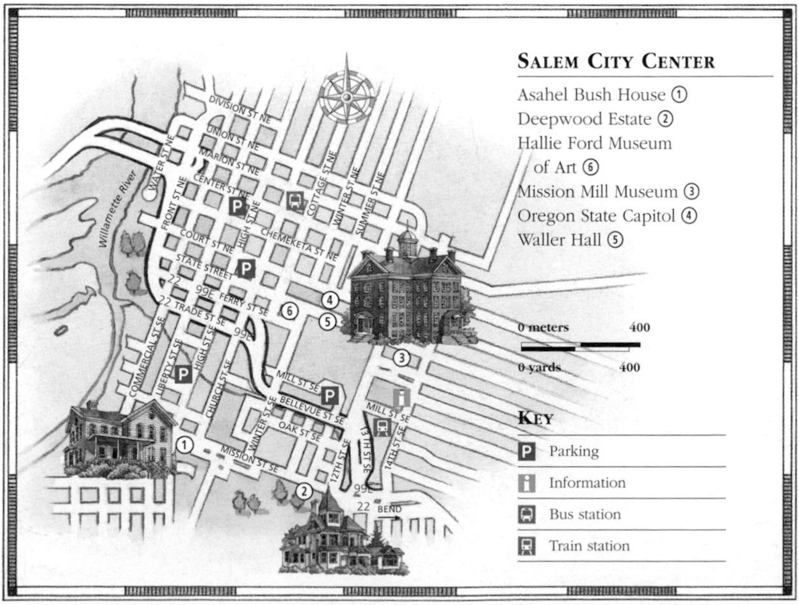
SALEM CITY CENTER
Asahel Bush House ①
Deepwood Estate ②
Hallie Ford Museum of Art ⑥
Mission Mill Museum ③
Oregon State Capitol ④
Waller Hall ⑤
0 meters 400
0 yards 400
KEY
Parking
Information
Bus station
Train station
Willamette River
DIVISION ST NE
UNION ST NE
MARION ST NE
CENTER ST NE
COURT ST NE
STATE STREET
FERRY ST SE
TRADE ST SE
CHEMEKETA ST NE
WATER ST NE
FRONT ST NE
HIGH ST NE
COTTAGE ST NE
WINTER ST NE
SUMMER ST NE
COMMERCIAL ST SE
LIBERTY ST SE
HIGH ST SE
CHURCH ST SE
MILL ST SE
BELLEVUE ST SE
OAK ST SE
MISSION ST SE
WINTER ST SE
12TH ST SE
13TH ST SE
14TH ST SE
BEND

Swimming pool fed by hot springs at the Warm Springs Reservation resort

Madras and Warm Springs ⑱

Road map 1 B3. *Madras* ℹ️ *274 SW 4th St, (541) 475-2350.*
W www.ci.madrasor.us
Warm Springs ℹ️ *1233 Veterans St, (541) 553-3333.*
W www.warmsprings.com

MADRAS IS A desert ranching town surrounded by rimrock and vast tracts of wilderness recreation lands. **Crooked River National Grassland** provides endless vistas as well as fishing and rafting opportunities on two US National Wild and Scenic Rivers – the Deschutes and the Crooked – that weave through the 112,000 acres (45,300 ha) of juniper and sage brush. **Cove Palisades State Park** surrounds Lake Billy Chinook, where deep waters reflecting the surrounding basalt cliffs are popular with boaters.

The Treaty of 1855 between the US government and the Wasco, Walla Walla, and Paiute tribes established lands for the tribes on the 640,000-acre (259,000-ha) Warm Springs Reservation, located on the High Desert plateaus and forested Cascade slopes of central Oregon. These Confederated Tribes preserve their heritage at the **Museum at Warm Springs** with a stunning collection of basketry and beadwork, haunting historic photographs that chronicle the hardships of assimilation, and videotapes of tribal ceremonies. The Tribes also manage a casino and a resort, where a large pool is heated by hot springs.

🎣 **Crooked River National Grassland**
10 miles (16 km) south of Madras, off Hwy 26. ⭕ *dawn–dusk daily.*
ℹ️ *813 SW Hwy 97, Madras.*
📞 *(541) 416-6640.*

🌿 **Cove Palisades State Park**
15 miles (24 km) southwest of Madras, off Hwy 97. 📞 *(541) 546-3412.* ⭕ *dawn–dusk daily.* ♿

🏛 **Museum at Warm Springs**
Hwy 26, Warm Springs. 📞 *(503) 553-3331.* ⭕ *9am–5pm daily.* ♿ 📷
W www.warmsprings.com/museum

Sisters ⑲

Road map 1 B4. 🚹 *900.* ℹ️ *164 N Elm St, (541) 549-0251.*
W www.sisterschamber.com

SISTERS IS A RANCHING town that cashes in on its cowboy history with Old West–style storefronts and wood sidewalks. The setting, though, is authentic – the peaks of the Three Sisters, each exceeding 10,000 ft (3,000 m), tower majestically above the town and the surrounding pine forests, alpine meadows, and rushing streams.

ENVIRONS: The McKenzie Pass climbs from Sisters to a 1-mile (1.6-km) summit amid a massive lava flow. The **Dee Wright Observatory** provides panoramic views of more than a dozen Cascades peaks and buttes and of the sweeping lava fields, which can be examined at close range on the half-mile (0.8-km) Lava River Interpretive Trail.

The cold and clear waters of the Metolius River flow through fragrant pine forests on the flanks of Mount Jefferson. Near Camp Sherman, a tiny settlement of cabins 14 miles (22.5 km) west of Sisters, the river bubbles up from springs beneath Black Butte. The view from the scenic overlook above the headwaters usually includes fly-fishing enthusiasts casting their lines into one of the state's best trout streams.

🎣 **Dee Wright Observatory**
Hwy 242, 15 miles (24 km) west of Sisters. ⭕ *mid-Jun–Oct: dawn–dusk daily.* ⚫ *Oct–mid-Jun.*

Galloping horses near Sisters, the towering peaks of the Three Sisters mountains visible in the distance

Bend's High Desert Museum, showcasing life in central and eastern Oregon

Smith Rock State Park ⓴

Road map 1 B4. ☏ (541) 548-7501. ◯ dawn–dusk daily. 🖪 🅦 www.smithrock.com

AT SMITH ROCK, the Crooked River flows beneath towering rock faces of welded tuff – volcanic ash that was compressed under intense heat and pressure. These unusually shaped peaks and pinnacles – with compelling names like Morning Glory Wall and Pleasure Palace – are a lure for risk-taking rock climbers, who ascend the sometimes more than 550-ft (168-m) sheer faces on over 1,300 climbing routes. The less intrepid can enjoy the spectacle from roadside viewpoints or from one of the many hiking trails that follow the base of the cliffs.

Bend ㉑

Road map 1 B4. 🏠 51,000. 🚌 63085 N Hwy 97, (541) 382-3221. 🅦 www.bendchamber.org

BUSY BEND, once a sleepy lumber town, is alluringly close to the ski slopes, lakes, streams, and the many other natural attractions of Central Oregon. While unsightly development is quickly replacing juniper- and sage-covered grazing lands on the outskirts, the old brick business district retains a good deal of small-town charm. Drake Park is a grassy downtown retreat on both banks of the Deschutes River, and **Pilot Butte State**

Scenic Viewpoint, atop a volcanic cinder cone that rises 500 ft (150 m) from the center of town, overlooks the High Desert and nine snowcapped Cascade peaks.

The **High Desert Museum** celebrates life in the rugged, arid High Desert terrain that covers much of central and eastern Oregon. Walk-through dioramas use dramatic lighting and sound effects in authentic re-creations of Native American dwellings, a wagon camp, a silver mine, and other scenes of desert settlement. Outdoors, a trail crossing the floor of a forest of ponderosa pine leads to replicas of a settler's cabin and a sawmill, and to natural habitats, including a trout stream and an aviary filled with hawks and other raptors.

🍂 Pilot Butte State Scenic Viewpoint
East end of Greenwood Ave. ☏ (800) 551-6949. ◯ dawn–dusk daily.

🏛 High Desert Museum
59800 S Hwy 97. ☏ (541) 382-4754. ◯ 9am–5pm daily. ● Jan 1, Thanksgiving, Dec 25. 🖪 🎦 🅗 🅦 www.highdesert.org

Newberry National Volcanic Monument ㉒

Road map 1 B4. ◯ Apr–Oct: dawn–dusk daily. 🖪 🅦 www.fs.fed.us

THE 55,000 ACRES (22,300 ha) of the Newberry National Volcanic Monument encompass eerie and bleak landscapes of black lava, as well as

sparkling mountain lakes, waterfalls, hemlock forests, and snow-capped peaks. Exhibits at the **Lava Lands Visitor Center** explain how Newberry Volcano has been built by thousands of eruptions that began about 600,000 years ago – the last eruption occurred in about AD 700 – and which, seismic activity suggests, may begin again. Other exhibits highlight central Oregon's cultural history. Well-marked roads and interpretive trails lead to major sites within the monument.

At Lava River Cave, a passage extends almost a mile (1.5 km) into a lava tube, a channel through which molten lava once flowed. At Lava Cast Forest, a paved loop trail transverses a forest of hollow molds formed by molten lava, which created casts around tree trunks. A road ascends into the 18-mile- (29-km-) wide crater, where Paulina and East Lakes sparkle amid pine forests. It then skirts a massive field of shiny black lava known as the Big Obsidian Flow as it climbs to 7,907-ft (2,454-m) summit of Paulina Peak, the highest point within Newberry Monument.

In addition to magnificent scenery, the monument provides opportunities for hiking, fishing, boating, and other recreational activities.

Lava Lands Visitor Center
58201 Hwy 97. ☏ (541) 593-2421. ◯ May 1–May 20: 9:30am–5pm Wed–Sun; May 21–Labor Day: 9:30am–5pm daily; Labor Day–mid-Oct: 9:30am–5pm Wed–Sun. ● mid-Oct–Apr.

A rock outcrop at the Newberry National Volcanic Monument

Cascade Lakes Highway 23

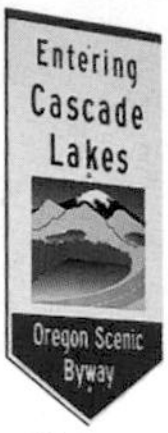

Highway sign

THIS LOOP IS OFTEN CALLED Century Drive because the circuit is just under 100 miles (160 km) long. A stunning display of forest and mountain scenery unfolds in this relatively short distance. Most memorable are the many vistas of sparkling lakes backed by craggy Cascade peaks. Trails into the deep wilderness, idyllic picnic and camping spots, lakes and streams brimming with trout and salmon, and ski slopes and rustic resorts are likely to tempt even the most time-pressed traveler to linger on this scenic byway for as long as possible.

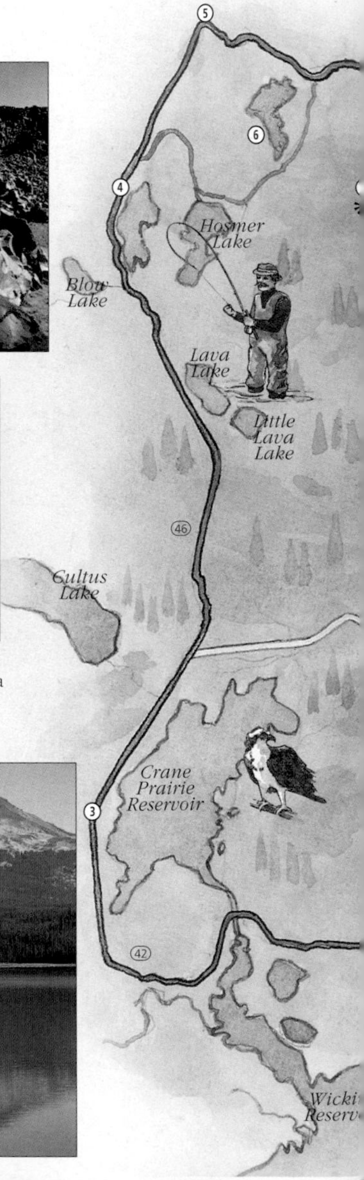

Mount Bachelor 7
Some of the best skiing and snowboarding in the Pacific Northwest is here, on Mount Bachlor's 71 runs. There are also numerous trails for cross-country skiing and snowshoeing.

Devils Garden 5
Astronauts trained on foot and in moon buggies for their historic 1969 moonwalk on this enormous 45-sq-mile (117-sq-km) lava flow.

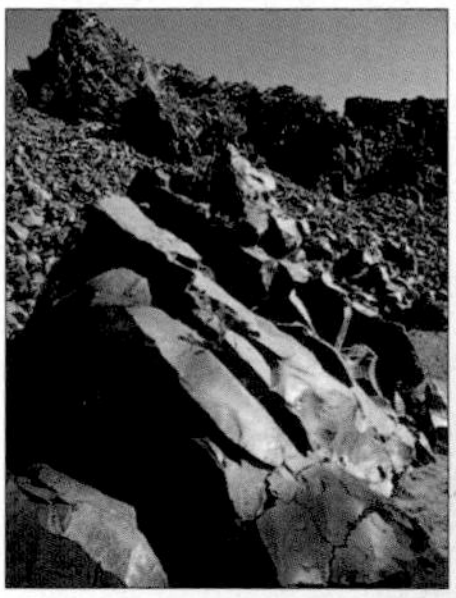

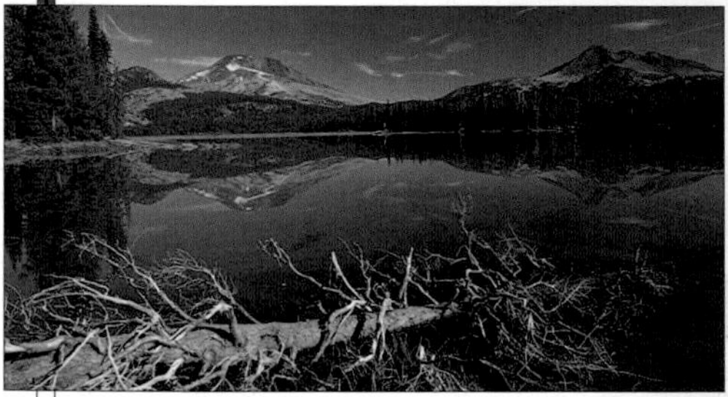

Sparks Lake 6
This large shallow trout lake, surrounded by mountains, lava formations, and meadow, was considered by photographer Ray Atkeson to be the most scenic place in Oregon.

Elk Lake 4
Conveniently located along the Cascade Lakes Highway, Elk Lake is a popular destination for sailing, windsurfing, and fishing. The store at the Elk Lake Resort rents canoes, motorboats, rowboats, and paddleboats.

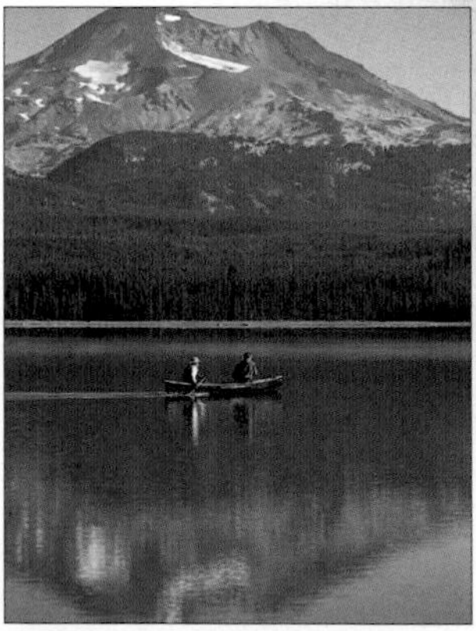

Osprey Observation Point 3
Crane Prairie Reservoir hosts a large colony of osprey that plunge from the sky like meteorites to pluck fish out of the water.

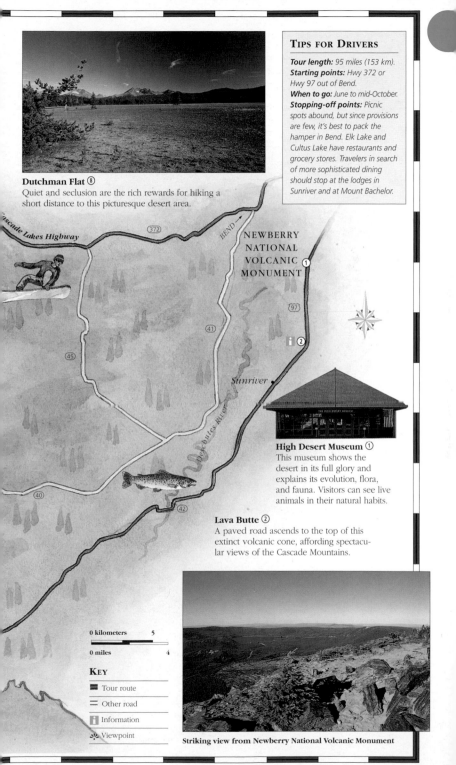

Dutchman Flat ⑧
Quiet and seclusion are the rich rewards for hiking a
short distance to this picturesque desert area.

Cascade Lakes Highway

372

BEND

NEWBERRY
NATIONAL
VOLCANIC
MONUMENT ①

97

ℹ ②

41

45

Sunriver

Deschutes River

40

42

High Desert Museum ①
This museum shows the
desert in its full glory and
explains its evolution, flora,
and fauna. Visitors can see live
animals in their natural habits.

Lava Butte ②
A paved road ascends to the top of this
extinct volcanic cone, affording spectacular views of the Cascade Mountains.

0 kilometers   5

0 miles   4

KEY

▬ Tour route

═ Other road

ℹ Information

🔱 Viewpoint

Striking view from Newberry National Volcanic Monument

Crater Lake National Park Tour ㉔

Chipmunk at Crater Lake

OREGON'S ONLY NATIONAL PARK surrounds a lake that, at 1,932 ft (589 m), is the deepest in the US and the seventh deepest in the world. Creation of Crater Lake began about 7,700 years ago when Mount Mazama erupted and then collapsed, forming the caldera in which the lake now sits. The crater rim rises an average of 1,000 ft (300 m) above the lake. On the drive that circles the lake, the many overlooks, 90 miles (144 km) of trails, and a beautiful lodge afford stunning views.

Merriam Point ④
This promontory is an excellent spot from which to admire the west side of the lake, with the cone-shaped Wizard Island and its surrounding black volcanic blocks.

The Watchman ③
This viewpoint, reached after a moderate climb, is named for its historic fire tower, and is the closest lookout to Wizard Island.

Wizard Island ②
Wizard Island is a small volcanic island in the shape of a cone jutting 764 ft (233 m) above the surface of the lake. At the summit is a crater 300 ft (90 m) across.

Crater Lake Lodge ①
This rustic hotel perched on the caldera rim has welcomed guests since 1915. Extensive renovations have restored the structural integrity of the building, once at risk of collapsing under its own weight and that of the 15 ft (4.5 m) of snow that can accumulate in winter. Magnificent views can be enjoyed from here.

Rim Village

Mazama Village

Tourists departing on a boat tour from Cleetwood Cove, on the north shore of the lake

Tips for Drivers

Tour length: *33 miles (53 km).*
Starting point: *Steel Information Center, on Rim Drive 4 miles (6.5 km) north of Rte 62.*
When to go: *Rim Drive is open from the end of June to mid-October, weather permitting.*
Stopping-off points: *Breakfast, lunch, and dinner are offered at Crater Lake Lodge; snacks are sold in Rim Village. Two-hour narrated boat trips (Jul–mid-Sep: 10am–4:30pm daily) depart from Cleetwood Cove. The cove is accessible only on foot.*

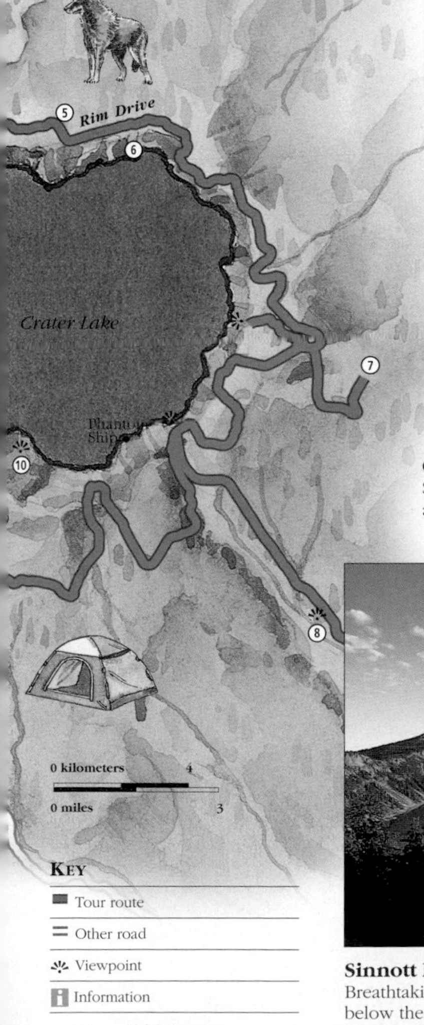

5 Rim Drive
6
Crater Lake
7
Phantom Ship
10
8
0 kilometers 4
0 miles 3
KEY
Tour route
Other road
Viewpoint
Information

Rim Drive [5]
On this 33-mile (53-km) circuit, spectacular vistas of the lake, the islands, and the surrounding mountains unfold at every turn.

Cleetwood Trail [6]
This 1-mile (1.6-km) trail, which drops a steep 700 ft (210 m), provides the only access to the lake. In summer, a boat tour departs from the dock at the base of the trail.

Mount Scott [7]
When weather allows, views from this peak – at 8,929 ft (2,722 m) the highest point in the park – extend as far as California's Mount Shasta, located 100 miles (160 km) to the south.

The Pinnacles [8]
An eerie landscape of pumice spires, known as fossil fumaroles, rises from the caldera's eastern base. Many of the spires are hollow.

Castle Crest – Wildflower Trail [9]
Spectacular wildflowers bloom in July and August alongside this easy-to-walk 0.4-mile (0.6-km) trail.

Sinnott Memorial Overlook [10]
Breathtaking views reward the short descent to this point just below the caldera rim, where park rangers give geology talks.

A park ranger giving a tour in the Oregon Caves National Monument

Oregon Caves National Monument ㉕

Road map 1 A5. 🚹 *19000 Caves Hwy, Cave Junction, (541) 592-2100.* ⭕ *Mar–Apr & Nov: 10am–4pm daily; May & Sep–Oct: 9am–5pm daily; Jun–Aug: 9am–7pm daily;* ⬤ *Dec–Feb.* 🈁 🅿 🆆 *www.nps.gov/orca*

VISITORS ON THE 70-minute guided tours of these vast underground caverns follow lighted trails past strange formations, cross underground rivers, squeeze through giant ribs of marble, and clamber up and down staircases into enormous chambers hung with stalactites. Discovered in 1874 by a hunter chasing his dog into a dark hole in the side of Elijah Mountain, the caves have been formed by the steady trickling of water over the past hundreds of thousands of years. Above ground, three trails cross a remnant old-growth coniferous forest and lead to an ancient and noble Douglas fir, famous for having the widest girth of any known tree in Oregon.

Jacksonville ㉖

Road map 1 A4. 🚘 *2,000.* 🚹 *185 Oregon St, (541) 899-8118.* 🆆 *www.jacksonvilleoregon.org*

IN THIS GOLD RUSH boomtown, time has more or less stood still since the 1880s, when Rich Gulch Creek ceased to yield gold and it was decided that main railroad lines would bypass the town.

The **Jacksonville Museum of Science and History** chronicles gold panning and

farming in the fertile hills and valley, and the town is a museum in itself. With more than 80 brick and wood-frame 19th-century buildings, Jacksonville has been designated a National Historic Landmark. A walking tour (a map is available from the information center in the old railroad depot) shows off the town's wealth of architecture and history. The **Beekman House** offers a glimpse of how the town's prosperous burghers once lived, and the estate of 19th-century photographer Peter Britt is the setting of the annual **Britt Festivals**, when dance and music concerts are performed beneath a canopy of stately Ponderosa pines.

🏛 **Jacksonville Museum of Science and History**
205 5th St. ☎ *(541) 773-6536.* ⭕ *10am–5pm Wed–Sat, noon–5pm Sun.* ⬤ *major hols.* 🈁 🚻
🚻 **Beekman House**
352 E California St. ☎ *(541) 773-6536.* ⭕ *10am–5pm Wed–Sat, noon–5pm Sun.* ⬤ *major hols.* 🈁 🚻
🎭 **Britt Festivals**
517 W 10th St, Medford.
☎ *(541) 773-6077.*
🆆 *www.brittfest.org*

Jacksonville's Beekman House, built during the Gold Rush

Ashland ㉗

Road map 1 A5. 🚘 *17,000.* 🚹 *110 E Main St, (541) 482-3486.*

AT FIRST GLANCE, it may be difficult to believe that every year some 350,000 theatergoers descend on this amiable town surrounded by farms and orchards. What draws them is the **Oregon Shakespeare Festival**, established in 1935, and now presenting, between February and November, an annual schedule of 11 plays by Shakespeare as well as by classic and contemporary playwrights. Aside from enjoying the performances, theater buffs can view props and costumes from past performances at the Festival Exhibit Center, and take detailed backstage tours of the festival's three venues: the 1,200-seat, open-air Elizabethan Theatre; the Angus Bowmer Theatre; and the modern New Theatre.

🎭 **Oregon Shakespeare Festival**
15 S Pioneer St. ☎ *(541) 482-4331.* 🆆 *www.osfashland.com*

A Renaissance stage set at the Oregon Shakespeare Festival

ENVIRONS: Many commercial outfitters launch raft and jet boat trips from Grants Pass, 40 miles (64 km) north of Ashland on I-5. The Rogue River rushes 215 twisting miles (346 km) through Siskiyou National Forest and other wilderness before reaching the Pacific Ocean. Elk, mountain lions, and bears are often seen roaming the riverbanks, and bald eagles fly overhead.

Steens Mountain Tour 28

Alpine lupines in a mountain meadow

SCENERY DOESN'T GET much more rugged and grand than it does here on this 9,700-ft (2,960-m) mountain. Steens Mountain is a fault-block, formed when land on two sides of a geological fault rose and fell to different levels. As a result, the west slope of this mountain rises gradually from sagebrush country through stands of aspen, juniper, and mountain mahogany, while the east face drops precipitously for more than a mile (1.6 km). Antelope, bighorn sheep, and wild horses roam craggy gorges and alpine tundra carpeted with wildflowers, and eagles and falcons soar overhead. The Steens Mountain National Back Country Byway traverses this remarkable landscape.

Tips for Drivers

Tour length: *58 miles (93.5 km).*
Starting point: *North Loop Road in Frenchglen.*
When to go: *The entire Steens Loop Road is closed from November to June due to snow cover, though snow squalls and lightning storms can occur in any season.*
Getting around: *This dirt and gravel road is steep in parts. It is not suitable for vehicles with low clearance.*
Stopping-off points: *Many scenic overlooks, picnic spots, and some campgrounds are located on the route. Frenchglen has lodging and restaurants.*

Donner und Blitzen River ①
An army officer named this rushing torrent "Thunder and Lightning" while attempting to cross it during a thunderstorm in 1864.

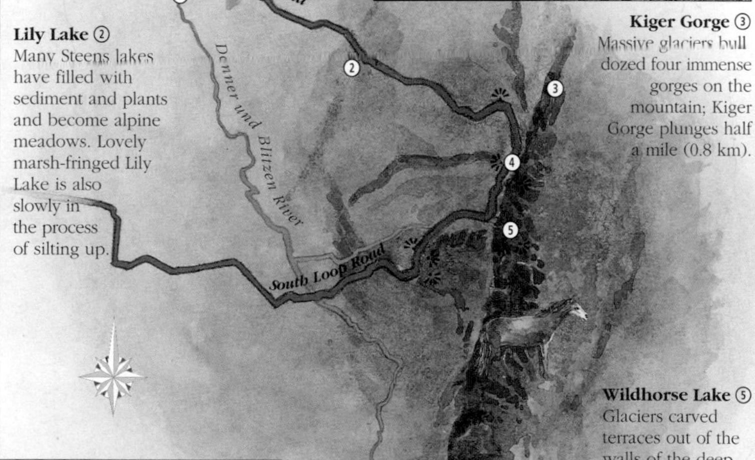
← BEND
Frenchglen
North Loop Road
Donner und Blitzen River
South Loop Road
0 kilometers 8
0 miles 6

Lily Lake ②
Many Steens lakes have filled with sediment and plants and become alpine meadows. Lovely marsh-fringed Lily Lake is also slowly in the process of silting up.

Kiger Gorge ③
Massive glaciers bulldozed four immense gorges on the mountain; Kiger Gorge plunges half a mile (0.8 km).

Wildhorse Lake ⑤
Glaciers carved terraces out of the walls of the deep gorge that encircles this sparkling lake.

East Rim Viewpoint ④
This perch is a full mile (1.6 km) above the alkali flats of the Alvord Desert; sitting in the rain shadow of the mountain, this desolate desert receives a mere 6 inches (15 cm) of rain a year.

Key

Tour route

Viewpoint

The seemingly endless desert landscape of the Jordan Valley

Jordan Valley ㉙

Road map 1 C4. 🏃 390. ℹ️ 676 SW 5th Ave, (541) 889-8012.

THIS SCRUFFY DESERT ranching settlement is one of only a few towns in sparsely populated Malheur County, where just 28,000 people inhabit 10,000 sq miles (25,900 sq km). Jordan Valley makes two claims to fame. A legacy of the Basque sheepherders who settled the town in 1890 is the ball court, built in 1915, for playing petola, a game that resembles American hardball. And a windswept, sagebrush-filled cemetery 17 miles (27 km) south of town on Hwy 95 is the final resting place of Jean Baptiste Charbonneau, son of the Indian guide Sacagawea *(see p37)*. Born in 1805, Charbonneau was taken across the country with the Lewis and Clark party, which his mother helped guide. Years later, he died of a chill at a stagecoach stop near Jordan Valley in 1866.

Malheur National Wildlife Refuge ㉚

Road map 1 C4. 🎫 (541) 493-2612. **Refuge and museum** ⃝ dawn–dusk daily. ⬤ major hols. **Visitors' center** ⃝ 7am–4:30pm Mon–Thu, 7am–3:30pm Fri; some weekends in spring & summer. ⬤ major hols. ♿

ONE OF THE NATION'S largest wildlife refuges, Malheur spreads across 186,500 acres (75,500 ha) of the Blitzen

Valley floor. More than 320 species of birds and 58 species of mammals inhabit the wetlands, meadows, and uplands, ensuring prime wildlife viewing for visitors. Sandhill cranes, tundra swans, snowy white egrets, white-faced ibis, pronghorn antelope, mule deer, and redband trout are among the most numerous of the refuge's denizens.

Spring and fall are the best times to view birds, which alight in the refuge on their annual migrations up and down the Pacific Flyway, a major north–south route for migrating North American waterfowl. A small museum houses specimens of birds commonly seen in the refuge. Starting at the center, the Central Patrol Road traverses the 40-mile (64-km) length of the refuge and provides access to the prime viewing spots. The P Ranch, at the south end, is the historic spread of Peter French, who settled the Blitzen Valley in the 1880s.

ENVIRONS: From the refuge, the 69-mile (111-km) **Diamond Loop National Back Country Byway** heads into sage-covered hills and red rimrock canyons. Along the route are Diamond Craters, a volcanic landscape formed between 17,000 and 25,000 years ago; the Round Barn, a distinctive 19th-century structure with a round stone corral surrounded by a circular paddock; and Diamond, a small, poplar-shaded ranch town where the number of guests staying at the hotel

determines whether the town's population exceeds the single digits.

🎯 **Diamond Loop National Back Country Byway**
ℹ️ 28910 Hwy 20 W, Hines.
🎫 (541) 573-4400.

Resting mule deer in the Malheur National Wildlife Refuge

John Day Fossil Beds National Monument ㉛

Road map 1 B3. ℹ️ Hwy 19, 40 miles (64 km) west of John Day, (541) 987-2333. ⃝ dawn–dusk daily; **Visitors' center (Sheep Rock unit)**: Mar–Memorial Day & Labor Day–Thanksgiving: 9am–5pm daily; Memorial Day–Labor Day: 9am–6pm daily; Thanksgiving–Feb: 9am–5pm Mon–Fri. ⬤ major hols. 🅆 www.nps.gov/joda

PREHISTORIC FOSSIL beds litter the John Day Fossil Beds National Monument, where sedimentary rocks preserve the plants and animals that flourished in jungles and savannas for 40 million years, between the extinction of the

Formations at John Day Fossil Beds National Monument's Sheep Rock unit

The magnificent Painted Hills at John Day Fossil Beds National Monument

dinosaurs and the beginning of the most recent ice age. The monument's 14,000 acres (5,700 ha) comprise three units: Sheep Rock, Painted Hills, and Clarno. At all three, trails provide opportunities for close-up observation of the fossil beds. Painted Hills presents the most dramatic landscapes: volcanic rock formations are vivid hues of red, pink, bronze, tan, and black. Clarno contains some of the oldest formations, dating back 54 million years and including some of the finest fossil plant remains on earth. At Sheep Rock, where formations date from 16 million to 6 million years ago, the visitors' center displays many important finds from the beds.

Enteledont skull and forelimb fossils

The fossil beds are named in honor of John Day, a fur trader from Virginia who arrived in Oregon in 1812 and for whom the John Day River is named, though Day himself apparently never actually set foot near the beds.

Pendleton 32

Road map 1 C3. 🏘 17,000. ℹ 501 S Main St, (541) 276-7411.

PENDLETON IS the largest town in eastern Oregon, and it has an outsized reputation for raucous cowboys and lawless cattle rustlers to match. Visitors may be disappointed to learn, however, that these more colorful days belong to the past. **Pendleton Woolen Mills** (see p76), known for its warm clothing and blankets, particularly its "legendary" blankets whose designs are a tribute to Native American tribes, is now the big business in town. The mill wove its first Indian trade blanket in 1895. Native Americans used these blankets not only as standard clothing items but also in ceremonies and trade among each other, where the blankets were used as a measure of value and credit.

Cowboy lore continues to come alive during the Pendleton Round-Up each September, when rodeo stunt performers and some 50,000 spectators crowd into town. Previous rodeos are honored in the photographs and other memorabilia at the **Round-Up Hall of Fame**.

The **Pendleton Underground Tours** reveal much about the town's notoriety. The tours begin in an underground labyrinth of opium dens, gaming rooms, and prohibition-era drinking establishments and include stops at the Cozy Room bordello and the cramped 19th-century living quarters of Chinese laborers.

Another chapter of local history is commemorated in the **Tamástslikt Cultural Institute**. Re-creations of historic structures and handsome exhibits of war bonnets and other artifacts depict the horse culture, seasonal migrations, forced resettlements, and current success of the Cayuse, Umatilla, and Walla Walla tribes, who have lived on the Columbia River plateau for more than 10,000 years.

🧶 **Pendleton Woolen Mills**
1307 SE Court Pl. ☎ (541) 276-6911. *Salesroom* ◯ May–Dec: 8am–5pm Mon–Sat, 11am–3pm Sun; Jan–Apr: 8am–5pm Mon–Sat. ● Jan 1, Dec 25. 🎟 9am, 11am, 1:30pm, 3pm Mon–Fri. ♿
ⓦ www.pendleton-usa.com

🏛 **Round-Up Hall of Fame**
1205 SW Court Ave.
☎ (541) 276-2553. ◯ May–Sep: 10am–5pm Mon–Sat; Oct–Apr: by appt. ● major hols.
ⓦ www.pendletonroundup.com

🎫 **Pendleton Underground Tours**
37 SW Emigrant Ave. ☎ (541) 276-0730. ◯ Mar–Oct: 9:30am–3pm Mon–Sat; Nov–Feb: call for hrs. ● major hols. ♿ ♿ ⓦ www.pendletonundergroundtours.org

🏛 **Tamástslikt Cultural Institute**
72789 Hwy 331. ☎ (541) 966-9748. ◯ 9am–5pm daily. ● Jan 1, Thanksgiving, Dec 25. ♿ ♿ ⓦ www.tamastslikt.com

ENVIRONS: The town of La Grande, 52 miles (84 km) southeast of Pendleton, is best known as the jumping-off point for trips into the scenic wilds of the Blue and Wallowa Mountains and Hells Canyon (see pp112–15).

In downtown La Grande, charming turn-of-the-19th-century buildings now house shops and cafés.

A rodeo rider at the popular Pendleton Round-Up

Elkhorn Drive National Scenic Byway Tour ㉝

Covered wagon of the type used by pioneers

THIS DRIVE THROUGH two mountain ranges takes in some of the finest scenery in Eastern Oregon. To the west, the route climbs across the Elkhorn Range of the Blue Mountains, where dense pine forests interspersed with crystal-clear lakes give way to historic gold-mining towns. To the east rise the snow-capped summits of the spectacular Wallowa mountain range, where dense wilderness surrounds Joseph – a delightful frontier town – and majestic Wallowa Lake.

Anthony Lakes ⑥
A string of mountain lakes sparkle amid forests of ponderosa pines. In winter, skiers and snowmobile enthusiasts glide across this hilly terrain on deep powder.

Granite ⑤
When pioneer gold mining days came to a close, the town of Granite changed from a boom-town into a ghost town.

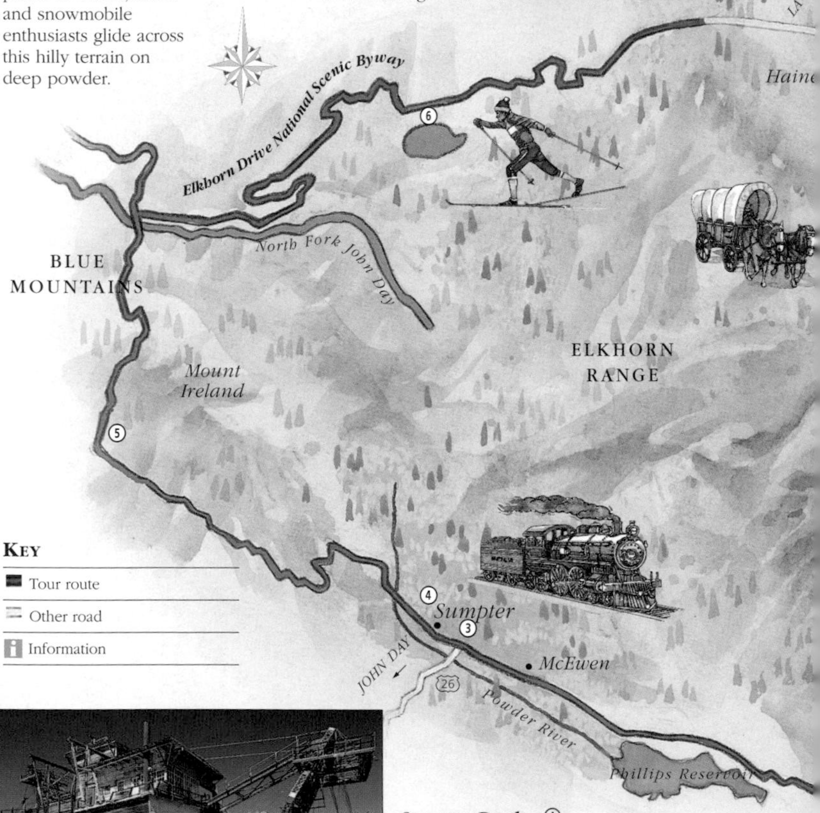
Elkhorn Drive National Scenic Byway
North Fork John Day
BLUE MOUNTAINS
Mount Ireland
ELKHORN RANGE
Sumpter
McEwen
JOHN DAY
26
Powder River
Phillips Reservoir
KEY
Tour route
Other road
Information

Sumpter Dredge ④
This massive dredge once dug its way across the valley floor in search of gold. The hulking wood and steel beast is now the centerpiece of a unique heritage site.

0 km 8
0 miles 5

TIPS FOR DRIVERS

Tour length: 83 miles (134 km).
Starting point: Baker City.
When to go: Summer and autumn. Snow often forces road closures until July.
Stopping-off points: Baker City's Geiser Grand Hotel (see p284) makes a fine dining stop. There are also several picnic sites along the route.

National Historic Oregon Trail Interpretive Center ①
Here, replicas of pioneer scenes, accompanied by the sounds of jangling oxen, re-create life on the Oregon Trail.

30

WALLOWA
MOUNTAINS

HELLS
CANYON

Baker City
ℹ ②

Baker City ②
Some rather grand downtown blocks and fine Victorian residences are reminders of the fame and prosperity that gold mining once brought to this now quiet ranching town.

Sumpter Valley Railway ③
A narrow-gauge steam train once again chugs along a historic route originally built to haul lumber and gold. Hawks and other wildlife usually provide an escort.

Joseph ㉞

Road map 1 C3. 🏘 1,100. ℹ Wallowa Mountains Visitor Center, Hwy 82, Enterprise, (541) 426-5546.

JOSEPH IS NAMED for Chief Joseph, leader of the Nez Percé people *(see p25)*. In 1877, he led his tribe on a 2,000-mile (3,200-km) flight to resist resettlement from their lands in the Wallowas; they were apprehended near the Canadian border.

The brick storefronts, snow-capped Wallowa Mountains, and outlying grasslands lend Joseph a frontier-town air still. These days, though, recreation enthusiasts outnumber ranchers, and artisans, particularly sculptors, have established galleries. The **Manuel Nez Percé Crossing Museum** has a fine collection of local bronzes, blankets, and baskets; **Wallowa County Museum** is devoted to Chief Joseph's famous retreat. Chief Joseph Days, held in July, feature a rodeo and carnival.

Bronze horse sculpture in Joseph

🏛 **Manuel Nez Percé Crossing Museum**
400 N Main St. 🅲 (541) 432-7235. ◻ Jun–Oct: 8am–5pm daily; Nov–May: 10am–4pm daily. 📷
🏛 **Wallowa County Museum**
110 S Main St. 🅲 (541) 432-6095. ◻ Memorial Day–3rd weekend Sep: 10am–5pm daily.

Restored historic corner building in Joseph, Oregon

Motorboat moored on the blue waters of Wallowa Lake

Wallowa Lake ㉟

Road map 1 C3.

THE CRYSTAL-CLEAR waters of this long glacial lake sparkle at the foot of the Wallowa Mountains, which form a 10,000-ft- (3,050-m-) high, 40-mile- (64-km-) long wall of granite. Though the lake was a popular tourist retreat as long as 100 years ago, the forested shoreline is remarkably unspoiled. Much of it falls within the boundaries of national forest lands and Wallowa State Park.

One of the few commercial structures on the lake is **Wallowa Lake Lodge**, a beautifully restored log building dating from the 1920s. It still provides accommodation and meals. The popular **Wallowa Lake Tramway** whisks riders up more than 8,000 ft (2,400 m) to the summit of Mount Howard, where spectacular views of the lake below and the Wallowa mountains can be enjoyed. Deep wilderness is only a short hike or pack trip away from the lake in the Eagle Gap Wilderness, which climbs and dips over some 400,000 acres (162,000 ha) of mountainous terrain to the west of the lake.

🌿 **Wallowa Lake State Park**
6 miles (10 km) south of Joseph off Hwy 82. 🅲 (541) 432-8855. ◻ dawn–dusk daily.
🆆 www.oregonstateparks.org
🚡 **Wallowa Lake Tramway**
59919 Wallowa Lake Hwy, Joseph. 🅲 (541) 432-5331. ◻ Jun–Sep: call for hrs. 📷

Hells Canyon National Recreation Area Tour 36

Local prickly pear cactus

Sᴏᴍᴇ ᴏꜰ ᴛʜᴇ ᴡɪʟᴅᴇsᴛ ᴛᴇʀʀᴀɪɴ in North America clings to the sides of craggy, 9,400-ft (2,865-m) peaks at Hells Canyon and plunges to the famed basin far below, where the Snake River rushes through the world's deepest river-carved gorge. Visitors are awed by the massive canyon walls rising 6,000 ft (1,830 m) and delight in the dense upland pine forests and delicate flower-covered alpine meadows – 652,000 acres (264,000 ha) in all. Much of the terrain is too rugged to cross, even on foot, making sections of the Snake River accessible only by boat. Many visitors settle for the stunning views from several lookouts, and not one is disappointed.

Hells Canyon National Recreation Area viewpoint

Buckhorn Lookout ①
One of several spectacular overlooks in the Hells Canyon area, this remote spot offers superb views of the Wallowa-Whitman National Forest and the Imnaha River canyon.

Nee-Me-Poo Trail ②
Hikers on this scenic trail follow in the footsteps of Chief Joseph and 700 Nez Percé Indians who, in 1877, embarked on an 1,800-mile (2,880-km) trek toward freedom in Canada *(see p25)*.

Hells Canyon Reservoir ⑥
Formed by Oxbow Dam to the south and Hells Canyon Dam to the north, this 25-mile- (40-km-) long reservoir is part of a huge power-generating complex on the Snake River. A road along the east shore pro-vides boaters and rafters with access to the river.

Imn

JOSEPH

Big Sheep Creek

North Pine Creek

BAKER CITY

350

86

Salmon River
Pittsburg Landing
493
Snake River
4240
Seven Devils Mountains
Hells Canyon Dam
454

TIPS FOR DRIVERS

Tour length: *214 miles (345 km), including all turnoffs.*
Starting point: *Oregon SR 350, 8 miles (13 km) east of Joseph.*
When to go: *Summer months only. Some roads are not suitable for every type of vehicle. For information, call the area's Visitor Center at (541) 426-5546.*
Stopping-off points: *Picnic areas are abundant. Imnaha offers restaurants and lodging.*

Imnaha River ③

A road from the city of Imnaha follows this frothy river through a pine-scented valley, passing isolated ranches and a fish weir where Chinook salmon can be seen swimming upstream on their annual migration from the distant Pacific Ocean.

KEY

- Tour route
- Other road
- [i] Information
- Viewpoint

0 kilometers 18

0 miles 14

Hat Point Road ④

A dizzying drive up a steep 23-mile (37-km) gravel road leads to Hat Point, which is located at an altitude of 7,000 ft (2,100 m).

Wild and Scenic River ⑤

A 31.5-mile (50.5-km) stretch of the Snake River, from Hells Canyon Dam to Upper Pittsburg Landing, is designated a Wild and Scenic River. Experienced guides pilot rafters over the many stretches of rapids. Searing temperatures and inhospitable terrain, as well as bears, rattlesnakes, and poison ivy, make an overland trek alongside the river less inviting.

HELLS CANYON ADVENTURES

A boat negotiating rapids on a trip on the Snake River

SEATTLE

Seattle at a Glance

Map of Seattle on a manhole cover

SEATTLE'S HISTORY, commerce, and quality of life are closely tied to its waterfront location on Puget Sound. The Klondike Gold Rush National Historical Park recalls the city's pivotal role as an embarkation point for the gold rush of 1897–8. The Seattle Aquarium and Odyssey Maritime Discovery Center explore Puget Sound's diverse natural habitat and its importance to Pacific Rim trade. Embracing both the past and the future, Seattle's architectural icons include a number of historic buildings, the once-futuristic Space Needle, and the provocative Experience Music Project.

Experience Music Project
This innovative museum celebrates rock 'n' roll from its beginnings to later influences (see pp146–7).

Space Needle
Built for the 1962 World's Fair, the 605-ft (184-m) Space Needle is Seattle's official landmark. A 43-second elevator ride whisks visitors to the observation deck and a 360-degree view (see pp144–5).

Odyssey Maritime Discovery Center
Opened in 1998, this cleverly designed museum on Seattle's working waterfront engages visitors with interactive exhibits showcasing the region's maritime and fisheries industries (see pp138–9).

Seattle Aquarium
Offering a window into Pacific Northwest marine life, this popular aquarium has an underwater glass dome which surrounds visitors with sharks, salmon, octopus, and other Puget Sound creatures (see p136).

◁ **Sailboats on Lake Union, Seattle**

Benaroya Hall
Home of the Seattle Symphony, this $118 million complex occupies an entire city block. Its 2,500-seat Taper Auditorium is internationally acclaimed for its superior acoustics (see p129).

0 meters 200
0 yards 200

Four Seasons Olympic Hotel
This stately hotel is listed on the National Register of Historic Places (see p128).

Seattle Art Museum
Designed by Venturi Scott Brown and Associates, this limestone and sandstone building houses 23,000 works of art, ranging from ancient Egyptian reliefs to contemporary American installations (see pp128–9).

Smith Tower
Once the world's tallest office building outside of New York City, this 42-story tower boasts the last manually operated elevators of their kind on the West Coast (see p124).

Pike Place Market
Dating from 1907, the oldest farmer's market in the country is a beloved Seattle landmark and a National Historic District (see p134).

Klondike Gold Rush National Historical Park
This indoor park located in the Pioneer Square Historic District celebrates Seattle's role in North America's last great gold rush (see p125).

PIONEER SQUARE
AND DOWNTOWN

T HE BIRTHPLACE of Seattle, Pioneer Square was the city's original downtown, established in 1852 when Arthur and David Denny arrived with a handful of fellow pioneers. Emerging from the ashes of the Great Fire of 1889, the rebuilt commercial area prospered as the 19th century drew to a close. By the time the much-touted Smith Tower opened in 1914, however, the city core had begun spreading north and Pioneer Square was less and less

Dragon, International District

a prestigious business address. Today, the revitalized Pioneer Square – a National Historic District – is a thriving arts center, with First Thursday gallery walks and venues for author readings. A short walk leads to downtown – home to the city's modern skyscrapers, upscale shops, and luxury hotels, as well as green spaces such as Freeway Park. Lending cultural panache is the boldly designed Seattle Art Museum and the state-of-the-art Benaroya Hall.

SIGHTS AT A GLANCE

Buildings and Shops
Bank of America Tower ❼
Benaroya Hall ❿
Elliott Bay Book Company ❸
Four Seasons
    Olympic Hotel ❽
Pacific Place ⓬
Pioneer Building ❷
Smith Tower ❶

Museums
Seattle Art Museum ❾

Parks and Districts
Freeway Park ⓫
International District ❻
Klondike Gold Rush
    National Historical Park ❺
Occidental Square ❹

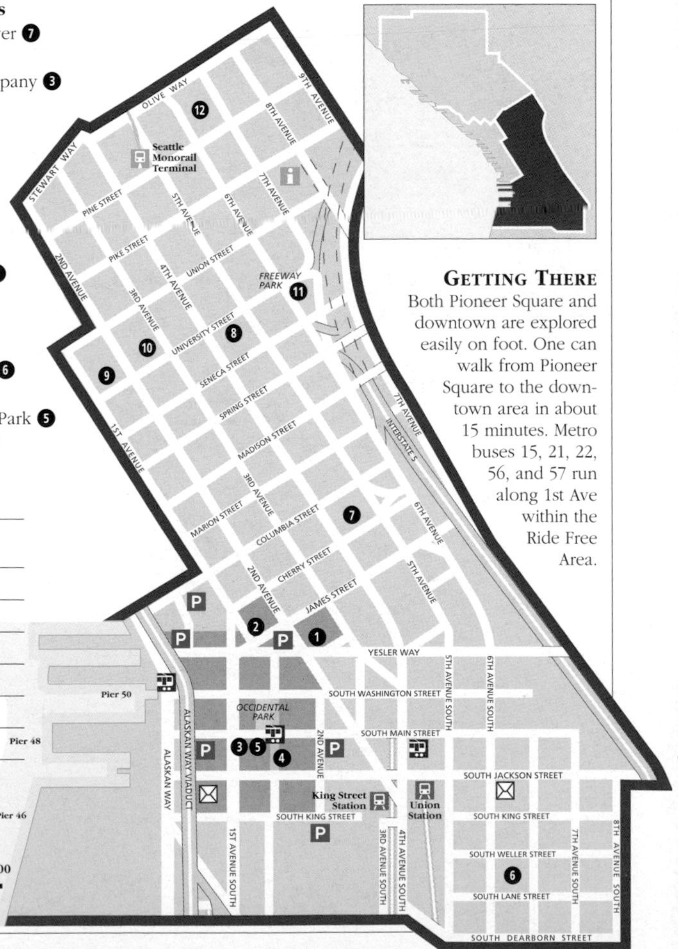

KEY

	Street-by-Street map *See pp122–3*
🚋	Streetcar
🚝	Monorail terminal
🚆	Train station
ℹ	Information
P	Parking
✉	Post office

0 meters   400
0 yards   400

GETTING THERE

Both Pioneer Square and downtown are explored easily on foot. One can walk from Pioneer Square to the downtown area in about 15 minutes. Metro buses 15, 21, 22, 56, and 57 run along 1st Ave within the Ride Free Area.

◁ Jonathan Barofsky's *Hammering Man* at the entrance to the Seattle Art Museum

Street-by-Street: Pioneer Square

Decorative manhole cover

PIONEER SQUARE, Seattle's first downtown and later a decrepit skid row, is today a revitalized business neighborhood and National Historic District. The tall totem poles gracing the square are reminders of the Coast Salish Indian village that originally occupied this spot. The grand Victorian architecture, social service missions, and upscale shops that line the bustling streets and cobblestone plazas are further reminders of the area's checkered past and recent transformation. Many of the buildings standing today were constructed in the years between the Great Fire of 1889 and the Klondike Gold Rush of 1897–8, both pivotal events in Seattle's history. While the buildings look much as they did a century ago, their tenants have changed dramatically. Where saloons, brothels, and mining company headquarters once flourished, art galleries, boutiques, and antique shops now reside.

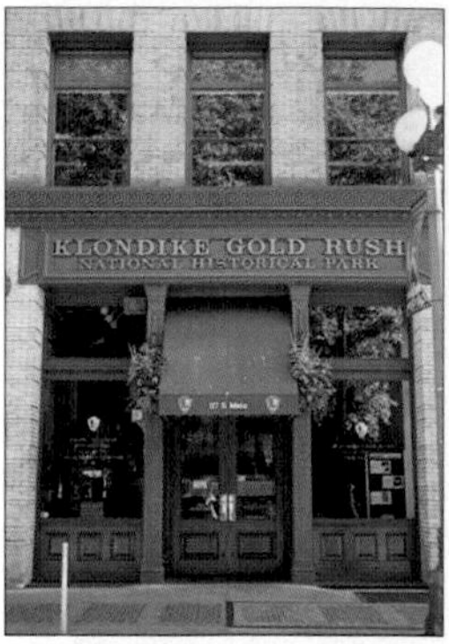
KLONDIKE GOLD RUSH
NATIONAL HISTORICAL PARK

★ Klondike Gold Rush National Historical Park
The park in this historical building is devoted to telling the story of the Gold Rush ❺

Elliott Bay Café

Elliott Bay Book Company
This Seattle institution occupies the 1891 stone-and-brick Globe Building, which has survived three fires, two earthquakes, and two explosions ❸

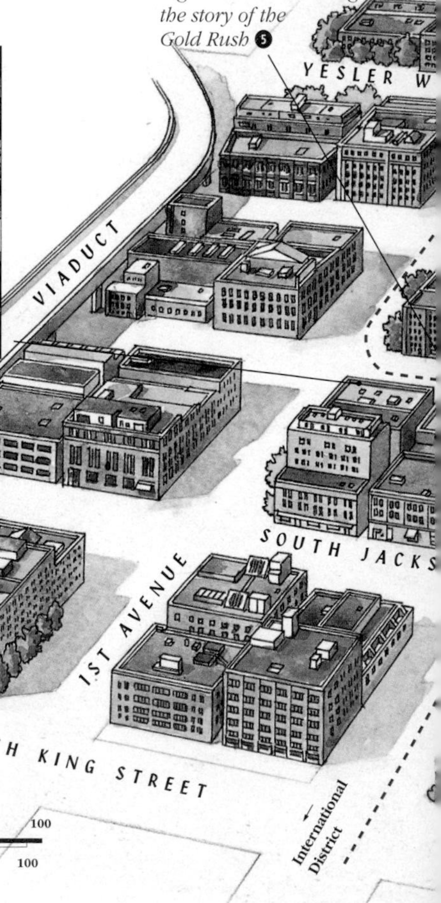
VIADUCT
ALASKAN WAY
1ST AVENUE
SOUTH KING STREET
International District

STAR SIGHTS

- ★ Klondike Gold Rush National Historical Park
- ★ Pioneer Building

0 meters 100
0 yards 100

KEY

- - - Suggested route

LOCATOR MAP
See Street Finder map 4

★ **Pioneer Building**
*Completed in 1892 in the Romanesque
Revival style, this building faces onto Pioneer
Place. Seattle's Underground Tour (see p124)
starts from here* ❷

Downtown ◄

2ND AVENUE

SOUTH WASHINGTON STREET

SOUTH MAIN STREET

REET

ccidental Walk

Occidental Square

The Smith Tower, an imposing
terra-cotta building and Seattle
landmark, is named after typewriter
tycoon Lyman C. Smith, who
commissioned the building in 1914.

Pioneer Place
*This small triangular park is
graced with a Tlingit totem
pole and an iron-and-glass
pergola, once marking the
entrance to the "finest underground restroom in the US." A
bust of Chief Seattle looms
above the fountain.*

Smith Tower ❶

506 2nd Ave. **Map** 4 D3. 📞 *(206) 622-4004*. 🚌 *39, 42, 136, 137*.
Observation deck ⭘ *mid-Apr–Oct: 11am–6pm daily; Nov–mid-Apr: 11am–4pm Sat–Sun*. ⬤ *Easter, Thanksgiving, Dec 25*. 🏷 *to observation deck*. ♿ *except observation deck*. 🎦 *for groups*. 🅦 *www.chineseroom.com*

WHEN IT OPENED on July 4, 1914, the 42-story Smith Tower was heralded as the tallest office building in the world outside New York City, and for nearly a half century it reigned as the tallest building west of Chicago.

Commissioned by rifle and typewriter tycoon Lyman Cornelius Smith, Seattle's first skyscraper is clad in white terra cotta. While its height – 522 ft (159 m) from the curbside to the top of the tower finial – is no longer its claim to fame, the city's landmark does boast the last manually operated elevator of its kind on the West Coast. For a fee, you can ride one of the gleaming brass-cage originals to the 35th-floor Chinese Room. The carved wood and porcelain-inlay ceiling and the ornate Blackwood furniture adorning this banquet room were gifts to Smith from the last empress of China. The deck here offers panoramic views of Mount Rainier, the Olympic and Cascade mountain ranges, and Elliott Bay.

The onyx and marble lobby, recently restored to its former glamour, is presided over by 22 carved chieftans.

Decorative brass elevator doors of the 1914 Smith Building

Pioneer Building ❷

608 1st Ave. **Map** 4 D3. 🚌 *15, 18, 21, 22*. **Underground tour** 📞 *(206) 682-4646*. 🎦 📷 *call for hrs & reservations*. 🅦 *www.undergroundtour.com*

COMPLETED IN 1892, three years after the Great Fire flattened the core business district, the Pioneer Building was voted the "finest building west of Chicago" by the American Institute of Architects. It is one of more than 50 buildings designed by Elmer Fisher *(see p148)* following the devastating fire. Still imposing without its tower, destroyed in a 1949 earthquake, the brick building

Sign for the Elliott Bay Book Company

houses offices and Doc Maynard's Saloon, starting point of the **Underground Tour**. This 90-minute walk offers a lively look at Seattle's colorful past and the original streets beneath the modern city, including the 1890s stores abandoned in the 1900s when engineers raised streets a full story. Beware: the tour's subterranean portion is musty and dusty.

Elliott Bay Book Company ❸

101 S Main St. **Map** 4 D3. 📞 *(206) 624-6600*. 🚌 *15, 18, 21, 22, 56*. 🚇 *Occidental Park*. ⭘ *9:30am–10pm Mon–Fri, 10am–10pm Sat, 11am–7pm Sun, noon–5pm public hols*. ⬤ *Thanksgiving, Dec 25*. ♿ *except café*. 🅦 *www.elliottbaybook.com*

READ, COMMANDS the red neon sign in the store window. Not that Seattle, a city of self-proclaimed bookworms and bibliophiles, needs any such encouragement. Occupying the site of Seattle's first hospital, run by Doc Maynard, Elliott Bay Book Company is an inviting warren of nooks and crannies, creaky wood floors, and cedar shelves lined with 150,000 titles, from new books to used and limited editions. The bookstore is also known for its excellent author-reading series.

THE GREAT SEATTLE FIRE

On June 6, 1889, in a cabinet shop near Pioneer Square, a pot of flaming glue overturned, igniting wood shavings. The tide, which the city's water system depended on, was low at the time, and little water came out of the hydrants initially. The fire spread rapidly, engulfing 60 city blocks before burning itself out. Miraculously, no one died in the blaze, and it came to be seen as a blessing in disguise. Sturdy brick and stone buildings were erected where flimsy wood structures once stood; streets were widened and raised; and the sewer system was overhauled. From the ashes of disaster rose a city primed for prominence as the 20th century approached.

The aftermath of the Great Seattle Fire of 1889, devastating to a city built of wood

The stately Smith Tower, once the tallest building outside New York

Occidental Square ➍

Occidental Ave between S Main & S Jackson Sts. **Map** 4 D3. 🚌 *15, 18, 21, 22, 56.* 🚋 *Occidental Park.*

THE BRICK-PAVED plaza known as Occidental Square offers relief from the busy traffic of Pioneer Square. The tree-lined pedestrian walk is flanked by upscale shops, galleries, and coffeehouses, many housed in attractive Victorian buildings.

Across South Main Street is Occidental Park, where the ambiance changes considerably because of the local contingent of homeless people and panhandlers. Of special note here are four cedar totem poles carved by Northwest artist Duane Pasco and the Fallen Firefighters' Memorial, a moving tribute to the 34 Seattle firefighters who have died in the line of duty since the Seattle Fire Department was founded in 1889.

The striking cedar totem poles in Pioneer Square's Occidental Park

Klondike Gold Rush National Historical Park ➎

117 S Main St. **Map** 4 D3. 📞 *(206) 553-7220.* 🚌 *15, 18, 21, 22, 56.* 🚋 *Occidental Park.* ⏰ *9am–5pm daily.* ● *Jan 1, Thanksgiving, Dec 25.* ♿ Ⓦ *www.nps.gov/klse*

IN 1895, GOLD was discovered in a tributary of the Klondike River, in the middle of the Canadian Yukon wilderness.

Exhibit at the Klondike Gold Rush National Historical Park

This discovery triggered a frenzied stampede, as 100,000 gold seekers from around the world rushed to the Klondike to find their fortunes.

The largest and closest US city to the gold fields, Seattle became the primary outfitting and embarkation point for the stampede north. Tens of thousands of miners passed through the city, purchasing $25 million worth of food, clothing, equipment, pack animals, and steamship tickets. While few Klondikers struck it rich during the Gold Rush of 1897–8, Seattle merchants made a fortune and established the city's reputation as the premier commercial center of the Pacific Northwest.

Established by Congress in 1976, Klondike Gold Rush National Historical Park comprises five units – three in Canada, one in Skagway, Alaska, and one in Seattle's Pioneer Square Historic District. Housed in the Union Trust Annex, the Seattle visitors' center celebrates the city's role in North America's last great gold rush. On display here are evocative black-and-white photographs and simulations of the "ton of provisions" that Canadian law required each prospector to bring with him, including 350 pounds (160 kg) of flour and 150 pounds (68 kg) of bacon. Personable park rangers staff the center, offering insights into this fascinating period in American history.

Open year-round, the park offers an expanded program in the summer. Activities include ranger-led walking tours of Pioneer Square, gold-panning demonstrations, and scheduled screenings of

Gold Rush–themed films in the 102-seat auditorium. (These films are shown at other times of the year by request.)

International District ➏

East of 6th Ave S, south of Yesler Way. **Map** 4 E4. 🚌 *7, 14, 36.* 🚋 *Jackson.*

LOCATED SOUTHEAST of Pioneer Square, the International District was settled by Asian Americans in the late 1800s. This bustling area continues to serve as the cultural hub for the city's Chinese, Korean, Japanese, Filipino, Vietnamese, and Laotian residents.

In addition to its fine ethnic restaurants, the area is home to **Uwajimaya** (600 5th Avenue South), the largest Asian market in the Pacific Northwest. The **Wing Luke Asian Museum** (407 7th Avenue South), a Smithsonian affiliate, is named after the first Asian Pacific American elected to office in the Pacific Northwest. The museum highlights the history, culture, and art of Asian Pacific Americans.

Items for sale at Uwajimaya, in Seattle's International District

The tall Bank of America Tower, dwarfing the Smith Tower

Bank of America Tower **⓻**

701 5th Ave. **Map** 4 D2.
📞 (206) 386-5151. 🚌 16, 358.
Observation deck 🕐 8:30am–
4:30pm Mon–Fri. ● public hols.
▣ to observation deck. ♿

T HE TALLEST BUILDING in
Seattle, the Bank of
America Tower (also known
as the "BOAT" and formerly
called Columbia Seafirst
Center) is the tallest building
– according to the number of
stories – west of the Mississippi River. Rising 1,049 ft
(320 m) above sea level, the
1.5 million-square-ft (139,500
sq-m), 76-story skyscraper
was designed by Chester
Lindsey Architects and
completed in 1985 at a cost of
$285 million. In 1998, it was
sold for $404 million.

A prestigious business
address for more than 5,000
Seattle-area workers, the
shimmering black tower also
attracts visitors to its 73rd-
floor observation deck, which
offers spectacular vistas of the
Cascade and Olympic moun-
tain ranges, Mount Rainier,
Lake Washington, and Puget
Sound, as well as views of
the city and its many suburbs.

The four-level retail atrium
houses shops, food vendors,
and, on the third floor, the
City Space art gallery, which
features the works of artists
who have been commissioned
for projects by the city.

Four Seasons Olympic Hotel **⓼**

411 University St. **Map** 4 D1.
📞 (206) 621-1700. 🚌 17, 19, 24,
26, 28. ♿ 🍴 🍸 🅿 See **Where to
Stay** p287.
Ⓦ www.fourseasons.com/seattle

W HEN IT DEBUTED in 1924,
the Olympic Hotel was
the place to see and be seen
– not surprising since the
bondholders who funded the
$4 million construction were
among the city's most socially
prominent citizens. Designed
by the New York firm of
George B. Post and Sons, the
Italian Renaissance–style
building features high, arched
Palladian windows, gleaming
oak-paneled walls, and
terrazzo floors laid by Italian
workmen who were sent to
Seattle for the task.

More than $800,000 was
spent on furnishings, including hundreds of antique mir-
rors, Italian and Spanish oil
jars, and bronze statuary. A
glamorous venue for parties,
weddings, and debutante
balls, the Olympic reigned as
the *grande dame* of Seattle
hotels for half a century
before losing her luster.

In 1979, the hotel was listed
on the US National Register of
Historic Places. A year later,
the Four Seasons hotel chain
assumed management of the
building and gave the hotel a
$62.5 million facelift – the
most costly hotel restoration
in the US at that time –
returning the landmark hotel
to her original grandeur and
celebrated status in Seattle.

**The striking modern façade
of the Seattle Art Museum**

Seattle Art Museum **⓽**

100 University St. **Map** 3 C2.
📞 (206) 654-3100. 🚌 174. 🕐
10am–5pm Tue–Wed & Fri–Sun, 10am–
9pm Thu. ● Mon (except some hols),
Jan 1, Thanksgiving, Dec 25. ▣ (free
1st Thu of month). 🚫 ♿ 🅿 ▣ ●
🅿 Ⓦ www.seattleartmuseum.org

T HERE'S NO MISSING the main
entrance of the Seattle Art
Museum – just look for the
giant *Hammering Man*. A
tribute to workers, Jonathan
Barofsky's 48-ft (15-m) ani-
mated steel sculpture "ham-
mers" silently and continuously
from 7am to 10pm daily, resting only on Labor Day.

The museum building is no
less impressive. Designed by
the Philadelphia firm Venturi
Scott Brown and Associates,
the bold limestone and sandstone building was completed
in 1991 at a cost of $62 million.

The museum's permanent
collection includes 23,000

The opulent interior of the Four Seasons Olympic Hotel

◁ **The Seattle skyline, framed by the Space Needle and Mount Rainier**

objects ranging from ancient Egyptian relief sculpture and wooden African statuary to Old Master paintings and contemporary American art.

Traveling exhibits are featured on the second floor. Permanent collections of Asian, African, and Northwest Coast Native American art figure prominently on the third floor. Highlights here include the 14-ft- (4-m-) tall red-cedar Native houseposts carved with bears and thunderbirds boasting 11-ft (3.5-m) wingspans, from the village of Gwa'yasdams in British Columbia. The fourth floor houses European and American art, including works by contemporary Pacific Northwest artists such as Morris Graves, Jacob Lawrence, and Dale Chihuly.

Also in this museum family is the Seattle Asian Art Museum, in Volunteer Park (see p153). Occupying the original home of the Seattle Art Museum, it houses extensive Asian art collections. The Seattle Art Museum's third venue – Olympic Sculpture Park, an outdoor "museum" on the north end of Seattle's waterfront – is slated for completion in 2004.

Benaroya Hall ⑩

200 University St. **Map** 3 C1.
[(206) 215-4700. **■** 174.
■ 12pm & 1pm Tue & Fri. **∅** **&**
▢ **▯** **w** www.benaroyahall.com

HOME OF THE SEATTLE Symphony and occupying an entire city block, the $118.1 million Benaroya Hall contains two performing halls, including the 2,500-seat Taper

Dale Chihuly's *Benaroya Hall Silver Chandelier*, one of a pair

Auditorium, acclaimed for its superior acoustics. The multi-level Grand Lobby, dramatic at night when lit, offers stunning views of Puget Sound and the city skyline.

Even if time doesn't permit attending a symphony performance, visitors can gain an appreciation of this magnificent facility by taking one of the excellent tours offered, learning how this acoustical masterpiece was created atop a railroad tunnel. Visitors can also admire Benaroya Hall's impressive private art collection, which includes *Echo*, Robert Rauschenberg's evocative 12-ft (3.5-m) mural painted on metal; *Schubert Sonata*, sculptor Mark di Suvero's towering steel wind vane; and Dale Chihuly's pair of chandelier sculptures – one silver, one gold – each with some 1,200 pieces of blown glass wired to a steel armature.

Within the hall's open space along 2nd Avenue is the Garden of Remembrance, a park commemorating Washington citizens killed in battle.

Freeway Park ⑪

Seneca St & 6th Ave. **Map** 4 D1.
■ 2, 13. **○** 6am–11:30pm daily. **&**

TUCKED INTO THE HEART of Seattle's bustling commercial district, and adjoining the Washington State Convention and Trade Center, 5-acre (2-ha) Freeway Park straddles the I-5, which runs through downtown. Inside the park, thundering waterfalls drown out the traffic roar, and shady footpaths invite leisurely strolling. Outdoor music concerts are held here in summer.

The light-filled circular atrium of the Pacific Place shopping center

Pacific Place ⑫

600 Pine St. **Map** 2 E5. **[** (206) 405-2655. **■** 7, 10, 11, 14, 43. **○** Jan–May: 9:30am–8pm Mon–Sat, 11am–6pm Sun; Jun–Dec: 10am–9pm Mon–Sat, 11am–6pm Sun (restaurant & cinema hrs vary). **Shops** ● Jan 1, Easter, Thanksgiving, Dec 25. **Restaurants & cinemas** ○ daily. **& ▮ ▢**
▯ **w** www.pacificplaceseattle.com

DOWNTOWN SEATTLE'S premier shopping, dining, and entertainment complex, Pacific Place houses dozens of upscale apparel, accessory, jewelry, and home and lifestyle stores, among them MaxMara, Coach, Cartier, Tiffany, and Pottery Barn. This five-level vertical mall also has four restaurants offering a variety of cuisines and an 11-screen, state-of-the-art cinema complex which can accommodate as many as 3,100 moviegoers, some in special love seats.

Benaroya Hall, grand home of the Seattle Symphony

PIKE PLACE MARKET AND THE WATERFRONT

ITUATED ABOVE THE SHORES of Elliott Bay, Seattle's Pike Place Market is both a venerable landmark and a veritable feast for the senses. Exuberant and engaging, this 9-acre (3.5-ha) National Historic District is known as much for its colorful personalities as it is for its abundance of local produce. Pike Street Hillclimb, a system of stairs and elevators, connects the market to Seattle's bustling waterfront, with its briny scents, squawking

Neon sign advertising fresh fish at Pike Place Market

sea gulls, fish and chip joints, and fine seafood restaurants. Marine activity abounds, as this working waterfront is the departure point for freighters, ferries, cruise ships, and harbor tour boats. The Bell Street Pier dazzles with the impressive Odyssey Maritime Discovery Center, while at Pier 57, the Seattle Aquarium showcases Pacific Northwest marine life. The adjacent Seattle IMAX Dome offers viewers the ultimate 3D experience.

SIGHTS AT A GLANCE

Aquariums
Seattle Aquarium ➏

Shops, Markets, and Restaurants
Athenian Inn ➍
Pike Place Market ➊
Pike Place Starbucks ➌
Upper Post Alley ➋
Ye Olde Curiosity Shop ➑

Ferry Terminal
Washington State Ferries Terminal ➎

Museums
Odyssey Maritime Discovery Center pp138–9 ➒

Theaters
Seattle IMAX Dome Theater ➐

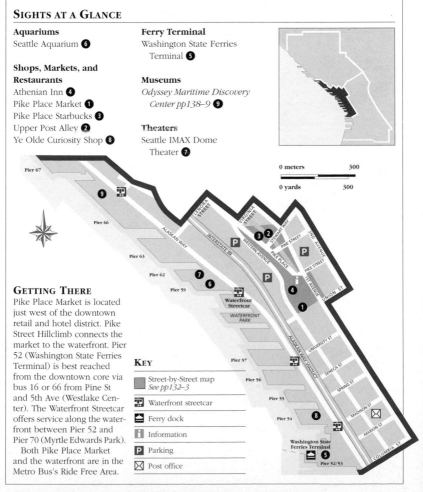

GETTING THERE
Pike Place Market is located just west of the downtown retail and hotel district. Pike Street Hillclimb connects the market to the waterfront. Pier 52 (Washington State Ferries Terminal) is best reached from the downtown core via bus 16 or 66 from Pine St and 5th Ave (Westlake Center). The Waterfront Streetcar offers service along the waterfront between Pier 52 and Pier 70 (Myrtle Edwards Park).
Both Pike Place Market and the waterfront are in the Metro Bus's Ride Free Area.

KEY

▨	Street-by-Street map *See pp132–3*
🚋	Waterfront streetcar
⚓	Ferry dock
ℹ	Information
🅿	Parking
⊠	Post office

◁ **Luscious locally grown cherries on display at a Pike Pike Market fruit stall**

Street-by-Street: Pike Place Market

Newsstand sign in Pike Place Market

PIKE PLACE MARKET is said to be the soul of Seattle. Established in 1907, it is the oldest continuously operating farmer's market in the US. Over the years, the market has mirrored national waves of immigration, with new arrivals from countries including Mexico, Ethiopia, and Cambodia flocking here to set up small businesses. Bustling with some 100 farmers, 200 artists and craftspeople, engaging street performers, and 500 residents, the district contains art galleries, ethnic and specialty groceries, bistros, and an eclectic mix of shops.

★ **Upper Post Alley**
This pedestrian walkway is lined with specialty shops, restaurants, and pubs. Its sister Lower Post Alley is home to similar businesses ❷

UPPER POST ALLEY

PIKE PLACE

PIKE PLAC

WESTERN AVENUE

Waterfront

Pike Place Starbucks
This building, a former feed store, is the site of the first Starbucks coffee shop, which opened in 1971. The Starbucks sign in the window sports the chain's original logo depicting a bare-breasted siren, based on a 16th-century Norse woodcut ❸

Athenian Inn
This historic restaurant in Pike Place Market is as well known for its appearance in the Tom Hanks movie Sleepless in Seattle *as it is for its seafood and diner-style sandwiches, which can be enjoyed while sitting at a booth overlooking Elliott Bay* ❹

STAR SIGHTS

★ Pike Place Fish

★ Rachel

★ Upper Post Alley

0 meters   40

0 yards   50

KEY

- - - Suggested route

Market sign and clock, c.1927, one of Seattle's oldest neon works

LOCATOR MAP
See Street Finder map 3

Newsstand
There are several news-stands in and around Pike Place Market, offering a wide range of US and international publications.

FIRST AVENUE

PIKE STREET

Downtown

LOWER POST ALLEY

★ **Rachel**
Rachel, an enormous piggy bank, stands at the main entrance to Pike Place Market. It was sculpted by Pacific Northwest artist Georgia Gerber and belongs to the Market Foundation, which uses the sculpture to raise money for low-income people.

★ **Pike Place Fish**
Fish-flinging fishmongers are a long-standing tradition at this Pike Place Market store.

Pike Place Market ❶

Bounded by Pike & Virginia Sts, from
1st to Western Aves. **Map** 3 C1.
📞 *(206) 682-7453.* 🚌 *15, 18.*
🕐 *9am–6pm Mon–Sat, 11am–5pm
Sun; may vary.* ⬤ *major hols.* ♿
📋 *Market Heritage Tour: 11am &
2pm Wed–Sun. Call (206) 682-7453
for details.*
🌐 www.pikeplacemarket.org

A wide selection of fish on display at Pike Place Fish, in the Main Arcade

THE HEART of Pike Place
Market is the **Main Arcade**
(1914) and the adjacent **North
Arcade** (1922). Here, low
metal-topped counters display
freshly picked seasonal fruit,
vegetables, herbs, and flowers
grown by local farmers. Shoppers at these lowstalls get to
"meet the producer,"
as promised by the
market's signature
green sign. Each
morning, the Mar-
ket Master, whose
role at the market
dates back to 1911,
does roll call,
assigning stalls
to farmers and
craftspeople
based on seniority.
This often results in vendors
selling their wares from a different stall each day.

**Fresh cut flowers from
a market flower stall**

Originally, the North Arcade
consisted of two "rows." The
Dry Row, along the west
wall, had no access
to running water. The
Wet Row, with access
to running water, was
also closest to the
exposed arcade
entrance and thus
the damp weather.
Today, craftspeople
sell from the dry
tables and farmers
from the wet tables,
the run-off still
being channeled
along a trough. Highstalls
leased by commercial green-
grocers on a permanent basis

are also to be found in the
Main Arcade. Both imported
and locally grown produce
are on offer here.

    Pike Place Fish, located in
the Main Arcade, is not Pike
Place Market's only seafood
vendor. It is, however, certainly the best known. Situated beneath the market's
landmark clock, this busy stall
always draws a crowd, thanks
to the loud, lively banter and
high-spirited antics of its fishmongers, who are amazingly
adept at tossing fish over the
heads of cheering spectators
to coworkers behind the
shop's counter. The repartee
is as fresh as the seafood,
which ranges from wild king
salmon and Dungeness crab
to rainbow trout and live
clams. Should tourists care to
buy, Pike Place Fish will ship
their seafood home.

    To the south of the arcades
is the **Economy Market**, a
1907 structure which was
incorporated into the market

THE HISTORY OF PIKE PLACE MARKET

Hungry for fresh produce and fair prices, Seattleites mobbed
Pike Place Market when it opened August 17, 1907, at Pike
Street and 1st Avenue, as an effort by the city council to elim-
inate "greedy middlemen" and allow farmers to sell directly to
the public. Sensing opportunity, local Frank Goodwin used
his Klondike gold to build permanent arcades. At its height
in the 1930s, hundreds of farmers sold their produce at the
market. But by World War II, it had fallen on hard times:
Japanese Americans made up to 80 percent of the sellers at
the wet tables; their internment *(see p40)* had a disastrous
effect. In the years that followed, the decline continued as
suburbs and super-
markets became
entrenched in the
American way of
life. By the late
1960s, developers
were lobbying to
tear it down. Ral-
lied by architect
Victor Steinbrueck,
Seattleites rebelled,
voting in 1971 to
make the market
an historic district.

**Local farmers selling their produce at
Pike Place Market, May 1912**

**One of many stands displaying
artwork at the market**

in 1916, and where, among other things, damaged goods were sold at a discount.

Across Pike Street are the **Corner Market** (1912) and **Sanitary Market** (1910) – two of the several buildings constructed during the market's first two decades as it prospered, and so named because horse-drawn carts were not allowed inside. Today all three market buildings house retail shops, restaurants, and cafés.

🐟 Pike Place Fish

Pike Place Market (Main Arcade). 📞 *(206) 682-7181.* 🕐 *6:30am– 6:30pm Mon–Sat, 7am–5pm Sun.* ♿ 🌐 *www.pikeplacefish.com*

A local clown entertaining visitors to Pike Place Market

Upper Post Alley ❷

Stewart to Virginia Sts between Pike Pl & 1st Ave. **Map** 3 B1. 🚌 *15, 18.* ♿

UPPER POST ALLEY has a decidedly European ambience. Along this brickpaved passageway are two of the city's favorite haunts. **The Pink Door** (1919 Post Alley) is an Italian trattoria identified only by an unmarked pink door. Come summer, the restaurant's terrace, with its impressive harbor view, is popular with locals – and tourists who happily stumble upon the elusive restaurant. Across the alley, **Kell's Irish Restaurant and Pub** (1916 Post Alley) pours Guinness and offers live Celtic music in cozy surroundings.

Above the shops of Upper Post Alley are condominiums and apartments, many housing the market's some 500 residents, many of whom are low-income seniors.

Pike Place Starbucks ❸

1912 Pike Pl. **Map** 3 B1. 📞 *(206) 448-8762.* 🚌 *15, 18.* 🕐 *6:30am–7pm Mon–Sat, 7am– 7pm Sun.* ♿

SEATTLE IS SAID to be the most caffeinated city in the US, a distinction Seattleites don't refute. To see where the coffee craze started, visit Pike Place Starbucks, birthplace of the omnipresent chain.

Opened in 1971, Starbucks Coffee, Tea and Spice was named after the first mate in Herman Melville's *Moby Dick*. The company's first logo – a voluptuous two-tailed mermaid encircled by the original name – still greets visitors at this small store.

In the early days, Starbucks did not brew or sell coffee by the cup; the focus then was on selling whole-bean coffee. Occasionally, the young company offered tasting samples in porcelain cups, creating a loyal clientele by educating customers on the finer points of quality coffee. A decade later, in 1982, inspired by the coffee culture of Milan, Italy, Starbucks opened its second location, also in Seattle. Today, visitors to the flagship store can choose from a long list of coffee drinks, as can the millions of other Starbucks customers around the world. Indeed, according to the company, 11 million customers visit Starbucks each week.

Starbucks' original sign, at its first location

The entrance to the Athenian Inn in Pike Place Market

Athenian Inn ❹

1517 Pike Pl (Main Arcade). **Map** 3 C1. 📞 *(206) 624-7166.* 🚌 *15, 18.* 🕐 *6:30am–6:30pm Mon–Sat.* ♿ *1st floor only.*

THE ATHENIAN INN has been in operation nearly as long as the market itself. Opened by three brothers in 1909, it evolved from a bakery and luncheonette to a tavern and, later, a restaurant. It was, in 1933, one of the first restaurants in Seattle to get a liquor license. Neither flashy nor fancy, this diner serves old-time favorites like corned beef hash, accompanied by generous helpings of local color. However, the best reason to visit the Athenian Inn is not for the food but for the view of Elliott Bay. Nab one of the wooden booths at the back of the restaurant and you will see the Duwamish waterway, with its impressive container-ship loading facility; West Seattle; Bainbridge Island; and ferries skimming across the bay.

If the inn seems oddly familiar as you pass by its U-shaped counter, that may be because of its supporting role in the 1993 movie *Sleepless in Seattle*.

The sign for Pike Place Market, high above the market's rooftop

Washington State Ferries Terminal at Pier 52, on Seattle's waterfront

Washington State Ferries Terminal ❺

Pier 52 off Alaskan Way. **Map** 3 C2.
🚌 *15, 18, 21, 22, 56.* 🚊 *Madison.*
Ferry schedules 📞 *(206) 464-6400 (recording).* ♿

BOTH A HIGHLY efficient transit system and a top tourist attraction, Washington State ferries transport 26 million residents and travelers a year. Seattle's main terminal is Colman Dock, located on the waterfront at the foot of Columbia Street.

The original wharf was built in 1882 by Scottish engineer James Colman to accommodate steamships. Destroyed seven year later in the Great Fire, it was immediately rebuilt to service Puget Sound's "mosquito fleet" of private ferries. It was also a bustling hub for ships bound for the northern gold fields during the gold rushes of the 1890s.

In 1908, Colman extended the dock, adding a domed waiting room and a clock tower. The elegant tower toppled four years later when the ocean liner *Alameda* rammed the pier. The tower's replacement met with similar misfortune when it was scorched in a 1914 pier fire.

Although not as architecturally interesting as its predecessors, the present terminal, which was built in 1964, does an admirable job accommodating the many passengers traveling to Bremerton and Bainbridge Island. The terminal also serves foot passengers traveling to Vashon Island.

A popular tourist activity is the 35-minute ferry ride to Winslow on Bainbridge Island, where galleries, shops, restaurants, and a waterfront park are all within walking distance of the ferry dock, making for a pleasant day trip.

The Seattle Aquarium exterior, as seen from the waterfront

Seattle Aquarium ❻

Pier 59 off Alaskan Way. **Map** 3 B1.
📞 *(206) 386-4320.* 🚌 *15, 18, 21, 22, 56.* 🚊 *Pike.* ◯ *Memorial Day–Labor Day: 9:30am–7pm daily; Labor Day–Memorial Day: 9:30am–5pm daily.*
📷 ♿ 🔳 *www.seattleaquarium.org*

ONE OF THE TOP aquariums in the country, the Seattle Aquarium offers a window into Pacific Northwest marine life, showcasing more than 400 species of animals, plants, and mammals indigenous to the area. Playful sea otters and seals cavort in pools; feeding time is especially entertaining.

The world's first aquarium-based salmon ladder – the fish jumping up the rungs to the maturing pond – explains the entire life cycle of the Pacific salmon. The aquarium's Discovery Lab invites children to touch starfish and hermit crabs and to examine live plankton through a high-resolution video microscope.

One of the highlights of the aquarium is its enormous underwater glass dome, surrounding visitors with 400,000 gallons (1,514,160 liters) of water inhabited by sharks, salmon, octopus, and other Puget Sound creatures.

A new exhibit, Life on the Edge, enables visitors to experience the tide-pool life of Washington's wild outer coast and Seattle's inland seas. Staffed by naturalists, the large exhibit pools include special touch zones for hands-on exploration.

The Pacific Coral Reef exhibit highlights reef fish, including sharks, and the complex array of habitats that exist at varying depths of this man-made reef.

Visitors can view kin of the giant eight-legged creatures living in Elliott Bay and Puget Sound in the aquarium's new octopus exhibit. The space is designed to have a beneath-the-dock atmosphere. Visitors look up at the octopus, which, when fully grown, may weigh as much as 100 lb (45 kg), with an arm span of more than 20 ft (6 m).

Sharks and other sea-dwellers on display at the Seattle Aquarium

The Waterfront Streetcar, linking attractions at downtown piers

Seattle IMAX Dome Theater ❼

Pier 59 off Alaskan Way. **Map** 3 B1.
📞 (206) 622-1868. 🚌 15, 18, 21, 22, 56. 🚋 Pike. ◐ 10am–8:30pm daily. ◐ Thanksgiving, Dec 25. ♿ (limited).
🖥 www.seattleimaxdome.com

LOCATED ADJACENT TO the Seattle Aquarium on Pier 59, the IMAX Dome wows visitors with its 3,600-sq-ft (334-sq-m), 180-degree domed screen and dramatic surround sound. The effect is such that viewers feel that they are part of the action – whether it be in the murky depths of the ocean or on the crest of a gigantic wave – rather than mere observers.

The 230-seat theater's long-standing feature film is the Academy Award–nominated *The Eruption of Mount St. Helens,* which takes viewers to the bottom of the crater, showing, in startling detail, the eruption of this volcano on May 18, 1980, and its devastating aftermath (*see pp192–3*). The film plays continuously from 10am onward every day.

For a small additional fee, visitors can also experience one of the other IMAX features showing at the theater. These range from wildlife films, such as those on the North American grizzly and polar bears, to sport action films, such as *Extreme,* showcasing daring athletes as they surf, snowboard, glacier climb, and otherwise stretch the limits of sport – always in spectacular settings.

Ye Olde Curiosity Shop ❽

Pier 54 off Alaskan Way. **Map** 3 C2.
📞 (206) 682-5844. 🚌 15, 18, 21, 22, 56. 🚋 Pike. ◐ 10am–8:30pm daily. ◐ Jan 1, Dec 25. ♿

THE QUINTESSENTIAL curio shop, this Seattle institution has been a fixture of the city's waterfront since 1899. Among the legendary curiosities are shrunken heads, a pig with three tails, and a well-preserved mummy that was discovered in the Arizona desert more than a century ago.

Sign for Ye Olde Curiosity Shop, a Seattle institution since 1899

Minute oddities include the Lord's Prayer engraved on a grain of rice and oil paintings on the heads of pins.

But there is much more to this tightly packed store than quirky curios. From its first days of business, this waterfront shop has been an Indian trading post. Today, Northwest Coast and Alaskan Native Americans continue to sell their crafts through the store which, over the years, has also provided a number of private collections and prestigious museums, including the Smithsonian Institute in Washington, DC, with Native American art and artifacts.

Joseph Edward Standley of Ohio started this family-run shop in 1899 – reportedly earning only 25 cents in the first three days. But Standley persevered. In 1909, he sold his ethnological collection, which had garnered a gold medal at Seattle's World Fair that year, to New York's Museum of the American Indian, for $5,000, establishing the shop with collectors.

IVAR'S ACRES OF CLAMS

A waterfront landmark since 1946, the seafood restaurant Ivar's Acres of Clams on Pier 54 was founded by Seattle-born Ivar Haglund (1905–85), a radio and television personality and self-promoter. Eighteen years before opening his popular restaurant, Haglund established Seattle's first aquarium, also on Pier 54, scooping the "exhibits" out of Puget Sound himself. Wearing his trademark captain's hat, Haglund entertained visitors by singing songs he had written about his favorite sea critters. The aquarium's other attraction was a fish-and-chips counter across from the seal cage. It was the seed for Haglund's foray into the

Hungry visitors and sea gulls – all are welcome at Ivar's

food-service business, an enterprise that grew to include three restaurants, nearly 30 fish bars throughout the Pacific Northwest, and Ivar's own brand of clam chowder. Known for his silly puns ("Keep Clam") remains the company motto) and frequent publicity stunts (he once hoisted a 16-ft/5-m salmon windsock to the flagpole atop stately Smith Tower), Haglund was – and remains – a colorful Seattle icon. Two months after his death in 1985, the city celebrated his 80th birthday with a boat parade in Elliott Bay. And each Independence Day, as Seattleites watch the lavish "Fourth of Jul-Ivar's" fireworks display over the bay, they remember with fondness the "firecracker" who started the tradition back in 1964.

Odyssey Maritime Discovery Center ❾

LOCATED ON THE HISTORIC SEATTLE WATERFRONT, at the Bell Street
Pier, the Odyssey is the US's first maritime discovery center.
Opened in 1998, it has evolved from a small visitor attraction created
by volunteers two decades previously to a popular tourist and educational site. The contemporary museum uses interactive exhibits and
engaging short films to explain how the maritime and fisheries industries contribute to the well-being and economy of the region. While
the entertaining, hands-on exhibits are geared primarily to children,
people of all ages enjoy this cleverly designed museum.

Upper
Level

Harbor Watch
*By using a radar screen or
the binoculars provided, visitors can identify and track
vessels in Elliott Bay while
listening in on US Coast
Guard communications.*

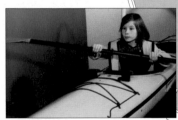

★ Sharing the Sound
*In this exhibit, dedicated to
Puget Sound, visitors can
paddle full-size kayaks
through virtual waters, dock
a small tanker, and learn
about Puget Sound.*

**Main
Entrance**

STAR SIGHTS

★ **Harvesting the Sea**

★ **Ocean Trade**

★ **Sharing the Sound**

Kid Skiff
*Young children can board
this playscape, the Kid Skiff,
put on a lifejacket, and
explore the world of
fishers and the many
different jobs people do
on a fishing boat.*

★ Harvesting the Sea

This gallery brings together information about catching, processing, and selling fish. Highlights include full-size models of the largest fish ever caught and interactive exhibits that invite visitors to experience the lives of crabbers and salmon fishers.

VISITORS' CHECKLIST

Bell St Pier 66, 2205 Alaskan Way. **Map** 3 A1. 📞 *(206) 374-4000.* 🚌 *15, 18, 21, 22, 56.* 🚋 *Bell.* 🕐 *10am–5pm Tue–Sat, noon–5pm Sun.* ⬤ *Mon, Jan 1, day before Thanksgiving, Thanksgiving, Dec 24 & 25.* 🅿 **Exhibits, lectures, films.** 🆆 www.ody.org

Pedal Prop

The Pedal Prop exhibit uses graphics, text, and interactivity to demonstrate the power required to propel a ship through the water. Visitors use foot pedals to spin a propeller that is 10 ft (3 m) in diameter.

GALLERY GUIDE

The center is laid out on two levels. The lower level houses the main galleries which feature hands-on exhibits for children. The upper level contains the Harbor Watch exhibits and offers good views of Elliott Bay.

KEY TO FLOORPLAN

- ☐ Harbor Watch
- ☐ Harvesting the Sea
- ☐ Ocean Trade
- ☐ Waterway
- ☐ Sharing the Sound
- ☐ Waterlink
- ☐ Main entrance hall
- ☐ Nonexhibition space

Lower Level

★ Ocean Trade

This gallery teaches visitors about Puget Sound's ocean trade and about how goods are packed, transported, and shipped. A mini-theater, a radio-controlled tugboat, and photographs bring the exhibits to life.

SEATTLE CENTER AND BELLTOWN

LOCATED NORTH OF downtown, the Seattle Center is the proud legacy of the city's second World's Fair, in 1962. Best known to tourists as the home of the Space Needle, the center boasts numerous cultural venues and excellent museums, including the innovative Experience Music Project, designed by architect Frank Gehry and funded by Microsoft

Hendrix gold record, EMP

billionaire Paul Allen *(see p159)*. Just to the south of the Seattle Center lies trendy Belltown, its hub stretching from Virginia to Vine Streets along 1st Avenue. Here, among the pricey condominiums, visitors will find high-end hair salons, upscale clothing boutiques, antique shops, home accessories stores, trendy restaurants, and a hip dot-com crowd.

SIGHTS AT A GLANCE

Museums and Theaters
Boeing IMAX Theater ❷
Children's Museum ❼
Experience Music Project pp146–7 ❺
Pacific Science Center ❶

Buildings
Austin A. Bell Building ❽
KeyArena ❻
Space Needle ❸
Virginia Inn ❾

Other Attractions
Seattle Monorail ❹

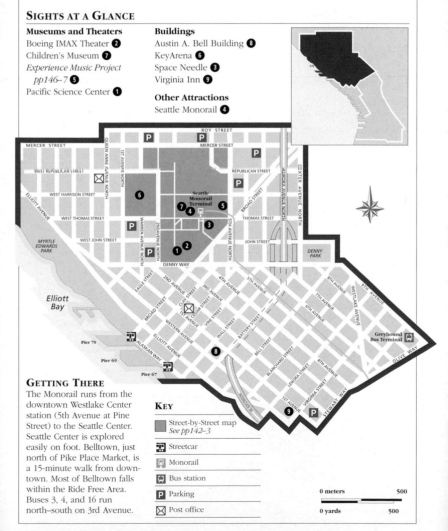

GETTING THERE

The Monorail runs from the downtown Westlake Center station (5th Avenue at Pine Street) to the Seattle Center. Seattle Center is explored easily on foot. Belltown, just north of Pike Place Market, is a 15-minute walk from downtown. Most of Belltown falls within the Ride Free Area. Buses 3, 4, and 16 run north–south on 3rd Avenue.

KEY

	Street-by-Street map See pp142–3
	Streetcar
	Monorail
	Bus station
P	Parking
⊠	Post office

0 meters 500
0 yards 500

◁ **The Space Needle, soaring above Frank Gehry's Experience Music Project building**

Street-by-Street: Seattle Center

THE SEATTLE CENTER GROUNDS have long been a lively gathering spot for city residents and visitors. In the 1800s, this prized parcel of land was the setting for Indian potlatches. In 1962, it was transformed into a fairground for the World's Fair – Century 21 Exposition *(see p145)*. Today, the 74-acre (30-ha) site is one of the most visited urban parks in the US.

Whale tail, *Neototems Children's Garden*

Strolling the pedestrian boulevards, you'll see several legacies of the World's Fair. Among the most notable and noticeable is the Space Needle, which now shares the spotlight with such innovative structures as the Experience Music Project. Performing arts companies, professional sports teams, and a children's museum all call Seattle Center home.

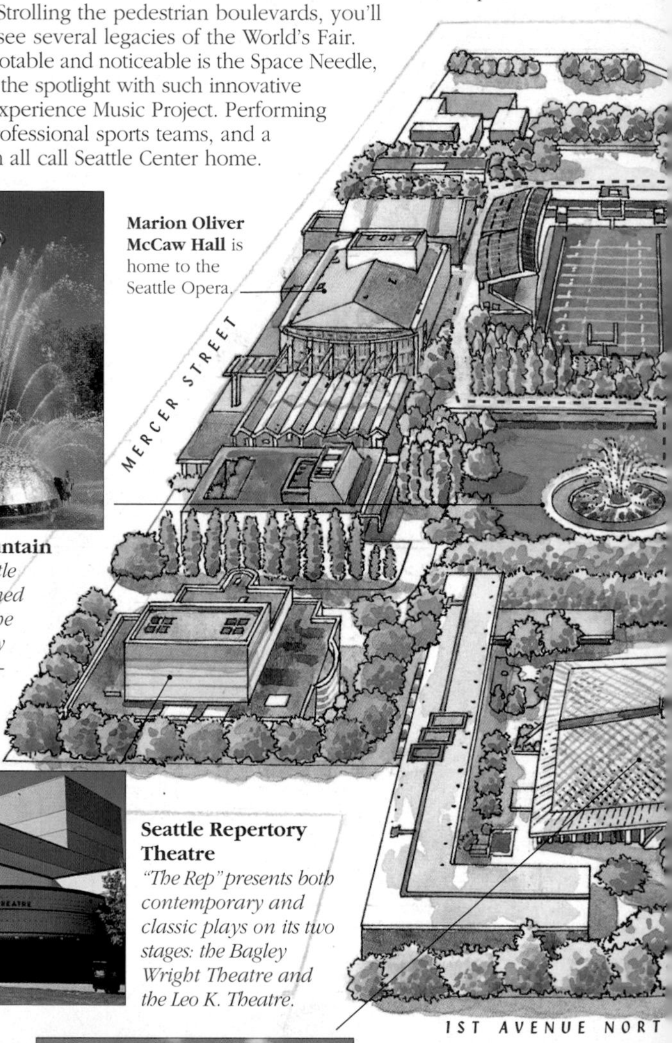

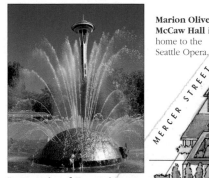

Marion Oliver McCaw Hall is home to the Seattle Opera.

MERCER STREET

International Fountain
At the heart of Seattle Center is a redesigned version (1995) of the fountain created by Shimizu and Kazu- yuki Matsushita for the 1962 World's Fair.

Seattle Repertory Theatre
"The Rep" presents both contemporary and classic plays on its two stages: the Bagley Wright Theatre and the Leo K. Theatre.

1ST AVENUE NORTH

KeyArena
Now a major sports venue, the arena was built in 1962 for Seattle's second World's Fair ❻

KEY

－－－ Suggested route

0 meters   40

0 yards   50

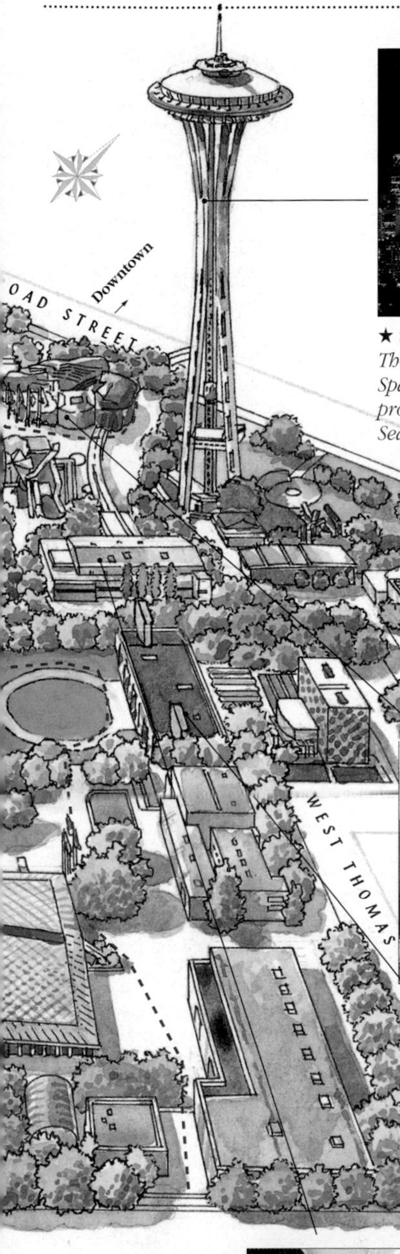

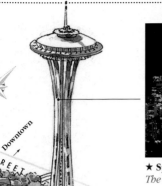

★ Space Needle
The once futuristic Space Needle is a prominent feature of Seattle's skyline ❸

LOCATOR MAP
See Street Finder map 1

Pacific Science Center
Interactive exhibits devoted to science, mathematics, and technology; two IMAX theaters; and a planetarium are housed in the center's five buildings ❶

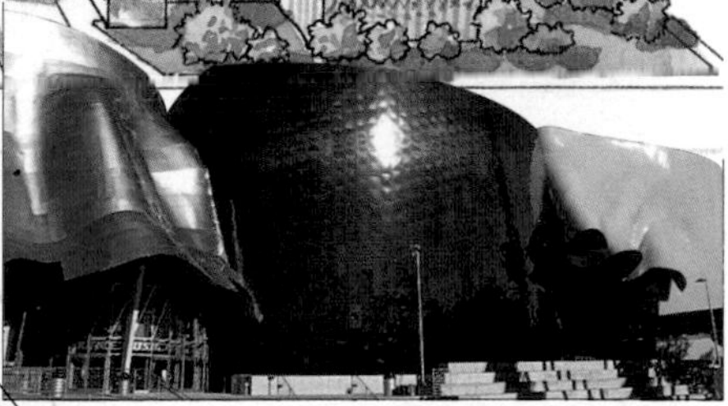

★ Experience Music Project
The concert space at this complex designed by Frank Gehry and known as the Sky Church contains the world's biggest video screen, measuring 40 ft (12 m) by 70 ft (21 m) ❺

Fisher Pavilion, facing the South Fountain Lawn, is a popular venue for trade shows and festivals.

★ Seattle Monorail
The monorail enters a tunnel within the Experience Music Project at the Seattle Center station using a global positioning satellite. The train is cantilevered as it hits the outbound curve ❹

STAR SIGHTS

★ Experience Music Project

★ Seattle Monorail

★ Space Needle

Butterfly murals above the entrance to the Pacific Science Center

Pacific Science Center **❶**

200 2nd Ave N. **Map** 1 B4. **(** *(206) 443-2001.* **🚇** *Seattle Center.* **🚌** *19, 24, 33.* **◯** *10am–5pm Mon–Fri (until 6pm mid-Jun–Labor Day); 10am–6pm Sat–Sun & public hols.* **●** *Thanksgiving, Dec 25.* **📷** *(additional charge for laser & IMAX shows).* **♿** **W** *www.pacsci.org*

A LEGACY OF THE 1962 Seattle World's Fair, the Pacific Science Center's buildings first served as the US Science Pavilion. Designed by Seattle-born Minoru Yamasaki (who also designed New York City's World Trade Center), the complex features six interconnected buildings surrounding five 110-ft (33.5-m) arches that rise majestically over reflecting pools and fountains. Made from white precast concrete, the buildings can perhaps best be described as "modern Gothic."

While enjoyed by all ages, the Pacific Science Center's hands-on science and math exhibits are especially appealing to kids. Among the most popular permanent exhibits are Dinosaurs: A Journey Through Time, which takes visitors back to the Mesozoic Era to meet lifelike robotic dinosaurs. In Body Works, visitors can test their reaction time or pedal the Calorie Bicycle to see how much energy they produce. In Tech Zone, they can challenge an industrial robot to a game of tic-tac-toe. Especially popular

with youngsters is the Kids Works exhibit, which allows budding meteorologists to see themselves on television.

In 1998, two new exhibits opened: Insect Village, which features huge robotic insects, as well as a mini-zoo, where brave visitors can touch a hissing cockroach or look a hairy tarantula in the eye, and the Tropical Butterfly House, inhabited by exotic free-flying butterflies.

The fun continues outside, where visitors can spin a 2-ton granite ball or ride the High Rail Bicycle perched 15 ft (4.5 m) above the ground on a one-inch (2.5-cm) rail. A planetarium, laser theater, and two IMAX theaters round out the Pacific Science Center's offerings.

Boeing IMAX Theater **❷**

200 2nd Ave N at Pacific Science Center. **Map** 1 C4. **(** *(206) 443-4629.* **🚇** *Seattle Center.* **🚌** *19, 24, 33.* **◯** *Jan–mid-Jun: 10am–5pm Mon–Fri, 10am–6pm Sat–Sun; mid-Jun–Labor Day: 10am–6pm daily; Labor Day–Dec 24: 10am–5pm Mon–Fri, 10am–6pm Sat–Sun; Dec 26–31:10am–6pm daily.* **●** *Thanksgiving, Dec 25.* **📷** **♿** **🖥**

R ESEMBLING A GIANT white orb, the 400-seat Boeing IMAX Theater was added to the Pacific Science Center campus in 1998. Designed by French architect Denis Laming, considered the "father of futuristic architecture" in France, it features a mammoth screen six stories tall and 80 ft (24 m) wide, as well as dramatic digital surround sound. The theater shows both regular IMAX and IMAX 3D films. Recent offerings included *Space Station 3D,* the first 3D space film.

The Boeing IMAX Theater, with its distinctive domed exterior

The magnificent Space Needle, the pride of Seattle

Space Needle **❸**

400 Broad St. **Map** 1 C4. **(** *(206) 905-2100.* **🚇** *Seattle Center.* **🚌** *3, 4, 16.* **◯** *Memorial Day–Labor Day: 8am–midnight daily; Labor Day–Memorial Day: 10am–10pm Sun–Thu, 10am–midnight Fri–Sat.* **♿** **🍴** **W** *www.spaceneedle.com*

W HAT STARTED AS a rough sketch on the back of a paper placemat has become Seattle's internationally recognized landmark and number one tourist attraction. Built for the 1962 World's Fair, the 605-ft (185-m) Space Needle was the brainchild of Edward Carlson, the fair's chairman, who was inspired by Germany's Stuttgart Tower. The final design by John Graham and Company, architects of the first shopping mall in the US, was approved just 18 months before the fair's opening date; the Space Needle was built in 12 months, for a relatively inexpensive $4.5 million. At the time, it was the tallest building west of the Mississippi River.

Supported by three curved steel legs, the needle's glass-enclosed tophouse features an observation deck and, below it, a revolving restaurant – the second in the world – turned by a one-and-a-half-horsepower motor.

The underground foundation, buried 30 ft (8 m) deep and stretching 120 ft (37 m) wide, took 467 cement trucks to fill – a mission that was accomplished in less than 12 hours. The tower is attached to the foundation with 72 30-ft- (9-m-) long bolts.

Solidly constructed, the Space Needle has weathered several earthquakes and has closed fewer than ten times in its four-decade history because of high winds. (While the structure itself can withstand winds up to 200 mph [322 km/h], its elevators can't.)

During the Seattle World's Fair, nearly 20,000 people a day rode the high-speed elevators to the top, enduring waits of up to three hours for the 43-second ride. Thankfully, the wait is much shorter today, and the view just as spectacular. Weather permitting, visitors can enjoy panoramic views of the Olympic and Cascade mountain ranges, Mount Rainier, Lake Union, Elliott Bay, and downtown Seattle.

In 1982, a "skyline level" was added 100 ft (30 m) above the ground. In 1999, on its 37th birthday, the Space Needle was proclaimed the city's official landmark by Seattle's Landmarks Preservation Board. And in 2000, a $20 million revitalization included construction of a glass pavilion, which encircles the base of the tower.

Seattle Monorail pulling into the Space Needle terminal

Seattle Monorail ●

Stations at Westlake Center (5th Ave & Pine St) & at Seattle Center (across from Space Needle). **Map** 1 C4–3 C1. **C** (206) 905-2620. ○ 7:30am–11pm Mon–Fri, 9am–11pm Sat–Sun; departs every 10 mins. 🍴 ♿ W www.seattlemonorail.com

B UILT FOR Seattle's second World's Fair in only ten months, its foundations

buried 25 ft (7.5 m) below street level, Seattle's Alweg monorail provided a link between the fairgrounds (now the Seattle Center) and downtown Seattle. At the time, it was described as a preview of the mass transit system of the future. Indeed, it was the first full-scale monorail system for mass transit in an urban center. Traveling between downtown and the foot of the Space Needle, the Monorail's high-speed trains carried 8 million passengers during the fair's six-month duration.

Today, this "futuristic" transit system is used by 2.5 million passengers per year, many of them locals who ride the Monorail to festivals, concerts, and sporting events at the Seattle Center. The fastest full-sized monorail system in the US, the Seattle Monorail covers the 1.2-mile (2-km) distance in 90 seconds, at a speed of up to 60 miles (97 km) per hour, zipping through the Experience Music Project, which was built around and over the Monorail's tracks.

SEATTLE WORLD'S FAIR

Officially known as the Century 21 Exposition, Seattle's second World's Fair was conceived as a way to commemorate the 50th anniversary of the Alaska-Yukon-Pacific Exposition held here in 1909. Billed as "America's Space Age World's Fair," the new exposition was dedicated to science and life in the 21st century. Ambitious plans and a desire to design a civic center that would be enjoyed by the community for generations to come pushed the original opening date back a few years, from 1959 to 1962.

Among the fair's most ambitious buildings and lasting legacies are the Space Needle, the Monorail, the US Science Pavilion (now the Pacific Science Center), and the Washington State Coliseum (now KeyArena). Designed to appear futuristic, in keeping with the Century 21 theme, the buildings now have a rather retro appeal, especially the Space Needle.

The fair drew 9,634,600 people. Today, more than four decades later, Seattleites and tourists continue to flock to the Seattle Center to enjoy a festival, cultural performance, or sporting event; visit a museum; or simply stroll the tree-lined, fountain-filled grounds.

Seattle's towering Space Needle under construction in 1961

The Space Needle's observation deck, offering stunning views

Experience Music Project [5]

OPENED IN 2000, the Experience Music Project (EMP) celebrates the past, present, and future of music, with rare memorabilia, interactive exhibits, a dynamic ride-like attraction, and live performance space – all housed in an exuberant structure that swoops and swirls at the base of the Space Needle. Designed by Frank Gehry, an architect with a penchant for atypical shapes and angles, innovative building materials, and bold colors, the building is said to resemble a smashed electric guitar. EMP was conceived by Microsoft cofounder Paul Allen *(see p159)* and his sister Jody Patton as a way to share with the public Allen's enormous collection of Jimi Hendrix artifacts. The vision broadened into creating a destination that would capture the essence of rock 'n' roll from its early roots to its later influences.

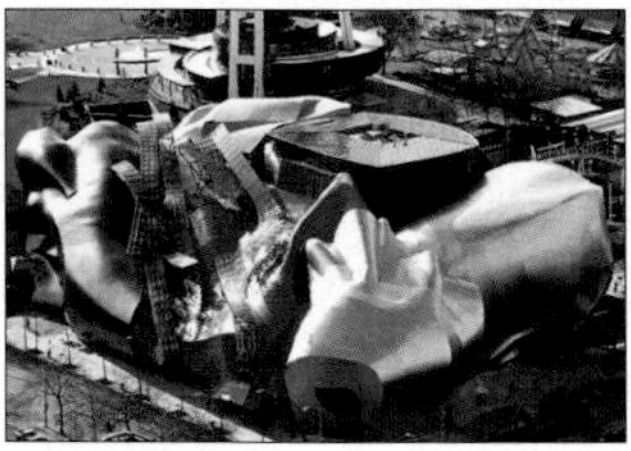

The Building
From the air, the seemingly random jumble of shapes and tortured metal designed by architect Frank Gehry takes form as the carcass of a smashed guitar.

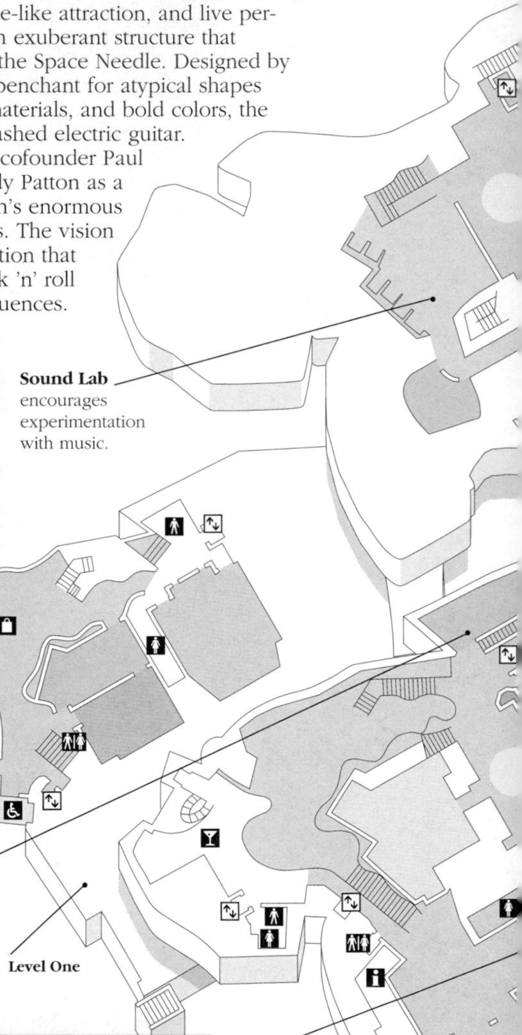

Sound Lab encourages experimentation with music.

The Northwest Passage exhibit explores the history of music in Seattle, including the evolution of jazz and rhythm and blues, the rise of punk, grunge, and hip-hop, and a retrospective on the riot grrrl movement.

Main Entrance

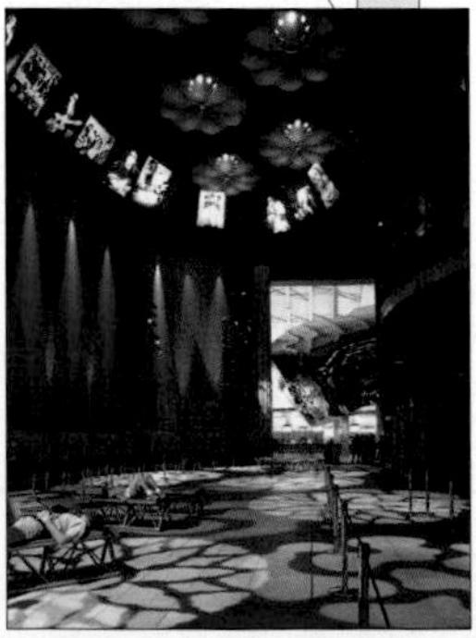

★ Sky Church
The "heart and soul" of EMP, this great hall is used as a performance space. Video screens, including the world's largest indoor one, and a state-of-the-art sound system enhance the many concerts held here.

STAR SIGHTS

- **★ Guitar Gallery**
- **★ Hendrix Gallery**
- **★ Milestones**
- **★ Sky Church**

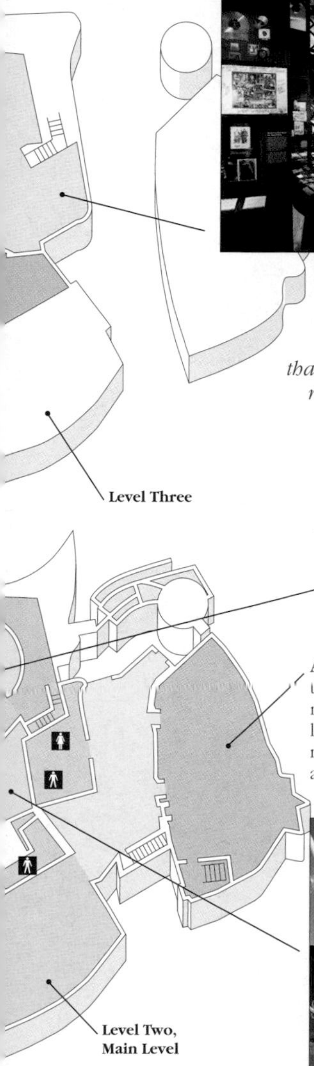

VISITORS' CHECKLIST

325 5th Ave N. **Map** 1 C4.
📞 *(206) 367-5483.* 🚉 *Seattle Center.* 🚌 *3, 4, 16.*
⏰ *Memorial Day–Labor Day: 9am–6pm Sun–Thu, 9am–9pm Fri–Sat; Labor Day–Memorial Day: 10am–5pm Sun–Thu, 10am–9pm Fri–Sat.* ● *Thanksgiving, Dec 25.* 🎟 🚫 ♿ 🎧
🍴 🍷 W www.emplive.com

★ **Milestones**
Musical milestones are celebrated in this space, along with the movements that made music history – from rhythm and blues to hip-hop.

Level Three

★ **Guitar Gallery**
In this gallery, famous guitars are on display, including one that belonged to Eddie van Halen.

Artist's Journey features exhibits that celebrate American popular music. It combines film, theatrical lighting, audio, special effects, and motion technology to offer visitors a unique musical experience.

🚶 🚶

🚶

Level Two, Main Level

MUSEUM GUIDE
EMP has three levels. The main galleries and exhibits are on Levels Two and Three. The lower level offers a theater for lectures, films, and classes; a digital lab offering access to the EMP digital collection; and a restaurant that serves regional American cuisine.

★ **Hendrix Gallery**
In this space devoted to the genius of Jimi Hendrix, exhibits trace his development as a virtuoso musician and highlight the influences that inspired him.

KEY TO FLOORPLAN

- ☐ Milestones
- ☐ On Stage
- ☐ Sound Lab
- ☐ Demo Lab
- ☐ Compaq Digital Lab
- ☐ JBL Theater
- ☐ Learning Labs
- ☐ Northwest Passage
- ☐ Play On
- ☐ Hendrix Gallery
- ☐ Artist's Journey lobby
- ☐ Artist's Journey
- ☐ Sky Church
- ☐ Special exhibits gallery
- ☐ Guitar Gallery
- ☐ Roots and Branches
- ☐ Nonexhibition space

KeyArena ❻

305 Harrison St. **Map** 1 B4.
📞 *(206) 684-7200.* **Event tickets**
📞 *(206) 733-9200.* 🅿 *Seattle
Center.* 🚍 *1, 2, 13, 14, 15, 18.* ♿
See **Shopping in Seattle** *p160.*

I N ITS FIRST LIFE, KeyArena
was the Washington State
Coliseum, offering Seattle
World's Fair visitors a glimpse
into the 21st century. Hailed
as an architectural masterpiece in 1962 for its shape
(a hyperbolic paraboloid)
and lack of interior roof
supports, this 4-acre (1.5-ha)
structure at the western end
of the Seattle Center was
designed by Paul Thiry (1904–
93), main architect of Seattle's
second World's Fair *(see p145),*
to last well into the 21st century as a sports and convention facility. Fairgoers fondly
recall the coliseum's giant glass
Bubbleator, which transported
150 passengers at one time
high up into the World of
Tomorrow exhibit.

After the fair, the futuristic
building was converted into a
sports arena. In 1964, it hosted
the Beatles' first Seattle concert and, since then, has
become one of the top big-
ticket concert venues on the
country's west coast.

In 1995, architectural firm
NBBJ led a $74 million renova-
tion in which the interior was
completely remodeled – the
plastic, wood, steel, copper,
and concrete from the gutted
interior either recycled in the
renovation or sold. Renamed,
the 17,000-seat KeyArena is
now home to Seattle's men's
and women's professional
basketball teams – the Super-
Sonics and the Storm – and the
Thunderbirds, a minor-league
hockey team, and a favored
venue for entertainment acts.

**A tricycle exhibit in Seattle's
Children's Museum**

Children's
Museum ❼

305 Harrison St. **Map** 1 B4.
📞 *(206) 441-1768.* ⏰ *10am–5pm
Mon–Fri, 10am–6pm Sat–Sun.*
● *Jan 1, Thanksgiving, Dec 25.*
🅿 *Seattle Center.* 🚍 *1, 2, 13, 14,
15, 18.* ♿ 🚻
🌐 *www.thechildrensmuseum.org*

W HILE THE ENTIRE Seattle
Center is a delight for
kids, the Children's Museum,
founded in 1979 by parents
and educators, is especially
popular with youngsters.
Located on the first level of
the Seattle Center's Center
House, the nonprofit
interactive museum features
eight permanent galleries,
one temporary gallery, and
three studio spaces.

Permanent exhibits include
Global Village, which intro-
duces young visitors to the cultures and lifestyles of contemporary Ghana, Japan, and the
Philippines. In the Mountain
Forest exhibit, kids learn about
Washington's natural environment as they hike through a
re-creation of a Pacific Northwest forest, complete with a

bat-inhabited cave, a waterfall, and flowing lava.

Pulleys, pipes, mazes, and
levers challenge hand-eye
coordination in Cog City. The
Time Trek exhibit allows
young visitors to experience
cooking over a fire as done
by the Mayans, riding in a
Chinese chariot of the Shang
Dynasty (1766–1027 BC),
and selecting a jury in
ancient Greece, the birthplace of modern democracy.
The museum also has an
interactive exhibit designed
especially for toddlers.

Three to four changing
exhibits throughout the year
guarantee that there is always
something new to see. The
museum also features an
artist-in-residence and drop-in
arts studio for kids – the first
of its kind in the region.

**Brick façade of the Austin A. Bell
Building, with its Gothic features**

Austin A. Bell
Building ❽

2326 1st Ave. **Map** 1 C5.
🚍 *15, 18, 21, 22, 56.* ● *to public.*

T HE AUSTIN A. BELL Building
was designed by Elmer
Fisher, Seattle's foremost commercial architect at the end of
the 19th century and designer
of more than 50 buildings in
the years surrounding the
Great Fire of 1889. While
most were in Pioneer Square,
including the still-standing
Pioneer Building *(see p124),* a
few Fisher-designed structures
graced the Belltown (then
Denny Hill) area, chief among
them this building.

The unique geometric roof of KeyArena, Seattle's central sports stadium

Combining Richardsonian, Gothic, and Italianate design elements, the handsome four-story brick structure was commissioned in 1888 by Austin Americus Bell, the wealthy son of Seattle pioneer William M. Bell, for whom Belltown is named. It was to be an apartment building and the young Bell's first major building project in the city. The 35-year-old entrepreneur did not live to see his building completed. Suffering from ill health and depression, Bell took his own life in 1889. His wife saw the project through to completion, and had Bell's name etched into the top of the building's façade. Its interior was destroyed by fire in 1981, but the exterior survived relatively unscathed.

Listed on the National Register of Historic Places, the Austin A. Bell Building now houses pricey condominiums on its upper three floors, a coffee shop and an upscale restaurant at street level.

The European-style Virginia Inn, a favorite pub among Belltown locals

Virginia Inn 9

1937 1st Ave. **Map** 3 B1.
 (206) 728-1937. 15, 18, 21, 22, 56. 11:30am–midnight Sun–Thu, 11:30am–2am Fri–Sat.

Located on the southern boundary of Belltown, the Virginia Inn has been a popular watering hole since before the area came to be called Belltown. Established nearly a century ago, it has operated continuously, first as a beer parlor for waterfront workers, right through the Prohibition period (1920–33), when it served as a cardroom and lunch spot.

In the 1970s, the pub began to attract an arty clientele, who joined the old-timers at the long elegant bar. Today, in keeping with the area's tradition of community spirit, the old-timers are acknowledged with special treatment of a sort: the price of their pints of beer has held steady at $1.25 since the current owners took over management of the pub in 1981. The Virginia Inn has since become known as Seattle's hottest art bar, with rotating exhibits by local artists adorning the walls.

A good place to sample a local microbrew (or one from its good selection of Belgian beers) and a tune from the juke box, the brick-and-tile Virginia Inn has something of a European feel to it – without the cigarette fumes, thanks to the pub's strict no-smoking policy.

A café-cum-laundromat, one of Belltown's many eclectic businesses

BELLTOWN HISTORY

With its broad avenues lined with hip clubs, chic restaurants, and eclectic shops, Belltown has been compared to Manhattan's Upper West Side. What Belltown conspicuously lacks is the one thing for which the rest of the city is famous: hills. This was not always the case. Originally home to a very steep slope, the area took on a new identity between 1905 and 1930 when Denny Hill was regraded and washed into Elliott Bay. In all, more than 50 city blocks were lowered by as much as 100 ft (30 m), turning Denny Hill into the Denny Regrade, a lackluster name for an unremarkable area of town inhabited by labor union halls, car lots, inexpensive apartments, and sailors' taverns. (Ironically, the intent of the regrade project was to encourage business development by making the area easier to navigate.)

For decades, the area's identity was its very lack thereof. This began to change in the 1970s when artists, attracted by cheap rents and abundant studio space, started moving to the Regrade. It was also during the 1970s that a neighborhood association renamed the area Belltown, after William M. Bell, one of the area's pioneers. By the 1980s, as Seattleites and suburbanites began taking an interest in cosmopolitan urban living, condominiums began appearing on Belltown's periphery. Fueled by the software boom of the 1990s, the area experienced a huge building boom, attracting well-paid high-tech types to its amenity-rich towers. Although today Belltown bears little resemblance to its early days, a few original structures remain; among them the Virginia Inn and the Austin A. Bell Building.

Belltown coffee shop sign

FARTHER AFIELD

SEATTLE'S OUTLYING AREAS offer plenty of opportunities for exploration and recreation. Immediately to the south sit two spectacular professional sports stadiums – the pride and joy of the US Northwest's baseball and football fans. To the east, two of Seattle's prominent hills, First and Capitol, offer notable museums, grand cathedrals, and an eclectic assortment of shops and restaurants. For active outdoor pursuits, Green Lake, Discovery Park, and Alki Beach all feature paths for strolling, jogging, biking, rollerblading, or hiking. Those wanting to go the distance can opt for the Burke-Gilman Trail, stretching from Fremont to Kenmore. The city is also home to Woodland Park Zoo, one of the top zoos in the US, and the University of Washington, the heart of the University District. Other Seattle neighborhoods, such as Ballard, Fremont, and Madison Park, each with its own distinct character, are ideal destinations for a day trip.

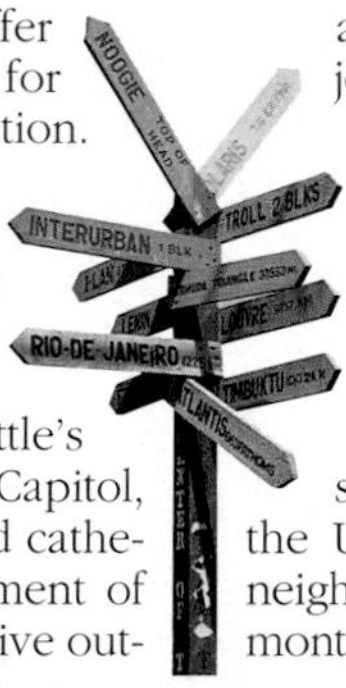

Signpost in Fremont

SIGHTS AT A GLANCE

Neighborhoods
Ballard [13]
Capitol Hill [4]
First Hill [3]
Fremont [12]
Madison Park [7]
University District [6]

Parks, Gardens, and Zoos
Alki Beach [15]
Burke-Gilman Trail [8]
Discovery Park [14]
Gas Works Park [9]
Green Lake [10]
Volunteer Park [5]
Woodland Park Zoo pp156–7 [11]

Sports Stadiums
Safeco Field [1]
Seahawks Stadium [2]

KEY

Central Seattle

Urban area

Major highway

Highway

Major road

5 miles = 8 km

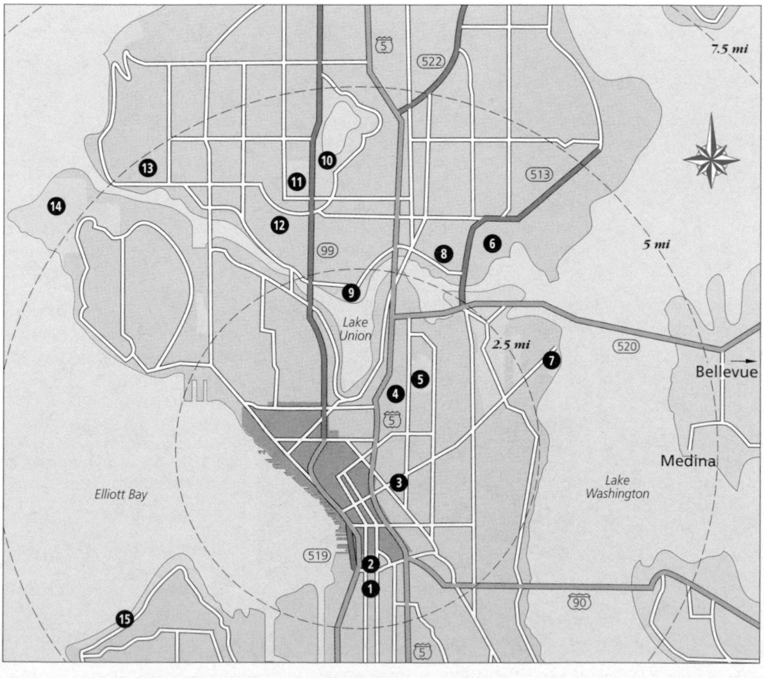

◁ **View of Puget Sound from the beach at Discovery Park, looking south**

Safeco Field ❶

S Atlantic St & 1st Ave S. **Map** 4 D5.
☎ *(206) 346-4000.* 🚍 *15, 18.*
🕐 *Apr–Oct: 10:30am, 12:30pm,
2:30pm daily (except days of afternoon
games; no 2:30pm tour on days of
evening games); Nov–Mar: 12:30pm
& 2:30pm Tue–Sun.* 🅿️ ♿

ALTHOUGH SEATTLE is a rainy
city, Seattle baseball fans
have not endured the disap-
pointment of a rainout since
the American League's Seattle
Mariners christened Safeco
Field on July 15, 1999. Its size
is impressive, encompassing
nearly 20 acres (8 ha) and
seating over 47,000 fans, who
enter the stadium through the
curved entranceway, behind
the field's home plate.

The stadium's state-of-the-
art retractable roof can cover
the playing field with a simple
push of a button. This massive
9-acre (3.5-ha) roof contains
enough steel to build a skyscraper 55 stories tall. Utility
came with a hefty price tag,
however – an unprecedented
$516 million. Designed by the
Seattle firm NBBJ and completed in 1999, Safeco Field
became the nation's most
expensive stadium ever built.

With its sweeping views of
the Seattle skyline, $1.3 mil-
lion in public art, and such
amenities as a children's play-
field and picnic patio, Safeco
Field provides an excellent
atmosphere in which to
watch a Major League ball-
game. While many games are
sold out, tourists may visit the
stadium by taking one of the
regularly scheduled tours.

Seahawks Stadium ❷

800 Occidental Ave S. **Map** 4 D4.
☎ *(206) 381-7555.* 🚍 *15, 18.*
🕐 *12:30pm & 2:30pm daily (except
days of major events).* **Events** ☎
(206) 381-7582. 🅿️ ♿
🌐 www.stadium.org

THE DESIGNERS of Seahawks
Stadium, which opened July
2002, were intent on factoring
the city's often inclement winter weather into its design. So
despite the harsh winds and
rains associated with winter
in Seattle, Seahawks Stadium
(named for its chief residents,
the National Football League's
Seattle Seahawks) was left
roofless. The end result is a
spacious, open-air stadium
with unobstructed views of
the Seattle skyline. With two
massive 760-ft (232-m) eaves,
nearly 70 percent of the 67,000
spectator seats are shielded
from falling rain. Some visiting
teams unfamiliar with Pacific
Northwest weather, however,
have found it to be an inhospitable environment.

Just as the stadium design
by Minneapolis-based Ellerbe
Becket is unconventional, so,
too, is the mix of art scattered
throughout the stadium, which
draws visitors from around
the world. Especially striking
are the four Native American–
inspired steel discs by New
Mexican artist Bob Haozous,
on the stadium's north tower.
The discs, each 24 ft (7 m)
in diameter, represent people's
interaction with and connection to the earth and nature.

**Entrance and rotunda of the
Frye Art Museum on First Hill**

First Hill ❸

Bounded by E Pike St, E Yesler Way,
12th Ave E & I-5. **Map** 4 E1.
🚍 *3, 4, 12.*

NICKNAMED PILL HILL for its
several hospitals and
numerous doctors' offices,
First Hill lies just east of downtown. A pedestrian-friendly
district (more than 40 percent
of its residents walk to work),
First Hill was Seattle's first
neighborhood, home to the
city's pioneer families. It still
boasts a number of the original mansions from Seattle's
earliest days.

First Hill's most recogniz-
able landmark is **St. James
Cathedral** (804 9th Avenue),
a parish church and the cathedral of the Catholic Archdio-
cese of Seattle. Designed by
the New York firm Heins and
LaFarge, the Italian Renaissance
structure dating to 1907 features two tall spires, which
are illuminated at night.

One block southeast of St.
James Cathedral, the **Frye Art
Museum** showcases the extensive art collection of Seattle
pioneers Charles and Emma
Frye, which features 19th- and
20th-century French, German,
and American paintings. Temporary exhibitions are held
throughout the year.

🏛 **Frye Art Museum**
704 Terry Ave. ☎ *(206) 622-9250.*
🕐 *10am–5pm Tue–Wed & Fri–Sat,
10am–8pm Thu, noon–5pm Sun.*
⬤ *Mon, Jan 1, Jul 4, Thanksgiving,
Dec 25.* 🅿️ ♿ 🖥 📷
🌐 www.fryeart.org

The brick and steel façade of Safeco Field, home of the Seattle Mariners

Capitol Hill 4

Bounded by Montlake Blvds E & NE, E Pike & E Madison Sts, 23rd Ave E & I-5. **Map** 2 F5. 🚌 *7, 9, 10.*

NORTHEAST OF downtown, lively Capitol Hill is a colorful and diverse urban neighborhood where no one blinks at spiked purple hair and multiple body piercings.

The district's commercial hub and major avenue is Broadway (East Roy to East Pike Streets). Referred to as the "living room of Capitol Hill," it offers shopping (from books to home accessories to vintage clothing), a number of ethnic restaurants, and bronze footsteps embedded in the sidewalk to teach passersby the tango and fox trot.

While people-watching is a major source of entertainment, Capitol Hill also features two vintage movie houses: the **Egyptian** (804 East Pine Street) and the **Harvard Exit** (807 East Roy Street). Both theaters specialize in independent and foreign films.

The hill is also home to **St. Mark's Episcopal Cathedral** (1245 10th Avenue East) (1931), belonging to the Diocese of Olympia. It is known for its magnificent Flentrop organ, installed in 1965 and consisting of 3,944 pipes that range in size from 1 inch (2.5 cm) to 32 ft (9.7 m).

The internationally acclaimed **Cornish College of the Arts** (710 East Roy Street) features a full roster of student exhibits and performances.

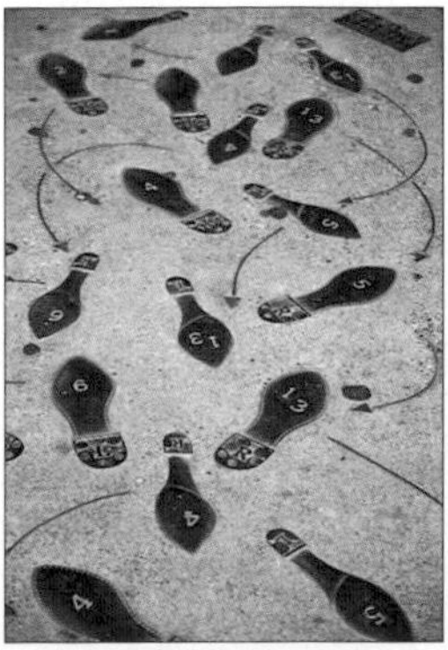

***Dance Steps on Broadway*, by Jack Mackie, in Capitol Hill**

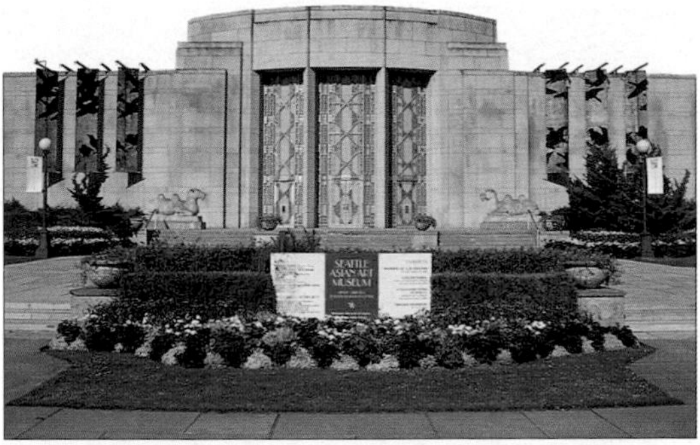

Volunteer Park's Seattle Asian Art Museum, in an historic Art Deco building

Volunteer Park 5

1247 15th Ave E. ☎ *(206) 684-4075.* 🚌 *7, 9, 10.* 🕐 *6am–11pm.*

LOCATED AT the north end of Capitol Hill, elegant Volunteer Park was designed in 1904–1909 by the Olmsted Brothers, the US's most famous landscape-architecture firm. The 48-acre (19.5-ha) park is named for the Seattle men who enlisted to fight in the Spanish-American War of 1898.

The Olmsteds' design called for an observation tower. The city obliged by building a 75-ft (23-m) brick water tower with an observation deck open to the public. A steep climb up the 106-step spiral staircase rewards visitors with spectacular views of the Space Needle, Puget Sound, and the Olympic mountain range.

A children's playground, wading pool, tennis courts, and bandstand make the park a favorite outing for families.

Volunteer Park is the site of the **Seattle Asian Art Museum**, located in a 1933 Art Deco building which formerly housed the Seattle Art Museum *(see pp128–9)*. The Seattle Asian Art Museum's renowned collection includes works from Japan, Korea, China, and Southeast Asia.

Highlights of the rotating collection include wood and lacquer furniture from imperial China and 14th-century Chinese sculpture. Other gems of the collection are the Korean ceramics and metalware, and bronze figures of Buddha and Bodhisattva that date back to the country's Unified Shilla dynasty (57–935).

Across from the museum is the **Volunteer Park Conservatory**, home to illegally imported plants confiscated by US customs. The conservatory consists of five houses. Four showcase bromeliads, palms, ferns, and cacti, respectively. The seasonal display house includes lilies, poinsettias, azaleas, and an European olive tree.

🏛 Seattle Asian Art Museum
1400 E Prospect St. ☎ *(206) 654-3100.* 🕐 *Memorial Day–Labor Day: 10am–5pm Tue–Wed, & Fri–Sun, 10am–9pm Thu; Labor Day–Memorial Day: 10am–5pm Wed & Fri–Sun, 10am–9pm Thu.* ● *Jan 1, Labor Day, Thanksgiving, Dec 25.* $ *by donation; free 1st Thu & Sat of month.* ♿ 🛍
[W] www.seattleartmuseum.org

🏛 Volunteer Park Conservatory
1400 E Galer St. ☎ *(206) 684-4743.* 🕐 *Memorial Day–Labor Day: 10am–7pm daily; Labor Day–Memorial Day: 10am–4pm daily.*
[W] www.cityofseattle.net/parks/parkspaces/volunteer

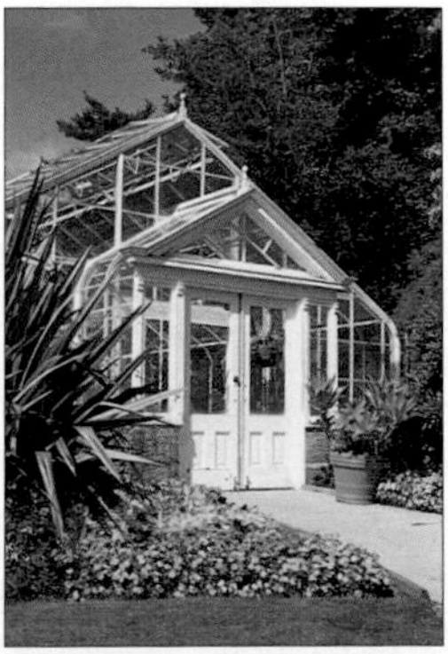

Summer flowers in one of the several gardens at Volunteer Park

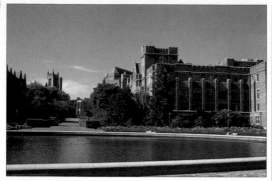

The University of Washington campus, with its mix of architectural styles

University District ❻

Bounded by NE 55th St, Portage Bay, Montlake Blvd NE & I-5. 🚌 *7, 25, 43, 70, 71, 72, 73.* ℹ️ *4014 University Way NE, (206) 543-9198.* 🕐 *8am–5pm Mon–Fri.*

Eclectic and energetic thanks to the vibrant youth culture surrounding a major university campus, the University District makes for an interesting half- or full-day excursion. The hub of the district is the University of Washington. The premier institution of higher learning in the Northwest US, this university is internationally known for its excellent research and graduate programs.

Located on the site of the 1909 World's Fair, the beautiful 693-acre (280-ha) parklike campus is home to more than 35,000 students and 218 buildings in a mix of architectural styles. Just inside the main campus entrance is the **Burke Museum of Natural History and Culture**, featuring dinosaur fossils and a notable collection of Northwest Native art. On the western edge of the campus sits the **Henry Art Gallery**, the first public art museum in the state of Washington. The museum has a special focus on photography and digital and projected media.

The university's main avenue is **University Way Northeast**, known to locals as "The Ave." Located just west of campus, it is lined with bookstores, pubs, inexpensive restaurants, and

shops. At the opposite end of the spectrum, University Village, located east of the campus, offers an upscale shopping and dining experience.

A must-see, especially spring through autumn, is the **Washington Park Arboretum**, a 230-acre (93-ha) garden and living plant museum, with 4,600 species, including 139 on the endangered list. The arboretum also features a Japanese garden with sculptures, carp-filled ponds, and an authentic teahouse open for ceremonies once a month.

Neo-gothic building, university campus

🏛 Burke Museum of Natural History and Culture

NE 45th St & 17th Ave NE. 📞 *(206) 543-5590.* 🕐 *10am–5pm daily, 10am–8pm 1st Thu of month.* 🔴 *Jan 1, Jul 4, Thanksgiving, Dec 25.* 🎟️ *(free 1st Thu of month; separate adm to some exhibits).* ♿ 🖼 🎁 🅿️ 🌐 *www.washington.edu/burkemuseum*

🏛 Henry Art Gallery

NE 41st St & 15th Ave NE. 📞 *(206) 543-2280.* 🕐 *11am–5pm Tue–Wed & Fri–Sun, 11am–8pm Thu.* 🔴 *Mon, Jan 1, Jul 4, Thanksgiving, Dec 24 & 25.* 🎟️ *(free 5–8pm Thu).* ♿ 🎁 *for groups.* 🖼 🎁 🅿️ 🌐 *www.henryart.org*

🌺 Washington Park Arboretum

2300 Arboretum Dr E. 📞 *(206) 543-8800.* **Visitors' center** 🕐 *10am–4pm.* **Grounds** 🔴 *7am–dusk.* 🎟️ *to Japanese Garden.* ♿ 🖼 🌐 *www.depts.washington.edu/wpa*

Madison Park ❼

Bounded by E Madison St, Lake Washington Blvd & Lake Washington. 🚌 *11.*

Seattle's lakeside community of Madison Park is one of the city's most affluent. Its tree-shaded streets, lined with charming older homes, most built between 1910 and 1930, are ideal for leisurely strolling.

The area was established in the early 1860s when Judge John J. McGilvra purchased 420 acres (170 ha) of land, cutting a road through the forest from downtown Seattle to his property, which was later named Madison Street after former US President James Madison (1751–1836). In the 1880s, McGilvra divided his land into lots, decreeing that only "cottages" could be built on them. He also set aside 24 acres (10 ha) for public use. This parcel of land is now known as Madison Park. By the end of the 19th century, this park had become the most popular beach in the city, complete with an ornate boathouse, piers, a wooden promenade, a greenhouse, and floating bandstands. Reminiscent of a friendly village, the neighborhood's commercial area today offers a number of popular restaurants, upscale boutiques, and home accessories shops.

Children playing on Madison Park's sandy lakeside beach

Burke-Gilman Trail ⑧

Numerous access points; main access point at Gas Works Park. ⊟ 25, 43.

WHEN THE SUN comes out in Seattle, cyclists, speed-walkers, joggers, rollerbladers, and lovers of the outdoors flock to the scenic Burke-Gilman Trail. Built on an old railway bed, this 12-mile (19-km) paved trail is used by more than one million people each year. It is both a popular recreation corridor and a pleasant, automobile-free commuter route for residents.

Although the Burke-Gilman Trail was recently extended west through Fremont (see p158) to 8th Avenue North-west, it officially begins at Gas Works Park, at the north end of Lake Union. From there, it follows the shores of Lake Washington, beginning at the University of Washington and extending all the way to the city of Kenmore, where it connects with the Sammamish River Trail.

A warning to pedestrians: bicyclists comprise roughly 80 percent of all trail users, making attentiveness and keeping to the right-hand side a must.

Gas Works Park ⑨

2101 N Northlake Way. [(206) 684-4075. ⊟ 26. ○ 4am–11:30pm daily.

HUGE RUSTY PIPES and pieces of decrepit machinery aren't typically found in a park. But Gas Works Park on Lake Union is anything but typical. Established in 1906 as a gasification plant by the Seattle Gas Company for extracting gas from coal, Gas Works was once a primary source of power for Seattle. Shut down in 1956, the plant's machinery and towers stood dormant until 1975, when the site was renovated into an award-winning park under the direction of landscape architect Richard Haag. With its renovation, Gas Works became the first industrial site in the world to be converted into a public park.

Stunning view of the Seattle skyline from Gas Works Park

Today, Gas Works Park is a scenic, 21-acre (8.5-ha) knoll offering vast recreational opportunities and magnificent views of Lake Union and downtown Seattle. Besides serving as a model for urban renewal, the park is a haven for kite flying, kayaking, picnicking, and viewing the July 4 fireworks.

Boaters enjoying an outing on Seattle's Green Lake

Green Lake ⑩

7201 E Green Lake Dr N. [(206) 684-4075. ⊟ 16, 26. ○ 24 hrs daily.

ON ANY GIVEN DAY – and especially a sunny one – Green Lake hosts a spirited parade of people, from joggers, walkers, cyclists, and skaters to bird-watchers, dog walkers, and pram-pushing parents. There's even an elderly gentleman who offers strolling Spanish lessons to those wanting to exercise both brain and body.

For wheeled sports, the 2.8-mile (4.5-km) asphalt path circling the lake is ideal.

Joggers and walkers can use the adjacent 3.2-mile (5-km) trail, which runs closest to the lake and has a crushed granite surface.

Attracting more than a million outdoor enthusiasts a year, this 324-acre (131-ha) park is populated by as many as 7,200 people a day on summer weekends. While kayaking, windsurfing, and paddleboating are popular pursuits during the warmer months, and boats can be rented at the lake, swimming may be restricted due to algae blooms and other problems caused by water stagnation.

Likened to New York's Central Park – albeit on a smaller scale – the lake and its surrounding park is a lively gathering spot for Seattle residents and a welcome recreational oasis in a high-density urban area. In addition to the lake, the park grounds include an indoor public pool, outdoor wading pool, tennis courts, soccer field, outdoor basketball court, baseball diamond, and pitch-and-putt golf course.

Jogger on the path that runs along Green Lake

Woodland Park Zoo ⑪

Sign for dragons of Komodo

Dᴇsɪɢɴᴇᴅ ɪɴ 1909 by city landscape consultant John Olmsted, Woodland Park Zoo is one of the oldest zoos on the West Coast and one of Seattle's major attractions. Of the nearly 300 animal species that reside at the 92-acre (37-ha) zoo, most live in environments that closely resemble their native habitats. Unlike typical zoo models where animals are grouped by species, Woodland Park creatures are grouped together in ecosystems. Five of the zoo's naturalistic habitats have won top honors from the American Zoo and Aquarium Association. Among these are the Elephant Forest – with its enormous elephant pool, Thai logging camp replica, and temple-like nighttime shelter – and the Trail of Vines, which includes the first open-forested canopy for orangutans to be created at a zoo.

★ **Tropical Rainforest**
The gorilla exhibit in the Tropical Rainforest includes the endangered western lowland gorilla, a gentle giant that can eat as much as 70 lbs (32 kg) of food each day.

★ **African Savanna**
Many species are found here, including zebras and springboks, which roam freely with the herd of imposing giraffes near a replica African village.

STAR SIGHTS
★ African Savanna
★ Dragons of Komodo
★ Northern Trail
★ Tropical Rainforest

Family Farm
A popular petting zoo is one of the features of the Family Farm, as is the recently added Bug World exhibit of creepy-crawlies.

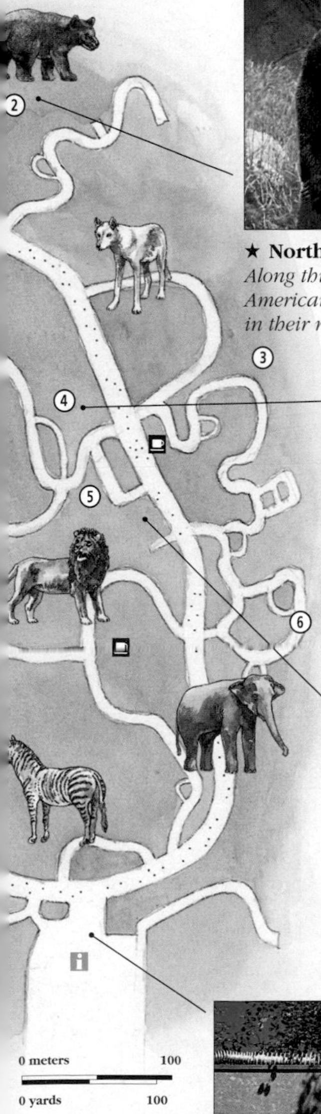

★ Northern Trail
Along this trail, indigenous North American animals can be viewed in their natural habitats.

Visitors' Checklist

5500 Phinney Ave N. ☎ *(206) 684-4800.* 🚌 5. 🕒 *mid-Mar–Apr: 9:30am–5pm daily; May–mid-Sep: 9:30am–6pm daily; mid-Sep–mid-Oct: 9:30am–5pm daily; mid-Oct–mid-Mar: 9:30am–4pm daily.* ♿ ☕ 🛍 [W] www.zoo.org

Conservation Yards East
In this exhibit area, endangered species such as the snow leopard are protected as part of the zoo's ongoing conservation efforts.

★ Dragons of Komodo
Housed in a customized multilevel enclosure, the enigmatic Komodo dragons are the world's largest lizards, with males averaging 9 ft (3 m) in length.

Main Entrance
A visitors' center at the main entrance provides detailed maps, fact sheets, and other information, such as animal feeding times.

Key

African Savanna (7)
Australasia (1)
Conservation Yards East (4)
Conservation Yards West (10)
Family Farm (8)
Northern Trail (2)
Temperate Forest (9)
Trail of Adaptations (5)
Tropical Asia: Elephant Forest (6)
Tropical Asia: Trail of Vines (3)
Tropical Rainforest (11)

People Waiting for the Interurban, an aluminum sculpture in Fremont

Fremont 🄫

Bounded by N 50th St, Lake Washington Ship Canal, Stone Way Ave N & 8th Ave NW. 🗺 *26, 28.*

I<small>N THE</small> 1960s, when it was a community of students, artists, and bohemians attracted by low rents, Fremont declared itself an "artists' republic." By the late 1990s, the neighborhood's character began to shift, after a high-tech firm settled its Seattle office here. However, Fremont has managed to hold on to cherished traditions, such as the Summer Solstice Parade and an outdoor cinema series, and today, it is still one of Seattle's funkiest districts.

Public art is a fixture of Fremont. A 13.5-ft- (4-m-) tall statue of Lenin towers above pedestrians at Fremont Place, and a 15-ft- (4.5-m-) tall Volkswagen-eating troll lurks under the north end of the Aurora Bridge. On 34th Street, near the drawbridge, sculptor Richard Beyer's *People Waiting for the Interurban* is

The historic landmark belltower in Ballard

The gigantic Fremont troll, waiting for unsuspecting cars

regularly clothed by locals. The dog's human face is modeled after an honorary mayor, with whom the artist had a dispute.

Ballard 🄭

Bounded by Salmon Bay, Shilshole Bay & Phinney Ridge. 🗺 *15, 17, 18.*

S<small>ETTLED BY</small> Scandinavian fishermen and loggers in 1853, Ballard was incorporated into Washington State in 1889 and annexed to Seattle in 1907. At the turn of the 19th century, Ballard was a mill town, producing an impressive three million wooden shingles a day. Many of the mill jobs were held by Scandinavian immigrants.

Located north of the shingle mills, Ballard Avenue was the commercial center of this then-booming area. Its buildings recall the area's industrial growth and Scandinavian heritage; many are open to the public. In 1976, King Carl XVI Gustav of Sweden read the proclamation establishing Ballard Avenue a Historic District.

The area's proud Scandinavian heritage is celebrated at the annual Norwegian Constitution Day Parade every May 17, at the excellent **Nordic Heritage Museum** (3014 Northwest 67th Street), and at the Bergen Place mural, located in Bergen Place Park and officially dedicated by

the king and queen of Norway in 1996.

In addition to welcoming royal visitors, Ballard greets the thousands of container ships, tugboats, fishing boats, and pleasure craft that make their way through the **Hiram M. Chittenden Locks** each year. Located at the west end of Ballard, the locks allow boats to travel between saltwater Puget Sound and freshwater Lake Union and Lake Washington. One of the city's major – and free – tourist attractions, the locks' grounds include 7 acres (3 ha) of botanical gardens.

🄫 Hiram M. Chittenden Locks

3015 NW 54th St. 📞 *(206) 783-7059.* **Grounds** ◯ *7am–9pm daily.* **Visitors' center** ◯ *May–Sep: 10am–6pm daily; Oct–Apr: 10am–4pm Thu–Mon.* 🚻 🅿 *2pm Thu–Mon (Dec–Feb by arrangement only).*

Discovery Park 🄮

3801 W Government Way. 📞 *(206) 386-4236.* 🗺 *24, 33.* **Park** ◯ *4am–11:30pm daily.* **Visitors' center** ◯ *8:30am–5pm Tue–Sun.* ◯ *major hols.* 🆆 *www.discoverypark.org*

L<small>OCATED ON</small> Magnolia Bluff, overlooking Puget Sound, 534-acre (216-ha) Discovery Park is Seattle's largest park. It occupies most of the former Fort Lawton site, a defensive base for soldiers during World Wars I and II and the Korean War. Built at the turn of the 20th century, the still-occupied Officers' Quarters are listed on the National Register of

The West Point Lighthouse, off the South Beach Trail, Discovery Park

Historic Places. A visitors'.
center at the east entrance
offers trail maps and interactive exhibits for kids.

Home to over 250 species
of birds and other wildlife,
the park offers more than 7
miles (11 km) of hiking trails,
including the 2.8-mile (4.5-
km) Loop Trail, which circles
the park and passes through
forests, meadows, and dunes.
For beach exploration, the park
has two very different habitats:
the rocky North Beach and
the sandy South Beach.

Discovery Park is also home
to the **Daybreak Star Cultural Center**. Operated by the
United Indians of All Tribes
Foundation, this cultural and
educational center houses a
collection of Native American
art. The annual summer Pow
Wow features some 500
dancers, 30 drum groups, arts
and crafts, and a salmon bake.

**🏛 Daybreak Star
Cultural Center**
Near north parking lot of Discovery
Park. 【 (206) 285-4425. 🖪
◯ 10am–5pm Mon–Sat, noon–
5pm Sun. &

**Rollerbladers on the paved path
alongside Alki Beach**

Alki Beach ⓯

1702 Alki Ave SW. 【 (206) 684-
4075. 🚌 37, 56.

WHEN THE FIRST European
settlers landed on Alki
Beach on a stormy November
day in 1851, they were welcomed by Chief Seattle and
his Duwamish tribe *(see p25)*.
Today, this lively beach is the
coolest place in town to be

A cyclist on Alki Beach, a stunning view of Seattle in the background

on a warm day. Reminiscent
of a southern California beach,
Alki welcomes beachcombers,
sunbathers, volleyball players,
picnickers, and people-watch-
ers. A 2.5-mile (4-km) paved
path attracts walkers, joggers,
rollerbladers, and bicyclists.

Alki Beach Park, which covers 135.9 acres (55 ha) of city
land, extends from Alki Point
to Duwamish Head, the mouth
of the Duwamish River.

Popular enough to be con-
nected to downtown Seattle
by a streetcar line built in 1902,
Alki Beach was the first municipal saltwater beach on the
West Coast. Swimmers then
and now experience water
temperatures ranging from
46 to 59°F (8 to 15°C).

In 1907, a small seawalled
amusement park called Luna
Park was built here. It was

destroyed by a fire in 1931,
but at low tide, pilings used
to anchor the amusement
park are still visible.

Alki Point, at the south end
of the beach, juts out into
Puget Sound. Visitors can
enjoy a picnic at the numerous picnic tables here. The
point also features a bath-
house dating from 1911 in
which can be found an art
studio, a 7-ft- (2-m-) tall
replica of New York's Statue
of Liberty, and a monument
commemorating the arrival of
the first white settlers. The
north end of the beach is
flanked by colorful cottages,

The beach offers spectacular views of Puget Sound, the
Olympic Mountains, the Seattle skyline, and of the ferries,
freighters, yachts, and sailboats that ply Elliott Bay.

THE MEN BEHIND MICROSOFT

Seattle is home to two of the world's wealthiest men and
most accomplished entrepreneurs. Bill Gates and Paul Allen
met at a prestigious Seattle prep school. Sharing a fascina-
tion for computers, the boys soon landed jobs with a company that paid them in computer time instead of cash. There
they pored over manuals and explored the computer system
inside and out. In 1973, Gates left for Harvard University but
kept in touch with Allen, with
whom he vowed to go into
business one day. By 1975,
Bill Gates was the US's most
successful college dropout,
having left Harvard to devote
his energies to the company
he founded with his friend.
Microsoft went on to become
the goliath of the computer
software industry. In 1985, its
headquarters settled in Redmond, a suburb of Seattle.
In 1986, the company began
public trading. Today, Microsoft employs over 40,000
people in 60 countries.

**Bill Gates, cofounder
of Seattle-based Microsoft**

Shopping in Seattle

SHOPPING AFICIONADOS WON'T BE DISAPPOINTED in Seattle. From 5th Avenue's ritzy boutiques to funky shops on Fremont's streets, you'll find plenty of irresistible buys. Without a car, you can shop until you drop downtown, at Pioneer Square, Pike Place Market, and Belltown, or hop on a bus and explore the shopping options farther afield.

Westlake Center shopping mall, in downtown Seattle

SHOPPING DISTRICTS

SEATTLE HAS SEVERAL interesting shopping districts. Upscale clothing boutiques, antique shops, and home accessory stores make their home in trendy Belltown *(see p141)*. Downtown *(see p121)*, chic boutiques mingle with top retailers and multilevel malls. At Pike Place Market *(see p134)* you'll find produce as well as antiques, art, crafts, jewelry, vintage apparel, and cookware. Pioneer Square *(see p121)* features bookstores, art galleries, antique shops, and a plethora of Oriental rug stores.

DEPARTMENT STORES AND SHOPPING CENTERS

SEATTLE-BASED **Nordstrom** opened its opulent flagship department store in 1998. Known for its wide selection of shoes, the fashion specialty store pampers shoppers with excellent customer service and, at this location, a luxurious full-service day spa. The **Bon Marche** department store downtown sells everything from linens and lingerie to loveseats and luggage. Downtown Seattle also has several notable malls. The poshest is **Pacific Place** *(see p129)*, a five-level complex

featuring dozens of upscale apparel, jewelry, and home accessory stores. Two blocks west, **Westlake Center** is home to top national and regional retailers and a sprawling food court. Barneys New York and Furla are among the prestigious retailers at **City Centre**. Located two blocks south of Pacific Place and Westlake Center, this classy mall boasts an impressive collection of contemporary glass art.

Located just outside downtown Seattle, **University Village** is the area's most high-end open-air shopping center. Locally owned specialty shops share the pedestrian-friendly Village with national retailers such as Barnes & Noble, Restoration Hardware, and Pottery Barn.

SPECIALTY SHOPS

YOU WILL FIND 150,000 titles and a cozy book-lined basement café at the **Elliott Bay Book Company** *(see p124)*. **Made in Washington**, which sells everything from smoked salmon to handmade pottery, offers one-stop shopping for top-quality, locally made merchandise and food items. The **REI** (Recreational Equipment Inc.) flagship store sells all kinds of outdoor gear, and features an indoor climbing wall. **Sur La Table** offers the latest culinary utensils and kitchenware. **Ye Olde Curiosity Shop** *(see p137)* is a jam-packed curiosity shop,

One of Seattle's many specialty shops, this one selling pottery

known for both its kitschy souvenirs and fine Native American crafts.

WHAT TO BUY

SMOKED SALMON, and coffee beans from small local roasting companies, such as Tully's, Seattle's Best, and Caffe Appassionato, are Seattle specialties. Handblown glass and pottery are popular souvenirs. More conventional items include Space Needle-inspired items, and bags with Pike Place Market motifs.

DIRECTORY

DEPARTMENT STORES AND SHOPPING CENTERS

Bon Marche
1601 3rd Ave. **Map** 3 C1.
(*(206) 506-6000.*

City Centre
1420 5th Ave. **Map** 3 C1.
(*(206) 624-8800.*

Nordstrom
500 Pine St. **Map** 3 C1.
(*(206) 628-2111.*

Pacific Place
600 Pine St. **Map** 2 E5.
(*(206) 405-2655.*

University Village
NE 45th St & 25th Ave NE.
(*(206) 523-0622.*

Westlake Center
400 Pine St. **Map** 3 C1.
(*(206) 467-3044.*

SPECIALTY SHOPS

Elliott Bay Book Company
101 S Main St. **Map** 4 D3.
(*(206) 624-6600.*

Made in Washington
1530 Post Alley. **Map** 3 C1.
(*(206) 467-0788.*

REI
222 Yale Ave N. **Map** 2 E4.
(*(206) 223-1944.*

Sur La Table
84 Pine St. **Map** 3 C1.
(*(206) 448-2244.*

Ye Olde Curiosity Shop
Pier 54 off Alaskan Way. **Map** 3 C2.
(*(206) 682-5844.*

Entertainment in Seattle

WITH SEATTLE'S VARIED OFFERINGS, from baseball to ballet, and book readings to Broadway musicals, visitors won't be lacking for entertainment. The city is home to one of the top opera companies in the US, a critically acclaimed symphony orchestra, and a Tony Award–winning repertory theater company.

Window of the Crocodile Café, a Belltown favorite for live music

INFORMATION

THE CITY'S DAILY newspaper, the *Seattle Times,* offers complete entertainment listings for the week in its Friday "Ticket" supplement. For daily listings, visit the newspaper's website at www.seattletimes. com/datebook.

BUYING TICKETS

TICKETS FOR SPORTING events and many performing arts events can be purchased through **Ticketmaster**. Half-price, day-of-show tickets for many theater, music, and dance performances are available through **Ticket/Ticket**, at the information booth located at the main entrance to the Pike Place Market. Ticket/Ticket accepts only cash and is open noon to 6pm, Tuesday through Sunday.

FREE EVENTS

FREE ART and literary events abound in Pioneer Square: First Thursday Gallery Walks through museums and galleries, as well as restaurants, bars, and shops, occur on the first Thursday evening of each month; and the Elliott Bay Book Company *(see p124)* hosts author readings several times each week.

THEATER

MANY OF SEATTLE'S performing arts venues are at the Seattle Center, including the respected **Seattle Repertory Theatre**, which presents nine plays from September to May, and the **Intiman Theatre**, which stages classic and contemporary plays March through December. The popular **Seattle Children's Theatre**, the second largest children's theater in the country, stages performances from September to June.

DANCE

INTERNATIONALLY acclaimed, the **Pacific Northwest Ballet** performs at Marion Oliver McCaw Hall. Its *Nutcracker* is a must see during the holiday season.

MUSIC

THE DISTINGUISHED **Seattle Symphony** performs September through June at the stunning **Benaroya Hall** *(see p129)*. The **Northwest Chamber Orchestra** performs in Benaroya's smaller Nordstrom Recital Hall September to May. Another high note on the Seattle classical music scene is the opening of the **Marion Oliver McCaw Hall**, home to the acclaimed **Seattle Opera**. For live blues, jazz, rock, and folk music, there are many venues to choose from in Pioneer Square, as well as in Belltown and Ballard.

Young musicians performing in downtown Seattle

SPECTATOR SPORTS

SPECTATOR SPORTS are big in Seattle. Seattleites are justifiably proud of their two new stadiums – Safeco Field *(see p152)*, home of the Seattle Mariners baseball team, and Seahawks Stadium *(see p152)*, where the National Football League's Seattle Seahawks play. The city's professional basketball teams – the Sonics and the Storm – play at the Seattle Center's KeyArena *(see p148)*. For sporting events tickets, call **Ticketmaster**.

Getting Around Seattle

S EATTLE MAY BE A HILLY CITY but its main tourist areas – Pioneer Square, downtown, Pike Place Market, the waterfront, Seattle Center, and Belltown – are relatively flat, close to each other, and easy to navigate on foot. The city's buses serve these areas and all Farther Afield sights and neighborhoods. A two-minute ride on the Monorail connects downtown to the Seattle Center.

STREET LAYOUT

I NTERSTATE-5 RUNS north–south through the middle of Seattle. In the downtown area, avenues run north–south, and streets run east–west. With only a few exceptions, avenues are numbered and streets are named (for example, 3rd Avenue and Spring Street). Many of Seattle's streets and avenues run one-way. For a good selection of local street maps, as well as state and recreational maps, visit **Metsker Maps of Seattle**, in Pioneer Square.

WALKING

S EATTLE IS A GREAT city for walking. Though it is quite hilly, the downtown area is compact enough to walk in its entirety, and locals are generally happy to offer directions. Keep in mind that jaywalking (crossing the street other than at designated crossings) is illegal in Seattle. Tourist offices provide free maps that will help visitors navigate the downtown area.

STOP FOR ME IT'S THE LAW

Traffic sign to help pedestrians

An old-fashioned streetcar running along Seattle's waterfront

BICYCLING

C YCLISTS MAY WISH to avoid Seattle's busy streets and head to one of the area's popular bike trails. The 12-mile (19-km) paved Burke-Gilman Trail (*see p155*) stretches from Fremont to Kenmore. Bike rental shops such as **All About Bike and Ski** and the **Bicycle Center of Seattle** are located near the trail. A 2.8-mile (4.5-km) path that encircles Green Lake (*see p155*) is ideal for shorter spins. **Gregg's Greenlake Cycle**, located beside the lake, rents touring, mountain, and hybrid bicycles, as well as inline and off-road skates.

TAXIS

T AXIS CAN USUALLY be flagged outside every major downtown hotel and attraction, as well as on main streets and at taxi stands, found at bus stations and the airport. Taxis can also be ordered by telephone. Fares start at $1.80, and increase at a rate of approximately $1.80 per mile.

PUBLIC TRANSIT

M ETRO TRANSIT offers inexpensive transportation throughout the city. Buses are equipped with wheelchair lifts. Between 6am and 7pm, bus transportation is free in

downtown Seattle. The Ride Free Area is delineated by Jackson Street to the south, 6th Avenue to the east, Battery Street to the north, and the waterfront to the west. Bus schedules are available from the **Seattle/King County Convention and Visitors Bureau** at the Washington State Convention and Trade Center (800 Convention Place) and from the Metro Transit customer service office at Westlake Station, on the mezzanine level. The **Metro Transit Rider Information** phone line provides route and other information.

Metro Transit also operates the George Benson Waterfront Streetcar, which travels between Pier 70's Myrtle Edwards Park south along the waterfront, through Pioneer Square, to the International District. The beautifully maintained Australian trolleys,

A Seattle taxi cab, a common sight on downtown streets

brought over from Melbourne in 1982, have mahogany and ash woodwork in the interior. Streetcars run approximately every 20 minutes from early morning to early evening and can accommodate riders with physical disabilities. Though the waterfront line is within the boundaries of the Ride Free Area, a one-zone fare – about $1.50 for adults and 50 cents for youth – must be paid or a valid transfer shown. If paying a cash fare, obtain a transfer, which will allow on-and-off privileges within a 90-minute period.

Another convenient and inexpensive way to travel within the city is the **Seattle**

The Seattle Monorail, linking downtown to the Seattle Center

Monorail *(see p145).* Linking downtown Seattle to the Seattle Center *(see pp142–3),* the Monorail operates Monday through Friday from 7:30am to 11pm, and Saturday through Sunday from 9am to 11pm. It departs every ten minutes from the station at Seattle Center (across from the Space Needle) and from Westlake Center, at 5th Avenue and Pine Street. The 1-mile (1.6-km) trip takes two minutes. During many special events, the monorail departs every five minutes or less.

FERRIES

SEVERAL OF Seattle's outlying areas can be reached via the **Washington State Ferries**, which offer scenic rides through the San Juan Islands and to other destinations around Puget Sound. Sail from downtown Seattle's Pier 52 to nearby Bremerton and Bainbridge Island, or from Pier 50 to Bremerton and Vashon Island. Ferries leaving from Pier 52 carry automobiles and passengers, whereas those from Pier 50 are passenger-only. Several private companies offer ferry rides along similar routes as well as narrated tours of the Seattle waterfront.

A Seattle bus stop sign

DRIVING

THE TRAFFIC in downtown Seattle can be daunting. To save wear and tear on your nerves, avoid driving during weekday rush hours, 7 to 9:30am and 3 to 7pm. Unless

posted otherwise, the speed limit on arterial (city) streets is 30 mph (48 km/h). The speed limit for non-arterial (residential) streets is 25 mph (40 km/h). A right-hand turn on a red light is permitted after coming to a full stop. Traffic circles (raised islands in intersections) are common in many neighborhoods. Drivers should yield to the motorist on the left, then proceed to the right.

Seat belts, safety seats for young children, and motorcycle helmets are mandatory. **American Automobile Association** members can obtain free maps and tour books from the Seattle office.

PARKING

PARKING downtown is generally expensive. However, one of the best-kept secrets is the underground parking garage beneath Pacific Place *(see p129),* where budget-savvy Seattleites park.

TOWING

IF YOUR CAR is towed from a street within the city limits, call the **Seattle Police, Auto Records Department.** Staff here will tell you which impound yard your car has been taken to. Be prepared to provide the car's license plate number and the location from which the vehicle was towed. If you are renting a car, be sure to carry the vehicle license number with you. If the car was towed from a private lot, call the number posted on the sign.

A local seaplane, offering visitors a bird's-eye view of Seattle

Washington State Ferries, linking Puget Sound communities

SEATTLE STREET FINDER

THE KEY MAP BELOW shows the area of Seattle covered by the *Street Finder* maps, which can be found on the following pages. Map references for sights, hotels, restaurants, shops, and entertainment venues given throughout the Seattle chapter of this guide refer to the grid on the maps. The first figure in the reference indicates which map to turn to (1 to 4), and the letter and number that follow refer to the grid reference on that map.

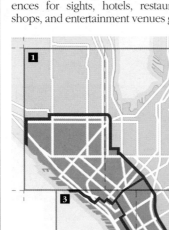

KEY TO STREET FINDER

	Major sight
	Minor sight
	Station building
🚊	Train station
🚌	Bus station – long distance
🚋	Streetcar
🚝	Monorail
P	Parking
ℹ	Information
✚	Hospital
🚓	Police station
✝	Church
⊠	Post office
⚓	Ferry boarding point
– –	Ferry route
‡‡‡	Railroad line
→	One-way street

0 meters 300
0 yards 300
SCALE OF MAPS 1–4

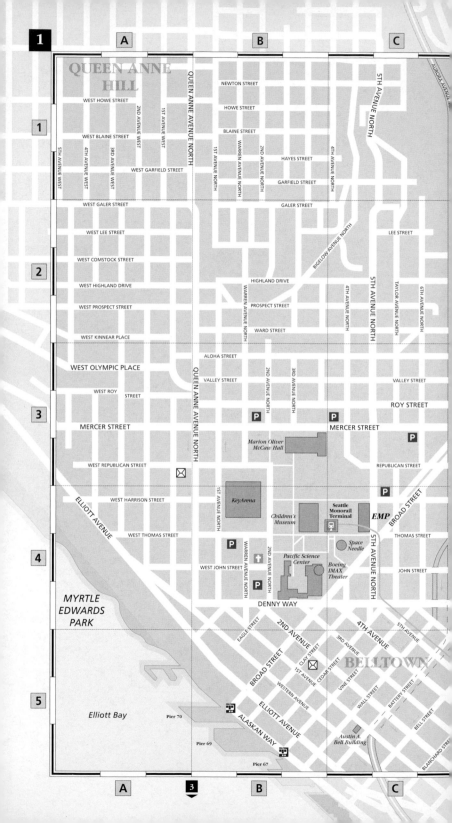

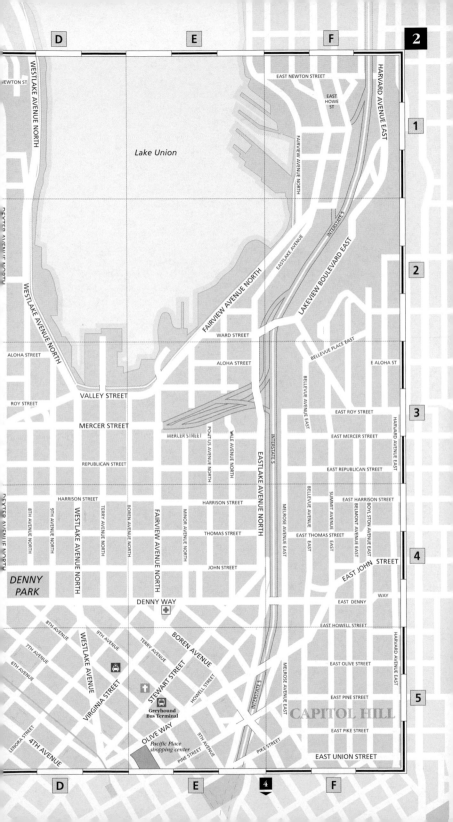

D | **E** | **F** | **2**

NEWTON ST

WESTLAKE AVENUE NORTH

EAST NEWTON STREET

EAST HOWE ST

HARVARD AVENUE EAST

FAIRVIEW AVENUE NORTH

1

Lake Union

DEXTER AVENUE NORTH

WESTLAKE AVENUE NORTH

EASTLAKE AVENUE

LAKEVIEW BOULEVARD EAST

INTERSTATE 5

2

WARD STREET

ALOHA STREET

FAIRVIEW AVENUE NORTH

ALOHA STREET

BELLEVUE PLACE EAST

E ALOHA ST

ALOHA STREET

BELLEVUE AVENUE EAST

ROY STREET

VALLEY STREET

EAST ROY STREET

HARVARD AVENUE EAST

3

MERCER STREET

MERCER STREET

PONTIUS AVENUE NORTH

YALE AVENUE NORTH

EASTLAKE AVENUE NORTH

EAST MERCER STREET

REPUBLICAN STREET

INTERSTATE 5

EAST REPUBLICAN STREET

HARRISON STREET

8TH AVENUE NORTH

9TH AVENUE NORTH

WESTLAKE AVENUE NORTH

TERRY AVENUE NORTH

BOREN AVENUE NORTH

FAIRVIEW AVENUE NORTH

MINOR AVENUE NORTH

HARRISON STREET

MELROSE AVENUE EAST

BELLEVUE AVENUE

SUMMIT AVENUE

BELMONT AVENUE EAST

BOYLSTON AVENUE EAST

EAST HARRISON STREET

EAST THOMAS STREET

4

THOMAS STREET

JOHN STREET

EAST JOHN STREET

DENNY
PARK

DEXTER AVENUE NORTH

DENNY WAY

EAST DENNY WAY

EAST HOWELL STREET

HARVARD AVENUE EAST

8TH AVENUE

7TH AVENUE

6TH AVENUE

WESTLAKE AVENUE

9TH AVENUE

VIRGINIA STREET

TERRY AVENUE

BOREN AVENUE

STEWART STREET

HOWELL STREET

MELROSE AVENUE EAST

EAST OLIVE STREET

EAST PINE STREET

CAPITOL HILL

5

Greyhound
Bus Terminal

OLIVE WAY

EAST PIKE STREET

LENORA STREET

4TH AVENUE

Pacific Place
shopping center

PINE STREET

9TH AVENUE

PIKE STREET

INTERSTATE 5

EAST UNION STREET

D | **E** | **▼ 4** | **F**

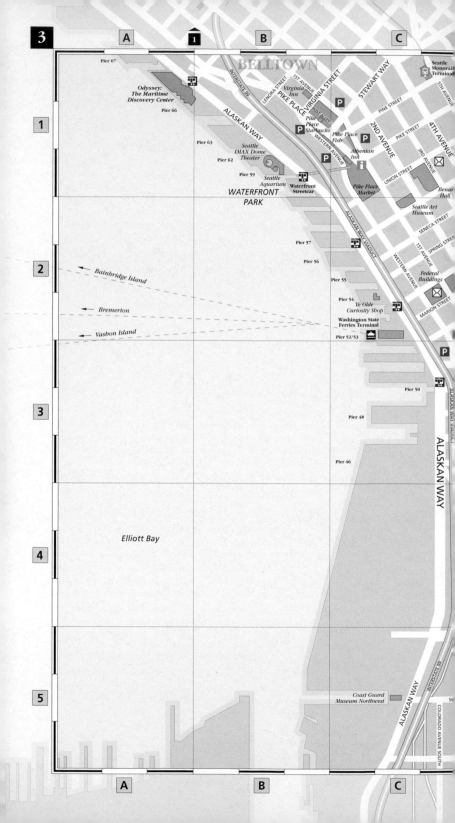

WASHINGTON

NAMED FOR THE FIRST PRESIDENT OF THE US, *Washington was the 42nd state to enter the Union, in 1889. Washington is located in the far northwestern corner of the country, sharing a border with Canada. Within its 68,139 sq miles (176,466 sq km) of land lies an extraordinary geographical diversity; each of the state's three distinct regions has its own geology, personality, and climate.*

The coastal region – bordered by the Pacific Ocean to the west, the Strait of Juan de Fuca to the north, Oregon to the south, and Puget Sound to the east – is dominated by the beautiful Olympic National Park and other great tracts of forest. Highlights include the charming Victorian seaport of Port Townsend, the spectacular views from the top of Hurricane Ridge, the expansive Crescent Lake, the towering moss-draped trees of the Hoh Rainforest, and miles of scenic coastline, which receive the highest amounts of rainfall in the state.

Western Washington contains the state's most populous areas, which lie in the corridor along Interstate-5, especially between Tacoma and Seattle. In the far northwest, scattered off the coast, are the San Juan Islands, with 247 days of sunshine a year.

The Cascade mountain range, which runs between western and eastern Washington, provides wonderful opportunities for skiing, hiking, and numerous other outdoor activities. Mount Rainier, the highest peak in the range, is Washington's most-visited attraction.

The dry, sunny eastern region, stretching from the Cascades to the Idaho border, contrasts with the dense, damp greenness of western Washington. Both the fertile Yakima Valley, the fifth largest producer of fruits and vegetables in the US, and the Walla Walla Valley are known for their many excellent wineries. Farther north, the magnificent Grand Coulee Dam harnesses the power of the mighty Columbia River to provide irrigation water for more than half a million acres (202,000 ha) of farmland.

Sea kayaks at Snug Harbor in Mitchell Bay, on the west side of San Juan Island

◁ Snow trekkers on the trail from Paradise to Camp Muir, Mount Rainier

Exploring Washington

W ASHINGTON'S MANY ATTRACTIONS are sprinkled liberally throughout the state, which consists of three distinct regions: coastal, western, and eastern. The Olympic Peninsula, in the coastal region, provides visitors with a choice of ocean, lake, forest, or mountain playgrounds. Western Washington's favorite islands, among them Bainbridge, Whidbey, and the San Juans, all offer charming towns, miles of terrain for cycling, and the opportunity to slip into "island time" for a day or two. A drive to the eastern region – at its best in late spring to mid-fall – leads to the western-themed Winthrop and the breathtaking peaks of North Cascades National Park.

Sailboats moored at Point Hudson marina, Port Townsend

SIGHTS AT A GLANCE

Tours

SEE ALSO

The dramatic metal cone of Tacoma's Museum of Glass

KEY

- ▬ Highway
- ▬ Major road
- ▬ Minor road
- ▬ Scenic route
- ☀ Viewpoint

Mount Rainier, as seen from Mount Rainier National Park

NORTH CASCADES NATIONAL PARK

18

19 **WINTHROP**

97

STEHEKIN

17

Lake Chelan

155

LAKE CHELAN

16

ALT 97

20 **GRAND COULEE DAM**

Banks Lake

LEAVENWORTH

15

US 97

Columbia River

395

2

SPOKANE

21

28

97

90

195

82

97

22 **YAKIMA VALLEY**

395

12

182

Snake River

24 **WALLA WALLA VALLEY WINE TOUR**

82

23 **WALLA WALLA**

GOLDENDALE OBSERVATORY STATE PARK

97

25

26

MARYHILL

GETTING AROUND

Bellingham, Seattle, Tacoma, and Olympia are all accessed by I-5, the state's main north–south interstate. I-90, the major east–west artery, leads from Seattle to Spokane. Five mountain passes and the Columbia Gorge link western and eastern Washington. US Hwy 2 crosses Stevens Pass to Leavenworth. State Hwy 20 (North Cascades Hwy), usually closed in winter, passes through Winthrop. Amtrak offers a rail service, and Greyhound, a bus service, to most of Washington's major cities. Washington State Ferries sail to destinations including around Puget Sound and the San Juan Islands.

0 kilometers   50

0 miles   40

Olympic Peninsula Tour ❶

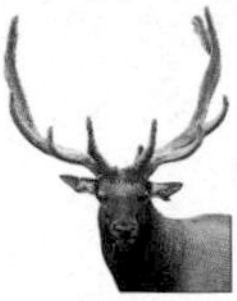

The shy Roosevelt elk

THE OLYMPIC PENINSULA, in the far northwestern corner of Washington, offers many opportunities for spectacular sightseeing. The centerpiece of the peninsula is Olympic National Park, a UNESCO biosphere reserve and World Heritage Site. Encompassing 923,000 acres (373,540 ha), the park contains mountains with snowcapped peaks, as well as lakes, waterfalls, rivers, and rainforests. Opportunities for outdoor activities abound in the peninsula; among the most popular pursuits are deep-sea– and fly-fishing, kayaking, white-water rafting, mountain biking, and bird-watching.

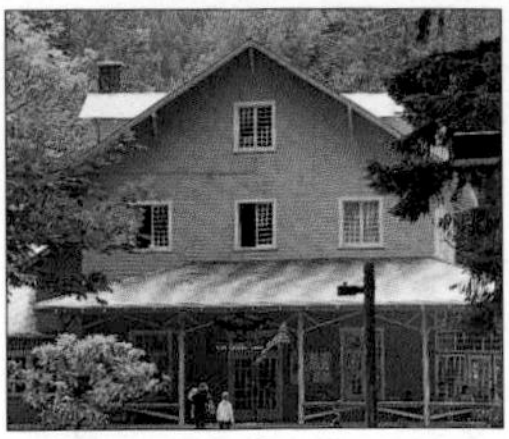

Lake Crescent ⑤
Lake Crescent Lodge is an historic resort on the shores of Lake Crescent. The lake's crystal-clear fresh water, which reaches a depth of 625 ft (190 m), makes it a favorite location for divers.

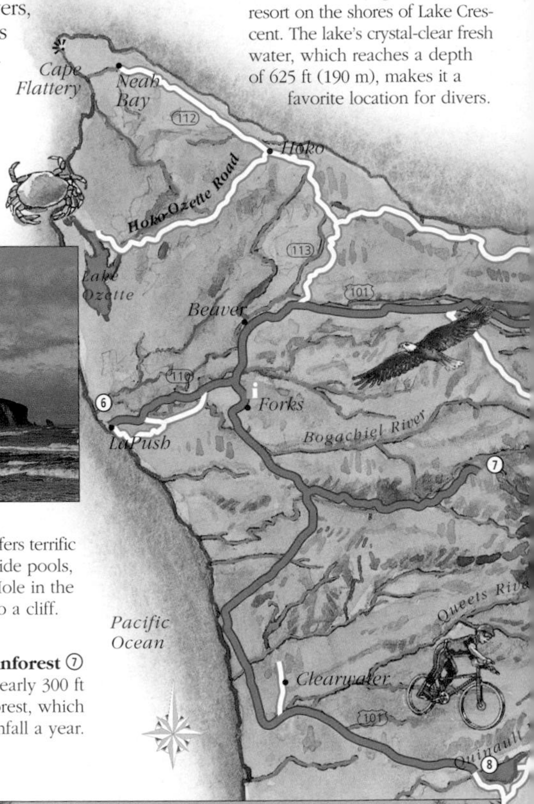

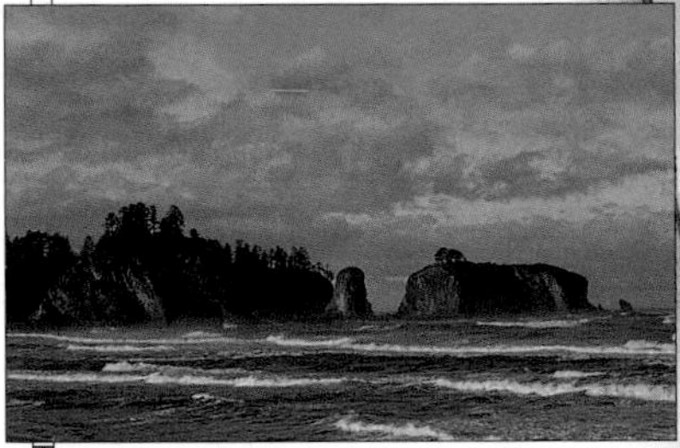

Rialto Beach ⑥
This 4-mile- (6.5-km-) long beach offers terrific views of the Pacific coast, with its tide pools, sea stacks, rocky islands, and the Hole in the Wall, a tunnel carved by waves into a cliff.

Hoh Rainforest ⑦
Ancient trees tower to nearly 300 ft (91 m) in this old-growth forest, which receives 14 ft (4 m) of rainfall a year.

0 kilometers 20

0 miles 15

KEY

- Tour route
- Other road
- Information
- Airport
- Ferry
- Viewpoint

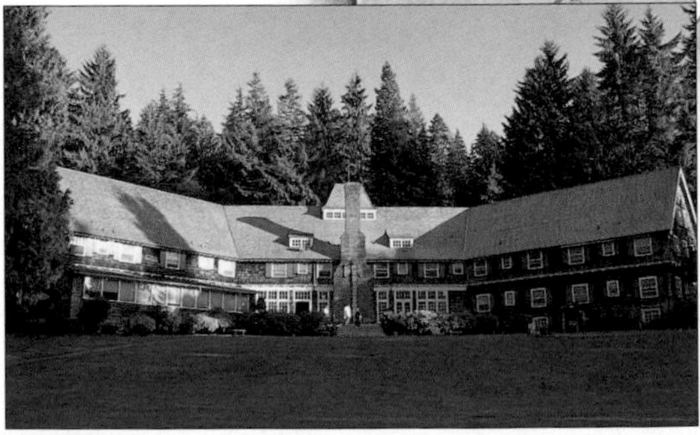

Lake Quinault ⑧
Snow-capped mountains encircle this lake and Lake Quinault Lodge.

Hurricane Ridge ④
The ridge's summit, at 5,230 ft (1,594 m), is covered with flowers in spring and offers panoramic views. Skiing and snowshoeing are popular winter activities here.

Sequim ③
Sitting in the rain shadow of the Olympic Mountains, Sequim features an elk viewing site and the Olympic Game Farm, home to endangered wild animals.

TIPS FOR DRIVERS

Tour length: 272 miles (438 km) including all detours off Hwy 101.
Starting point: Port Gamble on Hwy 104. Here, cross the Hood Canal Bridge to begin the tour.
Stopping-off points: As well as the numerous public campsites and lodges situated in or near Olympic National Park (see p289), a wide variety of restaurants and accommodations is to be found throughout this popular area.

Port Gamble ①
Located on the Kitsap Peninsula, this former logging town has retained its original New England Victorian–style homes, country store, and church. The 1982 movie *An Officer and a Gentleman* was filmed here.

Port Townsend ②
This seaport, a National Historic Landmark, is known for its Victorian architecture and vibrant arts community (*see pp176–7*). The town is also an excellent base from which to make kayaking, whale-watching, and cycling day trips.

Mount Olympus ⑨
With its West Peak rising 7,965 ft (2,428 m), this three-peaked, glacier-clad mountain is the highest in Washington's Olympic range.

Port Townsend ②

Shop sign, Port Townsend

Port Townsend was founded in 1851, almost 60 years after Captain Vancouver first saw its harbor and named it for his friend, the Marquis of Townshend. By the late 1800s, it was a bustling maritime community, with more ships in its port than in any other city in the US with the exception of New York. Convinced that Port Townsend would be the end point for a transcontinental railroad, residents went on a building spree, erecting lavish mansions and grand buildings in anticipation of its becoming the "New York of the West." That dream never materialized, but most of the original structures from that era have survived. The city today enjoys a booming tourism business, thanks to its Victorian buildings. Port Townsend is one of only three seaports on the National Registry as a historic landmark.

Ann Starrett Mansion, with its unusual eight-sided domed tower

Exploring Port Townsend

Port Townsend is easily explored on foot. Water Street, the Downtown Historic District's main boulevard, is lined with brick-and-stone buildings housing art galleries, upscale shops, and restaurants. Many of the city's Victorian homes, churches, and inns are in the Uptown Historic District, between Clay and Lincoln Streets. The center of the uptown business district is Lawrence and Tyler Streets. Maps and information about tours are available at the visitors' center.

🏛 Jefferson County Courthouse

1322 Washington St. ℂ (360) 385-9100. ◯ 8am–5pm Mon–Fri.
◉ public hols. ♿
The jewel of Port Townsend's Victorian architecture, this neo-Romanesque building was designed in 1892 by Seattle architect Willis A. Ritchie, who ordered its bricks be hauled west from St. Louis, rather than using the soft, local ones. The building's 124-ft- (38-m-) tall clock tower, its clockwork also dating to 1892, has long been a landmark for sailors.

Jefferson County Courthouse tower

🏛 Jefferson County Historical Society

540 Water St. ℂ (360) 385-1003.
◯ Mar–Dec: 11am–4pm Mon–Sat; 1–4pm Sun; Jan–Feb: 11am–4pm Sat, 1–4pm Sun.
◉ Thanksgiving, Dec 25.
🖼 ♿ partial. ◉
ⓦ www.jchsmuseum.org
Occupying the old City Hall (1891), this building once housed the town's fire station, jail, court room, and city offices. Today it is home to the city council, as well as an excellent museum that showcases the county's heritage through artifacts, archives, and photographs. Highlights of the exhibits include a display on the area's Native peoples.

🏛 Ann Starrett Mansion

744 Clay St. ℂ (360) 385-3205.
◯ noon–3pm daily. 🖼 for tour.
🎥 mandatory.
ⓦ www.starrettmansion.com
Built in 1889 by wealthy contractor George Starrett as a wedding gift for his bride, Ann, this grand Queen Anne–style mansion has received national recognition for its architecture, frescoed ceilings, and three-tiered spiral staircase topped by a domed ceiling. A National Historic Landmark, it now serves as a bed-and-breakfast.

🏛 Rothschild House

Franklin & Taylor Sts. ℂ (360) 385-2722. ◯ May–Sep:10am–5pm daily.
◉ Oct–Apr. 🖼 🎥 year-round by arrangement.
A departure from Port Townsend's more elaborate homes, this estate reflects the simplicity of the New England–style design that predated Victorian architecture. Built in 1868 for David C.H. Rothschild, it was donated by the sole remaining family member to the Washington State Parks and Recreation Commission in 1959. Restored and listed on the National Register of Historic Places, the house contains original furnishings.

⛪ St. Paul's Episcopal Church

1032 Jefferson St. ℂ (360) 385-0770. ◯ 9am–2pm Wed–Sat.
🕐 10am Wed; 8am, 10am Sun; 6:30pm 3rd Sat of month. ♿
The oldest surviving church in Port Townsend – and the oldest Episcopal church in

Union Wharf, jutting out from Port Townsend's waterfront

continuous use in Washington – the Gothic Revival–style St Paul's was built in 1865. Originally located below the bluff, the church was placed on logs and rolled to its present location in 1883 with the help of horses and a windlass.

🏛 Fire Bell Tower

Tyler & Jefferson Sts.

Located on the bluff overlooking downtown, the 1890 fire bell tower was once used to summon the town's volunteer fire fighters. The number of rings indicated which part of town the fire was in. The tower is placed first on Washington, DC's list of Ten Most Endangered Historic Treasures.

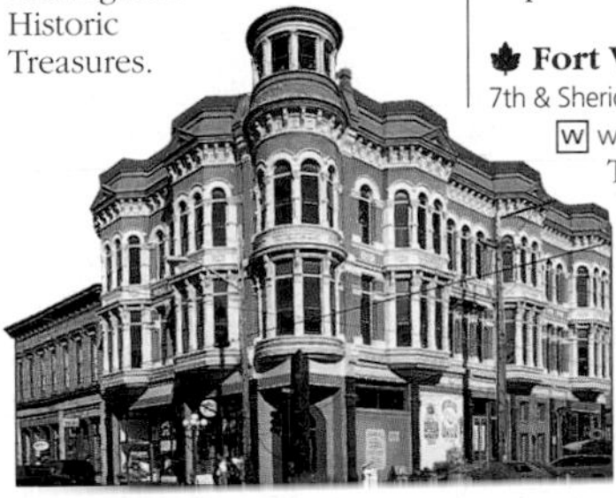

The prominent 1889 Hastings Building, today housing offices and upmarket shops

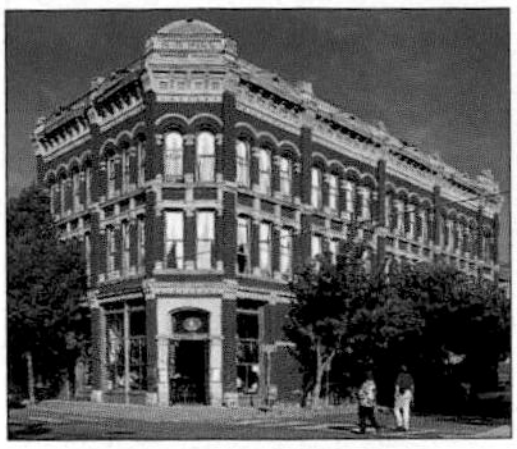

Water Street's N.D. Hill Building, used as a hotel since 1889

🏛 Haller Fountain

Taylor & Washington Sts.

Donated to the city in 1906 by city resident Theodore Haller, the fountain's centerpiece, a bronze maiden, made her debut in the Mexican exhibit at the 1893 World's Columbian Exposition in Chicago.

🌲 Fort Worden State Park

7th & Sheridan Sts. ☎ *(360) 344-4400.* [W] www.olympus.net/ftworden

This former military base is now a 440-acre (178-ha) state park. Visitors can explore the fort's bunkers and tour the **Commanding Officer's Quarters** (1904). A museum refurbished in late-Victorian style, it offers a glimpse into the lives of the officers in the early 20th century. The **Puget Sound Coast Artillery Museum** is devoted to harbor-defense operations from the late 1800s through World War II.

VISITORS' CHECKLIST

Road map 1 A2. 👥 *8,000.*
⛴ *from Keystone on Whidbey Island & from Edmonds.*
[i] *2437 E Sims Way, (888) 365-6978.* [W] www.ptguide.com

🏛 **Commanding Officer's Quarters** 🕒 *Mar–May & Sep–Oct: 1–4pm Sat–Sun; Jun–Aug: 10am–5pm daily.* 💲 ☎ *call for details.*

🏛 **Puget Sound Coast Artillery Museum** ☎ *(360) 385-0373.* 🕒 *Memorial Day–Labor Day: 10am–4pm daily; Apr–May & Sep–Oct: 11am–4pm Sat–Sun.* ● *Nov–Mar.* ♿

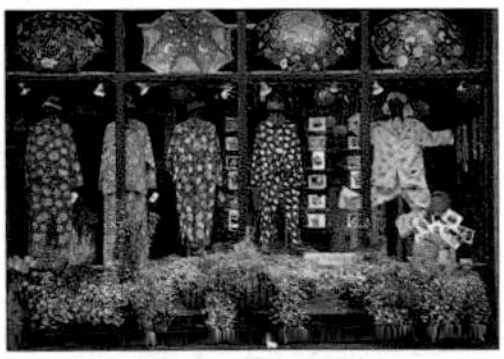

Store window display on Port Townsend's historic Water Street

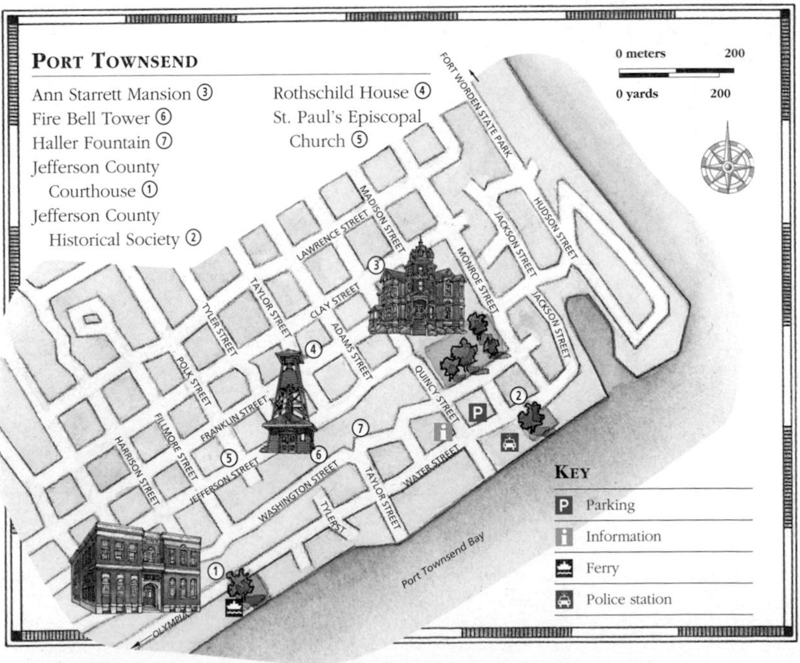
PORT TOWNSEND
Ann Starrett Mansion ③
Fire Bell Tower ⑥
Haller Fountain ⑦
Jefferson County Courthouse ①
Jefferson County Historical Society ②
Rothschild House ④
St. Paul's Episcopal Church ⑤
0 meters 200
0 yards 200
FORT WORDEN STATE PARK
HUDSON STREET
JACKSON STREET
MONROE STREET
MADISON STREET
LAWRENCE STREET
CLAY STREET
TAYLOR STREET
ADAMS STREET
TYLER STREET
POLK STREET
QUINCY STREET
FRANKLIN STREET
FILLMORE STREET
HARRISON STREET
JEFFERSON STREET
WASHINGTON STREET
TYLER ST
WATER STREET
OLYMPIA
Port Townsend Bay
KEY
Parking
Information
Ferry
Police station

San Juan Islands ❸

A Washington state ferry sailing from the mainland to the islands

Sᴄᴀᴛᴛᴇʀᴇᴅ ʙᴇᴛᴡᴇᴇɴ the Washington mainland and Vancouver Island, the San Juan archipelago consists of over 700 islands, 172 of them named. Ferries sail from Anacortes to the four largest islands: Lopez, Shaw, Orcas, and San Juan. Lopez is affectionately called "Slopez" because of its laid-back nature. Gently rolling roads, numerous stopping points, and friendly drivers make it a popular destination for cycling. Horseshoe-shaped Orcas, the hilliest island in the chain, offers breathtaking views from atop 2,409-ft (734-m) Mount Constitution. The best destination for walk-on passengers, San Juan Island is home to Friday Harbor, the largest town in the archipelago. The nationally renowned Whale Museum is located here. Primarily residential, Shaw Island does not offer visitor facilities.

Sailboats in the Channel
Sailors love the many harbors and good winds in the San Juan Channel.

★ **Roche Harbor**
A charming seaside village, Roche Harbor features a marina, Victorian gardens, a chapel, and the historic Hotel de Haro, built in 1886.

0 kilometers 2

0 miles 1

Sᴛᴀʀ Sɪɢʜᴛs

★ **Deer Harbor**

★ **Friday Harbor**

★ **Lopez**

★ **Roche Harbor**

Lime Kiln Point State Park
This state park, with its picturesque lighthouse, completed in 1919, is the only park in the US dedicated to whale-watching.

★ Deer Harbor
Sea kayakers flock to Deer Harbor and the other waters surrounding the islands of Orcas, Lopez, and San Juan.

VISITORS' CHECKLIST

Road Map 1 A1. 🚢 *Washington State Ferries from Anacortes or Sidney, BC, to the San Juan Islands.* 📞 *(206) 464-6400.* 🆆 *www.wsdot.wa.gov/ferries* 🛈 *PO Box 65, Lopez Island.* 📞 *(360) 468-3663.*

★ Lopez
Despite its gently rolling hills, Lopez is the flattest of the San Juan Islands, making it a popular destination for recreational cyclists.

★ Friday Harbor
The largest town in the San Juans, Friday Harbor offers a number of restaurants, inns, galleries, and shops – all within easy walking distance of the ferry dock.

KEY

▬	Major road
═	Minor road
‑ ‑	Ferry route
Ⓐ	Camping
✸	Viewpoint
✈	Airport
ℹ	Information

Bellingham ❹

Road map 1 A1. 🛬 *Bellingham Airport*. 🏠 *67,000*. 🚌 *(360) 671-3990*. 🌐 *www.bellingham.org*

O VERLOOKING Bellingham Bay and many of the San Juan Islands, Bellingham has been inhabited by the Lummi Indians for thousands of years. The area – consisting of the four original towns of Whatcom, Sehome, Bellingham, and Fairhaven – was settled in 1853 and consolidated in 1904. The town's historic architecture includes Old Whatcom County Courthouse (1308 East Street), the first brick building north of San Francisco, built in 1858, and the majestic City Hall, built in 1892 in the Victorian Second Empire style. The latter is now the heart of the **Whatcom Museum of History and Art**, a four-building campus that includes a children's museum. Highlights of the museum include exhibits on the Northwest Coast First Nations and on the birds of the Pacific Northwest.

South of downtown, the historic Fairhaven district is an artsy enclave of Victorian buildings housing galleries, restaurants, bookstores, and coffeehouses.

Just up the hill from downtown Bellingham sits the campus of **Western Washington University**, with its famous collection of outdoor sculptures, including artworks by

Boats journeying along the Skagit River in La Conner

internationally recognized American artists Richard Serra, Mark di Suvero, and Richard Beyer.

🏛 **Whatcom Museum of History and Art**

121 Prospect St. 📞 *(360) 676-6981.* 🕐 *noon–5pm Tue–Sun.* ***Children's Museum***: *noon–5pm Tue–Wed & Sun, 10am–5pm Thu–Sat.* 💲 *to Children's Museum.* 🚻 📷

🏛 **Western Washington University**

ℹ *S College Dr & College Way.* 📞 *(360) 650-3424.* ***Visitors' center*** 🕐 *mid-Sep–mid-Jun: 7am–8pm Mon–Fri; mid-Jun–mid-Sep: 7am–5pm Mon–Fri.* ⬤ *major hols.* 🚻 🌐 *www.wwu.edu*

Tower of Bellingham's former City Hall

ENVIRONS: South of Bellingham, Chuckanut Drive (Hwy 11) is a scenic 21-mile (34-km) loop with outlooks to Puget Sound and the San Juan Islands. Along the way are hiking and biking trails, restaurants, and oyster farms selling fresh oysters in season.

Fifty-five miles (88.5 km) east of Bellingham is 10,778-ft- (3,285-m-) high Mount Baker, where the ski and snowboarding season runs from November through April.

La Conner ❺

Road map 1 A2. 🏠 *750.* 🚢 ℹ *(888) 642-9284.* 🌐 *www.laconnerchamber.com*

L ONG ASSOCIATED in the minds of Washingtonians with tulips, the town of La Conner draws thousands to the Skagit Valley Tulip Festival. And although the town's famous fields are abloom with spectacular color come springtime, there is more to La Conner than flowers. A magnet for artists since the 1940s, this tiny town is a thriving arts community. The highly respected **Museum of Northwest Art** showcases works by Mark Tobey, Guy Anderson, Morris Graves, and Kenneth Callahan (all of whom were inspired by the Skagit Valley's unique light), as well as Dale Chihuly and other prominent Pacific Northwest artists.

Listed on the National Register of Historic Places, La Conner was founded in the early 1860s. It was originally called Swinomish, after the area's first residents, the Swinomish Indians. In 1869, wealthy merchant John Conner renamed the town after his wife, Louisa Ann Siegfried, by combining her first two initials and her married name. Louisa Ann was the town's first non-Indian woman resident. For a glimpse into her life – and those of other early settlers – visit the **Skagit County Historical Museum**.

🏛 **Museum of Northwest Art**

121 S 1st St. 📞 *(360) 466-4446.* 🕐 *10am–5pm Tue–Sun.* 💲 *(free 1st Tue of month).* 🚻 🌐 *www.museumofnwart.org*

🏛 **Skagit County Historical Museum**

501 4th St. 📞 *(360) 466-3365.* 🕐 *11am–5pm Tue–Sun.* 💲 🚻

Crab traps on a boat ready to set out from Bellingham Harbor

Whidbey Island ⑥

Road map 1 A2. ⚑ 60,000. ⛴
🛈 107 S Main St, Coupeville,
(360) 678-5434.

WHIDBEY ISLAND boasts five
state parks and two
charming seaside villages.
Coupeville's Victorian homes,
old barns, and quaint waterfront recall the town's beginnings. Nearby, the extensive
Ebey's Landing National Historical Reserve includes the
historic army post, **Fort Casey
State Park**. At the island's
south end, the arts community
of **Langley** has historic buildings, upscale shops, art galleries, and bed-and-breakfasts.

♣ Fort Casey State Park

SR 20, at Ebey's Landing.
🛈 (360) 678-4519. ◯ 8am–dusk.

Bainbridge Island ⑦

Road map 1 A2. ⚑ 22,000. ⛴ 🛈
590 Winslow Way E, (206) 842-3700.
ⓦ www.bainbridgechamber.com

A 35-MINUTE FERRY RIDE from
Seattle, Bainbridge Island
makes for an enjoyable outing.
Near the ferry terminal, a path
leads through Waterfront Park
to downtown Winslow's galleries, shops, and cafés. The
island's charming inns make it
a popular stop for travelers to
the Kitsap and Olympic Penin-
sulas. **Bloedel Reserve**, with
its colorful Japanese garden,
English landscape, and bird
refuge, is worth a visit.

♣ Bloedel Reserve

7571 NE Dolphin Dr. 🛈 (206) 842-
7631. ◯ 10am–4pm Wed–Sun;
reservations mandatory. 🌿 ♿

**Airplanes suspended in the air,
Great Gallery, Museum of Flight**

Museum of Flight ⑧

9404 E Marginal Way S, Seattle.
Road map 1 A2. 🛈 (206) 764-
5720. ◯ 10am–5pm daily. ●
Thanksgiving, Dec 25. 🌿 ♿ 🎦 ▯
📷 ⓦ www.museumofflight.org

THE WEST COAST'S largest air
and space museum, the
Museum of Flight takes visitors
on a fascinating journey right
through from the earliest days
of aviation to the Space Age.
The museum features 54
restored airplanes, nearly half
of them suspended from the
ceiling of the six-story Great
Gallery. Visitors can sit in the
cockpit of an SR-71 Blackbird
or F/A-18 Hornet, and board
the first Air Force One, the
US presidential jet.

The restored Red Barn,
Boeing's original 1910 airplane factory and a National
Historic Site, is part of the
museum. Its exhibits include
the world's first fighter plane.
The museum's new wing
houses its recently acquired
Champlin Fighter collection of
25 historical aircraft, mainly
from World Wars I and II.

Especially popular with visitors are the museum's eight
simulators. Among the most
challenging are the space-
docking simulators in which
participants try to link up with
the Hubble space telescope.
The museum's 268-seat William
M. Allen Theater features a
variety of air- and space-related
films. Weekend family workshops teach the fundamentals
of flying via hands-on activities such as paper airplane
building and kite making.

**Fighter planes from the US Air
Force, in the Museum of Flight**

Chateau Ste. Michelle ⑨

14111 NE 145th St, Woodinville.
Road map 1 A2. 🛈 (425) 415-3632.
◯ 10am–5pm daily. ● Jan 1, Easter,
Thanksgiving, Dec 25. ♿
🎦 10:30am–4:30pm daily. 📷
Summer concerts, cooking classes.
ⓦ www.ste-michelle.com

WASHINGTON'S OLDEST win-
ery, Chateau Ste. Michelle
is located on an 87-acre (35-ha)
wooded estate in Woodinville,
15 miles (24 km) northeast of
Seattle. This location produces
all Chateau Ste. Michelle's
white wines. (The red wines
are made in eastern Washington, where grapes for both
the white and red wines are
grown.) Complimentary cellar
tours and wine tastings are
offered daily. The winery's
summer concert series draws
top blues, jazz, classical, and
contemporary talents to its
outdoor grass amphitheater,
where concert-goers savor
wine and picnics while
enjoying the music.

Chateau Ste. Michelle, founded in 1934, Washington's oldest winery

The magnificent cascades of Snoqualmie Falls

Snoqualmie Falls ❿

Road map 1 B2.

THE MOST FAMOUS waterfall in the state, Snoqualmie Falls is Washington's second most visited tourist attraction after Mount Rainier. This 276-ft (84-m) waterfall on the Snoqualmie River draws one and a half million visitors each year. Long regarded as a sacred site by the Snoqualmie Indians and other local Native American tribes, the cascade also fascinated the naturalist John Muir who, in 1889, described it as the most interesting he had ever seen.

An observation deck 300 ft (91 m) above the river provides an excellent view of the thundering water. For a closer look, visitors can follow a steep half-mile (0.8 km) trail down to the river.

Tacoma ⓫

Road map 1 A2. 🏛 195,000. ✈ *Seattle-Tacoma International Airport.* ℹ *747 Market St, (253) 627-2836.* Ⓦ *www.cityoftacoma.org*

WASHINGTON'S third largest city, Tacoma was founded as a sawmill town in the 1860s. It prospered with the arrival of the railroad in the late 1880s, becoming a major shipping port for commodities important to a growing nation: lumber, coal, and grain. Many of the Pacific Northwest's railroad, timber, and shipping barons settled in Tacoma's Stadium District. This historic area, with its

stately turn-of-the-19th-century mansions, is named for Stadium High School, which is also known as the "Castle." Designed in the 1890s to be a luxury hotel, the French chateau–style building was converted in the early 1900s into a high school.

The undisputed star of the city's revitalized waterfront is the striking **Museum of Glass**. Opened in July 2002, this landmark building was designed by top Canadian architect Arthur Erickson to showcase contemporary art, with a focus on glass. The 75,000-sq-ft (6,968-sq-m) museum includes a spacious glass-blowing studio housed within a dramatic 90-ft (37-m) metal-encased cone.

The stunning Chihuly Bridge of Glass, a collaboration between Austin, Texas, architect Arthur Andersson and world-renowned Tacoma glass artist Dale Chihuly, serves as a pedestrian walkway linking the museum to downtown Tacoma and the innovative **Washington State History Museum**. Tales of Washington's past are related using interactive exhibits, high-tech displays, and theatrical storytelling by characters in period costume.

The spectacular new home of the **Tacoma Art Museum** was designed by architect Antoine Predock to be a dynamic cultural center and a showpiece for the city. The 50,000-sq-ft (4,645-sq-m), stainless-steel-wrapped museum boldly showcases

Sign denoting the old town of Tacoma

The imposing Stadium High School, in Tacoma's Stadium District

the growing collection of works from the 18th century to the present day. These include a large assembly of Pacific Northwest art, European Impressionist pieces, Japanese woodblock prints, American graphic art, and Chihuly glass. In keeping with its vision of creating a place that "builds community through art," the museum's facilities include the Bill and Melinda Gates Resource Center, providing visitors with access to a wide array of reference materials and state-of-the-art research equipment. As well, kids of all ages can make use of the in-house, interactive art-making studio, ArtWORKS.

Tacoma's most popular attraction is Point Defiance Park, ranked among the 20 largest urban parks in the US. Encompassing 700 acres

The modern stainless steel exterior of the Tacoma Museum of Glass

E.T. the walrus, at Point Defiance Zoo and Aquarium, Tacoma

(285 ha), its grounds include Fort Nisqually, the first European settlement on Puget Sound and a major fur-trading establishment; seven specialty gardens; a scenic drive; hiking and biking trails; beaches; a boat marina; and a picnic area. Fishing is permitted, and gear is available for rental.

Highlighting a Pacific Rim theme, the world-class **Point Defiance Zoo and Aquarium** is home to over 5,000 animals, including the only polar bears and beluga whales in Washington. A vantage point at the west end of the park offers terrific views of Mount Rainier, Puget Sound, and the Tacoma Narrows Bridge, one of the longest suspension bridges in the world.

🏛 **Museum of Glass**
1801 E Dock St. 📞 *(253) 284-4750 or (866) 468-7386.* ⏰ *10am–5pm Tue–Wed & Fri–Sat, 10am–8pm Thu, noon–5pm Sun.* 🌑 *Mon, Jan 1, Thanksgiving, Dec 25.* 📷 ♿ 🅿 🚻
🌐 *www.museumofglass.org*
🏛 **Washington State History Museum**
1911 Pacific Ave. 📞 *(253) 272-9747.* ⏰ *10am–5pm Tue–Wed & Fri–Sat, 10am–8pm Thu, noon–5pm Sun.* 🌑 *major hols.* 📷 ♿ 🚻 *for groups.*
🌐 *www.wshs.org*
🏛 **Tacoma Art Museum**
1123 Pacific Ave. 📞 *(253) 272-4258.* ⏰ *10am–5pm Tue–Wed & Fri–Sat, 10am–8pm Thu, noon–5pm Sun.* 🌑 *Mon, major hols.* 📷 *(free 3rd Thu of month).* ♿ *by arrangement.* 🎫 🚻
🚻 🌐 *www.tacomaartmuseum.org*
🦎 **Point Defiance Zoo and Aquarium**
5400 N Pearl St. 📞 *(253) 591-5337.* ⏰ *9:30am–between 4 & 7pm (depending on time of year, call for details) daily.* 🌑 *Jul 19, Thanksgiving, Dec 25.* 📷 ♿ 🚻 🅿
🌐 *www.pdza.org*

Environs: Just 11 miles (17 km) from Tacoma, across the Narrows on the Kitsap Peninsula, is the charming fishing village of **Gig Harbor**, named by Captain Charles Wilkes, who, from 1838 to 1842, charted the area from his gig. The community's boutiques, galleries, and waterfront restaurants reflect the proud Scandinavian and Croatian heritage of many of its 6,500 inhabitants.

The bastion at Fort Nisqually historic site in Point Defiance Park

Olympia ⑫

Road map 1 A2. 🏘 *43,000.* ℹ
103 14th Ave SW, (360) 586-3460.
🌐 *www.olympiachamber.com*

W**ASHINGTON'S STATE** capital since 1853, Olympia was named for its magnificent view of the Olympic Mountains. Located 60 miles (97 km) south of Seattle at the southern tip of Puget Sound, the city is known first and foremost for its lovely **State Capitol Campus**, dominated by the 28-story domed Legislative Building. With its stunning buildings, landscaped grounds (designed in 1928 by the Olmsted Brothers and known for their spectacular bulb and annual plantings),

fountains, and monuments, this capital campus is one of the most beautiful in the nation. The centerpiece is the **Legislative Building** (the Capitol). Its 287-ft (87-m) brick-and-sandstone dome is one of the tallest masonry domes in the world.

The **State Archives** stores Washington's historical records and artifacts. Visitors can view such treasures as documents from the Canwell Committee, which blacklisted suspected Communists in the 1950s.

Tree-lined streets, old homes, a picturesque waterfront, and a thriving cultural community all contribute to Olympia's charm. Tucked among downtown Olympia's historic buildings are restaurants, galleries, and shops. Within walking distance are attractions such as the lively **Olympia Farmers Market**, offering local produce, seafood, baked goods, and crafts, along with dining and entertainment.

Percival Landing (4th Avenue between Sylvester and Water Streets), a 1.5-mile (2.5-km) boardwalk along Budd Inlet, offers views of the Olympic Mountains, Capitol Dome, and Puget Sound.

State Capitol Campus
ℹ *103 14th Ave SW, (360) 586-3460.*
🌑 *Jan 1, Thanksgiving, Dec 25.* **Legislative Bldg** ⏰ *until Jan 2005,* 🚻
Campus: *10am–3pm daily;* **Temple of Justice**: *8am–5pm Mon–Fri.* ♿
🏛 **State Capital Museum**
211 W 21st Ave. 📞 *(360) 753-2580.* ⏰ *10am–4pm Tue–Fri; noon–4pm Sat.* 🌑 *major hols.* 📷 ♿
🌐 *www.wshs.org*
🏛 **State Archives**
1129 Washington St SE. 📞 *(360) 753-1801.* ⏰ *8:30am–4:30pm Mon–Fri.* ♿
🍎 **Olympia Farmers Market**
700 N Capitol Way. 📞 *(360) 352-9096.* ⏰ *Apr–Oct: 10am–3pm Thu–Sun; Nov–Dec: 10am–3pm Sat–Sun.* ♿ 🌐 *www.farmers-market.org*

The imposing Legislative Building on the State Capitol Campus, Olympia

Mount Rainier National Park ⑬

E STABLISHED IN 1899, Mount Rainier National Park encompasses 337 sq miles (872 sq km), of which 97 percent is designated Wilderness. Its centerpiece is Mount Rainier, an active volcano towering 14,410 ft (4,392 m) above sea level. Surrounded by old-growth forest and wildflower meadows, Mount Rainier was named in 1792 by Captain George Vancouver

Jeep with outdoor equipment

for fellow British naval officer Peter Regnier. Designated a National Historic Landmark District in 1997, the park, which features 1920s and 1930s National Park Service rustic architecture, attracts two million visitors a year. The summer draws hikers, mountain climbers, and campers; the winter lures snowshoers and cross-country skiers.

Mount Rainier Nisqually Glacier

Close to the Paradise entrance, the Nisqually Glacier is one of the most visible on Mount Rainier. Its last retreat was 1985–91.

Mount Rainier Narada Falls

One of the more spectacular and easily accessible cascades along the Paradise River, Narada Falls is just a short hike from Route 706. The falls plummet 168 ft (51 m).

OLYMPIA

Carbon River entrance

Ipsut Creek

Wonderland Trail

M O U N
R A I N I

Tahoma Vista

Cougar Rock

Narada Fa

Westside Road

706 Nisqually entrance

Longmire

Sunshine Point

STAR SIGHTS
★ Emmons Glacier
★ Paradise
★ Sunrise

National Park Inn

This small and cozy inn, located in Longmire and open year-round, is a perfect spot from which to enjoy the stunning view of Mount Rainier.

★ Emmons Glacier

*Emmons Glacier, on Mount Rainier's
eastern slope, is, at 43 sq miles (111 sq km),
the largest glacier in the lower 48 states.*

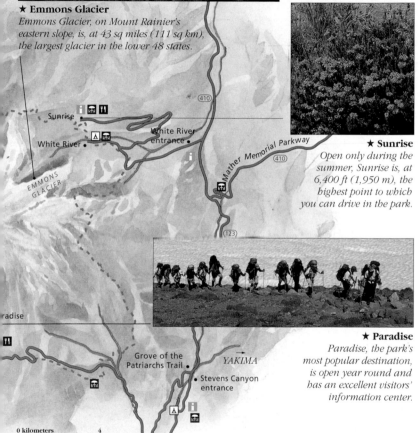

★ Sunrise

*Open only during the
summer, Sunrise is, at
6,400 ft (1,950 m), the
highest point to which
you can drive in the park.*

★ Paradise

*Paradise, the park's
most popular destination,
is open year round and
has an excellent visitors'
information center.*

0 kilometers   4

0 miles   2

KEY

▬	Minor road
═	Dirt or four-wheel-drive road
▪ ▪	Hiking trail
△	Camping
🏕	Picnic area
i	Information
☼	Viewpoint
🍴	Restaurant

GETTING AROUND

From the southwest (Hwy 706), enter the park via Nisqually gate.
Open year-round, this is the primary entrance in winter. Drive
6 miles (10 km) to Longmire, where facilities include an inn and
museum, and the Wilderness Information Center, open from late
May to October. The 12-mile (19-km) road between Paradise and
Longmire is steep and winding; drive carefully. Carry chains
when traveling by car during winter. Ashford Mountain Center
Shuttle (tel. 360/569-2604) and Rainier Shuttle (tel. 360/569-2331)
offer seasonal shuttle service to and tours of Mount Rainier.

Downhill skiing on the sparkling snow-covered slopes of Washington's Crystal Mountain

Crystal Mountain ⑭

Road map 1 B2. 【 (360) 663-2265.
◯ hrs vary depending on facility &
season; call for details. 🍴 ▢ 🛆
See **Where to Stay** p288.
🆆 www.skicrystal.com

LOCATED NEAR the northeast
corner of Mount Rainier
National Park and rising
above the town of the same
name, Crystal Mountain is
Washington's largest and only
destination ski area.

Attracted by reports of local
gold finds in the late 1800s,
the first visitors to the area
were miners intent on making
their fortunes. However, by
the end of World War I, these
claims had not yielded the
riches envisioned, and invest-
ment in this area then known
as the Summit Mining District
severely declined.

Its recreational attributes
were discovered in 1949
when attempts to put a chair
lift on Mount Rainier failed,
and a group of avid Puget
Sound skiers began looking
for another spot to develop as
a ski area. Crystal Mountain
opened for business in 1962,
receiving national attention
three years later when it
hosted the National Alpine
Championships, an event that
attracted skiing legends such
as Jimmie Heuga, Billy Kidd,
and Jean Claude Killy.

The ski area, with 50 named
runs, encompasses 2,300 acres
(930 ha), including 1,000 (405
ha) acres of backcountry

terrain. Ten lifts, including
two high-speed, six-passenger
chairs, transport more than
19,000 skiers per hour. Cross-
country skiers will also find
an extensive network of
challenging trails.

During summer, mountain
biking, hiking, and chair-lift
sightseeing are Crystal
Mountain's main
attractions. On
weekends,
high-speed lifts
whisk passen-
gers to the
6,872-ft (2,095-m)
summit and its
panoramic
views of the
Olympic and Cascade Moun-
tains, with Mount Rainier dominating the western horizon.
Herds of elk and black-tailed
deer grazing the grassy slopes
are often spotted from the lifts.

**Shop sign in the Bavarian-
themed village of Leavenworth**

**Snowboarding in the stunning
backcountry at Crystal Mountain**

Leavenworth ⑮

Road map 1 B2. 🏠 2,200.
🚻 220 9th St, (509) 548-5807.
🆆 www.leavenworth.org

CROSSING OVER the Cascade
Mountains from the west-
ern part of the state, first-time
visitors to Leavenworth
never fail to be
surprised to
encounter an
enchanting
Bavarian-style
village seem-
ingly straight out
of a fairy tale.
But this small
town was not
always so charming. In the
early 1960s it was a dying
logging town, with plenty of
drive-through traffic but no
real business to sustain it.
Inspired by Leavenworth's
spectacular mountain backdrop, a tourism committee
decided to develop a Bavarian
village theme to revitalize
the town. Buildings were
remodeled to echo Bavarian
architecture and, today, every
commercial building in town,
Starbucks and McDonald's
included, looks as though it
belongs in the Alps.

Leavenworth now bustles
with festivals, art shows, and
summer theater productions,
attracting more than a million
visitors each year. Among its
most popular festivals are
Fasching, a classic Bavarian
carnival held in February;
Maifest, with its 16th-century

costumes, maypole dances, Tyrolean Haflinger horses, and jousting; Oktoberfest, the traditional celebration of German beer, food, music, and live entertainment; and Christkindlmarkt, an open-air Christmas market similar to those in Germany. In addition to its many shops and restaurants featuring Bavarian specialties, the town also boasts the **Leavenworth Nutcracker Museum**, which showcases 4,500 nutcrackers from 38 countries, some dating back 500 years.

🏛 **Leavenworth Nutcracker Museum**

735 Front St. 📞 (509) 548-4573. ⏱ May–Oct: 2–5pm daily; Nov–Apr: 2–5pm Sat–Sun. 🎟 🎫 for groups by appt.

Leavenworth's traditional horse-drawn 13-barrel beer wagon

Lake Chelan ⑯

Road map 1 B2. 🏔 7,000. ℹ 102 E Johnson Ave, (509) 682-3503. 🌐 www.lakechelan.com

CHELAN, A RESORT town on the southeast end of Lake Chelan, has been a popular summer vacation destination for generations of western Washingtonians seeking the sunny, dry weather on the eastern side of the state. Basking in the rain shadow of the Cascade Mountains, the

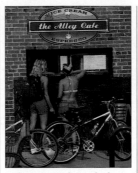

Cyclists stopping for a refreshment at the Alley Cafe in Chelan

town enjoys 300 days of sunshine each year.

Its namesake claims the distinction of being the third deepest lake in the country, reaching 1,500 ft (457 m) at its deepest point. Fed by 27 glaciers and 59 streams, the lake, which is less than 2 miles (3 km) wide, stretches for 55 miles (89 km). In the summer, it buzzes with activity: waterskiing, boating, snorkeling, fishing, and wind surfing.

Strolling through the town, visitors can admire the vintage **Ruby Theatre** (135 East Woodin Avenue). Listed on the National Register of Historic Places, it is one of the oldest continuously running movie theaters in the Northwest US. The 15 murals painted on area buildings are another highlight of the town. Depicting the agricultural, recreational, cultural, and ecological history of the Lake Chelan Valley, all contain

Sign welcoming visitors to Lake Chelan

an image – obvious in some murals, obscure in others – of an apple, a crop that thrives in the area's soil, fertile thanks to the glaciers that melted here thousands of years ago.

ENVIRONS: Manson, 9 miles (14 km) along the north shore from downtown Chelan, is a charming town. Along with shops, restaurants, and recreational activities, the town boasts the Scenic Loop Trail, offering easy exploration of the nearby orchards and hilly countryside. Many businesses offer free route maps.

Stehekin ⑰

Road map 1 B2. 🏔 70. ℹ 102 E Johnson St, (509) 682-3503. 🌐 9am–5pm Mon–Fri, hrs on weekends vary, call ahead. 🌐 www.stehekinvalley.com

AT THE NORTHERNMOST tip of Lake Chelan, nestled at the base of the North Cascade Mountains, rustic Stehekin invites travelers to slow down and savor life without the distractions of televisions or telephones. You won't find one single automated bank machine in this tiny community, but you will discover some of the most beautiful scenery in the state – accessible only by foot, horseback, plane, or boat.

For more than 100 years, the Lady of the Lake boat service has ferried passengers from Chelan to Stehekin. This ride takes four hours; faster options include the *Lady Express* (just over two hours) and the high-speed *Lady Cat*, which zips to Stehekin in an hour.

Bird-watching, biking, hiking, horseback riding, fishing, and rafting the Stehekin River are all popular summer activities in the Stehekin Valley; cross-country skiing and snowshoeing are popular in winter.

Rainbow Falls, a 312-ft (95-m) waterfall near Stehekin Landing, is worth a visit (call 509/682-4494 for tour details).

View of glacier-fed Lake Chelan, in its arid setting

North Cascades National Park Tour ⑱

THE NORTH CASCADES NATIONAL PARK is a breathtakingly beautiful ecosystem of jagged snowcapped peaks, forested valleys, and cascading waterfalls. Its many wonders can be accessed from the scenic North Cascades Highway, which bisects the park. With more than 300 glaciers, the 684,300-acre (276,935-ha) park is the most heavily glaciated region in the lower 48 states. It is home to a variety of animals, including bald eagles, beavers, gray wolves, and black and grizzly bears. The park and the adjacent Ross Lake and Lake Chelan National Recreation Areas attract over 400,000 visitors each year. The North Cascades Highway and the Lake Chelan National Recreation Area are linked by hiking trails to the quiet town of Stehekin on Lake Chelan, which is serviced by a ferry from Chelan *(see p187)*.

Mount Shuksan ④

NORTH CASCADES NATIONAL PARK (NORTH UNIT)

Baker Lake

③

New hale

ℹ ②

Skagit River

①

⑳ *Marblemount*

MOUNT BAKER

Cascades River Rd.

Marble Creek

Mount Shuksan ④
One of the state's highest mountains at 9,131 ft (2,783 m) and a dominant feature of the park, Mount Shuksan consists of a form of basalt known as Shuksan greenschist.

Gorge Creek Falls ③
Plunging 242 ft (74 m) into Gorge Lake, the Gorge Creek Falls are visible from an overlook just off the North Cascades Highway. A fully accessible, paved trail leads to the overlook.

North Cascades Visitor Center ②
Commanding an impressive view of the Picket Range, the visitor center, near Newhalem, offers interpretive displays, multimedia presentations, and daily ranger-guided programs in summer.

Skagit River ①
The second longest river in Washington, the Skagit is popular for steelhead and salmon fishing. The river has been dammed in three locations in the park, creating lakes and providing hydroelectric power for the state.

KEY

▬	Tour route
═	Other road
▪▪	Trail
⚹	Viewpoint
ℹ	Information

Diablo Lake 5

Diablo Lake owes its rich turquoise color to sediment from glacier-fed streams. Boat tours of Diablo Lake are offered Thursday to Monday in July and August; Saturday and Sunday in June and September.

Tips for Drivers

Tour length: *56 miles (90 km).*
Starting point: *State Route 20 (North Cascades Highway) at the entrance to Ross Lake National Recreation Area, approximately 5 miles (8 km) north of Marblemount.*
When to go: *Mid-Apr–mid-Oct, when all of Route 20 is open.*
Stopping-off points: *There are restaurants in Marblemount and Winthrop but in the park itself there are only picnic facilities. It is a good idea to bring along your own provisions. You can stock up on groceries and buy hot soup and coffee at the Skagit General Store in Newhalem.*

ROSS LAKE NATIONAL RECREATION AREA
6
Ruby Creek
North Cascades Highway
NORTH CASCADES NATIONAL PARK (SOUTH UNIT)
Rainy Pass
7
McAlester Trail / Rainbow Creek Trail
LAKE CHELAN NATIONAL RECREATION AREA
Glory
8
Stehekin
Lake Chelan
0 kilometers 15
0 miles 10

Ross Lake Overlook 6

At this lookout, dramatic vistas of 24-mile- (40-km-) long Ross Lake, created by the damming of Skagit River, come into view.

Washington Pass Overlook 7

This overlook, 5,477 ft (1,669 m) above ground level, offers heart-pounding views of the steep pass up Liberty Bell Mountain.

Rainbow Falls 8

Accessible on foot after a 20-mile (32-km) hike from Rainy Pass or a short hike from Stehekin, these spectacular falls are located on a creek leading into Lake Chelan.

The jagged peak of Glory Mountain's 7,228-ft- (2,203-m-) high summit

Horseback riders enjoying the scenery along a Winthrop trail

Winthrop **⓲**

Road map 1 B1. 🏔 *350.*
🅸 *202 Hwy 20, (509) 996-2125.*
🆆 *www.winthropwashington.com*

THE WILD WEST lives on in Winthrop. In the spring or fall, more than one astonished traveler has witnessed a genuine cattle drive – right down the main street.

The town was founded in 1891 by Guy Waring, a Boston-bred businessman whose Winthrop enterprises included the Duck Brand Saloon. The saloon, now home to the Winthrop Town Hall, is still standing, as is Waring's pioneer log house, which sits on the grounds of the **Shafer Museum**, along with other relics from the past.

By the 1960s, Winthrop resembled any other small, nondescript town in the American West before its merchants, eager to revive the local economy, "renovated" the town to give it an Old West ambience. A popular overnight and vacation destination for tourists exploring the North Cascades, the Winthrop area offers a wealth of outdoor recreation possibilities.

🏛 **Shafer Museum**
285 Castle Ave. 🅲 *(509) 996-2712.*
🅾 *Memorial Day–Labor Day: 10am–5pm Thu–Mon.*

Spokane **⓴**

Road map 1 C2. 🏔 *195,000.*
🛪 *Spokane International Airport.*
🅸 *301-801 W Riverside Ave, (509) 624-1341.* 🆆 *www.visitspokane.com*

WASHINGTON'S SECOND largest city, Spokane is the commerce and culture center for the Inland Northwest. Founded in 1873 by real estate developer James Nettle Glover, the city suffered a disastrous fire in 1889. It responded by rebuilding in brick and terra cotta. Many handsome reminders of the building boom remain.

Grand Coulee Dam **⓳**

CONSIDERED ONE OF THE modern engineering wonders of the world, Grand Coulee Dam is the largest concrete dam in North America and the third largest producer of electricity in the world. Spanning the mighty Columbia River – the second largest river in the US – it generates more power than a million locomotives, supplying electricity to 11 western states. Construction of the dam began in 1933 and took over nine years. The dam was built primarily to supply irrigation water to eastern Washington, where inadequate rainfall threatened the livelihood of the region's farmers.

VISITORS' CHECKLIST

Road map 1 C2. *Visitors' center* 🅲 *(509) 633-9265.*
🅾 *call for hrs.* 🅿
🆆 *www.grandcouleedam.org*

INSIDE THE DAM

The power plants house the generators and turbines.

Trash-racks prevent debris from entering the generators.

Four gantry cranes are located on the dam to move heavy equipment.

Lake Roosevelt

A third power plant featuring reversible pumps was added in the 1970s.

Irrigation Canal

Twelve irrigation pipes at the canal headworks pump water to Lake Roosevelt.

The dam, nearly a mile (1.6 km) long, towers almost 550 ft (152 m) above bedrock.

The spillway doubles as a screen in summer for spectacular nightly laser shows.

Columbia River

The concrete poured to build the dam amounts to almost 12 million cubic yards (9 million cubic m) – enough to build a 6-ft (2-m-) wide sidewalk around the equator.

View of the Spokane River, the town in the background

Regional history is showcased at the **Northwest Museum of Arts and Culture**. Nearby **Campbell House** (1898) is an interactive museum.

The smallest city ever to host a world's fair (Expo '74), Spokane's fair site is now **Riverfront Park**, a 100-acre (40-ha) expanse in the heart of the city that offers views of dramatic Spokane Falls. Other attractions are an IMAX theater and a 1909 carousel carved by Charles Looff, of Coney Island fame. A 37-mile (60-km) trail connects Riverside State Park.

🏛 Northwest Museum of Arts and Culture
2316 W 1st Ave. 📞 *(509) 456-3931.* ⏱ *11am–5pm daily (until 8pm Wed & Fri).* ■ *major hols* 📷 ♿ ☐ □
🔳 *www.northwestmuseum.org*

ENVIRONS: Just 6 miles (10 km) northwest of Spokane, **Riverside State Park** offers plenty of freshwater shoreline. The Bowl and Pitcher, with its suspension bridge and volcanic formations, is stunning.

♣ Riverside State Park
9711 W Charles St, Nine Mile Falls. 📞 *(509) 465-5064.*

Yakima Valley ❷

Road map 1 B2. 🛈 *10 N 8th St, Yakima, (509) 575-3010.*
🔳 *www.visityakima.com*

BOASTING RICH volcanic soil, an abundance of irrigation water, and 300 days of sunshine per year, the Yakima Valley is the fifth largest producer of fruits and vegetables in the US, and home to more than 30 regional wineries. Yakima is the valley's largest community and commercial hub. The **Washington's Fruit Place Visitor Center** offers free fruit samples and an overview of the state's fruit-growing industry.

For a taste of the valley's award-winning wines, drive ten minutes south of Yakima on I-82. Begin the wine tour at Exit 40 (Sagelands Vineyard), then continue on the Yakima Valley Highway.

Washington's Fruit Place Visitor Center
205-105 S 18th St, Yakima. 📞 *(509) 576-3090.* ⏱ *year-round: 10am–5pm Mon–Fri; May–Dec: also 10am–4pm Sat.* ♿

Luscious grapes on the vine in the wine-growing area of Yakima Valley

Walla Walla ❷❸

Road map 1 C3. 🚶 *30,000.*
🛈 *29 E Sumac St, (509) 525-0850.*
🔳 *www.wallawalla.org*

LOCATED IN THE southeast corner of the state, Walla Walla is a charming and pretty town – and a green oasis in the midst of an arid landscape. The town features a large number of National Register buildings, lovely parks, and a wealth of public art. **Whitman College**, one of the nation's top-rated liberal arts colleges, is just three blocks from downtown. The attractive campus is a delight to stroll, as is the surrounding neighborhood, with its tree-shaded streets lined with historic homes.

A popular destination for wine connoisseurs, the Walla Walla Valley offers more than 35 wineries (see pp192–3) – several right in the heart of downtown Walla Walla. Among the town's other claims to fame are its delicious sweet onions and its annual Hot Air Balloon Stampede, a rally of some 45 pilots, held in May. The stampede also features live music, antiques and arts-and-crafts booths, and various events.

For a historical perspective on the area, visit **Fort Walla Walla Museum**, a pioneer village consisting of 17 original and replica buildings, including a schoolhouse, jail, and train station, as well as the **Whitman Mission National Historic Site**. Here, the story of pioneer missionaries Marcus and Narcissa Whitman and their subsequent massacre by the Cayuse Indians is told. On weekends, the Living History Company honors the area's history through music and dance.

🏛 Fort Walla Walla Museum
755 Myra Rd. 📞 *(509) 525-7703.* ⏱ *Apr–Oct: 10am–5pm daily.* 📷 ♿ *(call ahead).* 📷 *by appt.*
🔳 *www.fortwallawallamuseum.org*
🏛 Whitman Mission National Historic Site
Hwy 12. 📞 *(509) 522-6360.* ⏱ *Jun–Sep: 8am–6pm daily; Oct–May: 8am–4:30pm daily.* ● *Jan 1, Thanksgiving, Dec 25.* 📷 ♿ *(except Monument Hill).* 🔳 *www.nps.gov/whmi*

Balloons over Walla Walla during the annual Hot Air Balloon Stampede

Walla Walla Valley Wine Tour ㉔

Walla Walla Valley grapes

ALTHOUGH GRAPE-GROWING in the Walla Walla Valley dates back to the mid-1800s, it wasn't until 1977 that the valley's first winery was established. Seven years later, the region was recognized as an American Viticultural Area. Today, the Walla Walla Valley boasts more than 35 wineries and 1,000 acres (405 ha) of vineyards.

Lying at the same latitude as the great wine-producing regions of France, the valley enjoys long, sunny days and cool evenings, which together with ideal soil conditions create the perfect environment for growing grapes. The region has won national and international recognition for its wines and is especially known for its reds – in particular, cabernet sauvignon, merlot, and syrah.

L'Ecole No. 41 ②
The cellars at this winery are located in a 1915 schoolhouse, colorfully depicted on the wine bottle labels.

① ② Lower Dry Creek Road (12)

YAKIMA

Walla Walla River

Woodward Canyon ①
This winery is known for its award-winning merlots, cabernets, and chardonnays

Goldendale Observatory State Park ㉕

1602 Observatory Dr, Goldendale. **Road map** 1 B3. (509) 773-3141. *Observatory* ☐ Apr–Sep: 2–5pm & 8pm–midnight Wed–Sun; Oct–Mar: 1–5pm & 7–9pm Sat, 1–5pm Sun. by donation. ☐ partial. **Library**.

PERCHED ATOP a 2,100-ft (640-m) hill, the Goldendale Observatory, with its 20-ft- (6-m-) diameter dome, has more than a dozen telescopes with which to observe the countryside and night sky. The highlight is a 24.5-inch (62-cm) reflecting Cassegrain, one of the largest telescopes in the US available for public viewing. During the day, visitors can enjoy great views of Mount Hood and the Klickitat Valley. By night, they can observe the sky from a location well away from city lights. Daily programs on telescopes and sky-watching are offered.

Maryhill ㉖

Road map 1 B3.

A REMOTE SAGEBRUSH bluff overlooking the Columbia River is where entrepreneur Sam Hill chose to build his palatial residence. In 1907, he purchased 7,000 acres (2,833 ha) here, with the vision of creating a utopian colony for Quaker farmers. He called the community Maryhill, in honor of his daughter, Mary. Utopia never materialized, however. No one wanted to live in such a desolate place, and Hill was persuaded to turn his unfinished mansion into a museum. The **Maryhill Museum of Art** houses the throne and gold coronation gown of his friend Queen Marie of Romania, 87 sculptures and drawings by Auguste Rodin, an impressive collection of Native art, and many other treasures. The beautifully landscaped grounds include a lovely picnic area.

At the original Maryhill town site, 2.5 miles (4 km) east of the museum, is a replica Stonehenge built by Hill to honor locals killed in World War I.

🏛 **Maryhill Museum of Art**
35 Maryhill Museum Dr, Goldendale. (509) 773-3733. ☐ Mar 15–Nov 15: 9am–5pm daily. 🎨 ☐ ☐ ☐

Mount St. Helens National Volcanic Monument ㉗

Road map 1 A3. (360) 449-7800. 🎨 🍴 ☐ Ⓦ www.fs.fed.us/gpnf/mshnvm

ON THE MORNING of May 18, 1980, Mount St. Helens literally exploded. Triggered by a powerful earthquake, the

Maryhill Museum of Art, overlooking the Columbia River Gorge

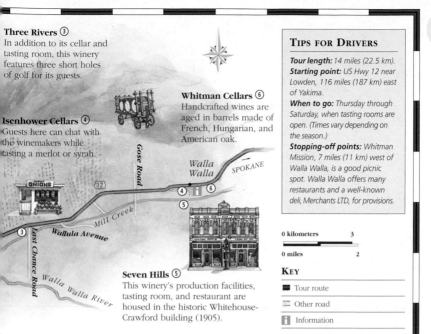

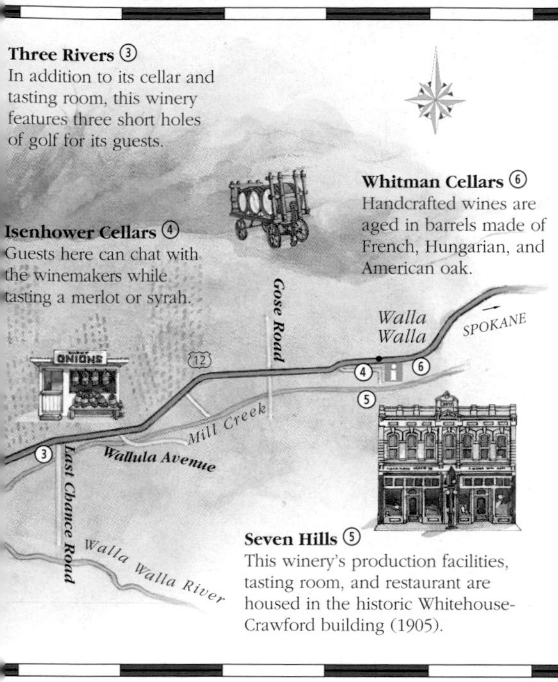
Three Rivers 3
In addition to its cellar and tasting room, this winery features three short holes of golf for its guests.
Whitman Cellars 6
Handcrafted wines are aged in barrels made of French, Hungarian, and American oak.
Isenhower Cellars 4
Guests here can chat with the winemakers while tasting a merlot or syrah.
ONIONS
Gose Road
Walla Walla
SPOKANE
12
Mill Creek
Wallula Avenue
Last Chance Road
Walla Walla River
Seven Hills 5
This winery's production facilities, tasting room, and restaurant are housed in the historic Whitehouse-Crawford building (1905).

Tips for Drivers

Tour length: *14 miles (22.5 km).*
Starting point: *US Hwy 12 near Lowden, 116 miles (187 km) east of Yakima.*
When to go: *Thursday through Saturday, when tasting rooms are open. (Times vary depending on the season.)*
Stopping-off points: *Whitman Mission, 7 miles (11 km) west of Walla Walla, is a good picnic spot. Walla Walla offers many restaurants and a well-known deli, Merchants LTD, for provisions.*

0 kilometers 3

0 miles 2

Key

Tour route

Other road

Information

Mount St. Helens and surrounding area after the 1980 explosion

conical peak erupted, spewing a cubic mile (4.17 cubic km) of rock into the air and causing the largest avalanche in recorded history. In the blink of an eye, the mountain lost 1,314 ft (400 m), and 234 sq miles (606 sq km) of forestland were destroyed. The eruption also claimed 57 human lives and those of millions of animals and fish.

Following the eruption, the US Congress created the 110,000-acre (44,000-ha) monument to allow the environment to recover naturally and to encourage research, recreation, and education. Roads and trails allow visitors to explore this fascinating region by car and on foot. On the mountain's west side, Highway 504 leads to five visitor centers. The first is the **Mount St. Helens National Volcanic Monument Visitor Center** (tel. 360/274-2100), at milepost 5, featuring interpretive exhibits of the mountain's history. **The Hoffstadt Bluffs Visitor Center** (tel. 360/274-7750), at milepost 27, gives visitors their first full view of Mount St. Helens and offers helicopter tours into the blast zone from May to September. The **Forest Learning Center** (tel. 360/414-3439), at milepost 33, open in the summer only, teaches about reforestation efforts. **Coldwater Ridge Visitor Center** (tel. 360/274-2131), at milepost 43, has a self-guided interpretive trail. **Johnston Ridge Visitor Center** (tel. 360/414-3439), at milepost 52, offers a close-up view of the crater and lava dome.

Fort Vancouver 28

Road map 1 A3. ☎ *(360) 696-7655.* 🕘 *Mar–Oct: 9am–5pm daily; Nov–Feb: 9am–4pm daily.* ● *Thanksgiving, Dec 24, 25 & 31.* $ ♿ *partial.* 📷 [W] www.nps.gov/fova

Between 1825 and 1849, Fort Vancouver was an important trading outpost for the British-based Hudson's Bay Company, the giant fur-trading organization *(see p38)*. Located close to major tributaries and natural resources, it was the center of political and commercial activities in the Pacific Northwest during these years. During the 1830s and 1840s, the fort also provided essential supplies to settlers. A National Historic Site, Fort Vancouver features accurate reconstructions of nine of the original buildings, including the jail, fur store, and wash house, all on their original sites. Guided tours and reenactments offer a window into the fort's past.

The three-story bastion, dating from 1845, at Fort Vancouver

VANCOUVER

Vancouver's Best

Inukshuk, English Bay

LIVELY AND LIVABLE, Vancouver is a young city with an eclectic sense of identity. The city's passion for the outdoors began with Stanley Park when it opened in 1888 and the love affair continues. The art and culture of coastal First Nations people is a source of pride, with totem poles and other artwork evident in the park and throughout the city. The cityscape reflects both old and new, from the century-old buildings of Gastown to Science World's geodesic dome, built for the 1986 world exposition. As the gateway to the Pacific Rim, Vancouver boasts the largest Asian population in North America; its Chinatown is the second largest in North America, after that of San Francisco.

Vancouver Art Gallery
Emily Carr's works are featured in the gallery, which has a lovely flower garden on its north side (see p211).

Vanier Park
Across English Bay from downtown, Vanier Park features a planetarium and two museums. Restored boats are docked in nearby Heritage Harbour (see pp220–21).

0 meters 800
0 yards 800

Granville Island Public Market
Bustling and bright, this former industrial site is a must-visit for its fresh produce stalls, baked goods, and arts-and-crafts tables. Enjoy a snack or meal here, accompanied by live entertainment provided by the market's numerous buskers (see p219).

Yaletown
Funky restaurants, brewpubs, and shops make Yaletown a great destination day or night (see pp220–21).

◁ **Marina on False Creek, Vancouver**

Canada Place
The Canada Place promenade offers a terrific view of Vancouver's port, busy with seaplanes, cruise ships, and harbor craft (see p202).

Harbour Centre
Enjoy panoramic views of Vancouver and beyond from The Lockout! observation deck, 553 ft (169 m) above the city (see p203).

Water Street
A world first, the cast bronze-and-gold steam clock was installed in 1977, instantly becoming one of the city's most beloved landmarks (see p203).

Chinatown
Straddling Pender Street, the classically proportioned Chinatown Millennium Gate was erected in 2002 as the gateway to historic Chinatown, with its 19th-century buildings and lively street market (see p204).

Science World
OMNIMAX shows inside the geodesic dome are just one of Science World's highlights (see p213).

Dr. Sun Yat-Sen Classical Chinese Garden
Built in the classical style of Chinese gardens, this serene enclave in Chinatown was the first full-sized example of its kind built outside China (see p205).

Waterfront, Gastown, and Chinatown

Pavilion at Dr. Sun Yat-sen Garden

Vancouver's waterfront, the city's birthplace, thrives with activity, the five-sailed roof of Canada Place at its helm. The harbor view from here is memorable, as is that from the Harbour Centre tower. Clustered near the waterfront are shops, restaurants, and some of Vancouver's most interesting attractions. Nearby Gastown began as a haven for gold-seekers, loggers, and a host of ruffians. This changed when, in 1885, Canadian Pacific Railway (CPR) chose the fledging town as its western terminus. After the Great Fire of 1886, the newly renamed Vancouver – a CPR marketing decision – settled into respectability. Boutiques and restaurants now occupy the area's historic buildings. Chinatown sprung up next door in what was then swampland. Today, its bustling sidewalks and night markets highlight an enduring presence.

Sights at a Glance

Museums and Galleries

Chinese Cultural Centre Museum and Archives [10]
Vancouver Police Centennial Museum [7]

Historic Buildings

Marine Building [1]
Waterfront Station [3]

Gardens and Viewpoints

Canada Place [2]
Dr. Sun Yat-Sen Classical Chinese Garden [9]
Harbour Centre [4]

Historic Squares, Streets, and Districts

Chinatown [8]
Maple Tree Square [6]
Water Street [5]

Key

Street-by-Street map *See pp200–201*
SkyTrain station
SeaBus terminal
[i] Information
[P] Parking
Police station

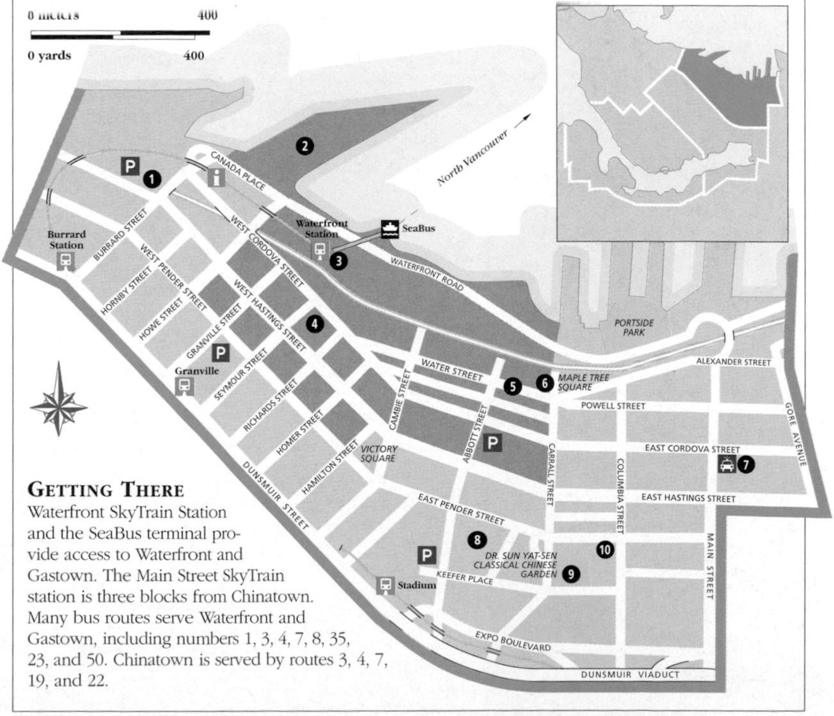

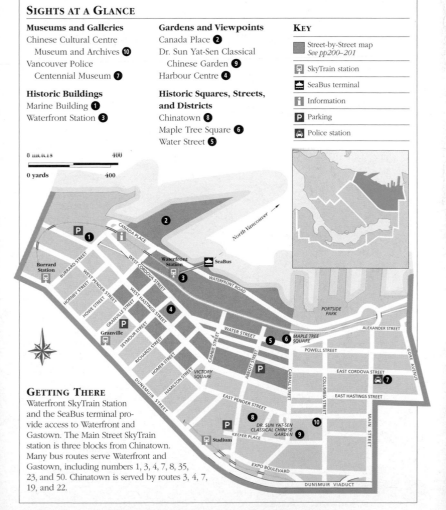

Getting There

Waterfront SkyTrain Station and the SeaBus terminal provide access to Waterfront and Gastown. The Main Street SkyTrain station is three blocks from Chinatown. Many bus routes serve Waterfront and Gastown, including numbers 1, 3, 4, 7, 8, 35, 23, and 50. Chinatown is served by routes 3, 4, 7, 19, and 22.

◁ **Reflections of the Art Deco Marine Building on the façades of downtown high-rises**

Street-by-Street: Waterfront and Gastown

The landmark steam clock

ONE OF VANCOUVER'S oldest areas, Gastown, which faces the waters of Burrard Inlet, is bounded by Columbia Street to the east and Burrard Street to the west. The district grew up around a saloon opened in 1867 by "Gassy Jack" Deighton, whose statue stands in Maple Tree Square. Gastown is a charming mix of cobblestone streets and restored 19th-century public buildings and storefronts. Chic boutiques and galleries line Water Street, and delightful restaurants and cafés fill the mews, courtyards, and passages. Visitors can watch the steam rise from the steam clock every 15 minutes, as well as be entertained by local street performers.

Canada Place
Canada Place is a waterside architectural marvel of white sails and glass that houses a hotel, two convention centers, and a cruise ship terminal ❷

The SeaBus, *a catamaran that ferries passengers across Burrard Inlet between the central Waterfront Station and Lonsdale Quay in North Vancouver, offers stunning views of the harbor.*

Waterfront Station
occupies the imposing 19th-century Canadian Pacific Railway building ❸

★ Harbour Centre
Harbour Centre is a modern high-rise building best-known for The Lookout!, a viewing deck 550 ft (167 m) above the city. On a clear day it is possible to see as far as Vancouver Island ❹

STAR SIGHTS
★ Harbour Centre
★ Water street

★ Water Street
Much of the quaint charm of Gastown can be seen here. Water Street boasts brick streets and cobblestones, as well as shops, cafés, and the famous steam clock ❺

LOCATOR MAP
See Street Fnder map 3

The steam clock is said to be the world's first steam-operated clock; it is based on an 1870s model and chimes every hour on the hour.

The Inuit Gallery
displays original Inuit art such as sculpture and prints.

"Gassy Jack" Statue
Gastown is named after "Gassy Jack" Deighton, an English sailor noted both for his endless chatter and for the saloon he opened here for the local sawmill workers in 1867.

KEY

- - - Suggested route

| 0 meters | 100 |
| 0 yards | 100 |

Shopping on West Cordova Street, with its wide range of small galleries and trendy boutiques, is a delightful experience.

Triangular Building
Reminiscent of New York's Flatiron Building, this striking structure, at the corner of Alexander and Powell Streets, was built in 1908–09 as a hotel. it now houses apartments.

Marine Building ❶

355 Burrard St. **Map** 3 A1.
🚇 *Waterfront.* 🚌 *17, 22.*
⛴ *SeaBus: Waterfront.*

Architects McCarter and Nairne described the Marine Building as "a great crag rising from the sea." Their design, built in 1929 in an extravagant Art Deco style near the waterfront, cost its Toronto developers $2.35 million before they went broke. The 25-story buff-brick tower, meant to house Vancouver's marine-related businesses, was sold in 1933 for a mere $900,000 to Ireland's Guinness family.

This now-beloved office building has seen $20 million worth of restoration and repair since the mid-1980s. Outside and in, it is the most impressive of all Vancouver's historic buildings. On the façade, terra-cotta marine fauna, including sea horses, frolic amid frothy waves. The main entrance, with its double revolving doors, features bronze grilles and brass bas-relief castings of starfish, crabs, and seashells. A 40-ft- (12-m-) high terra-cotta arch includes depictions of a jutting ship's prow and Canada geese.

The lobby is a dramatic step back in time, with aqua-green and blue tiles and carved maritime-inspired friezes. The elevator, inlaid with 12 varieties of BC hardwood, whisks visitors up to the second floor, from where there is a bird's-eye view of the lobby.

Entrance to the Art Deco Marine Building, with its bronze grilles

Canada Place, resembling a sailing ship setting out to sea

Canada Place ❷

999 Canada Pl. **Map** 3 B1.
🚇 *Waterfront.* 🚌 *1, 3, 4, 7, 8, 50.*
⛴ *SeaBus: Waterfront.* ⭕ *daily.* ♿

Built for Expo '86, Canada Place was the flagship pavilion of the Government of Canada. Today Canada Place is home to a cruise ship terminal, the Vancouver Trade and Convention Centre, Vancouver's World Trade Centre, and an upscale hotel.

The structure's five white Teflon-coated fabric "sails," aside from being a pleasing sight on the waterfront, make possible a huge interior area free of support structures. On the west side of the complex, a cooling fountain, shady trees, and ample outdoor seating provide an oasis in the heart of the bustling city.

The three-block, open-air Canada Place Promenade juts into Vancouver Harbour and offers a panorama of busy sea and air traffic. More than 2,800 cruise ships a year dock alongside the promenade en route to Alaska or Seattle. Every year on July 1 *(see p31)*, Canada Place hosts a spectacular celebratory fireworks display over the harbor; the promenade offers the best view in town.

The **CN IMAX Theatre**, at the north end of Canada Place, shows up to four different films daily on its five-story screen. The viewing experience is boosted by a 14,000-watt digital sound system.

CN IMAX Theatre
Canada Pl. 📞 *(604) 682-4629.* ⭕
11am–10pm daily. ⭕ *Dec 25.* 🎬 ♿

Waterfront Station ❸

601 W Cordova St. **Map** 3 B2.
🚇 *Waterfront.* 🚌 *1, 3, 4, 7, 8, 50.*
⛴ *SeaBus: Waterfront.* ♿ 🚻 📱

A busy transportation hub, Waterfront Station is the convergence point of the SeaBus, SkyTrain, and West Coast Express trains. Built by Canadian Pacific Railway, the current Waterfront Station is the third passenger train station built on the site *(see p211)*. The first cross-Canada passenger train pulled into the original timber station on May 23, 1887. The second

The grand columned entrance to Waterfront Station

station here was a chateau-style structure built in 1898–9.

The present-day building was designed by the firm of Barott, Blackader and Webster and completed in 1914. It was restored in 1976–7 to make the most of its expansive waiting area, arches, and columns. Murals circling the upper walls portray romantic versions of Canadian landscapes. Shops and cafés now occupy the former waiting room.

Outside the station is *Wounded Soldier*, a sculpture by Charles Marega (1871–1939), Vancouver's premier artist of his day. Marega also carved the two stone lions that guard the Stanley Park entrance to Lions Gate Bridge.

Viewing platform at Harbour Centre's The Lookout!

Harbour Centre ❹

555 W Hastings St. **Map** 3 B2.
📞 (604) 689-7304. 🚉 Waterfront.
🚌 23, 35. ⛴ SeaBus: Waterfront.
🕙 10am–6pm Mon–Sat. 🚻 🖥 📷

GLASS ELEVATORS glide 553 ft (169 m) up the tower of Harbour Centre to **The Lookout!**, an enclosed observation deck with a 360-degree view of Vancouver and informative plaques to help visitors identify the sights below. When this, the tallest building in British Columbia, opened on August 13, 1977, Neil Armstrong was a special guest. The first man on the moon left his footprint in cement as an official memento of the opening. A ticket to the deck is valid all day, so visitors often

return to watch the sun set over Vancouver Island, visible across the Strait of Georgia. Also at the top of tower is a revolving restaurant, turning a full circle in 90 minutes and providing fabulous views.

At street level, in Simon Fraser University's downtown campus, the small Teck Gallery showcases the work of Pacific Northwest artists, and offers an excellent view of the harbor. The two lower levels of Harbour Centre house a food fair, souvenir and clothing shops, and the well-stocked Simon Fraser University Bookstore.

The Lookout!
Harbour Centre. 📞 (604) 689-0421.
🕙 Apr–Sep: 8:30am–10:30pm daily;
Oct–Mar: 9am–9pm daily. 🚻 🚻 📷
🖥 📷 🖥 www.vancouverlookout.com

Water Street ❺

From Richards to Carrall Sts. **Map** 3 B2.
🚉 Waterfront. 🚌 1, 50. ⛴ SeaBus:
Waterfront.

WATER STREET, with its distinctive red-brick paving, is Gastown's main thoroughfare. Its turn-of-the-19th-century buildings house a mix of restaurants, nightclubs, boutiques, souvenir shops, rug merchants, offices, and First Nations art galleries.

Water Street was not always so popular, however. Having slipped into decline after

Water Street's steam clock, drawing a crowd every hour

World War I, it wasn't until the 1960s that the area's potential was again recognized and a wave of restoration and revival begun. By 1971, Water Street was designated an historic area. Old-fashioned street lamps, hanging flower baskets, and courtyards and mews enhance its historic flavor.

The world's first steam-operated clock stands 16 ft (5 m) tall, resplendent in bronze and gold, at the corner of Water and Cambie Streets. Erected in 1977, it strikes its Westminster chimes on the hour, every 15 minutes emitting a blast of steam supplied from steam vents beneath the sidewalk. Local horologist Raymond Saunders patterned its movements on an 1875 design.

THE GREAT FIRE OF 1886

On June 13, 1886, the lethal combination of a powerful westerly wind and sparks from a Canadian Pacific Railway brush fire near Drake and Homer Streets, in what is now Yaletown *(see pp220–21)*, burned through Vancouver's motley assortment of 1,000 wooden buildings. In 20 minutes, the city was devastated, barely two months after its incorporation. The raging fire – so hot it not only burned nearby St. James' Anglican Church but also melted its bell – killed at least 21 people; the exact number is unknown. Within 12 hours, rebuilding had begun. The Burns Block in Maple Tree Square *(see p204)* was built that same year and still exists.

City officials in front of a temporary city hall after the devastating fire of 1886

Statue of "Gassy Jack" Deighton in Gastown's Maple Tree Square

Maple Tree Square **❻**

Water St at Carrall St. **Map** 3 C2.
🚌 *1, 50.*

SEARCH AS YOU MIGHT, you won't find a maple tree in Gastown's Maple Tree Square. The famous tree, destroyed in the Great Fire of 1886 *(see p203)*, marked a popular meeting spot for local residents.

Standing in the square is Okanagan artist Vern Simpson's 6-ft- (1.8-m-) tall hammered copper statue of John "Gassy Jack" Deighton, for whom Gastown is named. Commissioned in 1970, the statue recognizes this voluble, or "gassy," entrepreneur's place in Vancouver history.

In 1867, Deighton built, near Maple Tree Square, the first watering hole on Burrard Inlet. Deighton apparently persuaded local millworkers to build the Globe Saloon in just 24 hours. Deighton died on May 29, 1875, at age 45, and was buried in an unmarked grave in New Westminster, some 13 miles (20 km) from Gastown.

The restored Gaoler's Mews in the square marks the residence of Constable Jonathan Miller, the town of Granville's first policeman, in 1871. The two adjacent small log prisoner cells had doors but no locks.

Vancouver Police Centennial Museum **❼**

240 E Cordova St. **Map** 3 C2.
📞 *(604) 665-3346.* 🚌 *3.* 🕐 *9am–3pm Mon–Fri; May–Sep: also 10am–3pm Sat.* ⬤ *major hols.* 🈴 📷 📹
🌐 *www.city.vancouver.bc.ca/police/museum*

OPENED IN 1986 to mark the centennial of the Vancouver police force and housed in the former (1932–80) Coroner's Court Building, this museum includes the city's original morgue. Step into the autopsy laboratory to view the forensic table where actor Errol Flynn was declared dead on October 14, 1959. Scenes for TV series *The X-Files* and *Da Vinci's Inquest* have been filmed here. A large mural depicts the colorful history of the police department; historical action settings re-create Vancouver crime scenes. Some 100 international police uniforms and 200 police hats are displayed, as well as street weaponry, prohibited weapons, antique firearms, and a Thompson submachine gun.

Chinatown **❽**

E Hastings to Union Sts, from Carrall to Gore Sts. **Map** 3 C3. 🚊 *Stadium.* 🚌 *3, 4, 7, 19, 22.* 🖋 *call (604) 658-8883.*

VANCOUVER'S CHINATOWN is older than the city itself. Pender Street, the main byway, is straddled near Taylor Street by Millennium Gate, a good

Chinatown's record-thin Sam Kee Building (1913)

spot from which to view architectural details of the area's restored buildings. The 1907 **Chinese Freemasons Building** (1 W. Pender St.) was once home to Dr. Sun Yat-sen. The 1913 **Sam Kee Building** (8 W. Pender St.) is the result of government expropriation of property in order to widen the street. In defiance, the owner erected the world's thinnest commercial building on the 5-ft- (1.5-m-) wide plot that was left. The 1889 **Wing Sang Building** (51–67 E. Pender St.), the oldest in Chinatown, had an opium factory at its rear.

Known for its traditional shops, tearooms, and restaurants offering *dim sum*, Chinatown is largely a daytime place. The exception is the open-air **Chinatown Night Market**, selling goods of all kinds.

Dragon atop a lamppost, Chinatown

🏮 **Chinatown Night Market**
E Pender & E Keefer Sts, Gore to Main Sts. 🕐 *May–Sep: 6:30–11pm Thu–Sun.*

The ornate Millennium Gate welcoming visitors to Chinatown

A classical pavilion at the Dr. Sun Yat-sen Chinese Garden

Dr. Sun Yat-Sen Classical Chinese Garden ❾

578 Carrall St. **Map** 3 B3.
☎ *(604) 662-3207.* 🚉 *Stadium.*
🚌 *4, 7, 19, 22.* 🕐 *call for hrs.*
● *Jan 1, Dec 25.* 📷 ♿ 🛒 🏠
🌐 *www.vancouverchinesegarden.com*

MODELED AFTER private gardens developed in the city of Suzhou during the Ming Dynasty, this is the first complete classical Chinese garden created outside China. A 52-member team of experts from Suzhou spent an entire year constructing the garden, building with materials shipped from China in more than 950 crates. No nails, screws, or power tools were used in constructing the buildings.

At first, the garden, named in honor of the founder of the Republic of China, seems a maze of walls within walls. Designed to appear larger than it really is, the garden is sprinkled with windows and moon gates – large circular openings in walls – that allow inviting glimpses of tiny courtyards wrapped around still smaller courtyards, miniature pavilions, intricate mosaic pathways, bridges, and galleries. Many of the plants and trees here symbolize human virtues: willow is a symbol of feminine grace; the plum and bamboo represent masculine strength. Small lakes and streams are surrounded by extraordinary rocks.

Chinese Cultural Centre Museum and Archives ❿

555 Columbia St. **Map** 3 C3.
☎ *(604) 658-8880.* 🚉 *Stadium, Main.* 🚌 *3, 19, 22.* 🕐 *11am–5pm Tue–Sun.* ● *Mon, Jan 1, Dec 25 & 26.* 📷 *(except to gallery).* ♿ 🛒
🌐 *www.cccvan.com*

THE THREE-STORY Chinese Cultural Centre Museum and Archives building, styled after the architecture of the Ming Dynasty (1368–1644), is an impressive sight. At the edge of its curving tiled roof stand a pair of ornamental dragons, protecting the building from harm.

The museum and archives opened in 1998 as part of the Chinese Cultural Centre complex (50 East Pender Street). At the Pender Street entrance, the intricate red-and-green China Gate, which was originally displayed at the Expo '86 China Pavilion in Vancouver, is a distinguishing landmark for the complex.

The museum and archives are significant additions to Chinatown. On the first floor is the To-Yick Wong Gallery, with exhibits of both established and up-and-coming artists.

On the second floor, permanent exhibits of artifacts and photos, such as From Generation to Generation, portray the history of BC's Chinese population from the Gold Rush of 1858 to the present. The Chinese Canadian Military Museum is also housed here. Exhibits recount the lives of Chinese-Canadian veterans of World War II.

On the third floor, the S.K. Lee Academy hosts seminars and symposiums to promote cross-cultural understanding.

The Ming Dynasty–style Chinese Cultural Centre building

VANCOUVER'S CHINESE COMMUNITY

Vancouver's Chinatown, home to over 35,000 people of Chinese descent, is the largest in North America after San Francisco's. The success of the community, which sprang up as a shantytown in the 1880s after 18,000 Chinese immigrated to BC to build the cross-Canada railway *(see p211)*, did not come easily. Chinatown's growth was seen as a threat to non-Asian seasonal workers. In 1885, a closed-door immigration policy became law. Many Chinese still came, but women were largely excluded; the men who stayed often supported families they would not see for decades. Racial tensions culminated in two major riots in Vancouver, in 1887 and 1907. The Chinese Immigration Act of 1923 caused BC's Chinese population to decline further. But by the 1940s, Vancouver's Chinatown was drawing tourists, prompting the government, in 1947, to grant Chinese Canadians citizenship and reopen immigration. Encouraged by this policy shift, Chinese immigrants ventured beyond Chinatown to settle in other areas of the city. Today, a second Chinatown is located in Richmond.

A Chinatown storefront with a variety of foodstuffs on display

Downtown Vancouver

DOWNTOWN VANCOUVER is a compact hub of activity, where shopping, business, and arts and culture all play a major role. In 1895, when Christ Church Cathedral opened at the corner of Burrard and Georgia Streets, its comforting lights could be seen in the harbor below. Today, the little church is almost buried by a cluster of office towers as the modern city grows around it. Neverthe-less, quiet enclaves, such as the court-yard at Cathedral Place, can still be found amid the hustle of pedestrians.

Stained glass, Christ Church Cathedral

The city's most famous landmark is in the center of downtown: the historic Fairmont Hotel Vancou-ver, which still hosts royalty and other celebrities from around the world. The Vancouver Art Gallery, with its important collection of paintings by Emily Carr and the Group of Seven, is located in a former courthouse overlooking Robson Square – a wonderful place to sit and watch the world pass by. Robson Street, which cuts through the heart of down-town, is known for its excellent shop-ping and numerous restaurants.

SIGHTS AT A GLANCE

Museums and Galleries
BC Sports Hall of Fame
  and Museum **9**
Science World **12**
Vancouver Art Gallery **5**

Churches and Buildings
BC Place Stadium **10**
Cathedral Place **2**
Christ Church
  Cathedral **1**

Fairmont Hotel Vancouver **3**
HSBC Building **4**
Plaza of Nations **11**
Vancouver Central Library **8**

Squares
Robson Square and
  Law Courts **6**

Shopping Streets
Robson Street **7**

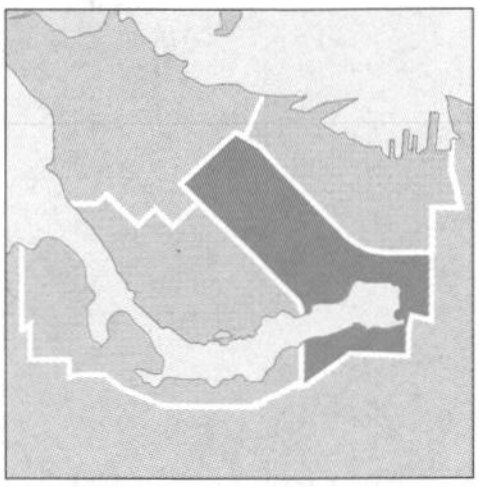

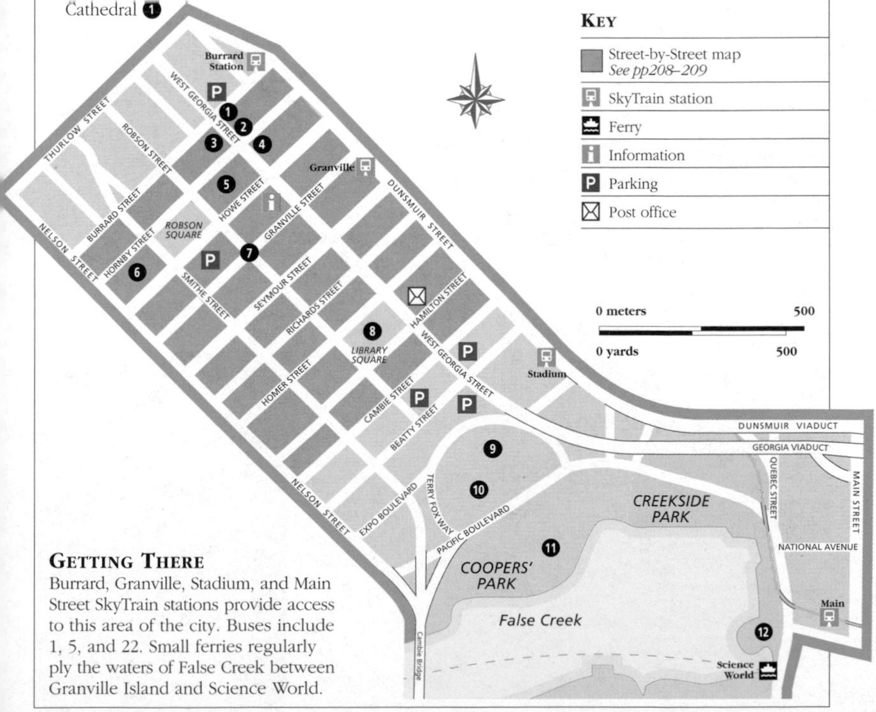

KEY

Street-by-Street map
See pp208–209

SkyTrain station

Ferry

Information

Parking

Post office

GETTING THERE
Burrard, Granville, Stadium, and Main Street SkyTrain stations provide access to this area of the city. Buses include 1, 5, and 22. Small ferries regularly ply the waters of False Creek between Granville Island and Science World.

◁ **Boats bobbing in a marina in False Creek against a backdrop of downtown apartment buildings**

Street-by-Street: Downtown

Justice, the Law Courts

VANCOUVER'S SMALL DOWNTOWN might have ended up an unlivable, daytime-only place crowded with office towers. That affliction has been avoided by preserving existing, often historic, apartment blocks, and by building new towers to accommodate inner-city dwellers. Although Vancouver is a relatively new city, it has taken care to preserve many of its historic buildings, which gives the downtown area a panache missing in many other North American city centers. A prime example is the Vancouver Art Gallery *(see p211)*, housed in the former provincial courthouse, designed in 1906 by the preeminent Victoria architect Francis Rattenbury.

Christ Church Cathedral
Stained-glass windows inside this cathedral, which was once a landmark for sailors, depict the lives of Vancouver heroes ❶

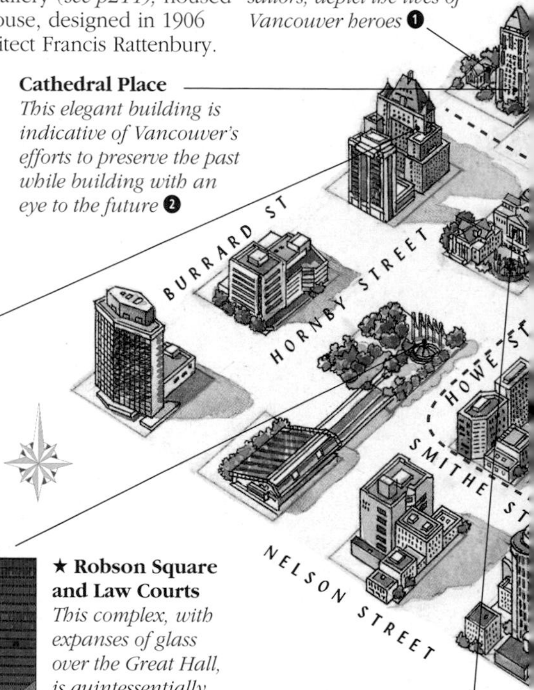

Cathedral Place
This elegant building is indicative of Vancouver's efforts to preserve the past while building with an eye to the future ❷

Fairmont Hotel Vancouver
An historic building and Vancouver landmark, this building dates back to the 1920s. Much of the hotel's interior today has been restored to its former glory ❸

BURRARD ST

HORNBY STREET

HOWE ST

SMITHE ST

NELSON STREET

★ **Robson Square and Law Courts**
This complex, with expanses of glass over the Great Hall, is quintessentially West Coast in style ❻

★ **Vancouver Art Gallery**
British Columbia's major artists are shown at this gallery, alongside exhibits by acclaimed international artists ❺

0 meters   100

0 yards   100

KEY

– – – Suggested route

HSBC Building
A stunning seven-story brushed aluminum pendulum swings gracefully in this building's tree-filled atrium ❹

LOCATOR MAP
See Street Finder map 2

WATERFRONT, GASTOWN & CHINATOWN

DOWNTOWN

GRANVILLE SOUTH & YALETOWN

Robson Street
Shops on this busy street are known worldwide as being the height of casual chic ❼

★ **Vancouver Central Library**
A coliseum is set in the heart of the city thanks to Moshe Safdie's innovative design ❽

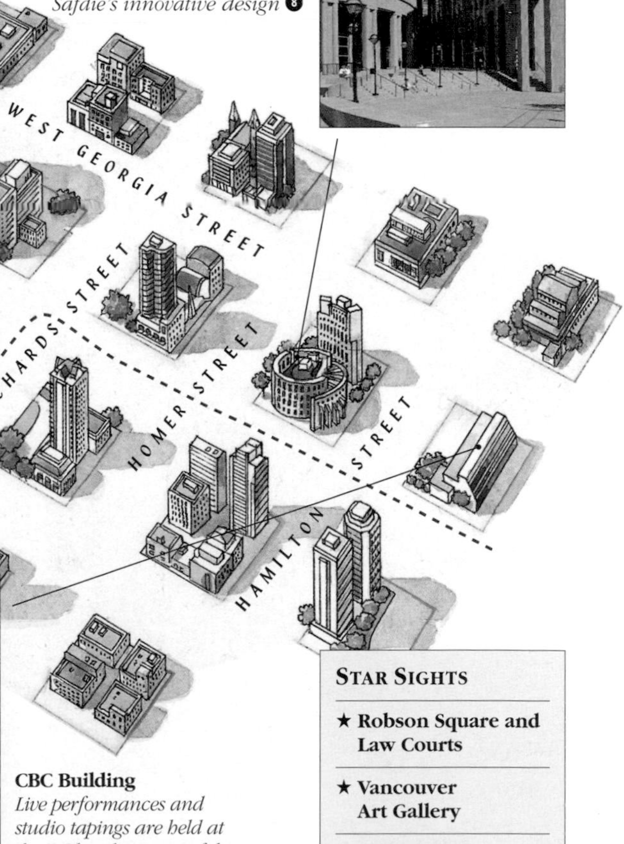

GRANVILLE STREET

WEST GEORGIA STREET

ROBSON STREET

...MOUR STREET

RICHARDS STREET

HOMER STREET

... STREET

HAMILTON STREET

CBC Building
Live performances and studio tapings are held at the BC headquarters of the public Canadian Broadcasting Corporation (CBC).

STAR SIGHTS

★ **Robson Square and Law Courts**

★ **Vancouver Art Gallery**

★ **Vancouver Central Library**

The stained-glass windows of Christ Church Cathedral

Christ Church Cathedral **❶**

690 Burrard St. **Map** 2 F2.
☎ *(604) 682-3848.* 🚇 *Burrard.*
🚌 *22.* ○ *10am–4pm Mon–Fri &
Sun for services.* ● *public,
non-religious hols.* ♿ 🎵 *Concerts.*
Ⓦ *www.cathedral.vancouver.bc.ca*

ORIGINALLY KNOWN as "the
light on the hill," Christ
Church Cathedral was once a
beacon for mariners entering
Vancouver's harbor. After
undergoing several expan-
sions since its consecration in
1895, the oldest surviving
church in Vancouver now sits
in the midst of the downtown
business center. Modeled after
a Gothic parish church by its
designer, Winnipeg architect
C.O. Wickenden, the interior
features arched ceiling beams
of Douglas fir. The sandstone
cathedral remains to this day
a quiet sanctuary.

In 1929, the church became
a cathedral and, in 1930, the
spacious chancel was added.
The overhead lanterns were
installed in 1937. Plans to
build a bell tower were halted
when a city by-law restricting
church bells was passed.

Thirty-two impressive
British- and Canadian-made
stained-glass windows feature
scenes from Old and New
Testament stories. Look for
several unique windows that
include images of Vancouver
people and places. Three
William Morris windows, on
permanent loan from the Vancouver Museum, are located
in the downstairs office vesti-
bule. To see them, use the
Burrard Street entrance.

The Casavant organ, made
from recycled materials after
World War II, is now deterio-
rating and awaits replacement.

Cathedral Place **❷**

925 W Georgia St. **Map** 2 F2.
☎ *(604) 684-0925.* 🚇 *Burrard.*
🚌 *22.* ○ *7am–7pm Mon–Fri, 9am–
5pm Sat.* ● *Sun & major hols.* ♿ 🅿

CATHEDRAL PLACE is a high-
rise makeover of the 1929
Art Deco Georgia Medical Dental Building that once stood
on this site. The 23-story postmodern tower was designed
by Paul Merrick Architects
and constructed in 1990–91.
Cathedral Place preserves
the stylistic ambience of its pre-
decessor. The sculpted figures
on the 11th-story parapet are
copies of the three famous
terra-cotta nurses dressed in
World War I uniforms that
graced the Medical Dental
building and were demol-
ished along with that building. Lions that adorned the
3rd-story parapet are now at
home at each of the entrances
to Cathedral Place. Eight gar-
goyles on the 16th-story parapet echo those of the Hotel
Vancouver across the street.
The exterior of Cathedral Place
is a collection of 20,000 pieces
of Kansas limestone, polished,
cut to shape, numbered, and
then hoisted by crane.

The Art Deco–inspired lobby
is dominated by the glass-and-
steel illuminated sculpture
*Navigation Device: Origin
Unknown,* by West Coast artist
Robert Studer. Some 17,000
pieces of Spanish granite are
set geometrically into the floor.
Behind the lobby is an outdoor
grassy courtyard offering welcoming benches and serenity.

**Cathedral Place, as seen from
the Vancouver Art Gallery**

**The copper-roofed Fairmont
Hotel Vancouver, a city landmark**

Fairmont Hotel Vancouver **❸**

900 W Georgia St. **Map** 2 F2. ☎ *(604)
684-3131.* 🚇 *Burrard.* 🚌 *22.* ♿
🍽 *10:30am & 1:30pm Sat by reservation.* 🅿 🍴 🍷 🅿 *See **Where to
Stay** p291.* Ⓦ *www.fairmont.com*

THE FIRST Hotel Vancouver
was built by the Canadian
Pacific Railway (CPR) in 1887,
two blocks east of where the
current Vancouver icon stands.
Construction of this hotel, the
fourth to bear the name, began
in the late 1920s but came to
a standstill after the stock market crash of 1929. When it was
finally completed in 1939,
the CPR closed the original
hotel and entered into a joint-
management contract for the
new hotel with rival Canadian
National Railway.

The building boasts a distinctive peaked green copper
roof, a Vancouver landmark
that has set the style for many
downtown office towers. Ten
craftsmen from ten countries
worked for 12 months to carve
the exterior stonework. Her-
mes, messenger of the gods
in Greek mythology, is carved
on the façade facing Georgia
Street. Also visible are boats,
trains, rams, winged goats,
and griffins, noteworthy for
their classic ugliness.

The hotel's lobby was
restyled in 1996 by Fairmont
Hotels, the current owners.
The $12-million renovation
restored the lobby according
to the original architectural
drawings. More than 8,000 sq
ft (743 sq m) of marble were
used in the renovations.

HSBC Building ❹

885 W Georgia St. **Map** 2 F2. 🚇
Burrard. 🚌 22. **Pendulum Gallery**
📞 (604) 688-3578. ⏰ 6am–6pm
Mon–Wed, 6am–9pm Thu–Fri, 8am–
6pm Sat. ⬤ Sun & major hols. ♿ 🛗
🏢 🅦 www.885westgeorgia.com

THE SKYLIT ATRIUM is a striking
entrance to the glass-and-
granite HSBC Building, a 24-
story tower which houses,
among others, offices of the
Hong Kong Bank of Canada. A
stunning seven-story kinetic
pendulum hangs from the ceiling. Swinging in a graceful 20
ft (6 m) arc 11,232 times each
day, the hollow 3,527-lb (1,600-
kg) brushed-aluminum sculpture by BC artist Alan Storey
is enhanced by the building's
postmodern Classicism style.
The Pendulum Gallery shows
include works of prominent
Canadian contemporary artists
and international photographers. Local musicians sometimes play the baby grand
piano next to the coffee bar.

**The magnificent pendulum
suspended in the HSBC Building**

Vancouver Art Gallery ❺

750 Hornby St. **Map** 2 F2. 📞 (604)
662-4719. 🚇 Burrard. 🚌 5.
⏰ daily. ⬤ Mon from Thanksgiving
to April 1, Jan 1, Dec 25. 🎞 (Thu
pm by donation). ♿ 🛍 🏢 🏢
🅦 www.vanartgallery.bc.ca

WHAT WAS ONCE British
Columbia's imposing
provincial courthouse now
houses the Vancouver Art

Logger's Culls (c.1935) by Emily Carr, Vancouver Art Gallery

Gallery. The building was
created in 1906 by Francis
Rattenbury, an architect known
for his Gothic design of Victoria's Parliament building and
Empress Hotel *(see pp248–9).*
The interior was modernized
in 1983 by Arthur Erickson,
another noted architect, who
designed the UBC Museum of
Anthropology *(see pp230–31).*
Among an impressive assortment of historical and modern
Canadian art, including works
by the Group of Seven, the
gallery houses the world's
largest collection of paintings
by one of Canada's best-loved
artists, Emily Carr. Born in
Victoria in 1871, Carr studied
the local Native cultures, cap-
turing their way of life and
the scenery of the western
coastline in her sketchbook.
She often depicted Haida artifacts such as totem poles in her
pictures. Her palette is dominated by the blues, greens, and
grays of the stormy West Coast.

Robson Square and Law Courts ❻

800 block Robson St. **Map** 2 F2–F3.
📞 (604) 660-8989. 🚇 Granville.
🚌 5. ⏰ 9am–4pm Mon–Fri.
⬤ Sat–Sun & major hols. ♿ 🍴

DESIGNED BY eminent BC
architect Arthur Erickson,
the four-level Robson Square
stretches several blocks. On
the south side of Robson Street,
on the square's first level, trees
and a waterfall provide a
shaded, soothing background
to Alan Chung Hung's red steel
sculpture, *Spring.* Steps to the
right of the waterfall lead to a
pool and parkette offering a
good view north. From here,
a walkway leads to the law
courts, built from 1974 to 1979.
Jack Harman's statue *Themis
Goddess of Justice* overlooks
the Great Hall. An impressive
but controversial (it is prone
to leaking) steel frame rises
four stories above the hall.

THE IRON ROAD

In 1886, Prime Minister John A. Macdonald fulfilled his
promise to build the Canadian Pacific Railway (CPR) to unite
the new Dominion of Canada. The Iron Road linked eastern
financial centers and the emerging lumber town of Vancouver.
The first cross-Canada
passenger train arrived
in Vancouver on May
23, 1887 *(see p202).* The
Iron Road was completed
at last. Progress came at
the price of many lives,
including those of over
600 Chinese laborers,
many of whom did the
most dangerous of jobs,
clearing and grading the
roadbed and securing
rail ties with gravel.

**The first cross-Canada passenger
train arriving in Vancouver in 1887**

One of the many specialty stores on Robson Street

Robson Street ❼

Map 2 E1. 🚇 *Burrard.* 🚌 *5.*
ⓦ www.robsonstreet.ca

O**NCE KNOWN AS** Robson-
strasse because of its multitude of German businesses,
Robson Street, named after former BC premier John Robson
(1889–92), today boasts restaurants from just about every
continent. Vancouver's urban
chic, international celebrities,
and tourists alike flock here,
making people-watching from
the vantage point of outdoor
cafés a popular pastime.

But above all, shopping is
the street's main attraction.
Accessories, soaps, chocolates, lingerie, men's wear,
souvenirs, even hologram
products are sold in the
stylish shops that stretch
along Robson Street from
Granville to Denman Streets.
A music megastore at the corner of Robson and Burrard
Streets is located in the old
Vancouver Public Library
building, constructed in 1957.
The structure, a sentimental

favorite among locals, is
famous for being Vancouver's
first modernist glass-curtain
building. Some traces of the
original structure can still be
seen despite the renovations.

All stores on Robson Street
are open seven days a week,
with extended evening hours.

Vancouver Central Library ❽

350 W Georgia St. **Map** 3 A3. 📞 *(604)
331-3603.* 🚇 *Granville, Stadium.* 🚌
5, 15, 17. 🕐 *10am–8pm Mon–Thu,
10am–5pm Fri–Sat, 1–5pm Sun.*
⬤ *major hols.* ♿ 🖥 🅿 *Author
readings, special events.*
ⓦ www.vpl.vancouver.bc.ca

I**MAGINATIVE and**
daring, the
design of the Van-
couver Central
Library was
inspired by a
Roman coliseum.
The wraparound,
sand-colored, pre-
cast concrete
colonnade occu-
pies a full city
block. The 9-
story library
building features
a dramatic con-
course, the ceiling soaring 6
stories overhead. The top two
floors are occupied by the
offices of the provincial government. Adjacent to the
library is a 21-story federal
government office tower.

Designed by Moshe Safdie
& Associates (designers of
the National Gallery of
Canada in Ottawa) with
Downs/Archambault Partners

**Percy Williams statue at
BC Sports Hall of Fame**

(designers of Canada Place,
see p202) and opened in 1995,
the building was decried by
some as not fitting into the
Vancouver cityscape. The
negative opinions have been
toppled by the unanimous
support the dramatic building
has subsequently received.

Engineered to high seismic
standards, the building is
also notable because it is not
cooled by air conditioning but
by an ecologically sound air
circulation system.

More than 1.2 million books
are housed in the 350,000-sq-
ft (32,500-sq-m) library space,
which draws over 6,000
people daily. The collection
is rounded off by another
1.2 million periodicals, videos,
CDs, and audio-cassettes,
among other materials.

Items are transported
through the building via
vertical and horizontal
conveyor belts.

On the impressive
concourse are several
cafés, where visitors
can pause for a
snack. During the
warmer months,
the outdoor plaza
is a popular meet-
ing place.

BC Sports Hall of Fame and Museum ❾

777 Pacific Blvd, Gate A. **Map** 3 A3.
📞 *(604) 687-5520.* 🚇 *Stadium.*
🚌 *15, 17.* 🕐 *May–Oct: 10am–5pm
daily; Nov–Apr: 10am–5pm Tue–Sun.*
⬤ *Dec 25.* 🎦 ♿ ☑
ⓦ www.bcsportshalloffame.com

C**ANADA'S LARGEST** sports
museum, the BC Sports
Hall of Fame and Museum is
housed in 20,000 sq ft (1,858
sq m) of space inside the BC
Place Stadium. Twenty galleries
showcase BC's sports history,
starting in the 1860s. The huge
collection of artifacts includes
medals, trophies, uniforms,
equipment, murals, and
photographs. Clever games
test visitors' knowledge.
Interactive displays provide
fascinating details of the lives
of famous athletes, such as
Olympic medalists sprinter

The elliptical coliseum-style colonnade of the Vancouver Central Library

Harry Jerome and skier Nancy Greene. A series of videos on the 1990s tell the exciting stories of the Vancouver Canucks' skate to the Stanley Cup finals, the BC Lions' Grey Cup victory, and Victoria's Commonwealth Games, all held in 1994.

Children will particularly enjoy the Participation Gallery, where they can run against the clock, rock climb, and see how fast they can pitch.

One of the most touching displays is that honoring runner Terry Fox (1958–81), who lost his leg to cancer. His run across Canada to raise money for cancer research was halted only by his death. The feat of another local sports hero, wheelchair athlete Rick Hansen, is also highlighted. To raise public awareness of the potential of people with disabilities, Hansen set out in 1987 to wheel 24,855 miles (40,000 km) around the world. Two years later, he had earned the well-deserved title of Man in Motion.

The enormous air-supported dome of BC Place Stadium

BC Place Stadium ⑩

777 Pacific Blvd. **Map** 3 A4. ☎ (604) 669-2300. ☐ Stadium. 🚌 15, 17. ☐ *hrs vary, depending on events.* ✎ ✿ ✉ *Jun–Aug: 11 am & 1pm Fri.* ☒ www.bcplacestadium.com

ITS WHITE-DOMED ROOF standing out in the city's skyline, BC Place Stadium was, when it opened 1983, Canada's first covered stadium and the largest air-supported dome in the world: the wafer-thin, strong-as-steel fiberglass fabric roof is held up by air pressure. The 10-acre (4-ha) stadium, consisting of enough cement to pour a sidewalk from Vancouver to Tacoma *(see p182)*, can convert in only hours from a football field seating 60,000 to a cozier concert bowl seating 30,000.

Decorative columns against the backdrop of the Plaza of Nations

Plaza of Nations ⑪

750 Pacific Blvd. **Map** 3 B4. ☎ (604) 682-0777. ☐ Stadium. 🚌 1, 5. ☐ *daily.* ✿ ❚❙ ▼ 🔗 ☒ www.plazaofnations.com

THE PLAZA OF NATIONS amphitheater was the epicenter of Expo '86, the World's Fair that drew over 22 million visitors. Overlooking False Creek, the outdoor area can accommodate 10,000 people. The glass walls of the complex provide unobstructed views and shelter from the elements. Several major events are held here, including the Alcan Dragon Boat Festival and Molson Indy Vancouver. Concerts are often held on the Plaza of Nations stage, which seats 750. A conference center, the 500-seat indoor Plaza Theatre, a nightclub, and a comedy club are also located here.

A walking and biking trail along False Creek passes by the Plaza of Nations, heading east to Science World and west to English Bay, offering scenic views of boats and birds.

Science World ⑫

1455 Quebec St. **Map** 3 C4. ☎ (604) 443-7443. ☐ Main. 🚌 3. ☐ *10am–5pm Mon–Fri, 10am–6pm Sat-Sun.* ● *Dec 25.* ✎ ✿ ☒ www.scienceworld.bc.ca

OVERLOOKING THE waters of False Creek, the 155-ft- (47-m-) tall steel geodesic dome built for Expo '86 now houses Science World, Vancouver's interactive science museum. The dome was designed by American inventor Richard Buckminster Fuller (1895–1983), who patented the geodesic dome in 1954. It is one of the city's most striking landmarks.

Science World hosts both traveling and permanent exhibitions. The latter include hands-on activities such as blowing square bubbles, wandering through the insides of a camera, and playing with magnetic liquids, making this a museum popular with children. In the Sara Stern Search Gallery, visitors can touch fur, bones, and animal skins. The Shadow Room encourages visitors to chase their own shadows. KidSpace Gallery features a huge kaleidoscope kids can crawl into, and a flying saucer. The Our World and Eureka! exhibits are especially educational, exploring themes of sustainability, motion, and energy. There is also a wide spectrum of laser shows.

Science World is renowned for its Alcan OMNIMAX Theatre, located in the dome. A five-story screen 88 ft (27 m) in diameter shows films on subjects ranging from bears to Sir Ernest Shackleton's epic 1914 Antarctic journey.

The futuristic geodesic dome atop Vancouver's Science World

GRANVILLE SOUTH AND YALETOWN

THE NEIGHBORHOODS of South Granville and Yaletown are separated by a drive across Granville Bridge or a nautical ride across False Creek. On the south shore, South Granville offers a mix of grocers, cafés and restaurants, and upscale shops – clear signs that people live as well as work here. The numerous commercial art galleries justify the local moniker "gallery row." Nearby Vanier Park and Kitsilano Beach are favorite recreational areas.

Glass marine reliquary vase

Since the early 1990s, Yaletown, on the north shore of False Creek, has seen a dramatic transformation. Once an underused warehouse district, it is now a magnet for high-tech companies and downtown dwellers. High-rises and converted warehouses lend a flair both ultramodern and charmingly historic. Terrace cafés, designer outlets, and interior design stores draw visitors in the day; nightclubs and brew pubs attract revelers come evening.

SIGHTS AT A GLANCE

Museums, Galleries, and Art Schools
Emily Carr Institute
    of Art and Design **2**
Granville Island Museums **5**

Studios and Markets
Granville Island
    Public Market **6**
Kids Market **3**
New-Small and Sterling
    Studio Glass **4**

Waterways and Ferries
False Creek **1**
Granville Island Market
    Ferries **7**

Beaches, Parks, and Neighborhoods
Sunset Beach **9**
Vanier Park **8**
Yaletown **10**

KEY

	Street-by-Street map See pp216–17
🚢	False Creek ferry
ℹ	Information
P	Parking
✚	Church

GETTING THERE
The area is reached by buses 1, 22, and 50. Granville Island is a ten-minute walk north of Granville Street and 4th Ave. Aquabus and False Creek Ferries link docks on False Creek to Granville Island.

0 meters   400
0 yards   400

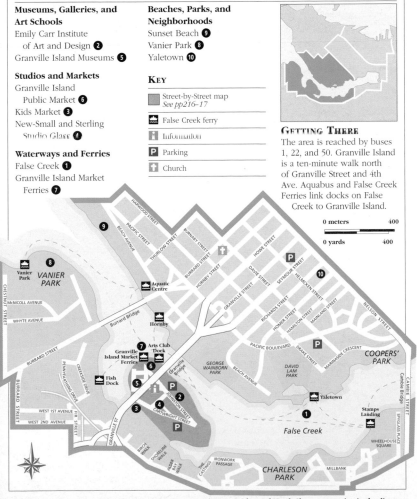

◁ **Bird's-eye view of Granville Island at night, the Burrard Street Bridge and North Shore mountains in the distance**

Street-by-Street: Granville Island

Granville Island Brewing Company sign

Granville Island had its beginnings in 1916, as an industrial area situated on land dredged from False Creek. For decades, heavy industry belched out noxious fumes. By the 1950s, the area was nearly abandoned. In 1972, the Canadian government, backed by City Hall, took over the site, with a plan to make it a people place, and, in 1979, a public market opened. Today, stores, known for the originality of their wares, galleries, studios, and restaurants are housed in brightly painted converted warehouses and tin sheds. Granville Island, which is not an island at all but a peninsula, is also home to music, dance, and theater.

Marina on False Creek, downtown buildings in the background

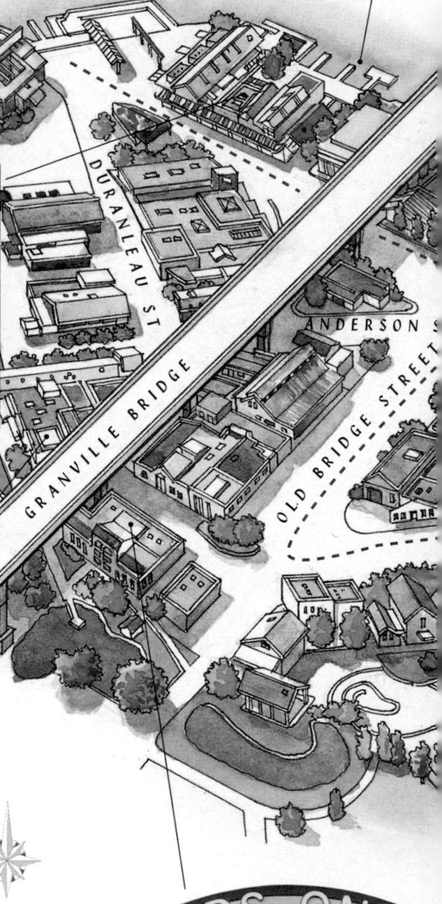

★ Granville Island Public Market
Enjoy a wonderful diversity of locally grown fruits and vegetables in the colorful displays that make this market Vancouver's most popular attraction 6

Granville Island Museums
These three small museums are favorites of train-lovers, ship-lovers, and fishing enthusiasts 5

Kids Market
The Kids Market is a child's fantasyland, with more than 20 shopkeepers selling everything from games and toys to pint-sized clothing 3

★ Emily Carr Institute of Art and Design

Named in honor of one of BC's major artists (see p28), this respected school is located in a former warehouse ❷

New-Small and Sterling Studio Glass

Look through the windows of this glass-blowing studio and marvel as molten glass is transformed into beautiful works of art ❹

LOCATOR MAP
See Street Finder maps 1 & 2

| 0 meters | 00 |
| 0 yards | 80 |

KEY

- - - Suggested route

STAR SIGHTS

★ **Emily Carr Institute of Art and Design**

★ **Granville Island Public Market**

One of the many of outdoor cafés and restaurants at Granville Island

View of False Creek, looking northeast toward Yaletown from Granville Island

False Creek ❶

Map 3 B4.

IN SPITE OF ITS NAME, False Creek is not a creek at all but a saltwater inlet in the heart of the city, extending east from Burrard Bridge to Science World *(see p213)*. In the 1850s, Captain G.H. Richards sailed up this body of water, which originally covered what is now Chinatown eastward to Clark Drive, hoping to find the Fraser River. Disappointed, he named it False Creek.

The mud flats Richards saw originally served as the winter fishing grounds of the Squamish people. By the late 1800s, sawmills had set up on the south shore, followed by the railyards of Yaletown *(see pp220–21)* on the north shore.

Today, paved seawalls flank both the north and south shores, allowing walkers, bicyclists, and rollerbladers to admire the views of downtown and the mountains.

Emily Carr Institute of Art and Design ❷

1399 Johnston St. **Map** 2 E5.
📞 *(604) 844-3075.* 🚌 *50.*
⛴ *False Creek Ferries, Aquabus.*
🕐 *10am–6pm daily.* ● *mid-Dec–Jan 1.* ♿ 🔲 www.eciad.bc.ca

THE UNPAINTED corrugated metal exterior of the famed Emily Carr Institute of Art and Design (ECIAD) is perfectly in keeping with the industrial ambience of Granville Island. Not surprisingly, industrial design is a major focus within

the school's three degree-granting programs. Over 4,000 artists and designers have been trained at ECIAD and its several predecessors.

The school moved into three abandoned industrial buildings on Granville Island in 1980. The original building, on the north side of Johnston Street, houses the **Charles H. Scott Gallery**, which hosts regional, national, and international exhibits of contemporary art that complement the institute's curriculum. Student shows are held in the **Concourse Gallery**.

The school's new addition on the south side of Johnston Street is a 58,00 sq ft (5,400 sq m) structure built for $14 million. A retractable roof can transform the concourse into an atrium within 45 seconds.

Well-known alumni of the school include painter Jack Shadbolt, cartoonist Lynn Johnston, and *Generation X* author Douglas Coupland.

Eric Metcalfe's Attic Project at Emily Carr Institute of Art and Design

Kids Market ❸

1496 Cartwright St. **Map** 2 D5.
📞 *(604) 689-8447.* 🚌 *50.*
⛴ *False Creek Ferries, Aquabus.*
🕐 *10am–6pm daily.* ● *Jan 1, Dec 25 & 26.* ♿ 🔲 www.kidsmarket.ca

CHILDREN WILL BE dazzled by the Kids Market: two floors filled with toys, games, gadgets, clothing, and jewelry. The more than 20 retailers here provide an eclectic shopping experience. There is also a Family Entertainment Centre, supervised play area, picnic area, and special events. Outside, Granville Island Waterpark is a joyful free-for-all of fountains, nozzles, and sprays.

Pousse-café vessels at New-Small and Sterling Studio Glass

New-Small and Sterling Studio Glass ❹

1440 Old Bridge St. **Map** 2 D5.
📞 *(604) 681-6730.* 🚌 *50.* ⛴ *False Creek Ferries, Aquabus.* 🕐 *10am–6pm daily.* ● *Jan–Mar: Mon; Jan 1, Dec 25 & 26.* ♿ 🔲 🗺
🔲 www.hotstudioglass.com

MANY OF the best-known glassblowers in BC have worked for New-Small and Sterling Studio Glass since it opened here in 1982. Visitors can watch owner David New-Small and apprentices create vases, bowls, and artwork using traditional techniques dating back hundreds of years.

The studio specializes in free-blown glass, made without molds using steel blowpipes and pontils. One of the studio's four furnaces keeps 150 lbs (70 kg) of glass molten at 2,000°F (1,100°C) around the clock. The others are fired as needed to heat and shape works in progress. Complicated pieces require a team of glassblowers.

The adjacent shop is one of the best-known glass galleries in Western Canada.

Granville Island Museums ❺

1502 Duranleau St. **Map** 2 D5.
☎ (604) 683-1939. 🚌 50.
🚢 False Creek Ferries, Aquabus.
🕐 10am–5:30pm daily. ⬤ Dec 25
& 26. 🎞 ♿ 🏛
🌐 www.granvilleislandmuseums.com

F̲ISHING, TRAINS, and seagoing
vessels, the three loves of
owner John Keith-King, come
together here. Fishing enthusiasts will enjoy the creels,
reels, and ice-fishing memorabilia. An entire wall with pull-
out drawers features over 500
exquisite hand-tied flies along
with photos of their creators.
A handwritten letter to the
museum from eminent BC
fly-fisher and author Roderick
Haig-Brown is also on display.

An excellent collection of
model ships, all handcrafted by
British Columbians, includes
fine examples of coastal working vessels such as tugboats
and fishing trawlers. A 13.5-ft-
(4-m-) long scale model of
HMS Hood, sunk by the German battleship *Bismark* in
1941, is a highlight of the military sector. A model of Captain
Nemo's submarine, from Jules
Verne's book *20,000 Leagues
Under the Sea,* heads up the
underwater contingent.

The model train museum
depicts the Kettle Valley train
trestle *(see p258),* with small,
intricately carved figures and
6,000 miniature trees. Steam-
powered trains fueled by
tiny pieces of coal whoosh
through elaborate dioramas.

**Working train diorama at
Granville Island Museums**

**Abundant fresh produce at
Granville Island Public Market**

Granville Island Public Market ❻

1689 Johnston St. **Map** 2 D4.
☎ (604) 666-6477. 🚌 50.
🚢 False Creek Ferries, Aquabus.
🕐 9am–6pm daily. ⬤ Jan: Mon;
Jan 1, Dec 25 & 26. ♿
🌐 www.granvilleisland.com

T̲HE GRANVILLE ISLAND Public
Market opened in 1979 in
a former industrial building.
Cleaned up and given new tin
cladding, the public market
building was the first renovated structure on the site
to open for business. Food
specialties at the market
include high-quality fresh
fruits and vegetables (many
of them organic), meats, fresh
pasta, cheese, breads and
baked goods, chocolates, and
herbs and spices. Flowers are
also a big draw.

At the rear of the market,
vendors sell the wares of local
artisans and craftspeople –
candles, custom jewelry, and
hats. Exhibitors are selected
for their high standards of
design and production.

A food fair on the market's
west side offers a variety of
ethnic cuisines. From the
benches outside on the wharf,
visitors take in one of the best
views of the False Creek
marina and docks, as well as
a spectacular view of downtown and the North Shore
mountains. Street performers –
from musicians to stilt-walkers
to magicians – entertain outside, adding to the market's
eclectic, vibrant ambience.

Granville Island Market Ferries ❼

Map 2 D4. *False Creek Ferries* 🛥
(604) 684-7781. *Aquabus* 🛥 (604)
689-5858. 🚌 50. 🅿 call for hrs.
⬤ Dec 25 & 26. 🎞 ♿ partial. See
Getting Around Vancouver p235.
🌐 www.granvilleislandferries.bc.ca
🌐 www.aquabus.bc.ca

A̲ RIDE ABOARD one of the
ferries that service
Granville Island and the
surrounding area is one of the
best ways to see the sights of
False Creek, such as Granville
Island, the Maritime and
Vancouver Museums, and the
Aquatic Centre. These small
boats offer a striking perspective of the city's downtown and west side.

Two ferry companies
operate from Granville Island.
False Creek Ferries' vessels,
launched in 1982, depart daily
from the wharf on the west
side of the Granville Island
Public Market. Routes cross
False Creek to the south foot
of Hornby Street and also go
to Vanier Park *(see pp220–21).*
Another route goes to Science
World *(see p213).* The fleet
now includes four 20-
passenger diesel ferries.

The **Aquabus** fleet dates
back to 1983. Ten small
vessels run three routes from
the ferry dock west of Granville Island Public Market. The
Hornby route takes passengers and bicyclists to the
southern foot of Hornby
Street. The Yaletown route
drops passengers at the
eastern foot of Davie Street.
A third route encompasses
Science World.

Both companies offer mini-
cruises, including sunset
cruises of False Creek, with
frequent departures. The
Aquabus evening cruise is
aboard the *Rainbow Hunter,*
a restored antique ferry.

**An Aquabus vessel, belonging to one
of two False Creek ferry services**

Vanier Park ❽

**A ship in the harbor at
the Maritime Museum**

Vanier Park is a calming oasis in the middle of the city.
Although it is relatively small, it feels spacious. Boats
sail by on English Bay, kites fly overhead, ferries dock
and depart, and pedestrians and cyclists pass through
on their way to Kitsilano Beach or Granville Island
(see pp216–19). Vanier Park was first inhabited by Coast Salish people. It is now the
home of the Vancouver Museum, the
H.R. MacMillan Space Centre, and
the Vancouver Maritime Museum. In late May, large
white tents are set up for the week-long Vancouver
International Children's Festival *(see p30)*. In
the summer months, the Bard on the Beach
Shakespearean Festival is a mainstay here.

Gateway to the Pacific Northwest
*This imposing giant red steel
sculpture by Alan Chung Hung
overlooks English Bay.*

HERITAGE
HARBOUR

ENGLISH
BAY

0 meters   150

0 yards   200

Sunset Beach ❾

Map 2 D3. 🚌 *1.*
🚢 *False Creek Ferries, Aquabus.*

The white sands of Sunset
Beach, which marks the
end of the English Bay seawall and the start of False
Creek, make an ideal place
to relax and do some serious
suntanning or swimming.
Summertime water tempera-
tures rise to 65°F (18°C), and
lifeguards are on duty from
mid-May to Labor Day.
  The western end of Sunset
Beach provides a good view
of the gray granite *Inukshuk,*
which sits at the foot of
neighboring English Bay
Beach. This Inuit statue by
Alvin Kanak, modeled on
traditional markers used by

the Inuit for navigation, is a
symbol of friendship.
  The **Vancouver Aquatic
Centre**, at the east end of the
beach, has a 164-ft- (50-m-)
long Olympic-size swimming
and diving pools, a sauna, a
whirlpool, and a steam room.
False Creek Ferries dock
behind the center, with routes
to Vanier Park, Granville
Island, and Science World.

Yaletown ❿

Map 2 F3. 🚇 *Stadium.* 🚌 *1.*
🚢 *False Creek Ferries, Aquabus.*

Warehouses have been
transformed into lofts,
outdoor cafés have sprung up
on old loading docks, and
high-rise buildings have filled

**Restaurant with outdoor seating
on a street in Yaletown**

in the horizon of Yaletown.
The area was first settled by
Canadian Pacific Railway
(CPR) train crews and labor-
ers after the CPR closed its
construction camp in Yale,

Vancouver Museum

The curved white roof of the Vancouver Museum resembles a Haida woven hat. The Crab, a stunning stainless steel sculpture by George Norris, presides outside. Canada's largest civic museum boasts seven re-creations of Vancouver's history, including an immigrant ship and a fur-trading post.

H.R. MacMillan Space Centre

Space lore is presented in child-friendly hands-on displays and multimedia shows at the space center. The popular Cosmic Courtyard is an interactive gallery that focuses on space exploration.

Vancouver Maritime Museum

The West Coast's rich maritime history is featured in this museum, from seagoing canoes to a 1928 police schooner.

KEY

🅿	Parking
☼	Viewpoint

BC, on completion of the transcontinental railway to Vancouver in 1887. Yaletown remained the decaying heart of the city's industrial activity until the early 1990s, when a development plan began its transformation into a lively urban community.

A multitude of Yaletown condominiums now house a youthful, sophisticated crowd. Along with new residents came a new look. Dirty and neglected industrial warehouses on Homer, Hamilton, and Mainland Streets have been given facelifts. The result is a landscape of bistros, restaurants, cafés, nightclubs, studios, galleries, hair salons, interior design stores, and international and local designer clothing outlets.

On Beach Avenue, the **Roundhouse Arts and Recreation Centre**, in a former CPR switching building, includes theater and gallery spaces and a host of community arts and athletics programs. It also houses the locomotive that pulled the first passenger train to Vancouver in 1887.

JOE FORTES, THE HERO OF ENGLISH BAY

Vancouver's "Citizen of the Century" was a simple man named Seraphim "Joe" Fortes. Born in Barbados in 1865, he arrived in Vancouver in 1885 and was soon a regular at the English Bay Beach. He taught thousands of children to swim. As the city's first appointed lifeguard, he is credited with saving more than 100 lives. Joe's cottage was located right by the beach at the site of today's Alexandra Park. The Joe Fortes Memorial Drinking Fountain in the same park was designed by Charles Marega and installed in 1926, four years after Joe's death.

Joe Fortes in front of his cottage

FARTHER AFIELD

BEYOND downtown Vancouver lie such memorable attractions as Stanley Park and the University of British Columbia Museum of Anthropology. Other intriguing sights are located in outlying cities, easily reached by car or public transit. The North Shore, once home to the Coast Salish people, consists of two cities. Lions Gate Bridge spans the First Narrows to West Vancouver,

Detail of a totem pole in Stanley Park

featuring 17 miles (28 km) of scenic shoreline. The bridge also leads to North Vancouver and the physical wonders of Capilano Canyon and Grouse Mountain. At the mouth of the Fraser River is fast-growing Richmond. With its Chinese malls and markets, this city superbly reflects Greater Vancouver's multicultural character. The riverside community of Steveston is noted for its historic cannery.

SIGHTS AT A GLANCE

Museums and Galleries
University of British Columbia Museum of Anthropology pp230–31 🟨 **9**
West Vancouver Museum and Archives **2**

Areas of Natural Beauty
Capilano Suspension Bridge and Park **3**
Grouse Mountain **4**
Marine Drive **1**
Stanley Park pp226–7 **7**

Markets
Lonsdale Quay Market **5**

Neighborhoods and Cities
Richmond **10**
Steveston **12**
West End **6**

Buildings
Chinese Buddhist Temple **11**
University of British Columbia **8**

KEY

⬛	Central Vancouver
⬜	Urban area
▬	Major highway
▬	Highway
═	Minor road
✈	Airport

5 miles = 8 km

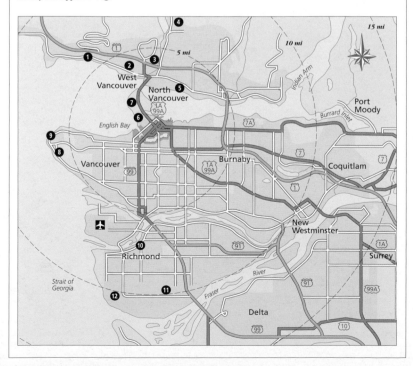

◁ **Siwash Rock, alongside the seawall in Stanley Park, Vancouver**

The Capilano Suspension Bridge, not for the fearful

Marine Drive ❶

250. **[** (604) 926-6614.
W www.westvanchamber.com

SCENIC MARINE DRIVE winds through West Vancouver and makes for an ideal day trip. Park Royal Shopping Centre, with its 250 stores, is the area's major mall. The nearby seaside village of Ambleside boasts a par three golf course on the Capilano Indian Reserve; a popular seawall walkway; and a park overlooking Burrard Inlet, which includes tennis courts, a paddling center, fitness circuit, skateboard park, and water-fowl pond. At the end of the Ambleside Sea Walk, Dundarave Pier offers a wonderful view of Vancouver and the Strait of Georgia. Both Ambleside and Dundarave are good places to shop and dine.

From here westward, Marine Drive clings to the rocky shoreline, buffered by cottages and some of Canada's priciest real estate.

At Lighthouse Park, an easy walk through old-growth forest leads to the Atkinson lighthouse, built in 1912.

Horseshoe Bay welcomes visitors with a park, a marina, and a Native art gallery. Ice cream and fish and chips are Horseshoe Bay specialties.

West Vancouver Museum and Archives ❷

680 17th St, West Vancouver.
[(604) 925-7295. 251, 252.
○ Jul–Aug: 11am–5pm Tue–Sun;
Sep–Jun: noon–4:30pm Tue–Sat.
● public hols & various other times;
call for details. (free Tue).

Atkinson Lighthouse, just off Marine Drive

SMALL AND INVITING, the West Vancouver Museum and Archives is housed in the stately former home of Gertrude Lawson, daughter of John Lawson, the first permanent white settler in West Vancouver. The stones of the 1938 house were brought from New Zealand as ballast on a sailing ship; others came from the Capilano River. After Gertrude died in 1989, the District of West Vancouver acquired the property. The house was restored and then opened in 1995 as a museum.

The museum's exhibits relate to West Vancouver heritage and community interests, such as local sporting history and historic toys. West Vancouver communities are sometimes profiled and decorative arts are particularly well represented. The gift shop sells arts and crafts by local artists and books on West Vancouver history and architecture.

Capilano Suspension Bridge and Park ❸

3735 Capilano Rd, North Vancouver.
[(604) 985-7474. 232, 236.
SeaBus. ○ mid-Apr–Oct: 8:30am–
8:30pm; Nov–mid-Apr: 9am–5pm.
● Dec 25. May–Oct. partial. **W** www.capbridge.com

THE FIRST Capilano Suspension Bridge, not much more than a hemp rope and cedar planks, was built in 1889 by Scotsman George Mackay and Squamish locals August and Willie Jack. Mackay was drawn by Capilano Canyon's wild beauty and built a cabin overlooking it. Access to the Capilano River below was almost impossible. It is said that Mackay built the bridge so that his son, who loved fishing, could reach the river.

The present bridge, dating to 1956 and the fourth to be constructed here, spans 450 ft (137 m). Secured by 13 tons of concrete, 230 ft (70 m) above the canyon floor, it is the longest such bridge in the world.

Nature lovers are drawn here by the views and the chance to wander through old-growth woods, past trout ponds and a 200-ft- (61-m-) high waterfall. Other highlights include Totem Park and the Big House, where Native artists carve poles and explain their techniques and heritage. The Living Forest exhibit teaches visitors about the West Coast rainforest; the bug boxes are especially popular with kids.

Costumed guides at the Capilano Suspension Bridge and Park

View of Vancouver from the top of Grouse Mountain

Grouse Mountain **❹**

6400 Nancy Greene Way. ☎ (604) 984-0661. 🚌 232, 236. ⛴ SeaBus. ⏰ 9am–10pm daily. ♿ 📶 🍴 🏛 W www.grousemountain.com

Fᴿᴼᴹ ᴛʜᴇ ꜱᴜᴍᴍɪᴛ of Grouse Mountain, visitors can experience British Columbia's dramatic landscape. On a clear day one can see as far as Vancouver Island in the west and the Columbia Mountains in the east.

The 2-mile (3-km) Grouse Grind trail, leading to the top of the 3,973-ft (1,211-m) mountain, lives up to its name. Most prefer to take the fully enclosed Skyride gondola.

Popular activities include skiing, skating, snowshoeing, and sleigh rides in the winter; mountain biking, hiking, forest walks, helicopter tours, and tandem paragliding in the summer. Ski and snowboarding schools, 12 ski runs, and equipment rentals are among the amenities here.

During the day, the Feasthouse invites visitors into a beautifully crafted cedar longhouse to learn about the cultures of Pacific Northwest First Nations. In the evening, legends come alive with a presentation that includes traditional Native cuisine, songs, and dances (see p310).

At the Refuge for Endangered Wildlife, an enclosed 2-acre (1-ha) natural habitat, home to two orphaned grizzly

The Skyride gondola, Grouse Mountain

bears, wildlife rangers give daily talks. The Theatre in the Sky presents a video that takes viewers on an aerial tour of British Columbia.

Lonsdale Quay Market **❺**

123 Carrie Cates Ct, North Vancouver. ☎ (604) 985-6261. ⛴ SeaBus. ⏰ daily; call for hrs. ● Jan 1, Dec 25. ♿ 📶 🍴 🍷 🏛 🚫 W www.lonsdalequay.com

Oᴘᴇɴᴇᴅ ɪɴ 1986, the striking concrete-and-glass building housing the Lonsdale Quay Market forms part of the North Shore SeaBus terminal. The market has a floor devoted to food, as well as an array of cafés and restaurants that serve a variety of ethnic cuisines. On the second floor, visitors will find specialty shops that sell handcrafted products, such as jewelry, pottery, and textiles; and Kid's Alley, a row of child-oriented shops. The complex also includes a five-star hotel, a pub, and a nightclub.

In the summer, music festivals are held outside on the adjacent Plaza Deck, overlooking the city and port. Musical offerings include jazz, folk, African, and Celtic performances.

The modern fountain at Lonsdale Quay, Vancouver in the distance

Sailboat on English Bay, West End high-rises in the background

West End **❻**

🚌 1, 5, 6. 🚉 Burrard.

Vᴀɴᴄᴏᴜᴠᴇʀ'ꜱ ᴡᴇꜱᴛ ᴇɴᴅ is the most densely populated residential area in Canada, yet it maintains a relaxed and spacious ambience, in part because of its proximity to Stanley Park and English Bay. Offering everything from beaches to hip urban streetlife, it is one of the best neighborhoods in Vancouver for strolling and taking in the delights of the city.

As one of Vancouver's earliest neighborhoods, the West End has preserved several important historic buildings, such as the exquisite turn-of-the-century **Roedde House**, home to Vancouver's first bookbinder and now a house-museum, and the ivy-clad Sylvia Hotel, built in 1911.

West End streets are generally busy with pedestrians at all hours of the day or night. Robson, Denman, and Davie Streets are the main West End thoroughfares, with Burrard Street as its eastern boundary. Among the many shops and restaurants on Robson Street (see p212) is the Robson Public Market. Denman Street reflects the beach culture of English Bay with its casual clothing boutiques and cafés. It is also popular with Vancouver's gay community. Although Davie Street is more residential, it too has many cafés and restaurants.

The West End also offers plenty of green space in amongst the high-rise apartments and heritage homes.

🏛 Roedde House

1415 Barclay St. ☎ (604) 684-7040. 🎟 By guided tour only. Call for hrs.

Stanley Park ❼

A MAGNIFICENT 1,000-ACRE (404-HA) PARK of tamed wilderness a short ride from downtown Vancouver, Stanley Park was originally home to Musqueam and Squamish peoples. In 1888, Lord Stanley, governor general of Canada, opened the park to all. More than eight million visitors a year make this Vancouver's top attraction. Many walk the 6.5-mile (10.5-km) perimeter seawall with its lovely views of the harbor, English Bay, and the Coast Mountains. Rollerblades and bicycles can be rented near the Denman Street entrance to the park. In addition to the Vancouver Aquarium, Stanley Park boasts rose gardens, a lake, a lagoon, and a totem pole display, as well as beaches, swimming pools, a children's farmyard, tennis courts, and a pitch-and-putt golf course.

***Girl in a Wetsuit* sculpture**

Siwash Rock
A natural volcanic formation jutting from the inlet beside the seawall, the rock has inspired many native legends. According to one, it is a young chief turned to enduring stone for his courage.

ENGLISH BAY

Park Drive

Prospect Point

Third Beach

Ferguson Point

Bridle Path

North Lag

Stanley Park Causeway

Second Beach

★ **Second Beach**
Second Beach is a hub of activity in the summer with a saltwater swimming pool, children's playground, picnic areas, and baseball diamond.

Lost Lagoon
is immortalized in the poetry of Pauline Johnson (1861–1913), the daughter of a Mohawk chief, who named it for its appearance of vanishing at low tide. It is now a permanent lake and wildlife sanctuary.

Lagoon Drive

KEY

☆	Viewpoint
ℹ	Information
⊞	Picnic area
≈	Path
·–	Seawall walk
⊞	Restaurant
P	Parking

Colorful flowerbeds in Stanley Park

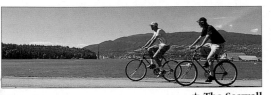

★ The Seawall

The Seawall winds around the rim of the park past Girl in a Wetsuit (see p226)*, a sculpture by Elek Imredy. This curious sculpture, which sits on an offshore rock, was introduced to the park in 1972.*

VISITORS' CHECKLIST

2099 Beach Ave. (604) 257-8400. Burrard. 23, 35. *24 hrs daily (not all sights).* *to some exhibits.* **Horse-drawn carriage tours** *(Mar–Oct)*, call (604) 681-5115. **Stanley Park Shuttle** *(Jun–Sep)*, call (604) 473-6205. **Special events,** call (604) 473-6204. www.seestanleypark.com

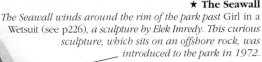

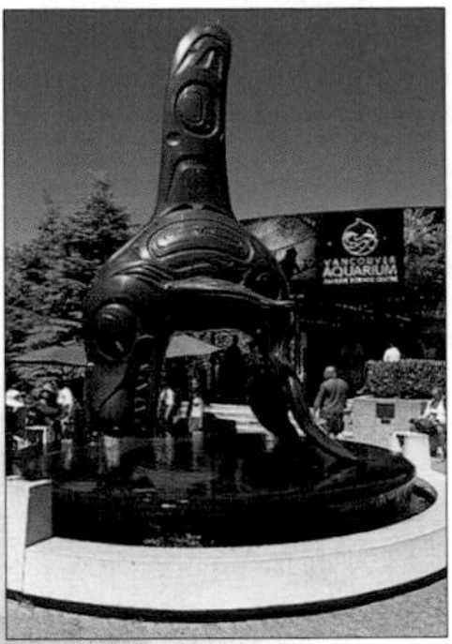

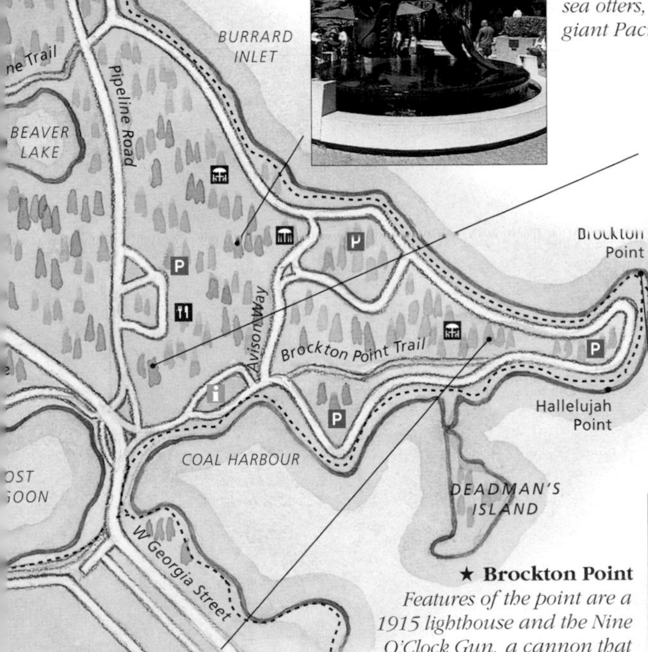

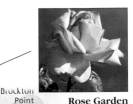

Vancouver Aquarium Marine Science Centre

Five surprisingly graceful white beluga whales are the stars of Canada's premier aquarium. The more than 165 displays also feature sea otters, wolf eels, and giant Pacific octopus.

Rose Garden

From April to September, the lovely formal Rose Garden, surrounded by a variety of perennial plantings, looks its very best.

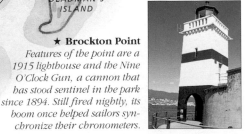

★ Brockton Point

Features of the point are a 1915 lighthouse and the Nine O'Clock Gun, a cannon that has stood sentinel in the park since 1894. Still fired nightly, its boom once helped sailors synchronize their chronometers.

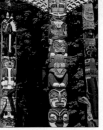

Totem Park

Situated beside Brockton Oval, where the city's first cricket match was played in the late 1800s, Totem Park displays eight totem poles. Created by the Haida, Kwakiutl, and other Aboriginal peoples, each totem tells its own story.

STAR SIGHTS

- ★ Brockton Point
- ★ Second Beach
- ★ The Seawall

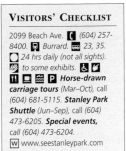

Walter C. Koerner Library, University of British Columbia

University of British Columbia ⓼

📞 *(604) 822-4636.* 🚌 *4, 10, 99 B-Line.* ♿ 🅿️ ⓦ *www.ubc.ca*

FOUNDED IN 1915, the University of British Columbia (UBC) is one of Canada's leading medical doctoral universities. Located a 30-minute drive from the heart of downtown Vancouver, the 988-acre (400-ha) campus is an eclectic mix of architecture, the range of which can be seen by comparing the 1923 **Main Library** with the **Walter C. Koerner Library**, whose construction began in 1996. The former is a combination of imposing stone walls and medieval-style detail; the latter, designed with the help of Arthur Erickson, is a striking combination of concrete and glass.

Campus highlights include the **UBC Botanical Garden**, with 70 acres (28 ha) of rare or unusual plants, and the Rose Garden, boasting 300 varieties.

The zinc-paneled **Chan Centre for the Performing Arts** (*see p233*) hosts classical and contemporary musicians, theater and opera productions, as well as film screenings. Works by leading Canadian and international contemporary artists are shown at the **Morris and Helen Belkin Art Gallery**. UBC's **Museum of Anthropology** (*see pp230–31*) is world-renowned. The **Pacific Museum of Earth** is a treasure chest of minerals and fossils, including an impressive collection of BC jade. The award-winning cedar-and-glass **First Nations Longhouse** resembles a traditional longhouse. The **Asian Centre** houses a photographic exhibit of Asian Canadians and one of North America's largest collections of rare Chinese books. The Japanese-style Nitobe Memorial Garden, part of the Botanical Garden, is at the rear of the building. Campus maps are available from kiosks at the bus loop, Student Union Building, and Chan Centre.

🌿 **UBC Botanical Garden**
6804 SW Marine Dr. 📞 *(604) 822-9666.* ⭕ *mid-Mar–mid-Oct: 10am–6pm; mid-Oct–mid-Mar: 10am–3pm.* 🎟️ ♿ *partial.* 🅿️ *Mar–Oct.* 🍴
🏛️ **Morris and Helen Belkin Art Gallery**
1825 Main Mall. 📞 *(604) 822-2759.* ⭕ *10am–5pm Tue–Fri, noon–5pm Sat–Sun.* ⬤ *Mon & major hols.* ♿
🎎 **Asian Centre**
1871 West Mall. 📞 *(604) 822-3114.* *Library* ⭕ *9am–8pm Mon–Thu, 9am–5pm Fri, noon–5pm Sat.*

University of British Columbia Museum of Anthropology ⓽

See pp230–31.

Richmond's Public Market

Richmond ⓾

👥 *165,000.* 📞 *(604) 271-8280 or (877) 247-0777.* 🚌 *98 B-Line.* ⓦ *www.tourismrichmond.com* ⓦ *www.city.richmond.bc.ca*

BUILT ON A GROUP of islands, Richmond was originally an isolated farming community settled by Europeans in the 1880s. Before that, the Coast Salish used the islands as temporary dwelling grounds, for fishing and collecting berries. Blueberry and cranberry are still important local crops, but Richmond today is predominantly a busy metropolis. Lulu Island, the largest island, is the site of the city proper.

Richmond is home to the second largest North American Asian community. **Yaohan Centre**, one of several Asian malls, sells everything from traditional Chinese herbs to the latest high-tech gadgetry to tae kwon do classes. Tea ceremonies, foot massages, and face readings are some of the less conventional offerings. The **Richmond Centre** combines mainstream shopping with Asian influences.

Richmond also offers international dining, art galleries, and live performances at the **Gateway Theatre**. Outdoor activities include year-round golfing and visiting the **Richmond Nature Park**, which features trails through forests, bogs, and pond habitats. Walking and cycling the West Dyke Trail are also popular activities.

🌿 **Richmond Nature Park**
11851 Westminster Hwy.
📞 *(604) 718-6188.*

The UBC's imposing Main Library, its clock tower a campus landmark

Restaurants lining the boardwalk along Steveston's waterfront

Chinese Buddhist Temple ⑪

9160 Steveston Hwy, Richmond.
(604) 274-2822. 98 B-Line, 403. 9:15am–5:15pm daily. (by donation).

THE GRACE OF Richmond's huge Chinese Buddhist Temple, completed in 1983 after much planning and fundraising by five Chinese immigrants, is immediately evident in the curved roof of golden porcelain tiles and the marble lions guarding the entrance. The temple's interior is richly adorned with sculptures of the Buddha, ornate murals, and sumptuous painting, woodwork, and embroidery. Visitors may encounter one of the daily ceremonies that take place and are welcome to observe the rituals.

Outside, a majestic stone path lined with Tang Dynasty lanterns and brilliant marigolds leads to the statue of the Maitreya Buddha. The

shade of twin gazebos and the restful sound of nearby fountains offer a soothing respite from the bustling city. The bonsai garden in the courtyard is a delight to stroll.

Steveston ⑫

(877) 247-0777. 401, 402.

THE VILLAGE of Steveston, in Richmond, offers visitors a peek into British Columbia's fishing and agricultural heritage. Steveston is proud of its past, which dates back to the the turn of the 19th century. The charming **Steveston Museum** is housed in the last of the original 350 Northern Banks that once operated in Western Canada. The **London Heritage Farm** features a restored 1880s farmhouse that overlooks the Fraser River.

Steveston's waterfront is home to Canada's largest commercial fishing fleet. Freighters and fishing boats share the mouth of the Fraser River as they head for the Strait of

Georgia. On Fisherman's Wharf, shoppers can purchase fish and seafood directly off the fishing boats. Restaurants overlooking the water serve equally fresh fare. Harbor cruises depart from the wharf for excursions up the Fraser River. A block away, on Moncton Street, art shops and souvenir galleries mingle with local businesses. A short walk from the village center is 44-acre (18-ha) **Garry Point Park**, with beaches that offer vistas of Vancouver Island.

A highlight of Steveston is the **Gulf of Georgia Cannery**. In the 1890s, 15 salmon canneries operated in Steveston, employing upwards of 10,000 men and women. Most of the Gulf of Georgia Cannery complex, a national historic site which includes an icehouse, a lead foundry, an artifact collection featuring machinery from the early 1900s, and a multimedia exhibit, sits on pilings built over the Fraser River. At its height, in 1897, the cannery produced over 2.5 million cans of salmon.

Steveston Museum
3811 Moncton St. (604) 271-6868. 9:30am–1pm & 1:30–5pm. Sun & major hols. by donation. 1st floor only. by appt.
London Heritage Farm
6511 Dyke Rd. (604) 271-5220. year-round: noon–4pm Sat–Sun; Jul–Aug 10am–4pm daily. 1st floor & tearoom only. by appt.
Gulf of Georgia Cannery
12138 4th Ave. (604) 664-9009. Jun–Aug: 10am–5pm daily; Apr–May & Sep–Oct: 10am–5pm Thu–Mon. Nov–May.

The intricately carved Chinese Buddhist Temple and gate

THE MIGHTY FRASER RIVER
The majestic Fraser River travels from Mount Robson Provincial Park to the Strait of Georgia, near Vancouver. It broadens at Hope, transforming the Fraser Valley into lush farmlands. Once in the Vancouver area, it splits into two arms. One million migratory birds settle by the river near Steveston each winter, making this a great bird-watching area. The Fraser is also the largest salmon river in the world, though overfishing has severely reduced its runs.

The spectacular, winding Fraser Canyon

University of British Columbia Museum of Anthropology ❾

FOUNDED IN 1947, this outstanding museum houses one of the world's finest collections of Northwest Coast Native peoples' art. Designed by Canadian architect Arthur Erickson in 1976, the museum is housed in a stunning building overlooking mountains and sea. The tall posts and huge windows of the Great Hall were inspired by the post-and-beam architecture of Haida houses and are a fitting home for a display of full-size totem poles, canoes, and feast dishes. Through the windows of the Great Hall, the visitor can see the magnificent outdoor sculpture complex, which includes two houses designed by contemporary Haida artist Bill Reid.

★ **The Great Hall**
The imposing glass and concrete structure of the Great Hall is the perfect setting for totem poles, canoes, and sculptures.

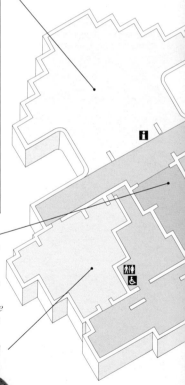

OUTDOOR HAIDA HOUSES AND TOTEM POLES

Set overlooking the water, these two Haida houses and collection of totem poles are faithful to the artistic tradition of the Haida and other tribes of the Pacific Northwest, such as the Salish, Tsimshan, and Kwakiutl. Animals and mythic creatures representing various clans are carved in cedar on these poles and houses, made between 1959 and 1963 by Vancouver's favorite contemporary Haida artist Bill Reid and Namgis artist Doug Cranmer.

Carved red cedar totem poles

Climbing Figures
These climbing figures are thought to have decorated the interior of First Nations family houses. Carved from cedar planks, the spare style is typical of Coast Salish sculpture.

STAR EXHIBITS

★ **The Great Hall**

★ **The Raven and the First Men by Bill Reid**

Ceramic Jug
This beautifully decorated jug was made in Central Europe in 1674 by members of the Anabaptist religious sect. The foliage motifs are in contrast to the freely sketched animals that run around the base.

★ The Raven and the First Men *(1980)*
Carved in laminated yellow cedar by Bill Reid, this modern interpretation of a Haida creation myth depicts the raven, a wise and wily trickster, trying to coax mankind out into the world from a giant clamshell.

VISITORS' CHECKLIST

6393 NW Marine Dr. *(604) 822-5087.* *99.* *mid-May–Aug: 10am–5pm Wed–Mon, 10am–9pm Tue; Sep–mid-May: 11am–5pm Wed–Sun, 11am–9pm Tue.* *Oct–May: Mon; Dec 25 & 26.*
www.moa.ubc.ca

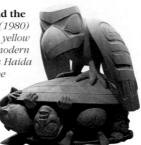

MUSEUM GUIDE
The museum's collections are arranged on one level. The Ramp gallery leads to the Great Hall, which features the cultures of Northwest coast First Nations peoples. The Visible Storage gallery contains artifacts from other cultures, and a range of 15th- to 19th-century European ceramics is housed in the Koerner Ceramics gallery.

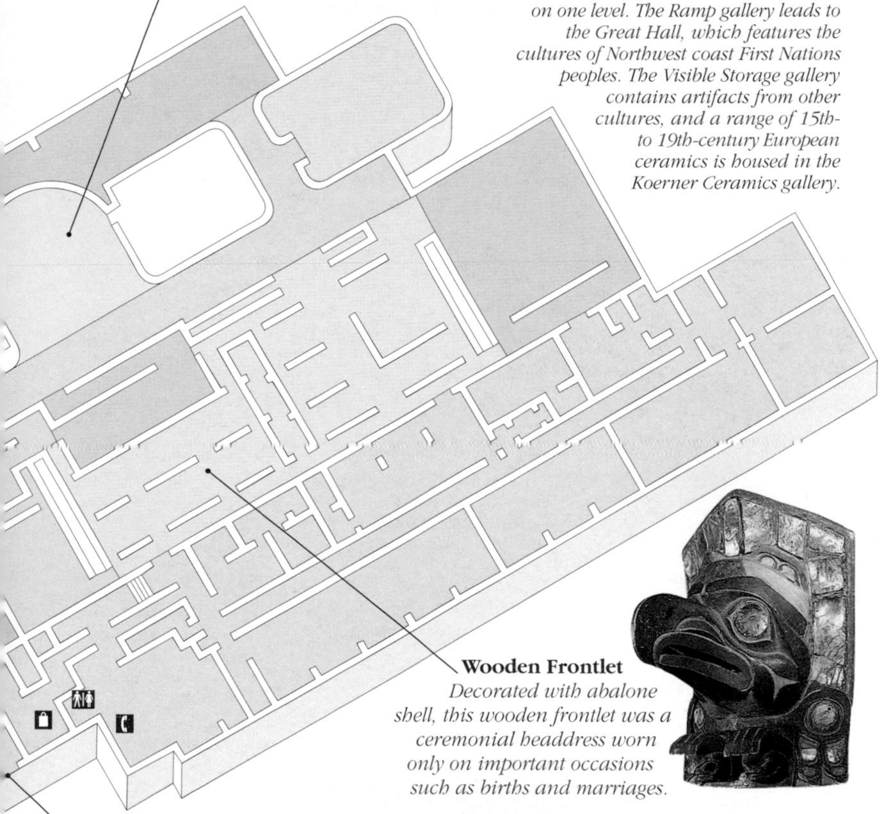

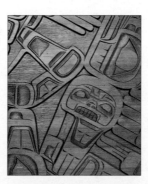

Wooden Frontlet
Decorated with abalone shell, this wooden frontlet was a ceremonial headdress worn only on important occasions such as births and marriages.

Red Cedar Carved Front Doors
This detail comes from the set of stunning carved red cedar doors that guard the entrance to the museum. Created in 1976 by a group of First Nations artists from the 'Ksan cultural center near Hazelton, the doors show the history of the first people of the Skeena River region in British Columbia.

KEY

- The Ramp gallery
- The Great Hall
- The Rotunda
- Visible storage/ Research collection
- Archeological gallery
- Koerner Ceramics gallery
- Temporary exhibition space
- Theatre gallery
- Nonexhibition space

Shopping in Vancouver

THE SHOPS IN VANCOUVER and surrounding areas showcase goods and fashions from every continent.
Funky boutiques and vintage clothing stores abound
in Gastown, as do shops specializing in Native art.
Other shopping districts also offer myriad goods, from
upscale furniture to kitchenware and speciality items.

**Window display at a clothing store
on Vancouver's Granville Island**

SHOPPING DISTRICTS

ROBSON STREET (see p212) is
Vancouver's major shop-
ping promenade.
Specialty shops and
boutiques line the
streets of Gastown,
Kitsilano, Kerris-
dale, Yaletown,
and Ambleside (see
p224). South Gran-
ville is home to
upscale clothing and
furnishing stores. Granville
Island (see pp216–19) offers
an array of shops and galleries, as well as a huge food
market. Visit Chinatown and
the Punjabi market around
Main Street and 49th Avenue
for ethnic shopping. Richmond
(see p228) is known for its
Asian shopping malls.

**Sign for Lonsdale
Quay Market**

DEPARTMENT STORES
AND SHOPPING CENTERS

MOST OF THE CITY'S shopping
centers are anchored by
major department stores. **The
Bay** sells quality Canadian and
international brand-name clothing, and its own clothing lines.
Sears on Robson features the
Roots and Kenneth Cole labels,
as well as big cosmetic houses.
    At the 140-store **Pacific Cen-
tre** and the 500-store **Metrotown**, BC's largest shopping
mall, goods range from brand-
name fashions to smoked BC
salmon. The smaller **Sinclair
Centre** features international
fashions in an Edwardian
Baroque–style building that
was formerly a post office.

On the North Shore, Lonsdale
Quay Market (see p225) offers
a harbor view as well as a food
market and boutiques, while
Park Royal Shopping Centre
(see p224) houses a multitude
of shops under two roofs.

SPECIALTY SHOPS

THE OUTLET STORE for Jax
and Koret brands,
Gastown's **Jax Fashions &
Fabrics** offers big discounts.
On the funkier side is **John
Fluevog** with unique
boot and shoe
designs for both
men and women.
Leone houses
sophisticated
boutiques, with
fashions from Yves
St. Laurent, Prada,
and Versace, among
others. Internationally known
Roots offers Canadian design
in casual and athletic wear,
as well as leather goods.
    The elegant selection at
Birks Jewellers includes,
along with fine jewelry, pens,
watches, crystal, and classic
gifts. The **Inuit Gallery**, one
of several stores in Gastown
specializing in Native art,
carries high-quality Inuit
prints and soapstone carvings,
and Northwest Coast First
Nations masks, bentwood
boxes, prints, and jewelry.
    Book-lovers will enjoy the
selection and personal service
at **Duthie Books**, one of
Vancouver's oldest and best-
loved independent bookstores.

**Store in Gastown selling western-
style boots and other leather goods**

DIRECTORY

DEPARTMENT STORES
AND SHOPPING CENTERS

The Bay
674 Granville St. **Map** 3 A2.
[(604) 681-6211.

Metrotown
4800 Kingsway, Burnaby.
[(604) 438-3610.

Pacific Centre
700 W Georgia St. **Map** 3 A2.
[(604) 688-7236.

Park Royal
Marine Dr at Taylor Way,
West Vancouver.
[(604) 925-9576.

Sears on Robson
701 Granville St. **Map** 3 A2.
[(604) 685-7112.

Sinclair Centre
757 W Hastings St. **Map** 3 A2.
[(604) 659-1009.

SPECIALTY SHOPS

Birks Jewellers
698 W Hastings St. **Map** 3 A2.
[(604) 669-3333.

Duthie Books
2239 W 4th Ave. **Map** 1 A5.
[(604) 732-5344.

Inuit Gallery
206 Cambie St. **Map** 3 B2.
[(604) 688-7323.

Jax Fashions & Fabrics
316 W Cordova St. **Map** 3 B2.
[(604) 684-7004.

John Fluevog
837 Granville St. **Map** 2 F3.
[(604) 688-2828.

Leone
757 W Hastings St. **Map** 3 A2.
[(604) 683-1133.

Roots
1001 Robson St. **Map** 2 F2.
[(604) 683-4305.

WHAT TO BUY

QUALITY CANADIAN-made
fashions, leatherwear, and
handbags are good buys in
Vancouver. First Nations and
Inuit art – including carvings,
prints, masks, and jewelry – is
available at many stores and
gallery shops. BC jade jewelry
is also popular, as are Cowichan knit sweaters. Traditionally smoked wild sockeye
salmon, often packaged in
decorative cedar boxes, is
another West Coast specialty.

Entertainment in Vancouver

ENTERTAINMENT IN VANCOUVER runs the gamut from world-class opera productions to amateur music concerts. Each year the city hosts folk music, jazz, theater, dance, comedy, literary, and film festivals, among others. Vancouver is one of Canada's top theater centers; homegrown talent mixes with performers from Europe and the US.

The Orpheum Theatre's spectacular gold-leaf interior, built in 1927

INFORMATION

THE CITY's two dailies, the *Vancouver Sun* and *The Province*, publish events listings on Thursdays. The free weekly *Georgia Straight* also has extensive listings. *Where Vancouver*, available at downtown hotels and tourist kiosks, lists events and shows.

BUYING TICKETS

TICKETS FOR MOST events can be purchased from **Ticketmaster** by phone or at one of its locations. Many venues also sell tickets directly. **Tickets Tonight**, in the main Tourist-info Centre *(see p234)*, sells full-price tickets for theater and sporting events, and half-price tickets for some performances on the day of. Discounted tickets must be bought in person; others can be bought online.

FREE EVENTS

THE VANCOUVER Central Library *(see p212)* hosts a variety of lectures and author readings; CBC *(see p209)* presents concerts and admits the public to many studio tapings. Annual and community festivals are listed in *Georgia Straight*.

THEATER

CLASSICS BY Shakespeare, Shaw, and others, along with modern US and Canadian plays, are features of the **Vancouver Playhouse Theatre Company**. The **Arts Club Theatre** owes its success to solid theatrical fare performed by BC's leading actors. A popular venue for musicals is the 1930 **Stanley Theatre**, now restored to its sassy vaudeville style. The small **Firehall Arts Centre** showcases culturally diverse contemporary theater and dance.

Summer events include plays at the open-air Theatre under the Stars (tel. 604/687-0174) in Stanley Park and the Bard on the Beach Shakespeare Festival (tel. 604/739-0559) in Vanier Park.

DANCE AND MUSIC

WITH ITS INSPIRING modern repertoire, **Ballet British Columbia** performs at the **Queen Elizabeth Theatre**, as does the **Vancouver Opera**, founded in 1958 and presenting four operas each year. The ornate 2,700-seat **Orpheum Theatre** hosts a variety of concerts, including classical, jazz, and pop. It is also home to the **Vancouver Symphony Orchestra**, whose series include classical and family concerts, often with internationally recognized guest musicians. The 1,200-seat **Chan Centre for the Performing Arts** *(see p228)* showcases musical recitals and opera ensembles. **Commodore**

Performer in one of Vancouver Opera's many productions

Ballroom, boasting a floating dance floor and table seating for 500, hosts an eclectic mix of local and international talent.

SPECTATOR SPORTS

SPORTING EVENTS such as BC Lions CFL football and Vancouver Canucks NHL hockey games take place at **BC Place Stadium** and **General Motors Place**. Vancouver Canadians Baseball is played at **Nat Bailey Stadium** in Queen Elizabeth Park.

Getting Around Vancouver

ALTHOUGH SOMEWHAT SPRAWLING, Vancouver is not so big as to be overwhelming. The Vancouver Touristinfo Centre, near Canada Place, provides information on sights, accommodation, and transit, as well as street maps. The various local tours on offer, such as the free tour of historic Gastown, are an excellent way of exploring the city.

CITY AND STREET LAYOUT

THE MANY BRIDGES spanning Vancouver's bodies of water can confuse visitors, as can the occurrence of "west" in the names of several areas in the city. The residential West End shares the downtown peninsula with the business and commercial district and with Stanley Park. The West Side stretches from Ontario Street, on the south side of False Creek, to the University of British Columbia and encompasses several neighborhoods, including Kitsilano and Kerrisdale. The community of West Vancouver is adjacent to North Vancouver, on the North Shore.

Before heading anywhere, it is wise to consult a good street map. The mountains, which are to the north, are a useful landmark for orientation.

Most streets run north–south and east–west, though some run on the diagonal. Some downtown streets are one-way. Outside the downtown core, avenues, divided east–west by Ontario Street, are numbered; north–south streets are named.

WALKING

MANY OF THE CITY'S attractions are within walking distance of the downtown core. Others are easily accessible by public transit. However, as the neighborhoods are somewhat scattered, it is often best to drive or use public transit to

The SeaBus heading from the North Shore to downtown Vancouver

get to a particular neighborhood and then walk around to soak up the atmosphere. Walking tours through various neighborhoods are available; for a tour of Gastown, contact **Walking Tours of Gastown**.

BICYCLING

VANCOUVER IS a great city for cycling, with bikeways covering more than 60 miles (100 km). Bikeways can be found at False Creek, Stanley Park, the University of British Columbia, and elsewhere in the city. The free brochure "Cycling in Vancouver" includes a map of bike routes. It is available at bicycle shops and bookstores, or by calling the **City of Vancouver Bicycle Hot Line**, which also provides details on where to rent bicycles.

Traffic-calming circles and other measures, such as cyclist-friendly sensors at traffic lights, slow vehicle traffic on city streets. Bicycle helmets are mandatory.

TAXIS

TAXIS ARE NUMEROUS in Vancouver and can be hailed on the street or ordered by telephone. Taxi fares start at $2.30 and increase at the rate of approximately $1.35 per half mile (1 km).

PUBLIC TRANSIT

THE GREATER Vancouver transportation authority, **TransLink**, operates an extensive public transit network. Transit maps are available for a minimal charge at major drugstores and supermarkets, some convenience stores, and the main location of the **Vancouver Touristinfo Centre**.

The SeaBus, a 400-seat catamaran, crosses Vancouver Harbour from the downtown Waterfront Station to Lonsdale Quay in North Vancouver every 15 to 30 minutes until around midnight.

SkyTrain, a driverless aboveground light rail system, travels between Waterfront Station and Surrey. Schedules vary, depending on the time of day and day of the week. Fares range from $2 to $4 and are based on a three-zone system. Tickets allow interchangeable travel on the SeaBus, SkyTrain, and

Vancouver taxi

buses, including TransLink trolleys. Children under the age of 4 ride free; those between the ages of 5 and 13, as well as people over age 65, pay a reduced fare. A transfer ticket is free and lasts for 90 minutes of travel in any direction. FareSaver books of ten tickets, usually available where transit maps are sold, provide a discount. An $8 day pass can be purchased at supermarkets and at SkyTrain ticket vending machines in the stations.

All trips after 6:30pm and on weekends and holidays are considered to be in one zone anywhere in the system.

The commuter rail service **WestCoast Express** runs during peak periods on weekdays between Mission and Vancouver, stopping at several outlying municipalities.

The free Stanley Park shuttle bus at Brockton Point, one of its many stops

The WestCoast Express, Sky-Train, SeaBus, and many of the bus routes are wheelchair accessible.

FERRIES

TWO FERRY COMPANIES operate ferries along False Creek: **False Creek Ferries** and **Aquabus** *(see p219)*. The ferries dock at Science World, Yaletown, the Vancouver Aquatic Centre, Granville Island, and Vanier Park. Fares range from $1 to $3.50. False Creek Ferries' day pass ($8 to $12) allows unlimited one-day travel. The Aquabus mini-tour pass ($3 to $6) offers round-trip travel with one stopover.

DRIVING

DESPITE SOME downtown congestion, traffic in Vancouver usually flows reasonably well. Streets are generally easy to navigate, although street signage is sometimes nonexistent. Some downtown streets limit left-hand turns to nonpeak hours. Right-hand turns on a red light are allowed after coming to a full stop, unless otherwise noted. Weekday rush hours are from 7 to 9:30am and 3 to 6pm. Friday's crush of cars may start even earlier and will be especially busy on the Friday of a long weekend.

The city speed limit is 30 mph (50 km/h). Some intersections are monitored by police cameras. Seat belts are mandatory, as are helmets for motorcyclists.

The **British Columbia Automobile Association** (BCAA) offers assistance, maps, and guidebooks to members of the Canadian or American Automobile Association.

PARKING

PAID PARKING is available in Vancouver's numerous parking lots. Metered street parking is also available. Keep a variety of change on hand, including quarters

The SkyTrain, linking downtown with Vancouver suburbs

A double-decker local sightseeing bus

and $1 coins. Credit cards are accepted for parking in many places. It may be less expensive to park in a lot and pay the day rate than to feed the meter throughout the day. Infractions ticketing is usually prompt and always expensive. Check posted street parking regulations; they may limit parking during rush hours or specify other parking regulations, such as a maximum of two hours' parking. Free street parking is generally available from 8pm to 6am. Again, check the posted parking regulations; they can vary. Some shopping malls and attractions offer free parking, although these are usually situated outside the downtown core.

TOWING

IF YOUR CAR IS TOWED from a city street, contact **Busters Towing**. Its main impound yard is located beneath the north end of Granville Street Bridge. If towed from a private lot, call the telephone number on the sign posted nearby.

An Aquabus ferry bringing passengers to Granville Island

VANCOUVER STREET FINDER

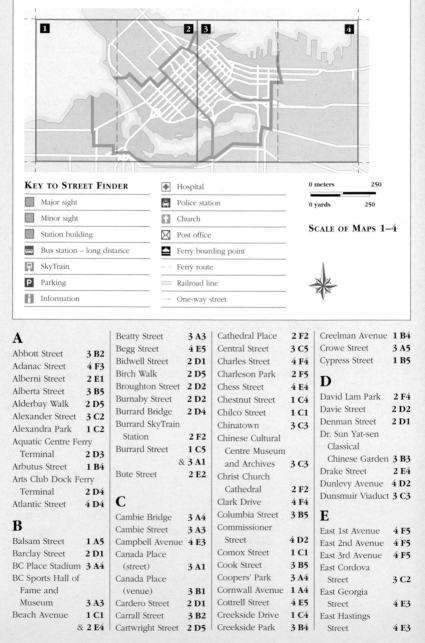

T HE KEY MAP BELOW shows the area of Vancouver covered by the *Street Finder* maps, which can be found on the following pages. Map references for sights, hotels, restaurants, shops, and entertainment venues given throughout the Vancouver chapter of this guide refer to the grid on the maps. The first figure in the reference indicates which map to turn to (1 to 4); the letter and number that follow refer to the grid reference on that map.

KEY TO STREET FINDER

■ Major sight	✚ Hospital
■ Minor sight	▣ Police station
■ Station building	✟ Church
🚌 Bus station – long distance	⊠ Post office
🚉 SkyTrain	⚓ Ferry boarding point
P Parking	− − Ferry route
i Information	═══ Railroad line
	⟶ One-way street

0 meters 250
0 yards 250

SCALE OF MAPS 1–4

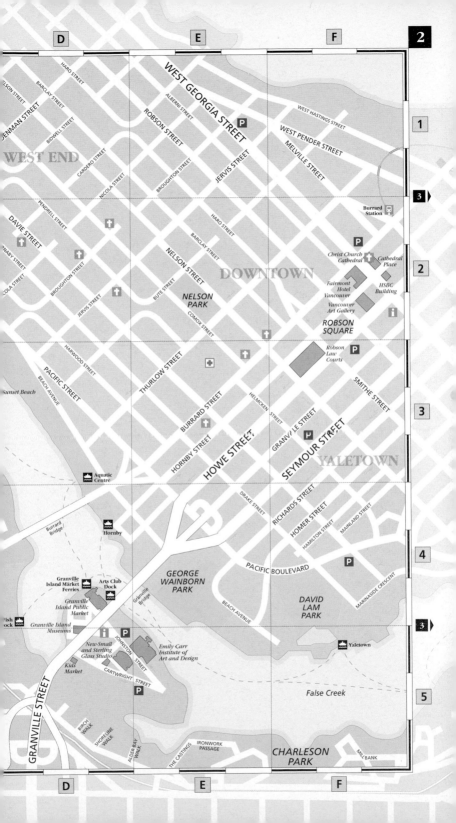

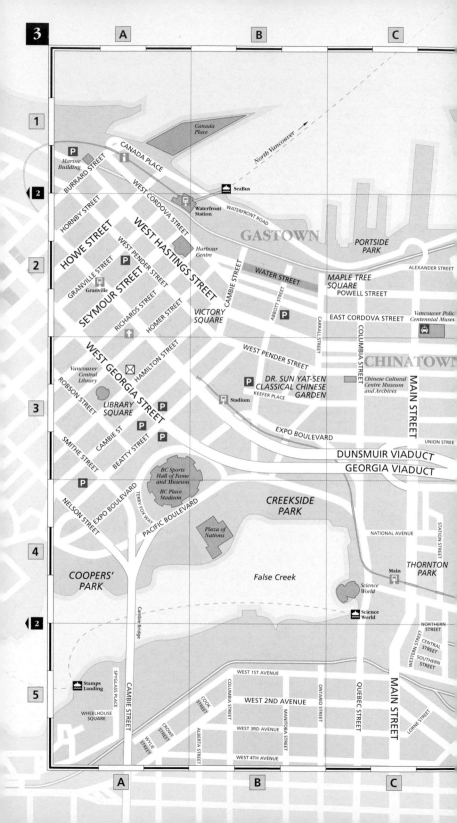

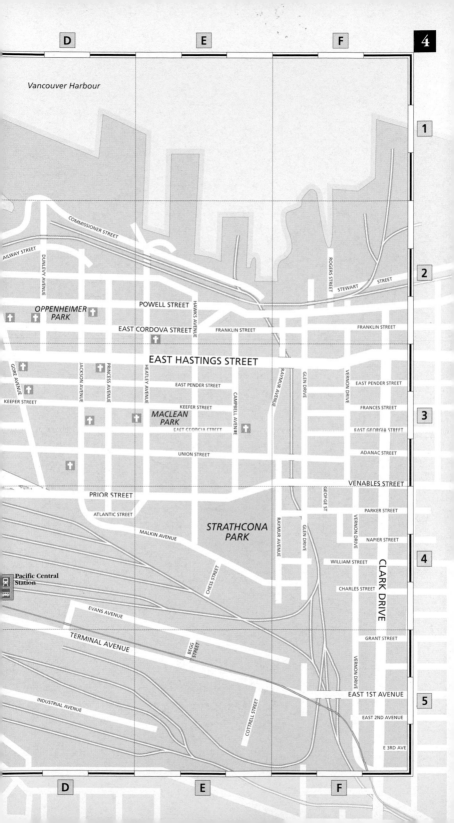

BRITISH COLUMBIA

B RITISH COLUMBIA IS ONE OF CANADA'S *most strikingly beautiful provinces. Tranquil islands grace its Pacific Ocean coastline while awe-inspiring mountain ranges on the mainland include the world-famous Rockies. Astounding natural vistas surround lively urban centers, from the large, modern cities of Vancouver and Victoria to small towns with historic pasts.*

Thousands of years before the first Europeans arrived, the 366,254-sq-mile (948,600-sq-km) area that is now British Columbia was home to First Nations tribes. Today, reconstructions of their cedar longhouses and semi-subterranean pit houses may be seen in museums.

Spanish and British ships explored the province's convoluted 16,800-mile (27,000-km) coastline from 1774 onward. In 1792, Captain George Vancouver – for whom the province's largest city was later named – was impressed, describing "innumerable pleasing landscapes." British Columbia joined the confederation of Canada in 1871, and the Canadian Pacific Railway arrived in Vancouver in 1887, joining the new West Coast province to the already established eastern ones and bringing waves of new settlers. BC was built on logging, mining, and fishing, and while these industries have seen hard times over the years, they continue to support many communities today. Tourism, however, is now ranked second in the province's economy, after forestry.

British Columbia offers travelers an impressive array of breathtaking scenery and experiences. Vancouver Island's sandy beaches and rugged wilderness are a short drive or ferry ride from the urban pleasures of Victoria and of Vancouver, from which popular ski hills are only minutes away. Inland, the Interior's many lakes provide glistening vistas and sunny playgrounds for watersports of all kinds. Nestled among the BC Rocky Mountains are historic mining towns, and provincial and national parks offering exciting winter skiing and summer hiking experiences. In the north, the Skeena River, the "river of mists," travels through ancient tribal lands, sprinkled with stunning First Nations totem poles. Prince Rupert is the port of call for the ferry to the remote, misty archipelago of Haida Gwaii, also known as the Queen Charlotte Islands.

The harbor in Masset on Graham Island, British Columbia

◁ Detail of totem pole at Skidegate, a Haida community in Haida Gwaii (Queen Charlotte Islands)

Exploring British Columbia

WILDLIFE VIEWING

Okanagan Valley sign

THE EXCEPTIONAL BEAUTY of British Columbia's coast, mountain ranges, forests, and lakes makes it a much-visited province. A wide variety of landscapes are to be found, from the northern Rockies with their bare peaks to the southern Okanagan Valley with its orchards and vineyards. To the west, Vancouver Island offers ancient rainforests and the impressive coastal scenery of the Pacific Rim National Park. Lying between the Pacific Ocean and the Coast Mountains, Vancouver is a stunningly attractive city, with good transportation links to the rest of the region. The province's temperate climate means that BC has more species of plants and animals than anywhere else in the country. Millions of visitors come here every year, drawn by a range of outdoor activities.

SIGHTS AT A GLANCE

Butchart Gardens ❷
Chemainus ❹
Cowichan District ❸
Dawson Creek ㉒
Fort Nelson ㉔
Fort St. John ㉓
Fort Steele
  Heritage Town ⑭
Glacier National Park ⑱
Gulf Islands ❻
*Haida Gwaii
  (Queen Charlotte
  Islands) pp272–3* ㉙
The Hazeltons ㉖
Kamloops ❾
Kelowna ❿
Kootenay National Park ⑰
*The Kootenays
  pp260–3* ⑬

Muncho Lake
  Provincial Park ㉕
Nanaimo ❺
*Pacific Rim National Park
  Reserve of Canada
  pp254–5* ❼
Prince George ㉑
Prince Rupert ㉘
The Purcell
  Mountains ⑮
Radium Hot Springs ⑯
Smithers ㉗
Summerland ⑪
Victoria pp246–51 ❶
Wells Gray
  Provincial Park ⑳
Whistler pp256–7 ❽
*Yoho National
  Park pp266–7* ⑲

Cruise and Tour

Cruise to Alaska pp274–5 ㉚
Okanagan Valley Tour ⑫

COAST
MOUNTAIN

TELEGRAPH
CREEK •

HAIDA
GWAII
(QUEEN
CHARLOTTE
ISLANDS)
㉙

㉚ CRUISE
TO ALASKA

㉘ PRINCE
RUPERT
⑯
KITIMAT • ㊲
PRINCE
RUPERT
㉖
THE
HAZELTON
SMITHER ㉗

Pacific
Ocean

• BELLA COOL

⑳

COAST
MOUNTAINS

⑲

VANCOUVER
ISLAND

①

WHISTLER ❽
VANCOUVER •
❼ NANAIMO ❺❻ GULF ISLAND
❹ CHEMAINUS
❸ COWICHAN DIST
❷ BUTCHART GARL
❶

PACIFIC RIM
NATIONAL
PARK
RESERVE OF   VICTORIA
CANADA

SEE ALSO

Tow Hill, Agate Beach, on Graham Island, Haida Gwaii

KEY

▬ Highway

▬ Major road

＝ River

❋ Viewpoint

Legislative Chamber in the provincial Parliament Buildings, Victoria

GETTING AROUND

Several major highways cross British Columbia: the Trans-Canada (Hwy 1), Crowsnest (Hwy 3), and Yellowhead (Hwy 16). The Coquihalla (Hwy 5) is a four-lane toll route between Hope and Kamloops. It is 45 miles (73 km) shorter than the Trans-Canada route. Hwy 97 links Dawson Creek with Whitehorse, in the Yukon. On Vancouver Island, Hwys 1, 4, and 19 are the main routes. VIA trains and Greyhound buses travel to many BC destinations.

㉕ **MUNCHO LAKE PROVINCIAL PARK**

㉔ **FORT NELSON**

Alaska Highway

Williston Lake

MANSON CREEK

㉓ **FORT ST. JOHN**

ROCKY MOUNTAINS

㉒ **DAWSON CREEK**

㉑ **PRINCE GEORGE**

Fraser River

Wooden waterwheel, Fort Steele Heritage Town

㉔ **WELLS GRAY PROVINCIAL PARK**

YOHO NATIONAL PARK

⑲

⑨ **KAMLOOPS**

⑱

OKANAGAN VALLEY TOUR

⑫ ⑩ **KELOWNA**

GLACIER NATIONAL PARK

⑰ **KOOTENAY NATIONAL PARK**

⑪ **SUMMERLAND**

RADIUM HOT SPRINGS ⑯

PURCELL MOUNTAINS

⑮ **FORT STEELE HERITAGE TOWN** ⑭

⑬ **THE KOOTENAYS**

km   100

miles   100

Picturesque and popular Whistler Village

Victoria ❶

Clock in the Bay Centre

A QUIET CITY, Victoria has an old-fashioned atmosphere, one enhanced by the hanging flower baskets that decorate the streets. Established as a Hudson's Bay Company fur-trading post in 1843 by James Douglas, Victoria had its risqué moments during its Gold Rush years (1858–63), when thousands of prospectors drank in its saloons. Established as the capital of British Columbia in 1871, Victoria was soon outgrown by Vancouver. Today, this multicultural city is still BC's political center, as well as a popular attraction for visitors.

Historic buildings along Yates Street, typical of Victoria's Old Town

Exploring Victoria

Many of Victoria's attractions are downtown and in Old Town, which is bordered by Wharf, Humboldt, Douglas, and Fisgard Streets. Plaques on historic buildings, now housing funky shops and cafés, offer insight into this area that was, in the 1800s, Victoria's commercial center. Downtown stretches from Inner Harbour to Quadra, Belleville, and Herald Streets. Historic Fort Street is home to Antique Row. The visitors' center provides details on walking tours, including lantern and cemetery tours.

❧ Inner Harbour
Foot of Government St.

Home to the Songhees, of the Coast Salish Nation, between 1858 and 1911, the Inner Harbour today is vibrant with boats, pedestrians strolling along the promenade, and street performers. Plaques along the walkway pay tribute to those who shaped the harbor's history. The promenade offers excellent views not only of the harbor but also of the Parliament Buildings and Empress Hotel, particularly in the reflecting sunlight of late afternoon.

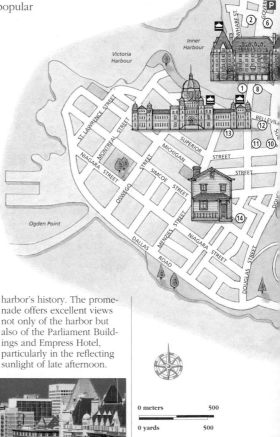

KEY

🚆	Train station
🚌	Bus station
🅿	Parking
⛴	Ferry
ℹ	Information

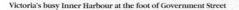

Victoria's busy Inner Harbour at the foot of Government Street

Bustling Bastion Square, dating back to the late 1880s

Bastion Square

Government St. ☐ *daily.* ⚫

This beautifully restored square faces Victoria's picturesque harbor and contains some of the city's oldest 19th-century buildings. What were once luxury hotels and offices, built during the boom era of the late 1800s, now house boutiques and gift shops. Restoration began in 1963 when it was discovered that the Hudson's Bay Company's fur-trading post Fort Victoria, established in 1843,

VISITORS' CHECKLIST

Road map 2 B5. 🏘 *79,000.* ✈ *Victoria Airport. 15 miles (25 km) north of city.* 🚆 *VIA, 450 Pandora Ave.* 🚍 *Pacific Coach Lines, 700 Douglas St.* ⛴ *BC Ferries.* 🛈 *812 Wharf St, (250) 953-2033.* 🎭 *Jazz Fest Int'l (mid-Jun); Victoria Shakespeare Festival (mid-Jul–mid-Aug); First Peoples Festival (early Aug).* 🅦 *www.city.victoria.bc.ca*

once stood on this site. Today, this pedestrian square includes the MacDonald Block building, built in 1863 in Italianate style, with elegant cast-iron columns and arched windows. The old courthouse, built in 1889, houses the BC Maritime Museum. In summer, both visitors and workers lunch in the courtyard cafés.

Market Square

560 Johnson St. ☎ *(250) 386-2441.* ☐ *10am–5pm daily.* ⚫ *Dec 25.* ⚫ *partial.*

Two blocks north of Bastion Square on the corner of Johnson Street, Market Square has some of the finest Victorian saloon, hotel, and store façades in the city. Most of the buildings date from the 1880s and 1890s, the boom period of the Klondike Gold Rush. After decades of neglect, the area received a much-needed face-lift in 1975. Today, the square is a shoppers' paradise, with a variety of stores selling everything from books and jewelry to musical instruments and other arts and crafts.

SIGHTS AT A GLANCE

Decorative banners lining Market Square, Victoria

🚇 Chinatown

Bounded by Pandora Ave & Store, Government & Herald Sts.

Victoria's Chinatown, the oldest in Canada and once its largest, is now the country's smallest, yet its vegetable markets, curio shops, and restaurants provide hours' worth of exploration. The ornate **Gate of Harmonious Interest** (Fisgard and Government Streets) leads into the two-block-square area that was at one time home to Chinese railroad laborers and their families (*see p211*).

Fan Tan Alley, possibly the world's narrowest street, was once filled with opium dens and gambling houses. Today, visitors will find an eclectic mix of shops here. From the alley, enter though the backdoor of **Chinatown Trading Co**. (551 Fisgard Street) to see artifacts from the district's earlier days, including those from a 19th-century gambling house.

The sunken knot garden behind City Hall at Centennial Square

♣ Centennial Square

Bounded by Fisgard, Douglas & Government Sts & Pandora Ave.

Created in 1963, Centennial Square is part of an effort to revitalize the city's downtown. Its centerpiece is a fountain with concrete "totems" adorned with mosaics by a local artist. Surrounding the public space are specialty shops, McPherson Playhouse – which opened in 1914 as the first Pantages Theatre and which has a beautiful baroque interior – a knot garden, and City Hall.

The Second Empire–style south wing of City Hall – its red brick façade and tin mansard roof exemplifying

The Second Empire–style City Hall, with its clock tower

this style – was built in 1878. In 1880, a fire station was added, and in 1891, a northeast wing. The clock, installed in the tower (1890) in 1891, is still wound once a week. In 1963, the interior of City Hall was completely renovated and an International Style west wing was added.

🚇 The Bay Centre

2-1150 Douglas St. 📞 *(250) 952-5680.* 🕐 *9:30am–6pm Mon–Wed & Sat, 9:30am–9pm Thu–Fri, 11am–5pm Sun.* ♿

The Bay Centre (formerly the Victoria Eaton Centre) sits behind the façades of several historic buildings on Government Street. The 1892 Driard Hotel was saved from demolition by a public campaign, as were the fronts of the 1910 Times Building and the 19th-century Lettice and Sears Building. Behind these and other elegant façades, more than 80 shops on four floors sell everything from fashion to handmade chocolates. In the atrium hangs a clock, its several faces displaying the time in various ports of the former British Empire.

🚇 St. Andrew's Cathedral

740 View St. 📞 *(250) 388-5571.* 🕐 *daily.* ✝ *8am & 12:10pm daily; 8am, 9:30am, 11am & 5pm Sun.* ♿

Built in 1892, this is the oldest Roman Catholic church in the area. The Victorian Gothic–style cathedral made of stone, slate, and brick features a 175-ft- (53-m-) tall spire – a Victoria landmark – and beautiful stained-glass windows. Works of local First Nations artists were introduced to the interior during the 1980s renovations. The altar was designed by Charles Elliott, of the Coast Salish Nation; the candles on either side of the pulpit are decorated with Native designs.

St. Andrew's Cathedral, Victoria's first Roman Catholic church

🚇 Fairmont Empress Hotel

721 Government St. 📞 *(250) 384-8111.* 🕐 *daily.* ♿ *See* **Where to Stay** *p295.*

Completed in 1905 to a Francis Rattenbury design and built on what was once mud flats and the site of the city's unofficial dump, the Empress Hotel is one of Victoria's best-loved

The central atrium in Victoria's Bay Centre, with its suspended clock

The entranceway to the grand Fairmont Empress Hotel

sights. Overlooking the Inner Harbour, the hotel dominates the skyline with its ivy-covered Gothic splendor. Visitors are welcome to experience the luxurious decor of the hotel's public bars and lounges, such as the Crystal Ballroom, with its Tiffany-glass dome. High tea, a popular Empress Hotel tradition, is served daily.

In front of the hotel stands a statue of Captain James Cook (see p36), who, though he explored much of BC's coast, ironically never saw Victoria.

Crystal Garden, home to all manner of tropical life

♣ Crystal Garden

713 Douglas St. (250) 381-1213. daily: call for hrs. Built in 1925 to house Canada's largest salt-water swimming pool, as well as ballrooms, and tearooms, the Crystal Garden was inspired by London's Crystal Palace and was designed by the preeminent Victoria architect Francis Rattenbury. The swimming pool has now been replaced by lush gardens whose junglelike foliage of palm and banana trees, orchids, and other tropical plants provides a refuge for many animals. There are rare monkeys, including pygmy marmosets, the world's

smallest at 4 inches (10 cm) when fully grown; tropical birds, such as toucans and flamingos; bats; lemurs; and iguanas. The koi pond is home to a variety of fish, among them giant goldfish. There are also hosts of colorful free-flying butterflies to see while taking tea in the conservatory.

🏛 Helmcken House

10 Elliot Sq. (250) 361-0021. May–Oct: 10am–5pm daily; Nov–Apr: call for hrs. The home of Hudson's Bay Company employee Dr. John Sebastian Helmcken was built in 1852 and is one of the oldest surviving houses in British Columbia. The young doctor, who later helped negotiate BC's entry into the Dominion of Canada, built the house with his wife using Douglas firs felled in the surrounding forest. Built using the post-on-sill method popular in French Canada, it was the first residence outside the secure boundaries of Fort Victoria. A second section was added to

HELMCKEN HOUSE HISTORIC SITE

Sign for Helmcken House

Wood-burning stove at the historic Helmcken House

the house in 1856, and a third in 1884. Together, the additions reflect the change in construction methods in the second half of the 19th century.

The simple but elegant dwelling contains many of the original furnishings, including the piano, which visitors are permitted to play. Other highlights include Dr. Helmcken's medical kit and equipment.

FROM FORT TO CAPITAL

James Douglas fell in love with Camosack, the area known to many now as Victoria, when he sailed into its harbor in 1842. As chief factor of the Hudson's Bay Company (HBC), he was there to establish a fur-trading post and fort, in part an effort to thwart American expansion into the region. Douglas was welcomed by the Lekwammen, ancestors of the Esquimalt and Songhee Nations. In 1843, Fort Camosack (later Fort Victoria) was established. By the end of the decade, the First Nations of the area had signed treaties, selling much of their land to the HBC. Small farms quickly sprung up, and the harbor was soon a busy port and a stopping-off point for prospectors in the 1858 gold rush. Victoria incorporated in 1862, four years later becoming capital of the Colony of British Columbia, the provincial capital once BC entered Confederation in 1871.

View of the growing community of Victoria, 1860

🍂 Thunderbird Park
Belleville & Douglas Sts.
This compact park, at the entrance to the Royal British Columbia Museum (see pp252–3), is home to an imposing collection of plain and painted giant totem poles. During the summer, Native artists carve these handsome totems in the Thunderbird Park Carving Studio. The poles show and preserve the legends of many different First Nations of the Northwest Coast. Also in the park, the Kwakwaka'wakw big house, built in 1952, is a replica of a 19th-century big house in Fort Rupert.

Giant totem poles, a signature feature of Thunderbird Park

🏛 Parliament Buildings
501 Belleville St. 📞 (250) 387-3046. ⬤ 8:30am–5pm daily. ⬤ Jan 1, Dec 25. ♿ ✏

Facing Inner Harbour, Victoria's many-domed Parliament Buildings are an impressive sight, particularly at night when the façades are

The spectacular main dome of the Parliament Buildings

illuminated by thousands of lights. This has been a tradition since 1956, though the buildings were first lit up as early as 1887, in celebration of Queen Victoria's diamond jubilee.

Designed by Francis Rattenbury in 1892, the buildings were completed in 1897, replacing the "Bird Cages," BC's first parliament buildings. (The carriage house on Superior Street behind the Parliament Buildings is the only remaining Bird Cage structure.) Rattenbury, a 25-year-old British architect who had arrived in British Columbia only the year before, won a national competition to design the buildings. He went on to design several of the province's landmarks, the Empress Hotel and Crystal Garden included.

The stone-and-marble buildings are home to the Provincial Legislature. The Legislative Chamber, where the assembly sits, is upstairs, off a small

gallery that boasts lovely stained-glass windows by William Morris. Visitors can view assembly sessions from the third-floor public galleries. A magnificent dome caps the nearby Lower and Upper Rotundas; the former, a perfect octagon, has a beautiful Italian mosaic floor.

British Columbia's history is depicted throughout the buildings. A statue of explorer Captain George Vancouver perches on top of the main dome. Inside, large murals painted during the Great Depression show scenes from BC history.

Carr House, where renowned artist Emily Carr lived as a child

🏛 Carr House
207 Government St. 📞 (250) 383-5843. ⬤ mid-May–mid-Oct: 10am–5pm daily. ✏ ♿ ✏ 🏠

Emily Carr, one of Canada's best-known artists (see p28), was born in 1871 in this attractive 1864 clapboard house.

Rooms are furnished in late 19th-century period style, with some original family pieces. Carr taught her first art classes to local children in the dining room. Carr's drawing of her father still sits on the mantel in the sitting room where, as an eight-year-old, she did her first sketches. Reproductions of Emily Carr's artwork hang in the Morning Room; the People's Gallery exhibits works of contemporary Canadian artists. The adjoining English garden showcases plants that were popular during the Victorian era.

🍂 Beacon Hill Park
Douglas St & Dallas Rd. 📞 (250) 361-0600. ⬤ daily. ♿

In the late 19th century, this delightful park was being used for stabling horses. In 1888, John Blair, a Scottish

The Legislative Chamber at Victoria's Parliament Buildings

A stately, centuries-old Garry oak tree in Beacon Hill Park

landscape gardener, redesigned the park to include two lakes and initiated extensive tree planting. Once a favorite haunt of artist Emily Carr *(see p28),* this peaceful 184-acre (74.5-ha) park, the oldest and largest in Victoria, is now renowned for its lofty old trees (including the rare Garry oaks, some of which are more than 400 years old); stretches of wild camas lilies, once highly valued by the area's First Nations; picturesque duck ponds; and a 100-year-old cricket pitch.

Art Gallery of Greater Victoria, shrine detail

⊞ Art Gallery of Greater Victoria

1040 Moss St. ☎ *(250) 384-4101.* ◯ *10am–5pm Mon–Wed, Fri–Sat, 10am–9pm Thu, 1–5pm Sun.* ☑ ☒ ☐
This gallery's eclectic collection is housed in an impressive Victorian mansion east of the downtown area. Inside, fine wood moldings, original fireplaces, and tall ceilings provide a stately home for an array of exhibits, including a wide-ranging collection of Chinese and Japanese painting, ceramics, and pottery. The gallery also has the only authentic Shinto shrine in North America.

The collection of contemporary Canadian paintings includes those of famous local artist Emily Carr *(see p28).* Executed between the 1900s and 1930s, Carr's paintings, with their haunting evocation of the stormy Northwest and the lives of Native peoples, are among the gallery's most popular exhibits. Carr's works, which include her writings, are rotated so that all pieces in the extensive collection can eventually be viewed.

♠ Craigdarroch Castle

1050 Joan Cres. ☎ *(250) 592-5323.* ◯ *mid-Jun–Labor Day: 9am–7pm daily; Labor Day–mid-Jun: 10am–4:30pm daily.* ● *Jan 1, Dec 25 & 26.*
Completed in 1890, Craigdarroch Castle was the pet project of respected local coal millionaire Robert Dunsmuir, who built it for his wife in return for her leaving her native Scotland. Although not a real castle, the design of this large house was based on a castle in Ayrshire, Scotland, and mixes several architectural styles, including Gothic and Romanesque Revival.

When the castle was threatened with demolition in 1959, a group of local citizens formed a society that successfully battled for its restoration. Today, the restored interior of the house is a museum that offers an insight into the lifestyle of a wealthy entrepreneur.

The castle is noted for having one of the finest collections of Art Nouveau lead-glass windows in North America, and many of the rooms and hallways retain their patterned wood parquet floors and carved paneling in white oak, cedar, and mahogany. Every room is filled with opulent Victorian furnishings from the late 19th century and decorated in deep greens, pinks, and rusts. Several layers of the paint have been painstakingly removed from the drawing room ceiling to reveal the original stenciled and hand-painted decorations beneath, which include wonderfully detailed butterflies and lions.

A tower at Craigdarroch Castle in the French Gothic style

⊞ Government House

1401 Rockland Ave. ☎ *(250) 387-2080.* ◯ *daily (gardens only).* ☒
The present Government House building was completed in 1959 after fire destroyed the 1903 structure, designed by Francis Rattenbury. The official residence of BC's lieutenant-governor, the house is closed to the public, but visitors can view 36 acres (14.6 ha) of stunning public gardens with lawns, ponds, an English country garden, and a Victorian rose garden. Marvelous views of the grounds can be enjoyed from Pearke's Peak, a mount formed from the rocky outcrops that surround the property and which contain rock gardens.

Government House, restored in 1959 with blue and pink granite

The Royal British Columbia Museum

THE ROYAL BRITISH COLUMBIA MUSEUM tells the story of this region through its natural history, geology, and peoples. The museum is regarded as one of the best in Canada for the striking way it presents its exhibits. The Natural History gallery on the second floor contains a series of imaginative dioramas re-creating the sights, sounds, and even smells of areas such as the Pacific seashore, the ocean, and the rainforest. Every aspect of the region's history, including a reconstruction of an early 20th-century town, is presented on the third floor. Visitors can experience the street life of the time in a saloon and in a cinema showing silent films. The superb collection of Native art and culture includes a ceremonial Big House.

Third Floor

19th-Century Chinatown
As part of an 1875 street scene, this Chinese herbalist's store displays a variety of herbs used in traditional Chinese medicine.

★ **First Peoples Gallery**
Made of cedar bark and spruce root in around 1897, this hat bears the mountain goat crest of the raven clan.

First Nations Ceremonial Masks
The mouse, raccoon, and kingfisher are carved on these masks belonging to the Mungo family, who wore them to dance on ceremonial occasions.

KEY TO FLOORPLAN

- ☐ First Peoples gallery
- ☐ Modern History gallery
- ☐ Feature exhibit
- ☐ Natural History gallery
- ☐ Museum theater
- ☐ National Geographic IMAX theater
- ☐ Nonexhibition space

Exterior of the Museum
The museum's main galleries opened in 1968. Previously the collections were displayed at several locations in and around the Parliament Buildings. The museum grounds include an archives building.

Modern History Gallery

A variety of streets, stores, and public buildings, from the 1700s to 1990s, are re-created in this gallery. Here, the Grand Hotel occupies an authentic wooden sidewalk.

Second
Floor

★ Natural History Gallery

A full-size prehistoric tusked mammoth guards the entrance to the Natural History gallery, which includes several lifelike dioramas that re-create British Columbia's coastal forests and ocean life since the last ice age.

⋏ Pacific Seashore Diorama

This diorama features sound, lighting, live sea creatures in tidal pools, and realistic animals such as this northern sea lion.

MUSEUM GUIDE

The main exhibits of the museum are housed on the second and third floors. The Natural History gallery, on the second floor, reconstructs a range of environments in displays ranging from the Open Ocean to the Boreal Forest. The third floor has the First Peoples and Modern History galleries.

First
Floor

STAR EXHIBITS

★ **First Peoples Gallery**

★ **Natural History Gallery**

★ **Pacific Seashore Diorama**

Main Entrance

Butchart Gardens ❷

Brentwood Bay, Vancouver Island.
[(250) 652-4422. **◯** 9am daily;
closing hrs vary by season. 🖼 🖳 🖵
🖿 🅆 www.butchartgardens.com

THESE BEAUTIFUL gardens were established in 1904 by Jennie Butchart, in the

The lily pond in the formal Italian garden at Butchart Gardens

excavated quarry left behind when her husband's cement company moved west to Victoria. The site, home to thousands of rare plants, is arranged into distinct areas, including a formal Italian garden and a lovely rose garden. In summer, the gardens are illuminated and play host to evening jazz and classical music concerts. Fireworks displays are held in the gardens on Saturday nights in summer.

Cowichan District ❸

Vancouver Island. 🚹 381A Hwy 1,
Duncan, (250) 746-4636.
🅆 www.cvrd.bc.ca

COWICHAN DISTRICT, on the south-central coast of Vancouver Island, consists of the Chemainus and Cowichan

Valleys. Cowichan means "warm land" in the dialect of the Cowichan people, one of largest First Nations groups in BC. The main freshwater lake on the island, Lake Cowichan offers great opportunities for swimming, canoeing, and fishing. Between the lake and the town of Duncan lies the **BC Forest Discovery Centre**. Its displays include a replica logging camp. Duncan, "City of Totems," has over 40 magnificent totem poles. **Quw'utsun' Cultural Centre** shares the heritage of the Cowichan tribes through tours and events.

🏛 BC Forest Discovery Centre
2892 Drinkwater Rd, Duncan. **[**
(250) 715-1113. **◯** Apr–mid-May &
Labor Day–mid-Oct: 10am–4pm daily;
mid-May–Labor Day: 10am–6pm daily.
● mid-Oct–Mar. 🖼 🖳 🖵 🖿
🅆 www.bcforestmuseum.com

Pacific Rim National Park Reserve of Canada ❼

THREE DISTINCT AREAS make up this reserve: Long Beach, the West Coast Trail, and the Broken Group Islands. Together they occupy an 80-mile (130-km) strip of Vancouver Island's west coast. The park is a world-famous area for whale-watching. Long Beach offers a range of hiking trails. The most challenging hike is the 46-mile (75-km) West Coast Trail, accessible from May to September. The Broken Group Islands can be reached by boat only.

The Broken Group Islands
This archipelago of some 100 islands and islets is popular with kayakers and scuba divers.

Schooner Trail is one of nine scenic and easy-to-follow trails through the coastal temperate rainforest.

The Wickaninnish Centre has viewing platforms for whale-watching.

Tofino

LONG BEACH

Port Albion

Ucluelet

Bamfi

Long Beach
The rugged, windswept sands of Long Beach are renowned for their wild beauty, with crashing Pacific rollers, unbeatable surfing opportunities, rock pools filled with marine life, and scattered driftwood.

🏛 **Quw'utsun'**
Cultural Centre
200 Cowichan Way, Duncan.
📞 *(250) 746-8119.* ⏲ *May–Sep: 9am–6pm daily; Oct–Apr: 10am–5pm daily.* ♿ 🚻 📷
🌐 www.quwutsun.ca

Chemainus ❹

Vancouver Island. 🏠 *4,000.*
ℹ *9796 Willow St, (250) 246-3944.*
🌐 www.chemainus.com

W HEN THE LOCAL sawmill closed in 1983, the picturesque town of Chemainus transformed itself into a major attraction with the painting of giant murals that depict the history of the region. Local and international artists continued the project, and today, 34 murals appear on specially built panels throughout the town, depicting events in the region's past.

Pleasure craft and fishing boats moored in Nanaimo Harbour

Nanaimo ❺

Road map 2 E4. 🏠 *79,000.*
ℹ *2290 Bowen Rd, (250) 756-0106.*
🌐 www.tourism.nanaimo.bc.ca

O RIGINALLY THE SITE of five Coast Salish villages, Nanaimo was established as a coal-mining town in the 1850s.

Its Old City Quarter contains many 19th-century buildings, including the Nanaimo Court House (31 Front Street), designed by Francis Rattenbury in 1895. In the **Nanaimo District Museum**, the most intriguing exhibit is a re-creation of Nanaimo's 1950s Chinatown, complete with wooden sidewalks, a general store, and an apothecary.

🏛 **Nanaimo District Museum**
100 Cameron Rd. 📞 *(250) 753-1821.*
⏲ *Victoria Day–Labor Day: 9am–5pm daily; Labor Day–Victoria Day: 9am–5pm Mon–Fri.* ♿ 📷 *by appt.*
🌐 www.nanaimo.museum.bc.ca

Gulf Islands ❻

Strait of Georgia. ℹ *(250) 754-3500.*
🌐 www.gulfislandsguide.com

T HEIR TRANQUILITY and natural beauty draw visitors to the Gulf Islands, where sightings of eagles and turkey vultures are common. Fishing charters and kayak tours provide views of otters, seals, and marine birds. The largest and most populated island, with about 10,000 residents, is **Saltspring**. In summer, visitors stroll around pretty Ganges Village. **Galiano's** nature preserve has many hiking trails; **Mayne's** tiny century-old museum recounts this island's history as a stopping-off point for Gold Rush miners and rumrunners. **North** and **South Pender Islands** are linked by a wooden bridge. Relics of a 5,000-year-old First Nations settlement have been found here. **Saturna**, the smallest and most remote of the islands, host a lamb barbecue each Canada Day *(see p31).* Visitors to **Gabriola** can view Snuneymuxw First Nations petroglyphs.

West Coast Trail
Stunning scenery, including moss-draped rainforest, sea stacks, and sea arches, is typical of this trail.

VISITORS' CHECKLIST

Hwy 4. 📞 *(250) 726-7721.*
⏲ *daily.* ♿ 📷 *Jun–Sep.* 🍴 🛒

KEY

— Major road

= Minor road

-- West Coast Trail

— National park boundary

— River

🔺 Camping

🏕 Picnic area

ℹ Information

🔭 Viewpoint

At the Nitinat Narrows,
a short ferry ride transports hikers on the West Coast Trail across this pretty waterway.

Port Renfrew

0 km   10

0 miles   10

Kayaks at Otter Bay on North Pender Island

Whistler ⑧

Whistler Valley tour trolley

Mild Pacific weather, reliable winter snow, and the greatest vertical rises of any ski runs in North America make Whistler one of the most popular skiing and snowboarding destinations in the world. Visitors flock in all seasons to the two side-by-side mountains of Whistler and Blackcomb, where winter activities include dog sledding, snowshoeing, and snowmobiling. In summer, hiking, mountain biking, canoeing, and horseback riding may be enjoyed around the five local lakes and at nearby wilderness locations such as Garibaldi Provincial Park.

One of a range of restaurant patios in Whistler Village

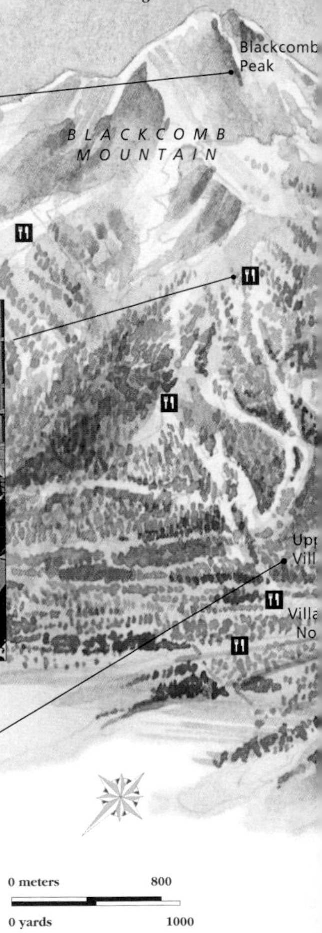

Blackcomb Peak

BLACKCOMB MOUNTAIN

Blackcomb Peak
The 7,490-ft- (2,284-m-) high Blackcomb Peak has more than 100 marked trails and five alpine bowls, two of which are glaciers. Its longest run covers a 7-mile (11-km) stretch.

Upp Vill

Villa No

The Rendezvous on Blackcomb Mountain
Snowboarders and skiers relax, refuel, and enjoy spectacular views at the Rendezvous restaurant and day lodge atop Blackcomb Mountain.

★ Fairmont Chateau Whistler
The Fairmont Chateau Whistler (see p295) is as much a tourist attraction as it is a hotel, with its art-filled lobby, luxurious tapestries and chandeliers, and rooftop garden terrace.

| 0 meters | 800 |
| 0 yards | 1000 |

Star Sights

★ **Alta Lake**

★ **Fairmont Chateau Whistler**

★ **Whistler Village**

Mountain biker in one of Whistler's many jump parks

VISITORS' CHECKLIST

Road map 2 B4. 🚶 10,000. ✈
🚌 ℹ️ *Tourism Whistler,
4010 Whistler Way, Whistler,
(604) 938-2769 or (800) 944-
7853 (in Canada & US) or
(800) 9447-8537.* 📅 🍴 🛍 🎭
Ⓦ www.mywhistler.com

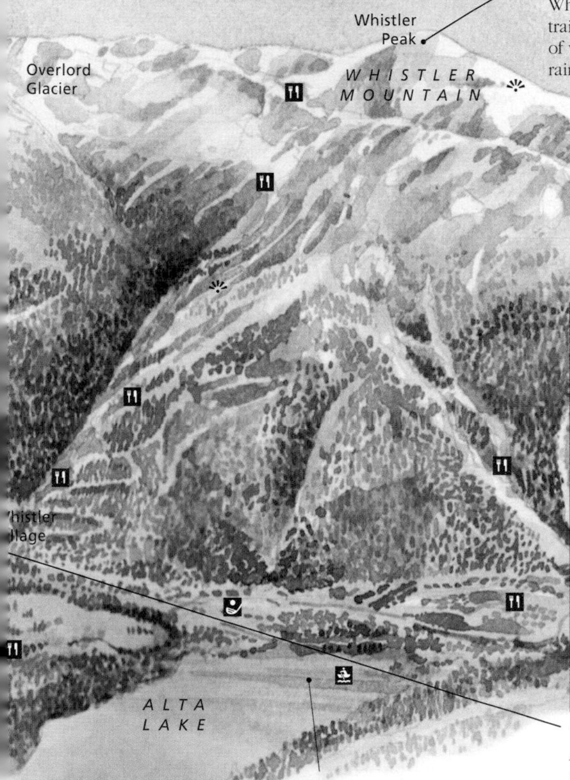

Whistler Peak
The 7,160-ft- (2,180-m-) high Whistler Peak has more than 100 trails, and seven alpine bowls, one of which is a glacier. Its skiable terrain covers 3,657 acres (1,463 ha).

Whistler Peak

Overlord Glacier

W H I S T L E R
M O U N T A I N

Whistler Village

A L T A
L A K E

★ Whistler Village
A tranquil pond proves a restful spot amid the bustle of Whistler Village, where hotels, restaurants, bars, and shops line the cobblestoned, car-free streets.

★ Alta Lake
Visitors come to this 1-mile- (1.6-km-) long lake – surrounded by forested mountains and 80 ft (24.5 m) at its deepest point – to swim, kayak, sailboard, and fish for rainbow and Dolly Varden trout. A number of hiking trails encircle the lake.

KEY

🍴 Restaurant
⛳ Golf course
🚣 Boating
❅ Viewpoint
ℹ️ Information

Kamloops 🟅

Road map 2 B4. 🏚 *83,000.*
ℹ️ *1290 W Hwy 1, (250) 374-3377.*
ⓦ *www.kamloopschamber.bc.ca*

KAMLOOPS – MEANING "where the rivers meet" in the language of the Secwepemc, or Shuswap, people – is situated at the confluence of the North and South Thompson Rivers. Nestled amid mountains and lakes, the city offers hiking, biking, skiing, river rafting, fishing, and golfing.

European settlement began here in 1812, with fur traders doing business with the Secwepemc. Remains of a 2,000-year-old village and re-created pit houses at the **Secwepemc Museum and Heritage Park** reflect the tribe's history.

US train robber Bill Miner arrived in Kamloops in 1904, on the run after committing Canada's first such robbery. Kamloops and trains have been linked ever since. The restored 1912 Steam Locomotive No. 2141, one of the few remaining operational steam engines, leaves the historic CN station on a tour that harks back to days of the Wild West. A train ride can also be taken at **Kamloops Wildlife Park**, home to threatened birds and animals.

Okanagan Valley wine

🏛 Secwepemc Museum and Heritage Park
355 Yellowhead Hwy. ⓒ *(250) 828-9801.* ⓞ *8:30am–4:30pm (days vary, call ahead).* ♿ 🚻

🦌 Kamloops Wildlife Park
Hwy 1, 10.5 miles (17 km) east of Kamloops. ⓒ *(250) 573-3242.* ⓞ *Jul–Aug: 8am–8:30pm; Sep–Jun: 8am–4:30pm daily.* ● *Dec 25.* 📷 ♿ 🚻

Mission Hill Estate Winery in Westbank, near Kelowna

Kelowna 🟊

Road map 2 B4. 🏚 *96,000.*
ℹ️ *544 Harvey Ave, (250) 861-1515.*
ⓦ *www.kelownachamber.org*

KELOWNA LIES ON the eastern shore of 56-mile- (80-km-) long Okanagan Lake. The Okanagan Valley's warm, dry climate has long attracted fruit growers, including Father Charles Pandosy, a French lay priest who arrived in 1859. Pandosy planted the area's first fruit trees at the Immaculate Conception Mission, the first non-Native settlement in the region. Today, the **Father Pandosy Mission** is a heritage site. Kelowna's peaches, apples, and cherries are plentiful, but its grapes make it the center of the largest and oldest wine-producing region in the province. Many of the Okanagan Valley's wineries are within a 30-minute drive of Kelowna. Wineries range from intimate to expansive; tours highlight grape-growing and harvesting methods. Orchard

tours may include wagon rides and visits to petting zoos.

Kelowna's lakefront parks and sandy beaches add to the enjoyment of fresh-fare restaurants. Okanagan Lake, golf courses, and trails for hiking, biking, and horseback riding offer recreational opportunities. In winter, the powder snow here makes **Big White Ski Resort** (tel. 250/765-3101) a major draw for skiers.

⛪ Father Pandosy Mission
3685 Benvoulin Rd. ⓒ *(250) 860-8369.* ⓞ *Easter–Thanksgiving: dawn–dusk daily.*

Ripe peaches from the orchards of Summerland, Okanagan Valley

Summerland 🟋

Road map 2 B4. 🏚 *11,000.*
ℹ️ *15600 Hwy 97, (250) 494-2686.*
ⓦ *www.summerlandchamber.bc.ca*

SUMMERLAND HAS BEEN synonymous with peaches since founder John Moore Robinson arrived in 1902 and persuaded farmers to turn to fruit growing. Today, its shops and town crier reflect an Old English theme.

The beautiful **Summerland Ornamental Gardens** overlook Okanagan Lake and Trout Creek Canyon. A viewpoint atop Giant's Head Mountain provides a lovely panorama.

Kettle Valley Railway, now a tourist attraction, operated here from 1915 to 1964. A 1924 Shay steam engine pulls two 1950 coaches and two open-air cars across the 238-ft- (73-m-) high Trout Creek Bridge.

🌿 Summerland Ornamental Gardens
4200 Hwy 97. ⓒ *(250) 494-6385.* ⓞ *8am–sunset daily.* 📷 ♿ 🚻
🚂 Kettle Valley Railway
18404 Bathville Rd. ⓒ *(250) 494-8422.* ⓞ *mid-May–mid-Oct: 10:30am & 1:30pm (days vary; call ahead).* 📷 ♿ 🚻 ⓦ *www.kettlevalleyrail.org*

Vineyard in the south Okanagan Valley sloping down to Okanagan Lake

Okanagan Valley Tour [12]

WINE ROUTE
Okanagan wine route

THE OKANAGAN VALLEY is actually a series of valleys, linked by a string of lakes, that stretches for 155 miles (250 km) – from Osoyoos in the south to Vernon in the north. The main towns here are connected by Highway 97, which passes through the desert landscape near Lake Osoyoos, and on to the lush green orchards and vineyards for which the valley is most noted. Mild winters and hot summers have made the Okanagan Valley one of Canada's favorite vacation destinations.

Tips for Drivers

Tour length: *143 miles (230 km).*
Starting points: *On Hwy 97 from Vernon in the north, Osoyoos in the south.*
When to go: *Blossom and fruit festivals are held in spring and summer, when roadside stalls offer a cornucopia of fruit. Wine tours are available year-round.*

Kelowna [4]
The largest city in the Okanagan, Kelowna lies on the shores of Okanagan Lake between Penticton and Vernon, and is the center of the wine- and fruit-growing industries.

KAMLOOPS
Lake Country
Monashee Mountains
97
97C
Okanagan Lake
Peachland
Naramata
Lake Skaha
3A
Okanagan Falls
VANCOUVER
NELSON
US BORDER

Vernon [5]
Surrounded by farms and orchards, Vernon owes its lush look to the expansion of irrigation in 1908.

Summerland [3]
This small but charming lakeside resort town boasts several 19th-century buildings and stunning views from the top of Giant's Head Mountain.

Penticton [2]
This sunny lakeside town is known for the long Okanagan Beach, windsurfing, and local winery tours, as well as for its Peach Festival, held every August.

O'Keefe Historic Ranch [6]
Founded by the O'Keefe family in 1867, this historic ranch displays original artifacts belonging to the family that lived here until 1977. The original log cabin remains, as does the church and store.

Osoyoos [1]
Visitors are drawn here by hot summers, the warm waters and sandy beaches of Lake Osoyoos, and the nearby pocket desert.

0 km 25
0 miles 25

Key

Tour route
Other road
Viewpoint

The Kootenays ⓭

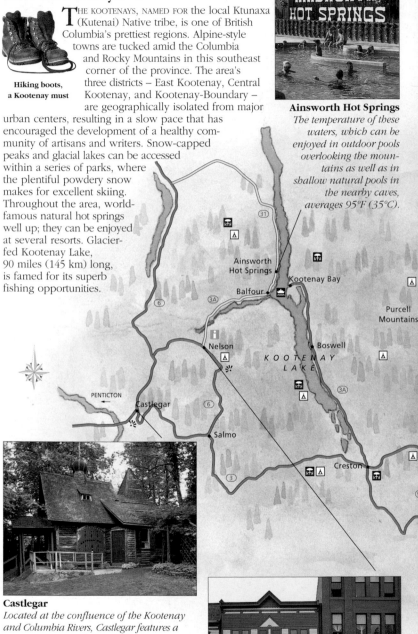

Hiking boots, a Kootenay must

THE KOOTENAYS, NAMED FOR the local Ktunaxa (Kutenai) Native tribe, is one of British Columbia's prettiest regions. Alpine-style towns are tucked amid the Columbia and Rocky Mountains in this southeast corner of the province. The area's three districts – East Kootenay, Central Kootenay, and Kootenay-Boundary – are geographically isolated from major urban centers, resulting in a slow pace that has encouraged the development of a healthy community of artisans and writers. Snow-capped peaks and glacial lakes can be accessed within a series of parks, where the plentiful powdery snow makes for excellent skiing. Throughout the area, world-famous natural hot springs well up; they can be enjoyed at several resorts. Glacier-fed Kootenay Lake, 90 miles (145 km) long, is famed for its superb fishing opportunities.

Ainsworth Hot Springs
The temperature of these waters, which can be enjoyed in outdoor pools overlooking the mountains as well as in shallow natural pools in the nearby caves, averages 95°F (35°C).

Ainsworth Hot Springs
Kootenay Bay
Balfour
Nelson
Boswell
K O O T E N A Y
L A K E
PENTICTON
Castlegar
Salmo
Creston
Purcell Mountains

Castlegar
Located at the confluence of the Kootenay and Columbia Rivers, Castlegar features a reconstructed Doukhobor village.

★ Nelson
With its steep streets, heritage buildings, and large community of artists, Nelson is a lovely town in which to stroll. It is also a good base for hiking, skiing, and other outdoor activities.

★ **Fernie**

This scenic town lies in one of the Kootenays' most popular areas for snow sports. In the 1880s, Fernie was reputedly cursed by an Indian chief when he was betrayed by its founder. In 1964, the curse was officially lifted by a peace pipe–smoking ceremony.

VISITORS' CHECKLIST

Hwy 3. ▮ *225 Hall St, Nelson, (250) 352-3433.* ▮ *2279 Cranbrook St N, Cranbrook, (250) 426-5914.* ▮ *Hwy 3 & Dicken Rd, Fernie, (250) 423-6868.* ▢ *all three offices: year-round: 9am–5pm Mon–Fri, Victoria Day–Labor Day: 10am–5pm Sat also.* ✕ *Cranbrook & Castlegar.* ⛴ *BC Ministry of Highways inland ferry service Kootenay Bay–Balfour, year-round, 6am–midnight daily; 35 mins; (250) 229-4215.* Ⓦ *www.th.gov.bc.ca/ bchighways/inlandferryschedule/ ferryschedule.htm* Ⓦ *www.bcrockies.com*

The Kootenay Bay–Balfour ferry, offering magnificent views of surrounding mountains from its decks

Kimberley · 95A

Fort Steele

M O U N T   F I S H E R

Cranbrook

Fernie · 3 · i

Moyie Lake Provincial Park

M O Y I E   L A K E

Crowsnest Highway · 93

0 kilometers   25
0 miles   15

KEY

▬	Major road
═	Minor road
⛴	Ferry
🅰	Camping
⛩	Picnic area
ℹ	Information
❀	Viewpoint

STAR SIGHTS

★ **Cranbrook**

★ **Fernie**

★ **Nelson**

★ **Cranbrook**

Panoramic views can be enjoyed just a short hike from this town, which lies between the Rocky and Purcell Mountains. This land, where the Ktunaxa once camped, has excellent cross-country ski and hiking trails.

Exploring the Kootenays

R USHING RIVERS, DEEP LAKES, and historic towns nestle
among the sheer mountains of the Kootenays,
a region at the southern end of the Canadian Rockies
in the southeast corner of British Columbia. The
Kootenays offer a wide range of outdoor activities,
including heli-skiing, rock climbing, river rafting, and
fly-fishing. Its horse ranches, ski lodges, and chartered
houseboats offer visitors comfortable accommodation
and opportunities for active and memorable vacations.

**Downhill skier on one of Fernie's
spectacular ski runs**

Fernie

Road map 2 C4. 🏃 *4,900.* 🚌 🚖
102 Commerce Rd, (250) 423-4395.
ⓦ *www.fernietourism.com*

F ERNIE IS AN ATTRACTIVE, tree-
lined town set amid the
pointed peaks of Crowsnest
Pass. The town owes its handsome appearance to a fire that
razed it in 1908. All buildings
constructed since are brick and
stone. Among several historic
buildings, the 1911 courthouse
stands out as BC's only
chateau-style courthouse.

Fernie boasts the best
powder snow in the Rockies;
the ski season runs from
November to April. The
Fernie Alpine Resort lifts
can transport 12,300 skiers
up the mountain every hour.

During the summer, magnificent mountain scenery can
be enjoyed from a variety of
hiking trails in Mount Fernie
Provincial Park. Boat trips on
the area's many lakes and
rivers are popular, as is fishing.
Helicopter sightseeing trips
take visitors close to the mountains to see the formations
and granite cliffs particular to
this region of the Rockies.

Cranbrook

Road map 2 C4. 🏃 *19,000.* ✈ 🚌
🚻 *2279 Cranbrook St N, (250) 426-
5914.* ⓦ *www.explorecranbrook.com*

C RANBOOK, LYING BETWEEN the
Purcell and Rocky Moun-
tain ranges, is the largest town
in southeast BC. A major
transportation hub, Cranbrook
is within easy reach of spec-
ular scenery. The area boasts
the highest density of grizzlies
in the Rockies. These, along
with the region's other wildlife, which includes elk,
wolves, and cougars, may be
spotted on the many trails in
the area. Hikers should exercise caution *(see pp320–21).*

The Canadian Pacific Railway
reached Cranbrook in 1898.
The **Canadian Museum of
Rail Travel** includes the magnificent Royal Alexandra Hall
Café with its high decorative
curved ceilings, and 12
restored luxury cars, including
the 1929 Trans-Canada Limited.

🏛 **Canadian Museum of
Rail Travel**
57 Van Horne St S. 📞 *(250) 489-3918.*
🔘 *Apr–mid-Oct: 10am–6pm daily;
mid-Oct–Mar: noon–5pm Tue–Sat.*
🖼 🚻 ✔ 🅿

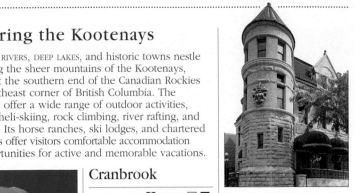

**Nelson's pink-brick and marble
City Hall, dating from 1902**

Nelson

Road map 2 C4. 🏃 *9,000.* 🚌
🚻 *225 Hall St, (250) 352-3433.*
ⓦ *www.city.nelson.bc.ca*

O NE OF THE MOST attractive
towns in southern British
Columbia, Nelson overlooks
Kootenay Lake. Established in
the 1880s as a mining town,
Nelson flourished with the
arrival of the railroad in the
1890s, becoming a center for
the transportation of ore and
timber. Many of the town's
public buildings and houses
were constructed between
1895 and 1920. In 1979, a $3
million municipal renovation
program helped restore the
historic façades of the downtown buildings.

The town has a thriving
cultural scene, with bookstores,
art galleries, cafés, and craft
shops. Visitors can enjoy the
short ride on Car 23, a 1906
streetcar that operated here
from 1924 to 1949. Restored
in 1992, it now travels along
Nelson's delightful waterfront.

The opulent dining car on a restored train at Cranbrook's rail museum

Exploring Nelson

Nelson's downtown, though hilly, is easily walkable. More than 350 historic buildings, from elegant mansions to elaborate commercial structures, give the city its unique style. Many of these restored buildings are part of Nelson's historic downtown walking tour. The visitors' center provides maps and guides for the tour.

🏛 Bank of Montreal
298 Baker St. ◉ *bank & major hols.* 🚹
When it opened in 1900, after a year under construction, the Bank of Montreal was considered one of the finest commercial buildings in the BC Interior. Its Italian influences include rounded window arches and detailed brickwork.

🏛 Mara-Barnard Block
421–431 Baker St. 🚹
This elaborate High Victorian building, with unusual bay windows on the second floor, housed the first branch of the Royal Bank of Canada to open in BC, in 1897.

🏛 K.W.C. Block
488–498 Baker St. 🚹
Built by three merchants, Kirkpatrick, Wilson, and Clements, in 1901, the K.W.C. Block is

the largest mercantile building in Nelson. The turret and window arches are noteworthy.

🏛 Houston Block
601–607 Baker St. 🚹
Nelson's first mayor, John Houston, commissioned architect A.E. Hodgins to design the grand Houston Block, built in 1899, to house a bank.

🏛 City Hall
502 Vernon St. 🕻 *(250) 352-5511.* ☐ *year-round: 8:30am–4:30pm Mon–Fri.* ◉ *major hols.* 🗹 🚹
Spokane pink brick and Kaslo marble make for a picturesque mixture of textures and patterns on the 1902 Post Office and Customs House, now Nelson City Hall.

🏛 Nelson Court House
310 Ward St. 🕻 *(250) 354-6165.* ☐ *year-round: 8:30am–4:30pm Mon–Fri.* ◉ *major hols.* 🗹 🚹
F.M. Rattenbury, designer of Victoria's Parliament Buildings *(see p250),* designed this fine example of Beaux Arts château architecture. Dating from 1909, it features a high pitched roof, towers, conical caps, gables, and paired windows.

Castlegar

Road map 2 C4. 🏔 *7,400.* ☒ 🖼
ℹ *1995 6th Ave, (250) 365-6313.*
Ⓦ *www.castlegar.com*

LOCATED AT THE confluence of the Kootenay and Columbia Rivers, Castlegar is a fisher's paradise. In the early 1900s, Doukhobors (Russian religious dissenters) fleeing persecution began arriving here in large numbers. The **Doukhobor Village Museum** showcases the group's culture with displays of traditional clothes, tools, and farm machinery in a re-created village. Set in lovely grounds with river views and accessed via a 470-ft- (143-m-) long suspension bridge, **Zuckerberg Island Heritage Park** features a Lakes Salish pit house and a Russian Orthodox chapel.

Statue of Tolstoy, Doukhobor Village

🏛 Doukhobor Village Museum
112 Heritage Way. 🕻 *(250) 365-6622.* ☐ *May–Sep: 10am–6pm daily.* 🗹 🚹
🏛 Zuckerberg Island Heritage Park
9th St at 7th Ave. 🕻 *(250) 365-5511.* ☐ *May–Aug daily.* 🗹 *by donation.* 🗹 🚹

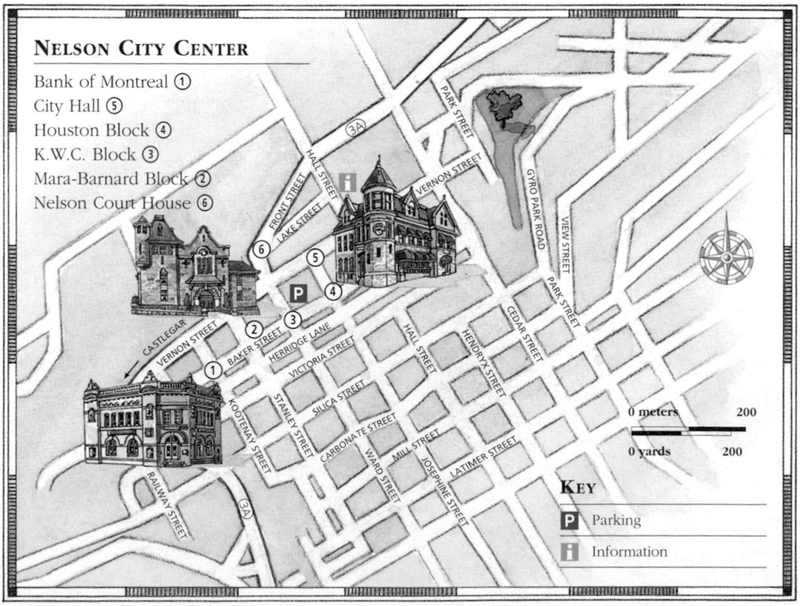

NELSON CITY CENTER

Bank of Montreal ①
City Hall ⑤
Houston Block ④
K.W.C. Block ③
Mara-Barnard Block ②
Nelson Court House ⑥

PARK STREET
3A
HALL STREET
IRONS STREET
LAKE STREET
VERNON STREET
GYRO PARK ROAD
VIEW STREET
PARK STREET
CEDAR STREET
HENDRYX STREET
HALL STREET
CASTLEGAR
VERNON STREET
BAKER STREET
HERRIDGE LANE
VICTORIA STREET
SILICA STREET
KOOTENAY STREET
STANLEY STREET
WARD STREET
CARBONATE STREET
MILL STREET
JOSEPHINE STREET
LATIMER STREET
RAILWAY STREET
3A

0 meters 200
0 yards 200

KEY
🅿 Parking
ℹ Information

19th-century barber's shop in Fort Steele Heritage Town

Fort Steele Heritage Town ⑭

Road map 2 C4. 🄲 *(250) 426-7352.* ⭘ *mid-May–mid-Oct: 9:30am–8pm daily.* 🅆 *www.fortsteele.bc.ca*

FORT STEELE is a re-creation of the mining supply town that was established at this site in 1864, when gold was discovered at Wild Horse Creek. Thousands of prospectors and entrepreneurs arrived by the Dewdney Trail, which linked the town of Hope to the gold fields. Originally called Galbraith's Ferry,

An historic dentist's sign in Fort Steele Heritage Town

the town was renamed after Samuel Steele, the North West Mounted Police superintendent who arrived in 1887 to restore peace between warring Ktunaxa Natives and European settlers. The town enjoyed a brief boom with the discovery of lead and silver, but the mainline railroad was routed through Cranbrook instead, and by the early 1900s, Fort Steele was a ghost town.

Today, there are more than 60 reconstructed or restored buildings, staffed by guides in period costume, including the general store, livery stable, and North West Mounted Police officers' quarters, where personal items such as family photographs, swords, and uniforms create the illusion of recent occupation. Demonstrations of traditional crafts such as quilting and ice cream-making are also held here. "Living history" dramas and musical comedy shows staged in the Wild Horse Theater are inspired by the town's history, and tours at the nearby Wild Horse Creek Historic Site include a chance to pan for gold.

The Purcell Mountains ⑮

Road map 2 C4. 🄷 *1905 Warren Ave, Kimberley, (250) 427-4838.*

THE RUGGED and beautiful Purcell Mountains face the Rockies across the broad Columbia River Valley. The region is one of the most remote in the Rockies and attracts hikers and skiers from around the globe. A high range of granite spires, called the Bugaboos, also draws mountain climbers. In the north of the Purcell range, the Purcell Wilderness Conservancy – one of the range's few accessible areas – covers a vast 167,000 acres (67,609 ha).

From the nearby town of Invermere, it is possible to access the Earl Grey Pass Trail, one of the most difficult trails in Canada, which extends

The Purcell Mountains, noted for remote rivers and forests

35 miles (56 km). It is named after Earl Grey, Canada's Governor General from 1904 to 1911, who chose the Purcell range as the place to build a vacation cabin for his family, in 1912. The trail he traveled followed an established route used by the Kinbasket Natives of the Ktunaxa First Nations tribe. Today the trail is notoriously dangerous; bears, avalanches, and fallen trees are just some of the hazards hikers may encounter along the way. Hiking along it requires skill and experience and therefore should not be attempted by novice hikers.

Radium Hot Springs ⑯

Road map 2 C4. 🄷 *400.* 🄲 *(250) 347-9331.* 🅆 *radiumhotsprings.com*

THE TOWN of Radium Hot Springs is famous for its mineral springs and is a good base for exploring nearby Kootenay National Park. In summer, flowerpots decorate the storefronts of the cafés and pubs on the main street, and the town has more visitors than residents. Many of the 1.2 million annual tourists come to bathe in the healing waters of the springs.

The nearby Columbia Valley Wetlands provide an important habitat for over 250 migratory waterfowl, such as Canada geese, great blue herons, and tundra swans. Fed by glacial waters, the Columbia River meanders through these extensive marshlands.

Fort Steele's Wasa Hotel, modeled on a popular 1904 East Kootenay resort

The dramatic peaks of the Rocky Mountains in Kootenay National Park

Kootenay National Park ⑲

Road map 2 C4. 🛈 *7556 Main St E, Radium Hot Springs, (250) 347-9505.* ⭕ *daily.* ***Visitors' center*** ⭕ *May 17–Jun 26: 9am–5pm daily; Jun 27–Sep 2: 9am–7pm daily.* 🅿 ♿ 🅿 W *www.parkscanada.gc*

KOOTENAY NATIONAL Park covers 543 sq miles (1,406 sq km) of the most diverse terrain in the Rockies. Much of this scenery can be seen from the Kootenay Parkway (Hwy 93), which cuts through the park from north to south following the Vermilion and Kootenay Rivers. Most of the park's attractions can be seen from the many short trails that lead from the highway.

The road winds westward through Sinclair Pass, where the high red walls of Sinclair Canyon, a limestone gorge, lead to the Sinclair Falls and the Redwall Fault. Here, rust-colored cliffs form a natural gateway across the highway.

Farther north, the magical Paint Pots, ocher and red pools formed from iron-rich mineral springs, are reached by a short trail from the road. Farther on lie the high limestone walls of the stunning Marble Canyon.

Glacier National Park ⑱

Road map 2 C4. 🛈 *Rogers Pass, (250) 837-7500.* ⭕ *daily.* 🅿 ♿ 🅿 W *www.parkscanada.qc.ca*

GLACIER NATIONAL PARK covers 520 sq miles (1,350 sq km) of wilderness in the Selkirk Range of the Columbia Mountains. The park was established in 1886, and its growth was linked to the expansion of the railroad, which was routed through Rogers Pass in 1885. Today, one of the park's most accessible trails follows an abandoned railroad line. Other trails here offer visitors spectacular views of the park's 420 glaciers, including the Great Glacier, now known as the **Illecillewaet Glacier**.

Glacier National Park contains rainforests, glacial lakes, streams, and waterfalls. During winter, snow falls almost daily, totaling as much as 75 ft (23 m) per season. The threat of avalanches in the park is serious; skiers and climbers are encouraged to obtain information about travel conditions before visiting.

The Rogers Pass line was eventually abandoned by the Canadian Pacific Railway because of the frequent avalanches, and a tunnel was built underneath it instead. The Trans-Canada Highway (Hwy 1) follows the route of the pass as it bisects the park en route to the lovely city of Revelstoke. From here, visitors may access the forests and jagged peaks of **Mount Revelstoke National Park**.

Illecillewaet Glacier, one of 420 glaciers in Glacier National Park

HOT SPRINGS HAVENS

The geology of the British Columbia Rockies has created numerous hot springs, formed naturally by groundwater seeping downward, coming into contact with hot rock 2–2.5 miles (3–4 km) below the earth's crust, and rising back to the surface at a very high temperature. The province's many hot springs resorts offer hot pools in the 100°F (38°C) range, as well as larger warm pools for swimming. The waters are rich in sulfates, calcium, and hydrogen sulfide and are said to benefit arthritis and rheumatism sufferers.

Roadside sign welcoming visitors to Radium Hot Springs

The ocher-colored Paint Pot pools in Kootenay National Park

Yoho National Park ⑲

Shooting star flower

INSPIRED BY THE BEAUTY of the area's mountains, lakes, waterfalls, and distinctive rock formations, this park was named Yoho for the Cree word meaning "awe and wonder." Yoho National Park lies on the western side of the Rockies range in British Columbia, near Banff and Kootenay National Parks. The park is ideal for climbing, hiking, canoeing, and cross-country skiing. It also is home to the Burgess Shale fossil beds, an extraordinary find of perfectly preserved marine creatures from the Cambrian period, over 500 million years ago. Access to the beds is by guided hike, limited to 15 people each trip.

WAPTA ICEFIELD

Emerald Lake
The rustic Emerald Lake Lodge provides facilities at this secluded spot in the middle of the park. The lake, named for the intense color of its waters, is a popular place for canoeing, walking, and horseback riding.

Natural Bridge
Found in the center of the park, over the waters of Kicking Horse River, Natural Bridge is a rock bridge formed by centuries of erosion, which have worn a channel through solid rock. The bridge is a short drive from Highway 1.

VANCOUVER, GLACIER NATIONAL PARK

KEY
— Highway
— Major road
— River
Ⓐ Campsite
🏠 Picnic area
ℹ Information
🌿 Viewpoint

Hoodoo Creek
Erosion created these mushroom-like towers of rock. A very steep one-mile (1.6-km) ascent should be tackled only by experienced hikers.

The Yoho Valley is noted for its stunning scenery, which includes the Takakkaw Falls.

Takakkaw Falls
Takakkaw means "it is wonderful" in the language of the local Native people, and these, with a drop of 833 ft (254 m), are among the most impressive falls in Canada. The falls can be accessed along the Yoho Valley Road.

Burgess Shale was declared a UN World Heritage Site so as to protect two fossil beds. Guided hikes here are by reservation only.

CALGARY, BANFF NATIONAL PARK

Kicking Horse River
This wild river rushes through Yoho alongside the original 1880s railroad. Today the tracks carry freight and the Rocky Mountaineer tourist train (see p332).

ANBURY LACIER

Lake O'Hara
Shadowed by the majestic peaks of Mounts Victoria and Lefroy, Lake O'Hara is astonishingly beautiful. Guests wishing to use the area's excellent hiking trails must book in advance, as access is limited so as to protect this fragile environment.

Helmcken Falls, crowned by a rainbow, in Wells Gray Provincial Park

Wells Gray Provincial Park ⑳

Road map 2 B4. **ℹ** Clearwater, (250) 674-3693. ○ call for hrs. **W** www.wellsgray.ca

WELLS GRAY Provincial Park, in the Cariboo Mountains, is not only one of the largest but also one of the most beautiful wildernesses in British Columbia, offering wonders comparable to the Rockies in eastern BC. The park, established in 1939, is distinguished by alpine meadows, thundering waterfalls, and glacier-topped peaks that rise as high as 8,450 ft (2,575 m). The Canadian National Railroad and Highway 5 follow the Thompson River along the park's western edge, and both routes provide stunning views.

From the Clearwater Valley Road, off Highway 5, there are several trails, from easy walks to arduous overnight hikes in remote country. A number of trails just minutes from the road lead to spectacular 450-ft (137-m) **Helmcken Falls**, the fourth highest waterfall in Canada. Nearby Mushbowl Bridge provides the best view of the fast-moving Murtle River and the giant holes it has carved into the surrounding rock.

In late August and early September, Chinook salmon leap in futile attempts to continue upstream past the dramatic **Bailey's Chute**.

Four lakes located throughout the park provide excellent opportunities for canoeing and angling.

Prince George ㉑

Road map 2 B3. 🏙 80,000. **ℹ** 1198 Victoria St, (250) 562-3700. **W** www.tourismpg.com

THE LARGEST TOWN in northeastern British Columbia, Prince George is a bustling supply-and-transportation center for the region. Two major highways pass through here: the Yellowhead (Hwy 16) and Highway 97, which becomes the Alaska Highway at Dawson Creek. Established in 1807 as Fort George, a fur-trading post at the confluence of the Nechako and Fraser Rivers, the town is well placed for exploring the province.

Prince George has all the facilities of a larger city, including its own symphony orchestra, several art galleries, and a new university specializing in First Nations, environmental, and forestry studies. The **Fraser-Fort George Regional Museum** lies on the site of the original fort, within the 65-acre (26-ha) Fort George Park. It contains a small collection of artifacts from Native cultures, European pioneers, and early settlers of the region.

An important center for the lumber industry, the town offers a range of free tours of local pulp mills, which take visitors through the process of wood production, from vast fields of young seedlings to hill-sized piles of planks and raw timber.

🏛 Fraser-Fort George Regional Museum
333 Becott Pl. 📞 (250) 562-1612. ○ Victoria Day–Thanksgiving: 10am–5pm daily; Thanksgiving–Victoria Day: 10am–5pm Wed–Sun. ● Jan 1, Dec 25 & 26. 🎟 by donation. ♿ **W** www.theexplorationplace.com

Dinosaur models in Fraser-Fort George Regional Museum

Dawson Creek ㉒

Road map 2 B3. 🏙 12,000. **ℹ** 900 Alaska Ave, (250) 782-9595. **W** www.tourismdawsoncreek.com

THE FORMERLY QUIET town of Dawson Creek was transformed by the construction of the Alaska Highway, which began in 1942 and swelled the town's population from 600 to 10,000. Designated as historic Mile Zero on the road to Fairbanks, 1,486 miles (2,391 km) to

Former grain elevator turned art gallery in Dawson Creek

the north, the city recognizes this distinction with the **Mile Zero post** at 10th Street and 102nd Avenue. Located at the corner of Highway 97 and the Alaska Highway, the red-and-white 1931 **Northern Alberta Railway Station** is now a museum and information center. The 4-acre (1.6 ha) site includes the Mile Zero stone cairn marking the official start of the Alaska Highway. Next to the railway station is a 1948 grain elevator annex that is now an art gallery. The conversion of elevator to gallery involved the removal of 10 tons of grain dust. Shows include the work of local artists as well as major traveling collections. On Saturday mornings from May to October, a farmers' market held across from the stone cairn sells local produce and crafts.

The Mile Zero post at Dawson Creek

At **Walter Wright Pioneer Village**, restored buildings and farm machinery recreate the agricultural community of Dawson Creek before the highway was built.

🏛 Walter Wright Pioneer Village

1901 Alaska Hwy. 📞 *(250) 782-7144.*
⏰ *mid-May–Aug: 8:30am–9pm daily.*
⏰ *Sep–mid-May.* 💰 *by donation.* ♿

Fort St. John ㉓

Road map 2 B2. 👥 *16,000.*
ℹ️ *9923 96th Ave, (250) 785-6037.*
🌐 *www.fortstjohnchamber.com*

THE CITY OF Fort St. John is located at Mile 47 of the Alaska Highway, among the rolling hills of the Peace River Valley. Fort St. John, originally one of six forts built in the area between 1794 and 1925, is the oldest non-Native settlement in British Columbia. At nearby Charlie Lake Cave, 10,000-year-old artifacts of the Paleo Indians have been found, making it the site of the earliest-known human activity in the province.

The area around Fort St. John is a unique ecosystem

in which moose, deer, elk, and black bears abound. During the 1942 construction of the Alaska Highway, the town's population increased dramatically, from 800 to 6,000. When completed, the highway turned Fort St. John into a busy supply center catering to visitors to the area and supporting the agriculture industry in the surrounding countryside.

The town boomed in the 1950s, when oil was found here in what proved to be the largest oil field in BC. The city's pride in its industrial heritage is reflected in its **museum**, which has a 140-ft- (43-m-) high oil derrick at its entrance and exhibits telling the story of the local oil industry. Other attractions include a honey-processing plant, with one of the world's largest glass beehives. A popular seasonal activity is watching the northern lights, very visible here.

Fort Nelson ㉔

Road map 2 B2. 👥 *4,200.* ℹ️ *5319 50th Ave S, (250) 774-2541.*
🌐 *www.northernrockies.org*

DESPITE THE GROWTH of the oil, gas, and lumber industries in the 1960s and 1970s, Fort Nelson retains the atmosphere of a northern frontier town. Before the building of the Alaska Highway in the 1940s, Fort Nelson was an important stop en route to Yukon and Alaska, and until the 1950s it was without telephones, running water, or electricity.

The steaming waters of the Liard River Hot Springs, Fort Nelson

Fur trading was the main activity until the energy boom; even today trappers continue to hunt beaver, wolf, and lynx, for both their fur and their meat.

This town at Mile 300 of the Alaska Highway has an air and bus service, a hospital, and good visitor facilities such as motels, restaurants, and gas stations. Local people are known for their friendliness, and during the busy summer months they run a program of free talks for visitors, describing life in the North.

The small **Fort Nelson Heritage Museum** displays photographs and artifacts that tell the story of the building of the Alaska Highway, and features a frontier-town general store and blacksmith's forge. The trappers log cabin behind the museum is also worth visiting.

The region has over a dozen parks, including **Liard River Provincial Park**; its hot springs are open year round. The area is a world-class cross-country skiing destination.

Lush farmland alongside the Peace River near Fort St. John

The green waters of Muncho Lake framed by mountains in Muncho Lake Provincial Park

Muncho Lake Provincial Park 25

Road map 2 A1. 📞 (250) 565-6340.
⭕ May–Oct: daily. 🅿️ to campsites.

ONE OF THREE provincial parks that were established after the building of the Alaska Highway in 1942, Muncho Lake occupies the most scenic section of the road. The park encompasses the bare peaks of the northern Rockies, whose stark limestone slopes incorporate the faults, alluvial fans, and fantastic rock formations that are a testament to thousands of years of glacial erosion. Flash floods are common here.

The highway skirts the eastern shoreline of the 7.5-mile- (12-km-) long Muncho Lake before crossing the Liard River, where the Mackenzie Mountains begin. In early summer, passing motorists are likely to see moose grazing in wildflower meadows. The park's bogs are popular with botanists eager to see the rare yellow Lady's Slipper orchid. The roadside also attracts great numbers of goats, sheep, and caribou, which are drawn by deposits of sodium, known as mineral licks.

Visitors may stay in the park at one of its 30 campgrounds or lodges in order to explore its 218,480 acres (88,420 ha) of wilderness. The deep waters of Muncho Lake offer a good supply of trout for anglers. Narrated boat tours of the lake are offered by Double G Service (tel. 250/776-3411).

The Hazeltons 26

Road map 2 A3. 🏠 6,500.
ℹ️ 4070 9th Ave, New Hazelton, (250) 842-6071.
🌐 www.village.hazelton.bc.ca

IN THE 1860s, pioneer communities were established at the confluence of the Skeena and Bulkley Rivers, 180 miles (290 km) east of Prince Rupert. Today, three villages at this location – Old, New, and South Hazelton – are known collectively as the Hazeltons. The towns, named for the hazel bushes covering the region's river-carved terraces, lie near the cliffs of Mount Rocher Déboulé, which tower over the area at 3,300 ft (1,005 m).

All the Hazeltons are charming, particularly Old Hazelton, where the old-fashioned storefronts offer a reminder of the days when the community was a bustling river terminus. The Old Hazelton walking tour shows off remnants of a Victorian steam engine from early forestry days, Skeena River paddlewheelers, the century-old St. Peter's Anglican Church, and the **Hazelton Pioneer Museum and Archives**, which portrays the early days of the initial settlement.

The highlight of the area is the **'Ksan Historical Village and Museum**, a replica of a Northwest Coast–style Gitxsan village. Gitxsan First Nations people have lived in the area for thousands of years, particularly along the beautiful Skeena River valley. Their culture and way of life were threatened by an influx of white settlers who arrived in the 1850s at Prince Rupert to work their way upriver to mine or farm, but the tribe has been recovering its traditions since the 1950s.

'Ksan totem poles at the 'Ksan Historical Village and Museum

Noted for their skill in creating carved and painted masks, totems, and canoes, Gitxsan elders are now schooling new generations in these skills at the 'Ksan village. Within the village complex are seven traditional longhouses, containing a carving school, totems, and a museum.

A 70-mile (113-km) self-guided driving tour winds through several First Nations villages, where one can see dozens of totem poles. Indeed, the Hazeltons are known as the "totem pole capital of the world." The area also abounds with recreational opportunities, including hiking and fishing.

🏛 **Hazelton Pioneer Museum and Archives**
4255 Government St, Hazelton.
☎ (250) 842-5961.
🏛 **'Ksan Historical Village and Museum**
High Level Rd, Hazelton. ❓ New Hazelton, (250) 842-5544. ⏱ mid-Apr–mid-Oct: 10am–4:30pm daily; mid-Oct–mid-Apr: 10am–4:30pm Mon–Fri.
🈂 ♿ 🎫 📷 🚻 Ⓦ www.ksan.org

A main street in Smithers, against a backdrop of steep mountains

Smithers ㉗

Road map 2 A3. 🏙 5,800.
❓ 1411 Court St, (250) 847-5072.
Ⓦ www.town.smithers.bc.ca

THE PICTURESQUE town of Smithers, located in the center of the fertile Bulkley Valley, is surrounded by the panoramic scenery of local mountain ranges over which the snow-crested 8,599-ft (2,621-m) Hudson Bay Mountain presides. Smithers is a year-round outdoor center

where Babine Lake is recommended for its plentiful rainbow trout and char, and rafters on the challenging Bulkley River twist past pine-lined shores through a beautiful canyon. A bicycle ride or hike along the forested 6-mile (9.5-km) Perimeter Trail may offer sightings of moose, deer, and grouse, while grizzly and black bears, mountain goats, and caribou live higher on the slopes. In winter, downhill, cross-country, and telemark skiing are predominant. Ski Smithers (tel. 250/847-2058) downhill resort features 18 runs and 1,750 ft (533 m) of vertical thrills. Snowmobiling and dog sledding are also popular.

Smithers' main street has an alpine theme, evident in the brick sidewalks, alpine-style storefronts, and *Alpenhorn Man*, a 7-ft (2-m) wooden statue of a man playing an alpenhorn. Nine colorful murals decorate the street, enhancing its shops and boutiques.

Prince Rupert ㉘

Road map 2 A3. 🏙 16,000. ❓ 100-215 Cow Bay Rd, (250) 624-5637.
Ⓦ www.tourismprincerupert.com

PRINCE RUPERT is the second largest urban center on BC's coast. Located on Kaien Island, at the mouth of the Skeena River, the city is encircled by forests and mountains, and overlooks the fjord-studded coastline. The harbor, busy with cruise ships, ferries, and fishing boats, is the main access point for the rugged Queen Charlotte Islands and Alaska.

A gift shop and gallery in Cow Bay, Prince Rupert

Like many of BC's major towns, Prince Rupert's development is linked to the growth of the railroad. Housed in the 1914 Grand Trunk Railroad Station, the **Kwinitsa Railway Museum** tells the story of businessman Charles Hay's big plans for the town, which were largely unfulfilled: he went down with the *Titanic* in 1912.

Tsimshian First Nations people were the area's first occupants; as recently as 150 years ago, the harbor was lined with their cedar houses and totems. The excellent **Museum of Northern British Columbia** focuses on Tsimshian history: museum tours showcase the culture over the past 10,000 years. In summer, a First Nations–led walking tour of nearby Laxspa'aws (Pike Island) provides information on five significant archeological and village sites 1,800 years old.

🏛 **Museum of Northern British Columbia**
100 1st Ave W. ☎ (250) 624-3207. ⏱ Jun–Aug: 9am–8pm Mon–Sat, 9am–5pm Sun; Sep–May: 9am–5pm Mon–Sat. ● Dec 25 & 26. 🈂 ♿ 🎫 🚻
Ⓦ www.museumofnorthernbc.com

One of the many renovated buildings by Prince Rupert's harbor

Haida Gwaii (Queen Charlotte Islands) 🄯

Balance Rock, Graham Island

HAIDA GWAII, also known as the Queen Charlotte Islands, is an archipelago of about 150 islands, many with unique ecosystems. For thousands of years they have been home to the Haida Nation, a people renowned for their carvings and sculptures made of silver, gold, cedar, and argillite (a black, slate-like stone found only on these islands). The remote Gwaii Haanas National Park Reserve and Haida Heritage Site protects ancient Haida villages nestled amid lush cedar and hemlock rainforest, home to distinctive species such as dusky shrews and short-tailed weasels. Bald eagles nest along the coast, and in spring, hundreds of migrating gray whales can be seen. Haida Gwaii offers some of the West Coast's finest fishing, kayaking, hiking, scuba diving, and whale-watching.

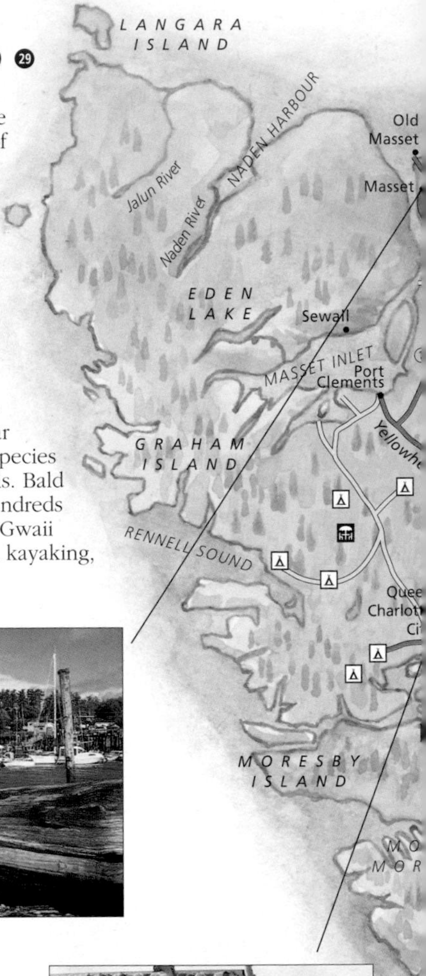

Masset
The oldest fishing community in Haida Gwaii, Masset is popular with both anglers and tourists. Its Delkatla Wildlife Sanctuary, an intertidal wetland and birdwatcher's paradise, is refuge to more than 140 recorded species, including large flocks of migrating shorebirds. In the nearby Haida village of Old Masset, traditional jewelers, carvers, and weavers work in home studios.

Queen Charlotte City
This quaint fishing village, also known simply as Charlotte, is a good base from which to explore the islands and take an ecotour or a paddling trip in a Haida canoe. Its tiny downtown offers cafés, hotels, and shops.

STAR SIGHTS

★ **Haida Gwaii Museum at Skidegate**

★ **Naikoon Provincial Park**

★ **Ninstints**

Tow Hill

HECATE STRAIT

Naikoon
National
Park

Tlell

PRINCE RUPERT

Skidegate

Sandspit

★ Naikoon Provincial Park
*Naikoon Provincial Park has breathtaking
views of Hecate Strait and Dixon Entrance,
and on clear days, Alaska is visible from here.
Remnants of shipwrecks dot the park's 60 miles
(100 km) of broad sandy beach. Tow Hill, at
the park's north end, is an ancient volcano
with a massive basalt cliff.*

Skidegate Inlet comprises the three communities of Skidegate,
Queen Charlotte City,
and Sandspit, and is one
of the prime fishing
locations on the
islands. In the spring,
gray whales can be seen
resting and feeding here.

LOUISE
ISLAND

K'uuna
(Skedans)

TANU
ISLAND

Hlk'yah Gaawga
(Windy Bay)

LYELL
ISLAND

Gwaii Haanas National Park
Reserve and Haida Heritage Site

BURNABY
ISLAND

KUNGHIT
ISLAND

SGAANG
GWAII

0 kilometers   20

0 miles   10

VISITORS' CHECKLIST

🚢 BC Ferries from Prince Rupert,
(250) 381-5453.
ℹ️ Gwaii Haanas National Park
Reserve & Haida Heritage Site,
(250) 559-8818.

KEY

━ Paved road

═ Dirt or four-wheel-drive road

╍ Hiking trail

🅰 Camping

🅿 Picnic area

✈ Airport

⛴ Ferry

╌ Ferry route

🔆 Viewpoint

ℹ Information

★ Haida Gwaii Museum at Skidegate
*The Haida Gwaii Museum celebrates
Haida culture, past and present.
Highlights here include argillite and
wood carvings, totems dating to 1878,
and Loos Taas, a 49-ft- (150-m-) long
dugout carved by Haida artist Bill Reid.*

★ Ninstints
*A UNESCO World Heritage Site since
1981, this Haida village on SGaang
Gwaii has more totems standing on
their original sites than does any other
Haida village.*

Cruise to Alaska ㉚

Continuing a tradition that began in 1880, cruise ships ply the Inside Passage, a protected waterway that runs along the BC coast to the inlets of Alaska. The waters are calmer than those of the open Pacific Ocean, so that whales and porpoises are often sighted. The popular cruises, many of which are combined with shore excursions, attract over one million passengers a year.

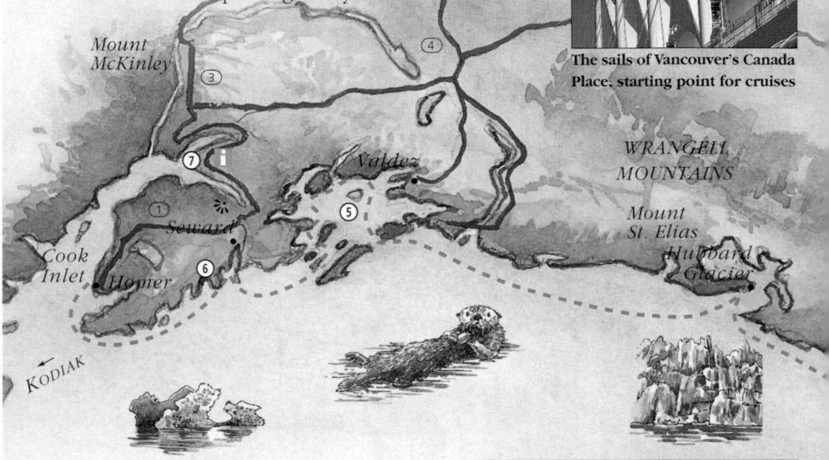
Mount McKinley
Valdez
WRANGELL MOUNTAINS
Mount St. Elias
Hubbard Glacier
Seward
Cook Inlet
Homer
KODIAK

The sails of Vancouver's Canada Place, starting point for cruises

Kenai Fjords National Park ⑥
In the Seward region, the glacier-carved fjords of Kenai are home to whales, sea lions, and tufted puffins.

Prince William Sound ⑤
More than 20 active tidewater glaciers are to be found at the sound, with its 3,000 miles (4,830 km) of coastline. A horned puffin colony lives here year-round and up to 5,000 bald eagles summer here.

Anchorage ⑦
Fabulous views of the Chugach Mountains can be enjoyed from Anchorage, situated on a broad peninsula in Cook Inlet. The Alaska Native Heritage Center here displays historic tableaux illustrating the daily lives of the region's First Nations tribes.

0 kilometers 200

0 miles 150

Key

- - Cruise route
▬ Major road
ℹ Information
✱ Viewpoint

Skagway ④

The boardwalk and false-fronted buildings of Skagway evoke the 19th century. The historic Klondike train, which steams through the cliff-hugging White Pass, starts here.

CRUISE TIPS

Starting point*: Canada Place and Ballantyne Pier cruise ship terminals, Vancouver.*
Cruise length*: to Sitka, 736 miles (1,184 km); to Skagway, 956 miles (1,538 km); to Seward, 1,443 miles (2,322 km).*
Highlights*: views of glaciers, mountains, and wildlife, as well as historic and scenic ports of call.*

Whitehorse
Alaska Highway

③

④

Atlin
Lake

③

Juneau ③

Alaska's capital is also its most beautiful city. Juneau is the gateway to the impressive 12-mile- (19-km-) long Mendenhall Glacier, which flows from the Juneau Icefield.

②

i
①

Prince Rupert

QUEEN CHARLOTTE
ISLANDS
(Haida Gwaii)

Gulf
of
Alaska

Sitka ②

Czarist icons and Russian dancers remind visitors of Sitka's Russian heritage.

Bella Bella

Ketchikan ①

Colorful 19th-century buildings and boardwalks, Tlingit clan houses, a prized totem collection, and an eagle population make this town unforgettable.

VANCOUVER
ISLAND

Vancouver

TRAVELERS' NEEDS

WHERE TO STAY 278-295

WHERE TO EAT 296-313

SHOPPING 314-315

OUTDOOR ACTIVITIES 316-321

WHERE TO STAY

WHETHER YOU are looking for a relaxing oceanside inn, a small and welcoming bed-and-breakfast, a low-key hostel, a convenient motel, or a perfectly appointed hotel room in the heart of the city, the Pacific Northwest offers accommodation to suit every taste and budget. In addition to this wide range of options, rustic lodges and guest ranches, usually located outside towns and cities and near

Hotel sign in Bavarian-themed Leavenworth, Washington

scenic areas, provide lodgings and unforgettable outdoor experiences. For those who love to camp, the numerous state, provincial, and national parks throughout the region offer a choice of campsites including smaller sites for rough camping. In order to help you select a place to stay, the listings in *Choosing a Hotel,* on pages 282–95, recommend more than 140 places, in all price ranges, each representing the best of its kind.

FINDING ACCOMMODATION

FOR ACCOMMODATION in Oregon, the **Oregon Tourism Commission** offers a handy online reservation service as well as a free publication called *Where to Stay in Oregon.* **Washington State Tourism** provides lodging and campground listings in its free booklet *Experience Washington,* which can be ordered by phone or downloaded from the Internet. **Tourism BC**'s *British Columbia Approved Accommodation* guide, available at no charge at tourist information centers, rates 700 BC government–inspected accommodations and campgrounds. Local bed-and-breakfast and inn agencies offer accommodation listings; check with the local visitors' center for details.

HOTELS

HOTELS IN THE Pacific Northwest's major destinations are counted among the world's best. Luxury chains, such as the Four Seasons, Radisson, and Westin, as well as numerous independents, are generally located downtown. They usually offer stylish decor, an upscale restaurant, a spa, and valet parking. Reservations are recommended, especially if you plan to visit during a holiday or a popular festival or event *(see pp30–33).*

If you are looking for personalized guest services and luxurious amenities, you may wish to investigate boutique

hotels – small, exclusive, independently owned hotels, usually situated in city centers and resort destinations.

All the major mid-range hotel chains, including Best Western, Holiday Inn, and Marriott, can be found in the larger cities of the Pacific Northwest and often in smaller towns near popular destinations. These chains provide rooms that are not only affordable but also standardized: no matter where the hotel is located, they offer clean, reliable accommodations as well as facilities that typically include a hotel restaurant, a swimming pool, and a fitness center.

MOTELS

MOTELS OFFER MUCH to travelers who are looking for simplicity and cleanliness. Most are located near busy highways and are a comfortable and inexpensive option as long as transportation into

the city is not an issue. Motels generally offer fewer amenities than hotels, although cable TV, private bathrooms, air conditioning, and ice and soda machines are standard. Reservations are usually not necessary.

BED-AND-BREAKFASTS AND INNS

THE PACIFIC Northwest prides itself on its many welcoming and charming bed-and-breakfasts. Guestrooms are typically located in a large house in which the host also resides. Accommodations range from rooms in historic Victorian homes with beautiful gardens, situated in residential city neighborhoods, to rooms in rustic log homes near the mountains, and everything in between.

As the name suggests, guests are served breakfast, often buffet-style. When reserving a room, inquire about other meals as well; some bed-and-

The Blue Gull Inn, a bed-and-breakfast in Port Townsend, Washington

◁ **Recreational vehicles in Washington's Mount Rainier National Park**

breakfasts also serve lunch and dinner. Most bed-and-breakfasts prohibit smoking, and some have restrictions on children and pets.

The **Oregon** and the **Washington Bed and Breakfast Guilds** provide extensive listings and information on bed-and-breakfasts in these two states. For visitors to British Columbia, the **Western Canada Bed and Breakfast Innkeepers Association** publishes a guide to accommodations that are approved by the agency. Like bed-and-breakfasts, inns come in all shapes and sizes, from small and rustic to large and luxurious.

Visitors to British Columbia may choose to stay at one of the province's numerous guest ranches, which include working cattle ranches. These properties offer a variety of activities, such as horseback riding and fishing, in a country setting, as well as the opportunity to participate in real ranch work. Visitors can choose from basic cabins, ski lodges, and luxury ranches featuring fireplaces, room service, air conditioning, hot tubs, and spa facilities. Contact the **BC Guest Ranchers' Association** for information.

HOSTELS

Hostels can be ideal for travelers on a budget. **Hostelling International** (HI) operates locations throughout the Pacific Northwest. HI memberships are available at a nominal fee (free for youths 18 years and younger) and entitle members to discounts on rooms, restaurant meals, car rentals, bus travel, airport shuttles, and more. Ask about other benefits at HI's regional offices.

A variety of accommodations are available: some hostels have kitchens, usually communal; many are dormitory-style and have shared bathrooms. Calling ahead to reserve a space is advisable.

A variety of hostels are centrally located within the metropolitan Seattle and Portland areas. There are also hostels, both HI and those

The heritage Gatsby Mansion in Victoria, BC, now a bed-and-breakfast

unaffiliated to HI, throughout Oregon and Washington.

In British Columbia, hostels are to be found in Vancouver, Whistler, Vancouver Island, and at major destinations in the BC Interior. Hostel-style accommodation is also available at the YMCA and YWCA in Vancouver and, in summer, at several universities and colleges, including the University of British Columbia.

For an online directory of hostels worldwide, visit **Hostels.com**.

CAMPGROUNDS

Throughout the Pacific Northwest, park facilities are basic – running water, flush or pit toilets, and a tenting area – although some sites have showers and running water. Privately owned tent, trailer, and recreational vehicle (RV) parks offer both simple sites with outhouses and full-service campgrounds with flush toilets, showers, electricity, and even playgrounds and games rooms.

In Oregon and Washington, some campgrounds accept reservations, whereas others are first come, first served. Campsites may be reserved up to a year in advance for certain weekends and holidays, such as July 4. Reservations for Oregon and Washington campsites can be made by contacting **Oregon State Parks** or **Washington State Parks**, or online at www.reserveamerica.com. Campgrounds at British Columbia's provincial and national parks fill up

quickly. Check the **BC Parks** website to determine which parks take reservations, and reserve with **Discover Camping** by phone or online.

PRICES

With so many accommodation options, prices vary tremendously and depend on the season and availability. During peak tourist months, May to September, and public holidays, prices are higher in the city and at seaside or lakeside accommodations. The best deals at these locations are to be found in the off-season, October to April. Ski resorts are on an opposite schedule, which means that mountain accommodations in mid-summer are readily available and prices quite affordable.

It is best to stay in cities on weekends, when hotels have almost no business clientele, and to stay at bed-and-breakfasts outside cities or popular weekend destinations during the week, when prices often drop considerably. Be sure to inquire about package deals – many hotels offer discounts on tours and entrance to attractions, restaurant and store coupons, as well as free airport and city shuttle service.

Increasingly, hotels offer discounts on room rates when bookings are made over the Internet. Reserving a room with an Internet booking agency *(see p280)* can also result in savings, especially on last-minute deals. As well, many hotels offer discounts to members of auto clubs, and to students, and seniors, so it is always a good idea to inquire about these discounts when calling to reserve a room. Watch for hidden costs such as parking fees and single-occupancy surcharges.

Oregon's hotel tax is 11.5 percent. Hotel tax in Seattle is 15.6 percent but varies throughout the rest of Washington. In British Columbia, prices are subject to a 7 percent federal Goods and Services Tax (GST); an 8 percent provincial hotel tax on rooms in properties with four or more units; and in certain municipalities, an additional tax of up to 2 percent. The GST is refundable to visitors who are not residents of Canada *(see p326)*.

How to Book

RESERVATIONS ARE recommended whatever the season, as festivals, conferences, and other events *(see pp30–33)* are held year-round throughout the Pacific Northwest. Campgrounds are especially popular during the summer, as are ski resorts in the winter. Most major hotels have toll-free reservation numbers and accept bookings by fax or Internet. Rooms can also be booked through Internet booking agencies, such as **Priceline.com** and **Expedia.com**.

If you have special requirements, such as a quiet room away from ice machines and elevators, make them known when you book your room. Reservations usually require a credit card number or a deposit the equivalent of one night's stay. Generally, refunds are made for cancellations if enough notice has been given; however, administration charges may apply. Notify the hotel if you expect to arrive later than 5pm or you may lose your reservations.

Travelers with Disabilities

HOTELS AND MOTELS in both the US and Canada are required by law to be wheelchair accessible, with

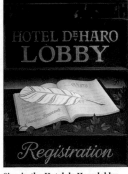

Sign in the Hotel de Haro lobby, Roche Harbor, San Juan Island

the exception of some in older buildings. The reality, however, is that this is not always the case. The vast majority of large private and chain hotels are equipped with the necessary facilities, including visual notification of the fire alarm and of incoming phone calls. Many also have suites designated specifically for people with disabilities. However, many of the older buildings and bed-and-breakfasts in the Pacific Northwest have narrow hallways that can obstruct wheelchairs and that are without ramps. As always, it is best to check in advance. In the US, the Society for Accessible Travel and Hospitality *(see p327)* provides travel tips and information about wheelchair access.

Many BC properties participate in the Access Canada program, which seeks to make traveling easier for seniors and people with

disabilities. Look for the Access Canada logo, which uses a numbered system from 1 to 4: 1 indicates accommodation suitable for active seniors and people with minor disabilities; 2, for seniors and people with moderate disabilities; 3, for people with advanced agility, hearing, mobility, and vision disabilities and independent wheelchair users; and 4, for those with severe disabilities.

Traveling with Children

CHILDREN ARE WELCOME in most hotels in the Pacific Northwest. Many hotels and motels offer family packages, services such as babysitting, and family games rooms. Call ahead to inquire about special rates and services for families and special accommodations for young children, such as cots, for which there is often a nominal fee of $10 to $15. It is advisable to inquire about a bed-and-breakfast's policy on accommodating children before booking a room.

Business Travelers

MANY HOTELS NOW provide travelers with access to fax machines and modems, and offer dual-line, direct-dial phone with voice mail, as well as fax and copier services. Larger hotels often maintain full-service business centers, which provide secretarial and courier services as well as Internet facilities.

The luxurious Fairmont Chateau Whistler, British Columbia

The Alaska Hotel in Dawson Creek, British Columbia, dating back to 1930

They may also have conference rooms that can be reserved in advance. If you plan to stay at an older property and wish to do business from there, make sure it has the facilities you require.

WHERE TO STAY IN PORTLAND

M OST OF THE MAJOR hotel chains are represented in downtown Portland. They provide good bases for visitors who want to feel the pulse of the city and visit its museums and cultural attractions. Downtown hotels are also in close proximity to

some of Portland's up-and-coming neighborhoods, such as the Pearl District. Most of the city's bed-and-breakfasts are located a bit farther afield.

WHERE TO STAY IN SEATTLE

S INCE SEATTLE'S DOWNTOWN is relatively small and many sights can be easily reached on foot, staying downtown is ideal for travelers. Accommodations in or near Pike Place Market are convenient for all the major shops and many rooms have stunning views of Elliott Bay and Puget Sound. Most of the major hotels are

clustered together and are within walking distance of many of the city's best bars and restaurants. Pioneer Square and Belltown, two neighborhoods flanking downtown, on the south and north respectively, offer more affordable accommodations. Still central though just outside the downtown area, Capitol Hill and Queen Anne Hill offer comfortable accommodations in neighborhood surroundings.

WHERE TO STAY IN VANCOUVER

M OST OF Vancouver's hotels are clustered in the downtown shopping and business districts, although there are also several near the airport. Bed-and-breakfasts are located downtown as well as in residential neighborhoods such as Kitsilano or Shaughnessy. As in most major cities, prices are generally highest downtown.

One of several resort hotels in popular Lake Chelan, Washington

---

DIRECTORY

TOURIST OFFICES

Oregon Tourism Commission
℡ (800) 547-7842.
ⓦ www.traveloregon.com

Tourism BC
℡ (800) 435-5622.
ⓦ www.hellobc.com

Washington State Tourism
℡ (360) 725-5052.
ⓦ www.tourism.wa.gov

BED-AND-BREAKFAST AND INN AGENCIES

BC Guest Ranchers' Association
℡ (250) 374-6836.

Oregon Bed and Breakfast Guild
℡ (800) 944-6196.
ⓦ www.OBBG.org

Washington Bed and Breakfast Guild
℡ (800) 647-2918.
ⓦ www.wbbg.com

Western Canada Bed and Breakfast Innkeepers Association
℡ (604) 255-9199.
ⓦ www.wcbbia.com

HOSTELS

Hostelling International Canada
℡ (604) 684-7101 or (800) 661-0020.
ⓦ www.hihostels.ca/ hostels/BC

Hostelling International Oregon Council
℡ (503) 239-0030.
ⓦ www.hiayh.org

Hostelling International Washington Council
℡ (206) 381-9926.
ⓦ www.hiayh.org

Hostels.com
ⓦ www.hostels.com

CAMPGROUND RESERVATIONS

BC Parks
ⓦ wlapwww.gov. bc. ca/bcparks

Discover Camping
℡ (604) 689-9025 or (800) 689-9025.
ⓦ www. discovercamping.ca

Oregon State Parks
℡ (800) 452-5687.
ⓦ www.prd.state.or.us

Washington State Parks
℡ (888) 226-7688.
ⓦ www.parks.wa.gov

RESERVATION AGENCIES

Expedia.com
ⓦ www.expedia.com

Priceline.com
ⓦ www.priceline.com

Choosing a Hotel

THESE HOTELS HAVE BEEN SELECTED ACROSS a wide price range for their good value, facilities, and location. They are listed by area and then by price category, with symbols denoting some of the amenities that may influence your choice. Map references for central Portland, Seattle, and Vancouver hotels have been added to help you locate these properties (see pp82–5, 166-9, 238-41).

	CREDIT CARDS	NUMBER OF ROOMS	RESTAURANT	CHILDREN WELCOME	GARDEN OR TERRACE

PORTLAND

OLD TOWN AND THE PEARL DISTRICT

EMBASSY SUITES $$$ 319 SW Pine St. **Map** 2 D4. ((503) 279-9000 or (800) 362-2779. **FAX** (503) 497-9051. w www.embassysuites.citysearch.com Centrally located, this family- and business-friendly hotel provides spacious suites and the convenience of many on-site amenities, including a day spa. 🛏 📺 🗏 🍸 🕯 🏊 🍴 ✆	AE DC MC V	276	■	●	

DOWNTOWN

HEATHMAN HOTEL $$$ 1001 SW Broadway. **Map** 1 C5. ((503) 241-4100 or (800) 551-0011. **FAX** (503) 790-7110. w www.heathmanhotel.com The award-winning Heathman Restaurant is a major draw, but guests also appreciate the comforts offered by this stylish hotel with a distinct European flavor. On display are city views and works by local artisans in each well-appointed room. 🛏 📺 🗏 🍸 🍴 ✆	AE DC MC V	150	■	●	
HILTON PORTLAND AND EXECUTIVE TOWER $$$ 921 SW 6th Ave. **Map** 1 C5. ((503) 226-1611 or (800) 445-8667. **FAX** (503) 220-2565. w www.portland.hilton.com In an ideal downtown location, this full-service hotel, popular with conventioneers, features a magnificent glass-ceilinged pool area and comfortable rooms with modern amenities. 🛏 📺 🗏 🍸 🕯 🏊 🍴 ✆	AE DC MC V	782	■	●	
WESTIN PORTLAND $$$ 750 SW Alder St. **Map** 1 C5. ((503) 294-9000 or (888) 627-8401. **FAX** (503) 241-9565. w www.westin.com/portland Superb service is the trademark of this recently built hotel. Plush guestrooms abound with all the amenities of equal appeal to business or vacation travelers. 🛏 📺 🗏 🍸 🕯 🍴 ✆	AE DC MC V	205	■	●	
GOVERNOR HOTEL $$$$ 611 SW 10th Ave. **Map** 1 B5. ((503) 224-3400 or (800) 554-3456. **FAX** (503) 241-2122. w www.govhotel.com This stately hotel is adorned with local Native art and murals depicting the Lewis and Clark expedition era. Some of its elegantly furnished rooms feature fireplaces and balconies. Complimentary wine receptions Monday to Thurday evenings. 🛏 📺 🗏 🍸 🕯 🍴 ✆	AE DC MC V	100	■		
PARAMOUNT HOTEL $$$$ 808 SW Taylor St. **Map** 1 B5. ((503) 223-9900 or (800) 663-1144. **FAX** (503) 223-7900. w www.paramounthotel.net The impressive lobby of this boutique hotel, featuring Italian marble countertops and bronze and glass artwork, conveys a feeling of opulence. This is continued in the guestrooms, where Biedermeier furnishings and panoramic views await. 🛏 📺 🗏 🍸 🕯 🍴 ✆	AE DC MC V	154	■		

FARTHER AFIELD

CLYDE HOTEL $ 1022 SW Stark St, Portland. ((503) 224-8000. **FAX** (503) 224-9999. w www.clydehotel.com The recent renovation of this 1912 hotel has retained the charm of its original features: mahogany panels and inlaid tiling, original doors in the rooms, and claw-foot bathtubs. Continental breakfast included. 📺 🗏	AE DC MC V	50		●	
MARK SPENCER HOTEL $ 409 SW 11th Ave, Portland. ((503) 224-3293 or (800) 548-3934. **FAX** (503) 223-7848. w www.markspencer.com Portland's arts community has a long-standing affinity with this charming hotel, which hosts performers and artists. Rooms come with fully equipped kitchens, popular with longer-stay guests. 🛏 📺 🗏	AE DC MC V	102		●	■
MACMASTER HOUSE BED AND BREAKFAST INN $$ 1041 SW Vista Ave, Portland. ((503) 223-7362 or (800) 774-9523. **FAX** (503) 224-8808. w www.macmaster.com This unique King's Hill B & B features an eclectic collection of furnishings – think sleigh- and four-poster beds, and claw-foot soaking tubs – and a great location adjacent to Washington Park.	AE MC V	6			■

Price categories, in US dollars, for a standard double room per night, including tax and service charges. (Prices may fluctuate depending on arrival date and availability; US$1 = CAN$1.50)
[$] under $100
[$][$] $100–$150
[$][$][$] $150–$200
[$][$][$][$] over $200

CREDIT CARDS
Indicates which credit cards are accepted: *AE* American Express; *DC* Diners Club; *MC* MasterCard/Access; *V* Visa.

RESTAURANT
Hotel restaurant or dining room also open to non-residents.

CHILDREN WELCOME
Child cots and a baby-sitting service available. Some hotel restaurants have children's portions and highchairs.

GARDEN OR TERRACE
Hotels with a garden, courtyard, or terrace.

Hotel	Credit Cards	Number of Rooms	Restaurant	Children Welcome	Garden or Terrace
MALLORY HOTEL [$][$] 729 SW 15th Ave, Portland. ☎ *(800) 228-8657.* [FAX] *(503) 223-0522.* [W] www.malloryhotel.com This 1920s-era, classic downtown property features crystal chandeliers and Old World charm. Rooms are bright and spotless, and pets are not only welcomed but registered, photographed, and entered in the Pet Pictoral Album. Continental breakfast included. 🅿 [TV] ☰ 🍸 🐕 ♿	AE DC MC V	136	■	●	
PORTLAND'S WHITE HOUSE BED AND BREAKFAST [$][$] 1914 NE 22nd Ave, Portland. ☎ *(503) 287-7131 or (800) 272-7131.* [FAX] *(503) 249-1641.* [W] www.portlandswhitehouse.com Looking remarkably similar to its famous East Coast namesake, this Greek Revival–style mansion offers elegant B & B amenities and a gourmet breakfast best enjoyed on the garden patio. 🅿 ☰	AE MC V	9		●	■
RAMADA INN ROSE QUARTER [$][$] 10 N Weidler St, Portland. ☎ *(503) 287-9900 or (800) 272-6232.* [FAX] *(503) 287-3500.* [W] www.the.ramada.com/portland13442 The usual reliable comfort and service of the well-known chain are offered at this inn, situated minutes from the Rose Garden Arena and the Coliseum. 🅿 [TV] ☰ 🍸 🛎 🏊 🏋 ♿	AE DC MC V	178	■	●	
BENSON HOTEL [$][$][$] 309 SW Broadway, Portland. ☎ *(503) 228-2000 or (888) 523-6766.* [FAX] *(503) 471-3920.* [W] www.bensonhotel.com This stately 1912 hotel, built by Portland lumber baron and philanthropist Simon Benson, is filled with marble and polished Russian walnut details, and its lobby boasts a lovely, ornate ceiling. Cozy robes are found in each classically furnished room. 🅿 [TV] ☰ 🍸 🛎 🏋 ♿	AE DC MC V	287	■	●	
FIFTH AVENUE SUITES HOTEL [$][$][$] 506 SW Washington St, Portland. ☎ *(503) 222-0001 or (866) 861-9514.* [FAX] *(503) 222-0004.* [W] www.5thavenuesuites.com Once the Lipman Wolfe Department Store, this historic boutique hotel was remodeled and re-opened in 1997. Now, its graceful interior in warm cream, yellow, and gold tones welcomes guests. A member of the Kimpton boutique hotels group. 🅿 [TV] ☰ 🍸 🛎 🏋 🐕 ♿	AE DC MC V	221	■	●	
FOUR POINTS SHERATON [$][$][$] 50 SW Morrison St, Portland. ☎ *(503) 221-0711 or (888) 627-8263.* [FAX] *(503) 484-1414.* [W] www.fourpointsportland.com Set on the Willamette River waterfront and handy for the Oregon Convention and World Trade Centers, this smart hotel offers well-appointed rooms, most with city views. 🅿 [TV] ☰ 🍸 🏋 ♿	AE DC MC V	140	■	●	
HOTEL LUCIA [$][$][$] 400 SW Broadway, Portland. ☎ *(503) 225-1717 or (877) 225-1717.* [FAX] *(503) 225-1919.* [W] www.hotellucia.com This hip hotel with sleek, stylish decor has recently opened, offering all the modern touches in its rooms: wireless Internet access, Aveda bath products, and top-notch mattresses. 🅿 [TV] ☰ 🛎 🏋 🐕 ♿	AE DC MC V	128	■	●	
HOTEL VINTAGE PLAZA [$][$][$] 422 SW Broadway, Portland. ☎ *(503) 228-1212 or (800) 263-2305.* [FAX] *(503) 228-3598.* [W] www.vintageplaza.com With rooms named for Oregon's many vineyards, this lovely hotel offers complimentary wine every evening. Reserve a top-floor suite and sleep under the stars in a room with wall-to-wall conservatory windows. A Kimpton boutique hotel. 🅿 [TV] ☰ 🍸 🛎 🏋 ♿	AE DC MC V	107	■	●	
PORTLAND MARRIOTT DOWNTOWN [$][$][$] 1401 SW Naito Pkwy, Portland. ☎ *(503) 226-7600 or (800) 228-9290.* [FAX] *(503) 221-1789.* [W] www.marriott.com This luxurious high-rise hotel, set riverside, features modern amenities in each room and soothing white-on-white decor. Rooms facing east have breathtaking views. 🅿 [TV] ☰ 🍸 🛎 🏊 🏋 ♿	AE DC MC V	503	■	●	
RIVERPLACE HOTEL [$][$][$][$] 1510 SW Harbor Way, Portland. ☎ *(503) 228-3233 or (800) 227-1333.* [FAX] *(503) 295-6190.* [W] www.riverplacehotel.com This lovely European-style hotel has light wood furnishings inside, a beautifully manicured garden outside. Room decor is soft and intimate. Complimentary on-site spa services. 🅿 [TV] ☰ 🍸 🛎 🏋 ♿	AE DC MC V	84	■	●	■

For key to symbols see back flap

Price categories, in US dollars, for a standard double room per night, including tax and service charges. (Prices may fluctuate depending on arrival date and availability; US$1 = CAN$1.50)
[$] under $100
[$][$] $100–$150
[$][$][$] $150–$200
[$][$][$][$] over $200

CREDIT CARDS
Indicates which credit cards are accepted: *AE* American Express; *DC* Diners Club; *MC* MasterCard/Access; *V* Visa.

RESTAURANT
Hotel restaurant or dining room also open to non-residents.

CHILDREN WELCOME
Child cots and a baby-sitting service available. Some hotel restaurants have children's portions and highchairs.

GARDEN OR TERRACE
Hotels with a garden, courtyard, or terrace.

OREGON

	Credit Cards	Number of Rooms	Restaurant	Children Welcome	Garden or Terrace
ASHLAND: *Ashland Springs Hotel* [$][$] 212 E Main St. ☎ *(541) 488-1700 or (800) 325-4000.* [W] www.ashlandspringshotel.com This beautifully renovated 1925 hotel is an Ashland landmark. Rooms are tastefully appointed with elegant French fabrics. Day spa services available. 🚗 [TV] ≡ 🍸 🛎 🏋 ♿	AE DC MC V	70	■	●	
ASHLAND: *A Midsummer's Dream Bed and Breakfast* [$][$][$] 496 Beach St. ☎ *(541) 552-0605 or (877) 376-8800.* [FAX] *(541) 552-5405.* [W] www.amidsummer.com This 1901 Victorian building now houses a romantic B & B set amid pretty gardens. All of the spacious, Shakespeare-themed rooms in this charming home feature king-size beds and fireplaces. 🚗 ♿	AE MC V	5			■
ASTORIA: *Rose River Inn Bed and Breakfast* [$][$] 1510 Franklin Ave. ☎ *(503) 325-7175 or (888) 876-0028.* [FAX] *(503) 325-7188.* [W] www.roseriverinn.com Simply furnished with European antiques and art, this lovely B & B is run by a hospitable Finn, Kati, who also offers massage treatments. Enjoy Finnish goodies with your morning coffee. 🚗 🐕	MC V	5		●	■
BAKER CITY: *Best Western Sunridge Inn* [$][$] 1 Sunridge Lane. ☎ *(541) 523-6444 or (800) 233-2368.* [FAX] *(541) 523-6446.* [W] www.bestwestern.com Comfort and a downtown location draw visitors to this reliable inn with spacious, spotless rooms. 🚗 [TV] ≡ 🍸 🛎 ≋ 🏋 ♿	AE DC MC V	156	■	●	
BAKER CITY: *Geiser Grand Hotel* [$][$] 1996 Main St. ☎ *(541) 523-1889 or (888) 434-7374.* [FAX] *(541) 523-1800.* [W] www.geisergrand.com This 1889 landmark building impresses upon entrance, with mahogany columns and an enormous stained-glass ceiling. The rooms are filled with oak furnishings and opulent fabrics. 🚗 [TV] ≡ 🍸 ♿	AE MC V	30	■	●	
BEND: *Inn of the Seventh Mountain* [$][$] 18575 SW Century Dr. ☎ *(541) 382-8711 or (800) 452-6810.* [W] www.innofthe7thmountain.com Situated on the banks of the Deschutes River, this resort makes a fine base for pursuing the area's many outdoor recreation offerings. The homey, condo-style accommodation ranges from simple bedroom units to fully equipped suites. 🚗 [TV] ≡ 🍸 🛎 ≋ 🏋 ♿	AE DC MC V	220	■	●	■
BEND: *Mount Bachelor Village Resort* [$][$] 19717 Mt Bachelor Dr. ☎ *(541) 389-5900 or (800) 452-9846.* [FAX] *(541) 388-7401.* [W] www.mtbachelorvillage.com Myriad activities are accessible from this upscale, full-service resort: on-site tennis courts and spa; hiking, running, and biking trails; skiing at Mount Bachelor. Choose from a selection of well-appointed condominiums. 🚗 [TV] ≡ 🍸 🛎 ≋ 🏋	AE DC MC V	130	■	●	
CANNON BEACH: *Webb's Scenic Surf Motel* [$][$] 255 Larch St. ☎ *(503) 436-2706 or (800) 374-9322.* [FAX] *(503) 436-1229.* [W] www.cannonbeach-oregon.com/lodging A family-friendly little property, right on the beach, that is ideal for travelers on a budget. Many of the rooms have kitchenettes and fireplaces. 🚗 [TV]	AE DC MC V	14		●	
CANNON BEACH: *Stephanie Inn* [$][$][$] 2740 S Pacific. ☎ *(503) 436-2221 or (800) 633-3466.* [W] www.stephanie-inn.com This oceanfront inn offers deluxe rooms with fireplaces, Jacuzzis, and stunning views of Haystack Rock. Buffet breakfast, wine, and hors d'oeuvres are all included. 🚗 [TV] ≡ 🍸 🛎 ≋ 🏋 ♿	AE DC MC V	50	■		■
COLUMBIA RIVER GORGE: *Timberline Lodge* [$][$][$] Timberline, Mount Hood. ☎ *(503) 622-7979 or (800) 547-1406.* [FAX] *(503) 622-0710.* [W] www.timberlinelodge.com This celebrated 1930s-era lodge, set midway up Mount Hood, was built using local stone and rough-hewn timber, adding greatly to its rustic ambience. Highlights include the handsome main staircase with animal carvings, and the atrium's huge rock fireplace. 🍸 ≋ ♿	AE DC MC V	70	■	●	■

CRATER LAKE NATIONAL PARK: *Crater Lake Lodge* $$$
565 Rim Village Dr. **(** *(541) 830-8700.* **FAX** *(541) 830-8514.*
W www.craterlakelodges.com This splendid 1915 lodge sits poised to take in spectacular lake views. Its magnificent Great Hall, detailed with Art Deco flourishes, is a reminder of a bygone era. The rooms are fully refurbished, some with claw-foot bathtubs. Closed November to mid-May.
AE DC MC V — 71

EUGENE: *Campbell House, A City Inn* $$
252 Pearl St. **(** *(541) 343-1119 or (800) 264-2519.* **FAX** *(541) 343-2258.*
W www.campbellhouse.com This B & B, in a restored Victorian house, extends gracious hospitality on landscaped grounds. Rooms range from small yet comfortable to spacious and honeymoon-worthy.
AE DC MC V — 18

EUGENE: *Excelsior Inn* $$
754 E 13th Ave. **(** *(541) 342-6963 or (800) 321-6963.* **FAX** *(541) 342-1417.*
W www.excelsiorinn.com This European-style inn, located close to the University of Oregon campus, offers beautifully furnished rooms, each named for a classical composer, with details such as hardwood floors and marble bathtubs. Complimentary full breakfast is included.
AE DC MC V — 14

HOOD RIVER: *Oak Street Hotel* $
610 Oak St. **(** *(541) 386-3845.* **FAX** *(541) 387-8696.* **W** www.gorgerentals.com/oakstreethotel
This quaint house offers homey but nicely appointed accommodation and a central location for exploring this popular windsurfers' hub. Reduced-price lift tickets at Mount Hood Meadows ski area available.
AE DC MC V — 8

HOOD RIVER: *Columbia Gorge Hotel* $$$
4000 Westcliff Dr. **(** *(541) 386-5566 or (800) 345-1921.* **FAX** *(541) 386-9141.*
W www.columbiagorgehotel.com This elegant cliff-top hotel has a well-earned reputation with guests who are romantics at heart. The complimentary five-course breakfast and afternoon champagne-and-caviar social can all be enjoyed overlooking the gorge.
AE DC MC V — 40

IMNAHA: *Imnaha River Inn Bed and Breakfast* $$
73946 Rimrock Rd, Imnaha. **(** *(541) 577-6002 or (866) 601-9214.* **FAX** *(541) 577-3070.*
W www.imnahariverinn.com This log-home B & B nestled in the Imnaha River Canyon is an outdoor-lover's dream, providing easy access to hiking, fishing, and hunting areas. Rooms are basic, some have decks.
— 7

JOSEPH: *Bronze Antler Bed and Breakfast* $$
309 S Main St. **(** *(541) 432-0230 or (866) 520-9769.* **FAX** *(541) 432-6219.*
W www.bronzeantler.com This small B & B charms with warm wood accents, copper-plated hardware, and hand-stenciled wall details. Rooms feature down comforters on the beds, and bidets in the ensuite bathrooms.
AE MC V — 3

LINCOLN CITY: *Ester Lee Motel* $$
3803 SW Hwy 101. **(** *(541) 996-3606 or (888) 996-3606.* **FAX** *(541) 996-6743.*
W www.esterlee.com Wood-burning fireplaces and Pacific Ocean views have earned this roadside motel with cottages a loyal following. Rooms in the older section are larger; most have kitchenettes.
MC V — 53

MCMINNVILLE: *McMenamin's Hotel Oregon* $
310 NE Evans St. **(** *(503) 472-8427 or (888) 472-8247.*
W www.mcmenamins.com Built in 1905, this historic hotel is a popular stop for tourists visiting the Oregon wine country. Rooms are furnished with antique oak pieces; some with shared bathrooms.
AE DC MC V — 42

MCMINNVILLE: *Youngberg Hill Vineyards and Inn* $$$
10660 SW Youngberg Hill Rd. **(** *(503) 472-2727 or (888) 657-8668.* **FAX** *(503) 472-1313.*
W www.youngberghill.com A winery and guesthouse in one, this Craftsman-style inn overlooks picturesque rolling hills covered with pinot noir grape vines. Rooms provide scenic views of Mounts Hood and Jefferson.
AE DC MC V — 7

SALEM: *Creekside Garden Inn* $
333 Wyatt Ct NE. **(** *(503) 391-0837 or (800) 949-0837.* **FAX** *(503) 391-1713.*
W www.marqueehouse.com This Mount Vernon Colonial mansion houses a B & B boasting garden-themed rooms decorated in lively colors. Enjoy the complimentary nightly social hour, when film classics are shown.
DC MC V — 5

SALEM: *Travelodge Salem Capitol Motel* $
1555 State St. **(** *(503) 581-2466 or (800) 578-7878.* **FAX** *(503) 581-2811.*
W www.travelodge.com This comfortable, quiet location is conveniently located for all the capital's major sights. Rooms have all the standard amenities; some include kitchenettes.
AE DC MC V — 42

For key to symbols see back flap

<table>
<tr><td>

Price categories, in US dollars, for a standard double room per night, including tax and service charges. (Prices may fluctuate depending on arrival date and availability; US$1 = CAN$1.50)
$ under $100
$$ $100–$150
$$$ $150–$200
$$$$ over $200

</td><td>

CREDIT CARDS Indicates which credit cards are accepted: *AE* American Express; *DC* Diners Club; *MC* Master Card/Access; *V* Visa.
RESTAURANT Hotel restaurant or dining room also open to non-residents.
CHILDREN WELCOME Child cots and a baby-sitting service available. Some hotel restaurants have children's portions and highchairs.
GARDEN OR TERRACE Hotels with a garden, courtyard, or terrace.

</td></tr>
</table>

		CREDIT CARDS	NUMBER OF ROOMS	RESTAURANT	CHILDREN WELCOME	GARDEN OR TERRACE

SEASIDE: *Shilo Inn Suites Hotel* — $ — AE DC MC V — 113 — ■ ● — —
30 N Prom St. (503) 738-9571 or (800) 222-2244. FAX (503) 738-0674.
www.shiloinns.com Set right on the beach, this hotel's prime location is its main draw. A long-time favorite with regulars, its rooms are cozy and lived in; suites have balconies, kitchens, and fireplaces.

SUNRIVER: *Sunriver Resort* — $$$ — AE DC MC V — 230 — ■ ● ■
1 Center Dr. (541) 593-1000 or (800) 801-8765. FAX (541) 593-5458.
www.sunriver-resort.com This full-service resort provides all the elements of a rejuvenating getaway, with golf, fitness center and spa, and a host of dining venues. Lodge rooms or private condos.

WALLOWA LAKE: *Heidi's Cabins* — $ — AE DC MC V — 8 — ● (Children Welcome)
59989 Mt Howard Lane, Wallowa Lake. (541) 432-0303. FAX (541) 432-0526.
www.heidiscabins.com Each unit in this rustic retreat is unique – some have stone fireplaces, some have sundecks with a lake view – but all are spacious and family friendly. Closed November to April.

WARM SPRINGS: *Kah-Nee-Ta High Desert Resort* — $$$ — AE DC MC V — 139 — ■ ● ■
6823 Hwy 8. (541) 553-1112 or (800) 554-4786. FAX (541) 553-1071.
www.kahneeta.com There's a wealth of things to do at this plush, new resort located on the Confederated Tribes of Warm Springs Reservation: try hiking, horseback riding, golfing, or kayaking. The on-site spa and casino round out the fun.

SEATTLE

PIKE PLACE MARKET AND THE WATERFRONT

PENSIONE NICHOLS — $$ — AE MC V — 12
1923 1st Ave. **Map** 3 C1. (206) 441-7125 or (800) 440-7125. FAX (206) 441-7125.
www.seattle-bed-breakfast.com This unique B & B is located near Pike Place Market. Its two suites offer amenities such as full kitchen, private bathroom, and balcony; the other ten rooms share bathrooms.

INN AT THE MARKET — $$$ — AE DC MC V — 70 — ■ ● ■
86 Pine St. **Map** 3 C1. (206) 443-3600 or (800) 446-4484. FAX (206) 448-0631.
www.innatthemarket.com Located in a landscaped courtyard off Pike Place Market, this lovely inn offers rooms with stunning views of Elliott Bay from floor-to-ceiling bay windows. Furnishings are elegantly simple and comfortable. Massage therapy sessions can be arranged.

SEATTLE CENTER AND BELLTOWN

MARQUEEN HOTEL — $$$ — AE DC MC V — 56 — ● (Children Welcome)
600 Queen Anne Ave N. **Map** 1 B3. (206) 282-7407 or (888) 445-3076. FAX (206) 283-1499
www.marqueen.com This quaint hotel close to the Seattle Center, Opera House, and theater district is small but classic. Each spacious room has a kitchenette and is appointed with hardwood floors, area rugs, and upscale amenities. Complimentary wine and shuttle to downtown

FARTHER AFIELD

ACE HOTEL — $$ — AE DC MC V — 30 — ● (Children Welcome)
2423 1st Ave, Seattle. (206) 448-4721. FAX (206) 374-0745. www.theacehotel.com
Groovy, minimalist decor and friendly service are the hallmarks of this modern hotel in Belltown. The hotel and its Cyclops Bar are popular with visiting musicians and artists. Half the guestrooms share bathrooms.

BEST WESTERN UNIVERSITY TOWER HOTEL — $$ — AE DC MC V — 155 — ■ ●
4507 Brooklyn Ave NE, Seattle. (206) 634-2000 or (800) 899-0251. FAX (206) 545-2103.
www.universitytowerhotel.com Conveniently located for the University of Washington, this recently redecorated, Art Deco–style property offers spotless rooms and complimentary deluxe continental breakfast.

CHAMBERED NAUTILUS BED AND BREAKFAST INN $$
5005 22nd Ave NE, Seattle. ☎ (206) 522-2536 or (800) 545-8459. FAX (206) 528-0898.
W www.chamberednautilus.com This 1915 Georgian Colonial home is set on a hill a short walk from the University of Washington campus. The antique-filled rooms boast cozy robes, fireplaces, and kitchens; many have porches. ⬛
AE MC V — 10

CHELSEA STATION ON THE PARK BED AND BREAKFAST $$
4915 Linden Ave N, Seattle. ☎ (206) 547-6077 or (800) 400-6077. FAX (206) 632-5107.
W www.bandbseattle.com Located just across from the Woodland Park Zoo south of downtown, this B & B has rooms with views of the garden or the Cascade Mountains; suites have ornamental fireplaces.
AE MC V — 9

GASLIGHT INN $$
1727 15th Ave, Seattle. ☎ (206) 325-3654. FAX (206) 328-4803.
W www.gaslight-inn.com On the quieter east side of Capitol Hill, this beautifully restored turn-of-the-19th-century inn has comfortable rooms and ample public space for displaying its stunning collection of Native art.
AE MC V — 16

ROOSEVELT HOTEL $$
1531 7th Ave, Bellevue. ☎ (206) 621-1200 or (800) 426-0670. FAX (206) 233-0335.
W www.westcoasthotels.com This elegantly restored hotel offers a great location for travelers on a budget, with comfy but unassuming rooms. Enjoy jazz piano performed nightly in the lobby.
AE DC MC V — 151

WALL STREET INN $$
2507 1st Ave, Seattle. ☎ (206) 448-0125 or (800) 624-1117. FAX (206) 448-2406.
W www.wallstreetinn.com This small inn offers comfortable Belltown lodging combining the benefits of both B & B and hotel service. Some rooms have views of Elliott Bay; five offer kitchenettes.
AE DC MC V — 20

WESTCOAST BELLEVUE HOTEL $$
625 116th Ave NE, Bellevue. ☎ (425) 455-9444 or (800) 325-4000. FAX (425) 455-2154.
W www.westcoasthotels.com This newly renovated hotel, convenient for local amenities and businesses, offers well-appointed facilities. Multiroom townhouse suites are ideal for groups or families.
AE DC MC V — 176

WESTCOAST VANCE HOTEL $$
620 Stewart St, Seattle. ☎ (206) 441-4200 or (800) 325-4000. FAX (206) 441-8612.
W www.westcoasthotels.com This 1920s-era hotel, with a relaxing, nostalgic ambience, is conveniently situated for all downtown amenities. Rooms are bright and comfortable.
AE DC MC V — 169

MARRIOTT SEA-TAC $$$
3201 S 176th St, Seattle. ☎ (206) 241-2000 or (800) 643-5479. FAX (206) 248-0789.
W www.marriott.com The five-story glass atrium provides drama at this large airport property. The rooms are comfortable and well appointed, with all the usual modern hotel amenities.
AE DC MC V — 459

MAYFLOWER PARK HOTEL $$$
405 Olive Way, Seattle. ☎ (206) 623-8700 or (800) 426-5100. FAX (206) 382-6996
W www.mayflowerpark.com This traditional hotel, situated adjacent to the Westlake Center, is ideally located for shoppers. The elegantly furnished rooms are small but abound in creature comforts.
AE DC MC V — 172

PARAMOUNT HOTEL $$$
724 Pine St, Seattle. ☎ (206) 292-9500 or (800) 325-4000. FAX (206) 292-8610.
W www.westcoasthotels.com/paramount Just steps from the noted Paramount Theatre and close to the best shopping downtown Seattle offers, this chateau-style property features spacious, smartly appointed rooms in pastel tones, fitted with modern furnishings.
AE DC MC V — 148

ALEXIS HOTEL $$$$
1007 1st Ave, Seattle. ☎ (206) 624-4844 or (866) 356-8894. FAX (206) 621-9009.
W www.alexishotel.com This lovely boutique hotel boasts luxurious Pacific Northwest–inspired decor and celebrated service. The hotel's guestrooms and public spaces are showcases for original works by local artisans. There is also an Aveda spa on-site.
AE DC MC V — 109

FOUR SEASONS OLYMPIC HOTEL $$$$
411 University St, Seattle. ☎ (206) 621-1700 or (800) 223-8772. FAX (206) 682-9633.
W www.fourseasons.com/seattle This award-winning hotel is Seattle's grandest property, apparent upon entrance into its elegant lobby, boasting marble countertops and plush rugs. Room decor is understated yet refined; service is top notch.
AE DC MC V — 450

For key to symbols see back flap

Price categories, in US dollars, for a standard double room per night, including tax and service charges. (Prices may fluctuate depending on arrival date and availability; US$1 = CAN$1.50)
$ under $100
$$ $100–$150
$$$ $150–$200
$$$$ over $200

CREDIT CARDS
Indicates which credit cards are accepted: *AE* American Express; *DC* Diners Club; *MC* Master Card/Access; *V* Visa.

RESTAURANT
Hotel restaurant or dining room also open to non-residents.

CHILDREN WELCOME
Child cots and a baby-sitting service available. Some hotel restaurants have children's portions and highchairs.

GARDEN OR TERRACE
Hotels with a garden, courtyard, or terrace.

	CREDIT CARDS	NUMBER OF ROOMS	RESTAURANT	CHILDREN WELCOME	GARDEN OR TERRACE
GRAND HYATT SEATTLE $$$$ 721 Pine St, Seattle. ((206) 774-1234 or (800) 233-1234. FAX (206) 774-6120. W www.grandseattle.hyatt.com Designed to appeal to high-tech professionals, this luxury hotel has state-of-the-art in-room facilities, such as digital concierge and complimentary Internet access, as well as stunning minimalist furnishings in its large, modern rooms.	AE DC MC V	450	■	●	
HOTEL MONACO $$$$ 1101 4th Ave, Seattle. ((206) 621-1770 or (800) 715-6513 . FAX (206) 621-7779. W www.monaco-seattle.com Upbeat furnishings – think bold stripes and modern fabrics – draw visiting artists and business travelers alike to this stylish hotel. Complimentary goldfish are available for company in your room. Enjoy gratis wine service 5–6pm.	AE DC MC V	189	■	●	
HYATT REGENCY BELLEVUE $$$$ 1100 5th Ave, Seattle. ((425) 462-1234. FAX (425) 646-7567. W www.hyatt.com This full-service luxury hotel, convenient to the high-tech corporate corridor, offers rooms decorated in soothing earth tones. Suites have boardroom-size tables and separate meeting rooms.	AE DC MC V	382	■	●	
W SEATTLE HOTEL $$$$ 1112 4th Ave, Seattle. ((206) 264-6000 or (877) 946-8357. FAX (206) 264-6100. W www.starwood.com/whotels This stylish hotel, known for its distinct roof-top steel-and-mesh pyramid, draws celebrities and other fashionable visitors. Rooms are decorated with a minimalist 1940s feel, and include deluxe amenities; some have floor-to-ceiling windows.	AE DC MC V	426	■	●	
WESTIN SEATTLE HOTEL $$$$ 1900 5th Ave, Seattle. ((206) 728-1000 or (888) 627-8513. FAX (206) 728-2259. W www.starwood.com/westin The two cylindrical towers of this hotel are distinct landmarks on the Seattle skyline. Rooms are ample and modern, most with views of Puget Sound or Lake Union.	AE DC MC V	865	■	●	
WASHINGTON					
CHELAN: *Campbell's Resort on Lake Chelan* $$ 104 W Wooden Ave. ((509) 682-2561 or (800) 553-8225. FAX (509) 682-2177. W www.campbellsresort.com Enjoying a prime beachfront location, this long-time local favorite offers a host of on-site facilities including spa and beach bar. Rooms are spacious and unfussy; a few have kitchens.	AE MC V	170	■	●	■
CHELAN: *Darnell's Lake Resort* $$ 901 Spader Bay Rd. ((509) 682-2015 or (800) 967-8149. FAX (509) 682-5872. W www.darnellsresort.com The huge variety of recreational activities offered is what makes this family-friendly resort on Lake Chelan so popular. Some units come with fully equipped kitchens.	MC V	48		●	■
CHELAN: *The Well Made Bed and Breakfast* $$ 324 W Highland Ave. ((509) 682-7278. This small B & B is a cozy alternative to the larger resorts so common in the area. Rooms are comfortable and tastefully decorated.	AE DC MC V	3			■
CRYSTAL MOUNTAIN: *Crystal Mountain Lodging Suites* $$$ 33000 Crystal Mountain Blvd. ((360) 663-2558 or (888) 668-4368. FAX (360) 663-0145. W www.crystalmtlodging-wa.com This year-round mountainside retreat comprises four chalets offering suites in a variety of sizes and styles, all with kitchens. Rates drop in the non-ski season (mid-April to November).	AE DC MC V	100		●	■
EASTSOUND: *Turtleback Farm Inn* $$ 1981 Crow Valley Rd, Orcas Island. ((360) 376-4914 or (800) 376-4914. FAX (360) 376-5329. W www.turtlebackinn.com Set on lush acreage overlooking its own duck pond, this converted farmhouse is a popular retreat. Rooms are decorated with antiques and lovely floral fabrics; many have claw-foot bathtubs.	MC V	11		●	■

EASTSOUND: *Rosario Resort and Spa* $$$
1 Rosario Way, Orcas Island. ☎ *(360) 376-2222 or (800) 562-8820.* [FAX] *(360) 376-2289.* [W] www.rosarioresort.com The former home of a local shipping magnate, this grandly decorated mansion is now an elegant, full-service hotel with rooms ranging from standard to luxurious. 🚗 [TV] ▤ 🍸 🏋 ♨ 🍴 ♿

AE DC MC V	127	■	●	■

FORKS: *Kalaloch Lodge* $$$
157151 Hwy 101. ☎ *(360) 962-2271 or (866) 525-2562.* [FAX] *(360) 962-3391.* [W] www.visitkalaloch.com Perched on a bluff overlooking the Pacific Ocean, this 1935 lodge is a firm Olympic National Park favorite, especially the 44 rustic self-catering cabins, many with Franklin-style wood-burning stoves. 🚗 🐕 ♿

AE MC V	64	■	●	■

FRIDAY HARBOR: *Friday Harbor House* $$$
130 West St, San Juan Island. ☎ *(360) 378-8455.* [FAX] *(360) 378-8453.* [W] www.fridayharborhouse.com This intimate, family-run hotel, situated above Friday Harbor ferry terminal, provides rooms decorated in tranquil earth tones. All offer fireplaces and full or partial views of the harbor. 🚗 [TV] ▤ ♿

AE DC MC V	20	■		

LEAVENWORTH: *Haus Rohrbach Pension* $$
12882 Ranger Rd. ☎ *(509) 548-7024 or (800) 548-4477.* [FAX] *(509) 548-6455.* [W] www.hausrohrbach.com Overlooking the town, this alpine-style B & B's ten whimsically named rooms are homey and offer either mountain or valley views. Enjoy the hearty, full breakfast and on-site spa facilities. 🚗 ♨

AE MC V	10			■

LEAVENWORTH: *Pine River Ranch* $$$
19668 Hwy 207. ☎ *(509) 763-3959 or (800) 669-3877.* [W] www.prranch.com Experience a down-home feel at this all-suites B & B set in the Cascades, where a full breakfast is delivered each morning. Snowshoes and mountain bikes are provided for outdoor enthusiasts. 🚗 [TV]

AE MC V	6			■

LEAVENWORTH: *Run of the River* $$$
9308 E Leavenworth Rd. ☎ *(509) 548-7171 or (800) 288-6491.* [W] www.runoftheriver.com Romance abounds at this atmospheric resort on the banks of the Icicle River. The emphasis is on privacy and intimacy in the cozily decorated rooms, popular with honeymooners. 🚗 [TV] ▤ ♨

AE DC MC V	6			■

LONGMIRE: *National Park Inn* $$
PO Box 108. ☎ *(360) 569-2275.* [FAX] *(360) 569-2770* Unlike the other historic lodge found in Mount Rainier National Park, this small rustic retreat with charming but basic rooms is open year round. Hiking, climbing, and snowshoeing excursions can be arranged. 🚗

AE DC MC V	25	■	●	

LOPEZ VILLAGE: *Edenwild Inn* $$
132 Lopez Rd, Lopez Island. ☎ *(360) 468-3238 or (800) 606-0662.* [W] www.edenwildinn.com Quiet and handy for village and island activities, this quaint inn is ideal for a romantic getaway. All the charmingly decorated rooms have private baths; three have fireplaces. 🚗 ▤ ♿

AE MC V	8			■

OLYMPIA: *West Coast Olympia Hotel* $$
2300 Evergreen Park Dr. ☎ *(360) 943-4000 or (800) 325-4000.* [FAX] *(360) 357-6604.* [W] www.westcoasthotels.com Centrally located and comfortably appointed, this hotel's selection of on-site dining venues plus live jazz performed in the lounge make it a solid choice. 🚗 [TV] ▤ 🍸 🏋 ♨ 🍴 ♿

AE DC MC V	190	■	●	

OLYMPIA: *Lighthouse Bungalow* $$
1215 E Bay Dr. ☎ *(360) 754-0389.* [W] www.lighthousebungalow.com Located on the shores of Puget Sound, this charming bungalow is perfect for families and groups, with two well-stocked units with fully equipped kitchens for self-catering: the upper deck sleeps up to ten guests, the lower sleeps up to three. ▤

AE DC MC V	2		●	■

PORT ANGELES: *Lake Crescent Lodge* $$$
416 Lake Crescent Rd. ☎ *(360) 928-3211.* [W] www.lakecrescentlodge.com Set on the shores of a fjord, this lodge makes a fine base for exploring Olympic National Park's northern areas. It may be worth upgrading to one of the cozy cottages as main lodge rooms can be a bit plain. Closed November to March. 🍸 ♿

AE DC MC V	52	■	●	■

PORT TOWNSEND: *Blue Gull Inn Bed and Breakfast* $$
1310 Clay St. ☎ *(360) 379-3241 or (888) 700-0205.* [FAX] *(360) 379-5498.* [W] www.bluegullinn.com Conveniently located a short walk from the town center, this circa-1868 inn treats its guests to a homey atmosphere, with rooms decorated in a cozy, country style. Afternoon tea and snacks are also included in the rate. 🚗 ▤

AE MC V	6			■

For key to symbols see back flap

Price categories, in US dollars, for a standard double room per night, including tax and service charges. (Prices may fluctuate depending on arrival date and availability; US$1 = CAN$1.50)
$ under $100
$$ $100–$150
$$$ $150–$200
$$$$ over $200

CREDIT CARDS
Indicates which credit cards are accepted: *AE* American Express; *DC* Diners Club; *MC* Master Card/Access; *V* Visa.

RESTAURANT
Hotel restaurant or dining room also open to non-residents.

CHILDREN WELCOME
Child cots and a baby-sitting service available. Some hotel restaurants have children's portions and highchairs.

GARDEN OR TERRACE
Hotels with a garden, courtyard, or terrace.

	CREDIT CARDS	NUMBER OF ROOMS	RESTAURANT	CHILDREN WELCOME	GARDEN OR TERRACE
PORT TOWNSEND: *Manresa Castle Hotel and Inn* $$ 7th & Sheridan St. (360) 385-5750 or (800) 732-1281. FAX (360) 385-5883. www.manresacastle.com Built as a residence for the city's first mayor, the Manresa Castle has been a hotel since the 1960s. The smallish rooms are comfy; the restaurant-lounge has been beautifully restored.	AE DC MC V	40	■	●	■
QUINAULT: *Lake Quinault Lodge* $$$ PO Box 7, Quinault. (360) 288-2900 or (800) 562-6672. FAX (360) 288-2901. www.visitlakequinault.com Styled along the lines of a grand park lodge, this 1926 property offers rooms retaining their original charm, but without intrusive modern amenities; only a few rooms have TVs.	AE MC V	92	■	●	■
ROCHE HARBOR: *Roche Harbor Village* $$$ 248 Reuben Memorial Dr, San Juan Island. (360) 378-2155. FAX (360) 378-6809. www.rocheharbor.com Lodging in this complex consists of the Hotel de Haro, a charming 1886 hotel where former US President Teddy Roosevelt once stayed; the McMillin Suites, offering luxury rooms; and the self-catering condominiums or Company Town cottages, suitable for families.	AE DC MC V	70	■	●	■
STEHEKIN: *North Cascades Stehekin Lodge* $$ 1 Stehekin Landing. (509) 682-4494. FAX (509) 682-8206. www.stehekin.com Hidden in the Cascade Mountains on Lake Chelan, this year-round lodge is accessible by ferry, float plane, or hiking trail only. No phones or TVs and a sole dining spot is the price paid for away-from-it-all tranquility.	AE MC V	28	■	●	■
TACOMA: *Chinaberry Hill Bed and Breakfast* $$ 302 Tacoma Ave N. (253) 272-1282. FAX (253) 272-1335. www.chinaberryhill.com/ruby.html In the heart of the historic Stadium district, this beautifully renovated Victorian mansion's rooms are romantic, spacious, and offer stunning views of Commencement Bay.	AE MC V	5			■
TACOMA: *Silver Cloud Inn* $$ 2317 N Ruston Way. (253) 272-1300 or (866) 820-8448. FAX (253) 274-9176. www.silvercloud.com This new hotel built on a pier amid Tacoma's waterfront bustle provides light-filled and spacious rooms, most with unobstructed water views, some with Jacuzzis.	AE DC MC V	90	■	●	
TACOMA: *Sheraton Tacoma* $$$ 1320 Broadway Plaza. (253) 572-3200 or (800) 325-3535. FAX (253) 591-4105. www.sheratontacoma.com Well situated for exploring the city and the Mount Rainier area, this hotel has tastefully decorated rooms with all the high-end amenities. A Kimpton boutique hotel.	AE DC MC V	319	■	●	
WALLA WALLA: *Best Western Walla Walla Suites Inn* $ 7 E Oak St. (509) 525-4700. FAX (509) 525-2457. www.bestwestern.com This modern, comfortable all-suites inn is handy for nearby wineries and restaurants, with rooms that are well appointed.	AE DC MC V	78		●	
WALLA WALLA: *Wine Country Inn* $$ 915 Alvarado Ter. (509) 386-3592 or (509) 525-1061. www.wallawallawinecountry.net As the name implies, this B & B's focus is on showcasing Washington state's wine bounty, with daily tastings offered. Each charming room occupies a whole floor.	AE MC V	3			■
YAKIMA: *Sun Country Inn* $ 1700 N 1st St. (509) 248-5650 or (800) 559-3675. FAX (509) 457-6486. This modest inn offers amenities such as complimentary breakfast, evening snacks, and on-site sauna and laundry facilities.	AE DC MC V	70		●	
YAKIMA: *A Touch of Europe Bed and Breakfast* $$ 220 N 16th Ave. (509) 454-9775 or (888) 438-7073. FAX (509) 452-1303. This intimate 1889 Victorian mansion is a popular romantic destination, offering three rooms decorated with antiques and rich fabrics.	AE MC V	3			■

YAKIMA: *Birchfield Manor Country Inn* $$$ AE DC MC V | 11 ●▪
2018 Birchfield Rd. ((509) 452-1960 *or* (800) 375-3420. FAX *(509) 452-2334*
www.birchfieldmanor.com This quaint inn offers accommodation in the
original manor house and the guest cottage, in a gracious pastoral setting.
All rooms have private bath; some with Jacuzzis and fireplaces.

VANCOUVER

WATERFRONT, GASTOWN, AND CHINATOWN

JOLLY TAXPAYER BED AND BREAKFAST $ AE MC V | 27 ▪
828 W Hastings St. **Map** 3 A2. ((604) 681-3550. FAX *(604) 681-3515.*
www.3.telus.net/jollytaxpayer This quaint B & B, housed in a restored 1904
heritage building, enjoys a great downtown location. There is also a
traditional British-style pub on-site.

DAYS INN DOWNTOWN $$ AE DC MC V | 85 ▪ ●
921 W Pender St. **Map** 3 A1. ((604) 681-4335 *or* (877) 681-4335. FAX *(604) 681-7808.*
www.daysinnvancouver.com Providing spotless, nicely appointed rooms,
this hotel's central location and handy services, such as complimentary
shuttle to cruise ship terminals, make it a popular choice.

DELTA VANCOUVER SUITES $$ AE DC MC V | 225 ▪ ● ▪
550 W Hastings St. **Map** 3 A2. ((604) 689-8188 *or* (800) 268-1133. FAX *(604) 605-8881.*
www.deltahotels.com This new hotel boasts state-of-the-art amenities in
the spacious rooms, geared mainly to business travelers. Convenient for
downtown trade and convention facilities.

FAIRMONT WATERFRONT $$$$ AE DC MC V | 489 ▪ ● ▪
900 Canada Pl Way. **Map** 3 A1. ((604) 691-1991 *or* (800) 441-1414. FAX *(604) 691-1896.*
www.thewaterfronthotel.com This harborfront property, a modern glass-
and-steel building tempered by terraced gardens, offers luxurious rooms,
most with majestic views of the mountains. A walkway links the hotel to
cruise ship terminals.

PAN PACIFIC VANCOUVER $$$$ AE DC MC V | 504 ▪ ●
999 Canada Pl Way. **Map** 3 A1. ((604) 662-8111 *or* (800) 663-1515. FAX *(604) 685-8690.*
www.panpacific.com This prestigious hotel shares spectacular harbor
frontage with the Vancouver Conference and Exhibition Centre, cruise ship
terminals, and the CN IMAX Theatre. Rooms are beautifully appointed. Also
home to the renowned Five Sails Restaurant.

DOWNTOWN

YWCA HOTEL $ AE MC V | 155 ●
733 Beatty St. **Map** 3 A3. ((604) 895-5830 *or* (800) 663-1424. FAX *(604) 681-2550.*
www.ywcahotel.com This immaculate, modern high-rise provides spotless
accommodation for solo or group travelers (both men and women). Complimentary access to nearby YWCA Health and Wellness Centre.

HAMPTON INN AND SUITES DOWNTOWN $$ AE MC V | 132 ▪
111 Robson St. **Map** 3 A3. ((604) 602-1008 *or* (877) 602-1008. FAX *(604) 602-1007.*
www.hamptoninnvancouver.com This modern hotel is well appointed with
guest facilities, and some of its rooms provide views of False Creek. Relax
in the roof-top Jacuzzi or quiet coffee lounge.

FAIRMONT HOTEL VANCOUVER $$$ AE DC MC V | 556 ▪ ●
900 W Georgia St. **Map** 2 F2. ((604) 684-3131 *or* (800) 441-1414. FAX *(604) 662-1929.*
www.fairmont.com Easily identified by its oxidized copper roof, this
landmark railway hotel offers a variety of services and amenities, such as
an in-house spa, dining areas, and shops, for an enjoyable stay in a quietly
elegant setting.

SUTTON PLACE HOTEL $$$ AE DC MC V | 397 ▪ ●
845 Burrard St. **Map** 2 F2. ((604) 682-5511 *or* (800) 961-7555. FAX *(604) 682-5513.*
www.suttonplace.com European touches lend charm to this lavishly
appointed hotel, offering plush rooms and a popular restaurant, Fleuri *(see
p309).* A full-service health center also on-site.

FOUR SEASONS HOTEL VANCOUVER $$$$ AE DC MC V | 376 ▪ ● ▪
791 W Georgia St. **Map** 3 A3. ((604) 689-9333. FAX *(604) 684-4555.*
www.fourseasons.com Situated at the top of the Pacific Centre Mall, this
luxury hotel prides itself on its reputation for excellent service and quiet
sophistication, as well as the award-winning Chartwell restaurant *(see
p309).*

Price categories, in US dollars, for a standard double room per night, including tax and service charges. (Prices may fluctuate depending on arrival date and availability; US$1 = CAN$1.50)
$ under $100
$$ $100–$150
$$$ $150–$200
$$$$ over $200

CREDIT CARDS
Indicates which credit cards are accepted: *AE* American Express; *DC* Diners Club; *MC* Master Card/Access; *V* Visa.

RESTAURANT
Hotel restaurant or dining room also open to non-residents.

CHILDREN WELCOME
Child cots and a baby-sitting service available. Some hotel restaurants have children's portions and highchairs.

GARDEN OR TERRACE
Hotels with a garden, courtyard, or terrace.

	CREDIT CARDS	NUMBER OF ROOMS	RESTAURANT	CHILDREN WELCOME	GARDEN OR TERRACE

WEDGEWOOD HOTEL $$$$
845 Hornby St. **Map** 2 F2. (*(604) 689-7777 or (800) 663-0666.* FAX *(604) 608-5348.*
W *www.wedgewoodhotel.com* This small, boutique hotel combines elegance and intimacy, with flowers, antiques, and original artwork on display. Its tastefully decorated rooms and attentive service add to the refined ambience. A spa and a cigar lounge are also on-site. 🛏 TV 🍽 Ⓨ 🛁 🐾 ♿

	AE MC V	83	■	●	■

GRANVILLE SOUTH AND YALETOWN

GRANVILLE ISLAND HOTEL $$
1253 Johnston St. **Map** 2 E5. (*(604) 683-7373 or (800) 663-1840.* FAX *(604) 683-3061.*
W *www.granvilleislandhotel.com* A deluxe yet casual boutique hotel matched in ambience to bustling Granville Island, this property offers unique rooms, some with wooden beams and soaker tubs. 🛏 TV 🍽 Ⓨ 🛁 🐾 🐕 ♿

	AE DC MC V	85	■	●	■

OPUS HOTEL $$$
322 Davie St. **Map** 2 F4. (*(604) 642-6787 or (866) 642-6787.* FAX *(604) 642-6780.*
W *www.opushotel.com* This hip Yaletown hotel exudes sophistication and opulence. The dramatically structured rooms are defined by five lifestyle-inspired design schemes, from traditionalist to sleek minimalist to edgy modern. 🛏 TV 🍽 Ⓨ 🛁 🐾 🐕 ♿

	AE DC MC V	97	■	●	

FARTHER AFIELD

GROUSE INN $
1633 Capilano Rd, N Vancouver. (*(604) 988-7101 or (800) 779-7888.* FAX *(604) 988-7102.*
W *www.grouseinn.com* A family-friendly motel with children's playground and pool, this comfortable inn is near the Lions Gate Bridge, with easy access to both downtown and North Shore attractions. 🛏 TV 🍽 🛁 ♒ ♿

	AE DC MC V	80	■	●	■

SYLVIA HOTEL $
1154 Gilford St, Vancouver. (*(604) 681-9321.* FAX *(604) 682-3551.*
W *www.sylviahotel.com* Built in 1912, this landmark brick and terra-cotta building by English Bay is a designated heritage structure, distinctive for the Virginia creeper ivy covering its exterior. The dark wood details and the plainly furnished rooms would appear to have seen better days. 🛏 TV Ⓨ

	AE DC MC V	119	■	●	

BEST WESTERN SANDS BY THE SEA $$
1755 Davie St, Vancouver. (*(604) 682-1831 or (800) 663-9400.* FAX *(604) 682-3546.*
W *www.rpbhotels.com* Located close to the beach at English Bay, this low-key hotel offers comfortable rooms with either mountain or water views.
🛏 TV 🍽 Ⓨ 🛁 🐾 🐕 ♿

	AE DC MC V	121	■	●	

THISTLEDOWN HOUSE BED AND BREAKFAST $$
3910 Capilano Rd, N Vancouver. (*(604) 986-7173 or (888) 633-7173.* FAX *(604) 980-2939.*
W *www.thistle-down.com* A 1920s, Craftsman-style heritage home, this quaint B & B is filled with handcrafted furnishings and surrounded with lovely gardens. The rate includes afternoon tea. 🛏

	MC V	5			■

FAIRMONT VANCOUVER AIRPORT $$$
3111 North Service Rd, Richmond. (*(604) 207-5200 or (800) 441-1414.*
FAX *(604) 248-3219.* W *www.fairmont.com* Located in Vancouver airport, guests can check in via the hotel desk or one of the satellite kiosks in the terminal. It offers deluxe soundproof rooms and an on-site spa.
🛏 TV 🍽 Ⓨ 🛁 ♒ 🐕 🐾 ♿

	AE DC MC V	392	■	●	

'O CANADA' HOUSE $$$
1114 Barclay St, Vancouver. (*(604) 688-0555 or (877) 688-1114.* FAX *(604) 488-0556.*
W *www.ocanadahouse.com* The national anthem "O Canada" was written in this 1897 house, now an award-winning, Victorian-style B & B with wraparound porch and English garden. Enjoy gourmet breakfasts and the hosts' attentive service, as well as a prime West End location. 🛏 TV

	MC V	6			■

BRITISH COLUMBIA

CHEMAINUS: *Olde Mill House Bed and Breakfast* $
9712 Chemainus Rd. ☏ *(250) 416-0049 or (877) 770-6060.* FAX *(250) 246-4457.*
Ⓦ www.oldemillhouse.ca An English garden with tall maples is the setting for
this elegant heritage home, very close to the well-known Chemainus murals
and theater. Rooms are uniquely and charmingly decorated. 🛏 📺 ▤ 🏠 🕭

| | AE MC V | 3 | | ● | ■ |

CLEARWATER: *Helmcken Falls Lodge* $$
6664 Clearwater Valley Rd. ☏ *(250) 674-3657.* FAX *(250) 674-2971.*
Ⓦ www.helmckenfalls.com Originally a lodge for hunting and fishing tours,
this building at the entrance to Wells Gray Provincial Park has grown into
various rustic accommodation options. The Main Lodge offers basic,
timbered rooms. Closed April, and mid-October to mid-December. 🛏

| | AE MC V | 21 | ■ | ● | ■ |

CRANBROOK: *Kootenay Country Comfort Inn* $
1111 Cranbrook St N. ☏ *(250) 426-2296 or (800) 862-2823.* FAX *(250) 426-3533.*
Ⓦ www.cyberlink.bc.ca/~motel A combination of modest prices, comfort, and
country-style decor make this property a hit. Whirlpool, sauna, and laundry
facilities are all on-site. 🛏 📺 ▤ 🏠

| | AE MC V | 36 | | ● | |

DAWSON CREEK: *Super 8 Motel* $
1440 Alaska Ave. ☏ *(250) 782-8899 or (888) 482-8884.* FAX *(250) 784-1988.*
Ⓦ www.super8.com This spotless motel, offering the standard amenities,
provides daily continental breakfast and newspaper. 🛏 📺 ▤ 🔆 🏠 🕭

| | AE DC MC V | 48 | | ● | |

FERNIE: *Best Western Fernie Mountain Lodge* $$
1622 7th Ave. ☏ *(250) 423-5500.* FAX *(250) 423-5501.*
Ⓦ www.bestwesternfernie.com This full-service hotel has the feel of a rugged
lodge, with outdoor hot tubs offering views of the Rocky Mountains.
Deluxe suites have fireplaces and Jacuzzis. 🛏 📺 ▤ 🍸 🔆 ♨ 🍴 🏠 🕭

| | AE DC MC V | 95 | ■ | ● | ■ |

FORT ST. JOHN: *Quality Inn Northern Grand* $
9830 100th Ave. ☏ *(250) 787-0521.* FAX *(250) 787-2648.*
Ⓦ www.choicehotels.ca Its smart, comfortable rooms make this modern,
downtown hotel a fine choice. 🛏 📺 ▤ 🍸 🔆 ♨ 🍴 🏠 🕭

| | AE MC V | 123 | ■ | ● | |

GALIANO ISLAND: *Island Time Bed and Breakfast* $$
952 Sticks Allison W. ☏ *(250) 539-3506 or (877) 588-3506.* FAX *(250) 539-3507.*
Ⓦ www.gulfislands.com/islandtime The oceanfront rooms in this West
Coast–style home have spacious decks for watching eagles, orcas, and sun-
rises; otherwise, relax in the hot tub overlooking the private beach. 🛏 📺

| | AE DC MC V | 3 | | | ■ |

GLACIER NATIONAL PARK: *Best Western Glacier Park Lodge* $$
Summit, Trans-Canada Hwy, Rogers Pass. ☏ *(250) 837-2126.* FAX *(250) 837-2130.*
Ⓦ www.glacierparklodgecanada.com Designer-decorated rooms and modern
amenities are found in this spacious lodge. Enjoy superb views of the
Selkirk Mountains, the Asulkan Glacier, or nature at play from the comfort
of the dining room or lounge. 🛏 📺 🍸 🔆 ♨ 🏠 🕭

| | AE DC MC V | 50 | ■ | ● | ■ |

HARRISON HOT SPRINGS: *Executive Hotel Harrison Hot Springs* $$
190 Lillooet Ave. ☏ *(604) 796-5555 or (888) 265-1155.* FAX *(604) 796-3731.*
Ⓦ www.harrisonhotsprings.com This hotel, located next to public hot springs and
handy for the beach, encourages pampering with its own spa, steam room,
and sauna. Rooms are spacious and comfortable. 🛏 📺 ▤ 🍸 🔆 🍴 🏠 🕭

| | AE DC | 88 | ■ | ● | ■ |

KAMLOOPS: *Plaza Heritage Hotel* $$
405 Victoria St. ☏ *(250) 377-8075 or (877) 977-5292.* FAX *(250) 377-8076.*
Ⓦ www.plazaheritagehotel.com Beautifully restored to a 1920s heritage style, each
room in this hotel is uniquely decorated, retaining the elegance of the original
furnishings and fixtures. A beer-and-wine shop is on-site. 🛏 📺 ▤ 🍸

| | AE DC MC V | 66 | ■ | ● | ■ |

KELOWNA: *Manteo Resort* $$$
3766 Lakeshore Rd. ☏ *(250) 860-1031 or (800) 445-5255.* FAX *(250) 860-1041.*
Ⓦ www.manteo.com A cluster of modern luxury rooms, suites, and villas are
offered for business or vacation travelers, as well as family groups, on the
shores of Okanagan Lake. 🛏 📺 ▤ 🍸 🔆 ♨ 🍴 🕭

| | AE DC MC V | 92 | ■ | ● | ■ |

MALAHAT: *Aerie Resort* $$$$
600 Ebedora Lane. ☏ *(250) 743-7115 or (800) 518-1933.* FAX *(250) 743-4766.*
Ⓦ www.aerie.bc.ca A luxurious, Mediterranean-style enclave with vistas of
southern Vancouver Island's mountain landscape, the Aerie Resort is the
ultimate retreat: impeccable service, plush rooms, its award-winning
restaurant, The Aerie *(see p311),* and an on-site spa. 🛏 📺 ▤ 🍸 ♨ 🍴

| | AE DC MC V | 29 | ■ | | ■ |

Price categories, in US dollars, for a standard double room per night, including tax and service charges. (Prices may fluctuate depending on arrival date and availability; US$1 = CAN$1.50)
[$] under $100
[$][$] $100–$150
[$][$][$] $150–$200
[$][$][$][$] over $200

CREDIT CARDS
Indicates which credit cards are accepted: *AE* American Express; *DC* Diners Club; *MC* Master Card/Access; *V* Visa.

RESTAURANT
Hotel restaurant or dining room also open to non-residents.

CHILDREN WELCOME
Child cots and a baby-sitting service available. Some hotel restaurants have children's portions and highchairs.

GARDEN OR TERRACE
Hotels with a garden, courtyard, or terrace.

	Credit Cards	Number of Rooms	Restaurant	Children Welcome	Garden or Terrace
MAYNE ISLAND: *Oceanwood Country Inn* [$][$][$] 630 Dinner Bay Rd. ☎ *(250) 539-5074.* [FAX] *(250) 539-3002.* [W] www.oceanwood.com Hidden among trees on 10 acres (4 ha) of waterfront, this island getaway comes with charming rooms and deep chairs by the fireplace to create a relaxing retreat. Breakfast included, licensed, gourmet dining on-site. Closed November to March.	MC V	12	■		■
NANAIMO: *Coast Bastion Inn* [$] 11 Bastion St. ☎ *(250) 753-6601 or (800) 663-1144.* [FAX] *(250) 753-4155.* [W] www.coasthotels.com Overlooking Georgia Strait, all rooms in this comfortable inn have great sea views. The hotel is well situated for the harborfront and seaplane terminals. [TV]	AE DC MC V	179	■	●	■
NELSON: *Inn the Garden Bed and Breakfast and Guesthouse* [$] 408 Victoria St. ☎ *(250) 352-3226 or (800) 596-2337.* [FAX] *(250) 352-3284.* [W] www.innthegarden.com A three-story Victorian home plus a smaller guesthouse, decorated with antiques and plants, make up the lodgings at this homey B & B. Relax in the lounge or the terraced garden.	AE MC V	7		●	■
PARKSVILLE: *Tigh-Na-Mara Resort* [$][$] 1095 Island Hwy E. ☎ *(250) 248-2072 or (800) 663-7373.* [FAX] *(250) 248-4140.* [W] www.tigh-na-mara.com This all-season, destination resort provides a variety of lodgings: log cottages, ocean-view condos, or new studios. Spa treatments and a variety of recreational activities are offered. [TV]	AE DC MC V	192	■	●	■
PENTICTON: *Penticton Lakeside Resort* [$][$] 21 Lakeshore Dr W. ☎ *(250) 493-8221 or (800) 663-9400.* [FAX] *(250) 493-0607.* [W] www.rpbhotels.com This lakeside resort, including a full-service hotel with dining and bar venues, convention center, and casino, is a destination in itself. Watersports rentals are available. [TV]	AE DC MC V	204	■	●	■
PRINCE GEORGE: *Esther's Inn* [$] 1151 Commercial Dr. ☎ *(250) 562-4131 or (800) 663-6844.* [FAX] *(250) 562-4145.* [W] www.esthersinn.com A slice of tropical life in the north. This South Seas–themed property offers spotless rooms; suites open onto two indoor garden courtyards. The tropical theme is further enhanced by hot tubs, lush plants, and pool waterslides. [TV]	AE DC MC V	126	■	●	■
PRINCE RUPERT: *Crest Hotel* [$][$] 222 1st Ave W. ☎ *(250) 624-6771 or (800) 663-8150.* [FAX] *(250) 627-7666.* [W] www.cresthotel.bc.ca Gorgeous views come with the location atop a bluff overlooking the harbor at this modern hotel. Beautiful public areas and attractive rooms belie the somewhat plain exterior. [TV]	AE DC MC V	102	■	●	
QUEEN CHARLOTTE CITY: *Dorothy and Mike's Guest House* [$] 3127 2nd Ave, Graham Island. ☎ *(250) 559-8439.* [FAX] *(250) 559-8439.* [W] www.qcislands.net/doromike The hosts of this centrally located guest house, long-time residents of the island, provide a resource library on the native Haida culture and wildlife. Rooms and suites are cozy. [TV]		8		●	■
RADIUM HOT SPRINGS: *Radium Resort* [$] 8100 Golf Course Rd. ☎ *(250) 347-9311 or (800) 667-6444.* [FAX] *(250) 347-6298.* [W] www.radiumresort.com This all-season resort affords spectacular views of the surrounding Rocky and Purcell mountain ranges while offering myriad recreational activities: golf, tennis, squash, bicycling, and more. Lodging is offered as one- to three-bedroom condos. [TV]	AE DC MC V	118	■	●	■
SALTSPRING ISLAND: *Anne's Oceanfront Hideaway* [$][$][$] 168 Simson Rd. ☎ *(250) 537-0851 or (888) 474-2663.* [FAX] *(250) 537-0861.* [W] www.annesoceanfront.com A relaxing spot, with stylishly appointed rooms, each with fireplace, reclining chairs, and bathroom with hydro-massage tub. The ocean view from the outside hot tub is stunning.	AE MC V	4			■

SMITHERS: *Hudson Bay Lodge* $
3251 Hwy 16 E. (*(250) 847-4581 or (800) 663-5040.* FAX *(250) 847-4878.*
W www.hblodge.com This family-owned, full-service hotel is located at the
base of Hudson Bay Mountain. The alpine-style decor and nicely appointed
rooms ensure a comfortable stay.

| | | 99 | ■ | ● | |

SOOKE: *Sooke Harbour House* $$$$
1528 Whiffen Spit Rd. (*(250) 642-3421 or (800) 889-9688.* FAX *(250) 642-6988.*
W www.sookeharbourhouse.com A picturesque inn by the sea combining a
hotel, fine dining restaurant *(see p312)*, spa, and art gallery. Each of the
luxurious, individually designed rooms has a private balcony and fireplace.
Enjoy complimentary breakfast and on-site spa services.

| | | 28 | ■ | ● | ■ |

TOFINO: *Middle Beach Lodge* $$
400 Mackenzie Beach Rd. (*(250) 725-2900.* FAX *(250) 725-2901.*
W www.middlebeach.com The unique assortment of accommodation this
property offers – a beach lodge, a headlands lodge, or self-contained
cabins – strives to offer a true Pacific Northwest experience, with timbered
buildings furnished with rustic pieces and stone fireplaces.

| | | 64 | ■ | ● | |

TOFINO: *Wickaninnish Inn* $$$$
Osprey Lane at Chesterman Beach. (*(250) 725-3100 or (800) 333-4604.*
FAX *(250) 725-3110.* W www.wickinn.com The original Tofino luxury oceanfront
property, this hotel boasts panoramic views of the ocean and nearby
islands from its perch at the tip of a rocky promontory. Its spacious rooms
have floor-to-ceiling windows and soaker tubs.

| | | 76 | ■ | ● | |

VICTORIA: *Quality Inn Downtown* $$
850 Blanshard St. (*(250) 385-6787 or (800) 661-4115.* FAX *(250) 385-5800.*
W www.victoriaqualityinn.com This spotless hotel has a superb location within
walking distance to all downtown and Inner Harbour sights. Enjoy the café,
popular English-style pub, and free parking.

| | | 56 | ■ | ● | |

VICTORIA: *Abigail's Hotel* $$$
906 McClure St. (*(250) 388-5363 or (800) 561-6565.* FAX *(250) 388-7787.*
W www.abigailshotel.com This charming inn epitomizes Old World charm
with its heritage Tudor architecture, colorful English gardens, and old-
fashioned hospitality. Enjoy complimentary gourmet breakfast in the dining
room and social hour hors d'oeuvres in the library.

| | | 23 | | | ■ |

VICTORIA: *Gatsby Mansion Inn and Restaurant* $$$
309 Belleville St. (*(250) 388-9191 or (800) 563-9656.* FAX *(250) 920-5651.*
W www.bellevillepark.com/gatsby.html This handsome, early 20th-century inn
offers bed and breakfast in elegant surroundings, featuring stained-glass
windows, and frescoed ceilings. There is a choice of topiary, rose garden,
or harbor views from the beautifully furnished rooms.

| | | 20 | ■ | ● | ■ |

VICTORIA: *Fairmont Empress* $$$$
721 Government St. (*(250) 384-8111 or (800) 257-7544.* FAX *(250) 381-4334.*
W www.fairmont.com A 1989 renovation restored this Inner Harbour
landmark to its original turn-of-the-19th-century grandeur. The "grand
duchess" of the Fairmont group is famed for its afternoon tea service; its
guestrooms are sumptuously appointed.

| | | 477 | ■ | ● | ■ |

WHISTLER: *Delta Whistler Resort* $$
4050 Whistler Way. (*(604) 932-1982 or (800) 515-4050.* FAX *(604) 932-7323.*
W www.deltawhistler.com Spectacular mountain views and spacious rooms
are the draws to this inn, which enjoys a great location steps from Whistler
Village and the Whistler and Blackcomb gondolas. Ski and bicycle rentals
are available on-site.

| | | 288 | ■ | ● | |

WHISTLER: *Fairmont Chateau Whistler* $$$$
4599 Chateau Blvd. (*(604) 938-8000 or (800) 606-8244.* FAX *(604) 938-2291.*
W www.fairmont.com The lobby's rich carpeting, First Nations art, and gold-
leaf domed ceiling convey an air of easy grandeur, reinforced by the
luxurious rooms and suites. Guests pamper themselves in the Vida spa or
in the restaurant's private wine room.

| | | 550 | ■ | ● | ■ |

WHISTLER: *Pan Pacific Whistler* $$$$
4320 Sundial Cres. (*(604) 905-2999 or (888) 905-9995.* FAX *(604) 905-2995.*
W www.panpac.com This exclusive resort offers lodging in studio, one-, and
two-bedroom suites. Rooms are lavishly appointed, each with fireplace and
soaker tub. On-site, find the West Coast Art Gallery and Best Spa services.

| | | 121 | ■ | ● | ■ |

WHERE TO EAT

THE PACIFIC NORTHWEST is known for its large number of coffee bars as well as the vast range of fresh local seafood it has to offer, from wild salmon to oysters, clams, and crab. Portland, Seattle, and Vancouver are all in the midst of a culinary revolution – small neighborhood, chef-owned restaurants are popping up on every block, showcasing a

Emblem of Starbucks, the coffee bar chain

broad array of fare and adding depth to the choices. Visitors can find a terrific French bistro neighbored by an affordable Thai noodle house and a mid-range Mediterranean seafood restaurant. Farm-fresh, local flavors mark the ingenious creations of the region's finest restaurants. Other eateries boast down-to-earth fare with the same freshness.

PACIFIC NORTHWEST CUISINE

INCREASINGLY, PACIFIC Northwest restaurants offer menus that highlight local produce, of which there is a wide variety. Oregon's climate is particularly conducive to growing wild mushrooms. Washington is perhaps best known for its apples, though it also grows many types of berries. In British Columbia, tree fruits, including apples, pears, peaches, cherries, and plums, often feature in its cuisine. As well, Pacific Northwest grapes and wineries are celebrated as some of the best in the world, so it is no surprise that many wine bars are opening throughout the region.

Seafood is very much the focus of Pacific Northwest cuisine. On just about every menu and in just about every type of restaurant, salmon, halibut, crab, mussels, clams,

Microbrewed beers of the Pacific Northwest

and oysters are on offer, whether in the form of cakes, chowder, or fish and chips. Smoked salmon, which has its origins in Native customs, is ubiquitous. Oysters are gaining in popularity not only on the local but also the national level. With so many varieties to choose from, making a meal of several types of oysters on the half shell while sipping a local beer at one of the many oyster bars is a popular pastime of locals and visitors alike.

Eating healthily in the region's restaurants is easy. Low-fat dishes are staples on most menus, as are vegetarian options, ranging from salads and wraps to Mongolian grills and Buddhist banquets. Native cuisine, using local ingredients such as seaweed, fern shoots, wild berries, oolichan (a small silvery fish), and caribou, can also be enjoyed, and is sometimes combined with traditional Native song and dance performances in an authentic setting.

Ivans, offering clams and other seafood to Seattle

TYPES OF RESTAURANTS

EATING ESTABLISHMENTS in the Pacific Northwest run the gamut, from five-star gourmet restaurants, bistros, and pubs to noodle houses and sushi bars to fast food and take-out. Coffee shops, bagel and bake shops, and ice-cream stores are all also easy to find.

Ethnic restaurants – French, Italian, Hungarian, Greek, Indian, and Caribbean to mention a few – are thriving and have given rise to a fusion cuisine unique to the West Coast. Asian restaurants are plentiful; there is usually at least one Thai and Japanese restaurant in every neighborhood. Sushi bars here are good as well, since the fish is so varied and fresh. Dining on authentic Japanese, Korean, Chinese, or Thai food in the Chinatown or International District found in all the major cities of the Pacific Northwest is inexpensive. Many Chinese restaurants serve *dim sum,* a traditional Chinese brunch.

ALCOHOL AND SMOKING

IT IS BECOMING more and more common for restaurants in the Pacific Northwest to ban smoking at their tables.

One of the many cafés in Seattle with both indoor and outdoor seating

However, where smoking is allowed, almost every restaurant has a designated non-smoking area. Patio seating may or may not be smoke-free. When reserving a table, be sure to note a preference.

Alcohol is available only in licensed establishments. Dining in taverns or certain parts of restaurants may be restricted. When they plan to order alcohol in any establishment, diners should always bring a valid form of picture identification, such as a driver's license or passport, as waitpersons are required by law to check the age of patrons who order alcohol. The legal drinking age in Washington and Oregon is 21, in British Columbia, 19.

HOURS

COFFEE SHOPS and restaurants serving full breakfasts open at 6 or 7am. With one on just about every downtown street corner, coffee shops are the best bet for a toasted bagel or pastry and a cup of coffee in the morning. Breakfast, which generally consists of some combination of pancakes, toast, eggs, omelets, sausages, and bacon, is typically served until 11am. On Sundays, brunch is served between 8am and 2pm at many restaurants that are not open for breakfast during the week.

Lunch hours are usually between 11:30am and 3pm. In the cities, many of the more upscale restaurants offer lunches that mirror the dinner menu in every aspect but

The Portland Brewing Company, Portland's successful microbrewery

Moe's Seafood Restaurant, Newport, Oregon, serving the catch of the day

price, making the midday meal a smart choice for travelers who want to dine at the best restaurants while on a budget.

Dinner hours run from 5pm to 9 or 10pm, later in busier areas and on weekends. Some exclusive restaurants open for dinner only. Almost all restaurants are open on Fridays and Saturdays, but it is not uncommon for them to be closed on Sundays and Mondays. Check with each establishment for specific times.

RESERVATIONS

RESERVATIONS are needed for the better or more popular restaurants and some will only accept reservations for parties of six or more. However, most restaurants do not require reservations. If booking more than a day in advance, confirm the booking the day of your reservation.

PRICES

DINNER ENTRÉES in Oregon and Washington cost between $8 and $12 at casual restaurants; between $20 and $40 at fine dining establishments. Taxes on foods and alcoholic beverages in Oregon and Washington vary from county to county; in the Seattle area, it is 9.1 percent. In BC, dinner entrées range from Can $12 to $20 at casual spots, from Can $25 to $34 at the more exclusive restaurants. Lunch costs from $7 to $20, breakfast $5 to $12. A tax of 7 percent is charged on meals and food. Alcoholic drinks are subject to a tax of 10 percent.

Sign at Granville Island, Vancouver

Brewpub sign in Seattle

PAYING AND TIPPING

NEARLY ALL restaurants accept major credit cards. Traveler's checks in US or Canadian currency are accepted with appropriate identification. Personal checks are usually not welcome.

At any sit-down restaurant with a waitperson, it is customary to tip 15 to 20 percent of the price of the meal, before tax. As a general rule, tipping 15 percent is about average; a 20 percent tip is generally given when service has been exceptionally good. When paying for the meal with a credit card, the tip amount can be added on the credit card slip. At coffee bars or cafeteria-style restaurants, a tip jar is often located near the cash register.

DRESS CODES

THE PACIFIC Northwest is, in general, a casual place. At most city restaurants, business-casual is appropriate: khakis and button-down shirts for men; a sweater or blouse and pants or skirt for women. Outside the cities, dress is often more casual, and most restaurants do not have dress codes. Usually, the more exclusive the restaurant, the more formal it is.

CHILDREN

WELL-BEHAVED children are welcome at most restaurants and many establishments cater especially to families with children. High chairs and booster seats are often available, as is a special kid's menu or portions.

What to Eat in the Pacific Northwest

Ripe cherry

THE DISHES PREPARED in the Pacific Northwest profit from an abundance of fresh local ingredients. Offerings from the sea, such as crabs, oysters, clams, and fish, and delicious vegetables and fruits from the Pacific Northwest's fertile valleys are an inspiration to the region's chefs, who draw on the best of Native, traditional American, and ethnic cuisines, including Japanese, Vietnamese, Chinese, Mexican, and Italian. The choices offered by the wide range of restaurants throughout the Pacific Northwest run the culinary gamut from wild-berry pancakes to pumpkin soup to refined ahi tuna.

Dungeness crab, *famous for its delicate meat, is usually served steamed with melted butter. It is harvested throughout the region in the crab season, which runs from mid-November to June.*

Bacon and eggs *is a classic North American breakfast dish. Eggs are prepared in a variety of styles and served with crispy bacon on the side.*

Wild blueberry pancakes, *a delicious type of breakfast pancake, are accompanied by wild berries and served with butter and maple syrup.*

Enchiladas, *a Mexican dish, are rolled corn tortillas, filled with cheese, beef, or chicken, and usually topped with a red chili sauce and melted cheese.*

Pho *is a traditional Vietnamese one-dish meal of hot, rich broth ladled over rice noodles and beef, accompanied by bean sprouts, fresh basil, chilies, and lime wedges.*

Spaghetti vongole, *a flavorsome Italian seafood dish, combines thin ribbon pasta with steamed clams, garlic, white wine, parsley, and, in some versions, tomatoes.*

Ahi tuna *is served rare in wafer-thin slices and accompanied by a pepper sauce or crust, usually with lightly cooked vegetables and rice on the side.*

Chili sauce

Herb sauce

Seafood sauce

Horseradish sauce

Oysters *are best enjoyed raw on the half-shell, accompanied by a variety of sauces, ranging from mild to tangy and sharp. Many types of oysters are cultivated throughout the region, and Washington state is one of North America's greatest oyster producers.*

Wild salmon *is one of the culinary delights of the Pacific Northwest, where salmon is always fresh. This firm and tasty fish lends itself well to many delicious methods of preparation, such as grilling on a cedar plank, poaching, or baking.*

Roast lamb *is delicious with roast potatoes and a sprig of rosemary as garnish. Lamb raised locally on British Columbia's Saltspring Island is world-renowned.*

Fillet of venison *is a choice cut of deer, caribou, elk, or moose, served in many ways, such as with a green peppercorn sauce and band noodles mixed with sliced zucchini.*

Pumpkin soup, *a thick and creamy soup made with pureed pumpkin, is garnished with roasted pumpkin seeds and often served with a toasted bagel on the side.*

T-bone steak, *usually served grilled and accompanied by a baked potato and corn on the cob or other vegetable, is a dish found on many menus of Pacific Northwest restaurants.*

Sautéed squash, *a popular side dish, is usually panfried in olive oil and often served with roasted or grilled meats and fish. This local vegetable comes in many varieties.*

Penne *are tubes of pasta which are prepared in a variety of ways. Here, they are tossed with tomatoes, mozzarella, olives, and fresh basil. Penne means "quills" in Italian.*

Dim sum, *a Chinese specialty, consists of a variety of small brunch dishes. Each contains morsels of meat, seafood, or vegetables, assembled into delicacies such as* har gow *(shrimp dumpling),* siu mai *(pork dumpling), and* cha siu bao *(barbecue pork bun).*

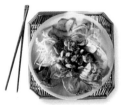

Lemongrass chicken salad *is a spicy Thai dish made with sliced chicken breast flavored with chili, lemongrass, and onion. It is often served on a bed of lettuce.*

Sushi *is a Japanese specialty consisting of fresh raw fish on cakes of vinegared cold rice, sometimes wrapped in seaweed. Pickled ginger and fiery wasabi complement the dish.*

WHAT TO DRINK

The Pacific Northwest is a coffee-lover's paradise: cafés seem to be on every street corner. Increasingly popular juice bars turn fresh fruits and vegetables into delicious and healthy beverages. Small local breweries – or microbreweries – produce a variety of stellar beers. Wine from the region's many excellent wineries can be sampled in bars and restaurants, and at the wineries themselves.

Biscotti *are crunchy Italian cookies baked in a variety of flavors, including chocolate. Traditional biscotti are baked with whole almonds. These sweets are the perfect accompaniment to a special coffee or a glass of sweet wine.*

Carrot juice

Beer

Caffe latte

Red wine

Choosing a Restaurant

THESE RESTAURANTS HAVE BEEN SELECTED across a wide price range for their value, good food, ambience, and location. They are listed by area, and within these by price. Most restaurants are wheelchair accessible and provide nonsmoking seating areas. Map references for central Portland, Seattle, and Vancouver listings are found on pages 82–5, 166–9, and 238–41 respectively.

	CREDIT CARDS	VEGETARIAN	OUTDOOR SEATING	CHILDREN WELCOME	LATE OPENING

PORTLAND

OLD TOWN AND THE PEARL DISTRICT

FONG CHONG RESTAURANT ⓢ
301 NW 4th Ave. **Map** 2 D3. 【 *(503) 228-6868.*
This Chinatown restaurant makes up for its well-worn interior by serving what is arguably the city's best *dim sum*.

	AE MC V	●		●	

DAN AND LOUIS OYSTER BAR RESTAURANT ⓢⓢ
208 SW Ankeny St. **Map** 2 D4. 【 *(503) 227-5906.*
A Portland landmark, this fish house is enjoyed by regulars for its Ankeny Street memorabilia and casual ambience. Oysters are served any way the diner likes, but do as the locals do and slurp them raw on the half shell.

	AE DC MC V	●	■	●	

DOWNTOWN

GOOD DOG/BAD DOG ⓢ
708 SW Alder St. **Map** 1 C5. 【 *(503) 222-3410.*
This fun and funky hangout, with photos of four-legged stars adorning the walls, has all types of low-fat hot dogs, including the Oregon Smokey, a local favorite made with blackstrap molasses.

	MC V	●		●	

BUSH GARDEN JAPANESE RESTAURANT ⓢⓢⓢ
900 SW Morrison St. **Map** 1 C5. 【 *(503) 226-7181.*
Claiming to be Portland's oldest Japanese restaurant, Bush Garden serves great *sushi* in a quiet setting. Groups can reserve a private *tatami* room.

	AE DC MC V	●		●	

ORITALIA ⓢⓢⓢ
750 SW Alder St. **Map** 1 C5. 【 *(503) 295-0680.*
Oritalia offers a menu full of Mediterranean-Asian fusion options, such as lamb curry and tuna *sashimi*, which work well together. The eclectic decor, with huge tentacled chandeliers, adds to the exotic ambience.

	AE MC V	●			■

SOUTHPARK SEAFOOD GRILL ⓢⓢⓢⓢ
901 SW Salmon St. **Map** 1 B5. 【 *(503) 326-1300.*
Full, bold Mediterranean flavors nicely accent the primarily seafood-based menu offerings at this chic restaurant with soaring ceilings and an industrial-elegant feel. A "small plates" menu is available in the lounge.

	AE DC MC V	●	■		

HEATHMAN RESTAURANT AND BAR ⓢⓢⓢⓢⓢ
1001 SW Broadway. **Map** 1 C5. 【 *(503) 790-7752.*
This award-winning, special-occasion restaurant features a menu of Pacific Northwest cuisine, which changes seasonally. Standout dishes include the *foie gras* cappucino and tuna *Rossini*. Live jazz Wednesday to Saturday. ♫

	AE DC MC V	●			

HIGGINS RESTAURANT ⓢⓢⓢⓢⓢ
1239 SW Broadway. **Map** 3 B1. 【 *(503) 222-9070.*
Diners savor creative regional cuisine cooked with classic French technique in this formal dining room. An abundance of fish and wild game is found on a menu that boasts highlights such as mussels steamed in hard cider.

	AE DC MC V	●			

FARTHER AFIELD

PASTINI PASTARIA ⓢ
1426 NE Broadway, Portland. 【 *(503) 288-4300.*
Pasta lovers can fill up on hearty helpings of a wide variety of classics, or other well-known Italian dishes, at this modern *trattoria*-style restaurant.

	AE MC V	●		●	

SAN FELIPE TAQUERIA ⓢ
6221 SE Milwaukie Ave, Portland. 【 *(503) 235-8158.*
A favorite lunch spot with locals, this unassuming *taqueria* (no-fuss eatery serving mainly burritos, tacos, and the like) offers tasty Mexican fare. The *gorditas* (puck-shaped tarts filled with a choice of meats) and *tortas* (Mexican sandwiches) are particularly good. ● *Sun, Mon.*

	MC V	●		●	

Price categories, in US dollars (US$1 = CAN$1.50), for a three-course meal and a half bottle of house wine, including taxes and service:
[$] under $25
[$][$] $25–$35
[$][$][$] $35–$50
[$][$][$][$] $50–$70
[$][$][$][$][$] over $70

CREDIT CARDS
Indicates which credit cards are accepted: *AE* American Express; *DC* Diners Club; *MC* MasterCard/Access; *V* Visa.

VEGETARIAN
A selection of vegetarian dishes available.

OUTDOOR SEATING
Garden, terrace, or courtyard with outside seating available.

CHILDREN WELCOME
Children's menu or portions; highchairs available.

LATE OPENING
Full meals or light menu served after 11pm.

Restaurant	Price	Credit Cards	Vegetarian	Outdoor Seating	Children Welcome	Late Opening
LE BISTRO MONTAGE 301 SE Morrison St, Portland. ☎ *(503) 234-1324.* Communal dining is key at this funky, Cajun eatery: patrons are seated together at long tables. Many dishes are variations of macaroni and cheese; desserts such as bread pudding are worth saving room for.	[$][$]		●		●	
BRIDGEPORT BREW PUB 1313 NW Marshall St, Portland. ☎ *(503) 241-3612.* This casual local hangout has a fine selection of pizzas, their crusts made with unfermented beer, and excellent microbrews (beers brewed in, and distinctive to, the region) on tap. Very family- and pet-friendly.	[$][$]	MC V	●	■	●	
BUCKMAN BISTRO 213 SE 12th Ave, Portland. ☎ *(503) 230-2381.* Many classic French bistro favorites, such as French onion soup and *daube de boeuf*, are found on the menu at this unpretentious spot, as well as highlights such as lamb shanks with white beans. No reservations accepted. Dinner only.	[$][$]	MC V	●			
DOTS CAFÉ 2521 SE Clinton St, Portland. ☎ *(503) 235-0203.* A great place for burgers and many types of French fries, this café is often filled with trendy locals hanging out amid the kitschy-cool 1970s decor. As a late-night dining spot, it is exclusively the domain of adults after 10pm.	[$][$]		●			■
PHO VAN 1012 NW Glisan St, Portland. ☎ *(503) 248-2172.* This bright, recently renovated Vietnamese restaurant serves stylish noodle fare and a particularly good version of its namesake soup, *pho.* ● *Sun.*	[$][$]	MC V	●		●	
SABURO'S SUSHI HOUSE 1667 SE Bybee Blvd, Portland. ☎ *(503) 236-4237.* Sellwood's tiny, excellent *sushi* spot is always packed with fresh-fish fanatics, and lineups are common. Signature dishes include creamy scallops and broiled *hamachi* collar (yellowtail fish neck). No reservations accepted. Dinner only.	[$][$]	AE MC V	●		●	
LITTLE WING CAFÉ 529 NW 13th Ave, Portland. ☎ *(503) 228-3101.* Filling sandwiches at lunchtime and inspired new-American fare at dinner keep this café, found in a renovated warehouse, in demand. In mild weather, sitting out front provides unlimited people-watching entertainment. ● *Sun.*	[$][$][$]	AE MC V	●	■	●	
OBA! RESTAURANTE 555 NW 12th Ave, Portland. ☎ *(503) 228-6161.* Contemporary Latin American flavors influence the menu offered at this modern, trendy restaurant. The subdued but intimate dining room has deep booths, low lighting, and a warming fireplace.	[$][$][$]	AE DC MC V	●			
RISTORANTE FRATELLI 1230 NW Hoyt St, Portland. ☎ *(503) 241-8800.* This romantic, traditional Italian restaurant presents a menu that emphasizes meat and fish over pasta. Desserts, including chestnut crepes stuffed with white chocolate mousse, are stellar. Dinner only.	[$][$][$]	AE DC MC V	●			
SIN JU 1022 NW Johnson St, Portland. ☎ *(503) 223-6535.* Soft colors, two waterfalls, and private *tatami* rooms set the stage for top-notch *sushi* and Japanese cuisine in the heart of the trendy Pearl District.	[$][$][$]	AE MC V	●			
BLUEHOUR 250 NW 13th Ave, Portland. ☎ *(503) 226-3394.* The sleekly modern interior provides the backdrop for some of Portland's best Pacific Northwest cuisine. The inventive menu offers dishes with a full, sensuous mix of textures and flavors. Dinner only. ● *Sun, Mon.*	[$][$][$][$]	AE DC MC V	●			

For key to symbols see back flap

<table>
<tr><td>

Price categories, in US dollars (US$1 = CAN$1.50), for a three-course meal and a half bottle of house wine, including taxes and service:
- **$** under $25
- **$$** $25–$35
- **$$$** $35–$50
- **$$$$** $50–$70
- **$$$$$** over $70

</td><td>

CREDIT CARDS
Indicates which credit cards are accepted: *AE* American Express; *DC* Diners Club; *MC* MasterCard/Access; *V* Visa.

VEGETARIAN
A selection of vegetarian dishes available.

OUTDOOR SEATING
Garden, terrace, or courtyard with outside seating available.

CHILDREN WELCOME
Children's menu or portions; highchairs available.

LATE OPENING
Full meals or light menu served after 11pm.

</td></tr>
</table>

	CREDIT CARDS	VEGETARIAN	OUTDOOR SEATING	CHILDREN WELCOME	LATE OPENING
GIORGIO'S **$$$** 1131 NW Hoyt St, Portland. 【 *(503) 221-1888.* Northern Italian cuisine incorporating local produce is served in a cozy dining room that is decidedly date-worthy. Homemade pastas and *gnocchi* are among the highlights of the menu. ● *lunch Sat; Sun, Mon.*	AE DC MC V	●	■		
COUVRON **$$$$$** 1126 SW 18th Ave, Portland. 【 *(503) 225-1844.* Unobtrusive service and a superb wine selection are the hallmarks of this classy Portland establishment. Its menu of inspired French cooking includes the signature dish of duck breast with a Sauterne sauce. ● *Sun, Mon.*	AE DC MC V	●			
MORTON'S OF CHICAGO **$$$$$** 213 SW Clay St, Portland. 【 *(503) 248-2100.* A fine spot for a blow-out steak dinner, this posh restaurant has the feel of a private club with its leather seats and windowless walls. The *filet mignon* and New York strip steaks are undisputed favorites. Dinner only.	AE DC MC V	●			
OREGON					
ASHLAND: *Alex's Plaza Restaurant* **$$$** 35 N Main St. 【 *(541) 482-8818.* An eclectic yet familiar menu that has a nice balance of meat and fish dishes – with favorites such as roast pork tenderloin – is offered in this restaurant housed in a historic brick building at the heart of Ashland Plaza.	AE MC V	●		●	
ASHLAND: *Peerless Restaurant* **$$$$$** 265 4th St. 【 *(541) 488-6067.* This lovely, light-filled restaurant is unique in offering a creative menu of Pacific Northwest cuisine that is both seasonal and sustainable (created with ingredients from producers using regenerative or organic processes). It also boasts an award-winning wine list. Dinner only. ● *Sun, Mon.*	AE DC MC V	●			
ASTORIA: *Wet Dog Café and Brew Pub* **$$** 144 11th St. 【 *(503) 325-6975.* Set on the Columbia River waterfront, this is a friendly and casual place to grab burgers, sandwiches, and other hearty American fare. On weekends, the brew pub becomes a popular spot, with a DJ and dancing.	AE MC V	●	■		
ASTORIA: *Baked Alaska* **$$$** 1 12th St. 【 *(503) 325-7414.* The nautical decor suggests the mood for fresh seafood and assorted game meats served at this pier-side restaurant. Great views of the Columbia River can be enjoyed from the floor-to-ceiling windows in the airy dining room.	DC MC V	●	■	●	
BAKER CITY: *Pizza á fetta* **$$** 1915 Washington St. 【 *(541) 523-6099.* Locals and visitors alike can be found enjoying gourmet pizzas, pastas, and other Italian-American favorites in the fun, friendly environment of this café, popular with families for its variety of children's menu options.	MC V	●		●	
BAKER CITY: *Geiser Grill* **$$$** 1996 Main St. 【 *(541) 523-1889.* Steaks, seafood, and pasta are served in this fine dining room in the historic Geiser Grand Hotel *(see p284)*, where an elegant ambience is created under a high stained-glass ceiling. Homemade desserts, such as peach cobbler and key lime pie, are very good.	AE DC MC V	●		●	
BEND: *Deschutes Brewery and Public House* **$$** 1044 NW Bond St. 【 *(541) 382-9242.* The home of many fine local microbrews, including Black Butte Porter, this quaint red-brick building also houses a casual restaurant serving good pub food, especially the hearty specialty sandwiches.	AE MC V	●		●	

BEND: *Merenda Restaurant and Wine Bar* $$$ 900 NW Wall St. ☎ *(541) 330-2304.* Rustic French and Italian dishes, grilled on a wood fire, are the specialties at this charming restaurant, popular for its stellar list of spirits and local wines – 80 selections by the glass. ♫ ● *Sun.*	AE DC MC V	●		●	
CANNON BEACH: *Wayfarer Restaurant* $$$ 1190 Pacific Dr. ☎ *(503) 436-1108.* This family-friendly restaurant serves a variety of seafood dishes, including crab cakes, salmon, and an award-winning clam chowder, in its contemporary, oceanfront dining room.	AE MC V	●		●	
CANNON BEACH: *Stephanie Inn Dining Room* $$$$ 2740 S Pacific St. ☎ *(503) 436-2221.* The dining room at this pleasant inn offers a four-course *prix fixe* menu of Pacific Northwest specialties, which change daily. Reservations required.	AE DC MC V	●			
EUGENE: *Oregon Electric Station Restaurant and Lounge* $$$ 27 E 5th Ave. ☎ *(541) 485-4444.* Located inside a 1912 train depot, this charming red-brick restaurant serves top-notch steak, fish, and pasta entrées and offers a lengthy wine list. Guests can dine aboard antique train cars, or *al fresco* on the front patio.	AE DC MC V	●	■	●	
EUGENE: *Willie's on 7th Avenue* $$$$ 338 W 7th Ave. ☎ *(541) 485-0601.* An eclectic menu focusing on local Oregon produce, with specialties such as locally raised lamb and quail, is served in the dining room of this renovated turn-of-the-19th-century home. ● *Sun.*	AE MC V	●	■	●	
HOOD RIVER: *Full Sail Brewing Company* $ 506 Columbia St. ☎ *(541) 386-2281.* Relax with windsurfers while sampling one of the brewery's many beers, accompanied by "small dishes" of pub fare for snacking.	AE MC V	●			
HOOD RIVER: *Pasquale's Ristorante* $$$ 102 Oak St. ☎ *(541) 386-1900 or (800) 386-1859.* The town's oldest vintage hotel, the Hood River Hotel, is the setting for this atmospheric restaurant with a cozy fireplace, offering a delightful fusion of Italian and Pacific Northwest cuisines. ● *Mon.*	AE MC V	●		●	
HOOD RIVER: *Mount Hood Railroad & Dinner Train* $$$$ 110 Railroad Ave. ☎ *(541) 386-3556.* Saturday-dinner and Sunday-brunch menus are offered onboard the four-hour rail excursion that winds through the landscape surrounding Mounts Hood and Adams. Passengers can enjoy classic dishes, such as prime rib and eggs Benedict, served in the restored vintage dining cars.	AE MC V	●		●	
JOSEPH: *Embers Brew House* $$ 206 N Main St. ☎ *(541) 432-2739.* A relaxed spot for Oregon microbrews accompanied by a tasty selection of pizzas, *calzones*, and burgers, this eatery offers diners the option of enjoying a meal on a large deck with lovely views of the Wallowa Valley.	AE MC V	●	■	●	
JOSEPH: *Outlaw Restaurant and Saloon* $$ 108 N Main St. ☎ *(541) 432-4321.* The menu in this relaxed and casual dining spot includes tried-and-true favorites such as steaks, pastas, and burgers. The kids will enjoy the in-house ice cream bar. Outdoor seating when weather permits. ● *Sun.*	AE MC V	●	■	●	
LINCOLN CITY: *McMenamin's Lighthouse Brew Pub* $$$ 4157 N Hwy 101, Suite 117. ☎ *(541) 994-7238.* The usual fine pub grub is offered at this location of the McMenamin's chain, situated in a shopping center. Ales with he-man names such as Liquidator, Terminator, and Hammerhead quench the toughest thirst.	AE DC MC V	●		●	
LINCOLN CITY: *Avanti Italian Cuisine* $$$$ 3521 SW Hwy 101. ☎ *(541) 996-8178.* This charming ocean-view restaurant offers a menu of dishes – mainly pasta and seafood – combining the vivid flavors of southern Italy.	AE DC MC V	●		●	
MCMINNVILLE: *Geraldi's Italian Eating Place* $$$ 226 E 3rd St. ☎ *(503) 472-7868.* This informal, family-friendly eatery serves a good selection of pastas, as well as other Italian classics, in its pleasant dining room. ● *Sun.*	AE MC V	●		●	

For key to symbols see back flap

<table>
<tr><td colspan="2">

Price categories, in US dollars (US$1 = CAN$1.50), for a three-course meal and a half bottle of house wine, including taxes and service:
Ⓢ under $25
ⓈⓈ $25–$35
ⓈⓈⓈ $35–$50
ⓈⓈⓈⓈ $50–$70
ⓈⓈⓈⓈⓈ over $70

</td><td>

CREDIT CARDS
Indicates which credit cards are accepted: *AE* American Express; *DC* Diners Club; *MC* MasterCard/Access; *V* Visa.

VEGETARIAN
A selection of vegetarian dishes available.

OUTDOOR SEATING
Garden, terrace, or courtyard with outside seating available.

CHILDREN WELCOME
Children's menu or portions; highchairs available.

LATE OPENING
Full meals or light menu served after 11pm.

</td></tr>
</table>

	CREDIT CARDS	VEGETARIAN	OUTDOOR SEATING	CHILDREN WELCOME	LATE OPENING

McMINNVILLE: *McMenamin's Hotel Oregon*   ⓈⓈⓈ   AE MC V   ●   ■   ●
310 NE Evans St. 【 *(503) 472-8427.*
This restored 1905 hotel is home to a terrific pub with a 40-ft- (13-m-) long bar, which also doubles as a dining area. Weekend brunch here is popular, as are the substantial sandwiches and soups.

SALEM: *Padington's Pizza Parlor*   ⓈⓈ   AE MC V   ●   ●
5255 Commercial St SE. 【 *(503) 370-7556.*
Locals and visitors flock to this family-run and family-friendly pizza place that is always bustling. Not licensed.

SALEM: *Roadhouse Grill and Saloon*   ⓈⓈⓈ   AE DC MC V   ●   ●
481 Lancaster Dr NE. 【 *(503) 375-0942.*
It must be the mix of well-presented American classics such as steaks, chops, and grilled chicken, accompanied by music from old-fashioned jukeboxes, that keep patrons coming back to this easy-going restaurant. ♬

SEATTLE

PIKE PLACE MARKET AND THE WATERFRONT

ATHENIAN INN   Ⓢ   AE DC MC V   ●   ●
1517 Pike Pl. **Map** 3 C1. 【 *(206) 624-7166.*
More renowned for its view than the food itself, this beloved old-timer in Pike Place Market offers friendly service along with its extensive menu of American fare (mainly fish dishes) and microbrews. ● *6:30pm.*

JACK'S FISH SPOT   Ⓢ   AE DC MC V   ■   ●
1514 Pike Pl. **Map** 3 C1. 【 *(206) 467-0514.*
This no-nonsense eatery is a must-try for some of the best fish-and-chips and chowder in the city. Seattle native and owner Jack Mathers is often on hand to assist customers with their selections. ● *5pm.*

BACCO CAFÉ AND JUICE BAR   ⓈⓈ   MC V   ●   ●
86 Pine St. **Map** 3 C1. 【 *(206) 443-5443.*
Follow the scent of baking waffles to this hidden gem decorated in vibrant Mediterranean tones. Fresh juices and hearty breakfast fare are the main draws, but the fresh sandwiches and salads are good, too. ● *3pm.*

DISH D'LISH   ⓈⓈ   AE DC MC V   ●   ●
1505 Pike Pl. **Map** 3 C1. 【 *(206) 223-1848.*
Enjoy terrific take-out from one of Seattle's most beloved food personalities, Kathy Casey. Everything, from the incredibly rich cakes to the macaroni and cheese, is tasty and satisfying. ● *6pm; Sun.*

VIRGINIA INN AND TAVERN   ⓈⓈ   AE MC V   ●   ■   ■
1937 1st Ave. **Map** 3 B1. 【 *(206) 728-1937.*
As well as being an atmospheric spot for dining on tasty fare, such as *tapenade* and chicken gumbo, this local centenarian is also a popular watering hole, which proudly displays a variety of local artists' works.

CAFÉ CAMPAGNE   ⓈⓈⓈ   AE DC MC V   ●   ■   ●
1600 Post Alley. **Map** 3 B1. 【 *(206) 728-2233.*
Although brunches here are exceptional, all the food is delicious at this snug, mellow French café (sister restaurant to the more pricey Campagne, upstairs), with a convivial long bar. Notable menu items include the steak *frites* and the tenderloin sandwich with gorgonzola *aioli*.

MATT'S IN THE MARKET   ⓈⓈⓈ   AE MC V   ●   ●
94 Pike St, Ste 32. **Map** 3 C1. 【 *(206) 467-7909.*
Tucked into the Corner Market Building, this tiny restaurant is celebrated for its po' boy sandwich fillings, catfish or oyster. Expect a warm, neighborly welcome. Not wheelchair accessible. ● *dinner Sun, Mon.*

THE PINK DOOR $$$ · AE DC MC V
1919 Post Alley. **Map** 3 B1. *(206) 443-3241.*
Decorated in "Italian Garage Sale" style, according to its owner, this lively *trattoria* serves up hearty, rustic fare. There's a free cabaret show Tuesday nights, but many diners like to simply relax on the patio overlooking Puget Sound. *Sun, Mon.*

PLACE PIGALLE $$$$ · AE DC MC V
81 Pike St. **Map** 3 C1. *(206) 624-1756.*
A perfect spot for a romantic evening, this classic bistro presents Pacific Northwestern cuisine with European and New Mexican influences; some of its imaginative fish dishes are award-winning. *Sun.*

VIVANDA $$$$ · AE MC V
95 Pine St. **Map** 3 C1. *(206) 219-6917.*
Seafood and Mediterranean flavors combine expertly in the imaginative menu offerings at this newcomer in Pike Place Market. The decor is hip and colorful, the view of Puget Sound outstanding.

SEATTLE CENTER AND BELLTOWN

PIZZERIA PAGLIACCI $$ · AE MC V
550 Queen Anne Ave N. **Map** 1 B3. *(206) 285-1232.*
The folks here at one of Seattle's most popular pizzerias stick to their tried-and-true recipe: New York–style pizza with a "thin and tangy" crust.

SAM'S SUSHI $$ · MC V
521 Queen Anne Ave N. **Map** 1 B3. *(206) 282-4612.*
This simple, no-nonsense Japanese emporium serves reliably good *sushi*, *gyoza* (pork dumplings), and *teriyaki*.

PESO'S $$$ · AE MC V
605 Queen Anne Ave N. **Map** 1 B3. *(206) 283-9353.*
This popular Mexican restaurant, decorated in *über*-cheesy style, fills up on weekends. The food packs a spicy punch, and is consistently good. Highlights include the meat dishes and the award-winning margaritas.

THE MELTING POT $$$$ · AE MC V
14 Mercer St. **Map** 1 B3. *(206) 378-1208.*
Although part of a growing chain, the Melting Pot is still a novel dining experience with its wide variety of savory and sweet fondue offerings. Non-fondue dishes are also available at this upscale dining venue.

FARTHER AFIELD

IVAR'S ACRES OF CLAMS $ · AE MC V
Pier 54, Alaskan Way, Seattle. *(206) 624-6852.*
A veritable Seattle institution, this classic fish-and-chips bar offers outstanding clam and salmon dishes. Many diners like to sit out on the dock and feed the seagulls their spare French fries.

MAMA'S MEXICAN KITCHEN $$ · AE MC V
2234 2nd Ave, Seattle. *(206) 728-6262.*
Locals love the unpretentious American-Mexican cuisine served amid Elvis kitsch and loud music at this eatery, in business for nearly 25 years. The outdoor patio is a great spot to enjoy a margarita.

NOODLE RANCH $$ · AE MC V
2228 2nd Ave, Seattle. *(206) 728-0463.*
This hip restaurant features a menu of innovative, Pan-Asian noodle dishes, such as the Mekong bowl with marinated chicken, *gyoza* (pork dumplings), and various *udon* noodle–based dishes. *Sun.*

TOI $$ · AE DC MC V
1904 4th Ave, Seattle. *(206) 219-6915.*
This trendy Thai spot tends to attract a stylish crowd that appreciates the menu of dishes blending new and traditional cooking styles, with offerings like grilled prawn *satay*. The bar is popular for people-watching.

ASSAGGIO RISTORANTE $$$ · AE DC MC V
2010 4th Ave, Seattle. *(206) 441-1399.*
The owner at this perennial favorite ensures a genial welcome along with generous portions of tasty northern Italian dishes. Specialties include *fusilli* with homemade sausage, and sturgeon with red grape sauce. *Sun.*

<table>
<tr><td>

Price categories, in US dollars (US$1 = CAN$1.50), for a three-course meal and a half bottle of house wine, including taxes and service:
$ under $25
$$ $25–$35
$$$ $35–$50
$$$$ $50–$70
$$$$$ over $70

</td><td>

CREDIT CARDS
Indicates which credit cards are accepted: *AE* American Express; *DC* Diners Club; *MC* MasterCard/Access; *V* Visa.

VEGETARIAN
A selection of vegetarian dishes available.

OUTDOOR SEATING
Garden, terrace, or courtyard with outside seating available.

CHILDREN WELCOME
Children's menu or portions; highchairs available.

LATE OPENING
Full meals or light menu served after 11pm.

</td></tr>
</table>

	CREDIT CARDS	VEGETARIAN	OUTDOOR SEATING	CHILDREN WELCOME	LATE OPENING
ELLIOTT'S OYSTER HOUSE $$$ Pier 56, 1201 Alaskan Way, Seattle. (206) 623-4340. This convivial seafood house on the waterfront has an interior distinguished by teak, copper, and rough-hewn timber. Locals and tourists alike sit at the 21-ft- (7-m-) long bar for local brews and raw oysters on the half shell.	AE MC V	●	■	●	
'OHANA $$$ 2207 1st Ave, Seattle. (206) 956-9329. The funky Tiki decor in this fun restaurant sets the mood for Polynesian fare and colorful drinks. Outstanding *sushi* is served at the bar.	AE DC MC V	●			■
WILD GINGER $$$ 1401 3rd Ave, Seattle. (206) 623-4450. Said by some to be Seattle's preeminent Pan-Asian fusion eatery, this well-loved spot does not disappoint. Its menu includes tangy soups and items from the popular Satay Bar, such as grilled scallops and boar meat.	AE DC MC V	●			■
CACTUS $$$$ 121 Park Lane, Kirkland. (425) 893-9799. Cactus is a fun, energetic Latin-American restaurant with a patio lounge that attracts Eastside revelers. Enjoy the Mexican nouvelle cuisine offerings, as well as a good *tapas* selection.	AE DC MC V	●	■		
DAHLIA LOUNGE $$$$ 2001 4th Ave, Seattle. (206) 682-4142. Constantly redefining Pacific Northwest cuisine, celebrity chef Tom Douglas serves sophisticated fare, such as *foie gras* with lavender-caramel and flat-iron steak, in his trendy, crimson-colored dining room. ● *Sun.*	AE DC MC V	●			■
FLYING FISH $$$$ 2234 1st Ave, Seattle. (206) 728-8595. A world of fresh fish dishes are found on the Asian-inspired seafood menu of this upbeat Belltown dining spot. The salt-and-pepper crab is a specialty.	AE DC MC V	●	■		■
KINGFISH CAFÉ $$$$ 602 19th Ave E, Seattle. (206) 320-8757. Lineups tend to form early at this upscale soul food restaurant – it doesn't accept reservations – by those wishing to enjoy savory Southern-style favorites such as grits and succotash, and the standout, catfish.	AE MC V	●		●	
PALACE KITCHEN $$$$ 2030 5th Ave, Seattle. (206) 448-2001. One of two Seattle establishments owned by chef Tom Douglas, this stark, wood-trimmed restaurant specializes in rotisserie meats, seafood, and robust American fare. Specialties include crab cakes and roast venison loin.	AE DC MC V	●		●	■
HERBFARM RESTAURANT $$$$$ 14590 NE 145th St, Woodinville. (425) 222-7103. Reputed to be the most extravagant dinner in the Pacific Northwest, each beautifully presented dish in this restaurant's nine-course meal is paired with a local wine to create a unique gastronomic experience. Reservations required.	AE DC MC V	●			
METROPOLITAN GRILL $$$$$ 820 2nd Ave, Seattle. (206) 624-3287. Long an establishment for Seattle's powerbrokers, this quietly luxurious steakhouse is a warm and sophisticated setting for enjoying what are possibly the best beef dishes in the city.	AE DC MC V	●			
WATERFRONT SEAFOOD GRILL $$$$$ 2801 Alaskan Way, Seattle. (206) 956-9171. This celebrated seafood house is full of sophistication – even the cocktails are chic. The Puget Sound views afforded from the pier-top dining room accompany dishes such as the specialty sesame seed–encrusted sea bass. ♫	AE DC MC V	●	■		

WASHINGTON

ASHFORD: *Alexander's Country Inn and Restaurant* $$$ MC V
37515 State Rd 706 E. ☎ *(800) 654-7615.*
The dining room of this country inn has a warm, inviting feel. House specialties include the rainbow trout (fresh from the on-site pond) and the homemade blackberry pie.

BELLINGHAM: *Pepper Sisters* $$$ MC V
1055 N State St. ☎ *(360) 671-3414.*
Centrally located in a historic commercial building, this cheerful bistro presents imaginative Southwestern fare, such as cilantro grilled salmon and spicy eggplant *tostada*. Dinner only. ● *Mon.*

CHELAN: *Banjo Creek Farms* $$$ AE MC V
Green Ave, Manson. ☎ *(509) 687-0708.*
Situated on a working farm just east of Chelan, this unique and fun dining experience offers a barbeque dinner, which includes rattlesnake meat appetizers and choice of entrées, accompanied by live bluegrass music. The horse-drawn carriage rides are popular with kids young and old. Dinner only.

CHELAN: *La LaGuna Restaurant* $$$ MC V
114 N Emerson St. ☎ *(509) 682-5553.*
This local favorite provides a menu loaded with seafood options, such as prawn and grilled halibut *fajitas*, along with more traditional Mexican fare. The *salsas* and salads are made fresh daily.

EASTSOUND: *Sunflower Café* $$$$ AE MC V
Prune Alley and A St, Orcas Island. ☎ *(360) 376-2335.*
A recent addition to the Eastsound restaurant scene, this hip café attracts locals and tourists alike with its menu of inventive Pacific Northwest fusion cuisine, beautifully presented, served in its simple but stylish dining room.

ELLENSBURG: *Valley Café* $$$
105 W 3rd Ave. ☎ *(509) 925-3050.*
With its unassuming façade, it might be easy to overlook this charming Art Deco bistro, but then you would miss the enticing menu loaded with locally raised meats and produce, as well as the pick of local wines.

FRIDAY HARBOR: *Fat Cat Café* $ AE DC MC V
275 A St, San Juan Island. ☎ *(360) 378-8646.*
Substantial helpings of American breakfast and lunch mainstays – eggs and hash browns, burgers and veggie wraps – are served here. Its outdoor patio offers what are possibly the most comfortable lounger seats on the island.

FRIDAY HARBOR: *The Place Next to the San Juan Ferry* $$$$ AE DC MC V
1 Spring St, San Juan Island. ☎ *(360) 378-8707.*
Diners can enjoy beautiful views of Friday Harbor while sampling classic dishes such as *filet mignon* and *bouillabaisse*. Works by local artisans are displayed throughout the dining area. Dinner only.

LEAVENWORTH: *Echo Bistro* $$$ AE DC MC V
911 Commercial St. ☎ *(509) 548-9685.*
This cheery restaurant, located in a turn-of-the-19th-century home, is popular for its mixed-grill items and handmade German sausage. A great selection of German brews is served in the large outdoor *biergarten*.

LEAVENWORTH: *Restaurant Österreich* $$$ AE MC V
633A Front St. ☎ *(509) 548-4031.*
This elegant restaurant is a step up from the many local schnitzel houses, with an award-winning menu of beautifully presented dishes – think edible flowers – of European, and particularly Bavarian, origin. Dinner only. ● *Mon, Tue.*

LOPEZ VILLAGE: *Love Dog Café* $$$ AE MC V
Village Center, Lopez Island. ☎ *(360) 468-2150.*
This pretty Italian restaurant serves hearty pastas and other rustic Italian fare. Fresh flowers and candlelight suggest romance, but families will enjoy the heaped portions and cozy yet casual atmosphere. ● *Wed.*

MAZAMA: *The Freestone Inn* $$$$ AE MC V
31 Early Winters Dr. ☎ *(509) 996-3906.*
The mountain views and massive stone hearth are as memorable as the food at the dining room of this luxury lakeside inn in the North Cascades. The chef uses the best of local products to create a seasonally changing menu.

For key to symbols see back flap

Price categories, in US dollars (US$1 = CAN$1.50), for a three-course meal and a half bottle of house wine, including taxes and service:
$ under $25
$$ $25–$35
$$$ $35–$50
$$$$ $50–$70
$$$$$ over $70

CREDIT CARDS
Indicates which credit cards are accepted: *AE* American Express; *DC* Diners Club; *MC* MasterCard/Access; *V* Visa.
VEGETARIAN
A selection of vegetarian dishes available.
OUTDOOR SEATING
Garden, terrace, or courtyard with outside seating available.
CHILDREN WELCOME
Children's menu or portions; highchairs available.
LATE OPENING
Full meals or light menu served after 11pm.

	CREDIT CARDS	VEGETARIAN	OUTDOOR SEATING	CHILDREN WELCOME	LATE OPENING
MOUNT ST HELENS: *19 Mile House* $$ 9440 Spirit Lake Hwy. (*(360) 274-8779.* At Milepost 19 on the Spirit Lake Highway sits this small restaurant overlooking the Toutle River, one of the few eateries in the Monument area. Noted for its delicious berry cobblers. ● *Nov–Apr.*	MC V	●		●	
OLYMPIA: *The Urban Onion* $$ 116 Legion Way. (*(360) 943-9242.* Inside the historic Olympian Hotel, this funky restaurant with tall windows and cozy booths offers a varied menu, with imaginative vegetarian fare dominating. Weekend breakfasts are popular.	AE MC V	●	■	●	
PORT TOWNSEND: *Sentosa Sushi* $$ 218 Polk St. (*(360) 385-2378.* A great place to dine on a variety of *sushi* and Pan-Asian noodle dishes in a relaxing setting, Sentosa's menu showcases the pick of the local fish and seafood bounty. Some vegan menu choices also offered.	AE MC V	●			
PORT TOWNSEND: *The Silverwater Café* $$$ 237 Taylor St. (*(360) 385-6448.* Outstanding soups and seafood dishes are the highlights here. Using the best of locally harvested products, chefs prepare creative Pacific Northwest cuisine, to be enjoyed in the light-filled and elegant dining room.	AE DC MC V	●		●	
SPOKANE: *Niko's II Greek and Middle Eastern Restaurant* $$$ 725 W Riverside Ave. (*(509) 624-7444.* The recently added wine bar enhances the already lively atmosphere at this upbeat spot. Stick with the more traditional dishes, such as *souvlaki* and *calamari* steaks, that Niko's has built its reputation on. ● *Sun.*	AE DC MC V	●		●	■
SPOKANE: *Paprika* $$$$$ 1228 S Grand Blvd. (*(509) 455-7545.* Paprika prides itself on its creative, seasonally changing menu, with highlight dishes such as braised rabbit with chestnuts. The artwork displayed here was created by the restaurant's sous-chef. ● *Sun, Mon.*	AE MC V	●		●	
TACOMA: *El Gaucho* $$$$$ 2119 Pacific Ave. (*(253) 272-1510.* This stylish steakhouse attracts a sophisticated crowd, with a menu that features sirloin steaks and seafood dishes. The cigar lounge is popular for martinis and after-dinner drinks. ♬	AE DC MC V	●			■
WALLA WALLA: *Merchants LTD* $$ 21 E Main St. (*(509) 525-0900.* A great spot for healthy and hearty breakfasts and lunches, this eatery covers the space of three red-brick storefronts along Main Street. It also has an in-house bakery and a gourmet groceries section. ● *Sun.*	AE MC V	●	■	●	
WALLA WALLA: *Grapefields* $$$ 4 E Main St. (*(509) 522-3993.* As with many restaurants in this area, Grapefields puts a strong focus on the region's wine offerings. It does a good job of matching Washington state's finest with light, elegant fare served in a stylish dining setting. ● *Sun.* ♬	AE DC MC V	●		●	
YAKIMA: *Grant's Brewery Pub* $$ 32 N Front St. (*(509) 575-2922.* Soak up the atmosphere in this historic building, formerly the Yakima train station. Better-than-average pub grub and some fine ales are served. ♬	AE MC V	●		●	
YAKIMA: *Birchfield Manor Restaurant* $$$$ 2018 Birchfield Rd. (*(509) 452-1960.* This charming Victorian inn *(see p291)* prides itself on the fine French country cuisine offered in the cozy dining room. Its European-trained chef presents six main dishes with well-considered wine choices.	AE DC MC V	●		●	

VANCOUVER

WATERFRONT, GASTOWN, AND CHINATOWN

FLOATA $$$
400-180 Keefer St. **Map** 3 C3. 【 *(604) 602-0368.*
There is plenty of room in this large Chinatown restaurant, even during the popular *dim sum* hours (busiest between 11am and 2pm). The emphasis is on seafood, but highlights also include Peking duck and the dessert buffet.

AE DC MC V ● ●

STEAMWORKS BREWING COMPANY $$$
375 Water St. **Map** 3 B2. 【 *(604) 689-2739.*
Housed on two floors of a stone building on the edge of Gastown, this popular spot serves good thin-crust designer pizzas, ahi tuna, and steamed shellfish. A variety of beers brewed in-house are offered on tap.

AE DC MC V ● ■ ●

DOWNTOWN

EZOGIKU NOODLE CAFÉ $
270 Robson St. **Map** 3 A3. 【 *(604) 685-9466.*
This small, trendy Japanese noodle house offers a short but popular menu: thick Sapporo-style *ramen* in *miso*, *shoyu* (soya), or *shio* (pork) broth; thin or chilled noodles; and *gyoza* (pork dumplings).

■

DIVA AT THE MET $$$$
645 Howe St. **Map** 3 A2. 【 *(604) 602-7788.*
A well-lit, multitiered dining room surrounds an open kitchen where chefs turn organic, local ingredients into modern dishes such as the restaurant's signature Alaskan black cod with fennel marmalade.

AE DC MC V ● ■ ●

FLEURI RESTAURANT $$$$
845 Burrard St. **Map** 2 F2. 【 *(604) 642-2900.*
Tucked inside the Sutton Place Hotel *(see p291)*, Fleuri is the perfect restaurant for special occasions. Its menu stresses innovative French cooking; highlights include the seafood buffet and the Chocoholic Bar.

AE DC MC V ● ●

CHARTWELL $$$$$
791 W Georgia St. **Map** 2 F2. 【 *(604) 844-6715.*
Walnut paneling and oak parquet floors provide a quietly dignified setting for fine dining. This restaurant, in the Four Seasons Hotel *(see p291)*, offers gourmet five-course tasting menus and a three-course pre-theater menu.

AE DC MC V ● ●

GRANVILLE SOUTH AND YALETOWN

BRIDGES $$$
1696 Duranleau St, Granville Island. **Map** 2 D4. 【 *(604) 687-4400.*
Bridges offers a choice of three dining experiences: a fine dining room upstairs; a more casual bistro and a lounge serving selections from local microbreweries downstairs. Upper floor dining area not wheelchair accessible.

AE DC MC V ● ■ ● ■

URBAN THAI $$$
1119 Hamilton St. **Map** 2 F4. 【 *(604) 408-7788.*
The menu at this funky spot combines elements of Thai and other Asian spicing and Western ingredients, resulting in notable dishes such as *osso bucco* Thai-style. More traditional offerings include chicken *satay* and curries.

AE MC V ● ■ ●

BLUE WATER CAFE AND RAW BAR $$$$
1095 Hamilton St. **Map** 2 F4. 【 *(604) 688-8078.*
This restaurant, situated in a 100-year-old converted warehouse, offers a menu that emphasizes locally harvested wild seafood, and features the city's largest selection of oysters.

AE DC MC V ● ■ ● ■

C RESTAURANT $$$$
1600 Howe St. **Map** 2 D4. 【 *(604) 681-1164.*
One of the city's most innovative venues for seafood, C presents entrées such as pan-roasted sablefish with black beluga lentils, which can be enjoyed while taking in the view of False Creek.

AE DC MC V ● ■

FARTHER AFIELD

HON'S WUN-TUN HOUSE $
1339 Robson St, Vancouver. 【 *(604) 685-0871.*
Enjoy fast, satisfying food at this restaurant specializing in Cantonese dishes to eat in or take out. Noted for the noodles, potstickers, and *dim sum*, it also offers a separate, fully vegetarian menu.

MC V ● ● ■

For key to symbols see back flap

Price categories, in US dollars (US$1 = CAN$1.50), for a three-course meal and a half bottle of house wine, including taxes and service:
$ under $25
$$ $25–$35
$$$ $35–$50
$$$$ $50–$70
$$$$$ over $70

CREDIT CARDS
Indicates which credit cards are accepted: *AE* American Express; *DC* Diners Club; *MC* MasterCard/Access; *V* Visa.

VEGETARIAN
A selection of vegetarian dishes available.

OUTDOOR SEATING
Garden, terrace, or courtyard with outside seating available.

CHILDREN WELCOME
Children's menu or portions; highchairs available.

LATE OPENING
Full meals or light menu served after 11pm.

	CREDIT CARDS	VEGETARIAN	OUTDOOR SEATING	CHILDREN WELCOME	LATE OPENING
PINK PEARL $$ 1132 E Hastings St, Vancouver. (604) 253-4316. A perennial favorite, this restaurant is often crowded with Chinese families enjoying outstanding *dim sum*. Dinner specialties include Peking duck.	AE MC V	●		●	
SAMI'S $$ 986 W Broadway Ave, Vancouver. (604) 736-8330. A distinctive fusion of North American and Indian cuisines, plus warm greetings and attentive service are to be found here. Try the minted mango and fresh ginger soup, or turkey satchels (pan-seared won tons).	MC V	●		●	
STEPHO'S SOUVLAKI GREEK TAVERNA $$ 1124 Davie St, Vancouver. (604) 683-2555. Both the quality and value of this lively West End restaurant are excellent. Traditional Greek fare, such as the ever-popular *souvlaki* and the roast lamb, is served in generous portions. Lineups are common at dinnertime.	AE MC V	●		●	
CIPRIANO'S RISTORANTE AND PIZZERIA $$$ 3995 Main St, Vancouver. (604) 879-0020. Cipriano's offers huge servings of pasta, pizza, and other northern Italian specialties in the intimate, softly-lit dining room. Especially good are the Caesar *alla Christina* salad and veal *Calabrese*. Dinner only. ● *Sun, Mon.*	V	●			
híwas FEASTHOUSE AND CULTURAL CENTRE $$$ 6400 Nancy Green Way, N Vancouver. (604) 980-9311. Set atop Grouse Mountain, this Native center presents an authentic five-course feast in a traditional longhouse accompanied by song, dance, and storytelling. Dinner ticket includes tram to and from mountain top. ● *Sun-Wed; Nov-Apr.*	AE DC MC V				
KIRIN SEAFOOD RESTAURANT $$$ 3 West Centre, 7900 Westminster Hwy, Richmond. (604) 303-8833. Enjoy Cantonese, Shanghai, and Szechuan specialties and award-winning *dim sum* at this restaurant popular with families. Excellent service.	AE DC MC V	●		●	
SALMON HOUSE ON THE HILL $$$ 2229 Folkestone Way, W Vancouver. (604) 926-3212. This restaurant, perched high in the hills of West Vancouver, is noted for its specialty, green alderwood–grilled BC salmon. The rustic yet elegant interior of wood and glass is adorned with First Nations art and artifacts.	AE DC MC V	●			
SUN SUI WAH SEAFOOD RESTAURANT $$$ 3888 Main St, Vancouver. (604) 872-8822. Glass awnings and a curved staircase welcome guests into a stunning interior. This restaurant offers an enticing *dim sum* selection; notable entrées include Alaska king crab and the house specialty, roast squab.	AE MC V	●		●	
VIJ'S $$$ 1480 W 11th Ave, Vancouver. (604) 736-6664. Expect lineups here, as no reservations are accepted and the food, a West Coast adaptation of various Indian cooking styles, is fabulous. Specialties include tea-braised halibut in ginger and black chickpea curry. Dinner only.	AE MC V	●		●	
HART HOUSE ON DEER LAKE $$$$ 6664 Deer Lake Ave, Burnaby. (604) 298-4278. An ideal venue for a special occasion, this traditional restaurant presents a menu full of West Coast offerings. The setting is pastoral: elegant dining areas in a Tudor mansion, situated in a lakefront park. ● *Mon.*	AE MC V	●	■		
RAINCITY GRILL $$$$ 1193 Denman St, Vancouver. (604) 685-7337. This popular West End fixture is well known for its commitment to using local produce. The Prince George lamb is a favorite on a menu built around regional seafood, meats, and organic vegetables.	AE DC MC V	●	■		

TOJO'S $$$$
777 W Broadway Ave, Vancouver. 【 (604) 872-8050.
Authentic Japanese cuisine and the ultimate in *sushi* is offered from the
hands of owner and master *sushi* chef Hidekazu Tojo. Try *omakase* (chef's
choice) for a tailored, imaginative meal. Dinner only. ● *Sun.*

		AE	●	■	●	
		MC				
		V				

WEST $$$$
2881 Granville St, Vancouver. 【 (604) 738-8938.
Behind the unassuming doorway on South Granville lies a spacious interior
with sleek, geometric decor and a menu featuring contemporary regional
fare. Near the Stanley Theatre, it's ideal for pre- and post-theater dining.

		AE	●			
		DC				
		MC				
		V				

BISHOPS $$$$$
2183 W 4th Ave, Vancouver. 【 (604) 738-2025.
Consistently listed as one of city's top restaurants, Bishop's combines
intimate dining and flawless service. Organic ingredients determine the West
Coast–themed menu, which changes weekly. Dinner only. ● *1st week of Jan.*

		AE				
		MC				
		V				

CINCIN RISTORANTE AND BAR $$$$$
1154 Robson St, Vancouver. 【 (604) 688-7338.
CinCin's imaginative menu emphasizes wood-fire grilled Italian specialties
with other Mediterranean touches. Try the *garganelli* with grain-fed veal
cheeks, or pumpkin *ravioli*. Not wheelchair accessible. ● *lunch Sat & Sun.*

		AE	●	■	●	■
		DC				
		MC				
		V				

FISH HOUSE IN STANLEY PARK $$$$$
8901 Stanley Park Dr, Vancouver. 【 (604) 681-7275 or (877) 681-7275.
This award-winning, contemporary seafood restaurant in beautiful Stanley
Park offers creative Pacific Northwest–inspired dishes, such as seared ahi
tuna with peppercorn sauce. Afternoon tea is also served.

		AE	●	■	●	
		DC				
		MC				
		V				

BRITISH COLUMBIA

COWICHAN BAY: *The Masthead Restaurant* $$$
1705 Cowichan Bay Rd. 【 (250) 748-3714.
This restaurant, housed in the historic original town hall, prides itself on a
menu built around local produce and seafood, and its selection of wines.
Its location right on Cowichan Bay provides lovely harbor views.

		AE	●	■		
		MC				
		V				

CRANBROOK: *Tuscany's Restaurant* $$
209 Van Horne St S. 【 (250) 417-0444.
Situated inside the Prestige Inn, this restaurant offers a menu that pairs
hearty main dishes with its bottomless Tuscana salad and warm sourdough
bread. The dessert offerings are popular.

		AE	●	■		
		DC				
		MC				
		V				

KAMLOOPS: *Chapters Viewpoint Restaurant* $$
610 W Columbia St. 【 (250) 374-3224.
This casual restaurant delivers on the views of the Kamloops landscape
implied by its name. The menu features steaks, seafood, and dishes
incorporating Navajo and Mexican flavors.

		AE	●	■	●	
		DC				
		MC				
		V				

KELOWNA: *de Montreuil* $$$
368 Bernard Ave. 【 (250) 860-5508.
This restaurant's contemporary, casual atmosphere is complemented by a
regularly changing menu that is inspired by the organic producers and
farms of the Cascade Mountain region.

		AE	●			
		DC				
		MC				
		V				

KELOWNA: *The Williams Inn* $$$
526 Lawrence Ave. 【 (250) 763-5136.
Vintage elegance abounds in this two-story restaurant located in a 1906
heritage building. The menu's emphasis is on classic European dishes in
addition to those with a regional focus. A good selection of local wines.

		AE	●	■		
		DC				
		MC				
		V				

MALAHAT: *The Dining Room at the Aerie* $$$$$
600 Ebedora Lane. 【 (250) 743-7115.
This upscale restaurant located inside the Aerie Resort *(see p293)* presents a
menu of beautifully prepared, European-inspired dishes, with an emphasis
on locally grown produce. Enjoy spectacular views of southern Vancouver
Island landscape from the dining room perched above the Malahat Summit.

		AE	●	■		
		DC				
		MC				
		V				

NANAIMO: *Mahle House Restaurant* $$$
2104 Hemer St. 【 (250) 722-3621.
This family-run restaurant, in a distinctive orange 1904 house just outside
Nanaimo, offers a menu incorporating vegetables and herbs harvested from
its own organic gardens, and locally raised venison and rabbit. ● *Mon, Tue.*

		AE	●			
		MC				
		V				

<table>
<tr><td colspan="6">Price categories, in US dollars (US$1 = CAN$1.50), for a three-course meal and a half bottle of house wine, including taxes and service:
$ under $25
$$ $25–$35
$$$ $35–$50
$$$$ $50–$70
$$$$$ over $70</td></tr>
</table>

CREDIT CARDS
Indicates which credit cards are accepted: *AE* American Express; *DC* Diners Club; *MC* MasterCard/Access; *V* Visa.

VEGETARIAN
A selection of vegetarian dishes available.

OUTDOOR SEATING
Garden, terrace, or courtyard with outside seating available.

CHILDREN WELCOME
Children's menu or portions; highchairs available.

LATE OPENING
Full meals or light menu served after 11pm.

	CREDIT CARDS	VEGETARIAN	OUTDOOR SEATING	CHILDREN WELCOME	LATE OPENING
NANAIMO: *Wesley Street Café* $$$ 321 Wesley St. ((250) 753-6057. Classic entrées with contemporary flavors, such as yam-crusted salmon filet, are on offer at this intimate café.	AE MC V	●		●	
NELSON: *All Seasons Café* $$ 620 Herridge Lane. ((250) 352-0101. This comfortable, busy restaurant featuring a tree-canopied patio is found in a restored heritage cottage on a downtown side street. Its diverse, West Coast menu matches a savvy wine list. Dinner only.	MC V	●	■	●	
PARKSVILLE: *Cedar Dining Room* $$$ 1095 E Highland Hwy. ((250) 248-1102 or (800) 663-7373. This elegant restaurant in the Tigh-Na-Mara Resort *(see p294)* presents a menu with a strong Pacific Northwest emphasis, including specialties such as seafood grill and roast rack of lamb. Also offers Sunday brunch.	MC V	●	■	●	
PENTICTON: *Granny Bogner's Restaurant* $$$ 302 W Eckhardt Ave. ((250) 493-2711. Located in a charming, wood-sided heritage house, this restaurant boasts crystal glassware and white linen on the table, and a variety of traditional European dishes on the menu. Not wheelchair accessible. ● *Mon.*	AE MC V	●	■		
PRINCE GEORGE: *Ric's Grill* $$$ 547 George St. ((250) 614-9096. A popular choice for steaks, this comfortable restaurant takes pride in offering Sterling Silver top sirloins, strip loins, tenderloins, and prime rib. There is also a variety of fish and pasta dishes, and a good wine selection.	AE MC V	●		●	
PRINCE RUPERT: *Cow Bay Café* $$ 205 Cow Bay Rd. ((250) 627-1212. It is best to book ahead at this busy 32-seat eatery with a view. Located on the wharf at Prince Rupert Harbour, its daily changing menu presents notables such as crab cakes and various homemade desserts. ● *Sun, Mon.*	AE MC V	●			
QUALICUM BEACH: *Beach House Café* $$$ 2775 W Island Hwy. ((250) 752-9626. This popular waterside restaurant is well situated for viewing beautiful sunsets. Its varied menu features dishes touched with Asian and German flavors, all served in the bright, airy dining room or on the inviting patio.	MC V	●	■	●	
SALTSPRING ISLAND: *Hastings House* $$$$$ 160 Upper Ganges Rd. ((250) 537-2362. A daily-changing five-course, regional menu is offered for dinner in the formal, wood-beamed dining room of this English manor overlooking Ganges Harbour. Saltspring Island lamb is a house specialty. ● *mid-Nov–mid-Mar.*	AE MC V	●	■		
SOOKE: *Sooke Harbour House* $$$$ 1528 Whiffen Spit Rd. ((250) 642-3421. A menu of regional classics, based strictly on wild seafood, free-range meat, and organic produce, has made this restaurant a frequent award winner. The wine list is equally good. Its stunning location affords great harbor views.	AE DC MC V	●		●	
SUMMERLAND: *Cellar Door Bistro* $$$ 17403 Hwy 97 N. ((250) 494-0451. This bistro, located in the Sumac Ridge Estate Winery, expertly pairs Okanagan wines with regional cuisine. Highlights include locally produced cheeses and its pastas and ice creams, made in-house.	AE MC V	●	■	●	
TOFINO: *The Pointe Restaurant* $$$$ Osprey Lane at Chesterman's Beach. ((250) 725-3100. This atmospheric dining room in the Wickaninnish Inn *(see p295)*, famed for its panoramic views, features a grand circular fireplace. Dungeness crab is a popular item on a menu that also includes venison.	AE DC MC V	●	■	●	

UCLUELET: *Matterson House* $ $
1682 Peninsula Rd. (250) 726-2200.
This small, charming restaurant, located in a historic house, serves a variety of breakfast, lunch, and dinner selections. Seafood dishes and in-house baked desserts and pastries are the specialties on offer.
MC V

VICTORIA: *Barb's Place* $
Fisherman's Wharf, 310 St Lawrence St. (250) 384-6515.
With open-air dining at picnic tables, this local favorite for dockside fish-and-chip dinners also serves steamed shellfish and burgers. ● mid-Oct–Feb.
MC V

VICTORIA: *J & J Wonton Noodle House* $ $
1012 Fort St. (250) 383-0680.
A family-style restaurant serving noodles made fresh daily, and featuring a variety of spicy Cantonese and Szechuan dishes. The kitchen window reveals chefs preparing such notables as braised beef hot pot. ● Sun, Mon.
MC V

VICTORIA: *Camille's* $ $ $
45 Bastion Sq. (250) 381-3433.
A historic brick building houses this charming, romantic two-room restaurant. The diverse, frequently changing menu could include locally raised seafood, wild game, ostrich, or emu. An extensive wine list.
AE MC V

VICTORIA: *Pescatore's Fish House and Oyster Bar* $ $ $
614 Humboldt St. (250) 385-4512.
Located on Victoria's Inner Harbour, Pescatore's takes full advantage of the sea's bounty. It offers fresh seafood dishes, a well-stocked oyster bar, and a variety of martinis, cocktails, and BC wines.
AE DC MC V

VICTORIA: *Süze Lounge and Restaurant* $ $ $
515 Yates St. (250) 383-2829.
This young and stylish spot features a reasonably priced, eclectic menu with Asian overtones. One of the city's few late-night eateries. Dinner only.
AE DC MC V

VICTORIA: *Il Terrazzo* $ $ $
555 Johnson St. (250) 361-0028.
This well-known restaurant is set in an original 1890 building and offers northern Italian cuisine such as veal *marsala* and grilled baby squid, as well as wood-fired-oven specialties. Brick fireplaces warm the courtyard terrace.
AE DC MC V

VICTORIA: *Empress Room* $ $ $ $
721 Government St. (250) 389-2727.
Enjoy the sumptuous interior and an impressive menu – a modern fusion of classic cuisine with Pacific Northwest influences – at this fine dining venue in the Fairmont Empress Hotel (see p295). Live harp music.
AE DC MC V

VICTORIA: *Victorian Restaurant* $ $ $ $ $
Delta Victoria Ocean Pointe Resort and Spa, 45 Songhees Rd. (250) 360-5800.
This hotel restaurant offers fine dining on West Coast cuisine. Panoramic city views from the floor-to-ceiling windows are especially dazzling at night when the Parliament Buildings are lit up. Dinner only. ● Jan.
AE DC MC V

WESTBANK: *Terrace Restaurant* $ $ $
1730 Mission Hill Rd. (250) 768-7611.
This outdoor stop at Mission Hill Family Estate Winery provides sweeping views of Okanagan Lake. The menu includes light, seasonal fare, nicely complemented by the winery's selections. Lunch only. ● Nov–May.
AE MC V

WHISTLER: *Chef Bernard's Café* $ $
4573 Chateau Blvd. (604) 932-7051.
Chef Bernard Casavant's tiny café dedicated to fresh foods is popular with locals and tourists alike for its friendly atmosphere, hearty breakfasts, and home-baked pecan cinnamon buns.
AE MC V

WHISTLER: *Tex Corleone's* $ $
4154 Village Green. (604) 932-7427.
A Western-style restaurant serving hearty chicken, ribs, and Chicago-style deep-dish pizza in an interior graced with Old West movie posters. Great fun for kids, who are offered crayons, coloring pages, and cowboy hats.
MC V

WHISTLER: *Trattoria di Umberto Restaurant* $ $ $ $
4417 Sundial Pl. (604) 932-5858.
The warmth of Tuscany is reflected in celebrity chef and Vancouver native Umberto Menghi's inviting decor and imaginative pasta choices. Highlights include *cioppino* (Italian fish chowder) and lamb shanks.
AE DC MC V

For key to symbols see back flap

SHOPPING IN THE PACIFIC NORTHWEST

DOWNTOWN DISTRICTS in the Pacific Northwest provide everything from the luxury goods offered by exclusive stores to bargains that can be picked up in flea markets. Outdoor gear manufactured by world-renowned local companies is popular. Shoppers can also purchase footwear and clothing to suit every taste; many secondhand shops sell vintage clothing and accessories. Other items to

Shop sign in Bellingham's Fairhaven District

shop for are antiques, books, and music from the chain stores and independents; fresh produce; smoked Pacific salmon; and first-class wines. Native American and First Nations jewelry, carvings, paintings, and other handicrafts and artwork are sold throughout the region in specialty shops, cultural centers, and galleries. Delicious Canadian maple syrup is widely available in British Columbia.

Store window filled with antiques in Portland's Sellwood District

SHOPPING HOURS

STORES ARE GENERALLY open seven days a week. Standard hours are from 9 or 10am to 6pm, though many stores and malls remain open until 9pm on certain nights. Sunday hours are usually noon to 5pm. Smaller stores often open at 10am, close at 6pm, and are closed on Sundays or Mondays. The busiest shopping days of the week are Fridays and weekends.

SALES

LOCAL NEWSPAPERS are a good source of information on upcoming sales. End-of-season sales can offer as much as 70 percent off the regular price. In the days – and in some cases, weeks – following Christmas, many stores offer huge discounts and specials.

PAYMENT

MOST STORES accept all major credit cards, with Visa and MasterCard being the most popular. "Direct payment" with bank debit cards at point-of-sale terminals are also widely used. Traveler's checks are readily accepted with proper identification, such as a valid passport or a driver's license.

Hat store at Vancouver's Granville Island, one of many specialty shops

In most US stores, foreign currency is not accepted, whereas many Canadian stores will accept both US and Canadian currencies. However, the exchange rate offered by stores is generally substantially lower than what a bank or currency exchange office will give. Personal checks are rarely accepted.

SALES TAX

SALES TAXES VARY depending on which state or province you are visiting, and in the US they can vary depending on where you are within a state. In Washington, taxes are in the 8 to 9 percent range (with Seattle's at 8.6 percent), though groceries are exempt. Out-of-state or foreign visitors to Seattle who have no sales tax at home are exempt, provided they show

Glasshouse, Seattle's oldest glassblowing studio, at Pioneer Square

ID such as a valid driver's license. In Oregon, there is no sales tax. In British Columbia, a 7.5 percent provincial sales tax (PST) and a 7 percent federal Goods and Service Tax (GST) apply to most goods; the major exception is basic food items. Taxes are usually added to the price at the time of purchase, so price tags rarely include taxes.

Visitors to Canada can apply for a GST rebate on some items within 60 days of the date of purchase *(see p326)*.

RETURNS

B E SURE you understand the store's return policy before you pay. Each store sets its own return and exchange policies; they are generally posted at the cash register. Some stores offer full refunds, while others maintain an all-sales-final policy or give an in-shop credit note rather than a refund.

Keep your receipt as a proof of purchase, should you decide to return the item or find that it is defective. Sale items are usually not returnable.

Fruit stall at Granville Island's public market, Vancouver

MARKETS

F ARMERS' MARKETS held in cities and rural communities across the Pacific Northwest sell locally grown fruits and vegetables. Apples, apricots, plums, cherries, berries, tomatoes, and zucchini are common offerings. Some markets also sell seafood, baked goods, flowers, crafts, and locally made souvenirs.

Markets range from large and sheltered, such as **Granville Island Public Market** *(see*

Wine shop at Chateau Ste. Michelle, one of Washington's top vineyards

p219) in Vancouver and **Pike Place Market** *(see pp132–5)* in Seattle, to medium-sized open-air markets, such as the **Saturday Market** in Portland's Old Town District *(see pp52–3)*, to small markets consisting of a few trucks parked in a lot or field. Many of the seafood merchants at these markets, particularly the larger ones, will ship fresh fish to your home.

Most of the larger markets are open year round, whereas many of the smaller markets may be seasonal, running from early spring to late fall.

OUTLET STORES

S HOPPERS CAN FIND great bargains at outlet malls, sometimes saving as much as 70 percent off the regular price.

Oregon is home to the **Columbia Gorge Factory Stores**, east of Portland in Troutdale. **Factory Stores @ Lincoln City**, the largest factory outlet center in the Pacific Northwest, offers tax-free shopping. Washington's 49-shop **Factory Stores at North Bend** is located east of Seattle.

British Columbia's outlet centers include the **Roots** and **Danier Leather** factory outlets in Burnaby, just east of Vancouver.

FINE WINES

T HE PACIFIC NORTHWEST produces world-class pinot noirs, chardonnays, and rieslings, as well as dessert wines, such as late harvest wines and flavorful icewines made from grapes that are picked

and crushed while frozen. Pinot gris and pinot blanc are also becoming increasingly important varieties.

Hundreds of wineries in Oregon's Willamette Valley *(see pp98–9)*, Washington's Yakima Valley *(see p191)*, the greater Puget Sound area, and British Columbia's Okanagan Valley *(see pp258–9)* offer guided tours and wine tastings. Most of the wineries also sell directly to the public.

Winegrowers' associations in Oregon, Washington, and British Columbia provide visitors with maps and guides to regional wineries, as well as information about special events, such as Washington Wine Month (March), the Oregon Wine and Art Auction, and the Okanagan Fall Wine Festival, in British Columbia.

Kite store to suit all tastes and winds, Lincoln City, Oregon

Outdoor Activities

THE DRAMATICALLY VARIED TERRAIN and beautiful landscapes of the Pacific Northwest make it an ideal region for a wide range of outdoor activities, from such peaceful pursuits as bird-watching, whale-watching, hiking, and fishing to more exhilarating sports such as skiing, snowboarding, scuba diving, and white-water rafting. For information about particular activities, equipment rentals, instruction, and guided tours, contact the state or provincial tourist offices.

Dune buggies on Oregon's sand dunes, near Florence

Kite-boarding on the Hood River, off the Columbia River Gorge

ADVENTURE SPORTS

THE DRAMATIC LANDSCAPE of the Pacific Northwest offers countless possibilities for thrill-seekers, such as hang gliding, paragliding, kite-boarding, hot-air ballooning, and sky-diving, to name just a few.

In Oregon, both Lakeview, in the south, and Cape Kiwanda, in the north, provide ideal conditions for hang gliding and paragliding, as does **Chelan Sky Park** in Washington. In British Columbia, the most popular spot for these sports is Malahat, north of Victoria, offering spectacular views of the Saanich Peninsula and Strait of Georgia. For more information about hang gliding and paragliding in BC, contact the **Hang Gliding and Paragliding Association of Canada**.

Hot-air ballooning offers another exciting way to get a bird's-eye view of the region. To float over Oregon's wine country in a balloon, contact **Vista Balloon Adventures**, or to see southern Oregon

from above, contact **Oregon Adventures Aloft**. In Washington, you can take a balloon ride over the Methow Valley and enjoy a champagne brunch with **Morning Glory Balloon Tours**, or fly over the Woodinville area vineyards with **Over the Rainbow**. In British Columbia, **Pegasus Ballooning** operates out of Surrey and **Fantasy Balloon Charters** is located at Langley Municipal Airport.

BEACHES

THE SHORELINES of the Pacific Northwest are among the most scenic in the world. Although the waters are cool, swimming offers refreshment during the summer months.

The **Oregon Dunes National Recreation Area**, between Florence and Coos Bay, comprises 32,000 acres (12,800 ha) of huge sand dunes, some more than 500 ft (150 m) tall. Higher than those of the Sahara Desert, these steep dunes are ideal for sandboarding. The Umpqua Scenic Dunes Trail, 30 miles (48 km) south of Florence and approximately

one mile (1.6 km) long, skirts the tallest dunes in the area. Enjoy the breathtaking views from the boardwalk's overlook, located 24 miles (39 km) north of North Bend.

Oregon's top beaches include Bandon, **Oswald West State Park**, **Cannon Beach**, and **Sunset Bay State Park** beaches, and the beaches of the **Samuel H. Boardman State Scenic Corridor**.

Deception Pass State Park beaches, in the Puget Sound area, are located in Washington's most popular state park. A 15-minute drive from downtown Seattle, **Alki Beach** *(see p159)* offers a panoramic view of the city's skyline and of Elliott Bay. Other particularly beautiful beaches in Washington include Dungeness Spit, the longest saltwater sand spit in North America, and the sandy and cliff-lined beaches in **Olympic National Park**.

In British Columbia, among the beaches that dot Vancouver's shoreline the most popular are English Bay, Sunset *(see p220)*, Kitsilano, Jericho, Locarno, Spanish Banks, and the Second and Third Beaches

Sunbathers at Kitsilano Beach on English Bay, Vancouver

Sandboarding at Oregon Dunes National Recreation Area

in Stanley Park *(see pp226–7)*. Visitors are also drawn to the tranquil and beautiful shores of the Gulf Islands *(see p255)*.

BIRD-WATCHING

THROUGHOUT THE YEAR, bird-watchers can sight gulls, sandpipers, plovers, and ducks along the coasts of Oregon and Washington and British Columbia boasts important migration habitats for waterfowl, shorebirds, and hawks. Contact the local **Audubon Society** chapter for information about birds and the many superb birding spots in the Pacific Northwest, such as Oregon's **Malheur National Wildlife Refuge**, Washington's Skagit River, and the **George C. Reifel Bird Sanctuary** in British Columbia.

CAMPING

NUMEROUS CAMPSITES are tucked away in wilderness areas, close to cities, and near beaches. All the region's national parks and most state and provincial parks offer excellent campgrounds.

In the high country, campgrounds are usually open from mid-June through August, and in lower elevations year-round. Space in most parks is available on a first-come, first-served basis. To reserve a spot in a state park in Oregon, call **Reservations Northwest**; in Washington, call **Washington State Parks**. In Canada, call **Parks Canada**, or to book in one of British Columbia's provincial parks, call **Discover Camping**'s reservation service.

CANOEING AND KAYAKING

CANOEING AND kayaking are both easy and environmentally friendly ways of seeing the Pacific Northwest's beautiful waters and abundant marine life.

Washington's Puget Sound and San Juan Islands are the most popular destinations for sea kayakers in the Pacific Northwest. White-water kayakers flock to the state's many rivers, and Lake Ozette in **Olympic National Park** is a hot spot for canoeists.

Off Oregon, the ocean's waters are generally too rough for kayaking, but the bays along the coast and the Lewis and Clark National Wildlife Refuge, on the Columbia River, provide calmer waters for paddlers. For listings of canoe and kayak outfitters in the US, visit the **Arcadian Outdoor Guide** website.

For information about many canoeing and kayaking destinations in British Columbia, contact the **Recreational Canoeing Association of BC** and **Whitewater Kayaking Association of BC**.

White-water kayaking on the fast-moving McKenzie River in Oregon

CAVING

WHETHER YOU ARE an experienced caver or simply interested in venturing into tubes of lava and limestone, there are thousands of caving possibilities in the region. Among the most popular are the Oregon Caves National Monument, Lava River Caves, and Sea Lion Caves in Oregon; Washington's Gardner Cave; and British Columbia's Cody and Horne Lake Caves.

Caves are largely unaffected by the climate outdoors, so although it may be warm outside, temperatures inside average 50°F (10°C) year-round. Be sure to wear warm clothing and comfortable footwear. For more information about exploring the caves of the Pacific Northwest, contact the **Cave Guiding Association of BC** or the **US National Caves Association**.

Mountain biking near Kamloops, in British Columbia's Interior

CYCLING AND ROLLERBLADING

CYCLING AND rollerblading are inexpensive and healthy ways of traveling around the cities and countryside of the Pacific Northwest. Most of the parks in the region have designated cycling trails as well as rental outlets for equipment; Portland, Seattle, Vancouver, and many other large cities have cycling paths.

Several companies offer long-distance cycling tours in the region, including **Pathfinders**, based in Oregon. **Bicycle Adventures** offers tours through Oregon, Washington, and Western Canada. Contact state and

Rollerbladers, cyclists, and walkers at Green Lake, Seattle

provincial tourist offices for details on tour operators. For maps of cycling trails in Oregon, contact the **Oregon Bicycle Map Hotline**; in Washington, contact the **Bicycle Hot Line**; and for maps and general information about cycling in British Columbia, contact **Cycling BC**.

Bicycles for rent at Friday Harbor, on Washington's San Juan Island

Most local tourist offices and bike rental shops will also have information about cycling and rollerblading.

ECOTOURISM

SEVERAL COMPANIES organize eco-tours, allowing travelers to enjoy the natural beauty of the Pacific Northwest's landscape while respecting local communities and the environment. Guided wilderness cruises, kayak tours around Washington's San Juan Islands, and llama treks through Silver Falls State Park in Salem, Oregon are among the ecotours available. To learn about the

impact of tourism, or for information about ecologically and socially responsible travel options, contact the **International Ecotourism Society**.

FISHING

THE PACIFIC NORTHWEST is a paradise for fishing enthusiasts. Pacific salmon, steelhead, perch, bass, trout, halibut, and sturgeon are among the region's catches.

For information on freshwater fishing in the US, contact the **Washington Department of Fish and Wildlife** or the **Oregon Department of Fish and Wildlife**. Most visitors' centers and fishing shops also provide details of local regulations.

In Canada, contact the **Sportfishing Institute** for information about sportfishing, **Fisheries and Oceans Canada** for saltwater fishing licenses, and **BC Fisheries** to obtain a BC Freshwater Fishing Regulations Synopsis.

Fishing for trout in Oregon's peaceful McKenzie River Valley

GOLFING

WITHIN THE PACIFIC Northwest, golfers can choose from golf courses with scenic backdrops of mountain vistas, coastal views, or cityscapes. Because of the mild climate, you can golf all year-round in many areas of the region.

Most of Oregon's golf courses are clustered in the areas around Portland and Bend-Redmond; there are also several along the coast. While a few of Washington's resorts maintain private courses, most of its cities offer public ones. British Columbia has more than 200 golf courses, from par 3s to 18-hole championship courses. To obtain listings of both private and public courses, contact state, provincial, or local tourism offices.

Golfers on one of the many courses in the Pacific Northwest

HIKING

HIKING TRAILS leading over mountains, through meadows and forests, and along seashores offer naturelovers everything from strenuous climbs to leisurely strolls. All the national, state, and provincial parks have well-marked trails of varying levels of difficulty. Visitors' centers and the **American Hiking Society** are good sources of information about hiking. The **Pacific Northwest Trail Association** offers information about the scenic 1,200-mile (1,931-km) trail, which runs from the Continental Divide to the Pacific Ocean.

Most of the more popular hikes in the Pacific Northwest require only minimal preparation, but if you plan to venture into little-known territory, plan to travel with a trained guide.

ROCK CLIMBING AND MOUNTAINEERING

THE PACIFIC Northwest's Cascade, Coast, and Rocky Mountain systems offer innumerable possibilities for rock climbing and mountaineering.

In Oregon, **Timberline Mountain Guides** offer instruction and guided climbs on rock, snow, and ice. Rock climbers will want to visit the world-renowned Smith Rocks State Park, near Redmond, to check out its 1,300 climbing routes, some of which are the toughest in the world.

Visitors to Washington can hire a guide or take lessons from outfits such as **Mazama Mountain Guides**, **Rainier Mountaineering**, and **Olympic Mountaineering**. The **Peshastin Pinnacles State Park** was created especially for rock climbers.

For information about climbing and mountaineering in British Columbia, contact the **Federation of Mountain Clubs of BC** or **BC Parks**.

Sailboats on Burrard Inlet, with West Vancouver in the background

WATERSPORTS

THE PACIFIC COASTLINE and the rivers and lakes of the Pacific Northwest attract enthusiasts of white-water rafting, scuba diving, swimming, boating, surfing, and windsurfing.

White-water rafting is one of the region's most popular sports, especially in the waters of the Cascades range. Destinations in Oregon include the Deschutes, Snake, and John Day Rivers; in Washington, the Wenatchee, Skykomish, and Methow Rivers; and in British Columbia, the Mackenzie River system. Basic training courses

Windsurfers on Hood River, near Oregon's Columbia River Gorge

are usually available for inexperienced rafters. To book a rafting trip in the US, contact **River Riders** or **Wildwater River Tours** in Washington. To find out about BC's outfitters, contact **BC Parks**. **Whistler River Adventures** offers rafting as well as jet-boating tours that whisk passengers close to waterfalls.

The coasts of the Pacific Northwest, and of Puget Sound and the San Juan Islands in particular, offer scuba divers thousands of miles of ocean flora and fauna. Visit **3 Routes** on the Internet to access comprehensive scuba diving directories for Oregon, Washington, and British Columbia. There are also many prime surfing spots along the Pacific coast, through the Strait of Juan de Fuca, and around the San Juan Islands.

For windsurfers, the Columbia River Gorge, a stretch of the Columbia River which forms a natural divide between Oregon and Washington, offers ideal conditions and beautiful scenery. The popular Columbia Gorge Sailpark in Oregon has a large shallow area for beginners. British Columbia's best windsurfing is near the town of Squamish,

a Coast Salish word meaning "strong wind." The sport is also popular on the Sunshine Coast, in White Rock, and at Jericho Beach in Vancouver.

WHALE-WATCHING

WHALE-WATCHING IS one of the most popular outdoor activities in the Pacific Northwest, particularly during the spring and summer. An offshore show, courtesy of more than 20,000 gray whales that migrate every year from Alaska to California and Mexico, can be seen from boats or from the shores of the Pacific Ocean in Oregon, Washington, and British Columbia. A number of charter companies run whale-watching cruises.

The best vantage points in Oregon include Cape Meares, Cape Lookout, Cape Kiwanda, Devil's Punchbowl, Cape Perpetua, Sea Lion Caves, Shore Acres State Park, Face Rock Wayside, Cape Blanco, Cape Sebastian, and Harris Beach State Park.

In Washington, orcas swim around the San Juan Islands and in the waters off Puget Sound; San Juan Island's **Lime Kiln Point State Park** is the only park in the US dedicated to whale-watching.

In British Columbia, of the dozens of companies that organize boat tours, most are Victoria-based. Both **Seacoast Expeditions** and **Five-Star Whale Watching** aim to minimize the negative impact of tourism on the whale populations. The shores of Vancouver Island's **Pacific Rim National Park Reserve** are world-famous for whale-watching.

White-water rafting the Nahatlatch River in southwestern British Columbia

WINTER SPORTS

THE PACIFIC NORTHWEST boasts some of the world's best snowboarding and downhill and cross-country skiing. Oregon's Mount Bachelor offers some of the best skiing in the US, and in the summer, you can snow ski down Mount Hood at Timberline Lodge, where the US Olympic Team practices. Most of Washington's 16 ski areas are in the Cascade Mountains, at locations such as Mount Baker, Stevens Pass, and Crystal Mountain *(see p186)*, though there are also a number of smaller ski areas in the eastern part of the state. In British Columbia, Whistler *(see pp256–7)* delights skiers with North America's longest vertical run, 7,000 acres (2,800 ha) of ski and snowboard terrain, more than 200 trails, and 12 alpine bowls. For details, contact **Tourism Whistler**.

In addition to snowboarding and skiing, other popular winter sports include ice skating, dogsledding, snowshoeing, snowmobiling, and heli-skiing (being lifted by helicopter to backcountry peaks for skiing or boarding off the beaten track).

SAFETY MEASURES

BOTH GRIZZLY and black bears live in the national parks of the BC Rockies. Although bear sightings are rare, visitors

Snowboarding the challenging Mount Hood Meadows, in Oregon

DIRECTORY

ADVENTURE SPORTS

Chelan Sky Park
((877) 440-7933.

Fantasy Balloon Charters
((604) 530-1974.

Hang Gliding and Paragliding Association of Canada
((416) 365-1947.
W www.hpac.ca

Morning Glory Balloon Tours
((509) 997-1700.

Oregon Adventures Aloft
((541) 582-1574 or (800) 238-0700.

Over the Rainbow
((206) 364-0995.

Pegasus Ballooning
((604) 533-2071.

Vista Balloon Adventures
((503) 625-7385.

BEACHES

Alki Beach
((206) 684-4075.
W www.cityofseattle.net/tour/alki.htm

Cannon Beach
((503) 436-2623.
W www.cannonbeach.org

Oregon Dunes National Recreation Area
((541) 271-3611.
W www.fs.fed.us/r6/siuslaw/oregondunes

BIRD-WATCHING

Audubon Society
((800) 542-2748.
W www.audubon.org

George C. Reifel Bird Sanctuary
((604) 946-6980.
W www.reifelbirdsanctuary.com

Malheur National Wildlife Refuge
((541) 493-2612.
W pacific.fws.gov/malheur

CAMPING

Discover Camping
((604) 689-9025 or (800) 689-9025.
W www.discovercamping.ca

Parks Canada
((604) 513-4777.
W www.parkscanada.gc.ca

Reservations Northwest
((800) 452-5687.
W www.oregonstateparks.org/reserve

Washington State Parks
(Reservations: (800) 226-7688.
W www.parks.wa.gov/RNW

CANOEING AND KAYAKING

Arcadian Outdoor Guide
W www.thetent.com

Recreational Canoeing Association of BC
((604) 437-1140.
W www.canoebc.ca

Whitewater Kayaking Association of BC
((604) 515-6376.
W www.whitewater.org

CAVING

Cave Guiding Association of BC
((250) 923-1311.

US National Caves Association
((866) 552-2837.
W www.cavern.com

CYCLING AND ROLLERBLADING

Bicycle Adventures
((360) 786-0989.

Bicycle Hot Line
(Washington)
((360) 705-7277.

Cycling BC
((604) 737-3034.

Oregon Bicycle Map Hotline
((503) 986-3556.

Pathfinders
((800) 778-4838.

ECOTOURISM

International Ecotourism Society
((802) 651-9818.
W www.ecotourism.org

FISHING

BC Fisheries
W www.bcfisheries.gov.bc.ca/rec/fresh/regulations/intro.html

Fisheries and Oceans Canada
((604) 666-0384.
W www.pac.dfo-mpo.gc.ca

Oregon Department of Fish and Wildlife
((503) 872-5268.
W www.dfw.state.or.us

Sportfishing Institute
((604) 270-3439.
W www.sportfishing.bc.ca

Washington Department of Fish and Wildlife
((360) 902-2200.
W www.wa.gov/wdfw

should observe the rules posted at campgrounds. A leaflet published by Parks Canada, entitled "You Are in Bear Country," gives safety tips for encounters with bears. The fundamental rules are: do not approach the animals, never feed them, and do not run. Bears have an excellent sense of smell, so when camping, be sure to store food or trash properly, inside a car or in the bear-proof boxes provided.

While less alarming, insects can be irritating. Take all possible measures to repel blackflies and mosquitos. Do not drink stream or river water without thoroughly boiling it first, as it may contain parasites.

When camping and hiking, be sure to bring a map, compass, flashlight or headlamp with spare bulbs and batteries; sunglasses and sunscreen; a first-aid kit, including antihistamines and bug repellent; a pocketknife; matches kept in a waterproof container and fire starter.

Sailing gear with flashlight, pocketknife, and other safety accessories

HIKING

American Hiking Society
☏ (301) 565-6704.
W www.americanhiking.org

Pacific Northwest Trail Association
☏ (877) 854-9415.
W www.pnt.org

ROCK CLIMBING AND MOUNTAINEERING

Federation of Mountain Clubs of BC
☏ (604) 878-7007.
W www.mountainclubs.bc.ca

Mazama Mountain Guides
☏ (509) 996-3194.

Olympic Mountaineering
☏ (360) 452-0240.
W www.olymtn.com

Rainier Mountaineering
☏ (888) 892-5462.
W www.rmiguides.com

Timberline Mountain Guides
☏ (541) 312-9242.
W www.timberlinemtguides.com

WATERSPORTS

River Riders
☏ (800) 448-7238.

3 Routes
W www.3routes.com/scuba/na

Whistler River Adventures
☏ (604) 932-3532 or (888) 932-3532.

Wildwater River Tours
☏ (253) 939-2151.

WHALE-WATCHING

Five-Star Whale Watching
☏ (250) 388-7223.
W www.5starwhales.com

Seacoast Expeditions
☏ (250) 383-2254.
W www.seacoastexpeditions.com

WINTER SPORTS

Tourism Whistler
☏ (800) 944-7853.
W www.mywhistler.com

NATIONAL PARKS

Crater Lake National Park
☏ (541) 594-3100.
W www.nationalparks.com

Kootenay National Park
☏ (250) 347-9505.
W www.britishcolumbia.com / Parks And Trails / Parks / AllParks

National Forest Service
☏ (202) 205-8333.
W www.fs.fed.us

National Park Service
☏ (510) 817-1300.
W www.nps.gov/parks.html

North Cascades National Park
☏ (360) 856-5700.
W www.nps.gov/noca

Olympic National Park
☏ (360) 565-3130.
W www.nps.gov/olym

Pacific Rim National Park Reserve
☏ (250) 726-7721.
W www.parkscanada.gc.ca

STATE AND PROVINCIAL PARKS

BC Parks
W wlapwww.gov.bc.ca/bcparks

Deception Pass State Park
☏ (360) 675-2417.
W www.parks.wa.gov/parks

Lime Kiln Point State Park
☏ (360) 378-2044.
W www.sanjuansites.com/thingstodo

Oregon State Parks
☏ (503) 378-6305.
W www.prd.state.or.us

Oswald West State Park
☏ (800) 551-6949.
W www.oregonstateparks.org

Peshastin Pinnacles State Park
W www.parks.wa.gov/parks

Samuel H. Boardman State Scenic Corridor
☏ (800) 551-6949.
W www.oregonstateparks.org

Smith Rocks State Park
☏ (541) 923-0702.
W www.smithrock.com

Sunset Bay State Park
☏ (800) 551-6949.
W www.oregonstateparks.org

Washington State Parks
☏ (360) 902-8844.
W www. parks.wa.gov/parks

SURVIVAL
GUIDE

PRACTICAL INFORMATION

Historic Columbia River Highway sign

THE PACIFIC NORTHWEST'S stunning scenery attracts visitors from around the world. Booming tourism – and in more recent years, ecotourism – has spawned an extensive network of facilities and services for visitors: internationally acclaimed accommodations and restaurants abound, while efficient transportation by air, land, and water takes travelers virtually anywhere they want to go. The following pages provide useful information for all travelers planning a trip to this region. Personal Health and Security *(see pp328–9)* recommends a number of precautions; Banking and Communications *(see pp330–31)* answers financial and media queries. There is also information on traveling to the region *(see pp332–3)* and driving once there *(see pp334–5)*.

TOURIST INFORMATION

MAPS AND information about sights, events, accommodations, and tours are available free of charge from the **Oregon Tourism Commission**, **Washington State Tourism**, and **Tourism British Columbia**. These agencies also provide either free reservation services for a wide range of accommodation or referrals to such services. Most communities in the Pacific Northwest also operate visitors' information centers or seasonal tourism booths, which offer information about local activities, lodgings, and restaurants.

ENTRY REQUIREMENTS

DUE TO CHANGING US immigration laws, visitors to Washington and Oregon who are traveling from outside the US should check current entry requirements with a US embassy or consulate before leaving. All visitors must have a valid passport, and visitors from most countries must have a non-immigrant visitor's visa. Citizens of Australia, New Zealand, South Africa, the UK, and many other European countries can visit the US without a visa if they plan to stay for fewer than 90 days.

Visitors to Canada must carry a valid passport, though a visa is not necessary for visitors from the US, EU, UK, and British Commonwealth countries. In your home country, the nearest Canadian consulate, embassy, or high commission will have current information on visa regulations. Visitors who are under the age of 18 and traveling alone must carry a letter from a parent or guardian giving them permission to do so.

All travelers who plan to stay in Canada or the US for 90 days or longer must have visas. If crossing the border by car, be prepared for customs personnel to do a search.

Canadian landed immigrants should check the regulations before traveling to the US – citizens of some Commonwealth countries that were formerly exempt from the visa requirement are now required to have a visa.

WHEN TO GO

IN DECIDING WHEN to go to the Pacific Northwest, visitors should first determine what they would like to do. The region's winter weather is ideal for skiing and other snow sports, while warmer weather suits hiking, cycling, fishing, and watersports. (See also

Crystal Mountain, Washington, a perfect winter ski destination

◁ **Hikers on the lower slopes of Mount Rainier, Washington** pp30–33 for details on seasonal events and weather in the Pacific Northwest.)

The peak tourist season extends from mid-May through September. In the metropolitan areas of Portland, Seattle, and Vancouver, spring is often quite rainy, with temperatures in the 60 to 69°F (16 to 21°C) range. Along the coast, mild summer temperatures average 77°F (25°C) and occasionally go as high as 85°F (29°C), which makes walking around these cities very comfortable. The central and eastern regions can be significantly hotter than the coast.

In early September, trees at the higher elevations begin to change color, making excursions out of the cities even more scenic. In September and early October, the weather in the three major cities, particularly in Seattle, can be quite dry and sunny.

Although the weather is generally clement along the coast, rain is not uncommon in other areas. It starts to get chilly again in the fall, toward the end of October.

Except in areas catering to skiers and other snow sports enthusiasts, winter is the least popular season to visit the Pacific Northwest. This makes it an ideal time of year for visitors who are looking for fewer crowds and more affordable hotel rates. Though snowfalls in the three main coastal cities are relatively rare, in the interior and eastern regions they can be frequent and heavy, making roads treacherous, if passable at all. If you plan to cross from west to east between late fall and early spring, inquire about road conditions beforehand.

TIME ZONES

THERE ARE TWO time zones in the Pacific Northwest: Pacific Standard Time (PST) and Mountain Standard Time (MST). Washington and most of British Columbia and Oregon lie within the Pacific time zone. Parts of Oregon, along the Idaho border, and parts of British Columbia, along the Alberta border, lie within the mountain time zone. The

Bikes and windsurfing gear in Hood River, Oregon

clocks are turned back one hour in October; in April they are turned forward one hour to Daylight Savings Time.

CUSTOMS ALLOWANCES

VISITORS 21 YEARS of age and over are permitted to enter the US with two pints (1 liter) of alcohol, 200 cigarettes, 50 cigars or 4 pounds (1.8 kg) of smoking tobacco, and gifts worth up to $100. Visitors to British Columbia who are 19 years of age or older are allowed up to 3.15 pints (1.5 liters) of wine or 2.4 pints (1.14 liters) of liquor, 200 cigarettes, 50 cigars, or 0.44 pounds (200 grams) of tobacco, and gifts worth up to $60.

In both countries, restricted items include meats, dairy products, and fresh fruits and vegetables. As well, travelers entering either country with more than $10,000 in cash or traveler's checks must declare the money to customs officials upon entry.

"Pioneers" at the National Historic Oregon Trail Interpretive Center

OPENING HOURS AND ADMISSION PRICES

MOST BUSINESSES are open weekdays from 9am to 5pm, but many in Seattle's, Portland's, and Vancouver's downtown districts stay open later. Many businesses are also open on Saturdays and, often, Sundays as well. Banks are generally open from 9 or 9:30am to 4:30 or 5pm, and some offer limited hours on Saturdays. Most attractions are open daily, except perhaps on public holidays (see p33). Phone ahead for opening hours; they are often shorter outside the summer season.

Most museums, galleries, and other attractions charge an admission fee, but discounts are widely available for families, children, students, and seniors. Check tourist brochures and local papers for discount coupons.

TAXES

TAXES VARY between states and provinces. In Oregon, hotel tax is 11.5 percent and there is no sales tax. Hotel tax in Seattle is 15.6 percent but varies throughout the rest of the state; and Washington's sales taxes are in the 8 to 9 percent range but do not apply to groceries.

In British Columbia, a 7.5 percent provincial sales tax (PST) and a 7 percent federal Goods and Service Tax (GST) apply to most goods and services. Hotel rooms are subject to GST, PST, and

A restaurant and wine bar in Portland's South Park Blocks

an additional 3 percent hotel tax. Travelers visiting Canada from other countries can apply for a GST rebate within 60 days of the date of purchase. GST on restaurant meals, drinks, tobacco, and transportation expenses are excluded. Refund forms are available at airports, duty-free stores, hotels, and most Canadian embassies. For more information, check the *GST Rebate for Visitors* pamphlet, available from the **Canada Customs and Revenue Agency**.

ETIQUETTE

Pacific Northwesterners' dress tends to be casual, practical, and dependent on the weather. Stricter clothing requirements apply in theaters, high-end restaurants, and other more formal places. Designated beaches allow topless and nude sunbathing.

ALCOHOL AND CIGARETTES

Alcohol is available only in government liquor stores, beer and wine stores, and licensed restaurants, bars, and clubs. Drinking alcohol in non-licensed public places is illegal, as is driving with an open bottle of alcohol. There are also strict laws against drinking and driving.

The minimum legal drinking age in Oregon and Washington is 21; in British Columbia, 19. Younger travelers are advised to carry photo identification, such as a passport or driver's license, should they need to prove they are of legal age to enter bars or clubs or to order alcohol in restaurants.

In Oregon and Washington, cigarettes can be sold only to people 18 or older; in British Columbia, 19 or older. It is illegal to smoke in public buildings and on public transportation. Some restaurants still permit smoking in designated areas, though these are becoming increasingly rare.

TIPPING

Tips and service charges are not usually added to restaurant bills. For service at restaurants, cafés, bars, and clubs, and for tour guides, a standard tip is 15 to 20 percent of the amount before taxes. Porters and bellhops should be tipped at least $1 per bag or suitcase; cloakroom attendants, $1 per garment; and chambermaids, a minimum of $1 to $2 per day.

TRAVELERS WITH DISABILITIES

The Pacific Northwest has some of the world's best facilities and recreational opportunities for travelers with physical disabilities. Most public buildings, hotels *(see p280)*, public transit, and entertainment venues are wheelchair accessible. However, some older buildings and smaller venues may not be. Taxi service is available for people with wheelchairs, and parking spaces closest to the entrance of most buildings are reserved for persons with disabilities (note that permits may be required).

The **Society for Accessible Travel and Hospitality** is an excellent source of information. To find out about barrier-free sports and recreation opportunities in British Columbia, contact **BC Disability Sports**.

SENIOR TRAVELERS

Reduced rates for attractions, hotels, transportation, and services are often available for seniors. Photo identification proving one's age may be required. Seniors are eligible for discounts with Amtrak and VIA rail services and with Greyhound bus services *(see p333)*. If discounts are not advertised, inquire when purchasing tickets. Also inquire about discounts for seniors' traveling companions.

For discounts and more information about traveling as a senior, contact the **American Association of Retired Persons**, in the US or Canada. For information about learning programs for people 55 years of age and older, contact **Elderhostel**.

TRAVELING WITH CHILDREN

The Pacific Northwest is extremely child-friendly, with many attractions suited to children, including zoos and a multitude of festivals,

Petting zoo at Port Townsend's farmers' market, Washington

Oregon Museum of Science and Industry, in Portland

events, and programs. The region's beaches and popular outdoor activities can entertain children year-round. Admission to attractions is often free for children under five who are accompanied by a parent. In most cities in the Pacific Northwest, children under five can also travel for free on public transportation when they are accompanied by a parent; there are often concession fares for older children.

Many hotels offer cribs, high chairs, even baby-sitting services, and restaurants generally welcome children. With more upscale establishments, you may wish to inquire in advance whether children are welcome. When renting a car, be sure to reserve a child's car seat in advance.

STUDENT TRAVELERS

A N INTERNATIONAL student identity card (ISIC), administered by the **International Student Travel Confederation**, entitles full-time students to discounts on travel as well as admission to movies, galleries, museums, theaters, and many other tourist attractions. The ISIC should be purchased in the student's home country; they are available at **STA Travel** and **Travel CUTS** (in the US and Canada only).

A wide range of bus and rail *(see p333)* discounts are available to students. Ask for a copy of the *ISIC Student Handbook*, for listings of places that offer discounts to cardholders, as well as travel tips.

Members of **Hostelling International** (HI) can stay at HI locations throughout the Pacific Northwest *(see p279)*. Ask about free shuttles and other amenities at HI's regional offices.

CONVERSION CHART

Imperial to Metric
1 inch = 2.5 centimeters
1 foot = 30 centimeters
1 mile = 1.6 kilometers
1 ounce = 28 grams
1 pound = 454 grams
1 pint = 0.6 liter
1 US pint = 0.5 liter
1 US quart = 0.9 liter
1 gallon = 4.6 liters
1 US gallon = 3.8 liters

Metric to Imperial
1 centimeter = 0.4 inch
1 meter = 3 feet 3 inches
1 kilometer = 0.6 mile
1 gram = 0.04 ounce
1 kilogram = 2.2 pounds
1 liter = 1.8 pints/1.1 US quarts

Bear in mind that 1 US pint (0.5 liter) is a smaller measure than 1 UK pint (0.6 liter).

ELECTRICITY

E LECTRICAL sockets accept two- or three-prong plugs and operate at 110 volts. You will need a plug adapter and voltage converter to operate 220-volt appliances such as hairdryers and rechargers. Batteries are universal and are readily available.

Standard North American plug

Personal Health and Security

Hospital sign

THE PACIFIC NORTHWEST prides itself on the safety of its towns and cities and on its welcoming attitude toward visitors. Street crime is rare, and police are a visible presence as they patrol the major cities on horseback, motorcycle, and foot. However, it is still wise to be vigilant and to find out from your hotel or a tourist information center which parts of town should be avoided. In the open countryside, bear in mind natural dangers, such as unexpectedly inclement weather and wild animals. Always heed local warnings.

GUIDELINES ON SAFETY

WHEN TRAVELING, it is advisable to take a few basic precautions and at all times to be aware of your surroundings.

Carry traveler's checks and small amounts of cash in a secure bag, purse, or pocket, and do not carry your wallet in a back pocket. Pickpockets and thieves, who are often well dressed and tend to work in pairs, target their victims in airports, malls, and other crowded areas.

Always watch your luggage carefully at airports and while checking in and out of your hotel. Although theft is rare in hotel rooms, ask at your hotel if you can store valuable items, such as jewelry, credit cards, or extra cash, in the hotel safe.

When you use an automated teller machine (ATM), choose one that is located in a well-lit, busy area and never let a stranger look over your shoulder or assist you in using your bank card.

Travelers with cars should park in well-lit garages or use valet parking if offered by the hotel, and avoid leaving valuable items in the car. Always lock the doors when you park the car and leave the glove compartment empty and open. It is also advisable to keep the car doors locked while driving.

MEDICAL MATTERS

MOST MAJOR CITIES in the Pacific Northwest have walk-in medical clinics, which are usually sufficient for minor injuries and ailments. Clinics and hospitals are listed in the Yellow Pages of the telephone directory. Without insurance, medical services can be expensive. Even with insurance, you may have to pay upfront for the medical treatment and seek reimbursement from your insurance company later.

Nonprescription painkillers and other medicines can be obtained from drugstores, many of which are open 24 hours a day. Prescription drugs can be dispensed only from a pharmacy. If you take a prescription drug, pack an extra supply, as well as a copy of the prescription. A first-aid kit is recommended when camping or trekking into remote areas.

If you have HIV or AIDS, call the embassy or consulate of the country to which you are traveling to find out about regulations regarding travelers with either of these conditions. The entry requirements can change at short notice.

EMERGENCIES

DIAL 911 if the emergency requires the fire department, police, or an ambulance; if you are not in a major city, dial 0. The call can be made free of charge from any telephone. Most hospitals have a 24-hour emergency room; be prepared for a long wait. Although they may be busy, public hospitals can be much less expensive than private ones. Hospitals in British Columbia will provide treatment to anyone, regardless of health care coverage; in the US, visitors must provide payment or proof of insurance coverage before receiving treatment.

NATURAL HAZARDS

BEFORE SETTING OFF to hike or camp, check with the appropriate state, provincial, or federal forest service for information on the conditions in the area and recommended safety precautions. Skiers and snowboarders should heed warning signs and stay on groomed runs and trails.

Moose warning sign

Marble Canyon   Cañon Marble

US national park sign for hikers

It is always best to be accompanied when engaging in any such outdoor activity. Insects are another hazard. While black flies, which are common in the spring, are annoying, they are relatively harmless. Mosquitoes, however, which are prevalent in the summer, can be carriers of the potentially fatal West Nile virus. Ticks, which can be carriers of Lyme disease, are found in dry, wooded areas. To protect yourself, use insect repellent and wear long sleeves, long trousers, and socks. If you are bitten and develop a rash or flu-like symptoms, seek medical attention immediately.

Heed the red-tide warnings that alert shellfish collectors to contamination. When

Avalanche warning sign

Compact first-aid kit, an essential item for travelers

Vancouver police officers on duty

camping, beware of cougars, wolves, coyotes, and bears (*see p318*). Leaving food out can attract dangerous wildlife and is illegal in many areas, as is feeding wild animals.

LAW ENFORCEMENT

THE PORTLAND and Seattle police departments are present in these cities on foot, on horseback, motorcycle, and in cars. Neighborhood security teams, made up of citizen volunteers, also patrol on foot in some areas. Outside metropolitan areas, there are county police and sheriff's offices to assist you. British Columbia is policed by the Royal Canadian Mounted Police (RCMP); some municipalities also have their own police forces. In addition, you are likely to see security officers from private security companies in airports and public places, and on Vancouver's downtown streets.

It is illegal to comment on or joke about bombs, guns, and terrorism in places such as airports, where it is possible to be arrested for an off-the-cuff remark.

Drinking and driving is taken very seriously in the Pacific Northwest, and it is illegal to carry open alcohol containers in a vehicle. Police checks for impaired drivers are increasingly common.

Narcotics users can face criminal charges, followed by moves for deportation; penalties are especially severe in the US.

LOST OR STOLEN PROPERTY

ALTHOUGH THE CHANCES of retrieving lost or stolen items are slim, it is nevertheless important to report missing items to the police as soon as possible. Be sure to obtain a copy of the police record in case you need it for an insurance claim.

Before leaving home, make photocopies of important documents such as your passport, driver's license, credit cards, and identification cards; keep one set of photocopies at home, another set with you.

Should you lose your passport, contact your nearest embassy or consulate. Visitors do not generally need a new passport if they are returning directly to their home country and so may be issued a temporary one. However, if you are traveling on to another destination, you will need to replace your permanent passport.

Report lost credit cards and traveler's checks as soon as you notice them missing; American Express, MasterCard, Visa, and Thomas Cook all have toll-free call centers open 24 hours a day, seven days a week. If you have a record of the traveler's checks' numbers, replacing them should be fairly straightforward and new ones are often issued within 24 hours. For items lost on public transit or in a taxi, contact the lost-and-found departments of the appropriate transit system or taxi company.

A park ranger

TRAVEL INSURANCE

TRAVEL INSURANCE is essential when traveling. Consider purchasing insurance for health and medical emergencies, trip cancellation and interruption,

theft, and loss of valuable possessions. A minimum of $1 million medical coverage is recommended, especially if you are traveling to the US. Insurance for luggage and travel documents can be arranged through a travel agent or the airline. Emergency dental, out-of-pocket, and loss-of-vacation expenses are generally covered by separate policies. Ask your travel agent or insurance company to recommend suitable insurance; also check with your credit card company (*see p330*).

DIRECTORY

EMERGENCIES

Police, Fire, Ambulance
[*In major cities call 911; elsewhere, dial 0.*

Hospitals
[*Call 411 for directory assistance.*

EMBASSIES AND CONSULATES

Links to US Embassies and Consulates Worldwide
w *travel.state.gov/links*

Links to Canadian Embassies, Consulates, and High Commissions Worldwide
w *www.dfait-maeci.gc.ca*

LOST OR STOLEN CREDIT CARDS AND TRAVELER'S CHECKS

American Express
[*(800) 554-2639 for credit cards, (800) 221-7282 for traveler's checks.*

MasterCard
[*(800) 307-7309.*

Thomas Cook
[*(800) 223-7373*

Visa
[*(410) 581-3836 or (800) 847-2911 for credit cards, (800) 227-6811 for traveler's checks.*

Banking, Local Currency, and Communications

Both in the US and Canada the unit of currency is the dollar, which is divided into 100 cents. Coins include denominations of 1 cent (penny), 5 cents (nickel), 10 cents (dime), 25 cents (quarter), and $1 (buck; in Canada it is often called a "loonie"). In Canada, there is also a $2 coin, a "toonie." Bank notes, or bills, are printed in denominations of $5, $10, $20, $50, and $100 in both countries, and in $500 and $1,000 in Canada, though these larger denominations are less common. In the US, a $2 bill is also in circulation, but it is uncommon. Plan to arrive with $50 to $100 in local currency and get small change as soon as possible for tipping and transportation.

Credit cards, a convenient method of payment for travelers

BANKS AND FOREIGN CURRENCY EXCHANGE

Most banks are open from 9 or 9:30am to 4:30 or 5pm, with many in downtown locations offering extended hours, especially on Fridays. Many banks are closed Saturdays, and all are closed Sundays and statutory holidays.

Exchange rates for foreign currency are posted in banks where exchange services are offered (usually the main branches of large banks) as well as at foreign exchange brokers, **American Express** and **Thomas Cook** being the most popular ones.

AUTOMATED TELLER MACHINES (ATMS)

Automated teller machines (ATMs) can be found in bank branches, shopping centers, gas stations, grocery stores, mini-marts, transit terminals, and airports. They offer one of the most convenient ways of obtaining local

An ATM, common throughout the Pacific Northwest

currency since you can, in most cases, use your debit card or a major credit card to withdraw cash. Consult with your bank, credit union, or credit card company before leaving home about which ATM systems will accept your bank card, and what fees and commissions will be charged on each transaction made outside your home country.

TRAVELER'S CHECKS

Traveler's checks provide one of the safest ways to carry money on a vacation. They are widely accepted at stores, hotels, and restaurants in major cities, but may be difficult to use in rural areas or areas less geared to tourism. Foreign currency checks can be exchanged at any bank and at some major hotels, but it is advisable to purchase checks in US or Canadian currency, depending on your destination. Choose small denominations, such as $10 or $20, as most retailers prefer not to part with large amounts of change. A passport or other photo identification is required to cash traveler's checks at a bank. Checks issued by American Express and Thomas Cook are the most popular and, as such, the most readily accepted. Rarely will a personal check be accepted.

CREDIT CARDS

Credit cards such as Visa, MasterCard, American Express, Discover, and Diners Club are widely accepted and can be used to pay for just about anything, from a cup of coffee to a hotel room.

Not only do credit cards allow you to carry a minimal amount of cash but they are often required when checking into a hotel or renting a car – many such businesses will insist on taking a credit card imprint as a form of deposit. Credit cards can be used to obtain cash advances at banks and ATMs, and can also be handy in emergency situations.

If your credit card company offers travel insurance, keep a copy of the statement of conditions and coverage with your travel documents. Before leaving home, be sure to note all emergency contact numbers connected with your credit card in case of loss or theft.

WIRING MONEY

In an emergency, visitors can have cash wired from home by way of electronic money transfer services offered by American Express, Thomas Cook, and **Western Union**.

POSTAL SERVICES

Post offices are generally open weekdays from 9am to 5pm. Stamped, addressed mail can be dropped into roadside mailboxes, which are blue in the US and red in Canada. Pick-up times are listed on the boxes. Most hotels will also accept letters and postcards at the front desk.

Mail sent within the US or Canada takes from one to five business days for delivery (longer if no zip or postal code is given); overseas mail up to seven business days. Courier companies and the priority services of the

US Postal Service and Canada Post offer speedier delivery. Priority mail costs more than regular mail but usually less than courier services.

TELEPHONES

PUBLIC PAY PHONES are virtually everywhere, including bars, restaurants, public buildings, gas stations, and street corners, and at rest stops outside urban areas. Local calls made from pay phones in the US cost 35 cents; in Canada, 25 cents. Most pay phones are operated by coins, though increasingly more accept phone cards and credit cards too. Any combination of coins, excluding pennies, can be used. Keep in mind that making phone calls from hotel rooms can be expensive; inquire about rates first. It is usually cheaper to use the pay phone in the lobby.

For local calls, dial the area code followed by the seven-digit number. For long-distance calls within North America, dial 1, followed by the area code and the local number. For calls outside North America, dial 011, followed by the country code (Australia: 61; New Zealand: 64; South Africa: 27; UK: 44), then the city or area code, then the local telephone number; or dial 0 for operator assistance.

Coin-operated pay phone

Vending machines in Seattle, dispensing a range of newspapers

CELL PHONES AND E-MAIL

CELL PHONES can be rented in many cities, or visitors can have their own mobiles tuned to local networks. Check with your cell phone service provider before leaving home. Your provider might also supply you with a cell phone compatible with the local system before you leave. E-mail and the Internet can now be accessed from many hotels and most public libraries, or from the ubiquitous local Internet café. Rates for computer use vary but are generally reasonable.

FAXES AND TELEGRAMS

FAXES CAN BE sent from most hotels and many business facilities. The most common service for sending telegrams is operated by Western Union, which has numerous locations throughout the Pacific Northwest.

COMMUNICATIONS AND MEDIA

NEWSSTANDS IN THE US carry most major international and national papers, including the *New York Times*, the *Wall Street Journal*, and *USA Today*. Local papers are available at sidewalk boxes, coffee shops, and convenience stores. The most widely read newspapers in Seattle are the *Seattle Times*, *Seattle Weekly*, and the *Seattle Post-Intelligencer*. In

Portland, it is the *Oregonian* and *Willamette Week*.

The US is famous for having a multitude of TV channels, provided by the four networks – ABC, CBS, FOX, and NBC – as well as by cable channels. CNN is a national 24-hour headline news station.

Various radio stations in the US offer local news bulletins and weather forecasts. National Public Radio is a good source of commercial-free news and entertainment; it is usually located along the FM band.

The *Globe and Mail* and the *National Post* are the national newspapers in Canada and are readily available at newsstands, as are major international papers. Vancouver's two dailies are the *Vancouver Sun* and *The Province*, and most smaller BC cities, including Victoria, have their own local papers.

The CBC, Canada's public broadcasting corporation, has local, national, and international television and radio programming. VTV, the Vancouver affiliate of CTV, Canada's largest private television broadcaster, airs news and other programs daily throughout the province.

AREA CODES

Oregon
Portland, Salem & Astoria **503/971**
Oregon, elsewhere **541**

Washington
Western Washington

- Seattle **206/564**
- Eastside **425/564**
- Southside, including Tacoma **253/564**
- Elsewhere **360/564**

Eastern Washington **509**

British Columbia
Vancouver/Lower Mainland **604**
BC, elsewhere **250**

DIRECTORY

American Express
((800) 346-3607.

Thomas Cook
((800) 287-7362
(for branch locations).

Western Union
(*In US & Canada:* (800) 325-6000.
In UK: 0800-833833.

TRAVEL INFORMATION

THE THREE MAJOR airports in the Pacific Northwest are conveniently located to serve the metropolitan areas of Portland, Oregon; Seattle, Washington; and Vancouver, British Columbia. But these urban centers can also be easily accessed by train, car, or bus on the region's excellent network of well-maintained highways. Train travel is

Passenger jet at takeoff

ideal for enjoying the picturesque landscape; buses are relatively inexpensive; and driving is particularly popular, as it enables travelers to visit many locations that would otherwise be difficult to reach. Once you have arrived in the Pacific Northwest, ferries and cruises provide a scenic way of traveling between coastal communities.

ARRIVING BY AIR

THE MAJOR AIRPORT in Washington is **Sea-Tac International Airport** (SEA), located between Seattle and Tacoma. In Oregon, **Portland International Airport** (PDX) is just a few miles outside the city proper. Most major carriers fly into these airports, though international passengers may need to stop in Seattle and transfer to another plane to fly into Portland.

United Airlines offers flights to the major cities of the Pacific Northwest, while **Alaska Airlines** and **Horizon Airlines** fly to these as well as to regional destinations. **San Juan Airlines** and **Kenmore Air** fly between Seattle and the San Juan Islands.

The point of arrival for most international visitors to British Columbia is **Vancouver International Airport** (YVR), which is served by Canada's major carrier, **Air Canada**, as well as other national airlines from around the world. **WestJet** is a low-cost national alternative that links up with other major airlines. Air Canada's regional division flies to most major BC destinations; smaller airlines, such as **Harbour Air**, serving the Gulf Islands, and **Hawkair**, serving northern BC, connect the province's smaller communities.

TRANSPORTATION FROM THE AIRPORT

TAXIS AND the less expensive shuttle buses are readily available at all of the three major international airports in the Pacific Northwest. Some hotels provide shuttle service;

ask when booking your room. The least expensive way to get into the cities from the airports is by public transit. The **MAX** light rail system is ideal for getting into Portland; **Gray Line** also offers an airport service. Seattle's **Metro Transit** buses run regularly from Sea-Tac Airport, and several share-ride shuttles are available. **TransLink** buses run regularly from the Vancouver airport, as does the **Vancouver Airporter** bus, traveling between the airport and downtown hotels.

TRAVELING BY BUS

ALTHOUGH THE BUS may be the slowest way of getting to the Pacific Northwest, it may also be the most economical way. **Greyhound** has bus routes throughout the region; **Gray Line**, **Maverick**, and **Pacific Coach Lines** offer sightseeing tours. Discounts are often available for children, students, and senior citizens.

A Greyhound bus, an economical way to travel long distances

TRAVELING BY TRAIN

IF YOU ARE TRAVELING from within the US or Canada, the train is a good way to get to the Pacific Northwest and to travel within it. **Amtrak** offers daily services to Washington and Oregon from the Midwest and California and has daily runs between Vancouver, Seattle, Portland, and Eugene, Oregon. **American Orient Express Railway** offers scenic trips in the Pacific Northwest aboard luxury cars.

In British Columbia, **VIA Rail**, Canada's national rail service, links Vancouver to Alberta and the rest of Canada. **BC Rail** travels to Whistler and Prince George, while **Rocky Mountaineer Railtours** takes

Union Station, Portland's Italian Renaissance–style train depot, opened 1896 a scenic route to Kamloops, continuing on to Jasper, Banff, or Calgary, in Alberta. Reserve seats through a travel agent or VIA Rail directly.

TRAVELING BY CAR

Washington State Ferries terminal, Port Townsend

O REGON, WASHINGTON, and British Columbia maintain an extensive network of highways. The major interstate through Oregon and Washington is I-5, running north to British Columbia and south to California. The best route to eastern Washington from Seattle is I-90; the most accessible route to eastern Oregon from Portland is I-84. The Trans-Canada Highway traverses British Columbia, linking it to the rest of the

Amtrak train, offering convenient travel and sightseeing at once

country. There are no tolls on roads leading into Portland and Seattle, and all US interstate highways are free; some BC highways have tolls. Speed limits and seatbelt laws are strictly enforced.

Travelers driving across the Canada-US border can choose from 16 crossings. Bring your passport and a current driver's license. In some cases, an International Driving Permit will be required. Rules governing border crossings are subject to change; check with the authorities before traveling.

TRAVELING BY FERRY

F ERRIES ARE an important, and scenic, mode of transportation in the Pacific Northwest. **Washington State Ferries** *(see p162)* travel regularly

between Washington's mainland and the Puget Sound and San Juan Islands, as well as to Sidney, British Columbia, 17 miles (27 km) north of Victoria.

In British Columbia, **BC Ferries** travel 25 routes along the Sunshine Coast, in the Gulf Islands, the Queen Charlotte Islands, the Discovery Coast Passage, and between the mainland and Vancouver Island. It has two terminals in the Vancouver area: one in Tsawwassen, the other in Horseshoe Bay. Unlike BC Ferries, the **Victoria Clipper** provides a route to Washington. It also travels from Victoria and Seattle to the San Juan Islands.

BC and Washington ferries carry both foot passengers and vehicles, and offer discounts to students and seniors.

DIRECTORY

AIRPORTS

Portland International Airport
(*(877) 739-4636.*

Sea-Tac International Airport
(*(206) 433-5288.*

Vancouver International Airport
(*(604) 207-7077.*

AIRLINES

Air Canada
(*(888) 247-2262.*

Alaska Airlines
(*(800) 252-7522.*

Harbour Air
(*(800) 665-0212.*

Hawkair
(*(800) 487-1216.*

Horizon Airlines
(*(800) 547-9308.*

Kenmore Air
(*(800) 543-9595.*

San Juan Airlines
(*(800) 690-0086.*

United Airlines
(*(888) 864-8331.*

WestJet
(*(888) 937-8538.*

TRANSPORTATION FROM THE AIRPORT

MAX (TriMet)
(*(503) 238-7433.*

Metro Transit
(*(800) 542-7876.*

TransLink
(*(604) 953-3333.*

Vancouver Airporter
(*(604) 946-8866.*

BUS COMPANIES

Gray Line
(*In Portland:*
(800) 422-7042.
In Seattle: (800) 426-7532.
In Vancouver:
(800) 667-0882.
In Victoria: (250) 388-5248.

Greyhound
(*In US: (800) 229-9424.*
In Canada: (800) 661-8747.

Maverick Coach Lines
(*(604) 940-2332.*

Pacific Coach Lines
(*(604) 662-8074.*

RAIL COMPANIES

American Orient Express Railway
(*(888) 759-3944.*

Amtrak
(*(800) 872-7245.*

BC Rail
(*(604) 986-2012.*

Rocky Mountaineer Railtours
(*(604) 606-7245.*

VIA Rail
(*(888) 223-3779 or*
(250) 386-3431.

FERRY COMPANIES

BC Ferries
(*(250) 381-5452 or*
(888) 223-3779.

Victoria Clipper
(*(800) 888-2535.*
In Seattle: (206) 448-5000.
In Victoria: (250) 382-8100.

Washington State Ferries
(*(800) 843-3779*
or (206) 464-6400 (for Seattle schedule).

Traveling by Car in the Pacific Northwest

D RIVING IS THE BEST WAY to explore the Pacific North-west, especially if you want to enjoy the spectacular beauty of more remote areas, such as Oregon's Hells Canyon, the mountains of Washington's Olympic Peninsula, or British Columbia's Okanagan Valley. In major cities, parking may be hard to find and traffic heavy during rush hours; tune into local TV or radio news for reports on traffic and road conditions, particularly if you visit in the winter. Rental cars are widely available at airports and in the cities and towns.

DRIVER'S LICENSE AND INSURANCE

I N THE US, you do not need an International Driving Permit if you are carrying a valid driver's license from the country in which you live. You must, however, carry proof of auto insurance, vehicle registration, and, if renting a car, the rental contract.

A valid driver's license from your own country entitles you to drive for up to six months in British Columbia. It is advisable to carry an International Driving Permit as well, in case you run into problems.

In Oregon, Washington, and BC, insurance coverage for drivers is compulsory. Before leaving home, check your own policy to see if you are covered in a rental car. Most rental agencies offer damage and liability insurance; it is a good idea to have both. Insurance can be purchased on arrival through the **British Columbia Automobile Association**; in the US, contact the **American Automobile Association**.

RULES OF THE ROAD

V EHICLES ARE DRIVEN on the right-hand side of the road in both the US and Canada. Right-hand turns on a red light are permitted after coming to a complete stop unless otherwise indicated.

Distances and speed limits are posted in miles in the US, and in kilometers in Canada. Speed limits vary from 25 mph (40 km/h) on neighborhood streets to a maximum of 65 mph (105 km/h) on major highways. Speed limits are strictly enforced. On most major highways in the Pacific Northwest, carpool lanes are available for vehicles with two or more passengers, to reduce pollution and traffic.

Four-way stops are common in the Pacific Northwest. The first car to reach the intersection has the right of way. At intersections with no stop signs, drivers must yield to the car on their right.

Coin-operated parking meter

Because traffic in and around Portland, Seattle, and Vancouver can be heavy, it is wise to avoid rush hours in these cities, generally between 7:30 and 9:30am and from 3:30 to 6pm on weekdays. On city streets, parking meters offer between 15 minutes and two hours of parking. Be sure to put money into the meter and to read all signs since parking enforcement officers are especially active within city limits.

Seat belts are compulsory throughout the Pacific Northwest for both drivers and passengers, and children weighing less than 40 lbs (18 kg) must be in the appropriate child seats. Cyclists and motorcyclists are required to wear helmets. Driving while intoxicated (which is defined as having a blood alcohol content of more than 0.08 percent) is a criminal offense. If you are involved in an accident, contact the local police. (In Canada, local policing may be done by the Royal Canadian Mounted Police, or RCMP, depending where you are.)

SAFETY ON THE ROAD

P OTENTIAL SAFETY hazards for drivers include gravel roads, which can become very slippery when wet, heavy snowfalls, black ice, and fog, which can be particularly thick along the coast. To be safe, always carry a spare tire, and salt or sand in winter, a flashlight, jumper cables, blankets, water, some emergency food, and a shovel. Before venturing out onto back roads, be sure to inquire about road conditions and weather forecasts and to have a full tank of gas. Refill the tank fairly often along the way as an extra precaution. If you know you will be driving on dirt roads or in treacherous conditions, you may want to rent a vehicle with four-wheel drive.

During the spring and summer, wildlife such as deer, bears, and moose have been known to rush out of the woods onto the roads.

The spectacular Columbia River Historic Highway, near Rowena, Oregon

Speed limit

Gas pump

Road conditions

Rest area

Wildlife

Signs will indicate where wildlife is most likely to appear; take extra care in these areas.

CAR RENTALS

CAR RENTAL AGENCIES such as **Alamo**, **Avis**, **Budget**, **Enterprise**, **Hertz**, **National**, and **Thrifty** are located within the cities and towns as well as at airports. To rent a vehicle in the US or Canada, you must be 21 years of age and have a valid driver's license. If you are younger than 25, you will likely have to pay a higher insurance premium. A major credit card is usually required, even when you are prepared to make a hefty cash deposit.

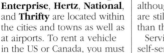
Sign for a rental car agency

Rent a car that suits your destination: a small car or sedan is appropriate for city sightseeing, but if you plan to cross mountain ranges, especially between October and April, you may want to request a sturdier, high-traction vehicle. Recreational vehicles (RVs) can also be rented but are more expensive and usually need to be reserved well in advance. Many outlets are reluctant to rent their cars if they know there is a risk of gravel roads chipping the paintwork, so if you plan to drive along back roads, you may be best off renting from an outlet in the backcountry.

FUEL

MOST VEHICLES in the US and Canada run on unleaded fuel, sold by the gallon in the US and by the liter in Canada. Fuel prices fluctuate, and are generally higher in Canada than in the US, although Canadian prices are still significantly lower than they are in Europe.

Service stations are usually self-serve (except in Oregon, where law prohibits self-serve), and many are closed at night. At full-serve stations, you remain in your car while an attendant fills up your gas tank and usually washes the windshield, making full-serve slightly more expensive. Be sure to keep your gas tank full when traveling through the mountains or in more remote areas.

ROADSIDE ASSISTANCE

EMERGENCY ROAD service is available 24 hours a day, 365 days a year, anywhere in the US or Canada. Members of the **American Automobile Association** and **Canadian** or **British Columbia Automobile Association** can call 1-800-222-4357. Be prepared to give your name, membership number and expiry date, phone number, type of vehicle, license plate number, exact location, and tow destination.

DIRECTORY

REPORTS ON ROAD CONDITIONS

in British Columbia
w www.bcnetwork.com/roadreport.html

in Oregon
(541) 889-3999 or (800) 977-6368.

in Washington
(206) 368-4499 or (360) 705-7075. Mountain Pass Report: (888) 766-4636.

CAR RENTALS

Alamo
(800) 327-9633.

Avis
(800) 331-1212.

Budget
(800) 527-0700.

Enterprise
(800) 325-8007.

Hertz
(800) 654-3131.

National
(800) 387-4747.

Thrifty
(800) 331-4200.

ROADSIDE ASSISTANCE

American Automobile Association
(407) 444-7000.

British Columbia Automobile Association
In Lower Mainland, BC: (604) 293-2222 or cell users: *222. In other areas of Canada & US: (800) 222-4357.

Canadian Automobile Association
(613) 247-0117.

(800) 222-4357 for 24-hr emergency road service.

A gas station, one of many on major highways and in towns and cities

General Index

Acknowledgments

Dorling Kindersley and International Book Productions would like to thank the following people whose contributions and assistance have made the preparation of this book possible.

MAIN CONTRIBUTORS

Stephen Brewer, a New York-based travel writer, is proud to have been born in Oregon, where he spends as much time as he can.

Constance Brissenden has explored beautiful British Columbia for more than 25 years. A freelance writer living in Vancouver, she has written 12 books on travel and history.

Anita Carmin, a Seattle native, specializes in travel writing. Her assignments have taken her from the ballrooms of Europe to a remote jungle lagoon on the Yucatan Peninsula.

ADDITIONAL CONTRIBUTORS
Allison Austin, Cora Lee

CARTOGRAPHY
VISU*TronX*, Ajax, Ontario, Canada

PROOFREADER
Garry Bowers

INDEXER
Barbara Sale Schon

FOR DORLING KINDERSLEY
PUBLISHING MANAGER
Helen Townsend

ART EDITOR
Ian Midson

CARTOGRAPHER
Caspar Morris

DTP DESIGNERS
Jason Little, Conrad Van Dyk

PICTURE RESEARCHER
Claire Bowers

PROOFREADER
Lucilla Watson

ADDITIONAL EDITORIAL AND DESIGN ASSISTANCE
Jacky Jackson, Jo Cowen, Marisa Renzullo

SPECIAL ASSISTANCE
The publisher would also like to thank the following for their assistance: Amy Buranski, Experience Music Project; Cindy Bjorklund and Tim Manns, National Park Service; Perry Cooper, Seattle Center; Ardie Davis, Domaine Serene; Courtney Hallam; Angelika Harris; Leslie Lambert, Nathalie Levesque, and Natalie Stone, National Archives of Canada; Donald Olson; Jeffrey Richstone; Dana Selover; Tammy Walker, Walla Walla Chamber of Commerce.

PHOTOGRAPHY PERMISSIONS
The publisher would also like to thank the following for their assistance and kind permission to photograph at their establishments:

American Advertising Museum; Capilano Suspension Bridge and Park; Catch the Wind Kite Shop; Christ Church Cathedral; End of Oregon Trail; Evergreen Aviation Museum; Experience Music Project; Fraser – Fort George Regional Museum; Governor Hotel; Granville Island Public Market; Helmcken House; Klondike Gold Rush National Historic Park; Multnomah County Library; Museum of Flight; National Historic Oregon Trail Interpretive Center; Oregon Maritime Center; Oregon Museum of Science and Industry; Pacific Place; Pioneer Place; Port Townsend Farmers Market; Portland Art Museum; Powell's City of Books; Seattle Aquarium; Seattle
Children's Museum; Tillamook County Creamery Association; Victoria Bay Centre; Victoria Parliament Buildings.

PICTURE CREDITS
Every effort has been made to trace the copyright holders; we apologize in advance for any unintentional omissions. We would be pleased to insert the appropriate acknowledgments in any subsequent edition of this publication.

Placement Key: t = top; tl = top left; tlc = top left center; tc = top center; tr = top right; cla = center left above; ca = center above; cra = center right above; cl = center left; c = center; cr = center right; clb = center left below; cb = center below; crb = center right below; bl = bottom left; b = bottom; bc = bottom center; bcl = bottom center left; br = bottom right; d = detail.

Works of art have been reproduced with the permission of the following copyright holders: Steve Badanes, Will Martin, Donna Walter, and Ross Whitehead *Fremont Troll*, 1990 158bl; Jonathan Barofsky *Hammering Man* 120, 128tr; Richard Beyer *People Waiting for the Interurban* 158t; Neototems Children's Garden, an artwork by Gloria Bornstein © 2002 142t; Dale Chihuly *Benaroya Hall Silver Chandelier* 1998 129t; CITY OF VANCOUVER: *Percy Williams* by Ann McLaren 1996 212c; *Captain John Deighton (Gassy Jack)* by Vern Simpson 1970 201c, 204tl; *The Crab* by George Norris 1968 221t; *Girl in a Wetsuit* by Elek Imredy 1972 226t; *Gate to the Northwest Passage* by Alan Chung Hung 1980 220c; *Inukshuk* by Alvin Kanak 1986 24t, 196tl; *Chinatown Millennium Gate* by Joe Y. Wai Architect, Inc. 2002. 204b; EXPERIENCE MUSIC PROJECT: gold record belonging to Jimi Hendrix 141t; Georgia Gerber, Rachel the market pig 133bl; Themis Goddess of Justice Jack Harman 1982 208tl; *Allow Me* by J. Seward Johnson, Jr. Life-size, bronze sculpture. Image release courtesy of The Sculpture Foundation info@tsfmail.com 1981 57t; © Raymond Kaskey 1985 *Portlandia* 63c; Eric Metcalfe *Attic Project* 218b; Jack Mackie *Dance Steps on Broadway* 1981 153bl; PORTLAND ART MUSEUM: courtyard artwork 58tr; Seattle Public Utilities decorative manhole cover 118d, 122tl; Alan Storey Broken Column 211c; *Logger's Culls*, c.1935, oil on canvas, Vancouver Art Gallery, VAG 39.1, photo: Trevor Mills 211t.

The publisher would like to thank the following individuals, companies, and picture libraries for permission to reproduce their photographs:

© ALASKA DIVISION OF TOURISM: 274b; © Joel Bennett 274cl; © Harold Wilson ADF & G 274cr; © White Pass & Yukon Railroad 275t; © Mark Wayne 275ca; 275cb; 275b. AMAZON.COM, INC: 41b. © AUTHENTIC HENDRIX, LLC: Chuck Boyd 28tr.

BC ARCHIVES: D-06009 28tl; C-06116 29c; PDP00289 34; PDP04222 35c; PDP03716 38c. BELLINGHAM/WHATCOM COUNTY CONVENTION AND VISITORS BUREAU: Jim Poth 16t; Island Mariner Cruises 21t; Keith Lazelle 21ca; Island Mariner Cruises 95br. THE BOEING COMPANY: 41c.

CHATEAU BENOIT: Ashley Smith 98b. CHATEAU STE. MICHELLE: 45b, 181b, 315t. CITY OF VANCOUVER ARCHIVES: Stuart Thomson photo CVA 99-2507 25br; C. Bradbury photo SGN 1551 36c; Harry T. Devine photo LGN 1045 203b; W. Chapman photo CVA 677-441 221b. CN IMAX THEATRE AT CANADA PLACE: 202t. CONVENTION & VISITORS ASSOCIATION OF LANE COUNTY OREGON: front endpaper b, Sea Lion Caves 20t; Sally McAleer 26cl; Darrel Lindblad 27cr; Norm Coyer 27tl; 86; 96l; Sally McAleer 96b; Sandland Adventures 96c; Michael Chafron 99c; Dianne Dietrick Leis 101t; Sandland Adventures 316t; Lon Beale 317t; Sally McAleer 317b; Randy Siner 318cr; Dick Dietrich 318b. COURTESY OF COLORADO HISTORICAL SOCIETY: CHS.J1449, William Henry Jackson 39c. CRYSTAL MOUNTAIN: Jeremy Martinson www.cascaonline.com 186t, 186b, 324b. CRYSTAL SPRINGS RHODODENDRON GARDEN: Barbara L. Darval 74tr.

DALE CHIHULY PHOTO: Stewart Charles Cohen 28bl. DAVID SUZUKI FOUNDATION: 29b. DENVER PUBLIC LIBRARY, WESTERN HISTORY COLLECTION: X-31120 25bl, X-31012 25bc, Z-244 37c. DOMAINE SERENE: 98c. DORST, ADRIAN: 255c.

© 2000 Experience Music Project: Stanley Smith 146t, 147t; Lara Swimmer 146b, 147b.

Fairmont Hotel Vancouver: 210tr. Fernie Alpine Resort: 261t, 262c. Four Seasons Olympic Hotel: Photos by Robb Gordon 119tr, 128b.

Governor Hotel: 48clb. Granville Island: 214. Granville Island Museums: 216bl, 219bl. Gunter Marx – Stock Photos: 2-3, 20cl, 22c–23c, 23b, 31t, 32t, 33b, 175t, 188t, 222, 254c, 254b, 255b, 256c, 267c, 268t, 270b, 273b, 319b.

Hells Canyon Adventures: Ed Riche 115b, 115c.

Imes, Chuck: Medford, OR 58tl.

John Day Fossil Beds National Monument: Courtesy of National Park Service and NWIA 111c.

Kamloops Tourism: 317c. Koocanusa Publications: 261b.

Courtesy of Leavenworth Chamber of Commerce: 33t. L'Ecole No. 41 Winery: Brent Bergherm 192tr.

Medicine Wheel Website Design: 190tl. Microsoft: 159br. Mount St. Helens National Volcanic Monument: 18b, 41t, 193cl. MSCUA, University of Washington Libraries: UW4215 117c, UW6991 124br, A. Curtis 63021 37c, UW10921 39t.

National Archives of Canada: E. Sandys C-011040 8; Thomas Mower Martin C-114455 9c; Theodore J. Richardson C-102057 24c–25c; William George Richardson Hind C-13978 24b; John B. Wilkinson C-150276 25t; Robert Petley C-103533 35b; Peter Rindisbacher C-001904 36cb; Alfred Jacob Miller C-000411 36t; Henry James Warre C-001621 37b, C-001623 38br; Charles William Jefferys C-70270 37t; Robert William Rutherford C-09870 38bl; Lady Frances Musgrave C-35986 40t; Edward Roper C-011035 195c, R9266-350 277c; 211br; Edward D. Panter-Downes C-009561 42; Washington F. Friend C-129778 43c; Capt. Francis G. Coleridge C-102427 323c. National Park Service: 19t, 23ca, 108t, 188b, 188c, 189bl, 189br, 189c. New-Small and Sterling Studio Glass Ltd: © David New-Small 215t; Photo: Erica Henderson 217c; © David New-Small, photo: Kenji Nagai 218c. Northern BC Tourism Association: 269br. Northern Rockies Regional

District & Town of Fort Nelson: Hank Schut 269tr.

Odyssey Maritime Discovery Center: 118cb, 138b, 138c, 139b, 139c, 139t. Oregon Coast Aquarium: 95bl. Orpheum Theatre: Photo: David Blue 233t.

Pike Place Market Preservation & Development Authority: 40br, 134bl.

Royal British Columbia Museum: 252b, 252cb, 252ca, 252t, 253c, 253b, 253t.

Seattle Center: Photo by Carson Jones 142t; 145br. Seattle Children's Theatre: Chris Bennion 161b. Seattle's Convention and Visitors Bureau: 123b, 138t. Southwest Washington Convention & Visitors Bureau: 193c.

Terra Galleria Photography: 189t. Terry Fox Foundation: Gail Harvey 29tl.

University of British Columbia Museum of Anthropology: 230b, 230cb, 231b, 231c.

Logger's Culls, c.1935, oil on canvas, Vancouver Art Gallery, VAG 39.1, photo: Trevor Mills 211t. Vancouver Opera: Tim Matheson 233b. Verve Music Group: Diana Krall photo: Bruce Weber 28b. Viewfinders: 30b, 31b, 66, 87b, 92br, 97b, 97t, 103b, 105b, 106b, 106c, 107b, 107t, 108b, 108c, 109b, 109c, 110tl, 111b, 114b, 114c, 115t, 174b, 174tr, 175b, 175t, 178tr, 179c, 179t, 183b, 191t, 192b, 320t.

Walla Walla Chamber of Commerce: 30t, 191b. Woodland Park Zoo: Dennis Conner 156ca, 157ca, 157t. World Pictures: 270t.

Elevation relief art modified by VISUTronX from: Mountain High Maps® Copyright © 1993 Digital Wisdom Inc.

Jacket: Corbis: Gunter Marx – Stock Photos: front cr; John McAnulty: bc; Bill Ross: main and spine; Corbis: Raymond Gehman: back br; Getty Images: Glen Allison: back tl.

All other images © Dorling Kindersley
For further information see www.dkimages.com